Time Out

Barcelona

timeout.com/barcelona

D0057307

Time Out Guides Ltd
Universal House
251 Tottenham Court Road
London W1T 7AB
United Kingdom
Tel: +44 (0)20 7813 3000
Fax: +44 (0)20 7813 6001
Email: guides@timeout.com
www.timeout.com

Published by Time Out Guides Ltd, a wholly owned subsidiary of Time Out Group Ltd.
Time Out and the Time Out logo are trademarks of Time Out Group Ltd.

© **Time Out Group Ltd 2011**
Previous editions 1996, 1998, 2000, 2001, 2002, 2003, 2004, 2005, 2006, 2007, 2008, 2009, 2010.

10 9 8 7 6 5 4 3 2 1

This edition first published in Great Britain in 2011 by Ebury Publishing.
A Random House Group Company
20 Vauxhall Bridge Road, London SW1V 2SA

Random House Australia Pty Ltd 20 Alfred Street, Milsons Point, Sydney, New South Wales 2061, Australia

Random House New Zealand Ltd 18 Poland Road, Glenfield, Auckland 10, New Zealand

Random House South Africa (Pty) Ltd Isle of Houghton, Corner Boundary Road & Carse O'Gowrie, Houghton 2198, South Africa

Random House UK Limited Reg. No. 954009

Distributed in the US and Latin America by Publishers Group West (1-510-809-3700)
Distributed in Canada by Publishers Group Canada (1-800-747-8147)

For further distribution details, see www.timeout.com.

ISBN: 978-1-84670-218-1

A CIP catalogue record for this book is available from the British Library.

Printed and bound by Firmengruppe APPL, aprinta druck, Wemding, Germany.

The Random House Group Limited supports The Forest Stewardship Council (FSC), the leading international forest certification organisation. All our titles that are printed on Greenpeace approved FSC certified paper carry the FSC logo. Our paper procurement policy can be found at http://www.randomhouse.co.uk/environment.

Time Out carbon-offsets its flights with Trees for Cities (www.treesforcities.org).

Contents

Introduction

Truth, too often, can turn into cliché. Seville has its flamenco, its bulls, its fiery tempers. Madrid has its suckling pig and its old-school pomp. Bilbao is tough and gritty, with a heart of gold. So far, so familiar. But by contrast, Barcelona's truths have been harder to distinguish. Ordered and chaotic, traditional and forward-thinking, it's been resistant to platitudes over the centuries, and remains a pleasingly elusive place.

Of all the unlikely commentators, Leon Trotsky nailed Barcelona as well as anyone. 'Like Nice in a hell of factories,' he wrote in 1916. 'Smoke and flames on the one hand, flowers and fruit on the other.' Granted, the factories have long gone, but their stamp on Barcelona's history has proven indelible: the locals now work almost as hard in banking and commerce as they once did in the textile mills, and Catalonia is still considered the powerhouse of Spain in many of the same ways. And the smoke and flames of those tumultuous decades still linger in the fervent nationalism and endless demonstrations about perceived wrongs committed by central government.

Despite its uncompromising bedrock, Catalonia has managed to be the font of much of the country's creativity. Working from his restaurant El Bulli, Catalan chef Ferran Adrià has had a profound effect on the world's restaurant culture, much as Salvador Dalí did with art and Antoni Gaudí with architecture. And while Picasso wasn't Catalan, he considered Barcelona his spiritual home and his artistic muse.

But although Barcelona's cultural figureheads continue to hold plenty of appeal, the city has more to offer than the creations of these famous residents. From the characterful medieval quarter to the elegant, 19th-century Eixample to the regenerated waterfront, the city rewards the curious pedestrian, its streets awash with beauties, curiosities and diversions. Indeed, the very urban fabric of Barcelona is deliriously vital: grand with medieval design, playful with impish street art and ablaze with Modernista colours and furbelows. Or, as Trotsky might have it, flowers and fruit.
Sally Davies, Editor

Barcelona in Brief

IN CONTEXT

The book's opening section covers the saga of repression and resilience that shaped Barcelona, from its role as dusty Roman barracks to its crowning as Capital of the Mediterranean in 2010. As well as an analysis of its current politics and likely fortunes in the near future, there's an extended feature on the local cuisine.
▶ *For more, see pp13-49.*

SIGHTS

Barcelona perhaps lacks a list of must-see venues to tick off and photograph, but to miss out on some of the exuberant buildings of the Modernistas would be an opportunity wasted. It's also well worth dipping into the city's fabulous set of museums, and taking in a selection of its ancient churches, elegantly landscaped parks and bleeding-edge architecture.
▶ *For more, see pp51-110.*

CONSUME

In this section of the guide, you'll find scores of places in which to slake your thirst and linger over lunch, along with a rundown of the best accommodation options – everything from deluxe five-star hotels to short-term apartment rentals. You'll also find an extensive list of Barcelona's more fascinating stores, along with essential information on where to buy a SIM card or have a shoe reheeled.
▶ *For more, see pp111-206.*

ARTS & ENTERTAINMENT

Barcelona's arts scene is accessible to non-Catalan speakers, thanks to its dance companies and its tradition of visual theatre, and this is the best city in Spain in which to hear live music, from Mozart to Muse. We also cover the city's finest festivals, the hottest nightclubs, the best cinemas and the most exciting galleries, and also detail the best family-friendly entertainments in town.
▶ *For more, see pp207-266.*

ESCAPES & EXCURSIONS

You may feel that there's plenty to keep you in the city. However, with mountains, beaches and vineyards just a short hop away, Catalonia has much to offer outside Barcelona. In an hour or two, you could be strolling around Cistercian monasteries, exploring Dalí's surreal estate, walking, cycling or driving through a network of leafy routes, or simply lounging on the beach.
▶ *For more, see pp267-290.*

Barcelona in 48 Hrs

Day 1 The Old City

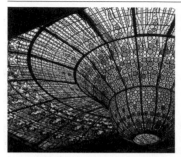

9AM Start the day with quiet stroll down La Rambla, the city's most famous boulevard, before the crowds, the living statues and the pickpockets arrive. Halfway along, duck into **Café de l'Opera** (*see p169*) for coffee and a breakfast *ensaïmada*, a spiral of flaky pastry dusted with icing sugar. It's a great way to start the day.

Another couple of hundred yards or so down La Rambla, heading towards the sea, you'll see the **Plaça Reial** off to your left. Turn in to admire its elaborate lampposts, an early council commission for Gaudí; then, exiting from its northern side, head right along C/Ferran to the grand Plaça Sant Jaume, skirting round the back of the Generalitat to the **Cathedral** (*see p56*).

You're now in the heart of the Barri Gòtic. Allow at least half an hour to mooch around its magnificent cloister and take the lift up to the roof for a great view of the city. Come out of the Cathedral and head east, crossing the Via Laietana to the **Palau de la Música** (*see p69*). Take a guided tour or simply marvel at the fantastical Modernista façade.

2PM Having worked up an appetite, head down into the Born proper (with a quick look at the roof of the **Mercat Santa Caterina** en route) and tuck into some tapas outside the magestic **Santa Maria del Mar** at **La Vinya del Senyor** wine bar (*see p174*). It's a skip and a hop to the **Museu Picasso** (*see p66*), an easy place to while away a couple of hours.

6PM After this, wander down to the Port Vell. For the best view over the harbour, go up to the rooftop café of the **Museu d'Història de Catalunya** (*see p77*), where you can sip an early evening beer before heading up to the modernised Barceloneta and the seafront.

9PM In this part of town, there are several excellent seafood restaurants: try **Can Majó** or **Kaiku** (for both, *see p157*). And if you can't bear to go home afterwards, then join the glossy crowd for a late-night cocktail at fashionable **CDLC** (*see p243*), on the fringe of the beach.

NAVIGATING THE CITY

Barcelona is a breeze to navigate. Many major sights are within walking distance of each other, and the natural enclosure formed by the sea and the mountains mean it's hard to get too lost. Remember that uphill is *muntanya* (mountain) and downhill is *mar* (sea) – locals often give directions with these terms.

As well as using your feet or the cheap, user-friendly metro and bus systems, you can get around with **Go Cars** (902 301 333, www.gocars.es), small yellow open-topped 'talking' cars. During the day from March to November, you can also get around by hiring a Trixi rickshaw (www.trixi.com), either hailing one on the street or calling 93 310 13 79. For full details on transport, *see pp292-295*.

PACKAGE DEALS

Articket (www.articketbcn.org, €22) gives free entry to seven major museums and galleries (one visit per venue over six

Day 2 Modernista Marvels

9AM To start a day of Modernisme, Barcelona's answer to art nouveau, have coffee and a pastry at the **Escribà** pâtisserie (La Rambla 83, 93 301 60 27), with its tiled façade, delicate stucco and wrought iron. From here, walk up to **Plaça Catalunya** and continue straight ahead for the elegant **Passeig de Gràcia**, a showcase for all things Modernista. Note the Gaudí-designed hexagonal paving tiles, along with Pere Falqués' elegant wrought-iron lamp-posts.

11AM Unless you get sucked into some of the street's blend of swanky boutiques and major chains, it's a five-minute walk to the contrasting masterpieces of the **Manzana de la Discòrdia** (*see p91* **Inside Track**). This block houses three extraordinary buildings designed by the holy trinity of Modernisme: Gaudí, Domènech i Montaner and Puig i Cadafalch. A five- to ten-minute walk further is Gaudí's **La Pedrera** (*see p97*). Backtrack to the Casa Batlló and take a metro train to Gaudí's most famous work, the spectacular **Sagrada Família** cathedral (*see p98*).

2PM Time for lunch. The area around the Sagrada Família is strangely bereft of decent restaurants, but the adjacent **Avda Gaudí** has several spots with pavement terraces for a *bocadillo* and a beer. Once you're done, continue along the avenue for the extravagant **Hospital Sant Pau** (*see p96*), an unsung Modernista tour de force by Domènech i Montaner, then take bus No.92 to Gaudí's unmissable **Park Güell** (*see p102* **Profile**).

9PM To complete a day of Modernisme, the deep-of pocket will love dinner at **Casa Calvet** (*see p160*), a great, if pricey, restaurant set in a Gaudí-designed townhouse. If money is more of an issue, you could plump for dinner in the charming **Els Quatre Gats** (*see p169*). The food is a little more ordinary, but the building is designed by Puig i Cadafalch and it's a former haunt of Picasso. Both are most easily reached by cab from Park Güell; and both also offer easy access to other nightlife options if you're not yet ready for bed.

---

months): Fundació Miró, MACBA, the MNAC, La Pedrera, the Fundació Tàpies, the CCCB and the Museu Picasso. It's available from participating venues, tourist offices and www.telentrada.com.

The good-value **Arqueoticket** (http://bcnshop.barcelonaturisme.com, €14) allows history buffs to visit five local archaeologically oriented museums. It's available from the museums and tourist offices, and is valid for unlimited visits for a year after purchase.

The **Barcelona Card** (www.barcelona card.com) allows unlimited transport on metro and buses, and gives discounts at sights, cable cars and airport buses. Costing €27 (€23 children aged 4-12, free under-4s) for a two-day pass, €33/ €28 for three days, €37.50/€30.50 for four days and €44/€34.50 for five days, it's sold at the airport, tourist offices, Sants station, Estació del Nord bus station, El Corte Inglés, various attractions and ww.barcelonaturisme.com.

Barcelona in Profile

THE BARRI GÒTIC

Medieval heart of the Old City, the Barri Gòtic is a spider's web of narrow alleyways and secluded squares and the best introduction to the city, combined with a wander down La Rambla, frenetic and shamelessly commercial, but with a certain charm.

For a taste of Barcelona's more grandiose architecture, Plaça Sant Jaume is flanked by the Renaissance palace of the Generalitat (Catalan government) and the neo-classical façade of the Ajuntament (City Hall).

▶ *For more, see pp52-61.*

THE BORN & SANT PERE

The Born's main artery, the Passeig del Born is a former jousting ground and one of Barcelona's prettiest boulevards, bookended by the magnificent wrought-iron 19th-century market building and the glorious 14th-century Santa Maria del Mar church. Highlights of the slightly scruffier San Pere are the swooping polychromatic roof of the Santa Caterina market, and the Modernista Palau de la Música.

▶ *For more, see pp62-69.*

THE RAVAL

Once a no-go area for tourists, the Raval is being transformed. Some of its gems have been around for years – Gaudí's medievalist Palau Güell was an early, brave attempt at gentrification. But others are newer: the revival began in 1995 with Richard Meier's monumental MACBA, housing the city's main collection of modern art, and carried on with the creation of the wide Rambla del Raval.

▶ *For more, see pp70-74.*

BARCELONETA & THE PORTS

The city's seafront was ignored until 1992, when it underwent a massive transformation for the Olympics. Despite initial resistance, it was wildly successful: the city now has seven kilometres of golden sands from bustling Port Vell to the upscale Port Olímpic and beyond. Inevitably, this is also where you'll find some of the city's best seafood restaurants.

▶ *For more, see pp75-80.*

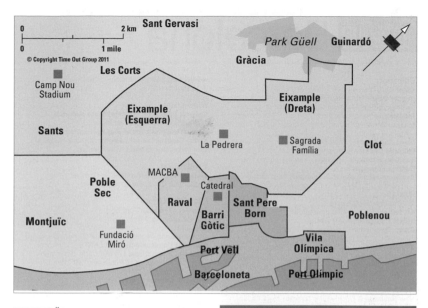

MONTJUÏC

In summer, the hill of Monjuïc is a few degrees cooler than the city below, and its many parks and gardens are excellent places for a shady picnic. There are also museums: the Fundació Joan Miró is as impressive for its Corbusier-influenced building as its collection.

▶ For more, see pp81-89.

THE EIXAMPLE

With the demolition of the medieval wall in 1854, the fields beyond the city became a blank canvas. The Eixample, with its grid layout, became a Modernista showcase, with buildings such as the Sagrada Família and Pedrera. Bisecting the area is the elegant Passeig de Gracìa; the area to its right is the fashionable Dreta, while to the left is the more down-at-heel Esquerra.

▶ For more, see pp90-99.

GRÀCIA & OTHER DISTRICTS

Beyond the Eixample lies low-rise Gràcia, an independent town swallowed up as the city spread but retaining its own identity. Other notable areas outside the centre include the forested Collserola hills and, to the north, the former industrial neighbourhood of Poblenou.

▶ For more, see pp100-110.

Time Out Barcelona

Editorial
Editor Sally Davies
Deputy Editor Anna Norman
Listings Editors Mary-Ann Gallagher, Helena Lizari
Proofreader Patrick Mulkern
Indexer William Crow

Managing Director Peter Fiennes
Editorial Director Ruth Jarvis
Business Manager Dan Allen
Editorial Manager Holly Pick
Assistant Management Accountant Ija Krasnikova

Design
Art Director Scott Moore
Art Editor Pinelope Kourmouzoglou
Senior Designer Kei Ishimaru
Group Commercial Designer Jodi Sher

Picture Desk
Picture Editor Jael Marschner
Acting Deputy Picture Editor Liz Leahy
Picture Desk Assistant/Researcher Ben Rowe

Advertising
New Business & Commercial Director Mark Phillips
International Advertising Manager Kasimir Berger
International Sales Executive Charlie Sokol

Advertising Sales (Barcelona) Hazel Walker, Maria Ntuk-Idem

Marketing
Sales & Marketing Director, North America & Latin America Lisa Levinson
Senior Publishing Brand Manager Luthfa Begum
Group Commercial Art Director Anthony Huggins
Marketing Co-ordinator Alana Benton

Production
Group Production Manager Brendan McKeown
Production Controller Katie Mulhern

Time Out Group
Director & Founder Tony Elliott
Chief Executive Officer David King
Group Financial Director Paul Rakkar
Group General Manager/Director Nichola Coulthard
Time Out Communications Ltd MD David Pepper
Time Out International Ltd MD Cathy Runciman
Time Out Magazine Ltd Publisher/MD Mark Elliott
Group Commercial Director Graeme Tottle
Group IT Director Simon Chappell

Contributors
Introduction Sally Davies. **History** Nick Rider, Sally Davies (*Profile* Mary-Ann Gallagher). **Barcelona Today** William Truini. **Architecture** Nick Rider, Sally Davies. **Catalan Cuisine** Colman Andrews. **Sightseeing** Nadia Feddo, Sally Davies, Stephen Burgen, William Truini (*On Yer Bike, Modernista Mansions* Mary-Ann Gallagher). **Hotels** Tara Stevens. **Restaurants** Sally Davies. **Cafés, Tapas & Bars** Sally Davies (*Pop Go the '80s* Suzanne Wales). **Shops & Services** Nadia Feddo (*The Retro Route* Suzanne Wales; *Finding an Outlet, Market Picks* Mary-Ann Gallagher). **Calendar** Sally Davies. **Children** Sally Davies. **Film** Sally Davies. **Galleries** Alx Phillips. **Gay & Lesbian** Dylan Simanowitz, Robert Rama (*The Party Circuit* Nadia Feddo). **Music & Nightlife** Katie Addleman (*Learn the Lingo* Alx Phillips; *Midnight Feasts* Mary-Ann Gallagher). **Performing Arts** Alx Phillips (*Pure Spectacle* Natasha Young). **Sport & Fitness** Daniel Campi (*Profile* Peterjon Cresswell). **Escapes & Excursions** Tara Stevens, Sally Davies. **Directory** Alx Phillips.

The Editor would like to thank Max Artigas, Tess O'Donovan, Nora Vos Lizari and all contributors to previous editions of *Time Out Barcelona*, whose work forms the basis for parts of this book.

Maps john@jsgraphics.co.uk, except: pages 336-337.

Cover photograph Grant Faint/Getty Images.
Back-cover photography Olivia Rutherford, Greg Gladman

Photography Elan Fleisher, except page 4 Nito; pages 5 (middle), 8 (bottom right), 9 (bottom), 40 (left), 51, 67, 78, 85, 91, 102, 121 (top), 124, 129 (bottom), 134, 143, 145, 165, 221, 215, 229, 235, 236, 239, 248, 249, 251, 253, 260, 266, 277, 281 Olivia Rutherford; pages 5 (top), 40 (right), 55, 99, 105 (right), 109, 110, 130, 168, 181, 216, 218, 222, 261, 269, 275 Natalie Pecht; page 5 (bottom) Ivonne Wierink; pages 6, 8 (top & bottom), 13, 35, 36 (right), 53, 63 (top right), 84, 101, 108, 141, 142, 149, 153, 166, 170, 171, 175, 179, 180, 182, 193, 240, 247, 265, 283, 289 Greg Gladman; pages 7, 287 Piotrwzk; page 14 akg-images/Ullstein Bild; pages 19, 20 Bridgeman Art Library; page 23 Gamma-Keystone/Getty Images; page 26 Getty Images; pages 9 (top), 31, 77, 79, 86, 87, 92, 107, 111, 112, 120, 136, 223, 246, 252, 255 Marc Goodwin; page 46 Winkelmann, Bernhard/StockFood; page 48 Alamy; page 73 Collectiu Lluna Vivent; page 163 Ivan Gimenez; page 184 Scott Chasserot; page 210 Lois Lammerhuber; page 213 Wijkmarkphoto; page 219 Ivan Moreno; page 263 Sportgraphic; page 267 Vladitto; page 271 ACT/Cablepress; page 279 Denis Babenko. The following images were provided by the featured establishments/artists: pages 93, 133, 190, 224, 257, 259.

About the Guide

GETTING AROUND

The back of the book contains street maps of Barcelona, as well as overview maps of the city and its surroundings. The maps start on page 319; on them are marked the locations of hotels (❶), restaurants (❶), and cafés, tapas bars and bars (❶). The majority of businesses listed in this guide are located in the areas we've mapped; the grid-square references refer to these maps.

THE ESSENTIALS

For practical information, including visas, disabled access, emergency numbers, lost property and local transport, please see the Directory. It begins on page 292.

THE LISTINGS

Addresses, phone numbers, websites, transport information, hours and prices are all included in our listings, as are selected other facilities. All were checked and correct at press time. However, business owners can alter their arrangements at any time, and fluctuating economic conditions can cause prices to change rapidly.

The very best venues in the city, the must sees and must-dos in every category, have been marked with a red star (★). In the Sights chapters, we've also marked venues with free admission with a FREE symbol.

THE LANGUAGE

Barcelona is a bilingual city: street signs, tourist information and menus may be in either Spanish or Catalan. For a language primer, see pages 308-309; there's help with restaurants on pages 144-145.

PHONE NUMBERS

The area code for Barcelona is 93. Even if you're in the city, you'll always need to use the code. From outside Spain, dial your country's international access code (00 from the UK, 011 from the US) or a plus symbol, followed by the Spanish country code (34) and the nine-digit number. So, to reach the Sagrada Família, dial +34 93 207 3031. For more on phones, see pages 303-304.

FEEDBACK

We welcome feedback on this guide, both on the venues we've included and on any other locations that you'd like to see featured in future editions. Please email us at guides@timeout.com.

Time Out Guides

Founded in 1968, Time Out has grown from humble beginnings into the leading resource for anyone wanting to know what's happening in the world's greatest cities. Alongside our influential weeklies in London, New York and Chicago, we publish more than 20 magazines in cities as varied as Beijing and Beirut, with *Time Out Barcelona* magazine published weekly in Catalan. (An English-language visitor's magazine is published biannually.) The company remains proudly independent, still owned by Tony Elliott four decades after he launched *Time Out London*.

Written by local experts and illustrated with original photography, our books also retain their independence. No business has been featured because it has advertised, and all restaurants and bars are visited and reviewed anonymously.

ABOUT THE EDITOR

Sally Davies has lived in Barcelona since 2001, and has edited and contributed to a number of books on Spain. She also writes on Spain for publications including *The Guardian*, *Sunday Times*, *Daily Telegraph* and *Evening Standard*.

A full list of the book's contributors can be found opposite. We've also included details of our writers in selected chapters throughout the guide.

WHENEVER, WHEREVER YOU NEED MONEY...

WE GET IT THERE IN 10 MINUTES*

CHOICE IS IN YOUR HANDS

1. Arrange for the person sending the money to visit a MoneyGram agent near them. After sending the money, they will give you a reference number.

2. Find your nearest MoneyGram agent at **www.moneygram.com** or anywhere you see the MoneyGram sign.

3. Give the reference number and your ID** to the MoneyGram agent.

4. Fill out one simple form to receive your money.

MoneyGram.
Money Transfer

900 81 16 32   www.moneygram.com

In Context

Mercat de Santa Caterina. *See p198*.

History

The fall and rise of Barcelona.

TEXT: NICK RIDER

Cultural, political and social diversity flourish in today's Barcelona, but things haven't always been that way. For long periods of its history, the city was the victim of attempts by governments in Madrid to absorb Catalonia within a unified Spanish state. Under several leaders, notably Philip V in the 17th century and Franco in the 20th, these attempts resulted in a policy aimed at stamping out any vestige of Catalan culture or independence. However, the region always re-emerged from such persecutions stronger and more vibrant, with a heightened desire to show the world its distinctive character – both socially and culturally.

Nick Rider wrote a PhD on 1930s Barcelona before becoming the first editor of Time Out Barcelona, *and has since written for several books on Spain.*

IN THE BEGINNING

The Romans founded Barcelona in about 15 BC on the Mons Taber, a hill between two streams that provided a good view of the Mediterranean; today, it's crowned by a cathedral. At the time, the plain around it was sparsely inhabited by the Laetani, an Iberian people who produced grain and honey, and gathered oysters. Then called Barcino, the town was smaller than Tarraco (Tarragona), the capital of the Roman province of Hispania Citerior, but it had the only harbour between there and Narbonne.

Like virtually every other Roman new town in Europe, Barcino was a fortified rectangle with a crossroads at its centre (where the Plaça Sant Jaume is today). It was an unimportant provincial town, but the rich plain provided it with a produce garden and the sea gave it an incipient maritime trade. It acquired a Jewish community soon after its foundation and became associated with Christian martyrs; among them was Santa Eulàlia, Barcelona's first patron saint. Eulàlia was supposedly executed at the end of the third century via a series of revolting tortures that included being rolled naked in a barrel full of glass shards down the alley called Baixada ('Descent') de Santa Eulàlia.

The people of Barcino accepted Christianity in AD 312, together with the rest of the Roman Empire, which by then was under growing threat of invasion. In response, the town's rough defences were replaced with massive stone walls in the fourth century, many sections of which can still be seen today. It was these ramparts that ensured Barcelona's continuity, making the stronghold desirable to later warlords.

Nonetheless, defences like these could not prevent the empire's disintegration. In 415, Barcelona, as it became known, briefly became capital of the kingdom of the Visigoths, under their chieftain Ataülf. They soon moved on southwards to extend their control over the whole of the Iberian peninsula, and for the next 400 years the town was a neglected backwater. The Muslims swept across the peninsula after 711, crushing Goth resistance; they made little attempt to settle Catalonia, but much of the Christian population retreated into the Pyrenees, the first Catalan heartland.

Then, at the end of the eighth century, the Franks drove south, against the Muslims, from across the mountains. In 801, Charlemagne's son, Louis the Pious, took Barcelona and made it a bastion of the *Marca Hispanica* (Spanish March), which was the southern buffer of his father's empire. This gave Catalonia a trans-Pyrenean origin entirely different from that of the other Christian states in Spain; equally, it's for this reason that the closest relative of the Catalan language is Provençal, not Castilian.

When the Frankish princes returned to their main business further north, loyal counts were left behind to rule sections of the Catalan lands. At the end of the ninth century, Count Guifré el Pilós (Wilfred 'the Hairy'; *photo p20*) managed to gain control over several of these Catalan counties from his base in Ripoll. By uniting them under his rule, he laid the basis for a future Catalan state, founding the dynasty of the Counts of Barcelona, which reigned in an unbroken line until 1410. His successors made Barcelona their capital, setting the seal on the city's future.

As a founding patriarch, Wilfred is the stuff of legends, not least of which is that he was the creator of the Catalan flag. The story goes that he was fighting the Saracens alongside his lord, the Frankish emperor, when he was severely wounded. In recognition of Wilfred's heroism, the emperor dipped his fingers into his friend's blood and ran them down the count's golden shield; thus, the Quatre Barres, four bars of red on a yellow background, also known as La Senyera. Recorded facts make this story highly unlikely, but whatever its origins, the four-stripe symbol was first recorded on the tomb of Count Ramon Berenguer II from 1082, making it the oldest national flag in Europe. What is not known is exactly in what way Wilfred was so notably hairy.

LAYING THE FOUNDATIONS

In the first century of the new millennium, Catalonia was consolidated as a political entity, and entered an age of cultural richness. This was the great era of Catalan Romanesque art, with the building of the magnificent monasteries and the churches of

World Class

Perfect places to stay, eat and explore.

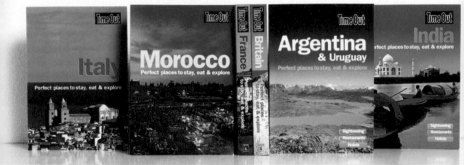

northern Catalonia, such as Sant Pere de Rodes near Figueres, and the painting of the glorious murals now housed in the Museu Nacional on Montjuïc. There was a flowering of scholarship, reflecting Catalan contacts with northern Europe and with Islamic and Carolingian cultures. In Barcelona, shipbuilding and trade in grain and wine grew, and a new trade developed in textiles. The city expanded both inside its old Roman walls and outside them, with *vilanoves* (new towns) appearing at Sant Pere and La Ribera.

The most significant addition, however, occurred in 1137, when Ramon Berenguer IV (1131-62) wed Petronella, heir to the throne of Aragon. In the long term, the marriage bound Catalonia into Iberia. The uniting of the two dynasties created a powerful entity known as the Crown of Aragon: each element retained its separate institutions, and was ruled by monarchs known as the Count-Kings. Ramon Berenguer IV also extended Catalan territory to its current frontiers in the Ebro valley. At the beginning of the next century, however, the dynasty lost virtually all its land north of the Pyrenees to France, when Count-King Pere I 'the Catholic' was killed at the Battle of Muret in 1213. This proved a blessing in disguise. In future years, the Catalan-Aragonese state became oriented decisively towards the Mediterranean and the south, and was able to embark on two centuries of imperialism that would be equalled in vigour only by Barcelona's burgeoning commercial enterprise.

EMPIRE-BUILDING

Pere I's successor was the most expansionist of the Count-Kings. Jaume I 'the Conqueror' (1213-76) joined the campaign against the Muslims to the south, taking Mallorca in 1229, Ibiza in 1235 and, at greater cost, Valencia in 1238 (which he made another separate kingdom, the third part of the Crown of Aragon). Barcelona became the centre of an empire that spanned the Mediterranean.

The city grew tremendously. In the middle of the 13th century, Jaume I ordered the building of a second wall along the line of La Rambla, roughly encircling the area between there and what is now the Parc de la Ciutadella; in doing so, La Ribera and the other *vilanoves* were brought within the city. In 1274, Jaume also gave Barcelona a form of representative self-government: the Consell de Cent, a council of 100 chosen citizens, an institution that would last for more than 400 years. In Catalonia as a whole, royal powers were strictly limited by a parliament, the Corts, with a permanent standing committee known as the Generalitat.

In 1282, Pere II 'the Great' sent his armies into Sicily; Catalan domination over the island would last for nearly 150 years, as the Catalan empire reached its greatest strength under Jaume II 'the Just' (1291-1327). Corsica (1323) and Sardinia (1324) were added to the Crown of Aragon, although the latter would never submit to Catalan rule and would, from then on, be a constant focus of revolt.

THE GOLDEN AGE

The Crown of Aragon was often at war with Arab rulers, but its capital flourished through commerce with every part of the Mediterranean, Christian and Muslim. Catalan ships also sailed into the Atlantic, to England and Flanders, their ventures actively supported by the Count-Kings and burghers of Barcelona and regulated by the first ever code of maritime law, known as the *Llibre del Consolat de Mar* (written in 1258-72). By the late 13th century, around 130 consulates ringed the Mediterranean, engaged in a complex system of trade.

Unsurprisingly, this age of power and prestige was also the great era of building in medieval Barcelona. The Count-Kings' imperial conquests may have been ephemeral, but their talent for permanence in building can still be seen today. Between 1290 and 1340, the construction of most of Barcelona's best-known Gothic buildings was initiated. Religious edifices such as the cathedral, Santa Maria del Mar and Santa Maria del Pi were matched by civil buildings such as the Saló de Tinell and the Llotja,

IN CONTEXT

'The Catalan Golden Age was an era of cultural greatness. Catalonia was one of the first areas in Europe to use its vernacular language.'

the old market and the stock exchange. As a result, Barcelona contains the most important collection of historic Gothic civil architecture anywhere in Europe.

The ships of the Catalan navy were built in the monumental Drassanes (shipyards), begun by Pere II and completed under Pere III, in 1378. In 1359, Pere III also built the third, final city wall along the line of the modern Paral·lel, Ronda Sant Pau and Ronda Sant Antoni. This gave the Old City of Barcelona its definitive shape. La Ribera, 'the waterfront', was the centre of trade and industry in the 14th century city. Just inland, the Carrer Montcada was where newly enriched merchants displayed their wealth in opulent Gothic palaces. All around were the workers of the various craft guilds, grouped together in their own streets.

The Catalan Golden Age was an era of cultural greatness. Catalonia was one of the first areas in Europe to use its vernacular language, as well as Latin, in written form and as a language of culture. Incipient Catalan literature was given a vital thrust by Ramon Llull (1235-1316). After a debauched youth, he experienced a series of religious visions and became the first man in post-Roman Europe to write philosophy in a vernacular language. Steeped in Arabic and Hebrew writings, Llull brought together Christian, Islamic, Jewish and classical ideas, and wrote a vast amount on other subjects – from theories of chivalry to poetry and visionary tales, in doing so effectively creating Catalan as a literary language. Catalan translations were undertaken from Greek and Latin. Chroniclers such as Ramon Muntaner recorded the exploits of Count-Kings and Almogàvers; in 1490, the Valencian Joanot Martorell published Tirant lo Blanc, a bawdy adventure widely considered the first European novel.

REVOLT AND COLLAPSE

But the prosperity of the medieval period did not last. The Count-Kings had overextended Barcelona's resources, and overinvested in far-off ports. By 1400, the effort to maintain their conquests, especially Sardinia, had exhausted the spirit and the coffers of the Catalan imperialist drive. The Black Death, which arrived in the 1340s, also had a devastating impact on Catalonia, intensifying the bitterness of social conflicts between the aristocracy, the merchants, the peasants and the urban poor.

In 1410, Martí I 'the Humane' died without an heir, bringing to an end the line of the Counts of Barcelona, unbroken since Wilfred 'the Hairy'. The Crown of Aragon was passed to a member of a Castilian noble family, the Trastámaras: Fernando de Antequera (1410-16). In the 1460s, the effects of war and catastrophic famine led to a sudden collapse into violent and destructive civil war and peasant revolt. The population was depleted to such an extent that Barcelona would not regain the numbers it had had in 1400 (40,000) until the 18th century.

In 1469, an important union for Spain initiated a woeful period in Barcelona's history; dubbed by some Catalan historians the Decadència, it led to the end of Catalonia as a separate entity. In that year, Ferdinand of Aragon (1479-1516) married Isabella of Castile (1476-1504), thereby uniting the different Spanish kingdoms, even though they would retain their separate institutions for another two centuries.

As Catalonia's fortunes declined, so those of Castile rose. In 1492, Granada, the last Muslim foothold in Spain, was conquered; Isabella decreed the expulsion of all Jews from Castile and Aragon; and Columbus discovered America. It was Castile's seafaring orientation towards the Atlantic, as opposed to the Mediterranean, that confirmed Catalonia's decline. The discovery of the New World was a disaster for

Ramon Berenguer. *See p15.*

Catalan commerce: trade shifted away from the Mediterranean, and Catalans were officially barred from participating in the exploitation of the new empire until the 1770s. The weight of Castile within the monarchy was increased, and it soon became the clear seat of government.

In 1516, the Spanish crown passed to the House of Habsburg, in the shape of Ferdinand and Isabella's grandson, Holy Roman Emperor Charles V. His son, Philip II of Spain, established Madrid as the capital of all his dominions in 1561. Catalonia was managed by viceroys, and the power of its institutions increasingly restricted, with a down-at-heel aristocracy and a meagre cultural life.

FEAR THE REAPERS

While Castilian Spain went through its 'Golden Century', Catalonia was left on the margins. However, worse was to come in the next century with the two national revolts, both heroic defeats that have since acquired a central role in Catalan mythology.

The problem for the Spanish monarchy was that Castile was an absolute monarchy and thus could be taxed at will, but in the former Aragonese territories, and especially Catalonia, royal authority kept coming up against a mass of local rights and privileges. As the Habsburgs' empire became entrenched in wars and expenses that not even American gold could meet, the Count-Duke of Olivares, the great minister of King Philip IV (1621-65), resolved to extract more money and troops from the non-Castilian dominions of the Crown. But the Catalans felt they were taxed quite enough already.

In 1640, a mass of peasants, later dubbed Els Segadors (the Reapers), gathered on La Rambla in Barcelona, outside the Porta Ferrissa (Iron Gate) in the second wall. The peasants rioted against royal authority, surged into the city and murdered the viceroy, the Marquès de Santa Coloma. This began the general uprising known as the Guerra dels Segadors, or the 'Reapers' War'. The authorities of the Generalitat, led by its president Pau Claris, were fearful of the violence of the poor; lacking the confidence to declare Catalonia independent, they appealed for protection from Louis XIII of France. French armies, however, were unable to defend Catalonia adequately, and in 1652 a destitute Barcelona capitulated to the exhausted army of Philip IV. In 1659,

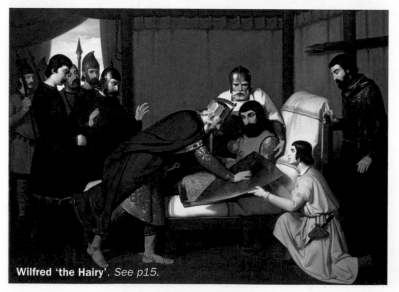

Wilfred 'the Hairy'. *See p15.*

France and Spain made peace with a treaty that gave the Catalan territory of Roussillon, around Perpignan, to France. Following the revolt, Philip IV and his ministers were magnanimous, allowing the Catalans to retain what was left of their institutions despite their disloyalty.

THE REIGN IN SPAIN

Fifty years later came the second of the great national rebellions – the War of the Spanish Succession. In 1700, Charles II of Spain died without an heir, and Castile accepted the grandson of Louis XIV of France, Philip of Anjou, as King Philip V of Spain (1700-46). But the alternative candidate, Archduke Charles of Austria, promised that he would restore the traditional rights of the former Aragonese territories, and won their allegiance. He also had the support, in his fight against France, of Britain, Holland and Austria.

But Catalonia had backed the wrong horse. In 1713, Britain and the Dutch made a separate peace with France and withdrew their aid, leaving the Catalans stranded, with no possibility of victory. After a 13-month siege in which every citizen was called to arms, Barcelona fell to the French and Spanish armies on 11 September 1714. The most heroic defeat of all, the date marked the most decisive political reverse in Barcelona's history, and is now commemorated as Catalan National Day, the Diada. Some of Barcelona's resisters were buried next to the church of Santa Maria del Mar in the Born, in the Fossar de les Moreres (Mulberry Graveyard), now a memorial.

In 1715, Philip V issued his decree of Nova Planta, abolishing all the remaining separate institutions of the Crown of Aragon and so, in effect, creating 'Spain' as a single, unitary state. Large-scale 'Castilianisation' of the country was initiated, and Castilian replaced the Catalan language in all official documents. In Barcelona, extra measures were taken to keep the city under control. The crumbling medieval walls and the castle on Montjuïc were refurbished with new ramparts, and a massive new citadel was built on the eastern side of the Old City, where the Parc de la Ciutadella is today. To make space, thousands were expelled from La Ribera and forcibly rehoused in the Barceloneta, Barcelona's first-ever planned housing scheme, with its barrack-like street plan unmistakably provided by French military engineers. The citadel became the most hated symbol of the city's subordination.

URBAN RENAISSANCE

Politically subjugated and without a significant ruling class, Catalonia nevertheless revived in the 18th century. Shipping picked up again, and Barcelona started a booming export trade to the New World in wines and spirits from Catalan vineyards, and textiles, wool and silk. In 1780, a merchant called Erasme de Gómina opened Barcelona's first true factory, a hand-powered weaving mill in C/Riera Alta with 800 workers. In the next decade, Catalan trade with Spanish America quadrupled; Barcelona's population had grown from 30,000 in 1720 to around 100,000 by the end of the 18th century.

The prosperity was reflected in a new wave of building in the city. Neo-classical mansions appeared, notably on C/Ample and La Rambla, but the greatest transformation was La Rambla itself. Until the 1770s, it had been a dusty, dry riverbed where country people came to sell their produce, lined on the Raval side mostly with giant religious houses and on the other with Jaume I's second wall. In 1775, the Captain-General, the Marqués de la Mina, embarked on an ambitious scheme to demolish the wall and turn La Rambla into a paved promenade. Beyond La Rambla, the previously semi-rural Raval was swiftly becoming densely populated.

Barcelona's expansion was briefly slowed by the French invasion of 1808. Napoleon sought to appeal to Catalans by offering them national recognition within his empire, but was met with curiously little response. After six years of turmoil, Barcelona's growing business class resumed its many projects in 1814, with the restoration of the Bourbon monarchy in the shape of Ferdinand VII (1808-33).

IN CONTEXT

GETTING UP STEAM

Ferdinand VII attempted to reinstate the absolute monarchy of his youth and reimpose his authority over Spain's American colonies, but failed to do either. On his death he was succeeded by his three-year-old daughter Isabella II (1833-68), but the throne was also claimed by his brother Carlos, who was backed by the country's most reactionary sectors.

To defend Isabella's rights, the Regent, Ferdinand's widow Queen María Cristina, was obliged to seek the support of liberals, and so granted a very limited form of constitution. Thus began Spain's Carlist Wars, which had a powerful impact in conservative rural Catalonia, where Don Carlos's faction won a considerable following, in part because of its support for traditional local rights and customs.

While this struggle went on around the country, a liberal-minded local administration in Barcelona, freed from subordination to the military, was able to engage in city planning, opening up the soon-to-be fashionable C/Ferran and Plaça Sant Jaume in he 1820s and later adding the Plaça Reial. A fundamental change came in 1836, when the government in Madrid decreed the Desamortización (or the 'disentailment') of Spain's monasteries. In Barcelona, where convents and religious houses still took up great sections of the Raval and La Rambla, a huge area was freed for development. La Rambla took on the appearance it roughly retains today, while the Raval, the main district for new industry in a city still contained within its walls, filled up with tenements and textile mills several storeys high.

In 1832, the first steam-driven factory in Spain was built on C/Tallers, sparking resistance from hand-spinners and weavers. Most of the city's factories were still relatively small, however, and the Catalan manufacturers were aware that they were at a disadvantage in competing with the industries of Britain and other countries to the north. Complicating matters further, they didn't even have the city to themselves. Not only did the anti-industrial Carlists threaten from the countryside, but Barcelona soon became a centre of radical ideas. Its people were notably rebellious, and liberal, republican, free-thinking and even utopian socialist groups proliferated between bursts of repression.

By this time, the Catalan language had been relegated to secondary status, spoken in every street but rarely written or used in cultured discourse. Then, in 1833, Bonaventura Carles Aribau published his *Oda a la Pàtria*, a romantic eulogy in Catalan of the country, its language and its past. The poem had an extraordinary impact and is still traditionally credited with initiating the Renaixença (Renaissance) of Catalan heritage and culture. The year 1848 was a high point for Barcelona and Catalonia, with the inauguration of the first railway in Spain, from Barcelona to Mataró, and the opening of the Liceu opera house.

SETTING AN EIXAMPLE

The optimism of Barcelona's new middle class was counterpointed by two persistent obstacles: the weakness of the Spanish economy as a whole, and the instability of their own society, which was reflected in atrocious labour relations. No consideration was given to the manpower behind the industrial surge: the underpaid, overworked men, women and children who lived in appalling conditions in high-rise slums within the cramped city.

One response to the city's problems that had almost universal support was the demolition of the city walls, which had imposed a stifling restriction on its growth. For years, however, the Spanish state had refused to relinquish its hold on the city. To find space, larger factories were established in villages around Barcelona, such as Sants and Poblenou, and in 1854 permission finally came for the demolition of the citadel and the walls. The work began with enthusiastic popular participation, crowds of volunteers joining in at weekends. Barcelona at last broke out of the space

IN CONTEXT

Profile Lluís Companys

Catalan nationalist, politician and war hero.

After beginning his political life early as an adolescent dissident, Lluís Companys rose to become the President of Catalonia, before he was shot by Franco's forces in 1940, aged 58. Companys is the only democratically elected incumbent president in Europe to have been executed by firing squad, and he has come to symbolise the savage Francoist repression of Catalonia, and remains a cult figure for Catalan nationalists.

Companys was a young law student in Barcelona during the first decade of the 20th century, when the Spanish government was threatened by trade unions and left-wing political entities. He would become devoted to causes of Catalan nationalism, socialism and republicanism: by the time of the Setmana Tràgica (*see p25*) in 1909, he had been arrested 15 times. Later, after intervening in a union dispute with the government in 1920, he was sent to prison in Menorca. Then, during the 1920s dictatorship of Miguel Primo de Rivera, he was imprisoned twice more: the first time for involvement in a plot to overthrow the government; and the second for protesting against the enforced exile of Francesc Macià, at that time the President of Catalonia.

Companys would succeed Macià as President in early 1934, when he proclaimed the short-lived but symbolic Estat Català (Catalan State).

IN MEMORIAM
A monument to Companys sits above the Arc de Triomf, at Ronda Sant Pere and the Passeig Lluís Companys.

He was sentenced to 30 years in prison, but was released in 1936 after a left-wing coalition triumphed in the elections that would spark the Spanish Civil War.

Companys remained in Barcelona at the head of the government until January 1939, just before the city fell to the Nationalist army. He then fled to France, where, with the assistance of the Spanish authorities, he was arrested by the Gestapo in August 1940. The Nazis sent him back to Barcelona, where an illegal court martial was held, and he was sentenced to death. His last words were: 'You kill an honourable man. For Catalonia!'

IN CONTEXT

it had occupied since the 14th century and spread outwards into its new
eixample (extension), built to a controversial plan by Ildefons Cerdà.

In 1868, Isabella II, once a symbol of liberalism, was overthrown by a progressive
revolt. During the six years of upheaval that followed, power in Madrid would be held
by the provisional government, a constitutional monarchy under an Italian prince and
subsequently a federal republic. However, workers were free to organise; in 1868,
Giuseppe Fanelli brought the first anarchist ideas, and two years later, the first
Spanish workers' congress took place in Barcelona. The radical forces were divided
between many squabbling factions, whereas the established classes of society felt
increasingly threatened and called for the restoration of order. The Republic proclaimed
in 1873 was unable to establish its authority, and succumbed to a military coup less
than a year later.

THE MIDAS TOUCH

In 1874, the Bourbon dynasty, in the person of Alfonso XII, son of Isabella II, was
restored to the Spanish throne. Workers' organisations were again suppressed.
The middle classes, however, felt their confidence renewed. The 1870s saw a frenzied
boom in stock speculation, known as the *febre d'or* (gold fever), and the real take-off of
building in the Eixample. From the 1880s, Modernisme became the preferred style of
the new district, the perfect expression of the confidence and impetus of the industrial
class. The first modern Catalanist political movement was founded by Valentí Almirall.

Barcelona felt it needed to show the world all that it had achieved, and that it was
more than just a 'second city'. In 1885, a promoter named Eugenio Serrano de
Casanova proposed to the city council the holding of an international exhibition,
such as had been held successfully in London, Paris and Vienna. Serrano was
a highly dubious character who eventually made off with large amounts of public
funds, but by the time that this became clear, the city fathers had fully committed
themselves to the event.

The Universal Exhibition of 1888 was used as a pretext for the final conversion of
the Ciutadella into a park. Giant efforts had to be made to get everything ready in time,
a feat that led the mayor, Francesc Rius i Taulet, to exclaim that 'the Catalan people
are the yankees of Europe'. The first of Barcelona's three great attempts to prove its
status to the world, the 1888 Exhibition signified the consecration of the Modernista
style, as well as the end of provincial, dowdy Barcelona and its establishment as a
modern-day city on the international map.

THE CITY OF THE NEW CENTURY

The 1888 Exhibition left Barcelona with huge debts, a new look and many reasons
to believe in itself as a paradigm of progress. The Catalan Renaixença continued,
and acquired a more political tone. A truly decisive moment came in 1898, when
the underlying weakness of the Spanish state was made plain over the superficial
prosperity of the first years of the Bourbon restoration. It was then that Spain was
forced into a short war with the United States, in which it lost its remaining empire
in Cuba, the Philippines and Puerto Rico.

Industrialists were horrified at losing the lucrative Cuban market, and despaired
of the ability of the state ever to reform itself. Many swung behind a conservative
nationalist movement: the Lliga Regionalista (Regionalist League), founded in 1901
and led by Enric Prat de la Riba and the politician-financier Francesc Cambó, promised
both national revival and modern, efficient government.

At the same time, however, Barcelona continued to grow, fuelling Catalanist
optimism. Above all, it had a vibrant artistic community, centred on Modernisme,
which consisted of great architects and established painters such as Rusiñol and
Casas, but also the penniless bohemians who gathered round them, among them the
young Picasso. These were drawn to the increasingly wild nightlife of the Raval, where

'Spain's neutral status during World War I gave a huge boost to the Spanish, and especially Catalan, economy.'

cabarets, bars and brothels multiplied at the end of the 19th century. Located around the cabarets, though, were the poorest of the working classes, for whom conditions had only continued to decline; Barcelona had some of the worst overcrowding and highest mortality rates in Europe. Local philanthropists called for something to be done, but Barcelona was more associated with revolutionary politics and violence than with peaceful social reform.

In 1893, more than 20 people were killed in a series of anarchist terrorist attacks, which included the notorious incident in which a bomb was hurled into the wealthy audience at the Liceu. The perpetrators acted alone, but the authorities seized the opportunity to round up the usual suspects – mainly local anarchists and radicals. Several of them, known as the 'Martyrs of Montjuïc', were later tortured and executed in the castle above the city. Retaliation came in 1906, when a Catalan anarchist tried to kill King Alfonso XIII on his wedding day.

Anarchism was still only in a fledgling state among workers during the 1900s. However, rebellious attitudes, along with growing republican sentiment and a fierce hatred of the Catholic Church, united the underclasses and led them to take to the barricades. The Setmana Tràgica (Tragic Week) of 1909 began as a protest against the conscription of troops for the colonial war in Morocco, but degenerated into a general riot, accompanied by the destruction of churches by excited mobs. Suspected culprits were summarily executed, as was the anarchist educationalist Francesc Ferrer, who was accused of 'moral responsibility', despite the fact that he wasn't even in Barcelona at the time.

These events dented the optimism of the Catalanists of the Lliga. However, in 1914, they secured from Madrid the Mancomunitat, or administrative union, of the four Catalan provinces, the first joint government of any kind in Catalonia in 200 years. Its first president was Prat de la Riba, who would be succeeded on his death in 1917 by the architect Puig i Cadafalch. However, the Lliga's plans for an orderly Catalonia were to be obstructed by a further surge in social tensions.

CHAMPAGNE AND SOCIALISTS

Spain's neutral status during World War I gave a huge boost to the Spanish, and especially Catalan, economy. Exports soared as Catalonia's manufacturers made millions supplying uniforms to the French army. Barcelona's industry was at last able to diversify from textiles into engineering, chemicals and other more modern sectors. The war also set off massive inflation, driving people in their thousands from rural Spain into the big cities. Barcelona doubled in size in 20 years to become the largest city in Spain, and also the fulcrum of Spanish politics. Workers' wages, meanwhile, had lost half their real value.

The chief channel of protest in Barcelona was the anarchist workers' union, the Confederación Nacional del Trabajo (CNT), constituted in 1910, which gained half a million members in Catalonia by 1919. The CNT and the socialist Union General de Trabajadores (UGT) launched a joint general strike in 1917, roughly co-ordinated with a campaign by the Lliga and other liberal politicians for political reform. However, the politicians soon withdrew at the prospect of serious social unrest. Inflation continued to intensify, and in 1919 Barcelona was paralysed for more than two months by a CNT general strike over union recognition. Employers refused to recognise the CNT, and the most intransigent among them hired gunmen to get rid of union leaders. Union activists

IN CONTEXT

replied in kind, and virtual guerrilla warfare developed between the CNT, the employers and the state. More than 800 people were killed on the city's streets over five years.

In 1923, in response both to the chaos in the city and a crisis in the war in Morocco, the Captain-General of Barcelona, Miguel Primo de Rivera, staged a coup and established a military dictatorship under King Alfonso XIII. The CNT was already exhausted, and it was suppressed. Conservative Catalanists, longing for an end to disorder and the revolutionary threat, initially supported the coup, but were rewarded by the abolition of the Mancomunitat and a vindictive campaign by the Primo regime against the Catalan language and national symbols.

This, however, achieved the opposite of the desired effect, helping to radicalise and popularise Catalan nationalism. After the terrible struggles of the previous years, the 1920s were actually a time of notable prosperity for many in Barcelona, as some of the wealth recently accumulated filtered through the economy. It was also, though, a highly politicised society, in which new magazines and forums for discussion – despite the restrictions of the dictatorship – found a ready audience.

A prime motor of Barcelona's prosperity in the 1920s was the International Exhibition of 1929, the second of the city's great showcase events. It had been proposed by Cambó and Catalan business groups, but Primo de Rivera saw that it could also serve as a propaganda event for his regime. A huge number of public projects were undertaken in association with the main event, including the post office in Via Laietana, the Estació de França and Barcelona's first metro line, from Plaça Catalunya to Plaça d'Espanya. By 1930, Barcelona was very different from the place it had been in 1910; it contained more than a million people, and its urban sprawl had crossed into neighbouring towns such as Hospitalet and Santa Coloma.

A pro-Franco Fascist march in 1931.

THE REPUBLIC SUPPRESSED

Despite the Exhibition's success, Primo de Rivera resigned in January 1930, exhausted. The king appointed another soldier, General Berenguer, as prime minister, with the mission of restoring stability. The dictatorship, though, had fatally discredited the old regime, and a protest movement spread across Catalonia against the monarchy. In early 1931, Berenguer called local elections as a first step towards a restoration of constitutional rule. The outcome was a complete surprise, for republicans were elected in all of Spain's cities. Ecstatic crowds poured into the streets, and Alfonso XIII abdicated. The Second Spanish Republic was proclaimed on 14 April 1931.

The Republic arrived amid real euphoria, especially in Catalonia, where it was associated with hopes for both social change and national reaffirmation. The clear winner of the elections in the country had been the Esquerra Republicana, a leftist Catalanist group led by Francesc Macià. A raffish, elderly figure, Macià was one of the first politicians in Spain to win genuine affection from ordinary people. He declared Catalonia to be an independent republic within an Iberian federation of states, but later agreed to accept autonomy within the Spanish Republic.

The Generalitat was re-established as a government that would, potentially, acquire wide powers. All aspects of Catalan culture were then in expansion, and a popular press in Catalan achieved a wide readership. Barcelona was also a small but notable centre of the avant-garde. Miró and Dalí had already made their mark in painting; under the Republic, the Amics de l'Art Nou (ADLAN, Friends of New Art) group worked to promote contemporary art, while the GATCPAC architectural collective sought to bring rationalist architecture to the city.

In Madrid, the Republic's first government was a coalition of republicans and socialists led by Manuel Azaña, its overriding goal to modernise Spanish society through liberal-democratic reforms. However, as social tensions intensified, the coalition collapsed, and a conservative republican party, with support from the traditional Spanish right, secured power shortly after new elections in 1933. For Catalonia, the prospect of a return to right-wing rule prompted fears that it would immediately abrogate the Generalitat's hard-won powers. On 6 October 1934, while a general strike was launched against the central government in Asturias and some other parts of Spain, Lluís Companys, leader of the Generalitat since Macià's death the previous year, declared Catalonia independent. The 'uprising' turned out to be something of a farce, however: the Generalitat had no means of resisting the army, and the new 'Catalan Republic' was rapidly suppressed. The Generalitat was suspended and its leaders imprisoned.

Over the following year, fascism seemed to become a real threat for the left, as political positions became polarised. Then, in February 1936, elections were won by the Popular Front of the left across the country. The Generalitat was reinstated, and in Catalonia the next few months were peaceful. In the rest of Spain, though, tensions were close to bursting point; right-wing politicians, refusing to accept the loss of power, talked openly of the need for the military to intervene. In July, the stadium on Montjuïc was to be the site of the Popular Olympics, a leftist alternative to the 1936 Olympics in Nazi Germany. On 18 July, the day of the Games' inauguration, army generals launched a coup against the Republic and its left-wing governments, expecting no resistance.

UP IN ARMS

In Barcelona, militants from the unions and leftist parties, on alert for weeks, poured into the streets to oppose the troops in fierce fighting. Over the course of 19 July, the military were worn down, and finally surrendered in the Hotel Colón on Plaça Catalunya (by the corner with Passeig de Gràcia, the site of which is now occupied by the Radio Nacional de España building). Opinions have always differed as to who could claim most credit for this remarkable popular victory: workers' militants have suggested it

IN CONTEXT

'Barcelona also had the sad distinction of being the first major city in Europe to be subjected to sustained intensive bombing.'

was the 'people in arms' who defeated the army, while others stress the importance of the police remaining loyal to the Generalitat throughout the struggle. A likely answer is that they actually encouraged each other.

Tension released, the city was taken over by the revolution. Militias of the CNT, different Marxist parties and other left-wing factions marched off to Aragon, led by streetfighters such as the Durruti and García Oliver, to continue the battle. The army rising had failed in Spain's major cities but won footholds in Castile, Aragon and the south, athough in the heady atmosphere of Barcelona in July 1936 it was often assumed their resistance could not last and the people's victory was near inevitable.

Far from the front, Barcelona was the chief centre of the revolution in republican Spain, the only truly proletarian city. Its middle class avoided the streets, where, as Orwell recorded in his *Homage to Catalonia*, everyone you saw wore workers' clothing. It became a magnet for leftists from around the world, drawing writers André Malraux, Ernest Hemingway and Octavio Paz. All kinds of industries and public services were collectivised, including cinemas, the phone system and food distribution. Ad hoc 'control patrols' of the revolutionary militias roamed the streets supposedly checking for suspected right-wing agents and sometimes carrying out summary executions, although this was condemned by many leftist leaders.

The alliance between the different left-wing groups was unstable and riddled with tensions. The communists, who had some extra leverage because the Soviet Union was the only country prepared to give the Spanish Republic arms, demanded the integration of these loosely organised militias into a conventional army under a strong central authority. The following months saw continual political infighting between the discontented CNT, the radical Marxist party Partit Obrer d'Unificació Marxista (POUM) and the communists. Co-operation broke down totally in May 1937, when republican and communist troops seized the telephone building in Plaça Catalunya (on the corner of Portal de l'Àngel) from a CNT committee, sparking the confused war-within-the-civil-war witnessed by Orwell from the roof of the Teatre Poliorama. A temporary agreement was patched up, but shortly afterwards the POUM was banned, and the CNT excluded from power. A new republican central government was formed under Dr Juan Negrín, a socialist allied to the communists.

After that, the war gradually became more of a conventional conflict. This did little, however, to improve the Republic's position, for the nationalists under General Francisco Franco and their German and Italian allies had been continually gaining ground throughout it all. Madrid was under siege, and the capital of the Republic was moved to Valencia, and then to Barcelona, in November 1937.

Catalonia received thousands of refugees, as food shortages and the lack of armaments ground down morale. Barcelona also had the sad distinction of being the first major city in Europe to be subjected to sustained intensive bombing – to an extent that has rarely been appreciated – with heavy raids throughout 1938, especially by Italian bombers based in Mallorca. The Basque Country and Asturias had already fallen to Franco, and in March 1938 his troops reached the Mediterranean near Castellón, cutting the main Republican zone in two. The Republic had one last throw of the dice, in the Battle of the Ebro in the summer of 1938, when for months the Popular Army struggled to retake control of the river. After that, the Republic was exhausted. Barcelona fell to the Francoist army on 26 January 1939. Half a million refugees fled to France, to be interned in barbed-wire camps along the beaches.

THE FRANCO YEARS

In Catalonia, the Franco regime was iron-fisted and especially vengeful. Thousands of Catalan republicans and leftists were executed, among them Generalitat president Lluís Companys; exile and deportation were the fate of thousands more. Publishing, teaching and any other public cultural expression in Catalan, including even speaking it in the street, were prohibited, and every Catalanist monument in the city was dismantled. All independent political activity was suspended, and the entire political and cultural development of the country was brought to an abrupt halt.

The epic nature of the Spanish Civil War is known worldwide; more present in the collective memory of Barcelona, though, is the long *posguerra* or post-war period, which lasted for nearly two decades after 1939. During those years, the city was impoverished, and food and electricity were rationed; Barcelona would not regain its prior standard of living until the mid 1950s. Nevertheless, migrants in flight from the still more brutal poverty of the south flowed into the city, occupying precarious shanty towns around Montjuïc and other areas in the outskirts.

The Franco regime was subject to a UN embargo after World War II. Years of international isolation and attempted self-sufficiency came to an end in 1953, when the country was at least partially re-admitted to the western fold. Even a limited opening to the outside world meant that foreign money finally began to enter the country, and the regime relaxed some control over its population. In 1959, the Plan de Estabilización ('Stabilisation Plan'), drawn up by Catholic technocrats of Opus Dei, brought Spain definitively within the western economy, throwing its doors wide open to tourism and foreign investment. After years of austerity, tourist income at last brought the Europe-wide 1960s boom to Spain and set off change at an extraordinary pace.

After the years of repression and the years of development, 1966 marked the beginning of what became known as *tardofranquisme*, 'late Francoism'. Having made its opening to the outside world, the regime was losing its grip, and labour, youth and student movements began to emerge from the shroud of repression. Nevertheless, the Franco regime never hesitated to show its strength. Strikes and demonstrations were dealt with savagely, and just months before the dictator's death, the last person to be executed in Spain by the traditional method of the garrotte, a Catalan anarchist named Puig Antich, went to his death in Barcelona. In 1973, however, Franco's closest follower, Admiral Carrero Blanco, was assassinated by a bomb planted by the Basque terrorist group ETA, leaving no one to guard over the core values of the regime.

GENERALISIMO TO GENERALITAT

When Franco died on 20 November 1975, the people of Barcelona took to the streets in celebration; by evening, there was not a bottle of cava left in the city. But no one knew quite what would happen next. The Bourbon monarchy was restored under King Juan Carlos, but his attitude and intentions were not clear. In 1976, he charged a little-known Francoist bureaucrat, Adolfo Suárez, with leading the country to democracy.

The first years of Spain's 'transition' were difficult. Nationalist and other demonstrations continued to be repressed by the police with considerable brutality, and far-right groups threatened less open violence. However, political parties were legalised, and June 1977 saw the first democratic elections since 1936. They were won across Spain by Suárez's own new party, the Union de Centro Democratico (UCD), and in Catalonia by a mixture of socialists, communists and nationalists.

It was, again, not clear how Suárez expected to deal with the demands of Catalonia, but shortly after the elections he surprised everyone by visiting the president of the Generalitat in exile, veteran pre-Civil War politician Josep Tarradellas. His office was the only institution of the old Republic to be so recognised, perhaps because Suárez astutely identified in the old man a fellow conservative. Tarradellas was invited to return as provisional president of a restored Generalitat; he arrived amid huge crowds in October 1977.

IN CONTEXT

The following year, the first free council elections since 1936 were held in Barcelona. They were won by the Socialist Party, with Narcís Serra appointed as mayor. The party has retained control of the council ever since. In 1980, elections to the restored Generalitat were won by Jordi Pujol and his party, Convergència i Unió (CiU), who held power for 23 years.

Inseparable from the restoration of democracy was a change in the city's atmosphere after 1975. New freedoms – in culture, sexuality and work – were explored, and energies released in a multitude of ways. Barcelona began to look different too, as the dowdiness of the Franco years was swept away by a new Catalan style: postmodern, high-tech, comic strip, minimalist and tautly fashionable. This emphasis first began underground, but it was soon taken up by public authorities and, above all, the Ajuntament, as a part of its drive to reverse the policies of the regime. The technocrats in the socialist city administration began to 'recover' the city from its neglected state, and in doing so enlisted the support of the Catalan artistic elite. No one epitomises this more than Oriol Bohigas, the architect and writer who was long the city's head of culture and chief planner. A programme of urban renewal was initiated, beginning with the open spaces, public art and low-level initiatives, such as the campaign in which hundreds of historic façades were given an overdue facelift.

This ambitious, modern approach to urban problems acquired greater focus after Barcelona's bid to host the 1992 Olympic Games was accepted, in 1986. Far more than just a sports event, the Games were to be Barcelona's third great effort to cast aside suggestions of second-city status. The exhibitions of 1888 and 1929 had seen developments in the Ciutadella and on Montjuïc; the Olympics provided an opening for work on a citywide scale. Taking advantage of the investment the Games would attract, Barcelona planned an all-new orientation towards the sea, in a programme of urban renovation of a scope unseen in Europe since the years after World War II.

Inseparable from all this was Pasqual Maragall, mayor of Barcelona from 1982 to 1997, a tireless 'Mr Barcelona' who appeared in every forum to expound his vision of the role of cities. He intervened personally to set guidelines for projects and to secure the participation of major international architects. In the process, Barcelona, previously a byword for modern blight, was turned into a reference point in urban affairs.

ENDGAMES

The Olympic Games were held in July and August 1992 and universally hailed as a success. The cultural legacy of the Games remains strong, with landmarks such as Frank Gehry's Fish now major tourist attractions. However, Pasqual Maragall, was to stand down amid surprise in 1997, and went on to become the Socialist candidate for President of the Generalitat in 1999. He would not succeed until 2003, when he enjoyed a muted triumph in the regional elections. Maragall took control of the Generalitat in return for a commitment to push for an Autonomy Statute. In this he was partly successful, but many felt he should have pushed for more devolution of power, and he stepped down for the elections in November 2006; in his place the Partit dels Socialistes del Catalunya (PSC) chose as candidate Andalucía-born José Montilla.

Those elections also failed to bring home an absolute winner; further negotiations resulted in the same tripartite coalition as in the previous election, therefore giving the presidency to Montilla, the first ever non-Catalan President of the Generalitat. Over at City Hall, meanwhile, Maragall had been replaced with smooth-talking Joan Clos. His successor, Jordi Hereu, brought the Socialist Party to another (slim) victory in the local elections of May 2007, having also formed a coalition with the 'eco-communists' (ICV), though not, this time, with Esquerra Republicana (ERC), the Republican left. The Spanish general elections held in March 2008 saw a return of José Luis Zapatero and his Socialist party for a second term, but the regional Socialists, under Montilla, ceded control of the Generalitat to the CiU and new President Artur Mas in the Catalan elections of 2010.

Barcelona Today

The city faces down the economic crisis with difficulty.

TEXT: WILLIAM TRUINI

On the face of it, Barcelona is weathering the ongoing economic slump better than other areas of Spain. Unemployment rates in the Catalan capital continue to be about half the staggering 21 per cent found generally in the country and, although the local economy remains sluggish, the second half of 2010 saw a small but much welcome increase in the number of new businesses setting up shop in the city.

However, it's hard to ignore signs that Barcelona's resilience is wearing thin. It's not uncommon, for example, to see stalled or abandoned building projects around town, most prominently in Plaça Catalunya, where the façade of a long-vacant, eight-storey former bank was recently graced with defiant, giant-lettered graffiti: 'This isn't a crisis, it's called Capitalism.' Also telling is the Ajuntament's decision to fence off a series of emblematic public spaces that previously provided improvised shelter to a small but growing number of the homeless, such as the arcaded periphery of La Boqueria market (to be closed at night) and the highly visible, exterior nooks of the MACBA.

'The city's self-esteem was given a boost when it was officially chosen to be the seat of the Euro-Mediterranean Association.'

General discontent with the state of things, at any rate, was well reflected in the Catalan parliamentary elections held in late 2010. The incumbent socialists, in power for the past seven years, suffered a resounding defeat – their worst loss since the restoration of democracy. Victory went to the conservative Catalan nationalists, Convergència i Unió (CiU), who rode into power just a few seats shy of an absolute parliamentary majority. Led by the square-jawed, family man Artur Mas, CiU in many ways reflects the quintessence of present-day Catalonia: pro-business and proudly nationalistic but opportunistically vague on the hot subject of the moment, mainly whether Catalan independence from the rest of Spain should be taken seriously or not. CiU is by no means a new player in the field, having reigned supreme in Catalonia for 23 years straight prior to the socialists' stint in office. The party's victory thus marks a return to a well-trodden path at a time of considerable economic uncertainty.

INDEPENDENCE PAYS

The recent elections also saw the political debut of Joan Laporta, the popular former president of Barça, who ran on a one-themed ticket: immediate Catalan independence. Surprisingly (or perhaps not so, given the incredible success Barça enjoyed under his stewardship), Laporta's self-created independence party won four parliamentary seats, stealing votes from the likewise pro-independence but leftist party, Esquerra Republicana (ERC). In yet another sign of Catalan ambiguity on the subject of independence, ERC, long-time veterans of Catalan politics, were severely chastised in the same elections, losing more than half their seats. The hubbub about Catalan nationhood has in part been fuelled by a recent, unofficial referendum on the subject held in Catalonia. Although the turnout was lower than expected at around 30 per cent, those who did vote were a whopping 95 per cent in favour of independence. Spain's government dismissed the independence vote as illegitimate, but the campaign stirred deep feelings, particularly in these dire economic times. Economics, in fact, was the sole message of Laporta's single-minded run, his argument being that it simply didn't make economic sense for Catalonia to remain within Spain. Catalonia, in effect, pays out more money to Spain than it gets back, to the tune of 22,000 million euros a year.

Catalan *seny*, or common-sense, however, generally takes a much less hard-line approach to the drive for greater autonomy, which explains the massive support for the middle of the road nationalism of CiU. In this respect, many Catalans recognise it would be folly to truncate ties with what is by far the largest market for Catalunya's goods and services: the rest of Spain. Even so, these are special times, and as Spain tightens its belt and squeezes funds from where it can, the question of independence, gradual or otherwise, is not something that is going to vanish from public discourse any time soon.

Whether or not Barcelona ends up a bona fide national capital in its own right, the city's self-esteem was given a boost not so long ago when it was officially chosen to be the seat of the Euro-Mediterranean Association, an organisation made up of 43 different European and Mediterranean countries in Europe, Africa, Asia Minor and the Middle East. The title has so far meant little more than an annual gathering in the city to discuss pan-Mediterranean issues, but being capital of the Med sits well with Barcelona's image of itself. Indeed, the title harks back to the golden days of the 13th century, when the metropolis ruled the Mediterranean through an astute combination of naval, military and commercial prowess. This time around, however, the primary objectives are to promote mutual prosperity through peaceful exchange and deal with the increasingly severe environmental problems facing the sea.

How Barcelona itself is dealing with the downturn, meanwhile, is still very much a work in progress. During two decades of roaring development, some attention was paid to embellishing low-income peripheral zones with sculptures and parks, and opening up and modernising some of the city's inner neighbourhoods, but the real money went into shiny, high-end real estate schemes. While the economic winds were favourable, complaints were few and far between. But after the market went into a tailspin, people began wondering why the city hadn't spent more on social services, public housing and neighbourhood facilities. So what next?

NEW FACES

The economic downturn has thrown into high relief what's currently most remarkable about the city, as well as the challenges confronting it. For starters, the crisis has shone the spotlight on one of Barcelona's newest and most visible faces: massive, non-European immigration. While the city owes its existence to immigration of one kind or another, never before in its 2,000-year history have so many people from outside Europe come here to live. During the recent boom, people poured in from around the planet, with China, South America, Pakistan, North Africa and the Philippines providing the largest number of newcomers. The proportion of foreign residents in the long-notorious but recently revamped Raval has gone from around five per cent to almost 50 per cent in just 15 years, and is now home to more than 70 different nationalities.

Unemployment has hit the newest arrivals hard, with the jobless rate climbing to well over 20 per cent in the Raval. As times have become tougher, the number of incoming immigrants has declined sharply, but those already here have begun to find their voice. Immigrant associations have started to call for more social services. Moroccan-born Mohammed Chaib, meanwhile, became the first Muslim elected to the Catalan Parliament, supported in part by the 300,000 Muslims who now live in Catalonia.

The enormous change in cultural and racial composition of significant zones of the city has generated relatively little social tension. That said, a striking new feature of the Catalan elections in late 2010 was the openness by which some rightwing parties, such as Plataforma per Catalunya (PxC) and Partido Popular de Catalunya (PPC), campaigned

against immigration. Just a few years ago, such brazen political incorrectness, not to mention racism, would have been unthinkable. During the run-up to the recent election, the PPC posted a mock video game on its website, portraying the party's leader as a Lara Croft-like heroine who won points by gunning down immigrants. While PxC failed to win representation, the PPC increased the number of their total seats by four.

CIVIL DISOBEDIENCE

Although xenophobia is very much a minority sentiment, in some areas of Barcelona, particularly the Old City, there's a tangible sense that civilised life is being overwhelmed on various fronts. Fingers are pointed at the hordes of all-night revellers (fuelled in part by illegal street vendors of canned beer, known as *lateros*), the mounds of rubbish and the non-stop, year-round tourist presence.

Of particular concern for image-conscious Barcelona has been the jump in street prostitution on and around La Rambla. To deal with the situation, the city council has encouraged the opening of discreet brothels and tried to relocate the pick-up zone to other, less central areas and, as mentioned above, has decided to fence off La Boqueria at night. But with more than a million people walking down La Rambla each week, it seems unlikely that such a lucrative beat will be abandoned. And one can't help wondering whether the media hysterics over the prostitutes' unabashed presence stems in part from a wish to hide the fact that Barcelona is similarly guilty of selling itself, in a degrading way, to souvenir shops and multinational chains.

One consequence of Barcelona's continued international popularity is that it has become a victim of its own success. Ironically, this means the formerly permissive city has had to start prohibiting the very things it promotes. It started with the so-called 'civic laws' passed a few years ago, which made it illegal to drink alcohol in the street. These laws coincided with a licensing clampdown that resulted in the closure of a number of classic bars, and the strict prohibition of live music anywhere but in bars with music licences. A freeze was also placed on the granting of any new licences for bars and restaurants in the Old City. Perhaps most ironically, a number of squares are being remodelled to reduce their user-friendliness, such as the Plaça George Orwell, colloquially know as the 'Plaça del Trippy', whose bench-like steps are being removed to prevent people from sitting around and hanging out, Barcelona-style. Whether all these measures will help Barcelona lead a more wholesome lifestyle is yet to be seen.

LOOKING AHEAD

On green matters, Barcelona is beginning to face up to the huge environmental challenges that confront any large metropolis. The city's famous capacity for civic action has been visible in the huge increase in regular cyclists making use of its bike lanes and of the hugely popular municipal bike-share scheme, Bicing. For a number of years, a municipal ordinance has required that all new buildings must be fitted with solar panels for thermally heating water; city-wide organic waste recycling was also recently incorporated into the well-established recycling of paper, glass, metal and plastic trash. And the city has opened an attractive, environmental education centre, the Fàbrica del Sol, in the former headquarters of the defunct gas factory in Barceloneta.

Finally, crisis or no crisis, Barcelona continues to build striking new buildings, which mostly fall into one of two categories: cutting-edge structures to further the city's bid to become a leading player in the knowledge economy, such as Zaha Hadid's Spiralling Tower and Enric Massip-Bosch's slender high-rise wedge Torre Diagonal Zero Zero, both near the Fórum; and extraordinary hotels designed to keep the city in the fast track of the luxury tourism industry. Foremost in this latter category is the W Hotel on Barceloneta beach. Ricardo Bofill originally planned the building to be much taller, but the Ajuntament managed to rein in the building's size and demand that the Port, which owns and leases the hotel's land, build a spacious new beachside promenade leading up to the huge glass structure. As always, the city knows how to cut deals.

Architecture

*Innovation galore, from Modernisme
to modern urban design.*

TEXT: NICK RIDER & SALLY DAVIES.

Architecture is sometimes regarded as Catalonia's greatest contribution to art history. Catalan craftsmen have been famed since the Middle Ages for their use of fine materials and skilled finishings, while Catalan architects have long been both artists and innovators: traditional Catalan brick-vaulting techniques were the basis of visionary structural innovations that allowed later architects to span larger spaces and build higher structures. Contemporary Catalan architects such as Ricardo Bofill and Enric Miralles have inherited the international prestige of their forebears.

Unlike many European cities, Barcelona has never rested on its architectural laurels or tried to preserve its old buildings as relics. Contemporary buildings are often daringly constructed alongside or even within old ones, a mix of old and new that characterises some of the most successful recent projects seen in Barcelona, such as Arato Isozaik's dramatically modern, Louvre-style entrance plaza to the Casaramona textile factory at the CaixaForum. Barcelona's citizens take a keen interest in their buildings, and tourists are encouraged to do the same: a range of architectural guides is available, some in English, and informative leaflets on building styles are offered (in English) at the city's tourist offices.

Sant Pau del Camp.

ROMAN TO GOTHIC

The Roman citadel of Barcino was founded on the hill of Mons Taber, just behind the cathedral, which to this day remains the religious and civic heart of the city. It left an important legacy in the fourth-century city wall, fragments of which are visible at many points around the Old City. Barcelona's next occupiers, the Visigoths, left little, although a trio of fine Visigothic churches survives in nearby Terrassa.

When the Catalan state began to form under the counts of Barcelona from the ninth century, its dominant architecture was Romanesque. The Pyrenean valleys hold hundreds of fine Romanesque buildings, notably at Sant Pere de Rodes, Ripoll, Sant Joan de les Abadesses and Besalú, but there are very few in Barcelona. On the right-hand side of the cathedral (if you're looking at the main façade) sits the 13th-century chapel of Santa Llúcia, eventually incorporated into the later building; the church of Santa Anna is tucked away near Plaça Catalunya; and the Born is home to the Capella d'en Marcús, a tiny travellers' chapel. But the city's greatest Romanesque monument is the beautifully plain 12th-century church and cloister of **Sant Pau del Camp** (*see p74*), part of a larger monastery.

By the 13th century, Barcelona was the capital of a trading empire and had started to grow rapidly. The settlements – called *ravals* or *vilanoves* – that had sprung up outside the Roman walls were brought within the city by the building of Jaume I's second set of walls, which extended west to La Rambla. This commercial growth and political eminence set the scene for the great flowering of the Catalan Gothic style, which saw the construction of many of the city's most important civic and religious buildings. The cathedral was begun in 1298, in place of an 11th-century building. Work began on the **Ajuntament** (Casa de la Ciutat; *see p56*) and the **Palau de la Generalitat** (*see p59*), later subject to extensive alteration, in 1372 and 1403 respectively. Major additions were made to the Palau Reial of the Catalan-Aragonese kings, especially the **Saló del Tinell** of 1359-62. And the great hall of **La Llotja** (the Stock Exchange) was built between 1380 and 1392.

The Catalan Gothic style is distinguished from classic northern Gothic by its relative simplicity. It also gives more prominence to solid, plain walls between towers and columns, rather than the empty spaces between intricate flying buttresses that were the hallmarks of the great French cathedrals, with the result that Catalan buildings appear much larger. On the façades, as much emphasis is given to horizontals as to verticals; octagonal towers end in cornices and flat roofs, not spires. And the decorative intricacies are mainly confined to windows, portals, arches and gargoyles. Many churches have no aisles but only a single nave; the classic example of this style is the beautiful **Santa Maria del Pi** in Plaça del Pi, built between 1322 and 1453.

The Catalan Gothic style went on to establish a historic benchmark for Catalan architecture: simple and robust, yet elegant and practical. Sophisticated techniques were developed as part of the style: the use of transverse arches supporting timber roofs, for instance, allowed the spanning of great halls uninterrupted by columns, a system used in Guillem Carbonel's Saló del Tinell. The **Drassanes**, built from 1378 as the royal shipyards (and now the Museu Marítim; *see p78*), is really just a very beautiful shed, but its enormous parallel aisles make it one of the city's most imposing spaces.

Around this time, La Ribera (nowadays known as Sant Pere and the Born) was the commercial centre of the city. Its pre-eminence resulted in the construction of **Santa Maria del Mar** (*see p69*), the magnificent masterpiece of Catalan Gothic built between 1329 and 1384. The building's superb proportions are based on a series of squares imposed on one another, with three aisles of almost equal height. The interior is staggering in its austerity.

The architecture of medieval Barcelona, at least that of its noble and merchant residences, can be seen at its best along **Carrer Montcada**, next to Santa Maria. Built by the city's merchant elite at the height of its confidence and wealth, this line of buildings conforms to a very Mediterranean style of urban palace and makes maximum use of space. A plain exterior faces the street with heavy doors opening into an imposing patio; on one side, a grand external staircase leads to the main rooms on the first floor (*planta noble*), which often have elegant open loggias.

MARKING TIME

By the beginning of the 16th century, a period of political and economic downturn, the number of patrons for new city buildings declined. The next 300 years saw plenty of construction, but rarely in any distinctively Catalan style; as a result, these structures have often been disregarded.

The Church also built lavishly around this time. Of the Baroque convents and churches along La Rambla, the **Betlem** (1680-1729), at the corner of C/Carme, is the most important survivor. Later Baroque churches include **Sant Felip Neri** (1721-52) and **La Mercè** (1765-75; *see p56*). Another addition, after the siege of Barcelona in 1714, was new military architecture, since the city was encased in ramparts and fortresses. Examples include the **Castell de Montjuïc** (*see p84*), the buildings in the **Ciutadella**, and Barceloneta.

One more positive 18th-century alteration was the conversion of La Rambla into a paved promenade, a project that began in 1775 with the demolition of Jaume I's second wall. Neo-classical palaces were built alongside: **La Virreina** and the **Palau Moja** (at the corner of C/Portaferrisa) both date from the 1770s. Also from that time, but in a less classical style, is the **Gremial dels Velers** (Candlemakers' Guild) at Via Laietana 50, with its two-colour stucco decoration.

However, it wasn't until the closure of the monasteries in the 1820s and '30s that major rebuilding on La Rambla could begin. Most of the new constructions were in international, neo-classical styles. The site that now holds the **Mercat de la Boqueria** was first remodelled in 1836-40 as Plaça Sant Josep to a design by Francesc Daniel Molina, based on the English Regency style of John Nash; it's now buried beneath the 1870s market building, but its Doric colonnade can still be detected. Molina also

IN CONTEXT

'The interplay between the Eixample's straight lines and the disorderly tangle of the older city became an essential part of the city's identity.'

designed the **Plaça Reial** (*see p55*), begun in 1848. Other fine examples include the colonnaded Porxos d'en Xifré, blocks built in 1836 opposite the Llotja on Passeig Isabel II by the Port Vell.

BIRTH OF THE MODERN CITY

In the 1850s, Barcelona was able to expand physically, with the demolition of the walls, and psychologically, with economic expansion and the cultural reawakening of the Catalan Renaixença. One of the characteristics of modern Barcelona was clearly visible from the start: audacious planning. The city eventually expanded outwards and was connected to Gràcia and other outlying towns through the **Eixample** (*see pp90-99*), designed by Ildefons Cerdà. An engineer by trade, Cerdà was influenced by socialist ideas, and concerned with the poor condition of workers' housing in the Old City.

With its straight lines and grids, Cerdà's plan was closely related to the visionary rationalist ideas of its time, as was the idea of placing two of its main avenues along a geographic parallel and a meridian. Cerdà's central aim was to alleviate overpopulation while encouraging social equality by using quadrangular blocks of a standard size, with strict building controls to ensure they were built only on two sides, to a limited height, and with a garden. Each district would be of 20 blocks, with all community necessities.

However, this idealised use of space was rarely achieved, with private developers regarding Cerdà's restrictions as pointless interference. New buildings exceeded planned heights, and all the blocks from Plaça Catalunya to the Diagonal were enclosed. Even the planned gardens failed to withstand the onslaught of construction. Still, the development of the Eixample did see the refinement of a specific type of building: the apartment block, with giant flats on the principal floor (first above the ground), often with large glassed-in galleries for the drawing room, and small flats above. In time, the interplay between the Eixample's straight lines and the disorderly tangle of the older city became an essential part of the city's identity.

MODERNISME

The art nouveau style was the leading influence in the decorative arts in Europe and the US between 1890 and 1914. In Barcelona, its influence merged with the cultural and political movement of the Catalan Renaixença to produce what became known as Modernisme (used here in Catalan to avoid confusion with 'modernism' in English, which refers to 20th-century functional styles).

For all Catalonia's traditions in building and the arts, no style is as synonymous with Barcelona as Modernisme. This is due to the huge modern popularity of Antoni Gaudí, its most famous practitioner, and to its mix of decoration, eccentric unpredictability, dedicated craftsmanship and practicality. Modernisme can also be seen as matching certain archetypes of Catalan character, as a passionately nationalist expression that made use of Catalan traditions of design and craftwork. Artists strove to revalue the best of Catalan art, showing interest in the Romanesque and Gothic of the Catalan Golden Age; Domènech i Montaner combined iron-frame construction with distinctive brick Catalan styles from the Middle Ages, regarding them as an 'expression of the Catalan earth'.

Art nouveau had a tendency to look at both the past and future, combining a love of decoration with new industrial techniques and materials. Even as they constructed a nostalgic vision of the Catalan motherland, Modernista architects experimented with

Sagrada Familia. *See p41.*

IN CONTEXT

Casa Batlló.

new technology. Encouraged by wealthy patrons, they designed works made of iron and glass, introduced electricity, water and gas piping to building plans, were the first to tile bathroom and kitchen walls, made a point of allowing extensive natural light and fresh air into all rooms, and toyed with the most advanced, revolutionary expressionism.

Catalan Modernista creativity was at its peak from 1888 to 1908. The Eixample is the style's display case, with the greatest concentration of art nouveau in Europe, but Modernista buildings can be found in innumerable other locations: in streets behind the Avda Paral·lel and villas on Tibidabo, in shop interiors and dark hallways, in country town halls and in the cava cellars of the Penedès.

International interest in Gaudí often eclipses the fact that many other remarkable architects and designers worked at the same time. Indeed, Modernisme was much more than an architectural style: the movement also included painters such as Ramon Casas, Santiago Rusiñol and Isidre Nonell, sculptors Josep Llimona, Miquel Blay and Eusebi Arnau, and furniture-makers such as the superb Mallorcan Gaspar Homar. More than any other form of art nouveau, Modernisme extended into literature, thought and music, marking a whole generation of Catalan writers, poets, composers and philosophers. It found its most splendid expression in architecture, but Modernisme was an artistic movement in the fullest sense of the word. In Catalonia, it took on a nationalistic element.

GAUDÍ'S VISION

Although Antoni Gaudí i Cornet is widely regarded as the genius of the Modernista movement, he was really an unclassifiable one-off. His work was a product of the social and cultural context of the time, but also of his individual perception of the world, together with a deep patriotic devotion to anything Catalan.

Gaudí worked first as assistant to Josep Fontseré in the 1870s on the building of the **Parc de la Ciutadella** (*see p69*); the gates and fountain are attributed to him. Around the same time, he designed the lamp-posts in the Plaça Reial, but his first major commission was for **Casa Vicens** (*see p101*) in Gràcia, built between 1883 and 1888. An orientalist fantasy, the building is structurally conventional, but Gaudí's use of surface material stands out in the neo-Moorish decoration, multicoloured tiling and superbly elaborate ironwork on the gates. His **Col·legi de les Teresianes** convent school (1888-89) is more restrained, but the clarity and fluidity of the building are very appealing.

In 1878, Gaudí met Eusebi Güell, heir to one of the largest industrial fortunes in Catalonia. The pair shared ideas on religion, philanthropy and the socially redemptive role of architecture, and Gaudí produced several buildings for Güell. Among them were **Palau Güell** (1886-88; *see p74*), an impressive, historicist building that established his reputation, and the crypt at **Colònia Güell** outside Barcelona, one of his most structurally experimental and surprising buildings.

In 1883, Gaudí became involved in the design of the **Sagrada Família** (*see p91*, which had been started the previous year. From 1908 until his death in 1926, he worked on no other projects, a shabby, white-haired hermit producing visionary ideas that his assistants had to interpret into drawings (on show in the museum alongside). Gaudí was profoundly religious, and part of his obsession with the building came from a belief that it would help redeem Barcelona from the sins of secularism and the modern era.

Although he lived to see the completion of only the crypt, apse and Nativity façade, with its representation of 30 species of plants, the Sagrada Família became the testing ground for Gaudí's ideas on structure and form. As his work matured, he abandoned historicism and developed free-flowing, sinuous expressionist forms. His boyhood interest in nature began to take over from more architectural references, and what had previously provided external decorative motifs became the inspiration for the actual structure of his buildings.

In his greatest years, Gaudí combined other commissions with his cathedral. **La Pedrera** (*see p97*), which he began in 1905, was his most complete project. The building has an aquatic feel about it: the balconies resemble seaweed, while the undulating façade is reminiscent of the sea, or rocks washed by it. The **Casa Batlló** (*see p92*), on the other side of Passeig de Gràcia, was an existing building that Gaudí remodelled in 1905-07; the roof looks like a reptilian creature perched high above the street. The symbolism of the façade is the source of speculation: some link it to the myth of St George and the dragon, but others say it's a celebration of carnival, with its harlequin-hat roof, wrought-iron balcony 'masks' and confetti-like tiles. This last element was the work of Josep Maria Jujol, who many believe was an even more skilled mosaicist than his master.

Gaudí's fascination with natural forms found full expression in the **Park Güell** (1900-14; *see p101*), for which he blurred the distinction between natural and artificial forms in a series of colonnades winding up a hill. These paths lead up to the large central terrace projecting over a hall; a forest of distorted Doric columns planned as the marketplace for Güell's proposed 'garden city'. The terrace benches are covered in some of the finest examples of *trencadís* (broken mosaic work), again mostly by Jujol.

BEYOND THE MASTER

Modernista architecture received a vital, decisive boost around the turn of the 19th century from the Universal Exhibition of 1888. The most important buildings for the show were planned by Lluís Domènech i Montaner (1850-1923), who was both far more prominent than Gaudí as a propagandist for Modernisme in all its forms and far more of a classic Modernista architect. Domènech was one of the first Modernista architects to develop the idea of the 'total work', working closely with teams of craftsmen and designers on every aspect of a building. His admirers dubbed him 'the great orchestra conductor'.

IN CONTEXT

Most of the Exhibition buildings no longer exist, but the **Castell dels Tres Dragons** in the Parc de la Ciutadella has survived. Designed as the Exhibition restaurant (it's now the Museu de Zoologia), the building demonstrated many key features of Modernista style: the use of structural ironwork allowed greater freedom in the creation of openings, arches and windows; while plain brick, instead of the stucco usually applied to most buildings, was used in an exuberantly decorative manner.

Domènech's greatest creations are the **Hospital de la Santa Creu i Sant Pau** (*see p96*), built as small 'pavilions' within a garden to avoid the usual effect of a monolithic hospital, and the **Palau de la Música Catalana** (*see p69*), an extraordinary display of outrageous decoration. He also left impressive constructions in Reus, notably the **Casa Navàs** and **Casa Rull** mansions, and the amazing pavilions of the **Institut Pere Mata**, a psychiatric hospital and forerunner of the Hospital de Sant Pau.

Third in the trio of leading Modernista architects was Josep Puig i Cadafalch (1867-1957), who combined traditional Catalan touches with a neo-Gothic influence in such buildings as the **Casa de les Punxes** ('House of Spikes'; officially the Casa Terrades; *see p91*) in the Diagonal. Nearby on Passeig de Sant Joan, at No.108, is another masterpiece: the **Casa Macaya**, its inner courtyard inspired by the medieval palaces of C/Montcada. Puig was also responsible for some of the best industrial architecture of the time, an area in which Modernisme excelled. The **Fàbrica Casaramona**, near the Plaça Espanya, was built as a textile mill and now houses the CaixaForum (*see p84*); outside Barcelona, he also designed the extraordinary **Caves Codorníu** wine cellars. But his best-known work is the **Casa Amatller** (*see p92*), between Domènech's **Casa Lleó Morera** and Gaudí's Casa Batlló in the extraordinary **Manzana de la Discòrdia**.

Modernisme caught on with extraordinary vigour all over Catalonia, but some of its most engaging architects are little known internationally. Impressive apartment blocks and mansions were built in the Eixample by Joan Rubió i Bellver (**Casa Golferichs**, Gran Via 491), Salvador Valeri (**Casa Comalat**, Avda Diagonal 442) and Josep Vilaseca. North of Barcelona is La Garriga, where MJ Raspall built exuberant summer houses for

Pavelló de la República.

'Budgets were limited, so the public funds were initially concentrated not on buildings but on the gaps between them.'

the rich and fashionable families of the time; there are also some dainty Modernista residences in coast towns, such as Canet and Arenys de Mar. Some of the finest Modernista industrial architecture is in Terrassa, designed by the municipal architect Lluís Moncunill (1868-1931). And Cèsar Martinell, another local architect, built co-operative cellars that are true 'wine cathedrals' in Falset, Gandesa and many other towns in southern Catalonia.

THE 20TH CENTURY

By the 1910s, Modernisme had become too extreme for Barcelona's middle classes; Gaudí's later buildings were met with derision. The new 'proper' style for Catalan architecture was Noucentisme, which stressed the importance of classical proportions. However, it produced little of note: the main buildings that survive are those of the 1929 Exhibition, Barcelona's next 'big event' that served as the excuse for the bizarre, neo-Baroque **Palau Nacional** (now home to the MNAC; *see p86*). The Exhibition also brought the city one of the most important buildings of the century: Ludwig Mies van der Rohe's German Pavilion, the **Pavelló Barcelona**, rebuilt near its original location in 1986. Its impact at the time was extraordinary; even today, it seems modern in its challenge to the conventional ideas of space.

Mies van der Rohe had a strong influence on the main new trend in Catalan architecture of the 1930s, which, reacting against Modernisme and nearly all earlier Catalan styles, was quite emphatically functionalist. Its leading figures were Josep Lluís Sert (1902-83) and the GATCPAC collective (Group of Catalan Architects and Technicians for the Progress of Contemporary Architecture), who struggled to introduce the ideas of Le Corbusier and of the International Style. Under the Republic, Sert built a sanatorium off C/Tallers and the Casa Bloc, a workers' housing project at Passeig Torres i Bages 91-105 in Sant Andreu.

In collaboration with Le Corbusier, GATCPAC also produced a plan for the radical redesign of the whole of Barcelona as a 'functional city', the Pla Macià of 1933-34. Drawings for the scheme present a Barcelona that looks more like a Soviet-era new town in Siberia, and few regret that it never got off the drawing board. In 1937, Sert also built the Spanish Republic's pavilion for that year's Paris Exhibition, since rebuilt in Barcelona as the **Pavelló de la República** (*see p110*) in the Vall d'Hebron. However, his finest work came much later in the shape of the **Fundació Joan Miró** (*see p82*), built in the 1970s after he had spent many years in exile in the United States.

BARCELONA'S NEW STYLE

The Franco years had an enormous impact on the city. As the economy expanded at breakneck pace in the 1960s, Barcelona received a massive influx of migrants, in a context of unchecked property speculation and minimal planning controls; the city became ringed by a chaotic mass of high-rise suburbs. Another legacy of the era are some ostentatiously tall office blocks, especially on the Diagonal and around Plaça Francesc Macià.

When a democratic city administration took over at the end of the 1970s, there was much to be done. A generation of architects had been chafing at Francoist restrictions. However, the tone set early on – above all by Barcelona's chief planner Oriol Bohigas, who has continued to design individual buildings as part of the MBM partnership with Josep Martorell and David Mackay – was one of 'architectural realism', with a powerful

IN CONTEXT

combination of imagination and practicality. Budgets were limited, so the public's hard-earned funds were initially concentrated not on buildings but on the gaps between them: public spaces, a string of modern parks and squares, many of which were to incorporate original artwork. From this quiet beginning, Barcelona placed itself at the forefront of international urban design.

Barcelona's renewal programme took on a more ambitious shape with the 1992 Olympics. The third and most spectacular of the city's great events, the Games were intended to be stylish and innovative, but they were also designed to provide a focus for a sweeping renovation of the city, with emblematic new buildings (such as Lord Foster's **Torre de Collserola**; *see p104*) and infrastructure projects linked by clear strategic planning.

The three main Olympic sites are quite different. The **Vila Olímpica** (*see p80*) had the most comprehensive masterplan: drawn up by Bohigas and MBM themselves, it sought to extend Cerdà's grid down to the seafront. The main project on **Montjuïc** (*see pp81-89*) was the transformation of the 1929 stadium, but there's also Arata Isozaki's Palau Sant Jordi and its space-frame roof. **Vall d'Hebron** was the least successful of the three sites, but Esteve Bonell's Velòdrom is one of the finest (and earliest) of the sports buildings, built in 1984 before the Olympic bid had even succeeded.

AFTER THE OLYMPICS

Not content with the projects completed by 1992, the city continued to expand through the '90s. Post-1992, the focus shifted to the Raval and the Port Vell ('Old Port'), then to the Diagonal Mar area in the north of the city. Many of the striking buildings here are by local architects such as Helio Piñón and Albert Viaplana, whose work combines elegant lines with a strikingly modern use of materials. Examples range from the controversial 1983 **Plaça dels Països Catalans** to transformations of historic buildings such as the Casa de la Caritat (now the **CCCB – Centre de Cultura Contemporània**; *see p72*) and all-new projects including **Maremagnum** in the port.

Other contributions to post-Olympic Barcelona were made by foreign architects: notable examples include Richard Meier's bold white building for **MACBA** (*see p72*), Norman Foster's **Torre de Collserola** communications tower (*see p104*) and Frank Gehry's **Fish** sculpture overlooking the beach (*see p80*). More recently two venerable buildings have been remodelled: the last stage of Italian architect Gae Aulenti's interior redesign of the Palau Nacional on Montjuïc created the expanded **Museu Nacional d'Art de Catalunya** (*see p86*) and the **CosmoCaixa** building in Tibidabo (*see p105*), which again converted a 19th-century hospice into a science museum. Also undergoing a major facelift, the Mudéjar-style arches of **Las Arenas** bullring (*see p82*) are being converted by Richard Rogers into a shopping and leisure centre.

Of late, architectural projects have become increasingly circumscribed by commercial imperatives, sometimes causing tensions between local traditions and the globalisation of commerce. The huge changes to the cityscape linked to the Fòrum Universal de les Cultures 2004 are a particular case in point. The area at the mouth of the Besòs river, near where Avda Diagonal meets the sea, was transformed for the occasion, most notably by the construction of a triangular building, the **Edifici Fòrum** (*see p109*), designed by Herzog and de Meuron (of Tate Modern fame). Nearby, Enric Miralles, also known locally for his redesign of the **Mercat de Santa Caterina** (*see p64*) and the **Gas Natural building** in Barceloneta, created a fiercely modern and rather soulless park, the **Parc de Diagonal Mar** (*see p109*). **Parc Central de Poblenou** (*see p108*), the work of Jean Nouvel – who also designed the 38-storey Torre Agbar in the same neighbourhood – has been a much more popular addition to the area, and combines futurism with nature to provide playfulness and much-needed shade.

Whether this fourth stage in the re-imagining of the city can be linked to those outbursts of Barcelona's architectural creativity in the service of urban planning is debatable. While the value of many of these buildings is unquestionable, some see the dark hand of big business behind the latest developments and dismiss the new expansions connected to the Fòrum as more about making money than art. It's also telling that many of Barcelona's most recent landmark buildings are five-star hotels, such as Richard Rogers' **Hesperia Tower** on the road out to the airport, or Ricard Bofill's **W Hotel** (*see p125*). Still, whatever the motives behind the city's latest reinvention, no one is denying the unique, dynamic air of its current urban fabric.

Torre Agbar.

IN CONTEXT

Catalan Cuisine

*How Catalonia became the
foodiest region of Spain.*

TEXT: COLMAN ANDREWS

It's not an accident that the most exciting contemporary cuisine in Spain is coming out of Catalonia. The proximity of France probably had a significant influence on the development of modern cooking in the region, as it did in the similiarly proximate Basque Country on the other side of the peninsula, but more important was the long-term nature of Catalan food. The Basques have a strong culinary tradition and excellent raw materials, but their signal dishes were developed largely in cultural isolation. Catalonia, by contrast, is historically cosmopolitan, and its kitchens have been influenced over the centuries not only by invaders and visitors – the Carthaginians, the Romans, the Moors, the Visigoths and, more recently, the Italians and the French – but also by dishes and products that came here by way of Catalan military and trade excursions all over the Mediterranean.

There's an exotic, almost baroque quality to Catalan food. Unlikely combinations of ingredients and unusual methods of preparation are old news in Catalonia, and the Catalans have long since turned them into a genuine cuisine: not just a collection of interesting specialities but a complex system of techniques and philosophies with a unique cultural identity.

Colman Andrews, co-founder of Saveur magazine, is the author of Catalan Cuisine and Ferran: The Inside Story of El Bulli and the Man Who Reinvented Food.

INTO THE SPOTLIGHT

When I wrote *Catalan Cuisine* back in the late 1980s, I subtitled it *Europe's Last Great Culinary Secret*. It was certainly that in those days; almost nobody outside the region knew anything about the way locals cooked and ate. That's no longer true. Two Catalan sauces, *romesco* and *allioli*, have become staples in Mediterranean-style restaurants around the globe; the names (and flavours) of such other local specialities as *calçots*, *suquet* and *crema catalana* (for all, *see p149* **Catalan Dishes**) are increasingly well known far from Spain; and an establishment near the Catalan beach town of Roses, Ferran Adrià's El Bulli (*see p167*) – though not obviously Catalan in style – has been dubbed the best restaurant in the world.

Contemporary Catalan cooking dates back more than a generation. Its pioneer was the late Josep Mercader, proprietor of what was then the Motel Ampurdan, just below the French border in Figueres. (Still run by his family, the place is now called the Hotel Empordà, and the dining room is still superb.) Mercader was trained in classic French cooking, but he started reimagining Catalan dishes, lightening and transforming them: turning the roasted vegetables called *escalivada* into a mousse, for instance, and transforming *crema catalana* into ice-cream. Non-cooking restaurateurs such as Ramon Cabau in Barcelona and Lluís Cruanyas, first in the Costa Brava town of Sant Fellu de Guixols and then also in Barcelona, hired bright young chefs and encouraged them in the same direction. Female chefs including Montse Guillén, Toya Roqué and Rosa Grau introduced refinement to tradition. And in the foothill town of Sant Celoni, self-taught chef Santi Santamaria earned a sterling reputation by treating local ingredients with French respect.

By the early 1990s, in Barcelona and to the north, in the Costa Brava/Empordà region and up into the Pyrenees, the modern Catalan culinary movement was in full flower. The emergence of the '*vanguardia*' cooking of Ferran Adrià, the Roca brothers (at their Celler de Can Roca in Girona; *see p290*) and others only fuelled the fires, bringing new levels of imagination and enthusiasm to local kitchens. Catalonia became quite possibly the most bracingly original place to eat in Europe.

THE BASICS

What are the characteristics of traditional Catalan cuisine and, by extension, of the contemporary creations based on it? To begin with, there are the *sofregit* and the *picada* (*see p149* **Catalan Dishes**), the bookends of traditional Catalan cooking. The former becomes the foundation for soups, stews, rice and noodle dishes, and for most traditional sauces; it's the first thing in the pot. The latter gets stirred in a few minutes before the dish in question has finished cooking, at which point it seems to fill in all the gaps of flavour and texture. The savoury aroma of a sauce made with a *sofregit* and a *picada*, no matter what the other ingredients, is definitive of Catalan cuisine, and unmistakable when you walk into a dining room where traditional fare is being served.

Some *picada* recipes call for unsweetened chocolate, and some involve nutmeg and/or cinnamon. These and other 'sweet' spices are commonly used in savoury dishes, part of what accounts for the cuisine's medieval character. The Catalans also mix fruit with meat or fowl: duck or goose with pears, and apples stuffed with ground pork are specialities of the Empordà, and *allioli* thickened with puréed apple or quince is a common accompaniment to roasted rabbit or pork in the Pyrenees. At times, Catalan cooking seems almost Moroccan or Persian. Local cooks also combine seafood and poultry and/or meat in the class of dishes called *mar i muntanya*, or 'sea and mountain'.

Contemporary Catalan chefs like to play with these concepts. Xavier Sagristà at Mas Pau near Figueres (www.maspau.com) serves a little block of crisp-skinned boneless chicken garnished with dressed crab meat; Barcelona chef Carles Gaig has created a salad of poached crayfish and strips of chicken breast with asparagus tips, dressed with pistachio oil; and Santi Santamaria goes high-low, combining cured pork

IN CONTEXT

'The most extravagant expression of mar i muntanya *is an old Empordanese creation, almost impossible to find today.'*

neck with Iranian caviar. The most extravagant expression of *mar i muntanya*, though, is an old Empordanese creation, almost impossible to find today, called *es niu*, or 'the nest'. This is a mysterious, earthy-sweet potful of thrush, quail or other small game birds, along with cuttlefish and their ink, dried cod, sausages or pork meatballs, and a fairly bizarre but well-loved Catalan ingredient called *tripa de bacallà*, the gelatinous air bladder (not literally the tripe) of salt cod. All this is long-cooked with potatoes and sometimes eggs, then served with *allioli*. The late Catalan author Manuel Vázquez Montalbán, who was both a communist and a gastronome, once memorably compared *es niu* to 'Catalan sexual acts and acts of political affirmation... [like] the storming of the Bastille, the assault on the Winter Palace.'

OUT OF THE DARKNESS

Catalan cuisine isn't all dark stews and unusual combinations. All the typical 'Mediterranean' vegetables – tomatoes, aubergines, marrow – are much appreciated, and legumes of all kinds are part of the daily diet. Artichokes, asparagus, cabbage, spinach and Swiss chard are common; turnips, especially the little carrot-shaped black ones grown in the Pyrenees, are popular in northern Catalonia; and wild mushrooms are practically worshipped. It's impossible to imagine Catalan cuisine without garlic. It's an essential part of every *picada* and many *sofregits*, but also, beyond that, one of the most popular ways of cooking many kinds of seafood and offal is to sauté them in olive oil with garlic and parsley. And, of course, garlic appears on almost every traditional table in the form of *allioli*, considered pretty much an essential condiment for grilled and roasted meats, simply cooked fish, vegetables, hearty soups, and most of Catalonia's popular rice and noodle dishes.

Grape Expectations

Catalonia's love affair with wine.

Around 25 years ago, an all-Catalan wine list would have been brief. It would have listed cava and a handful of decent reds and whites from the Penedès region; probably a white from a single producer in Alella, near Barcelona; a celebrated dessert wine made near the beach resort of Sitges; and, just possibly, an example or two of the unusual fortified wine called *vi ranci*, literally 'rancid wine' (for its sourish character), from an obscure region called the Priorat. Anything else would have been for local consumption only, not deserving of a wider audience.

Today, the Penedès is almost as well known for table wines – many of them produced by the massive Torres firm, under various labels – as for sparklers. The Priorat has turned into one of the most famous wine regions in Europe, notable for its full-bodied (and pricey) reds. The Empordà *denominación*, which encompasses much of the Costa Brava, is Spain's most exciting up-and-coming wineland. And bottlings from areas that few outside the immediate vicinity had even heard of a couple of decades ago – Conca de Barberà, Costers del Segre, Montsant, Pla de Bages, Terra Alta – are finding space on wine-shop shelves and in restaurant cellars all over the world.

For better or for worse, many of the newer wines of Catalonia are based on classic French varieties, which means they are intense and extracted and full of oak. Chardonnay, cabernet sauvignon, merlot, sauvignon blanc, pinot noir, syrah: you'll find them all here, but naturally some of them are better than others. More interesting are the whites made from indigenous varieties such as macabeo, perallada and especially xarel·lo, the three traditional cava grapes, and from garnatxa blanca (grenache blanc). A usually insipid cultivar known as picpoul in southern France but called picapoll in Catalonia produces an unexpectedly charming white in Pla de Bagès. For reds, ull de llebre (hare's eye), the local name for tempranillo, yields some pleasant wines, but the great successes are garnatxa and carinyena (carignan). The latter is at the heart of many of the Priorat's finest reds, and both grapes do very well in the area, in neighbouring Montsant and in the Empordà, where the results are less concentrated but often more elegant. Add together all these varieties and you'll end up with an all-Catalan wine list that would be unrecognisable from a quarter-century ago.

Sights

Parc Güell. *See p102.*

The Barri Gòtic

Roman relics and medieval monuments mark out the city centre.

The central third of the Old City's triptych, the Barri Gòtic (Gothic Quarter) contains the best-preserved medieval quarter in Europe, dotted with some astounding Roman remains. Neither as glacially cool as the Born or as bohemian as the Raval, it's nonetheless an essential port of call. Save for the dramatic destruction of a huge part of the medieval core for the construction of C/Jaume I and C/Ferran (1849-53) and Via Laietana (1909), its ancient splendour has survived the last 500 years or so virtually intact.

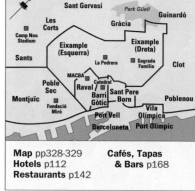

Map pp328-329	Cafés, Tapas
Hotels p112	& Bars p168
Restaurants p142	

History is written in stone here; the wealth of historical remains is such that visitors soon become as blasé as the locals about the large sections of Roman wall they might encounter at the back of a curry house, in a café or in a lift-shaft leading down to the metro.

THE HISTORIC QUARTER

The first settlement of this 2,000-year-old city was a Roman camp set up on the gentle hill of Mons Taber, the highest vantage point on the coastal plains. Now the imposing square of Plaça Sant Jaume, this is where the Roman forum was built, at the crossroads of the main thoroughfares of the *cardo maximus* and the *decumanus*, which roughly correspond to the lines traced by C/Call to C/Llibreteria and C/Bisbe to C/Ciutat today. Dominating the forum was the **Temple Romà d'August**, four columns of which can still be seen in C/Paradis. The square now hosts the municipal government (**Ajuntament**) and Catalan regional government (**Generalitat**) buildings and forms the civic heart of the city. It has also been the stage for demonstrations, speeches and key political moments, such as the proclamation of the Catalan republic in 1931.

Leading off the square, C/Bisbe has one of the area's most photographed features: the neo-Gothic **Pont dels Sospirs** (Bridge of Sighs).

About the author

Nadia Feddo has lived in Barcelona since 1995, and works as a freelance journalist and professional tour guide.

It's a pastiche from 1928, when the idea of this area as a 'Gothic Quarter' took off. Other alterations from the same period include the decorations on the Casa dels Canonges (once a set of canons' residences, and now Generalitat offices), on the other side of the bridge. Further down C/Bisbe is the Plaça Garriga i Bachs and Josep Llimona's monument to the martyrs of 1809, dedicated to the *barcelonins* who rose up against Napoleon and were executed.

In C/Santa Llúcia, in front of the **cathedral**, is the Casa de l'Ardiaca; originally a 15th-century residence for the archdeacon (*ardiaca*), it has a superb tiled patio. The broad square at the foot of the steps leading up to the cathedral is Plaça Nova, which houses an antiques market every Thursday (*see p204*) and is a traditional venue for festivals, concerts and *sardana* dancing (*see p57* **You Put Your Left Leg In**). At ground level, on the south-east corner of the square is *Barcino*: a 'visual poem' by Joan Brossa installed in 1994, it refers to the ancient name for Barcelona, supposedly given by the Carthaginians after Hannibal's father, Hamil Barca. Directly above is the Roman aqueduct; the final archway of the city's two aqueducts dating from the first century AD is preserved inside the tower that defended the north-eastern side of the gate; one of these has been externally rebuilt.

SIGHTS

Fast forward two millennia to the opposite side of Plaça Nova, dominated by one of the first high-rise blocks in the city: the **Col·legi d'Arquitectes** (Architects' Association) is decorated with a graffiti-style sand-blasted triptych of Catalan folk scenes, designed by Picasso while in self-imposed exile in the 1950s, and executed by Norwegian artist Carl Nesjar. The middle section depicts the *gegants* (giant figures who lead festival processions) and figures holding palm branches; the left-hand section (on C/Arcs) symbolises the joy of life, while the right-hand section (on C/Capellans) depicts the Catalan flag. There are also two interior friezes depicting a *sardana* dance and a wall of arches. When Picasso heard that Joan Miró was being considered for the commission, he said that he could easily 'do a Miró', hence the style.

In front of the cathedral, on the right as you leave, the **Museu Diocesà** houses an excellent collection of religious art. Around the side of the cathedral, meanwhile, is the little-visited but fascinating **Museu Frederic Marès**.

Further along is the 16th-century Palau del Lloctinent (Palace of the Viceroy); recently restored, it was the local headquarters for the Spanish Inquisition, from where the unfortunates were carted off to the Passeig del Born to be burnt. Once part of the former royal palace (Palau Reial Major, not to be confused with the Palau Reial in Pedralbes), the building has another exit to the medieval palace square,

the well-preserved Plaça del Rei. The square houses the **Museu d'Història de Barcelona** and includes some of Barcelona's most historically important buildings: the Escher-esque 16th-century watchtower (Mirador del Rei Martí) and the Capella de Santa Àgata, which houses the very stone where the breasts of Saint Agatha were allegedly laid when the Romans chopped them off in Catania. Parts of the palace are said to date back to the tenth century; there have been many remarkable additions to it since, notably the 14th-century Saló del Tinell, a medieval banqueting hall that is a definitive work of Catalan Gothic. It is here that Ferdinand and Isabella are said to have received Columbus on his return from America.

The narrow streets centred on C/Call once housed a rich Jewish ghetto (*call*), although the street names were Christianised after the 1391 pogrom. At the corner of C/Sant Domènec del Call and C/Marlet is the medieval **synagogue**, now restored and open to the public. Proving the regenerated interest in the Call, in 2008 the Centre d'Interpretació del Call research centre opened in Placeta Manuel Ribé (93 256 21 00, closed Mon & Tue) as part of the Museu d'Història de Barcelona; it has a small selection of medieval Jewish artefacts on display.

Near the centre of the Call is the beautiful little Plaça Sant Felip Neri and its fine Baroque church, whose façade was damaged by Italian bombing during the Civil War. Over 200 people were killed, many of them refugee children on a Sunday outing. This square is another 20th-century invention; the shoemakers' guild building (now housing the **Museu del Calçat**) was moved here in 1943 to make way for the Avda de la Catedral, while the nearby tinkers' guild was moved earlier last century, when Via Laietana was driven through the district.

Close by are the attractive Plaça del Pi and Plaça Sant Josep Oriol, where you'll find great bars and artisanal markets. The squares are separated by **Santa Maria del Pi**, one of Barcelona's most distinguished Gothic churches, with a magnificent rose window and spacious single nave. Opposite is the

Museu d'Història de Barcelona.

SIGHTS

SIGHTS

Walk Roman Remains

Walk the paths of the ancient empire.

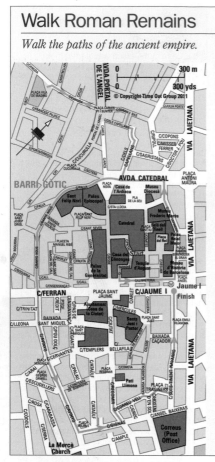

DURATION: 45 MINUTES

The Roman settlement of Barcino has had an unappreciated impact on the two millennia of life that followed its beginnings. Many of Barcelona's most familiar streets – C/Hospital, even Passeig de Gràcia – follow the line of Roman roads, and the best way to get an idea of the Roman town is to walk the line of its walls. Along the way sit all kinds of Roman remains, poking out from the buildings that have incorporated them or been built over them by medieval builders and those who followed them.

A good place to start your walk is at **C/Paradís**, between the cathedral and Plaça Sant Jaume, where a round millstone set into the paving marks what was believed to be the precise centre of the Mons Taber. It's here that you'll find the remains of the **Temple Romà d'August** (*see p60*). Where C/Paradís meets the Plaça Sant Jaume was where Barcino's two main streets once met; the road on the left, **C/Llibreteria**, began life as the Cardus Maximus, the main road to Rome. Just off this road is the Plaça del Rei and the **Museu d'Història de Barcelona**; below is the largest underground excavation of a Roman site in Europe.

Rejoining C/Llibreteria, turn left at **C/Tapineria** to reach **Plaça Ramon Berenguer el Gran** and the largest surviving stretch of ancient wall, incorporated into the medieval Palau Reial. Continue along Tapineria, where you'll find many sections

17th-century neo-classical retailers' guildhall, with its colourful 18th-century graffiti.

Snaking up to C/Portaferrissa from the Plaça del Pi is C/Petritxol. One of the most charming streets of the Barri Gòtic, it is known for its traditional *granges* offering hot chocolate and cakes, and also houses the **Sala Parés** (*see p226*), the city's oldest art gallery; Rusiñol, Casas and the young Picasso all exhibited here. On the other side of C/Portaferrissa, heading up C/Bot, is the Plaça Vila de Madrid, where you'll find the excavated remains of a Roman necropolis and a new information centre (93 256 21 22, closed Mon & Tue), along with a rare expanse of city-centre grass (fenced off). Between here and the Plaça Catalunya is the little Romanesque church of **Santa Anna**, begun in 1141 and containing an exquisite 14th-century cloisterHead back

along C/Santa Anna to emerge on the city's most crowded shopping street, the pedestrianised Portal de l'Àngel, crammed with high-street chains and the odd curiosity such as the Santa Anna drinking fountain, decorated with scowling bearded faces, which dates from 1356 and was later covered in Noucentista painted tiles. It's located to the rear of the **Real Cercle Artístic**, housed in the Palau Pignatelli and now home to **Dalí Barcelona**.

From here, duck into C/Duran i Blas to see four arches from a Roman aqueduct embedded into a wall and exposed in 1988 when the neighbouring building was demolished; they date from the first century AD and brought water from the River Besòs. Back out on Portal de l'Àngel, the end of the street is signposted by the famous five-storey-high **Cottet**

of Roman building, to **Avda de la Catedral**. The massive twin-drum gate on C/Bisbe, while often retouched, has not changed in its basic shape, at least at the base, since it was the main gate of the Roman town. To its left you can see fragments of an aqueduct, and at its front Joan Brossa's bronze letters, spelling out 'Barcino'.

If you take a detour up C/Capellans to **C/Duran i Bas**, you can see another four arches of an aqueduct. Heading left and straight over the Avda Portal de l'Àngel is the Roman necropolis in **Plaça Vila de Madrid**, with the tombs clearly visible. In accordance with Roman custom, these had to be outside the city walls.

Returning to the cathedral, turn right into **C/Palla**. A little way along sits a large chunk of Roman wall, only discovered in the 1980s when a building was demolished. C/Palla runs into **C/Banys Nous**; at No.16 is a centre for the disabled, inside which is a piece of wall with a relief of legs and feet (the public are free to enter). At No.4 is **La Granja** (*see p169*), a lovely old café with yet another stretch of Roman wall at the back; beyond this is the junction with **C/Call**, the other end of the *cardus*, and so the opposite side of the Roman town from Llibreteria-Tapineria. The staff of the clothes wholesalers at C/Call 1 are also used to people wandering in to examine their piece of Roman tower.

Carry on across C/Ferran and down **C/Avinyó**, the next continuation of the perimeter. Two sides of the cave-like dining room at the back of **El Gallo Kiriko**, the Pakistani restaurant that now occupies No.19, are actually formed by portions of the Roman wall.

From **C/Milans**, take a left on to **C/Gignás**. By the junction with **C/Regomir** are remains of the fourth sea gate of the town, which would have faced the beach and the Roman shipyard. Take a detour up C/Regomir to visit one of the most important relics of Barcino, the **Pati Llimona**; then continue up **C/Correu Vell**, where there are more fragments of the old city wall, to reach one of the most impressive relics of Roman Barcelona in the small, shady **Plaça Traginers**: a Roman tower and a corner of the ancient wall, in a remarkable state of preservation despite having had a medieval house built on top of it. Finally, turn up **C/Sots-Tinent Navarro**, which boasts a massive stretch of Roman rampart, before finally ending the walk at Plaça de l'Àngel.

thermometer, added in 1956 by the optician's shop beneath and greatly admired at the time as a technological marvel. Just a few metres away is the entrance to C/Montsió, which holds the world-famous **Els Quatre Gats** café (*see p169*), the legendary haunt of Picasso and other artists and bohemians. It's housed in Puig i Cadafalch's richly sculpted Casa Martí.

Back on the seaward side of the Barri Gòtic, if you walk from Plaça Sant Jaume up C/Ciutat, to the left of the Ajuntament, and turn down the narrow alley of C/Hércules, you'll come to Plaça Sant Just. This fascinating old square holds a recently restored Gothic water fountain from 1367 and the church of **Sants Just i Pastor**, built in the 14th century on the site of a chapel founded by Charlemagne's son Louis the Pious, but now looking rather unloved inside.

The once-wealthy area between here and the port became more rundown throughout the 20th century. It has a different atmosphere from the northern part of the Barri Gòtic: shabbier and less prosperous. The city authorities made huge efforts to change this, particularly in the 1990s, when new squares were opened up: Plaça George Orwell on C/Escudellers, known as the 'Plaça del Tripi (Trippy)' by the youthful party crowd that hangs out there, and Plaça Joaquim Xirau, off La Rambla. Another tactic was the siting of parts of the Universitat Pompeu Fabra on the lower Rambla.

Just above is the **Plaça Reial** (*photo p56*), known for its bars, cheap backpacker hostels and rather scuzzy atmosphere at night. It's still a popular spot for a drink or an outdoor meal (provided you don't mind the odd drunk and are

SIGHTS

prepared to keep an eye on your bags). An addition from the 1840s, the *plaça* has the **Tres Gràcies** fountain in the centre, and lamp-posts designed by the young Gaudí. It's the only work he ever did for the city council.

The grand porticoes of a number of the buildings around the church of **La Mercè**, once merchants' mansions, stand as testament to the former wealth of the area before the building of the Eixample. The Plaça de la Mercè itself was only created in 1982, with the destruction of the houses that used to stand here; the 19th-century fountain was moved here from the port. There's also a dwindling number of lively *tascas* (small tapas bars) on C/Mercè. Beyond C/Ample and the Mercè, you emerge from narrow alleys or the pretty Plaça Duc de Medinaceli on to the Passeig de Colom, where a few shipping offices and ships' chandlers still recall the atmosphere of decades gone by. On Passeig de Colom stands the monolithic **Capitanía General**, the army headquarters. The façade has the dubious distinction of being the one construction in Barcelona that's directly attributable to the dictatorship of Primo de Rivera.

FREE Ajuntament (City Hall)

Plaça Sant Jaume (93 402 73 64, www.bcn.cat). *Metro Jaume I or Liceu.* **Open** *Office* 8.30am-2.30pm Mon-Fri. *Visits* 10am-1.30pm Sun. **Admission** free. **Map** p329 C6.

Around the left-hand corner of the City Hall's rather dull 18th-century neo-classical façade sits the old entrance, in a wonderfully flamboyant 15th-century Catalan Gothic façade. Inside, the building's centrepiece (and oldest part) is the famous Saló de Cent, where the Consell de Cent (Council of One Hundred) ruled the city between 1372 and 1714. The Saló de Cròniques is filled with Josep Maria Sert's immense black-and-gold mural (1928), depicting the early 14th-century Catalan campaign in Byzantium and Greece under the command of Roger de Flor. Full of art and sculptures by the great Catalan masters from Clarà to Subirachs, the interior of the City Hall is open on Sundays. The Ajuntament is also open from 11am to 8pm on certain holidays, such as the Mercè (24 Sept), Santa Eulàlia (12 Feb) and Sant Jordi (23 Apr).

★ Catedral

Pla de la Seu (93 342 82 60, www.catedral bcn.org). Metro Jaume I. **Open** *Combined ticket* 1-5pm Mon-Fri; 2-5pm Sat, Sun. *Without combined ticket (Church & Cloister)* 8am-12.45pm, 5-7.30pm daily. *(Museum)* 10am-12.30pm, 5.15-7pm daily. **Admission** *Combined ticket* €5. *Church & cloister* free. *Museum* €2. *Lift to roof* €2.50. *Choir* €2.20. **No credit cards. Map** p329 C5/D5.

The construction of Barcelona's Gothic cathedral began in 1298. However, thanks to civil wars and plagues, building dragged on at a pace that makes the Sagrada Família project look snappy: although the architects remained faithful to the vertical Nordic lines of the 15th-century plans, the façade and central spire were not finished until 1913. Indeed, the façade continues to cause problems: although it's one of the newest parts of the building, it's crumbling, and roughly a third of it is being taken down and painstakingly rebuilt with the same Montserrat stone that was used for the original. For the time being, the building is shrouded in scaffolding, plastic and signs asking visitors to 'Sponsor a Stone'.

Plaça Reial. *See p55.*

You Put Your Left Leg In...

Dancing the sardana.

After the transporting passion and sweat of flamenco, or the athletic leaps of the Aragonese *jota*, Catalonia's emblematic folk dance can look a bit, well, wimpy. Not surprisingly, the gentle, bobbing steps of the *sardana* get a lot of stick from other regions of Spain: the mere mention of the word can result in hoots of derision, swiftly followed by an impression of a shuffling geriatric groping for the Zimmer frame. But, as any aficionado will tell you, the joy of the *sardana* is not in watching but in taking part. It's a dance of co-existence and solidarity, not spectacle.

In theory, anyone is allowed to join in a *sardana*. In practice, it's not a good idea to barge in on a circle beyond your level: choose carefully, and make sure you break into the left of a man so as not to commit the gaffe of breaking up a couple. Dancers don the traditional *tabarner espadrille* with ribbons, and join hands in a circle to begin the series of tiny, intricate steps forward and back, crossing to the left and right. Except for formal occasions, all their street shoes and belongings are piled up in the

middle, so they are, in best disco tradition, dancing around their handbags.

Sardanes, which can be lengthy, consist of interchanging sequences of eight *curts* (short sets), when dancers hold their arms low, and 16 *llargs* (long sets), when arms are held aloft. One person in the ring takes charge of counting the sets, but the dance is also accompanied by a traditional band known as a *cobla*. This consists of 11 musicians playing 12 instruments: double bass, trumpets and trombones, alongside reed instruments known as the *tible* and *tenora*; the drummer also plays the recorder. To follow the structure of the *sardana*, listen out for the *flabiol* (recorder) flourishes, which mark the introduction and the counterpoints for the dancers.

Sardanes are a stock feature of all traditional Catalan festivals and also take place every weekend in front of the cathedral (Jan-Aug, Dec noon-2pm Sun; Sept-Nov 6-8pm Sat, noon-2pm Sun) and in Plaça Sant Jaume (Oct-July 6-8pm Sun). For more information and details of classes, see www.fed.sardanista.cat.

SIGHTS

Inside, the cathedral is a cavernous and slightly forbidding place, but many paintings, sculptures and an intricately carved central choir (built in the 1390s) all shine through the gloom. The cathedral is dedicated to the city's patron saint Eulàlia, an outspoken 13-year-old martyred by the Romans in AD 303; her remains lie in the dramatically lit crypt, in an alabaster tomb carved with torture scenes from her martyrdom (being rolled in a nail-filled barrel down what is today the Baixada de Santa Eulàlia, for instance). To one side, there's a lift to the roof; take it for a magnificent view of the Old City.

The glorious, light-filled cloister is famous for its 13 fierce geese – one for each year of Eulàlia's life – and half-erased floor engravings, detailing which guild paid for which side chapel: scissors to represent the tailors, shoes for the cobblers and so on. The cathedral museum, housed in the 17th-century chapterhouse, includes paintings and sculptures by Gothic masters Jaume Huguet, Bernat Martorell and Bartolomé Bermejo.

A combined ticket (*visita especial*) has a timetable intended to keep tourists and worshippers from bothering one another. From 1-4.30pm, the entry fee is obligatory; however, ticket-holders have the run of the cloister, church, choir and lift, and can enter some chapels and take photos (normally prohibited).

FREE Centre Cívic Patí d'en Llimona
C/Regomir 3 (93 268 47 00). Metro Jaume I.
Open *Exhibitions* 10am-9pm Mon-Fri; 10am-2pm, 4-8pm Sat. Closed Aug. **Admission** free.
Map p329 C6.
From the street, peer through the glass paving slabs and windows to see the excavated foundations of a round defence tower that dates from the earliest Roman settlement, along with the remains of a Roman bath and house that stood against one of the gates of the city wall. In the 15th century, a luxury villa was built on the site; the courtyard still contains various capitals with carved faces from this period. The civic centre's cultural offerings include photography shows, workshops, theatre shows and poetry readings.

Dalí Barcelona Real Cercle Artístic
C/Arcs 5 (93 318 17 74, www.dalibarcelona.com).
Metro Jaume I or Liceu. **Open** 10am-10pm daily.
Admission €10; €7 reductions; free under-7s.
Credit AmEx, MC, V. **Map** p328 C4.
This private collection of Dalí sculptures looks right at home amid the dramatic red velvet curtains and high, Gothic arches of the ground floor and basement of the Palau Pignatelli. In his later years Dalí signed his name to almost anything, but these 44 pieces were moulded by his own hands in wax by the pool at his house in Port Lligat and show he was

BARCEL⊙NA M⊙DERNISME R⊙UTE

New Guided Visits !!

Domènech i Montaner's Hospital de Sant Pau
Daily visits in English at 10 am, 11 am, 12 am, and 1 pm

Domènech i Montaner's Palau Montaner
Visits in English every Saturday at 10'30 am

...and Gaudí's Pavellons Güell
Saturdays and Sundays at 10'15 am and 12'15 pm

More information at 933 177 652 and www.rutadelmodernisme.com

 Ajuntament de Barcelona   Institut del Paisatge Urbà i la Qualitat de Vida    RUTA DEL MODERNISME

just as accomplished at sculpting as painting. Broadly divided into themes such as eroticism, Don Quixote and mythology, they include such gems as a small bronze that is simultaneously a swan, a dragon and an elephant or an erotic vision of Quixote's Dulcinea. The collection is supplemented by over 600 drawings, sketches, lithographs and photographs. A free, related temporary exhibition space (in which items are for sale) has recently included shows by his niece, Lali Bas Dalí, and his muse, Amanda Lear. Upstairs is the home of the Royal Art Circle and visitors are welcome to view its exhibitions, for some of which entry is free.

Museu del Calçat (Shoe Museum)

Plaça Sant Felip Neri 5 (93 301 45 33).
Metro Jaume I. **Open** 11am-2pm Tue-Sun.
Admission €2.50; free under-10s. **No credit cards. Map** p329 C5.

Housed in what was once part of the medieval shoemakers' guild premises, this quirky museum details the cobbler's craft, from practical Roman sandals to tottering '70s platform boots. The earlier examples are reproductions, while those from the 17th century to the present day are originals, including clogs, swagged musketeers' boots and even celebrity footwear, such as the tiny shoes of diminutive cellist Pau Casals.

Museu Diocesà

Avda de la Catedral 4 (93 315 22 13,
www.cultura.arqbcn.cat). Metro Jaume I.
Open 10am-2pm, 5-8pm Tue-Sat; 11am-2pm Sun. **Admission** €6; €3 reductions; free under-8s.
No credit cards. Map p328 D4.

A hotchpotch of religious art, including some 14th-century alabaster virgins, altarpieces by Bernat Martorell and wonderful Romanesque murals. The building itself is also something of a mishmash; it includes the Gothic Pia Almoina, an almshouse and soup kitchen founded in 1009, stuck on to a Renaissance canon's residence complete with Tuscan columns, which in turn was built inside an octagonal Roman defence tower. The museum also has space for two temporary exhibitions, which generally showcase the work of local artists, photographers and architects.

★ Museu d'Història de Barcelona (MUHBA)

Plaça del Rei 1 (93 256 21 00, www.museu
historia.bcn.cat). Metro Jaume I. **Open** *Apr-Sept*
10am-8pm Tue-Sun. *Oct-Mar* 10am-2pm, 4-7pm
Tue-Sat; 10am-8pm Sun. **Guided tours** by appointment (Sat, Sun). **Admission** *All exhibitions* €7; €5 reductions; free under-16s.
Free to all 3-8pm Sun. *Temporary exhibitions*
€2; €1.40. **No credit cards. Map** p329 D5.

Stretching from the Plaça del Rei to the cathedral are some 4,000sq m (43,000sq ft) of subterranean Roman excavations – streets, villas and storage vats for oil and wine, all discovered by accident in the late 1920s when a whole swath of the Gothic Quarter was dug

up to make way for the central avenue of Via Laietana. The excavations continued until 1960; today, the labyrinth can be reached via the Casa Padellàs, a merchant's palace dating from 1498, which was laboriously moved from its original location in C/Mercaders to allow the construction of Via Laietana.

Admission also allows access to the Capella de Santa Àgata, with its 15th-century altarpiece by Jaume Huguet, and the Saló del Tinell, at least when there's no temporary exhibition. This majestic room began life in 1370 as the seat of the Catalan parliament and was converted in the 18th century into a Baroque church, which was dismantled in 1934. The Rei Martí watchtower is closed to the public. Tickets for the museum are valid for all seven MUHBA sites).

★ Museu Frederic Marès

Plaça Sant Iu 5-6 (93 310 58 00, www.museu
mares.bcn.cat). Metro Jaume I. **Due to reopen**
April 2011. Map p329 D5.

Kleptomaniac and general magpie Frederic Marès (1893-1991) 'collected' everything he laid his hands on, from hairbrushes to opera glasses and gargoyles. Unlike most private 19th-century collectors, Marès didn't come from a wealthy family, but spent every penny he earned as a sculptor and art professor on broadening his hoardings. Even when the Ajuntament gave him a palace in which to display his collection (and house himself), it wasn't enough; the overflow eventually spread to two other Marès museums in Montblanc and Arenys de Mar.

The exhibits here are divided into three main sections. The basement, ground floor and first floor are devoted to sculpture dating from the Pre-Roman era to the 20th century, including a vast array of polychromed religious carvings, tombs, capitals and entire church portals, exquisitely carved. On the second floor sits the Sentimental Museum, with objects from everyday life; look out for the Ladies' Room, filled with fans, sewing scissors and perfume flasks, and the Entertainment Room, with mechanical toys, puppets and a room dedicated to smoking paraphernalia. Also on the second floor, comprising the third main collection, is a room devoted to photography, and Marès' study and library. It's now filled with sculptures, many of them his own. Note that the museum is closed for refurbishment until spring 2011.

FREE Palau de la Generalitat

Plaça Sant Jaume (93 402 46 17, www.gencat.
cat/generalitat/eng/guia/palau). Metro Jaume I or
Liceu. **Guided tours** every 30-40mins approx,
10am-1pm, 2nd & 4th weekend of mth.
Admission free. **Map** p329 C5.

Like the Ajuntament, the Palau de la Generalitat has a Gothic side entrance that opens out on to C/Bisbe with a beautiful relief depicting St George (Sant Jordi), patron saint of Catalonia, made by Pere Johan in 1418. Inside the building, the finest features are the first-floor Pati de Tarongers (Orange Tree Patio), which was to become the model for many Barcelona patios,

SIGHTS

and the magnificent chapel of Sant Jordi of 1432-34, the masterpiece of Catalan architect Marc Safont. The Generalitat is traditionally open to the public on Sant Jordi (St George's Day, 23 April), when its patios are spectacularly decorated with red roses, but queues are long. It normally also opens on 11 September (Catalan National Day) and 24 September (La Mercè). The guided tours are generally in Spanish or Catalan; call ahead for an English-speaking guide.

Sinagoga Shlomo Ben Adret

C/Marlet 7 (93 317 07 90, www.calldebarcelona. org). Metro Jaume I or Liceu. **Open** *June-Oct* 10.30am-7pm Mon-Fri; 10.30am-3pm Sat, Sun. *Nov-May* 10.30am-6pm; 10.30am-3pm Sat, Sun. **Admission** €2; under-15s free. **Credit** DC, MC, V. **Map** p329 C5.
The main synagogue of the Call until the pogrom of 1391, this tiny basement building lay abandoned for many years, until its rediscovery and restoration in 1996. Now a working synagogue once again, one of the two rooms is a place of worship with several interesting artefacts; the other houses the 14th-century dyeing vats used by the family that lived here until their status as crypto-Jews was discovered. The façade of the building, slightly skewing the street, fulfils religious requirements by which the synagogue has to face Jerusalem; the two windows constructed at knee height allow light to enter from that direction.

FREE Temple Romà d'August

C/Paradis 10 (93 256 21 00). Metro Jaume I. **Open** *Apr-Sept* 10am-8pm Tue-Sun. *Oct-Mar* 10am-2pm, 4-7pm Tue-Sat; 10am-8pm Sun. **Admission** free. **Map** p329 D5.
Four stunning fluted Corinthian columns dating from the first century BC soar out of their podium in the most unlikely of places: a back patio of the Mountaineering Centre of Catalonia. Part of the rear corner of the temple devoted to the Roman emperor Augustus (who after his death was elevated to the pantheon), the columns were discovered and isolated from the structure of a medieval building in 1835. The current layout is actually a slight fudging of the original as the right-hand column resided separately in the Plaça del Rei until it was slotted next to the other three in 1956. Opening hours can vary, so call ahead.

LA RAMBLA

Whether you catch it on a Saturday night full of sombrero-wearing stags or early in the morning when the kiosk-holders are bursting open their fresh stacks of newspapers, one thing is for sure: you won't get La Rambla to yourself. And indeed, why would you want to? In the absence of any great buildings or museums, it's the people who provide the spectacle: from flower-sellers to living statues, operagoers to saucer-eyed clubbers, market shoppers to tango dancers, all human life is here.

However, there's no escaping the fact that, these days, it's mostly tourists who walk the golden mile from Plaça Catalunya down to the harbour. The business of extracting as much of their money as possible, whether by fair means or foul, has had an inevitable impact on the character of the boulevard, filling it with fast food outlets, short-stay apartments, identikit souvenir shops and pickpockets. After a lot of bad press, the council is desperately trying to smarten up the city's famous boulevard, and the prostitutes, sex shops, card sharps and fortune tellers are gradually being squeezed out. Even the famous human statues and street artists have been subjected to quality control.

La Rambla started life as a seasonal riverbed, which explains both its snaking trajectory, broadening out at the sea end, and also its name, which derives from *ramla*, an Arabic word for sand. The river ran along the western edge of the 13th-century city; after it became an open sewer, it was gradually paved over, although the distinctive wave-patterned paving slabs were not added until after the Civil War.

From the Middle Ages to the Baroque era, many churches and convents were built along here, some of which have given their names to sections of the road. Descending from Plaça Catalunya, La Rambla is successively called Rambla de Canaletes, Rambla dels Estudis (or dels Ocells), Rambla de Sant Josep (or de les Flors), Rambla dels Caputxins and Rambla de Santa Mònica. For this reason, many people refer to it in the plural as Les Rambles (Las Ramblas in castellano).

La Rambla also served as the meeting ground for city and country dwellers in this era – on the far side of these church buildings lay the still scarcely built-up Raval, 'the city outside the walls', and rural Catalonia. At the fountain on the corner with C/Portaferrissa, colourful tiles depict the city gateway that once stood here (*porta ferrissa* means 'iron gate'). The space by the gates became a natural marketplace; from these humble beginnings sprang La Boqueria (*see p198*).

La Rambla took on its present form between approximately 1770 and 1860. The second city wall came down in 1775, and La Rambla was paved and turned into a boulevard. But the avenue only acquired its final shape after the closure of the monasteries in the 1830s, which made land available for new building. No longer on the city's edge, La Rambla became a wide path through the city's heart.

As well as having five names, La Rambla is divided into territories. The first part – at the top, by Plaça Catalunya – was long the territory of shoeshiners and groups of men who came to play chess and hold informal debates, although the sparse new single-seat benches have made it a markedly less sociable place to sit these days.

La Rambla

The Font de Canaletes drinking fountain is beside them; if you drink from it, goes the legend, you'll return to Barcelona. Here, too, is where Barça fans converge to celebrate their triumphs.

This part segues into the Rambla dels Ocells; it's named after its ranks of cacophonous bird (*ocell*) stalls, although they're slowly being weeded out by the Ajuntament in an attempt to raise the tone of the boulevard. Next comes perhaps the best-loved section, known as Rambla de les Flors for its line of flower stalls. To the right is the **Palau de la Virreina** exhibition and cultural information centre, and the superb Boqueria market.

A little further down is the Pla de l'Os (or Pla de la Boqueria), the centrepoint of La Rambla, with a pavement mosaic created in 1976 by Joan Miró and recently restored to its original glory. On the left, where more streets run off into the Barri Gòtic, is the extraordinary **Bruno Quadros** building (dating from 1883; a former umbrella shop, it is decorated with roundels of open parasols and a Chinese dragon carrying a Peking lantern.

The lower half of La Rambla is initially more restrained, flowing between the sober façade of the **Liceu** opera house and the more fin-de-siècle (architecturally and atmospherically) **Café de l'Opera** (*see p169*). On the right is C/Nou de la Rambla (where you'll find Gaudí's neo-Gothic **Palau Güell**, partially closed for renovation until at least

2010; *see p74*); the promenade then widens into the Rambla de Santa Mònica, an area which has long been a haunt of prostitutes. Clean-up efforts have reduced their visibility, and various renovations – including the 1980s addition of an arts centre, the **Centre d'Art Santa Mònica** – have done much to dilute the seediness of the area, but single males walking at night can still expect to be approached.

Across the street is the unintentionally hilarious **Museu de Cera** (Wax Museum; *see p217*) and, at weekends, numerous stalls selling bric-a-brac and craftwork. Then it's a short hop to the port, and the Columbus column.

FREE Arts Santa Mònica
La Rambla 7 (93 567 11 10, www.artssanta monica.net). Metro Drassanes. **Open** 11am-9pm Tue-Sun. **Admission** free. **Map** p329 A7.
In a controversial move, the Generalitat appointed new director Vicenç Altaió to pump up the lacklustre visitor numbers for this contemporary art space. Altaió has created 'a multidisciplinary centre for art, science, thought and communication', although detractors fear that the governmental hijacking of the management will mean diluted programming. After remodelling, the museum reopened to the public in spring 2009; stunts included an 'itinerant musical action', which involved dragging a piano (with pianist), topped by a pair of actors, down La Rambla.

Museu de l'Eròtica
La Rambla 96 bis (93 318 98 65, www.erotica-museum.com). Metro Liceu. **Open** June-Sept 10am-9pm daily. Oct-May 10am-8pm daily. **Admission** €9; €8-€7 reductions; under-15s free. **Credit** MC, V. **Map** p328 B4.
Despite being a condom's toss from the red-light district, the Erotic Museum is a surprisingly limp affair. Expect plenty of filler in the form of Kama Sutra illustrations and airbrushed paintings of naked maidens, with the odd fascinating item such as studded chastity belts or a Victorian walking stick topped with an ivory vagina.

Palau de la Virreina
La Rambla 99 (93 316 10 00, www.bcn.cat/cultura). Metro Liceu. **Open** noon-8pm Tue-Sun. **Admission** free. **Map** p328 B4.
This classical palace, with Baroque features, takes its name from the widow of an unpopular viceroy of Peru, who commissioned it and lived in it after its completion in the 1770s. The Virreina now houses the city cultural department, and has information on events and shows as well as strong programming in its two gallery spaces. On the first floor, Espai 2 is devoted to exhibitions of contemporary art, while the free downstairs gallery, named after local photographer Xavier Miserachs, is focused on photography and hosts Barcelona's prestigious annual photo competition: the FotoMercè, held during the Mercè in September.

SIGHTS

The Born & Sant Pere

Chichi boutiques and religious treasures.

The most uptown area of downtown, the **Born** is a curious blend of the ecclesiastical, the elegant and the edgy, and now commands some of the highest property prices in the city. Label-happy coolhunters throng the primped pedestrian streets, where museums, restored 13th-century mansions and churches alternate with cafés, galleries and boutiques.

Regeneration has come more slowly for the neighbouring area of **Sant Pere**, which maintains a slightly grungier feel despite the municipal money-pumping. Still, there have been recent large-scale improvements, such as the long Plaça

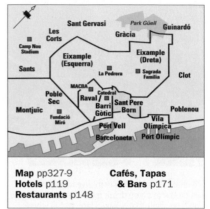

Map pp327-9	Cafés, Tapas
Hotels p119	& Bars p171
Restaurants p148	

Pou de la Figuera and the spectacularly reinvented Santa Caterina market. Both districts together are still sometimes referred to as **La Ribera** (the Waterfront), a name that recalls the time before permanent quays were built, when the shoreline reached much further inland and the area was contained within the 13th-century wall.

SIGHTS

AROUND LA RIBERA

La Ribera is demarcated to the east by the **Parc de la Ciutadella** and to the west by Via Laietana, both products of historic acts of urban vandalism. The first came after the 1714 siege, when the victors, acting on the orders of Philip V, destroyed around 1,000 houses, hospitals and monasteries to build a fortress: the Ciutadella (citadel). The second occurred when the Via Laietana was driven through the district in 1907, in line with the theory of 'ventilating' unsanitary city districts by creating wide avenues; it's now a traffic-choked canyon. There are plans to turn over some of Via Laietana's car lanes to pedestrians, but these are temporarily thwarted by the economic crisis.

From the park's north corner, the grand gateway to the area is the **Arc de Triomf**, an imposing, red-brick arch built by Josep Vilaseca as the entrance for the 1888 Universal Exhibition.

On the west side, the Josep Reynés sculptures adorning the arch represent Barcelona hosting the Exhibition, while the Josep Llimona ones on the east side depict prizes being awarded to the Exhibition's most outstanding contributors. Leading down to the park is the grand palm-lined boulevard of Passeig Lluís Companys, adorned with street lamps and carved stone benches by Pere Falqués. Once inside the park, it's easy to while away a morning, particularly if combined with a trip to the **Zoo** (*see p218*).

The area north of C/Princesa is centred around the tenth-century Benedictine monastery of Sant Pere de les Puelles (open for Mass only), which still stands, if greatly altered, in Plaça de Sant Pere. By the main façade, the superb Modernista wrought-iron drinking fountain was designed by Pere Falqués. For centuries, this area was Barcelona's main centre of textile production; to this day, Sant Pere Més Baix, Sant Pere Més Alt and the streets around them contain many

Parc de la Ciutadella. *See p69.*

textile wholesalers and retailers. Look out for the four low-slung Modernista warehouses of the Serra i Balet velvet manufacturers on neighbouring C/Ortigosa.

The area may be medieval in origin, but its finest monument is an extraordinary piece of Modernisme – the **Palau de la Música Catalana**, on C/Sant Pere Més Alt. Less often noticed on the same street is a curious feature, the Passatge de les Manufactures, a 19th-century arcade that passes inside a building between C/Sant Pere Més Alt and C/Ortigosa.

Sant Pere has been renovated with the gradual opening up of a continuation of Avda Francesc Cambó, which now swings around to meet with C/Allada-Vermell, a wide street that was formed when a block was demolished in 1994. Providing the area with some much-needed open space, the large square of Pou de la Figuera, between C/Sant Pere Més Baix and C/Carders, was completed in 2008 and houses gardens maintained by the neighbours themselves, playgrounds and a football pitch. The **Mercat de Santa Caterina**, one of the city's oldest markets, was rebuilt to a Gaudiesque design by Enric Miralles.

In the eastern corner of the market, by the recently created square of Joan Capri, is the **Espai Santa Caterina** (93 256 21 00, open as market – mornings Mon-Wed, Sat & all day Thur, Fri; free), which houses a portion of the archaeological remains discovered during the market's remodelling. Viewed through a glass floor are Bronze Age buildings, layered beneath a Christian necropolis, and the foundations of the medieval Convent of Santa Caterina, which became the headquarters of the Consell de Cent (an embryonic form of the democratic Barcelona government) and, later, the Inquisition.

Another nearby convent is the Sant Agustí, now a civic centre, on C/Comerç. The entrance contains *Deuce Coop*, a magical 'light sculpture' by James Turrell. Commissioned in the 1980s by the Ajuntament, it's turned on after dark. Almost next door is **Museu de la Xocolata** (*see p217*).

'Born' originally meant 'joust' or 'list', and in the Middle Ages, and for many centuries thereafter, the neighbourhood's main artery, the Passeig del Born, was the focal point of the city's festivals, processions, tournaments, carnivals and the burning of heretics by the Inquisition. At one end of the road is the old Born market, a magnificent 1870s wrought-iron structure that used to be Barcelona's main wholesale food market but closed in the 1970s. Plans to turn the structure into a library were thwarted by the discovery of perfectly preserved medieval remains. The foundations of buildings razed by Philip V's troops were discovered to contain hundreds of objects, some domestic and some, like rusty bombs, suggesting the traumas of the period. Work is under way and ultimately the remains will be incorporated into a cultural centre and museum, although progress is painfully slow.

Museu Picasso. *See p66.*

Walk Parc de la Ciutadella

A stroll around the city's oldest park.

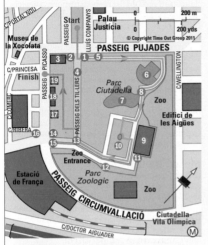

DURATION: 40 MINUTES

Ciutadella Park is named after the hated Bourbon citadel that occupied this site from 1716 to 1869, and the park came into being after the anti-Bourbon revolution of 1868, when General Prim announced that the area could be reclaimed for public use. The garrison fort was gleefully pulled down by hundreds of volunteers. Later, pleasure gardens were built to host the 1888 Universal Exhibition, handsome reminders of which are scattered around the park.

The grandiose Arc de Triomf to the north of the park was built to mark its entrance, and is flanked by the first of the two 'Statues of Progress' erected for the Exhibition: **Commerce** (❶) is represented on the left, and **Industry** (❷) on the right. Through the entrance is Domènech i Montaner's red-brick-and-tile **Castell de Tres Dragons** (❸) on the right – this served as the exhibition café and later the zoology part of the **Natural History Museum**, which is due to reopen in the Fòrum building (*see p109*) in 2011. Stretching ahead is the wide, leafy **Passeig dels Til·lers** (Linden-Tree Boulevard; ❹) and, to the left, Antoni Clavé's modern **Centenary Homage to the Universal Exhibition** (❺).

Continue along this path to **La Cascada** (❻), an extravagant waterfall. It was designed by Josep Fontseré, assisted by a young and unknown Antoni Gaudí.

From here the path south leads past a pretty **boating lake** (❼) on the right and, on the left, a scale model of a **mammoth** (❽). The original plan was that the much-loved mammoth would be joined by 11 other scale models of prehistoric species, but the writer and geologist behind the idea, Norbert Font i Sagué, died before the plan could be realised.

Continuing south on this path are the **Catalan parliament** (❾) buildings on the left, and the elegant Patio de Armes garden on the right. This was designed by JC Forestier in 1917, and its centrepoint is Josep Llimona's weeping woman, **Disconsolate** (❿). At the far end of the parliament buildings, next to the former entrance to the zoo, is the **Monument to Walt Disney** (⓫), a group of leaping deer.

Turn right and soon you'll see the **Monument to the Catalan Volunteers** (⓬) on the left. The plaque reads 'To the Catalans killed in France and around the world in defence of freedom, 1914-1918/1939-1945'. The plaque was replaced with another, mentioning only the First World War, during Franco's rule, and the naked torso adorned with a puritanical fig-leaf, which is there to this day. Beyond this is the entrance to the zoo, in front of which stands an imposing equestrian **statue of General Prim** (⓭), the driving force behind the park. Gracing the columns either side of the park entrance beyond Prim are the other two 'Progress' statues, **Agriculture** (⓮) and **Seamanship** (⓯). Just outside the entrance is the one of the **Wallace Fountains** (⓰), freshly painted and recently transplanted here from the top right corner of the park. Philanthropist Sir Richard Wallace donated 12 of these wrought-iron drinking fountains to the city in the 19th century, but only five remain.

Instead of leaving this way, turn right up the Passeig dels Til·lers where you'll see the **Umbracle** (Shade House; ⓱). This elegant slatted wooden building, also by Fontseré, houses palms and tropical plants, though it has been closed for a while pending restoration. Beside it is the neoclassical former home of the geological section of the Natural History Museum (⓲), and then, alongside the exit leading to Passeig Picasso, the iron-and-glass, Eiffel-inspired **Hivernacle** (Winter House; ⓳).

SIGHTS

Palau de la Música Catalana. *See p69.*

Off the Passeig del Born is C/Montcada, one of the unmissable streets of old Barcelona. A medieval Fifth Avenue, it's lined with a succession of merchants' mansions, some of the greatest of which house the **Museu Barbier-Mueller d'Art Precolombí** and the **Museu Picasso**; the Museu Tèxtil moved uptown to the newly created Disseny Hub Barcelona in the Palau Reial de Pedralbes (*see p104*) in late 2008. Its former home is now called **DHUB Montcada** (C/Montcada 12, 93 256 23 00, www.dhub-bcn.cat, closed Mon, admission €3) and is used for temporary exhibitions.

At the far upper end of C/Montcada is the Placeta d'en Marcús, with its small 12th-century Capella d'en Marcús, built as part of an inn. It was founded by Bernat Marcús, and said to have been the base for the *correus volants* ('flying runners'), Europe's first postal service by horse. The streets nearby were filled with workshops supplying anything from candles to hemp, and these trades are commemorated in the names of many of the streets.

At the other end of the Passeig from the market stands the greatest of all Catalan Gothic buildings, the spectacular basilica of **Santa Maria del Mar**. Opposite the main doors is a recently renovated 13th-century drinking fountain with gargoyles of an eagle and a dragon; on the east side is a funnel-shaped red-brick square, built in 1989 on the site where, it's believed, the last defenders of

the city were executed after Barcelona fell to the Spanish army in 1714. Called the Fossar de les Moreres (Mulberry Graveyard), the square is inscribed with a patriotic poem by Frederic Soler, and nationalist demonstrations converge here every 11 September for Catalan National Day. The red 'eternal flame' sculpture is a more recent, and less popular, addition.

From here, narrow streets lead to the Plaça de les Olles, or the grand Pla del Palau and another symbol of La Ribera, **La Llotja** (The Exchange). Its neo-classical outer shell was added in the 18th century, but its core is a superb 1380s Gothic hall, sadly closed to the public, but open doors mean you can often peer inside. Until the exchange moved to Passeig de Gràcia in 1994, this was the oldest continuously functioning stock exchange in Europe.

Museu Barbier-Mueller d'Art Precolombí

C/Montcada 14 (93 310 45 16, www.barbier-mueller.ch). Metro Jaume I. **Open** 11am-7pm Tue-Fri; 11am-8pm Sat, Sun. **Admission** €3.50; €1.70 reductions; free under-16s. Free 3pm-8pm every Sun; all day 1st Sun of mth. **Credit** (shop only) AmEx, MC, V. **Map** p329 E6.

Located in the 15th-century Palau Nadal, this world-class collection of pre-Columbian art was ceded to Barcelona in 1996 by the Barbier-Mueller Museum in Geneva. The Barcelona holdings focus solely on the Americas, representing most of the styles from the ancient cultures of Meso-America, Andean America and the Amazon region. Dramatically spotlit in black rooms, the frequently changing selection of masks, textiles, jewellery and sculpture includes pieces dating from as far back as the second millennium BC running through to the early 16th-century (demonstrating just how loosely the term 'pre-Columbian' can be used).

Museu Picasso

C/Montcada 15-23 (93 256 30 00, www.museupicasso.bcn.cat). Metro Jaume I. **Open** (last ticket 30mins before closing) 10am-8pm Tue-Sun. **Admission** *All exhibitions* €10; €6 reductions. *Temporary exhibition only* €6; €3 reductions; free under-16s. Free (permanent exhibition only) 3-8pm Sun, & all day 1st Sun of mth. **Credit** MC, V. **Map** p329 E6.

When it opened in 1963, the museum dedicated to Barcelona's favourite adopted son was housed in the Palau Aguilar. Nearly five decades later, the permanent collection of some 3,500 pieces has now been spread across five adjoining palaces, two of which are devoted to temporary exhibitions.

By no means an overview of the artist's work, the Museu Picasso is a record of the vital formative years the young Picasso spent nearby at La Llotja art school (where his father taught), and later hanging out with Catalonia's fin-de-siècle avant-garde.

C/Montcada

Santa Maria del Mar.

Those looking for hits like *Les Demoiselles d'Avignon* (1907) and the first Cubist paintings from the time (many of them done in Catalonia), as well as his collage and sculpture, will be disappointed. The founding of the museum is down to a key figure in Picasso's life, his friend and secretary Jaume Sabartés, who donated his own collection for the purpose. Tribute is paid with a room dedicated to Picasso's portraits of him (best known is the Blue Period painting of Sabartés wearing a white ruff), and Sabartés's own doodlings. The seamless presentation of Picasso's development from 1890 to 1904, from deft pre-adolescent portraits to sketchy landscapes to the intense innovations of his Blue Period, is unbeatable, then it leaps to a gallery of mature Cubist paintings from 1917. The *pièce de résistance* is the complete series of 58 canvases based on Velázquez's famous *Las Meninas*, donated by Picasso himself after the death of Sabartés, and now stretching through the Great Hall. The display ends with linocuts, engravings and a wonderful collection of ceramics donated by Picasso's widow. *Photo p64.*
▶ *The new annual carnet gives unlimited access for €11 (€15 families) – and you avoid the queues.*

★ Palau de la Música Catalana

C/Sant Francesc de Paula 2 (93 295 72 00, www.palaumusica.org). Metro Urquinaona. **Open** *Box office* 10am-9pm Mon-Sat; 10am-1hr before performance Sun. *Guided tours* 10am-3.30pm daily. *Aug* 10am-6pm daily. **Admission** €12; €10 reductions; free under-12s. **Credit** MC, V. **Map** p328 D3.
Commissioned by the nationalistic Orfeó Català choral society, this jawdropping concert hall was intended as a paean to the Catalan *renaixença* and a showcase for the most outstanding Modernista workmanship available. Domènech i Montaner's façade is a frenzy of colour and detail, including a large allegorical mosaic representing the members of the Orfeó Català, and floral tiled columns topped with the busts of Bach, Beethoven and Palestrina on the main façade and Wagner on the side. Inside, a great deal of money has been spent improving the acoustics, but visitors don't really come here to feast their ears: the eyes have it.
Decoration erupts everywhere. The ceiling is an inverted bell of stained glass on which the sun bursts out of a blue sky; 18 half-mosaic, half-relief Muses appear out of the back of the stage; winged horses fly over the upper balcony. The carved arch over the stage represents folk and classical music: the left side has Catalan composer/conductor Anselm Clavé sitting over young girls singing 'Flors de Maig', a traditional Catalan song, while the right has Wagnerian Valkyries riding over a bust of Beethoven.
By the 1980s, the Palau was bursting under the pressure of the musical activity going on inside it, and a church next door was demolished to make space for Òscar Tusquet's extension, a project which, combined with the extensive renovations to

the old building, spanned over 20 years. Rather than try to compete with the existing façade, the new part has subtler, organic motifs in ochre brick – particularly striking are the frilled mushroom gills on the underside of the circular tower.
Guided tours are available in English every hour and start with a short film of the Palau's history. Be sure to ask questions: the guides are knowledgeable, but unless prompted, they tend to concentrate mainly on the triumphs of the renovation. *Photo p67.*
▶ *Liked this? Domènech i Montaner's Hospital de la Santa Creu i Sant Pau (see p91) is equally ornate.*

★ FREE Parc de la Ciutadella

Passeig Picasso (93 413 24 00). Metro Arc de Triomf or Barceloneta. **Open** 9am-sunset daily. **Admission** free. **Map** p327 H11/J11.
There's so much going on in this extensive park – the zoo, the Natural History Museum, Catalan parliament buildings, a school, a church, a boating lake, a bandstand – that it's sometimes hard to find a plain, old-fashioned patch of grass. On a sunny Sunday you'll have to fight with hordes of picnicking families, bongo players and dogs for a bit of the green stuff; even then it will be distinctly worn from serving as a back garden to the space-starved inhabitants of the Old City. *See also p65* **Walk.** *Photo p63.*

★ FREE Santa Maria del Mar

Plaça de Santa Maria (93 310 23 90). Metro Jaume I. **Open** 9am-1.30pm, 4.30-8pm Mon-Sat; 10am-1.30pm, 5-8.30pm Sun. **Admission** free. **Map** p329 E6.
One of the most perfect surviving examples of the Catalan Gothic style, this graceful basilica stands out for its characteristic horizontal lines, plain surfaces, square buttresses and flat-topped octagonal towers. Its superb unity of style is down to the fact that it was built relatively quickly, with construction taking just 55 years (1329 to 1384). Named after Mary as patroness of sailors, it was built on the site of a small church known as Santa Maria d'Arenys (sand), for its position close to the sea. In the broad, single nave interior, two rows of perfectly proportioned columns soar up to fan vaults, creating an atmosphere of space around the light-flooded altar. There's also superb stained glass, especially the great 15th-century rose window above the main door. The original window fell down during an earthquake, killing 25 people. The incongruous modern window at the other end was a 1997 addition, belatedly celebrating the Olympics.
It's perhaps thanks to the group of anti-clerical anarchists who set the church ablaze for 11 days in 1936 that its superb features can be appreciated – without the wooden Baroque furniture that clutters so many Spanish churches, the simplicity of its lines can emerge. On Saturdays, the basilica is in great demand for weddings, and it's a traditional venue for concerts: look out for a Requiem Mass at Easter and Handel's *Messiah* at Christmas.

SIGHTS

The Raval

From Genet, slumming, to gentrification.

In the early 20th century, the Raval was notorious for its seedy theatres, brothels, anarchist groups and dosshouses. Despite decades of costly transformation – which, among other additions, have seen the arrival of a huge modern art gallery (the **MACBA**) and a four-star hotel (the **Barceló**; *see p123*) – the old red-light district still retains a busy crew of prostitutes, transsexuals and drug addicts. Many of these unshiftable locals could have stepped straight from the pages of Jean Genet's *The Thief's Journal*, a chronicle of the time the writer spent here as a teenage rent boy during the 1920s.

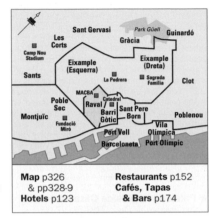

Map p326	**Restaurants** p152
& pp328-9	**Cafés, Tapas**
Hotels p123	**& Bars** p174

The area north of C/Carme (here we've described it as 'Upper Raval') has seen the most changes thanks to gentrification. These days it buzzes with art galleries and bars. The 'Lower Raval' still has a seedy port feel, but is worth the trip to see a couple of architectural gems: Gaudí's **Palau Güell** and the Romanesque **Sant Pau del Camp** church.

INTRODUCING THE RAVAL

Ever on the margins, Raval (*arrabal* in Spanish) is a generic word adapted from the Arabic *ar-rabad*, meaning 'outside the walls'. When a defensive wall was built down the north side of La Rambla in the 13th century, the area now sandwiched between Avda Paral·lel and La Rambla was a sparsely populated green belt of garden plots. Over the centuries, the land was to absorb the functional spillover from the city in the form of monasteries, churches, religious hospitals, prisons and virtually any noxious industry that citizens didn't want on their doorstep. When industrialisation arrived in the 18th century, the area became Barcelona's working-class district.

This was also the part of town where most land was available; yet more was freed up after the government dissolved the monasteries in the Desamortización ('Disentailment') of 1836, and early industries, mainly the textile mills, took the space. Workers lived in crowded slums devoid of ventilation or running water, and malnutrition, TB, scrofula and typhus kept the average life expectancy to a mere 40 years.

It's no coincidence that the city's sanatoriums, orphanages and hospitals were based here.

Widely known as the Quinto, or 'Fifth District', this was also where the underclass forged the centre of revolutionary Barcelona, and a breeding ground for anarchists and other radicals. Innumerable riots began here, and entire streets became no-go areas after dark. Heroin's arrival in the late 1970s caused extra problems; the semi-tolerated petty criminality became threatening and affected tourism.

Since the 1980s, city planners have done their best to open up the Raval by turning the area into something of a cultural theme park, installing or rebuilding a slew of high profile cultural institutions. Spurred on by the approaching 1992 Olympics, the authorities made a clean sweep of the Lower Raval. Whole blocks with links to prostitution or drugs were demolished, and many of the displaced families were transferred to housing estates on the edge of town, out of sight. A sports centre, a police station and office blocks were constructed, and some streets were pedestrianised.

However, the planners were caught by surprise by the sudden mass arrival of non-

SIGHTS

European immigrants into the area, starting in the 1990s. These new residents have perhaps done more to transform the Raval than any of the council's best laid plans. By 2006, more than half the *barrio*'s residents were from outside Spain, the majority from Pakistan and Ecuador. The Raval is now one of the most ethnically diverse places in Europe, with more than 70 different nationalities calling it home. Shop signs appear in a babel of languages, plugging everything from halal meat to Bollywood films and cheap calls to South America.

Despite this immigration, the council continued with its ambitions to revive the area. The most dramatic plan was to create a *'Raval obert al cel'* ('Raval open to the sky'), the most tangible result of which is the sweeping, palm-lined Rambla del Raval, completed in 2000. L'Illa de la Rambla del Raval, also known as the Illa Robador, is a mega-complex halfway up the new *rambla* that includes a hotel, offices, housing, shops and the Filmoteca (due for completion at the end of 2010). The nondescript housing blocks were completed by 2007, while new office space and a luxury hotel opened in 2008. The hotel was designed, in the words of its architect Pere Puig, as 'a cylindrical lamp to shed light on a dark neighbourhood'; however, after local complaints of light pollution, the building was instead coated in steel mesh, ostensibly to protect its guests' privacy. Whatever the case, the shiny armour of a high-end hotel in the middle of a once working-class district is a telling symbol of the growing disconnect in the city between tourism and local neighbourhood life.

The facelift has also raised prices. Alongside the immigrants, a wealthier community of arty western expats and university students have begun to arrive, dotting the area with galleries,

Antic Hospital de la Santa Creu.
See p72.

SIGHTS

shops and cafés. In and around C/Lluna you'll find a good number of small, inviting boutiques stocking locally designed clothes; C/Ferlandina has its share of boho cafés, and old industrial spaces along C/Riereta now serve as studios to more than 40 artists.

Despite its gentrification, the Raval has not lost its associations with crime and sleaze. Take care, particularly after dark in the area down towards the port. That said, as long as you exercise the usual precautions – staying off badly lit sidestreets, not flaunting your new digital camera – the Raval can make for a fascinating wander.

THE UPPER RAVAL

From La Rambla, signposts for the MACBA carefully guide visitors along the gentrified 'tourist corridors' of C/Tallers, C/Elisabets and C/Bonsuccès to a playground of cafés, galleries and boutiques. The centre of the Upper Raval is the Plaça dels Àngels, where the 16th-century Convent dels Àngels houses both the FAD design institute and a gigantic almshouse, the Casa de la Caritat, converted into a cultural complex housing the **MACBA** and the **CCCB**.

When the clean, high-culture MACBA opened in 1995, it seemed to embody everything the Raval was not, and was initially mocked as an isolated and isolating social experiment. Over the years, though, the square has become an

---

INSIDE TRACK
FORTUNE'S WHEEL

A circular wooden panel, a coat of arms and a slot for alms are all that remain on the façade of the **Casa de la Misericòrdia** at C/Ramalleres 17. Founded as a hospice in 1583, it later became the Casa Provincial de Maternitat i Expòsits (Maternity and Abandoned Children's Home), run by nuns. From 1853 to 1931, the foundling wheel behind the panel provided a means of leaving very young children in the nuns' care, anonymity intact. The infant would be placed on the revolving surface, a screen would close behind it and the nuns would hang a label round its neck stating the date of entry.

unofficial home to the city's skateboarders, and the surrounding streets have filled with restaurants and boutiques. There are now university faculties of philosophy, geography and history across from the CCCB, and thousands of students are also changing the character of the place.

Below here, C/Hospital and C/Carme meet at the Plaça Pedró, where the tiny Romanesque chapel (and ex-lepers' hospital) of Sant Llàtzer sits. From La Rambla, the area is accessed along either street or through the Boqueria market, itself the site of the Sant Josep monastery until the Desamortización. Behind the Boqueria is the **Antic Hospital de la Santa Creu**, which took in the city's sick from the 15th century until 1926. It now houses the Massana Arts School and a small neighbourhood library, as well as the much larger Catalan National Library, the headquarters of the Institute of Catalan Studies and **La Capella**, an attractive exhibition space.

C/Carme is capped at the Rambla end by the 18th-century Església de Betlem (Bethlehem), with its serpentine pillars and geometrically patterned façade. Its name features on many shop signs nearby; older residents still refer to this part of the Raval as Betlem.

MACBA

FREE Antic Hospital de la Santa Creu & La Capella

C/Carme 47-C/Hospital 56 (no phone). Metro Liceu. **Open** *9am-11pm Mon-Sat. La Capella (93 442 71 71) noon-2pm, 4-8pm Tue-Sat; 11am-2pm Sun.* **Admission** free. **Map** p328 A4.

This was one of Europe's earliest medical centres. There was a hospital on the site as early as 1024, but in the 15th century it expanded to centralise all the city's hospitals and sanatoriums (with the exception of the Santa Margarida leper colony, which remained outside the city walls). By the 1920s, it was hopelessly overstretched, and its medical facilities were moved uptown to the Hospital Sant Pau. One of the last patients was Gaudí, who died here in 1926; it was also where Picasso painted one of his first important pictures, *Dead Woman* (1903).

The buildings combine a 15th-century Gothic core with Baroque and classical additions. They're now given over to cultural institutions, among them the Massana Arts School, a neighbourhood library, the Catalan National Library (the second largest in Spain), the Institute of Catalan Studies and the Royal Academy of Medicine, which hosts occasional concerts. Highlights include a neo-classical lecture theatre complete with revolving marble dissection table (open 10am-2pm Mon-Fri), and the entrance hall of the Casa de Convalescència, tiled with lovely Baroque ceramic murals telling the story of St Paul; one features an artery-squirting decapitation scene. La Capella, the hospital chapel, was rescued from a sad fate as a warehouse and sensitively converted into an exhibition space for contemporary art. The courtyard is a popular spot for reading or eating lunch. *Photo p71.*

★ CCCB (Centre de Cultura Contemporània de Barcelona)

C/Montalegre 5 (93 306 41 00, www.cccb.org). Metro Catalunya. **Open** *11am-8pm Tue, Wed, Fri-Sun; 11am-10pm Thur.* **Admission** *1 exhibition* €4.50; €3.40 reductions & Wed. *2 exhibitions* €6; €4.50 reductions; free under-16s. Free to all 1st Wed of mth; 8-10pm Thur; 3-8pm Sun. **Credit** MC, V. **Map** p328 A2.

Spain's largest cultural centre was opened in 1994 at the Casa de la Caritat, a former almshouse, built in 1802 on the site of a medieval monastery. The massive façade and part of the courtyard remain from the original building; the rest was rebuilt in dramatic contrast, all tilting glass and steel, by architects Piñon and Viaplana, known for the Maremagnum shopping centre (*see p185*). The CCCB's exhibitions can lean toward heavy-handed didacticism, but there are occasional gems.

MACBA (Museu d'Art Contemporani de Barcelona)

Plaça dels Àngels 1 (93 412 08 10, www.macba. cat). Metro Catalunya. **Open** *Late June-24 Sept 11am-8pm Mon, Wed; 11am-midnight Thur, Fri;*

Moon Walks

An overlooked street blasts off into the partysphere every full moon.

In the heart of what was previously a neglected, dark side of the city, **C/Lluna** has enjoyed a steady rejuvenation in recent years with the arrival of more and more artistic talent. Taking a cue from its name, 'Moon Street' has begun to stage lively street parties on full moon nights. **Lluna Vivent** ('Living Moon') as the event has been christened, showcases an eclectic group of artisan-oriented shops, workshops, associations, bars and restaurants located on and around the pedestrian street.

The moon-fests include numerous happenings staged by the participating organisations. Previous parties saw **Taller Paloma** (C/Paloma 8) holding a volunteer fashion show of its cool, unique designs dreamed up by a French and Belgian duo. Male and female volunteers looking to strut their stuff should sign up to select their apparel between 5 and 7pm for such shows, which normally take place out on the street from C/Paloma to C/Lluna.

Over at the **NGO Agermanament** (C/Lluna 22), meanwhile, moonwalkers can quell their hunger with dishes from Cameroon, while the nearby **Almazen** (C/Guifré 9) stages a freestyle, open-mic night for anyone hit by the sudden need to let out an amplified howl. Original audiovisuals might be projected on to the street at **Antidoto 28** (C/Ferlandina 28), and those looking to slake their thirst can head to **El Balcón de Aquiles** (C/Leó 9), a bar that has revived the traditional serving of free tapas with drinks.

Other notable participants include **Imanol Ossa – Design Art Studio** (C/Lleó 6), who designs highly creative lamps and furnishings from recycled materials such as piano keys and bicycle fenders; **Del Través** (C/Lluna 13), a charming workshop-cum-showroom of upcycled apparel subjected to 'textile alchemy', according to designer

Fiona Capdevila; holy housewife ironing-board sculptures by Karol Bergeret at **Tallers de Ideas** (C/Sant Vincenç 33); irresistible woven works at **Colorin Colorado** (C/Lluna 7); and one-of-a-kind clothing at **Novedades** (C/Peu de la Creu 24), which has in the past hosted a homemade headgear competition.

Most of the spaces participating in the street party are also open during normal shopping times, or can be visited by appointment. For detail of events, visit the website www.llunavivent.blogspot.com.

10am-8pm Sat; 10am-3pm Sun. *Late Sept-23 June* 11am-7.30pm Mon, Wed-Fri; 10am-8pm Sat; 10am-3pm Sun. **Admission** *Permanent collection* €6; €4.50 reductions. *Permanent & temporary exhibitions* €7.50; €6 reductions. *Temporary exhibitions* €6; €4.50 reductions. *Annual pass* €10. **Credit** MC, V. **Map** p328 A2. If you're used to being soft-soaped by eager-to-please art centres, you'll have to make a bit of a mental

adjustment to accommodate the cryptic minimalism of the MACBA, where art is taken very seriously indeed. Yet if you can navigate the fridge-like interior of Richard Meier's enormous edifice, accept that much of the permanent collection is inaccessible to the uninitiated, tackle shows that flutter between the brilliant and baffling, and, most importantly, are prepared to do your reading, a trip to the MACBA can be extremely rewarding.

SIGHTS

Since its inauguration in 1995, the MACBA has transformed itself into a power player on the city's contemporary arts scene. Its library/study centre and auditorium host an extensive programme that includes accessibly priced (or free) concerts, conferences and cinema, while two floors of exhibition rooms offer a spacious showcase for large-scale installations and exhaustive, multidisciplinary shows. La Capella, a former medieval convent across the square, is free to enter, and provides a project space for specially commissioned works.

The permanent collection sits on the ground floor of the main building, and is rooted in the second half of the 20th century. Media, sound and performance art experimentalists of the 1960s and '70s, including Bruce Nauman, Joan Jonas and John Cage, are well represented, as are Spanish and Catalan artists such as Antoni Muntadas, Antoni Tàpies and the Dau al Set group.

Temporary shows at MACBA take the form of highly ambitious research projects. Until the end of April 2011, Are You Ready For Television? scrutinises the relationship between art and television. The smaller-scale shows here can be delightfully offbeat, such as that dedicated to Düsseldorf-based gallery owner Konrad Fischer, who gave Sol LeWitt and Dan Flavin their first shows in Europe. Others showcase low-key artists, particularly locals, with equal enthusiasm.

▶ *There are daily guided tours in English (times vary according to exhibition), included in the cost of admission.*

THE LOWER RAVAL

The lower half of the Raval, from C/Hospital down, is generally referred to as the Barrio Chino (or simply 'el Xino'). The nickname was coined in the 1920s by a journalist likening the neighbourhood to San Francisco's Chinatown, and referred to its underworld feel rather than to any Chinese population. In those days, drifters filled the bars, and cheap hostels lined streets such as Nou de la Rambla, alongside high-class cabarets and brothels for the rich, and cheap porn pits for the poor. A glimpse of the old sleaze can still be found in and around bars such as Bar Pastís and Marsella (also known as the 'absinthe bar'; *see p177*), while a small and appropriately seedy square is named after Jean Genet.

Just beneath C/Hospital in the Plaça Sant Agustí lies one of the Raval's more arresting pieces of architecture; the unfinished 18th-century church of Sant Agustí (No.2, no phone, Mass 11am, 1pm & 8pm Mon-Fri, 11am Sat, 11am, noon & 8pm Sun). The stone beams and jags protruding from its left flank on C/Arc de Sant Agustí and the undecorated sections of the Baroque façade show how suddenly work stopped when funding ran out.

Inside, the Capella de Santa Rita is packed on her feast day, which is 22 May; Rita is the patron saint of lost causes, and it is to her that the unhappy and unrequited bring their red roses to be blessed.

C/Nou de la Rambla, the area's main street, is home to Gaudí's first major project: the medievalist townhouse Palau Güell, at No.3. Nearby in C/Sant Pau is a Modernista landmark, Domènech i Montaner's Hotel España, and at the end of the same street sits the Romanesque church of Sant Pau del Camp. Iberian remains dating to 200 BC have been found next to the building, marking it as one of the oldest parts of the city. At the lower end of the area were the Drassanes (shipyards), now home to the Museu Marítim (*see p78*). Along the Avda Paral·lel side of this Gothic building lies the only large remaining section of Barcelona's 14th-century city wall.

FREE Palau Güell

C/Nou de la Rambla 3-5 (93 317 39 74, www. palauguell.cat). Metro Drassanes or Liceu. Open From May 2011. Map p329 A6.
A fortress-like edifice shoehorned into a narrow six-storey sliver, the Palau Güell was Gaudí's first major commission, begun in 1886 for textile baron Eusebi Güell. After major structural renovation, it is expected to fully reopen in 2011, when once again visitors will be able to look around the subterranean stables, with their exotic canopy of stone palm fronds on the ceiling, and the vestibule with ornate mudéjar carved ceilings from which the Güells could snoop on their arriving guests through the jalousie trellis-work. At the heart of the house, the spectacular six-storey hall, complete with musicians' galleries and topped by a dome is covered in cobalt honeycomb tiles. Visitors will also be shown a short video about the building. The antidote to this dark and gloomy palace lies on its roof terrace, decorated with a rainbow forest of 20 mosaic-clad chimneys.
▶ *For more on Gaudí, see pp40-41.*

★ Sant Pau del Camp

C/Sant Pau 101 (93 441 00 01). Metro Paral·lel. Open 10am-1.30pm, 4-7pm Mon-Sat. Mass 8pm Sat (Spanish); noon Sun (Catalan). Admission Visits €3; €2 reductions; free under-14s. Mass free. No credit cards. Map p326 E11.
The name St Paul in the Field reflects a time when the Raval was still countryside. In fact, this little Romanesque church is over 1,000 years old; the date carved on its most prestigious headstone – that of Count Guifré II Borrell, son of Wilfred 'the Hairy' and inheritor of all Barcelona and Girona – is AD 912. The church's impressive façade includes sculptures of fantastical flora and fauna along with human grotesques. The tiny cloister is another highlight, with its extraordinary Visigoth capitals, triple-lobed arches and central fountain.

Barceloneta & the Ports

The Olympic Games and times of change.

The 1992 Olympic Games were the catalyst for Barcelona's most notable transformation (and there have been many). Barcelona had famously 'turned its back on the sea' until some sharp city planners finally spotted the potential of its Mediterranean location. From industrial slum to leisure port, Barcelona's shoreline transformation is the result of two decades of development. The clean-up has extended to the whole seven kilometres of city seashore: this stretch is now a virtually continuous strip of modern construction, bristling with new docks, marinas, hotels, cruise-ship terminals, ferry harbours and leisure areas.

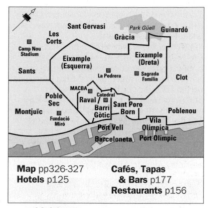

Map pp326-327	Cafés, Tapas
Hotels p125	& Bars p177
	Restaurants p156

The seafront got a second blast of wind in its sails from the 2004 Fòrum, which spawned a huge new swimming and watersports area, resculpted beaches and a park. The final grand project at the far end of Barcelona's waterfront is a state-of-the-art but controversial marine zoo, with four different ecosystems. The economic crisis, however, has put this on the backburner until at least 2014.

PORT VELL

The initial focus of the Olympic makeover was the area rechristened Port Vell (Old Port). Tearing out the railroad, warehouses and waste dumps that cut the city off from the sea, developers carved out a palm-lined promenade ringing a luxury yacht marina in what was Barcelona's main port in medieval times. In those days the city was the dominant naval power in western Mediterranean trade. Nearby are the Drassanes Reials (Royal Shipyards). Now home to the **Museu Marítim**, the shipyards remain among the finest pieces of civilian Gothic architecture in Spain.

Barcelona's power was dealt a blow when Christopher Columbus sailed westwards and found what he thought was the East. Soon, the Atlantic became the important trade route and Barcelona went into recession. Still, the city commemorates Columbus with the **Monument a Colom**. Prosperity returned in the 19th century, when the city became the base for the Spanish industrial revolution. Trade continues to boom at the Moll d'Espanya (Wharf of Spain), an artificial island linked to the bottom of La Rambla by the undulating wooden Rambla de Mar footbridge designed by Viaplana and Piñón. The island is home to the **Maremagnum** mall (*see p185*), an **IMAX** cinema (*see p223*) and **L'Aquàrium**.

At Columbus's feet, both the **Golondrinas** and the **Catamaran Orsom** pleasure boats begin their excursions out to sea. To the right, beyond the busy ferry and cruise ports, is the grandly named Porta d'Europa, the longest drawbridge in Europe, which curtains off the vast container port. Big as it is, plans are under way to enlarge the container port by diverting the mouth of the River Llobregat a mile or so to the south, which will double the port area in size by 2050. Andreu Alfaro's enormous *Onas* (Waves) greatly cheers up the gridlocked roundabout of Plaça de la Carbonera, where a grim basin of coal marks the spot where steamboats once refuelled.

Parallel with the Passeig de Colom, the refurbished Moll de la Fusta (Wood Wharf) boulevard was built after the city sea walls were demolished in 1878. The wooden pergolas, one of which is topped by Javier Mariscal's popular fibreglass *Gamba* (Shrimp), are all that remain of some ill-fated restaurants and clubs. Traffic noise and congestion have been greatly reduced by passing the coastal motorway underneath the boulevard.

Just over the grassy slopes stands the *Ictineo II*; it's a replica of the world's first combustion-powered submarine, created by Narcis Monturiol and launched from Barcelona port in 1862. Roy Lichtenstein's pop art *Barcelona Head* signposts the marina, with more than 450 moorings for leisure boats, and the **Palau de Mar**, the only remaining warehouse from the area's industrial past, now converted into offices, restaurants and the **Museu d'Història de Catalunya**. The adjoining Moll del Dipòsit (Warehouse Wharf)

Museu d'Història de Catalunya.

is crammed at the weekends with a craft market and immigrants selling knock-off goods.

Catamaran Orsom

Portal de la Pau, Port de Barcelona (93 221 82 83, www.barcelona-orsom.com, www.barcelona speedboat.com). Metro Drassanes. **Sailings** (approx 1hr 30mins) *Oct-Apr* call to confirm times. *May-Sept* noon, 3pm, 6pm daily. **Tickets** €12.50; €9.50 reductions; free under-4s. **Credit** AmEx, MC, V. **Map** p326 F12.
Departing from the jetty just by the Monument a Colom, this 23m (75ft) sail catamaran is the largest in Barcelona – it chugs up to 80 seafarers around to the Nova Bocana harbour area before unfurling its sails and peacefully gliding across the bay. There are evening jazz/chill out cruises at 6pm and 8pm at weekends from July to August (€14.90, €12.90 reductions; free under-4s) and a new speedboat trip runs to the Fòrum and back (50mins, €10.95, €9.50 reductions; free under-4s).

Las Golondrinas

Moll de Drassanes (93 442 31 06, www. lasgolondrinas.com). Metro Drassanes. **Sailings** Approximately hourly until sunset, depending on weather and demand. **Tickets** *Drassanes to breakwater & return* €6.50; €2.60 reductions; free under-4s. *Drassanes to Port Fòrum & return* €13.50; €5-11 reductions; free under-4s. **Credit** MC, V. **Map** p326 F12.
Since the 1888 World Exhibition, the 'swallow boats' have chugged around the harbour, giving passengers a bosun's eye-view of Barcelona's rapidly changing seascape. The traditional double-decker pleasure boats serve the shorter port tour (boats depart around every 40 minutes), while the more powerful catamarans tour as far as the Port Fòrum. Opening hours tend to be a bit erratic, so do check the website beforehand if possible. The Cine Mar tours (€25) at 10pm daily, from late July to late August, show black-and-white films from the silent era with an authentic live piano accompaniment.

★ Monument a Colom

Plaça Portal de la Pau (93 302 52 24). Metro Drassanes. **Open** *May-Sept* 9am-8.30pm daily. *Oct-Apr* 9am-6.30pm daily. **Admission** €3; €2 reductions; free under-4s. **Credit** MC, V. **Map** p326 F12.
Inspired by Nelson's Column, and complete with eight majestic lions, the Christopher Columbus monument was designed for the Universal Exhibition of 1888. Positioned at the base of La Rambla, the monument allegedly marks the spot where Columbus docked in 1493 after his discovery of the Americas, and the carvings illustrate key moments in his voyages. Columbus's white hair comes courtesy of the city pigeons, so take appropriate cover if you decide to take the tiny lift up inside the column to the vertiginous viewing platform.

On Your Bike Barceloneta & the Ports

A gentle ride along the waterfront.

Start your ride outside the **Monument a Colom**, dedicated to Christopher Columbus. Start riding along the **Moll de la Fusta** (with the port to your right) either using the designated bike path on the upper level or, if there's not too much pedestrian traffic, along the prettier lower level that skirts the waterfront.

When you reach Roy Lichtenstein's *Barcelona Head* statue at the end of Via Laietana, veer right to continue along the boulevard that runs past the **Museu d'Historia de Catalunya** and the marina, **Passeig Joan de Borbó**. This is also the threshold to the salty, seaside *barrio* of Barceloneta. Turn left into the **C/Maquinista** and continue for a minute or so and soon you'll hit the **Mercat de Barceloneta**, one of the city's

striking new indoor markets and a good place for a snack or tapa. Cross the square in front of the market and continue walking down the **C/Baluard** to the waterfront (be careful at the crossroads on this stretch). Turn right at the top and then breeze all the way down the promenade to the tall, sail-shaped **W Hotel** (*see p125*; you can't miss it). On its far side is a *plaça* with unrestricted views into the big blue.

In the opposite direction the beach promenade offers smooth two-wheeled sailing for another couple of kilometres. If you don't mind a bit of sand under your wheels, you could even venture right out as far as the **Fòrum** complex, from where you and your bike can get on the metro to head back into town.

► For details of bike hire, *see p295*.

Museu d'Història de Catalunya
Plaça Pau Vila 3 (93 225 47 00, www.mhcat.net). Metro Barceloneta. **Open** 10am-7pm Tue, Thur-Sat; 10am-8pm Wed; 10am-2.30pm Sun. **Admission** *All exhibitions* €5; €4 reductions; free under-7s & over-65s; free to all 1st Sun of mth. *Permanent exhibition* €4; €3 reductions. *Temporary exhibitions* €3; €2 reductions. **Credit** MC, V. **Map** p326 H12.
With exhibits spanning from the Lower Paleolithic era right up to Jordi Pujol's proclamation as

President of the Generalitat in 1980, the Catalan History Museum offers a virtual chronology of the region's past. There are two floors of text, film, animated models and reproductions of everything from a medieval shoemaker's shop to a 1960s bar. Hands-on activities, such as trying to lift a knight's armour or irrigating lettuces with a Moorish water wheel, add a little pzazz to the rather dry early history; to exit the exhibition, visitors walk over a huge 3-D map of Catalonia. Every section has a decent introduction in English; the reception desk can offer in-

SIGHTS

The Beaches. *See p80.*

depth English-language museum guides free of charge, and the English website is also very complete. Excellent temporary exhibitions typically examine recent aspects of regional politics and history while the huge rooftop café terrace has unbeatable views over the city and marina.
▶ *For an overview of Catalonia's past turn to the History chapter (see pp14-31).*

★ Museu Marítim
Avda Drassanes (93 342 99 20, www.mmb.cat). Metro Drassanes. Closed until 2013. **Map** p326 F12.
Even if you can't tell a caravel from a catamaran, the excellent Maritime Museum is worth a visit, as the soaring arches and vaults of the vast former *drassanes* (shipyards) represent one the most perfectly preserved examples of civil Gothic architecture in Spain. In medieval times, the shipyards sat right on the water's edge and were used to dry-dock, repair and build vessels for the royal fleets. The finest of these was Don Juan de Austria's galley, from which he commanded the fleet at Lepanto that defeated the Ottoman navy in 1571: a full-scale replica is the mainstay of the collection.

With the aid of an audio guide, the maps, mastheads, nautical instruments, multimedia displays and models show you how shipbuilding and navigation techniques have developed over the years. The admission fee also covers the beautiful 1917 *Santa Eulàlia* schooner docked nearby in the Moll de la Fusta, and the Maritime often has some interesting temporary exhibitions. Note that the museum is closed for renovation until 2013.

Teleféric del Port
Torre de Sant Sebastià (93 441 48 20). Metro Barceloneta. **Open** *June-Sept* 11am-8pm daily. *Oct-Feb* 11am-5.30pm daily. *Mar-May* 11am-7pm daily. **Tickets** €9 single; €12.50 return; free under-6s. **No credit cards. Map** p326 G13.
These rather battered cable cars do not appear to have been touched – except for the installation of lifts – since they were built for the 1929 Expo. They provide sky-high views over Barcelona on their grinding, squeaking path from the Sant Sebastià tower at the very far end of Passeig Joan de Borbó to the Jaume I tower in front of the World Trade Center; the final leg ends at the Miramar lookout point on Montjuïc. Make sure you go late in the day to avoid long queues.

BARCELONETA

Fishing tackle shops are moving out and cocktail bars are moving into the area. The tight-knit seaside community of Barceloneta ('Little Barcelona') is metamorphosing from a working-class neighbourhood dependent on fishing and heavy industry into a node of leisured bucket-and-spade tourism with ever greater numbers of bars, restaurants and homes converted into short-stay holiday flats.

And there is more to come. As part of the Pla de Barris initiative, more than €16 million are being pumped in to improve buildings and sanitary conditions and open up the cramped interior to the main promenades; there is even talk of a new *rambla*, connecting the recently remodelled market square to the beach. It looks good on paper, but many residents are suspicious of the motives behind this vision of a shiny new Barceloneta, fearful that it's simply a municipal push to transform a neglected slice of beachfront real estate into a tourist playground.

Controversy is not new to Barceloneta. When the old maritime *barri* of La Ribera was demolished in 1714 to make way for the citadel, thousands were made homeless and forced to live in slums on the beach. The question of where to put them was solved by the broad tongue of silt that had built up after the construction of a breakwater in 1474; by the 18th century, it was solid enough to build on, and in 1753, the new district of Barceloneta was born. Military engineer Juan Martín Cermeño laid out narrow rows of cheap workers' housing set around a parade ground (now the market square). The two-storey houses became home to fishermen, sailors and dockers.

With the arrival of factories and shipbuilding yards in the 19th century, the area soon became so overcrowded with workers that the houses were split in half and later in quarters. These famous *quarts de casa* typically measured no more than 30 square metres (320 square feet), had no running water until the 1960s and often held families of ten or so. Most were later built up to six or more levels, but even today, many of the flats remain cramped and in bad condition despite their brightly painted façades.

Since the Olympic clean-up, Barceloneta has had a higher profile, and current redevelopment includes university housing, Enric Miralles's glass-covered Gas Natural headquarters and, in the heart of the neighbourhood, the new market designed by Josep Miàs, a choppy composition of slats, undulating steel, solar panels and wrought iron recycled from the original 1884

Booked Up

Lending libraries for beach-goers.

In this era of ten-kilo luggage allowances, and with every possible frippery – ranging from just-in-case hiking boots to any toiletry fancier than soap – removed from suitcases everywhere, Ken Follett and his ilk have understandably taken a bit of a knock. Given the choice between 500g of Noah Gordon and a change of clothes, most people will plump for the latter.

Keen to improve the lot of their international visitors, and to bolster the attractions of Barcelona's artificial shoreline at the same time, the people at the city council have established two *biblioplatges*, beach libraries, for the use of tourists, who merely need to provide valid ID. The libraries stock around 200 novels, in various languages, along with kids' books and comics, magazines and a selection of newspapers from around the world.

Running alongside these services, and also incalculably useful for visitors with kids and small baggage allowances is the *ludoplatja*, which lends buckets and spades, sand moulds, watering cans and the like. The adults, meanwhile, can help themselves to volleyball balls and nets, beach boules and frisbees courtesy of the *esportplatja*.

The services are open daily from 11am to 7pm at the Centre de la Platja underneath the boardwalk below the Hospital del Mar in July and August, and at the Bac de Roda breakwater from July to September.
► For more, see www.bcn.cat/platges

SIGHTS

structure. The new market and large central square have acted as a catalyst for small businesses that cater to the increasingly international local population with new restaurants, food shops and boutiques.

The area has also been the beneficiary of a staggering amount of sculpture, particularly around the main promenade of **Passeig Joan de Borbó**. Lothar Baumgarten's *Rosa dels Vents* (Wind Rose) has the names of Catalan sea winds embedded in the pavement, and, at the other end of Passeig Joan de Borbó is Juan Muñoz's disturbing sculpture of five caged figures known as *Una habitació on sempre plou* (A Room Where It Always Rains). Monuments within the quarter include the 18th-century church of Sant Miquel del Port, with a muscular sculpture of the Archangel Michael on the façade and the Font de Carmen Amaya at the sea end of C/Sant Carles, a fountain dedicated to the gypsy flamenco dancer born in 1913 in the Somorrostro, a long-gone beach slum.

Follow the yachts moored along the Moll de la Barceloneta down to the small remaining fishing area by the clock tower (previously a beacon to guide ships into port), which is the emblem of the neighbourhood. Further down, the road leads to the Nova Bocana development, which is currently under construction. The complex will combine high-end leisure facilities and offices and is dominated by Ricardo Bofill's Hotel Vela, a towering sail-shaped luxury hotel. If you head left where Passeig Joan de Borbó passes the beach, you'll reach Rebecca Horn's tower of rusty cubes, *Estel Ferit* (Wounded Star), which pays homage to the much-missed *xiringuitos* (beach restaurants) that lined the sands in pre-Olympic days. The **Passeig Marítim** esplanade runs north from here, and is a popular hangout for skaters and strollers.

THE BEACHES

Barcelona never had much of a beach culture until the 1992 Olympics opened the city's eyes to the commercial potential of its location. What little sand there was before then was grey and clogged with private swimming baths and *xiringuitos* that served seafood on trestle tables set up on the sand; the rest was given over to heavy industry and waste dumps, cut off from the rest of the city by a strip of rail track, warehouses and factories.

For the grand Olympic makeover, the beaches were swiftly cleared and filled with tons of golden sand, imported palm trees and landscaped promenades. Visitors flocked, but the city beaches have become a victim of their own popularity, and keeping them clean is something of a Sisyphean task for the city council. Dubbed the 'Bay of Pigs' by the papers, the most central area has been subjected to a massive clean-up campaign with more beachfront toilets, extra bins, and endless posters and loudspeaker announcements reminding people to pick up their rubbish.

Of the seven city beaches, the most southerly is **Platja de Sant Sebastià**, running from the W Hotel (*see p125*) and popular with nudists. Next is **Platja de Sant Miquel**, which gets crowded in the summer months; it's popular with gays. **Platja de Barceloneta** provides a sandy porch for restaurants and nightclubs. The covered walkway is home to tables where old men play dominoes with all the aggressiveness of a contact sport; it also houses the new beach centre (93 224 75 71), with a small beach library that lends magazines and papers (some in English) along with beach toys and ID tags for children from June to September.

After the Port Olímpic and just down from the Ciutadella-Vila Olímpica metro station, **Platja de Nova Icària** is much broader, with plenty of space for volleyball and beach tennis, while **Platja de Bogatell** boasts the hippest *xiringuito,* with torches and loungers out at night from May to October. Further north, **Platja de Mar Bella** is all about sport, with the sailing club Base Nàutica, basketball nets, volleyball courts, table-tennis tables and a half-pipe for BMXers and skaters. It also has a small beach library (*see p79* **Booked Up**).

The most remote beaches are the quiet **Platja Nova Mar Bella**, which is mostly used by local families, and the newer **Platja Llevant**, which opened to the public in 2006 when the Prim jetty was removed and the platform for the future marine zoo was built.

VILA OLÍMPICA

At the far end of the Passeig Marítim, the gateway to the Port Olímpic is heralded by the twin skyscrapers of the Hotel Arts (*see p125*) and the Torre Mapfre, and Frank Gehry's shimmering copper *Fish* sculpture.

The large square of land behind these three was once an area of industry, but by the 1980s it had fallen into disuse and presented the perfect blank slate for the model neighbourhood of the Olympic Village for the Games in 1992. Based on Cerdà's Eixample grid, it provided parks, a cinema, four beaches, a leisure marina and accommodation for 15,000 athletes.

The lack of cafés and shops, however, leaves it void of distinctive Mediterranean charm. Most social activity takes place in the Port Olímpic. The empty boulevards do, however, lend themselves to sculpture, including a jagged pergola on Avda Icària by Enric Miralles and Carme Pinós.

Montjuïc

A playground for culture aficionados.

The mists of time obscure the etymology of the name 'Montjuïc', but one widely accepted educated guess is that 'juïc' comes from the old Catalan word meaning Jewish. It was here that the medieval Jewish community buried their dead; some of the excavated headstones are to be found in the **Castell de Montjuïc**, soon to be reincarnated as the International Peace Centre.

Today, the **Cementiri Sud-Oest** still stands on the sea-facing side of the hill, but Montjuïc nowadays is thought of as a huge playground, with parks, cable-cars, museums and a Greek-style

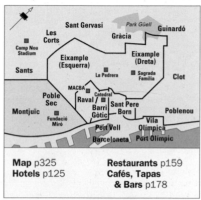

Map p325	**Restaurants** p159
Hotels p125	**Cafés, Tapas**
	& Bars p178

amphitheatre. The hill itself is often used as a stage set; at **Montjuïc de Nit** (*see p157*), performances and workshops of every stripe run late into the night.

(*see p157*)

INTRODUCING MONTJUÏC

If Montjuïc is undersubscribed, it's largely because the city's constantly remodelled infrastructure has passed it by. It's relatively inaccessible; to the uninitiated, the only way up seems to be from Plaça d'Espanya and the grandiose Avda Reina Maria Cristina or the vertigo-inducing cable car, although the funicular from Paral·lel is easy and convenient. Plans to convert Montjuïc into the Central Park of Barcelona involve opening up access from Poble Sec, with broad boulevards and escalators leading up to Avda Miramar.

The castle occupies a prime defensive position, with a commanding view of both the sea and the city. In reality, however, its vantage point has been used to attack the city, not to defend it. Catalan mythology has it that it was built by Philip V, after Barcelona fell to his forces in 1714, in order to keep an eye on his unwilling and rebellious subjects. In fact it was built 43 years before Philip was born and, although it has become a symbol of Spanish

About the author
Stephen Burgen is a former Spain correspondent for The Times. *He currently writes for the* Guardian *and works as an editor and translator.*

oppression, in 1706 the people rallied to its defence and that of its Austrian garrison against attacks from Bourbon forces. The most violent attack launched from the fortress was not in fact the work of fascists or their precursors, but was ordered by the progressive Catalan general Joan Prim i Prats, who to this day has an entire Barcelona *ramb la* named in his honour. Some 460 houses were damaged or destroyed in the bombardment that Prim launched on 7 September 1843. The Franco years cemented the role of the fortress as a symbol of oppression, particularly after the Republican president Lluís Companys was executed by firing squad there in 1940 (*see p23* **Profile**). Earlier in the Civil War, however, the Republicans themselves executed some 58 people in the castle.

The 1929 Exhibition was the first attempt to turn the hill into a leisure area. Then, in the 1940s, thousands of immigrant workers from the rest of Spain settled on the hill. Some squatted in precarious shacks, while others rented brick and plaster sheds laid out along improvised streets. These *barraques* thrived until the last few stragglers moved out in the 1970s, although the area still attracts intermittent waves of illegal tent and hut dwellers. Energetic visitors can follow the same steep routes these residents once took home,

Walk The Best of Montjuïc

The verdant pleasures of the city's favourite hill.

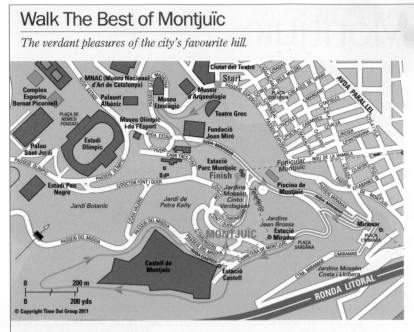

SIGHTS

DURATION: 90 MINS

From the **Teatre Grec** gardens, take the gateway to the right of the amphitheatre. From here, the **Escales del Generalife** lead up to the **Fundació Miró**. Named after the water gardens of Granada's Alhambra palace, this is a series of trickling fountains, flanked by stone steps, olive trees and benches for quiet contemplation. Instead of taking the steps, turn right into the **Jardins Laribal**, designed – like the Escales – by French landscape architect Jean-Claude Nicolas Forestier at the start of the 20th century. Ahead lie the **Colla de l'Arròs** rose gardens, at their best in late spring. From here, a long pergola leads up to the **Font del Gat** (Fountain of the Cat), a clearing on the slope with a small restaurant designed by Josep Puig i Cadafalch, and the rather modest fountain itself.

With your back to the restaurant, follow the path east towards the Miró and you will arrive at a clearing, in the middle of which stands Josep Viladomat's bronze *Noia de la Trena* (Girl with a Plait). Straight ahead is the stone *Repòs*, also created by Viladomat, a scaled-up version of a Manolo Hugué figure, undertaken when Hugué was too ill to finish the commission.

Turn right on to the Avda Miramar. Opposite the Miró museum you'll find a flight of steps leading up and around to the **Tres Pins nursery**, where plants for the city's municipal parks and gardens are grown. From here the Avda Miramar runs seaward, past the **Plaça Dante Alighieri**,

straight up C/Nou de la Rambla or C/Margarit in Poble Sec; the stairway at the top leaves you just a short distance from the **Fundació Joan Miró** and the Olympic stadium area.

The long axis from Plaça d'Espanya is still the most popular access to the park, with the climb now eased by a sequence of open-air escalators. In the centre of Plaça d'Espanya is a monument designed by Josep Maria Jujol

(who created the wrought-iron balconies on La Pedrera), with representations of the rivers Ebre, Tagus and Guadalquivir. Where Paral·lel meets Plaça d'Espanya is the **Las Arenas** bullring. The last bull met its fate here in the 1970s; until 2003, the arena lay derelict. Lord Rogers is currently overseeing a huge regeneration project, to be completed at an unspecified date, which will turn the ring into

Fira, the trade show area, with pavilions from 1929 and newer buildings used for conventions. To the left, the former Palau d'Esports is now the **Barcelona Teatre Musical**, hosting large-scale musical theatre. Further up, the rebuilt **Pavelló Mies van der Rohe** contrasts sharply with the neo-classical structures nearby. Across the street, Josep Puig i Cadafalch's Modernista factory has been converted into the excellent **CaixaForum** cultural centre. Further up the hill is **Poble Espanyol**, a model village designed in 1929 to showcase Spanish crafts and architecture.

Presiding over it all is the bombastic Palau Nacional, originally built as a temporary exhibition space for the Expo, and now home to the **MNAC (Museu Nacional d'Art de Catalunya)**, housing Catalan art from the last millennium. At night, the scene is illuminated by a water-and-light spectacular, the **Font Màgica**, still operating with its complex original mechanisms. Other nearby buildings erected for the 1929 Expo have been converted into the **Museu d'Arqueologia de Catalunya** and the **Ciutat del Teatre** (Theatre City) complex. From the same period are the nearby **Teatre Grec** (Greek theatre), used for summer concerts during the **Grec Festival**, and the beautifully restored Jardins Laribal, designed by French landscape architect Jean-Claude Nicolas Forestier. At the top of the garden is the Font del Gat information centre. The **Museu Etnològic**, a typical 1970s construction, sits just below it.

If walking isn't your thing, another way up the hill is via the funicular railway, integrated with the city's metro system and leaving from Paral·lel station. A more circuitous ascent is by the **Teleféric del Port** cable car across the harbour to Miramar, a peaceful spot with unrivalled views across the city – though the tranquillity was somewhat disturbed by the opening of the swish Hotel Miramar in 2006.

Montjuïc's Anella Olímpica (Olympic Ring) is a convergence of diverse constructions all laid out for the 1992 Olympic Games. The little-used Estadi Olímpic, although entirely new, was built within the façade of a 1929 stadium by a design team led by Federico Correa and Alfonso Milà. The horse sculptures are copies of the originals by Pau Gargallo. Next to it is the most original and attractive of the Olympic facilities, Arata Isozaki's Palau Sant Jordi indoor arena. Its undulating façade evokes Gaudí, and its high-tech interior features a transparent roof. In the hard, white *plaça* in front rises Santiago Calatrava's remarkable, Brancusi-inspired communications tower.

Across the square is the city's best swimming pool, the **Piscines Bernat Picornell**, while further down is the INEFC

---

where a bronze statue of the poet was presented by the city's Italian residents in 1921 to mark the 600th anniversary of Dante's death. In front of Dante, and in contrast to his stern salute, stands Josep Llimona's curvaceous and coquettish *Bellesa* (Beauty).

At the end of this road is the **Miramar** area, with its hotel (*see p127*), fronted by formal gardens, and the station for the cable car over the port; slightly south and below it are the **Costa i Llobera** cactus gardens. Backtracking slightly, a road leads behind the hotel up the hill towards the castle, passing the Jardins de Joan **Brossa** en route. These were created on the site of the old fairground, and some of the stone statues from the time (such as Charlie Chaplin) are still in place. Just outside the gardens is the much-photographed Sardana, an uplifting representation of the Catalan national dance. Cross the road here to walk up via the fountains and ceramic mosaics of the recently spruced-up **Mirador de l'Alcalde**. From here, the Camí del Mar, with great views out to sea, runs alongside the castle to the **Mirador del Migdia**, which has a wonderful outdoor café (*see p179* **La Caseta del Migdia**) far from the madding crowds and one of the few places in Barcelona where you can watch the sun set.

Take the path around the landward side of the castle, turning left just before the cable car station and following the steps and paths that wiggle down to the **Mossèn Cinto gardens**. These specialise in bulbs (daffodils, hyacinths and tulips) and various types of water lilies, with a series of terraced ponds running down the hillside to a small lake.

Exit from the lower side of the gardens Paral·lel and the metro.

---

a circular leisure complex while restoring the existing neo-Mudéjar façade. The vision encompasses a 'piazza in the sky' – a giant roof terrace that will allow for alfresco events and offer panoramic views over Barcelona. In a city already well endowed with shopping centres, this has the makings of a white elephant.

On the other side of the square, a pair of Venetian-style towers announce the start of the

SIGHTS

physical education institute, by architect Ricardo Bofill. Walk across the road and you look over a cliff on to a rugby pitch and an equestrian area offering pony rides; the cliff itself is a favourite with rock-climbers.

The many parks and gardens include the **Jardins Mossèn Costa i Llobera**, which abound in tropical plants, but particularly cacti, and are set just below Miramar on the steep flank nearest the port. Not far above are the **Jardins del Mirador**, which afford a spectacular view over the harbour. These gardens are also the starting point for a new path for pedestrians and cyclists, running precariously below the castle and leading to an outdoor café, **La Caseta del Migdia** (*see p179*). One of the newest parks is the nearby **Jardins de Joan Brossa**, featuring humorous, hands-on contraptions where children can experiment with sounds by bouncing on musical rubber pads, or talking through wooden speakers. Walk down towards the funicular station and you'll reach the enchanting **Jardins Cinto Verdaguer**, with ponds filled with lotus flowers and water lilies. All these gardens play an adjunct role to the creative biospheres of the **Jardí Botànic**, just above the Olympic stadium, sharply designed and finally maturing into an important scientific collection.

CaixaForum.

★ FREE CaixaForum

Casaramona, Avda Francesc Ferrer i Guàrdia 6-8 (93 476 86 00, www.fundacio.lacaixa.es). *Metro Espanya.* **Open** 10am-8pm Mon-Fri, Sun; 10am-10pm Sat. **Admission** free. **Map** p325 B9.
One of the masterpieces of industrial Modernisme, this former yarn and textile factory was designed by Puig i Cadafalch and will celebrate its centenary in 2011. It spent most of the last century in a sorry state, briefly acting as a police barracks before falling into dereliction. Fundació La Caixa, the charitable arm of Catalonia's largest savings bank, bought it and set about rebuilding. The original brick structure was supported, while the ground below was excavated to house a strikingly modern entrance plaza by Arata Isozaki, a Sol LeWitt mural, an auditorium, a bookshop and a library. In addition to the permanent contemporary art collection, there are three impressive spaces for temporary exhibitions – often among the most interesting shows to be found in the city.
▶ *Other notable Puig i Cadafalch buildings in the city include the Els Quatre Gats café (see p169) and the Casa Amatller (see p92).*

FREE Castell de Montjuïc

Castell de Montjuïc, Ctra de Montjuïc 66 (93 256 44 45, www.bcn.cat/castelldemontjuic). *Metro Paral·lel then funicular & cable car.* **Open** Apr-Sept 9am-9pm daily. Oct-Mar 9am-7pm daily. **Admission** free. **Map** p325 C12.
The Military Museum closed down in 2009 and its contents were moved to Figueres. The castle is now set to become an International Peace Centre, even though the remit of this is still undecided. For now, visitors can stroll through the castle, climb the battlements for fabulous views, or picnic in the wide moat. There's a café in the Plaça de Armes.

FREE Cementiri Sud-Oest

C/Mare de Déu de Port 54-58 (93 484 19 70). *Bus 38.* **Open** 8am-6pm daily. **Admission** free.
Designed by Leandro Albareda in 1880, this enormous necropolis sits at the side of the motorway, as a daily reminder to commuters of their own mortality. The cemetery was originally divided into four sections: one for Catholics, one for Protestants, one for non-Christians and a fourth for aborted foetuses. It now stretches over the south-west corner of the mountain, with family tombs stacked five or six storeys high. Many, especially those belonging to the gypsy community, are a riot of colour and flowers. The Fossar de la Pedrera memorial park remembers the fallen of the International Brigades and the Catalan martyrs from the Civil War. There is also a Holocaust memorial and a mausoleum to the former president of the Generalitat, Lluís Companys.

The cemetery is much visited, particularly on All Saints' Day, when the roads are clogged with cars. Eventually, it will provide a new home for the city's collection of funeral carriages.

SIGHTS

Font Màgica de Montjuïc.

★ Font Màgica de Montjuïc

Plaça Carles Buïgas 1 (93 316 10 00). Metro Espanya. **Shows** *(every 30 mins) May-Sept* 9.30-11pm Thur-Sun. *Dec-Apr* 7-9pm Fri, Sat. Closed Oct, Nov. **Map** p325 B9.

Still in possession of its original plumbing, the 'magic fountain' works its wonders with 3,600 pieces of tubing and more than 4,500 light bulbs. On summer evenings, the multiple founts swell and dance to anything from the *1812 Overture* to Freddie Mercury and Montserrat Caballé's *Barcelona*, showing off a kaleidoscope of pastel colours.

★ Fundació Joan Miró

Parc de Montjuïc s/n (93 443 94 70, http://fundaciomiro-bcn.org). Metro Paral·lel then Funicular de Montjuïc or 50,55 bus. **Open** *July-Sept* 10am-8pm Tue, Wed, Fri, Sat; 10am-9.30pm Thur; 10am-2.30pm Sun. *Oct-June* 10am-7pm Tue, Wed, Fri, Sat; 10am-9.30pm Thur; 10am-2.30pm Sun. **Guided tours** *Temporary exhibitions* 11.30am Sat. *Permanent exhibition* 11.30am Sun. **Admission** *All exhibitions*

€8.50; €6 reductions. *Temporary exhibitions* €4; €3 reductions; free under-15s. **Credit** MC, V. **Map** p325 C11.

Josep Lluís Sert, who spent the years of the Franco dictatorship as dean of the School of Design at Harvard University, designed one of the greatest museum buildings in the world on his return. Approachable, light and airy, these white walls and arches house a collection of more than 225 paintings, 150 sculptures and all of Miró's graphic work, plus some 5,000 drawings. The permanent collection, highlighting Miró's trademark use of primary colours and simplified organic forms symbolising stars, the moon, birds and women, occupies the second half of the space. On the way to the sculpture gallery lies Alexander Calder's rebuilt Mercury Fountain, originally seen at the Spanish Republic's Pavilion at the 1937 Paris Fair. In other works, Miró is shown as a cubist (*Street in Pedralbes*, 1917), naive (*Portrait of a Young Girl*, 1919) and surrealist (*Man and Woman in Front of a Pile of Excrement*, 1935). In the upper galleries, large, black-outlined paintings from Miró's final years precede a room of works with political themes. *Photo p86*.

★ Jardí Botànic

C/Doctor Font i Quer (93 426 49 35, www.jardibotanic.bcn.cat). Metro Paral·lel then Funicular de Montjuïc or 50, 55 bus. **Open** *Nov-Jan* 10am-5pm daily. *Feb-Mar, Oct* 10am-6pm daily. *Apr-May, Sept* 10am-7pm daily. *June-Aug* 10am-8pm daily. **Admission** €3.50; €2.60 reductions; free under-16s. Free after 3pm Sun & all day last Sun of mth. **No credit cards. Map** p325 B11.

INSIDE TRACK
CEMETERY TOURS

If your Spanish is up to it, there are guided tours of the **Cementiri Sud-Oest** at 11.15am on the second and fourth Sundays of the month, visiting 37 graves and tombs of artistic and historic interest.

SIGHTS

INSIDE TRACK ALL CHANGE

Be warned that the main road leading up to and around Montjuïc from Plaça Espanya changed its name in 2010 from Avda Marquès de Comillas to Avda Francesc Ferrer i Guàrdia, but you'll still see the former name around the place.

After the original 1930s botanical garden was disturbed by the construction for the Olympics, the only solution was to build an entirely new replacement. This opened in 1999, housing plants derived from seven global regions with a climate similar to that of the Western Mediterranean. Everything about the futuristic design, from the angular concrete pathways to the raw sheet steel banking (and even the design of the bins), is the complete antithesis of the more naturalistic, Gertrude Jekyll-inspired gardens of England. It is meticulously kept, with plants tagged with Latin, Catalan, Spanish and English names, along with the date of planting, and has the added advantage of wonderful views across the city. A small space plays host to occasional exhibitions and useful, free audio guides lead visitors through the gardens.

FREE Jardins de Joan Brossa

Plaça Dante (010, www.bcn.cat/parcsijardins).
Metro Paral·lel then Funicular de Montjuïc or 50,
55 bus. **Open** 10am-sunset daily. **Admission**
free. **Map** p325 C11.

Set in 5.2 hectares of the former fairground, Montjuïc's latest park is part forest, with 40 species of tree, and part urban playground. As well as a climbing frame, there are various oversized wooden instruments and creations designed for children, allowing them to play tunes and pump water.

FREE Jardins Mossèn Costa i Llobera

Ctra de Miramar 1 (010, www.bcn.cat/
parcsijardins). Metro Paral·lel then Funicular de
Montjuïc or 50, 55 bus. **Open** 10am-sunset daily
(but see below). **Admission** free. **Map** p325 D12.
The port side of Montjuïc is protected from the cold north wind, creating a microclimate that is two degrees centigrade warmer than the rest of the city – allowing some 800 species of the world's cacti to flourish here. This extraordinary collection has been closed to the public for some time while funding for essential maintenance is sought.

★ MNAC (Museu Nacional d'Art de Catalunya)

Palau Nacional, Parc de Montjuïc (93 622 03 76,
www.mnac.cat). Metro Espanya. **Open** 10am-
7pm Tue-Sat; 10am-2.30pm Sun. **Admission**
(valid 2 days) *Permanent exhibitions* €8.50; €6
reductions. *Temporary exhibitions* €5.50-€3.50.
Combined ticket with Poble Espanyol €12. Free
over-65s, under-16s and 1st Sun of mth. **Credit**
AmEx, MC, V. **Map** p325 B10.
'One museum, a thousand years of art' is the slogan of the National Museum, and the collection provides a dizzying overview of Catalan art from the 12th to the 20th centuries. In recent years, the museum has

Fundació Joan Miró. *See p85.*

On Your Bike Montjuïc

Meander around the delightful sculpture garden.

You will need the legs of Miguel Indurain to get up to Montjuïc's higher slopes, but you can take your bike on the funicular (from the Paral·lel metro station). Once at the top, take the right hand exit and you'll come out on the Avda del Miramar. Turn right and follow the signs to the Jardins de Joan Brossa. Once inside the gate, follow the path that snakes though a delightful array of interactive sculptures and gadgetry. Once on the other side, turn right on to the Ctra Montjuïc. At this point you might need to wheel your bike a short way up to the Plaça de la Sardana – the location of the monument to Catalonia's national dance.

Just beyond this, take the C/Tarongers downhill and turn left at the bottom, whooshing past the Jardí de Petra Kelly to the Passeig Olímpic. Here are the Estadi Olímpic, the Palau de Sant Jordi and Santiago Calatrava's telecommunications tower. Swing left and round the stadium to the Avda de l'Estadi. Soon you'll arrive at the rear of the MNAC. Here, you can cut through gardens and lift your bike down an escalator to the front entrance. Continue to the other side and follow the curving Passeig de Santa Madrona to the entrance of the Grec amphitheatre. Any downhill road will lead you back to Avda Paral·lel, where you can return to the Paral·lel metro stop on a bike lane.

For details of bike hire, *see p295*.

added an extra floor to absorb the section of the Thyssen-Bornemisza collection that was previously kept in the convent in Pedralbes, along with the mainly Modernista holdings from the former Museum of Modern Art in Ciutadella park, a fine photography section, coins and the bequest of Francesc Cambó, founder of the autonomist Lliga Regionalista, a regionalist conservative party.

The highlight, however, is the Romanesque collection. As art historians realised that scores of solitary tenth-century churches in the Pyrenees were falling into ruin – and with them, extraordinary Romanesque murals that had served to instruct villagers in the basics of the faith – the laborious task was begun of removing the murals from church apses. The display here features 21 mural sections arranged in loose chronological order. A highlight is the tremendous *Crist de Taüll*, originally from the 12th-century church of Sant Climent de Taüll. Even 'graffiti' scratchings (probably by monks) of animals, crosses and labyrinths have been preserved. The museum has also recently acquired a major 13th-century Romanesque mural from the cathedral at La Seu d'Urgell.

The excellent Gothic collection starts with some late 13th-century frescoes that were discovered in 1961 and 1997, when two palaces in the city were being renovated. There are carvings and paintings from local churches, including works by the indisputable Catalan masters of the Golden Age, Bernat Martorell and Jaume Huguet. The highlight of the Thyssen collection is Fra Angelico's *Madonna of Humility* (c1430), while the Cambó bequest contains some wonderful Old Masters. Also unmissable is the Modernista collection, which includes Ramon Casas' mural of himself and Pere Romeu on a tandem, which decorated Els Quatre Gats. The rich collection of decorative arts includes original furniture from Modernista houses. *Photo p88*.
▶ *Visit the original site of Ramon Casas' tandem mural at Els Quatre Gats; see p169.*

Museu d'Arqueologia de Catalunya
Passeig de Santa Madrona 39-41 (93 423 21 49, www.mac.cat). Metro Poble Sec. **Open** 9.30am-7pm Tue-Sat; 10am-2.30pm Sun. **Admission** €3; €2.10 reductions; free under-16s, over-65s. **No credit cards. Map** p325 C10.

The time frame for this archaeology collection starts with the Palaeolithic period, and there are relics of Greek, Punic, Roman and Visigothic colonisers, up to the early Middle Ages. A massive Roman sarcophagus is carved with scenes of the rape of Persephone, and an immense statue of Aesculapius, the god of medicine, towers over one room. A few galleries are dedicated to the Mallorcan Talayotic cave culture, and there is an exemplary display on the Iberians – the pre-Hellenic, pre-Roman inhabitants of south-eastern Spain. An Iberian skull with a nail driven through it effectively demonstrates a

MNAC. *See p86.*

typical method of execution from that time. The display ends with the marvellous, jewel-studded headpiece of a Visigoth king. One of the best-loved pieces, inevitably, is an alarmingly erect Priapus, found during building work in Sants in 1848 and kept under wraps 'for moral reasons' until 1986.

Museu Etnològic
Passeig de Santa Madrona 16-22 (93 424 68 07, www.museuetnologic.bcn.cat). Metro Poble Sec. **Open** *June-Sept* 10am-6pm Tue-Sat; 11am-8pm Sun. *Oct-May* 10am-7pm Tue, Thur, Sat; 10am-2pm Wed, Fri-Sat; 10am-2pm, 3-8pm Sun. **Admission** €3.50; €1.70 reductions; free under-12s. Free 3-8pm Sun & all day 1st Sun of mth. **No credit cards.** **Map** p325 B10.

The Ethnology Museum houses a vast collection of items, from Australian Aboriginal boomerangs to rugs and jewellery from Afghanistan, although the most comprehensive collections are from Catalonia. Of the displays upstairs, most outstanding are the Moroccan, Japanese and Philippine exhibits, although there are a number of interesting pre-Columbian finds. The attempts to arrange the pieces thematically, however, are not altogether successful: a potentially fascinating exhibition called 'Taboos', for instance, offers a rather limp look at nudity in different cultures.

Museu Olímpic i de l'Esport
Avda Estadí 60 (93 292 53 79, www.fundacio barcelonaolimpica.es). Metro Paral·lel then Funicular de Montjuïc or 50,55 bus. **Open** *Apr-Sept* 10am-8pm Tue-Sat; 10am-2.30pm Sun. *Oct-Mar* 10am-6pm Tue-Sat; 10am-2.30pm Sun. **Admission** €4.50; €2.50 reductions; free under-14s & over-65s. **Credit** (over €10) V. **Map** p325 B11.

Opened in 2007 in a new building across from the stadium, the Olympic and Sports Museum gives an overview of the Games (and, indeed, all games), from Ancient Greece to the present day. As well as photographs and film footage of great sporting moments and heroes, there are an array of related objects (Ronaldinho's boots, Mika Häkkinen's Mercedes), along with a collection of opening ceremony costumes and Olympic torches on show. Perhaps more entertaining are the interactive displays, including one that compares your effort at the long jump with those of the pros.

Pavelló Mies van der Rohe
Avda Francesc Ferrer i Guàrdia 13 (93 423 40 16, www.miesbcn.com). Metro Espanya. **Open** 10am-8pm daily. **Admission** €4.50; €2.30 reductions; free under-18s. **Credit** (shop only) MC, V. **Map** p325 B9.

Mies van der Rohe built the Pavelló Alemany (German Pavilion) for the 1929 World Exhibition not as a gallery but as a simple reception space, which was sparsely furnished with his trademark steel-framed 'Barcelona Chair'. The pavilion signified a founding monument of modern rationalist architecture, with its flowing floor plan and revolutionary use of materials. Even though the original pavilion was demolished following the exhibition, a fine replica was built on the same site in 1986, the simplicity of its design setting off the warm tones of the marble, and the expressive Georg Kolbe sculpture in the pond.

Poble Espanyol
Avda Francesc Ferrer i Guàrdia 13 (93 508 63 00, www.poble-espanyol.com). Metro Espanya. **Open** *Village & restaurants* 9am-8pm Mon; 9am-2am Tue-Thur; 9am-5am Fri, Sat; 9am-midnight Sun. *Shops* Dec-May 10am-6pm daily. June-Aug 10am-8pm daily. Sept-Nov 10am-7pm daily. **Admission** €8.90; €5.60-€6.60 reductions;

€20 family ticket; free under-4s. *Night ticket*
€5.50. *Combined ticket with MNAC* €12.
Credit AmEx, MC, V. **Map** p325 A9.
Built for the 1929 World Exhibition and designed by
the Modernista architect Josep Puig i Cadafalch, this
composite Spanish village may appear charming
or kitsch, depending on your personal tastes, and
features reproductions of traditional buildings and
squares from every region in Spain. The cylindrical
towers at the entrance are copied from the walled
city of Ávila and lead on to a typical Castilian main
square; from here, visitors can explore a tiny whitewashed street from Arcos de la Frontera in
Andalucía, then head to the 16th-century House of
Chains from Toledo. There are numerous bars and
restaurants along the way, including a flamenco
tablao and more than 60 shops selling Spanish crafts.
Outside, street performers recreate snippets of
Catalan and Spanish folklore.

Telefèric de Montjuïc (cable car)

*Estació Funicular, Avda Miramar (93 318 70 74,
www.tmb.net). Metro Paral·lel then Funicular de
Montjuïc or 50,55 bus.* **Open** *Nov-Feb* 10am-6pm
daily. *Mar-May, Oct* 10am-7pm daily. *June-Sept*
10am-9pm daily. **Tickets** *One way* €6.30; €4.70
one-way reductions. *Return* €9; €6.30 reductions;
free under-4s. **No credit cards. Map** p325 C11/D11.
The rebuilt system features eight-person cable cars
that soar from the funicular up to the castle.

Pavelló Mies van der Rohe.

POBLE SEC & PARAL·LEL

Poble Sec, the name of the neighbourhood
between Montjuïc and the Avda Paral·lel,
means 'dry village'; it was 1894 before the
thousands of impoverished workers who
lived on the flanks of the hill celebrated the
installation of the area's first water fountain
(which is still standing today in C/Margarit).

These days, Poble Sec is a friendly,
working-class area of quiet, relaxed streets
and leafy squares, with an increasingly
Latin American flavour, reflecting the large
immigrant population that comes from
Ecuador and elsewhere. Around 27 per
cent of the 40,000 people in Poble Sec
have arrived over the past five years.

On the stretch of the Paral·lel opposite the
city walls, three tall chimneys stand amid
modern office blocks. They are all that remains
of the Anglo-Canadian-owned power station
known locally as La Canadença ('The Canadian'),
the centre of the city's largest general strike in
1919. Beside the chimneys, an open space has
been created and dubbed the Parc de les Tres
Xemeneies (Park of the Three Chimneys).

Towards the Avda Paral·lel are some
distinguished Modernista buildings, which
local legend maintains were built for *artistas*
from the nude cabarets by their sugar daddies.
At C/Tapioles 12 is a beautiful, narrow, wooden
Modernista door with particularly lovely
writhing ironwork, while at C/Elkano 4 is La
Casa de les Rajoles, known for its mosaic façade.

The name Paral·lel derives from the fact
that the avenue coincides exactly with 41° 44'
latitude north, one of Ildefons Cerdà's more
eccentric conceits. This was the centre of
Barcelona nightlife in the early 20th century,
and full of theatres, nightclubs and music halls.
A statue on the corner with C/Nou de la Rambla
commemorates Raquel Meller, a legendary star
of the street who went on to big-screen success.
She now stands outside Barcelona's notorious
live-porn venue, the Bagdad. There are grand
plans to revive this as a theatre district.

Refugi 307

*C/Nou de la Rambla 169 (93 256 21 22,
www.museuhistoria.bcn.cat). Metro Paral·lel.*
Open (guided tour & by appointment only)
11am, noon, 2pm (Catalan), 1pm (Spanish) Sat, Sun.
Admission €3. **No credit cards. Map** p325 D11.
Around 1,500 Barcelona civilians were killed during
the air bombings of the Civil War, a fact that the
government has long silenced. Poble Sec was hit
particularly hard, and a large air-raid shelter was
built partially into the mountain at the top of C/Nou
de la Rambla; this is one of some 1,200 in the city.
Now converted into a museum, it's worth a visit; the
tour takes about 45 minutes.

SIGHTS

The Eixample

Grand boulevards and fabulous Modernista buildings.

SIGHTS

From an aerial perspective, it is the Eixample (pronounced esh-*am*-pluh) that gives Barcelona its distinctive appearance: the middle section of the city looks as if it has been stamped with a sizzling waffle iron. This extraordinary city plan, the Expansion (*eixample* in Catalan, or *ensanche* in Spanish) of Barcelona into an orthogonal grid of identical blocks, was designed as an extendable matrix for future growth, gradually developing to connect the city with the outlying villages of Gràcia, Sarrià, Les Corts, Sant Gervasi and Sant Martí de Provençals. In essence, it unifies the city as we know it today. Visitors to Barcelona tend to focus on the Old City and its medieval quarter, but fans of architecture and, in particular, Modernisme – the Catalan answer to art nouveau – will do well to spend a day strolling along the elegant boulevards of the Eixample.

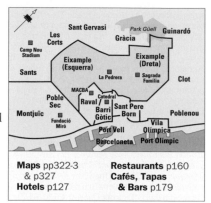

Maps pp322-3	Restaurants p160
& p327	Cafés, Tapas
Hotels p127	& Bars p179

INTRODUCING THE EIXAMPLE

The Eixample was Europe's first expansive work of urban planning, necessitated by the chronic overcrowding of old Barcelona – which, by the 1850s, had become rife with cholera and crime, tightly corseted by its much-hated city walls. It was eventually decided the walls must come down, whereupon the Ajuntament held a competition to build an ambitious urban zone on the sloping fields outside the city's ramparts. The competition was won by municipal architect Antoni Rovira i Trias, whose popular fan-shaped design can be seen at the foot of the statue of him in the Gràcia plaça that bears his name. The government in Madrid, however, vetoed the plan, choosing instead the work of social idealist Ildefons Cerdà, a military engineer.

Cerdà's plan, reflecting the rationalist mindset of the era, was for a grid of uniform blocks with chamfered corners (known as *illes* in Catalan, *manzanas* in Spanish). It would stretch from Montjuïc to the Besòs river, criss-crossed by the diagonal highways of Avda Diagonal and Avda Meridiana – meeting at Plaça de les Glòries, which was to become the hub of the modernised city. The ideas were utopian: each block was to be built on only

two sides and be no more than two or three storeys high; the remainder of the space to contain gardens, their leafy extremes joining at the crossroads and forming a quarter of a bigger park. Predictably, however, developers made a travesty of Cerdà's plans, and a concrete orchard of gardenless, fortress-like, six- or seven-storey blocks grew up instead.

Fortunately, the period of construction coincided with Barcelona's golden age of architecture: the city's bourgeoisie employed Gaudí, Puig i Cadafalch, Domènech i Montaner and the like to build them ever more daring townhouses in an orgy of avant-garde one-upmanship. The result is extraordinary but can be tricky to negotiate on foot: the lack of open spaces and similarity of many streets can cause confusion. The city council, meanwhile, is attempting to make the area more approachable by reclaiming pavement space for pedestrians, repaving roads with noise absorbent materials and reducing traffic.

The overland railway that ran down C/Balmes was the dividing line of the neighbourhood. The fashionable **Dreta** ('Right') side contains the most distinguished Modernista architecture, the main museums and the shopping avenues. The **Esquerra** ('Left') was built slightly later;

it contains some less well-known Modernista sights. Other subdivisions of the Eixample include the wealthy Sagrada Família area, and the scrappier residential neighbourhoods of Sant Antoni, near the Raval, and Fort Pienc, to the south of Glòries.

In its entirety, the Eixample covers about nine square kilometres. However, most of the sights of interest are within a few blocks of the grand central boulevard of **Passeig de Gràcia**, which ascends directly from the city's central square of Plaça Catalunya. Incorporating some of Barcelona's finest Modernista buildings, it is the showpiece of the **Quadrat D'Or** (Golden District) – a square mile of open-air museum between C/Muntaner and C/Roger de Flor that contains 150 protected buildings, many of them Modernista gems.

THE DRETA

The central boulevard of Passeig de Gràcia has always been the Eixample's most desirable address, and is where you'll find Modernisme's most flamboyant townhouses. The three most famous are Gaudí's humpbacked **Casa Batlló** (No.43), Puig i Cadafalch's **Casa Àmatller** (No.41) and Domènech i Montaner's **Casa Lleó Morera**, a decadently melting wedding cake of a building (partially defaced during the architecturally delinquent Franco era) on the corner of C/Consell de Cent at No.35. These buildings are collectively known as the Manzana de Discòrdia.

As the area surrounding Passeig de Gràcia is one of the wealthiest parts of the city, it's not surprising that it's also extraordinarily rich in privately owned art collections and museums; these include **Fundación Alorda Derksen** and **Fundació Suñol**, along with the **Museu**

Casa Àmatller. See p92.

Egipci de Barcelona, the **Fundació Francisco Godia**, the **Fundació Vila Casas** (Espai VolART, C/Ausiàs Marc 22, 93 481 79 85) and the **Fundació Antoni Tàpies**. The area is equally well-provided with shops, with a mix of boutiques, international designers and high-street brands jostling for space along the golden retail belts of Passeig de Gràcia, the parallel Rambla de Catalunya and the central section of the Avinguda Diagonal.

For most visitors, however, the crowning glory of the Eixample experience is the darkly beautiful **Sagrada Família**. Whether you love it or hate it (George Orwell called it 'one of the most hideous buildings in the world'), it has become the city's emblem and a sine qua non of Barcelona tourist itineraries. A less famous masterpiece, in the shape of Domènech i Montaner's **Hospital de la Santa Creu i Sant Pau**, bookends the northerly extreme of the Avda Gaudí. A few blocks south, there's more welcome green space in the **Parc de l'Estació del Nord** and, on C/Marina, one of Barcelona's weirdest museums – the macabre **Museu de Carrosses Fúnebres**.

The streets above the Diagonal boast some striking Modernista buildings, such as Puig i Cadafalch's 1901 **Palau Macaya** at Passeig de Sant Joan 108. Other buildings of interest include the tiled **Mercat de la Concepció** on C/Aragó, designed by Rovira i Trias, and the turret-topped **Casa de les Punxes** (*photo p92*); the work of the prolific Puig i Cadafalch, the latter combines

---

INSIDE TRACK MASTERPIECES OF MODERNISME

The three most famous Modernista buildings sit on the block known rather strangely as the **Manzana de Discòrdia**. It's a Catalan appropriation of the Spanish word *manzana* (rather than the usual Catalan word *illa*), which puns on the double meaning of 'block' and 'apple', and alludes to the fatal choice of Paris when judging which of a bevy of divine beauties would win the golden Apple of Discord. If the volume of camera-toting admirers is anything to go by, the fairest of these Modernista lovelies is surely Gaudí's **Casa Batlló**, permanently illuminated by flashbulbs.

---

elements of Nordic Gothic with Spanish plateresque. Moving down C/Roger de Llúria, you pass the **Casa Thomas** and the **Palau Montaner**, both designed by Lluís Domènech i Montaner, and on reaching C/Casp you arrive at one of Gaudí's lesser-known works, the **Casa Calvet**. To the right is the egg-topped **Plaça de Braus Monumental**: the city's last active bullring is now mainly frequented by tour buses from the Costa Brava, and out of season hosts tatty travelling circuses. Not far from the bullring, at C/Lepant 150, is the ultra-modern concert hall of **L'Auditori de Barcelona**, which also houses the newly reopened **Museu de la Música**.

FREE Casa Àmatller

Passeig de Gràcia 41 (93 496 1245, www. amatller.com). Metro Passeig de Gràcia. **Open** 10am-8.30pm daily. *Guided tour* noon Fri. **Admission** free; guided tour €10; free under-12s **Map** p322 G8.

Built for chocolate baron Antoni Àmatller, this playful building is one of Puig i Cadafalch's finest creations. Inspired by 17th-century Dutch townhouses, its distinctive stepped Flemish pediment is covered in shiny ceramics, while the lower façade and the doorway are decorated with lively sculptures by Eusebi Arnau. These sculptures include chocolatiers at work, almond trees and blossoms (which is a reference to the family name), and Sant Jordi slaying the dragon.

Besides chocolate, Àmatller's other great love was photography. His daughter later converted the family home into an art institute and archive for her father's vast collections, from which excellent selections are on display in the ground floor exhibition space. The guided tour of the house lasts around an hour and includes the ornate entrance hall, Antoni Àmatller's period photography studio and a tasting of Àmatller chocolate in the original kitchen. The façade of the building is currently undergoing restoration, and will be sheathed in unphotogenic green netting until at least 2011. *Photo p91.*

▶ *For more on Josep Puig i Cadafalch, see p42.*

FREE Casa Àsia

Avda Diagonal 373 (93 238 73 37, www.casa asia.org). Metro Diagonal. **Open** 10am-8pm Tue-Sat; 10am-2pm Sun. **Admission** free. **Map** p322 G6.

This cultural centre for Asia and the Asian Pacific is housed in the jaw-droppingly ornate Palau Baró de Quadras, designed by Puig i Cadafalch in 1904. If you can tear your eyes away from the building's array of lavish carvings and mosaics, there are a variety of excellent temporary exhibits covering anything from modern Chinese abstract art to Iranian graphics. The underlying function of this organisation, however, is the promotion of Asian culture in Barcelona, with language courses, interna-

Casa de les Punxes. *See p91.*

tional conferences and cinema seasons (often subtitled in English). It also features an excellent multimedia library on the fourth floor, which allows visitors to hire CDs, DVDs and books if you can show your passport or ID card.

▶ *The centre also runs Festival Asia; see p213.*

★ Casa Batlló

Passeig de Gràcia 43 (93 216 03 06, www. casabatllo.cat). Metro Passeig de Gràcia. **Open** 9am-8pm daily. **Admission** €17.80; €14.25 reductions; free under-11s. **Credit** AmEx, MC, V. **Map** p322 G8.

In one of the most extreme architectural makeovers ever seen, Gaudí and his long-time collaborator Josep Maria Jujol took an ordinary apartment block and remodelled it inside and out for textile tycoon Josep Batlló between 1902 and 1906. The result was one of the most impressive and admired of all Gaudí's creations. Opinions differ on what the building's remarkable façade represents, particularly its polychrome shimmering walls, its sinister skeletal balconies and its humpbacked scaly roof. Some say it's the spirit of carnival, others a Costa Brava cove. However, the most popular theory, which takes into account the architect's deeply patriotic feelings, is that the façade depicts Sant Jordi and the dragon – the idea being that the cross on top is the knight's lance, the roof represents the back of the beast, and the balconies below are the skulls and bones of its hapless victims.

The chance to explore the interior (at a cost) offers the best opportunity of understanding how Gaudí, sometimes considered the lord of the bombastic and overblown, was really the master of tiny details – from the ingenious ventilation in the doors to the amazing natural light reflecting off the inner court-

SIGHTS

Profile Museu del Modernisme

A new museum that showcases Catalonia's most famous design movement.

For all of Catalonia's traditions in building and the arts, no style is as synonymous with the region as Modernisme. This is in part due to the huge modern popularity of its most famous practitioner, Antoni Gaudí, and to its mix of decoration, eccentric unpredictability, craftsmanship and practicality.

In recent times, however, the exquisite craftsmanship has been all but forgotten, and instead Modernisme has been seen as synonymous with just architecture. The MNAC (*see p86*) contains some spectacular art and furniture from the period, but only now, with the 2010 opening of the **Museu del Modernisme Català** (for listing, *see p97*), has it had a showcase to itself.

The style that would become known as Modernisme (not to be confused with modernism, which refers to 20th-century functional styles) came about from a merging of the cultural and political movement of the Catalan Renaixença with art nouveau – without doubt the leading influence in the decorative arts in Europe and the US between 1890 and 1914.

Modernisme can also be seen as matching archetypes of Catalan character, as a passionately nationalist

expression that made use of Catalan traditions of design and craftwork, showing interest in the Romanesque and Gothic art of the Catalan golden age.

Inaugurated in spring 2010, the museum, formed from a private collection, includes work by all the heavyweights. There is a Gaudí-designed kissing chair, some extravagant ecclesiastical pieces by Puig i Cadafalch, tiled bedheads by Gaspar Homar, marble sculptures by Josep Llimona and paintings by Santiago Rusiñol, Joaquim Mir and Ramon Casas. The furniture created by lesser-known craftsmen also includes some stunning pieces, with a collection of marquetry escritoires.

Walk Modernisme

Stroll around the Eixample's finest architecture.

SIGHTS

DURATION: 90 MINS

The tour begins with the **Casa Comalat** by Valeri i Pupurull, which has the unusual distinction of two façades. The front (Avda Diagonal 442) features 12 voluptuously curvy stone balconies, complete with ornate wrought-iron railings, while the more radical back façade (C/Còrsega 316) is a colourful harlequin effect.

Almost opposite on Avda Diagonal is Puig i Cadafalch's sombre **Palau Baró de Quadras**, now home to the **Casa Àsia** exhibition space (*see p92*), and his **Casa Terrades** (Nos.416-20), known as La Casa de les Punxes (House of Spikes) because of its pointed turrets and gables. Look out for the individual entrances and staircases that Puig i Cadafalch built for each of the family's three daughters.

Turn down C/Girona and right on C/Mallorca to see Barenys i Gambús's fantasy **Casa Dolors Xiró** at No.302, followed by two Domènech i Montaner masterpieces: the **Casa Josep Thomas** (No.291) and the **Palau Ramón de Montaner** (No.278). Double back a few steps and turn downhill on to C/Roger de Llúria. On the corner at No.80 is Fossas i Martinez's spike-topped **Casa Villanueva**; opposite at No.82, columns of stained-glass windows mark Granell i Manresa's **Casa Jaume Forn**. A few steps further down C/Roger de Llúria at No.85, the **Queviures Murrià** grocery retains Ramon Casas' original decoration. On the right at No.74, meanwhile, is the stained-glass and floral decoration of the **Farmàcia Argelaguet**, one of many local Modernista pharmacies.

Retrace your steps up to the corner again, and turn right on to C/València. Continue for three blocks, and at No.339 you'll find a stunning corner building by Gallissà i Soqué, the **Casa Manuel Llopis i Bofill**. The façade is a blend of red brick and white sgraffito by Josep Maria Jujol; the neo-Mudéjar turrets, ceramics and keyhole shapes take their inspiration from the Alhambra in Granada.

Backtrack and turn left on C/Girona. At No.86 is the **Casa Isabel Pomar**, Rubió i Bellver's eccentric sliver of a building that squeezes in a neo-Gothic pinnacle, lively red brickwork and a staggered gallery window on the first floor. This contrasts with the spacious feel of Viñolas i Llosas's **Casa Jacinta Ruiz** (No.54). Glass galleries are a characteristic feature of Modernista houses, but here the jutting windows form the pivot for the design and give a three-dimensional effect. Further down, turn right on Gran Via, to another extravagant Modernista pharmacy, **Farmàcia Vilardell** (No.650), and Salvat i Espasa's elegant **Casa Ramon Oller** (No.658).

From there, head left down C/Pau Claris and left again on to C/Casp. At No.22, **Casa Llorenç Camprubí**, Ruiz i Casamitjana's intricate stonework is a delight, but the real treasure at No.48. Gaudí's **Casa Calvet** may seem conventional, but closer study reveals characteristic touches: the columns framing the door and gallery allude to the bobbins used in the owner's textile factory, while the wrought ironwork depicts a mass of funghi surrounded by stone flowers. The corbel beneath the gallery interweaves the Catalan coat of arms with Calvet's initial 'C'.

yard's azure walls, and the way the brass window handles are curved so as to fit the shape of a hand. An apartment is open to the public, and access has been granted to the attic and roof terrace: the whitewashed arched rooms of the top floor, originally used for laundering and hanging clothes, are among the master's most atmospheric spaces.

Fundación Alorda Derksen

C/Aragó 314 (93 272 62 50, www.fundacion ad.com). Metro Girona or Passeig de Gràcia. **Open** By appt only. Closed Aug. **Admission** €5; €3 reductions. **No credit cards. Map** p323 H8.

A garden furniture mogul might seem at first glance to be an unlikely art collector, but Manuel Alorda and his wife Hanneke Derksen proved that there is

no conflict between decking and painting when they opened this impressive gallery, dedicated to 21st-century art, in April 2008.

Fundació Antoni Tàpies

C/Aragó 255 (93 487 03 15, www.fundaciotapies. org). Metro Passeig de Gràcia. **Open** 10am-7pm Tue-Sun. **Admission** €7; €5.60 reductions; free under-16s. **Credit** MC, V. **Map** p322 G8.

Antoni Tàpies exploded on to the art scene in the 1950s when he began to incorporate waste paper, mud and rags into his paintings, eventually moving on to the point where his works included whole pieces of furniture, running water and girders. Today, he's Barcelona's most celebrated living artist, and his trademark scribbled and paint-daubed

Turn right down C/Girona on to C/Ausiàs Marc, part of the Quadrat d'Or. At Nos.37-39, the graceful arches and beautifully restored sgraffito of **Cases Tomàs Roger** are the work of Modernista architect Enric Sagnier. At No.31 is the **Farmàcia Nordbeck**, with a dark wood and stained-glass exterior. The last stop before Plaça Urquinaona is the **Casa Manuel Felip** (No.20), designed by a little-known architect, Fernández i Janot, with sumptuous stonework and slender galleries connecting the first two floors.

pieces are sought after for everything from wine bottle labels to theatre posters.

The artist set up the Tàpies Foundation in this, the former Montaner i Simon publishing house, in 1984, dedicating it to the study and appreciation of contemporary art. In a typically contentious act, Tàpies crowned the building with a glorious tangle of aluminium piping and ragged metal netting (*Núvol i Cadira*, or 'Cloud and Chair'). The building remains one of the earliest examples of Modernisme to combine exposed brick and iron, and is now a cultural centre and museum dedicated to the work and life of the man himself, with exhibitions, symposiums, lectures and films.

▶ *There are normally works by Tàpies on display at the MACBA; see p72.*

Fundació Francisco Godia

C/Diputació 250 (93 272 31 80, www.fundacion fgodia.org). Metro Passeig de Gràcia. **Open** 10am-8pm Mon, Wed-Sun. **Admission** €6.50; €3.25 reductions; free under-5s. **Credit** MC, V. **Map** p322 F8.

Recently transplanted from a first-floor flat to the Casa Garriga Nogués – a Modernista masterpiece in its own right – this vast private art collection now has enough room to breathe, with two floors of exhibition space. Godia was a Formula 1 driver for Maserati in the 1950s who funnelled his considerable fortune into an impressive collection of medieval religious art, historic Spanish ceramics, sculpture and modern painting. The permanent collection resides on the upper floor and largely consists of medieval sculptures and paintings, including Alejo de Vahía's *Pietà* and a Baroque masterpiece by Luca Giordano, along with some outstanding Romanesque sculptures. The inaugural temporary exhibition on the ground floor showcases Godia's contemporary collection, with pieces by Ramon Casas, Eduardo Chillida, Picasso, Antoni Tàpies and Joan Miró.

FREE Fundació Joan Brossa

C/Provença 318 (93 467 69 52, www.fundacio-joan-brossa.cat). Metro Diagonal or Verdaguer. **Open** 10am-2pm, 3-7pm Mon-Fri. Closed Aug. **Admission** free. **Map** p322 G7.

Polymathic artist Joan Brossa (1919-98) left fingerprints all over his home city, both in physical sculptures such as the letters spelling 'Barcino' by the cathedral or the *Illusory Clock* outside the Poliorama Theatre on La Rambla, and also in his vast legacy of poems, plays and tireless campaigning for the Catalan language, the Espai Escènic Joan Brossa theatrical space in the Born, and the founding of the Dau-al-Set avant-garde art movement in 1948. The permanent collection here fills three white rooms with some 35 of Brossa's visual and object poems, along with posters, manuscripts, books, photographs and screenings of some of his short films.

Fundació Suñol

Passeig de Gràcia 98 (93 496 10 32, www. fundaciosunol.org). Metro Diagonal. **Open** 4-8pm Mon-Sat. **Admission** €5; €2.50 reductions; free under-13s. **No credit cards. Map** p322 G7.

Opened in 2007, the foundation's two floors house the contemporary art collection of businessman Josep Suñol. There are 100 works on show at a time, including painting, sculpture and photography, shuffled every six months (in January and July) from an archive of 1,200 pieces amassed over 35 years. The collection includes historic – and predominantly Catalan and Spanish – artists of the avant-garde: Picasso, Miró and Pablo Gargallo, with international input from Giacometti, Man Ray and Warhol.

With superfluities removed, including labels, and chronology abandoned, works are arranged in careful, coherent compositions, by style, colour or even

SIGHTS

INSIDE TRACK
BREATHING SPACE

In 1985, the ProEixample was set up to reclaim some 50 of the courtyards that were proposed in Ildefons Cerdà's original plans, so that everybody living in the area should be able to find an open space within 300 metres of their home. Two of the nicest examples are the fake beach around the Torre de les Aigües water tower (C/Llúria 56) and the patio at Passatge Permanyer (C/Pau Claris 120).

---

mood, in serene interlinking rooms. Helpful English-speaking staff and a pamphlet aid visitors; an additional information booklet costs €2. Nivell Zero offers a large exhibition space to younger avant-garde artists, with shorter-term installations, poetry cycles and multimedia projects.

★ Hospital de la Santa Creu i Sant Pau

C/Sant Antoni María Claret 167 (93 291 90 00, www.santpau.cat). Metro Sant Pau Dos de Maig. **Map** p323 L5.

When part of the roof of the gynaecology department collapsed in 2004, it was clear restoration work was needed on the century-old Modernista 'garden city' hospital. In 2009, the last of the departments was transferred to the modern Nou Sant Pau building to the north, and there are tentative plans to turn part of the old complex into a museum of Modernisme. Scaffolding and builders will be on site for the next decade or so, but the renovations will be gradual and the complex still open to visitors who come to admire Domènech i Montaner's masterpiece.

A UNESCO World Heritage Site, the hospital is made up of 20 pavilions, abundantly adorned with the colourful Byzantine, Gothic and Moorish flourishes that characterise the architect's style and set in peaceful gardens that spread over nine blocks in the north-east corner of the Eixample. It's set at a 45° angle from the rest of Ildefons Cerdà's grid system, so that it catches more sun: Domènech i Montaner built the hospital very much with its patients in mind, convinced that aesthetic harmony and pleasant surroundings were good for the health. The public enjoy free access to the grounds, and guided tours (93 317 76 52, €10; €5 reductions) in English are held daily at 10am, 11am, 12pm and 1pm.

FREE Museu de Carrosses Fúnebres

C/Sancho de Avila 2 (93 484 17 10). Metro Marina. **Open** 10am-1pm, 4-6pm Mon-Fri; 10am-1pm Sat, Sun. **Admission** free. **Map** p327 K10.

Visiting what must be the most obscure museum in Barcelona hasn't got any easier. You'll need to ask at the reception desk of the Ajuntament's funeral service and, eventually, a security guard will take

you down to a perfectly silent and splendidly shuddersome basement housing the world's largest collection of funeral carriages and hearses, dating from the 18th century through to the 1950s. There are ornate Baroque carriages and more functional berlins and landaus, and a wonderful '50s silver Buick. The white carriages were designed for children and virgins; there's a windowless black-velour mourning carriage for the forlorn mistress, ensuring both her presence and anonymity. The vehicles are manned by ghoulish dummies dressed in period gear whose eyes follow you around the room, making you glad of that security guard. The museum is supposed to be moving to the cemetery on Montjuïc some day, although progress is, naturally, funereal.

Museu de la Música

L'Auditori, C/Padilla 155 (93 256 36 50, www. museumusica.bcn.cat). Metro Glòries. **Open** 10am-6pm Mon, Wed-Sat; 10am-8pm Sun. **Admission** €4; €3 reductions; free under-16s, over-65s. **Credit** AmEx, MC, V. **Map** p327 K9.

Finally rehoused in the Auditori concert hall in 2007 after six years in hibernation, the Music Museum's collections comprise over 1,600 instruments, displayed like precious jewels in red velvet and glass cases, along with multimedia displays, interactive exhibits and musical paraphernalia. With pieces spanning the ancient world to the modern day, and including instruments from all corners of the world, the museum's high note is the world-class collection of 17th-century guitars. Temporary exhibitions so far have concentrated on famous Catalan musicians, including the partnership between pianist and composer Enric Granados and cellist Pau Casals.

Museu Egipci de Barcelona

C/València 284 (93 488 01 88, www.museu egipci.com). Metro Passeig de Gràcia. **Open** 10am-8pm Mon-Sat; 10am-2pm Sun. **Admission** €11; €8 reductions; free under-5s. **Credit** AmEx, MC, V. **Map** p322 G7.

One of the finest collections of Ancient Egyptian artefacts in Europe, this collection is owned by prominent Egyptologist Jordi Clos and spans 3,000 years of Nile-drenched culture. Exhibits include religious statuary, such as the massive baboon heads used to decorate temples, everyday copper mirrors and alabaster headrests, and some rather moving infant sarcophagi. Outstanding pieces include some painstakingly matched fragments from the Sixth Dynasty Tomb of Iny, a bronze statuette of the goddess Isis breastfeeding her son Horus, and mummified cats, baby crocodiles and falcons. Another highlight is a 5,000-year-old bed, which still looks comfortable enough to sleep in. On Friday and Saturday nights, there are dramatic reconstructions of popular themes, such as the mummification ritual or the life of Cleopatra, for which reservations are essential. The museum entry fee is waived for guests staying at Hotel Claris, which is also owned by Clos.

Museu del Modernisme Català

C/Balmes 48 (93 272 28 96, www.mmcat.cat).
Metro Passeig de Gràcia. **Open** 10am-8pm Mon-Sat; 10am-2pm Sun. **Admission** €10; €7-€5 reductions; free under-5s. **Credit** AmEx, MC, V.
Map p322 G8.
See p93 **Profile.**

Museu del Perfum

Passeig de Gràcia 39 (93 216 01 21, www.museu delperfum.com). Metro Passeig de Gràcia. **Open** 10.30am-1.30pm; 4.30-8pm Mon-Fri; 11am-2pm Sat. **Admission** €5; €3 reductions; free under-5s. **No credit cards. Map** p322 G8.
In the back room of the Regia perfumery sit some 5,000 scent bottles, cosmetic flasks and related objects. The collection is divided in two. One displays all manner of unguent vases and essence jars in chronological order, from a tube of black eye make-up from pre-dynastic Egypt to Edwardian atomisers and a prized double-flask pouch that belonged to Marie Antoinette. The second section exhibits perfumes from brands such as Guerlain and Dior; some are in rare bottles, among them a garish Dalí creation for Schiaparelli and a set of golliwog flasks by Vigny Paris. The museum's most recent additions include a collection of 19th-century perfumed powder bottles and boxes.

FREE Parc de l'Estació del Nord

C/Almogávers 27-61 (no phone). Metro Arc de Triomf. **Open** 10am-sunset daily. **Admission** free. **Map** p327 J10/K10.
Otherwise known as Parc Sol i Ombra (meaning 'Sun and Shadow'), this small but well-used park is perked up by three pieces of landscape art in glazed blue and white ceramic by New York sculptor Beverly Pepper. Along with a pair of incongruous white stone entrance walls, *Espiral Arbrat* (Tree Spiral) is a spiral bench set under the cool shade of lime flower trees, while *Cel Caigut* (Fallen Sky) is a 7m (23ft) ridge rising from the grass. The colourful tiles recall Gaudí's *trencadís* smashed-tile technique.

★ La Pedrera (Casa Milà)

C/Provença 261-265 (93 484 59 00, www.caixa catalunya.cat/obrasocial). Metro Diagonal. **Open** Jan-Feb, Nov-Dec 9am-6pm daily. *Mar-Oct* 9am-8pm daily. **Admission** €11; €6 reductions; free under-13s. **Credit** MC, V. **Map** p322 G7.
Described variously as rising dough, molten lava and a stone lung, the last secular building designed by Antoni Gaudí, the Casa Milà (popularly known as La Pedrera, 'the stone quarry') has no straight lines. It is a stupendous and daring feat of architecture, and the culmination of the architect's experimental attempts to recreate natural forms with bricks and mortar (not to mention ceramics and even smashed-up cava bottles). Now a UNESCO World Heritage Site, it appears to have been washed up on shore, its marine feel complemented by collaborator Josep Maria Jujol's tangled balconies, doors of twisted kelp ribbon, sea-foamy ceilings and interior patios as blue as a mermaid's cave. When it was completed in 1912, it was so far ahead of its time that the woman who financed it as her dream home, Roser Segimon, became the laughing stock of the city – hence the 'stone quarry' tag. Its rippling façade led local painter Santiago Rusiñol to quip that a snake would be a better pet than a dog for the inhabitants. But La Pedrera has become one of Barcelona's best-loved buildings, and is adored by architects for its extraordinary structure; it is supported entirely by pillars, without a single master wall, allowing the vast, asymmetrical windows of the façade to invite in great swathes of natural light.

SIGHTS

On Your Bike The Eixample

Scoping it out from the saddle.

Starting at **Plaça Catalunya**, head up the **Passeig de Gràcia**, taking in the ornate lampposts and Modernista façades. While the street doesn't have cycle paths, buses and bikes are hived off into the side lanes, which does make for a more peaceful ride.

Once you get to **La Pedrera** (*see above*), turn right along C/Provença and take the first left at C/Pau Claris. You can window-shop here at **Vinçon** (*see p205*), the city's top design emporium, or continue along to the gorgeous – and free – **Casa Àsia** (*see p92*), located at the next crossroads.

Here, pick up the Avda Diagonal bike lane, heading right for eight blocks, and turn left on C/Sicilia, as far as C/Mallorca.

Once there, you'll hit the **Sagrada Família** (*see p98*). In front of the Nativity façade, take the C/Marina four blocks south (a cycle lane begins once you cross the Diagonal again) to the **Monumental**, Barcelona's now-defunct bullring. Turn right into the Gran Via. Continue for five blocks until you reach the Passeig de Sant Joan, where you can sprint clear downhill to the **Arc de Triomf**. Scoot under it and down the pedestrianised Passeig de Lluís Companys (there are bike lanes here) to the entrance to the **Ciutadella** park (*see p69*). Pedal into the park, find a shady tree and pass out.

► For details of bike hire, *see p295*.

Sagrada Família.

SIGHTS

There are three exhibition spaces at Casa Milà. The first-floor art gallery hosts free shows of work by a variety of eminent artists, while the upstairs space is dedicated to giving visitors a finer appreciation of Gaudi: accompanied by an audio guide (included in the admission price) you can visit a reconstructed Modernista flat on the fourth floor, with a sumptuous bedroom suite by Gaspar Homar, while the attic, framed by parabolic arches worthy of a Gothic cathedral, holds a museum offering an insightful overview of Gaudi's career. Best of all is the chance to stroll on the roof of the building amid its *trencadís*-covered ventilation shafts: their heads are shaped like the helmets of medieval knights, which led the poet Pere Gimferrer to dub the spot 'the garden of warriors'.

★ Sagrada Família

C/Mallorca 401 (93 207 30 31, www.sagrada familia.org). Metro Sagrada Família. **Open** *Apr-Sept 9am-8pm daily. Oct-Mar 9am-6pm daily.* **Admission** €12; €10 reductions; free under-11s. *Guided tour* €4. *Lift to spires* €2.50. **Credit** (shop only) MC, V. **Map** p323 K7.

'Send Gaudi and the Sagrada Família to hell,' wrote Picasso – and while it is easy to see how some of the religious clichés of the building and the devotional fervour of its creator might annoy an angry young Cubist, Barcelona's iconic temple still manages to inspire delight in equal measure.

Gaudi dedicated more than 40 years (the last 14 of them exclusively) to the project, and is buried beneath the nave. Many consider the crypt and the Nativity façade, which were completed in his lifetime, as the most beautiful elements of the church. The latter, facing C/Marina, looks at first glance as

though some careless giant has poured candle wax over a Gothic cathedral, but closer inspection shows every protuberance to be an intricate sculpture of flora, fauna or human figure, combining to form an astonishingly moving stone tapestry depicting scenes from Christ's early years.

Providing a grim counterpoint to the excesses of the Nativity façade is the Passion façade on C/Sardenya, where there are bone-shaped columns and haunting, angular sculptures by Josep Maria Subirachs that show the 12 stations of the cross. The vast metal doors, which are set behind the sculpture of the flagellation of Jesus, are particularly arresting, covered in quotations from the Bible in various languages. The Glory façade on C/Mallorca, the final side to be built and the eventual main entrance, is currently shooting up behind the scaffolding and is devoted to the Resurrection, a mass of stone clouds and trumpets emblazoned with quotations from the Apostles' Creed.

The most amazing thing about the Sagrada Familia project, however, is that it is happening at all. Setbacks have ranged from 1930s anarchists blowing up Gaudi's detailed plans and models, to lack of funds. The ongoing work is a matter of conjecture and controversy, with the finishing date expected to be somewhere within the region of 25-30 years; it was hoped the masterpiece would be completed in 2026 to coincide with the 100th anniversary of Gaudi's death, although this now seems unlikely. It's still something of an improvement on the prognosis in the 1900s, when construction was expected to last several hundred years; advanced computer technology is now being used to shape each intricately designed block of stone offsite to speed up the process. The latest tribulation to the

architects is the municipal approval of plans to build the AVE bullet train tunnel just a few feet away from the temple's foundations.

An estimated five million tourists visit the Sagrada Família each year, with more than half of them paying the entrance fee. (A combination of ticket revenues and charitable donations funds the continuing construction work, on which spending currently runs to about €1 million a month.) A ticket allows you to wander through the interior of the church, a marvellous forest of columns laid out in the style of the great Gothic cathedrals, with a multi aisled central nave crossed by a transept. The central columns are fashioned of porphyry – perhaps the only natural element capable of supporting the church's projected great dome, which is destined to rise 170m (558ft).

An admission ticket also gives visitors access to the museum in the basement, with displays on the history of the construction, original models for sculptural work and the chance to watch sculptors working at plaster-cast models through a large window.

INSIDE TRACK ORIENTATION

In the grid-like streets of the Eixample it can be hard to get your bearings, but directions are often given in a handy code – 'mar' (sea) or 'muntanya' (mountain) refer to the bottom or top of the area, while 'Besos' and 'Llobregat' (the rivers to the right and left of the Eixample) give you some guidance about which side you should be heading for.

THE ESQUERRA

When Cerdà designed the Eixample, he consciously tried to avoid creating any upper- or lower-class side of town, imagining each of his homogeneous blocks as a cross-section of society. This vision of equality did not come to pass, however, and the left (west) side of the tracks was immediately less fashionable than the right; eventually it was to become the repository for the sort of city services the bourgeoisie didn't want ruining the upmarket tone of their new neighbourhood.

A huge slaughterhouse was built at the eastern edge of the area (and was only knocked down in 1979, when it was replaced by the Parc Joan Miró). Also here is the busy Hospital Clínic, an ugly, functional building that covers two blocks between C/Corsega and C/Provença; to visit a market frequented by locals rather than tourists, try the Ninot, by the clinic. On C/Entença, a little further out, was the grim, star-shaped La Model prison. It has since been relocated out of town and replaced by subsidised houses and offices. The vast **Escola Industrial** on C/Comte d'Urgell, formerly a Can Batlló textile factory, was redesigned in 1909 as a centre to teach workers the methods used in the textile industry. Another building worth seeing is the central **Universitat de Barcelona** building on Plaça Universitat, completed in 1872. It is an elegant construction with a pleasant, cloister-like garden.

The Esquerra also contains a number of Modernista jewels, such as the **Casa Boada** (C/Enric Granados 106) and the **Casa Golferichs** (Gran Via 191), built in 1901 by Joan Rubió i Bellver, one of Gaudí's main collaborators, and now a civic centre. Beyond the hospital, the Esquerra leads to Plaça Francesc Macià, centre of the business district and a gateway to the Zona Alta. In recent years, ProEixample (*see p96* **Inside Track**) has restored many of its interior patios and reduced the traffic lanes in several streets. In a turnaround of fortunes, the lower left side of the Eixample has also become home to the 'Gaixample', an affluent gay neighbourhood where the rainbow flag flies from many a restaurant, bar and hairdresser's.

Parc Joan Miró (Parc de l'Escorxador)
C/Tarragona/ C/Aragó 2 (no phone). Metro Espanya. **Open** 10am-sunset daily. **Map** p325 C8.
Covering an area the size of four city blocks, the old slaughterhouse (*escorxador*) was demolished in 1979 to provide some much-needed parkland, although there's little greenery. The rows of palms and pines are dwarfed by Miró's sculpture *Dona i Ocell* (Woman and Bird) getting its feet wet in a cement lake; there's also a good playground for small kids.

SIGHTS

Gràcia & Other Districts

A runaway town holds onto its distinctive character.

The inexorable expansion that began when Barcelona's walls were demolished in the 19th century ate away at the fields that once separated **Gràcia** from its neighbour. By 1897, Barcelona had all but swallowed up the fiercely independent conurbation, and, amid howls of protest from its populace, the town was annexed.

Still, it retains its character and continues to draw visitors – as do neighbourhoods such as **Les Corts** (where football pilgrims head to the Camp Nou); **Tibidabo**, with its monster science museum, the CosmoCaixa; and **Poblenou**, scene of the most energetic attempts at urban regeneration.

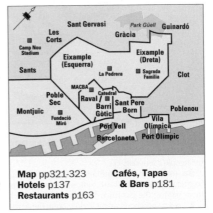

Map pp321-323	**Cafés, Tapas**
Hotels p137	**& Bars** p181
Restaurants p163	

GRACIA

Gràcia's reputation as a breeding ground for political insurgency came from the effects of industrial expansion. Centred around the 17th-century convent of Santa Maria de Gràcia, it was a village in 1821, with 2,600 residents. But by the time it was annexed 78 years later, its population had risen to 61,935; it had become the ninth largest town in Spain, and a hotbed of Catalanism, republicanism and anarchism.

Dissent has been a recurring feature in Gràcia's history. Streets boast names such as Llibertat, Revolució and Fraternitat, and for the 64 years preceding the Civil War, there was a satirical political magazine called *La Campana de Gràcia*, named after the famous bell in Plaça Rius i Taulet. However, few vestiges of radicalism remain. Sure, the *okupa* squatter movement inhabits a relatively high number of buildings in the area, but the middle-class population has been waging an increasingly successful campaign to dislodge them.

Gràcia is both 'alternative' and upmarket, and anything bigger than a shoebox costs a

fortune to rent or buy. For many, though, it's the only place to be in Barcelona. As a result it radiates a youthful chic, with buzzy bars, yoga centres and practitioners of shiatsu, acupuncture and every form of holistic medicine, as well as piercing and tattoo parlours, dotted among the antique shops and *jamonerías*. The *barri* is a favourite hangout of the city's bohemians: there are numerous workshops and studios, and the many small, unpretentious bars are often frequented by artists, designers and students.

The neighbourhood really comes into its own for a few days in mid August, when its famous *festa major* grips the entire city and all Barcelona converges here to party. Residents spend months preparing startlingly original home-made street decorations, and there is fierce competition for the accolade of best decorated street. Open-air meals are laid on for the residents of Gràcia, bands are dotted on every street and films are screened in *plaças* and bars, while old-timers sing along to *habaneros* (shanties) and resident squatters pogo to punk bands.

Much of Gràcia was built in the heyday of Modernisme, including the district's splendid main street, C/Gran de Gràcia. Many of the buildings are rich in nature-inspired curves and fancy façades, but the finest example of architecture is Lluís Domènech i Montaner's Casa Fuster at No.2, now a luxury hotel (*see p137*). Gaudí's disciple Francesc Berenguer was responsible for much of the civic architecture, most notably the Mercat de la Llibertat (Barcelona's oldest covered market, still proudly adorned with Gràcia's old coat of arms) and the old Casa de la Vila (Town Hall) in Plaça Rius i Taulet.

However, the district's most overwhelming Modernista gem is one of Gaudí's earliest and most fascinating works: the **Casa Vicens** of 1883-88, which is hidden away in C/Carolines. The building is a private residence and not open to visitors, but the castellated red brickwork and colourful tiled exterior inspired by Indian and Mudéjar influences should not be missed; notice, too, the spiky wrought-iron leaves on the gates. One of Gaudí's last works, the extraordinary **Park Güell** is a short walk away, across the busy Travessera de Dalt and up the hill. This is worth the effort (there are escalators at certain points), not only for the architecture but for the magnificent view of Barcelona and the sea.

Photography aficionados should also visit the **Fundació Foto Colectània**. Just off C/Sants is

C/Sant Medir, the starting point for the *barri's* **Festa de Sant Medir** (*see p208*), held in mid March every year, where local representatives canter around in horse-drawn carriages throwing sweets to the children.

ᴿᴿᴱᴱ Fundació Foto Colectània

C/Teodor Roviralta 47-51, Zona Alta (93 212 60 50, www.cosmocaixa.com). Bus 17, 22, 58/ FGC Avda Tibidabo. **Open** *July-mid Sept 10am-8pm daily. Mid Sept-June 10am-8pm Tue-Sun.* **Admission** €3; €2 reductions; free under-3s & 1st Sun of mth. *Planetarium, Toca Toca!* €2; €1.50 reductions; free under-8s. **Credit** MC, V.

This private foundation is dedicated to the promotion of the photography of major Spanish and Portuguese photographers from the 1950s to the present. It also has an extensive library of Spanish and Portuguese photography books.

★ ᴿᴿᴱᴱ Park Güell

C/Olot (Casa-Museu Gaudí 93 219 38 11). Metro Lessseps or Vallcarca (for top entrance) or bus 24, 92. **Open** *Park 10am-sunset daily. Museum Apr-Sept 10am-7.45pm daily. Oct-Mar 10am-5.45pm daily.* **Admission** *Park* free. *Museum* €5.50; €4.50 reductions; free under 11s. **No credit cards. Map** p323 H2/H3/J2/J3. *See p102* **Profile.**

SANTS

Sants, or at least the immediate environs of Estació de Sants, which is all that most visitors see of the area, stands as a monument to the worst of 1970s urban design. To coincide with the arrival of the overdue high-speed AVE train connection with Madrid, the station has undergone a makeover. The place is no longer shabby, but it's not one that you would want to hang around, and few people do. When they step outside, most take one look at the forbidding Plaça dels Països Catalans, a snarl of traffic around a roundabout whose centrepiece looks like a post-Miró bus shelter, and make a hasty exit.

However, for those with time to spare, Sants merits investigation for historic, if not aesthetic, reasons. Mid August is one of the better times to visit: following the Festa Major de Gràcia, Sants launches its own, lower-key, version, and

Plaça Rius i Taulet.

SIGHTS

Profile Park Güell

The exuberant charm of a world heritage site.

Gaudí's brief for the design of what became Park Güell (*see p101*) was to emulate the English garden cities so admired by his patron Eusebi Güell: to lay out a self-contained suburb for the wealthy, but also to design the public areas. (This English influence explains the anglicised spelling of 'Park'.) The original plan called for the plots to be sold and the properties designed by other architects. But the idea never took off – perhaps because it was too far from the city, or because it was too radical – and the Güell family gave the park to the city in 1922.

The fantastical exuberance of Gaudí's imagination remains breathtaking. Visitors were once welcomed by two life-size mechanical gazelles, a typically bizarre religious reference by Gaudí to medieval Hebrew love poetry, although these were unfortunately destroyed in the Civil War. The two gatehouses that remain were based on designs the architect made for the opera *Hänsel and Gretel*, one of them featuring a red and white mushroom for a roof.

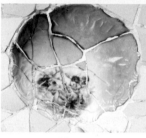

IN THE PINK
Designed by Gaudí student Francesc Berenguer, the pink Torre Rosa is now the Casa-Museu Gaudí. Tours, some in English, are available.

From here, walk up a splendid staircase flanked by multi-coloured battlements, past the iconic mosaic lizard sculpture, to what would have been the main marketplace. Here, 100 palm-shaped pillars hold up a roof, reminiscent of the hypostyle hall at Luxor. On top of this structure is the esplanade, a circular concourse surrounded by benches in the form of a sea-serpent decorated with shattered tiles – a technique called '*trencadís*', perfected by Gaudí's talented assistant Josep Maria Jujol.

The park itself, now a UNESCO World Heritage Site, is magical, with twisted stone columns supporting curving colonnades or merging with the natural structure of the hillside. Its peak is marked by a large cross, and offers an amazing panorama of Barcelona and the sea beyond.

the *barri* sheds its drab industrial coat in favour of street parties, decorations and music.

Sants was originally built to serve those who arrived after the town gates had shut at 9pm, with inns and blacksmiths to cater for latecomers. In the 19th century, though, it became the industrial motor of the city. Giant textile factories such as Vapor Vell (which is now a library), L'Espanya Industrial (now the **Parc de l'Espanya Industrial**) and **Can Batlló** (still a workplace) helped create the wealth that the likes of Eusebi Güell spent on the Modernista dream homes that still grace the more salubrious areas of the city. The inequality did not go unnoticed. The *barri* was a hotbed of industrial action; the first general strike in Catalonia broke out here in 1856, only to be violently put down by the infamous General Zapatero (known as the 'Tiger of Catalonia').

Most routes of interest start and finish at the Plaça de Sants, which lies halfway up the high street of C/Sants and where Jorge Castillo's *Ciclista* statue is to be found. Also worth a look are the showy Modernista buildings at Nos.12, 130, 145 and 151, all designed by local architect Modest Feu.

Returning to the Plaça de Sants and taking C/Olzinelles, you'll find the quaint Plaça Bonet i Mixi and the Parroquia de Santa Maria del Sants church, from which it is believed the *barri* got its name. This is the focal point for locals around Easter, when Semana Santa (Holy Week) grips Spain. Following C/Sants in the direction of Montjuïc, the road changes to C/Creu Coberta, an old Roman road that was once known as the Cami d'Espanya or 'the road to Spain'. Following C/Creu Coberta further, you'll find the large, lively and colourful Mercat d'Hostafrancs, where there's also a stop for the tourist bus. Further along still is C/Sant Roc and the Modernista-inspired Església de l'Angel Custodi.

FREE Parc de l'Espanya Industrial

C/Muntadas 1-37 (no phone). Metro Sants-Estació. **Open** 10am-sunset daily. **Admission** free. **Map** p325 B7.

During the 1970s, the owners of the old textile factory announced their intention to use the land to build blocks of apartments. The neighbourhood's residents, though, put their collective foot down and insisted on a park, which was eventually laid out in 1985. The result is a puzzling space, designed by Basque Luis Peña Ganchegui, with little in the way of greenery. Ten watchtowers overlook a boating lake with a statue of Neptune in the middle, which is flanked by a stretch of mud used mainly by dog walkers; by the entrance, children can climb over Andrés Nagel's *Drac*, a massive and sinister black dragon sculpture.

Les Corts

Another village engulfed by the expanding city in the 19th century, Les Corts ('cowsheds' or 'pigsties'), remains one of the most Catalan of the city's *barris*. Rows and rows of unlovely apartment blocks have stamped out almost any trace of its bucolic past, although the Plaça de la Concòrdia, a quiet square dominated by a 40-metre (131-foot) bell tower, remains. This is an anachronistic oasis housing the civic centre Can Deu, formerly a farmhouse and now home to a great bar hosting jazz acts every other Thursday. The area is much better known, though, for what happens every other weekend, when tens of thousands pour in to watch FC Barcelona, whose Camp Nou takes up much of the west of the neighbourhood. Note that at night the area is the haunt of transvestite prostitutes and their kerb-crawling clients.

★ Museu FC Barcelona

Avda Aristides Maillol, access 9, Les Corts (93 496 36 00/08, www.fcbarcelona.com). Metro Collblanc, Les Corts or Maria Cristina. **Open** *Apr-Sept* 10am-8pm Mon-Sat; 10am-2.30pm Sun. *Oct-Mar* 10am-6.30pm Mon-Sat; 10am-2.30pm Sun. **Admission** €19; €15.50 reductions; free under-6s. **Credit** MC, V. **Map** p321 A3.

Camp Nou, where FC Barcelona has played since 1957, is one of football's great stadiums – a vast cauldron of a ground that holds 98,000 spectators. That's a lot of noise when the team is doing well, and an awful lot of silence when it isn't. If you can't get there on match day but love the team, it's worth visiting the club museum. The excellent audio-guided tour of the stadium takes you through the players' tunnel to the dugouts and then, via the away team's changing room, on to the President's box, where there is a replica of the European Cup, which the team won at Wembley in 1992, in Paris in 2006 and in Rome in 2009. The club museum commemorates the glory years, making much of the days when the likes of Kubala, Cruyff, Maradona, Koeman and Lineker trod the hallowed turf, with pictures, video clips and souvenirs spanning the century that has passed since the Swiss businessman Johan Gamper and the Englishman Arthur Witty first founded the club. Last tour begins an hour before closing time.

▶ *For match tickets, see p262.*

TIBIDABO & COLLSEROLA

Before car pollution blurred the horizon, it was said that you could see Mallorca from Tibidabo. The mountain takes its name from the Devil's temptation of Christ, when he took Jesus to the top of a mountain and offered him all before him, with the words '*tibi dabo*' (Latin for 'To thee I will give'). This gave rise to the name of the dominant peak of the Collserola massif, with its sweeping views of, if not Mallorca, at least the whole of the Barcelona conurbation stretching to the sea: a tempting offer, given the present-day price of the city's real estate.

Crowning the peak, the neo-Gothic Sagrat Cor church has become one of the city's most recognisable landmarks, visible for miles. At weekends, thousands of people head to the top of the hill in order to whoop and scream at the funfair. Now the only one in the city, it's been running since 1921 and has changed little since: the rides are creaky and old-fashioned, but very quaint. The marionette show is also a survivor from the early days; a more recent addition is Spain's first freefall ride, where visitors are dropped 38 metres (125 feet) in 2.8 seconds. Within the funfair, the Museu d'Autòmats showcases a fine collection of fairground coin-operated machines from the early 1900s.

Getting there on the **Tramvia Blau** (Blue Tram) and then the **funicular railway** is part of the fun; between the two is Plaça Doctor Andreu, a great place for an alfresco drink. For the best view of the city, either take a lift up Norman Foster's tower, the **Torre de Collserola**, or up to the *mirador* (viewpoint) at the feet of Christ atop the Sagrat Cor.

The vast **Parc de Collserola** is more a series of forested hills than a park, its shady paths through holm oak and pine opening out to spectacular views. It's most easily reached by FGC train on the Terrassa-Sabadell line from Plaça Catalunya or Passeig de Gràcia, getting off at Baixador de Vallvidrera station. A ten-minute walk up into the woods (there's an information board just outside the station) will take you to the Vil·la Joana, an old *masia* covered in bougainvillea and containing the **Museu Verdaguer** (93 204 78 05, www. museuhistoria.bcn.cat, open 10am-1.30pm Sat, Sun, admission free) dedicated to 19th-century Catalan poet Jacint Verdaguer, who used this as his summer home. Just beyond the Vil·la Joana is the park's information centre (93 280 35 52, open 9.30am-3pm daily), which has free basic maps and more detailed maps for sale. Most of the information is in Catalan, but staff are helpful. There's also a snack bar.

Funicular de Tibidabo

Plaça Doctor Andreu to Plaça Tibidabo (93 211 79 42). FGC Avda Tibidabo then Tramvia Blau. **Open** as funfair (*see p218*), but from 15mins earlier, until 15mins later. **Tickets** €4; free under-90cm. **No credit cards.**
This art deco vehicle offers occasional glimpses of the city below as it winds through the pine forests up to the summit. The service has been operating since 1901, but only according to a complicated timetable. If it's not running, take the FGC line from Plaça de Catalunya to Peu del Funicular, get the

funicular up to Vallvidrera Superior, and then catch the 111 bus to Tibidabo (a process not half as complicated as it sounds). Alternatively, it's nearly an hour's (mostly pleasant) hike up from Plaça Doctor Andreu for those who are feeling energetic.

Torre de Collserola

Ctra de Vallvidrera al Tibidabo (93 211 79 42, www.torredecollserola.com). FGC Peu Funicular then funicular. **Open** as funfair, see p219. **Admission** €5; €3 reductions; free under-90cm. **Credit** AmEx, MC, V.
Just five minutes' walk from the Sagrat Cor is its main rival, and Barcelona's most visible landmark. Norman Foster's communications tower was built in 1992 to transmit images of the Olympics around the world. Those who don't suffer from vertigo attest to the wonderful views of Barcelona and the Mediterranean from the top.

ZONA ALTA

Zona Alta (the 'upper zone', or 'uptown') is the name given collectively to the series of smart neighbourhoods – including Sant Gervasi, Sarrià, Pedralbes and Putxet – that stretch out across the lower reaches of the Collserola hills. The handful of tourist sights found here include the Palau Reial de Pedralbes (not to be confused with the Palau Reial Major in the Barri Gòtic), with its gardens and museums, the **Museu de les Arts Aplicades**, the **CosmoCaixa** science museum and the **Pedralbes Monastery**. The monastery is still worth a visit, even though the religious paintings from the Thyssen-Bornemisza collection have been moved to the revamped Museu Nacional d'Art de Catalunya (MNAC; *see p86*). The centre of Sarrià and the streets of old Pedralbes around the monastery retain a flavour of the sleepy country towns these once were.

For many downtown residents, the Zona Alta is a favourite place to relax in the parks and gardens that wind in to the hills. At the end of Avda Diagonal, next to the functional Zona Universitària (university district), is the Jardins de Cervantes, with its 11,000 rose bushes, the striking *Rombes Bessons* (Twin Rhombuses) sculpture by Andreu Alfaro and, during the week, legions of picnicking students, continuing in the scholastic traditions of the founder of Catalan literature, Ramon Llull.

From the park, a turn back along the Diagonal towards Plaça Maria Cristina and Plaça Francesc Macià will take you to the city's main business and shopping district. Here, the small Turó Parc is a semi-formal garden, good for writing postcards amid inspirational plaques of poetry. The Jardins de la Tamarita, which lies at the foot of Avda Tibidabo, is a pleasant dog-free oasis with a

SIGHTS

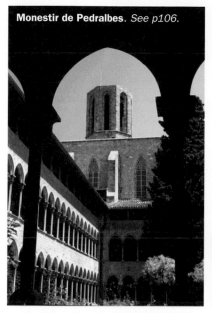

Monestir de Pedralbes. *See p106.*

SIGHTS

playground, while further up at the top of the tramline is the little-known Parc de la Font de Racó, full of shady pine and eucalyptus trees. A fair walk to the north-east, an old quarry has been converted into a swimming pool, the **Parc de la Creueta del Coll**.

Gaudí fans are rewarded by a trip up to the **Pavellons de la Finca Güell** at Avda Pedralbes 15; its extraordinary and rather frightening wrought-iron gate features a dragon into whose gaping mouth the foolhardy can fit their heads. Once inside the gardens, via the main gate on Avda Diagonal, look out for a delightful fountain designed by the master himself. Across near Putxet is Gaudí's relatively sober **Col·legi de les Teresianes** (C/Ganduxer 85-105), while up towards Tibidabo, just off Plaça Bonanova, rises his Gothic-influenced Torre Figueres (or Torre Bellesguard).

CosmoCaixa

C/Isaac Newton 26 (93 212 60 50, www. fundacio.lacaixa.es). Bus 60/FGC Avda Tibidabo. **Open** 10am-8pm Tue-Sun. **Admission** €3; €2 reductions; free under-7s. *Planetarium* €2; €1.50 reductions; free under-7s. **Credit** MC, V.
Said to be the biggest science museum in Europe, CosmoCaixa doesn't, perhaps, make the best use of its space. A glass-enclosed spiral ramp runs down an impressive six floors, but represents a long walk to reach the main collection five floors down. Here

you'll find the Flooded Forest, a reproduction of a flora- and fauna-filled corner of Amazonia, and the Geological Wall, along with temporary exhibitions.

From here onwards, it's on to the Matter Room, which covers 'inert', 'living', 'intelligent' and then 'civilised' matter: in other words, natural history. However, for all the fanfare that is made by the museum about taking exhibits out of glass cases and making scientific theories accessible, many of the displays still look very dated. Written explanations often tend towards the impenetrable, containing phrases such as 'time is macroscopically irreversible', and making complex those concepts that previously seemed simple.

On the plus side, the installations for children are excellent: the Planetarium pleases those aged five to eight, and the wonderful Clik (ages three to six) and Flash (seven to nine) introduce children to science through games. Toca Toca! ('Touch Touch') educates children on which animals and plants are safe and which to avoid. One of the real highlights, for both young and old, is the hugely entertaining sound telescope outside on the Plaça de la Ciència.

Disseny Hub Barcelona (DHUB)

Palau Reial de Pedralbes, Avda Diagonal 686 (93 280 16 21, www.dhub-bcn.cat, www. museuceramica.bcn.cat). Metro Palau Reial. **Open** 10am-6pm Tue-Sun. **Admission** €5; €3 reductions; free under-16s. Free 3-6pm Sun & all day 1st Sun of mth. **No credit cards. Map** p321 A2.

In 2008, the Museu Tèxtil, previously located in the Born, joined the ceramic and decorative arts museums in the Palau Reial de Pedralbes, built in the 1920s and briefly used as a royal palace. The museums are now collectively known as the Disseny Hub Barcelona. The Textile Museum provides a chronological tour of clothing, from its oldest piece, a man's Coptic tunic from a seventh-century tomb, through to Karl Lagerfeld's creations. There are many curiosities – such as an 18th-century bridal gown in black figured silk and the world's largest collection of kidskin gloves, but the real highlight is the fashion collection, from Baroque to 20th century, one of the finest of its type anywhere.

The Museum of Decorative Arts is informative and fun, and looks at the different styles informing the design of artefacts in Europe since the Middle Ages. A second section is devoted to post-war Catalan design of objects as diverse as urinals and man-sized inflatable pens.

The Ceramics Museum is equally fascinating, showing how 13th-century Moorish ceramic techniques were developed after the Reconquista with the addition of colours (especially blue and yellow) in centres such as Manises, in Valencia, and Barcelona. Upstairs is a section on 20th-century ceramics, with a room devoted to Miró and Picasso.

★ Monestir de Pedralbes

Baixada del Monestir 9 (93 256 21 22). FGC Reina Elisenda. **Open** *Apr-Sept* 10am-5pm Tue-Sat; 10am-8pm Sun. *Oct-Mar* 10am-2pm Mon-Sat; 10am-8pm Sun. **Admission** €7; €5 reductions; free under-16s. Free 1st Sun of mth and Sun 3-8pm. **No credit cards.**

In 1326, the widowed Queen Elisenda of Montcada used her inheritance to buy this land and build a convent for the Poor Clare order of nuns, which she soon joined. The result is a jewel of Gothic architecture; an understated single-nave church with fine stained-glass windows and a beautiful three-storey 14th-century cloister. The place was out of bounds to the general public until 1983, when the nuns, a closed order, opened it up as a museum (they escape to a nearby annexe).

The site offers a fascinating insight into life in a medieval convent, taking you through the kitchens, pharmacy and refectory, with its huge vaulted ceiling. To one side is the tiny chapel of Sant Miquel, with murals dating from 1343 by Ferrer Bassa, a Catalan

---

INSIDE TRACK
THE SINGER FROM SANTS

Opera fans may be interested in visiting one of Sants' oldest streets: the tiny commercial thoroughfare of **C/Galileu**, where tenor José Carreras was born at No.1 in 1946.

---

painter and student of Giotto. In the former dormitory next to the cloister is a selection of illuminated books, furniture and items reflecting the artistic and religious life of the community. The admission charge includes an audio-guide. *Photo p105.*

▶ *Tickets are valid for the Museu d'Història de Barcelona (see p59) and the Refugi 307 (see p89).*

FREE Parc de la Creueta del Coll

C/Mare de Déu del Coll 77 (no phone). Metro Penitents. **Open** 10am-sunset daily. **Admission** free.

Created from a quarry in 1987 by Josep Martorell and David Mackay, the team that went on to design the Vila Olímpica, this park boasts a large swimming pool complete with a 'desert island' and a charming sculpture by Eduardo Chillida: a 50-ton lump of curly granite suspended on cables, called *In Praise of Water.*

Pavellons de la Finca Güell

Avda Pedralbes 7 (info 93 317 76 52, www.rutadelmodernisme.com). Metro Palau Reial. **Open** *Tours* in English 10.15am, 12.15pm Sat, Sun. **Admission** €6; €3 reductions; free under-11s. **No credit cards. Map** p321 A3.

Industrial textile businessman Eusebi Güell bought what is now Palau Reial in 1882 as a summer home, contracting Gaudí to remodel the entrance lodges and gardens for the estate. In 1883, they began to build what would be one of Gaudí's first projects in Barcelona for the Güell family. This was also the first project on which Gaudí used his signature *trencadís* (mosaic motif).

The huge gardens were accessed by three entrances, of which only two remain. The Porta del Drac (Dragon's Gate), the most impressive, used to be the private entrance for the Güell family. It was connected to the Güell home in Barcelona by a private, walled road exclusively for their use when the family travelled between the city and the country. Nowadays, the gatehouses belong to the University of Barcelona. The family of Güell's original groundsman still lives in the same small house on the site.

The Pavellons must be visited with a guide, and tours are offered in Spanish and English. Really, though, it isn't much of a tour, lasting for about 25 minutes with a look at nothing more than the gate and the stables.

Tramvia Blau

Avda Tibidabo (Plaça Kennedy) to Plaça del Funicular (93 318 70 74, www.tmb.cat). FGC Avda Tibidabo. **Open** *Nov-Mar* 10am-6pm Sat, Sun. *Apr-June* 10am-8pm daily. *July, Aug* 10am-8pm Mon-Fri. *Sept, Oct* 10am-8pm Sat, Sun. **Frequency** 20mins. **Tickets** €2.80 single; €4.30 return. **No credit cards.**

Barcelonins and tourists have been clanking 1,225m (4,000ft) up Avda Tibidabo in the 'blue trams' since

SIGHTS

Modernista Mansions

Local summer villas that have been put to good use as community centres.

In the last decades of the 19th century, it was all the rage for wealthy local families to commission fashionable architects to build their summer villas in the country villages around Barcelona. These villages – Sarrià, Sant Gervasi, Horta and Les Corts – have long since been swallowed up by the urban sprawl, and most of the villas have been demolished to make way for dull apartment blocks. However, a handful of these mostly Modernista mansions survived; many of them have been converted into neighbourhood community centres, whose busy programmes of activities run from concerts to film screenings.

The wonderfully elegant **Vil·la Florida** (C/Muntaner 544, 93 254 62 65, www.bcn.cat/villaflorida), in the smart neighbourhood of Sant Gervasi, was extensively remodelled in the early 1900s by a wealthy wine merchant from Tarragona. Decorated with swooping Modernista ironwork and flanked by a storybook tower, it is surrounded by leafy gardens where immaculately coiffed old ladies dip their toes in a pristine paddling pool (part of a refreshing foot spa circuit). Puppet shows and concerts geared towards kids take place on Sundays, when the restaurant is filled with families enjoying lunch on the shady terrace.

Further east, in equally smart Sarrià, the 19th-century **Vil·la Amèlia** (C/Eduardo Conde 22-42, 93 256 27 20) was built as a plush summer retreat for an affluent merchant, who named it after his wife. The mansion is the buzzy neighbourhood civic centre, set amid gardens filled with palm trees and pools, yet surprisingly little known. Among the activities arranged by the centre are outdoor cinema screenings (films are shown in their original language, with subtitles), and a summer 'beach' for families with young children.

Little has survived of the old village of Les Corts, now a bland residential suburb, but the delightful **Can Deu** (Plaça de la Concòrdia 13, 93 410 10 07, www.cccandeu.com), a Modernista townhouse, presides over the neighbourhood's prettiest historic square. Inside, the original Modernista tiles, stained glass and woodwork have been preserved in the appealing café, and you can sip *vermut* on the magnificent terrace. There are regular jazz concerts, including popular 'Piano Obert' amateur sessions on Friday nights.

SIGHTS

Vil·la Florida.

1902. When the tram isn't running, a rather more prosaic bus (No.195) takes you up – or you can walk it in 15 minutes.

POBLENOU & BEYOND

In its industrial heyday, Poblenou was known as 'little Manchester' due to its concentration of cotton mills. Now, the old mills and other factories are being bulldozed or remodelled as the district is rebranded as a technology and business district, snappily tagged 22@, which will exist side by side with the innumerable garages, exhaust fitters, wheel balancers and car washes that are a feature of the *barrio*.

The main drag, the pedestrianised Rambla de Poblenou, dating from 1886, is a much better place for a relaxing stroll than its busy central counterpart, and gives this still-villagey area a heart. Meanwhile, a bone's throw away, the city's oldest and most atmospheric cemetery, the Cementiri de Poblenou, shows that most *barcelonins* spend their death as they did their life: cooped up in large, high-rise blocks. Some were able to afford roomier tombs, many of which were built at the height of the romantic-Gothic craze at the end of the 19th century. A leaflet or larger guide (€15) sold at the entrance suggests a route around 30 of the more interesting monuments.

Nearby, Plaça de les Glòries finally seems ready to fulfil its destiny. The creator of the

Eixample, Ildefons Cerdà, hoped that the square would become the new centre of the city, believing his grid-pattern blocks would spread much further north than they did and shift the emphasis of the city from west to east. Instead, it became little more than a glorified roundabout on the way out of town. Nowadays, it's best known for its huge commercial shopping complex and the bustling market Mercat Els Encants (www.encantsbcn.com, open Mon, Wed, Fri, Sat from 7.30am), which has everything from kitchen sinks to dodgy DVDs. From here, a wide and relatively quiet stretch of Diagonal is filled with joggers, cyclists and in-line skaters as it leads towards the sea.

Els Encants is already casting about for a new home – the Monumental bullring has been tipped as a possible site – as work is about to begin on remodelling the ghastly, traffic-choked Glòries, partly to open up the land around the hugely phallic **Torre Agbar**, and to form a gateway to Diagonal Mar and the new commercial and leisure area on the shoreline, known as the Fòrum.

The Torre Agbar, designed by French architect Jean Nouvel and owned by the Catalan water board, has been a bold and controversial project. A concrete skyscraper with a domed head and a glass façade, it's not unlike London's famed Gherkin. Nouvel says its design reflects the Catalan mentality: the concrete represents stability and severity; the glass, openness and transparency. At 144 metres (472 feet), it's Barcelona's third highest building (behind the two Olympic towers) and contains no fewer than 4,400 multiform windows. Remarkably, it has no air-conditioning: the windows let the breeze do the job. Nouvel claims Gaudí as the inspiration for the multicoloured skin – it has 4,000 LED lights that change colour at night – of a building that has already polarised public opinion and come to dominate the district. Ask any taxi driver to take you to *el supositori* (the suppository) and they'll know you mean the Torre Agbar.

The walled **Parc Central del Poblenou**, also designed by Nouvel, opened in 2008. It's one of a number of high-design gardens in Barcelona and features giant plants, an island, a cratered lunar landscape and a perfumed garden. It opened to decidedly mixed reviews from the locals: aesthetically pleasing though it may be, only time will tell if the park takes on a life of its own and if the hundreds of weeping willows can survive the rigours of the Mediterranean climate.

Another breath of fresh air is the **Parc del Clot**. Just beyond it is the Plaça de Valentí Almirall, with the old town hall of Sant Martí and the 17th-century former Hospital de Sant

Parc Central del Poblenou.

Pont de Calatrava.

Joan de Malta somewhat at odds with the buildings that have mushroomed around them. Further north, up C/Sagrera, the entrance to an old truck factory now leads to the charming **Parc de la Pegaso**. The area also has a fine piece of recent architecture, the supremely elegant **Pont de Calatrava**. Designed by Santiago Calatrava, it links to Poblenou via C/Bac de Roda.

Diagonal Mar

To many people, the Diagonal Mar development represents the worst hypocrisy of the Barcelona authorities: pure venality dressed up as philanthropy. The stalking horse for the five-star hotels and luxury apartments that were to come was the Fòrum, a six-month cultural symposium held in 2004. Its tangible legacy is the enormous conference halls and hotels that draw many wealthy business clients into the city, together with a scarcely believable increase in real-estate values. More recently, the Fòrum has benefited the city's youth, with its wide-open spaces providing an excellent venue for one of Barcelona's biggest music festivals, Primavera Sound (*see p237*).

If you're approaching from the city, the first sign of this resurgent *barri* is **Parc de Diagonal Mar**, containing an angular lake decorated with scores of curling aluminium tubes and vast Gaudían flowerpots. Designed by the late Enric Miralles (he of Scottish

Parliament fame), the park may not be to most *barcelonins'* taste, but flocks of seagulls have found it an excellent roosting spot. Just over the road from here is the Diagonal Mar shopping centre, a still woefully undervisited three-storey mall of high-street chains, cinemas and the grand Hotel Princesa, a triangular skyscraper designed by architect, designer, artist and local hero Oscar Tusquets.

The **Edifici Fòrum** (*photo p110*) a striking blue triangular construction by architects Herzog and de Meuron (responsible for London's Tate Modern), is the centrepiece of the €3-billion redevelopment. The remainder of the money was spent on the solar panels, marina, new beach and the Illa Pangea, an island 60 metres (197 feet) from the shore, accessible only by swimming. The building itself is to house the **Museu de Ciències Naturals** (Natural History Museum), transplanted here from the Born, at some point in 2011. Soon the Fòrum will be joined by Zaha Hadid's nearby Spiralling Tower, an extraordinary construction like a hastily stacked pack of cards, which will serve as a university building.

It's all a far cry from the local residential neighbourhood, Sant Adrià de Besòs, a poor district of tower blocks that includes La Mina, an area rife with drug-related crime. It's hoped that the new development will help regenerate the area, best known for its **Feria de Abril** celebrations in April (*see p210*) – the Andalucian community's version of the more famous annual celebrations in Seville.

HORTA & AROUND

Once a picturesque little village, Horta still remains aloof from the city that swallowed it in 1904. Originally a collection of farms (its name means 'market garden'), the *barrio* is peppered with old farmhouses, such as Can Mariner on C/Horta, dating back to 1050, and the medieval Can Cortada at the end of C/Campoamor, which is now a huge restaurant set in beautiful grounds. An abundant water supply also made Horta the place where much of the city's laundry was done: a whole community of *bugaderes* (washerwomen) lived and worked in lovely C/Aiguafreda, where you can still see their wells and open-air stone washtubs.

To the south, joined to Gràcia by Avda Mare de Déu de Montserrat, the steep-sided neighbourhood of Guinardó, with its steps and escalators, consists mainly of two big parks. **Parc del Guinardó**, a huge space designed in 1917 (making it Barcelona's third oldest park), is full of eucalyptus and cypress trees, and a relaxing place to escape.

The Vall d'Hebron is a leafy area located just above Horta in the Collserola foothills. Here,

SIGHTS

Edifici Fòrum. *See p109.*

In 1791, the Desvalls family, owners of this marvellously leafy estate, hired Italian architect Domenico Bagutti to design scenic gardens set around a cypress maze, with a romantic stream and a waterfall. The mansion may be gone (replaced with a 19th-century Arabic-influenced building), but the gardens are remarkably intact, shaded in the summer by oaks, laurels and an ancient sequoia. Best of all, the maze, an ingenious puzzle that intrigues those brave enough to try it, is also still in use. Nearby stone tables provide a handy picnic site. On paying days, last entry is one hour before sunset.

THE OUTER LIMITS

L'Hospitalet de Llobregat lies beyond the district of Sants, integrated within the city's transport system but nevertheless a distinct municipality, and one with its own identity. It is the second biggest city in Catalunya and has one of the highest population densities in Europe. The area also boasts a rich cultural life, with good theatrical productions at the **Teatre Joventut** (C/Joventut 10, 93 448 12 10, www.l-h.es/webs/teatreJoventut) and a schedule of excellent art exhibitions at the **Tecla Sala Centre Cultural**.

Sant Andreu is another vast residential district in the north-east of the city, and was once a major industrial zone. Apart from the Gaudí-designed floor mosaic in the Sant Pacià church on C/Monges, there's little reason to venture here, unless you have an historical interest in Josep Lluís Sert's rationalist Casa Bloc, originally workers' residences from the brief Republican era.

The name of Nou Barris, across the Avda Meridiana, translates as 'nine neighbourhoods', but the area is a collection of 11 former hamlets. The council has compensated for the area's poor housing (many of the 1950s tower blocks have fallen into disrepair) with the construction of public facilities such as the Can Dragó, a sports centre incorporating the biggest swimming pool in the city, and Parc Central. The district is centred on the roundabout at Plaça Llucmajor, which also holds Josep Viladomat's bold *La República*, a female nude holding aloft a sprig of laurel as a symbol of freedom. The renovation of the nearby Seu de Nou Barris town hall has brightened up an area in urgent need of a revamp, but it's not quite a tourist draw yet.

formerly private estates have been put to public use; among them are the chateau-like Palauet de les Heures, now a university building. The area was one of the city's four major venues for the Olympic Games and consequently is rich in sporting facilities, including public football pitches and tennis courts, as well as cycling and archery facilities at the Velòdrom. It's also the home to one of Barcelona's major concert venues. Around these environs there are several striking examples of street sculpture, including Claes Oldenburg's *Matches* and Joan Brossa's *Visual Poem* (in the shape of the letter 'A').

The area also conceals the rationalist **Pavelló de la República**, built in 1992 as a facsimile of the emblematic rationalist pavilion of the Spanish Republic designed by Josep Lluís Sert for the Paris Exhibition in 1937, and later to hold Picasso's *Guernica*. Here, too, is the **Parc del Laberint**, dating back to 1791 and surrounded by a modern park. More modern still is the Ciutat Sanitària, Catalonia's largest hospital; a good proportion of *barcelonins* first saw the light of day here.

Parc del Laberint
Passeig dels Castanyers 1 (93 413 24 00, www.bcn.cat/parcsijardins). Metro Mundet.
Open 10am-sunset daily. **Admission** €2.17; €1.38 reductions; free under-5s, over-65s; free Wed, Sun. **No credit cards.**

FREE Tecla Sala Centre d'Art
Avda Josep Tarradellas 44, Hospitalet de Llobregat (93 338 57 71, www.teclasala,net). Metro Torrassa.
Open 11am-2pm, 5-8pm Tue-Sat; 11am-2pm Sun. **Admission** free.
Tecla Sala is an old textile factory now housing a vast library and excellent gallery, which exhibits a varied mix of national and international artists.

Consume

Blow by Le Swing. *See p193.*

Hotels

Thanks to the recession, it's now cheaper to stay in Barcelona.

The economic crunch is being felt everywhere. However, it's hit Spain particularly hard, thanks in no small part to a weak pound that's kept the Brits' belts tightened. However, the economic downturn has had its flipside here in the city. Barcelona's popularity during the last decade and a half has seen it grow rather too big for its boots, with hotel prices reaching excruciating levels. But thanks to the slowdown, Barcelona's hoteliers have had to rethink their modus operandi. Nowadays, the travelling masses want to see quality at a fair price: while there are still plenty of luxury options for those who can afford it, creativity in the mid-range is starting to boom with rooms ranging between €80 and €150 a night. These days there are even some bargains at the top end, particularly at weekends and during the holiday months.

STAYING IN THE CITY

The glut of top-end accommodation means that hotels are continually revising their rates, and bargains are there for the taking: it's well worth doing a little extra research. At the budget end, many *hostales* are situated in fabulous old buildings with elaborate doorways and grand staircases, though the rooms aren't always so elegant. There's also been a rise in boutique B&Bs, bright places with en-suite bathrooms, internet access and other modern essentials.

With the city's growing niche as a conference capital, booking ahead is strongly advised. High season runs year round and finding somewhere to lay your head at short notice can be tough. Hotels generally require you to guarantee your booking with credit-card details or a deposit; it's always worth calling a few days before arrival to reconfirm the booking (get it in writing if you can; many readers have reported problems) and check the cancellation policy. Often you will lose at least the first night. *Hostales* are more laid-back and don't always ask for a deposit.

To be sure of a room with natural light or a view, ask for an outside room (*habitació/habitación exterior*), which will usually face the street. Many of Barcelona's buildings are built around a central patio or airshaft, and the inside rooms (*habitació/habitación interior*) around them can be quite gloomy, albeit quieter. However, in some cases (especially in the Eixample), these inward-facing rooms look on to large, open-air patios or gardens, which benefit from being quiet and having a view.

Hotels listed under the expensive and moderate brackets all have air-conditioning as standard. Air-conditioning is increasingly common even in no-frills places, however, and around half the *hostales* in the budget listings are equipped with it.

The law now prohibits smoking in communal areas in hotels. As a result, some hotels have banned smoking altogether, and many have the majority of floors/rooms as non-smoking.

Theft can be a problem, especially in lower-end establishments. If you're sleeping cheap, you might want to travel with a padlock to lock your door, or at least lock up your bags. Check to see if youth hostel rooms have lockers if you're sharing. Use hotel safes where possible.

> ❶ Red numbers given in this chapter correspond to the location of each hotel as marked on the street maps. *See pp321-327.*

Star ratings & prices

Accommodation in Catalonia is divided into two official categories: hotels (H) and *pensiones* (P). To be a hotel (star-rated one to five), a place must feature en-suite bathrooms in every room. Ratings are based on physical attributes rather than levels of service; often the only difference between a three- and a four-star hotel is the presence of a meeting room. *Pensiones*, usually cheaper and often family-run, are star-rated one or two, and are not required to have en-suite bathrooms (though many do). *Pensiones* are also known as *hostales*, but, confusingly, are not youth hostels; those are known as *albergues*.

For a double room, expect to pay €50-€75 for a budget *pensión*, €80-€180 for a mid-range spot and €200 upwards for a top-of-the-range hotel. However, prices vary depending on the time of year; always check for special deals. All bills are subject to seven per cent IVA (value added tax) on top of the basic price; this is not normally included in the advertised rate, but we've factored it into the prices listed here. Breakfast is not included unless stated.

Internet rates given are per 24 hours.

Booking Agencies

Barcelona Hotel Association

Via Laietana 47, 1º-2ª, Barri Gòtic (93 301 62 40, www.barcelonahotels.es). Metro Urquinaona or Jaume I. **Open** *Sept-June* 9am-6pm Mon-Fri; *July, Aug* 8.30am-2.30pm Mon-Fri. **Map** p328 D3.

The website of this hoteliers' organisation lists 264 hotels and apartments in all categories, ranging from luxury destinations to affordable places to stay. Clicking on this site will give you the chance to take advantage of a number of special offers and last-minute rates around the year. However, you will need to give your credit-card details, to secure your reservation online. Although information is available in the office, reservations cannot be made in-house. So the best way to book is to visit the website.

Barcelona On-Line

C/Valencia 352, Eixample (93 343 79 93, www.barcelona-on-line.es). Metro Passeig de Gràcia. **Open** 9am-7pm Mon-Fri. **Map** p326 G7.

At this highly professional agency, you can book hostel, hotel rooms and private apartments online, on the telephone or at the office. Staff are multilingual and the service is free, but there may be a fee to pay if you cancel your booking less than 48 hours before you are scheduled to arrive. If you are making apartment reservations, then you will need to make a prepayment.

Viajes Iberia

Plaça de Sants 12, Eixample (93 431 90 00, www.viajesiberia.com). Metro Plaça de Sants. **Open** *Sept-June* 9.30am-1.30pm, 4.30-7.30pm Mon-Fri (*July, Aug* until 8pm); 9.30am-1.30pm Sat. **Credit** AmEx, DC, MC, V. **Map** p321 A7.

This agency can book a room at many of Barcelona's hotels and some *pensiones*. The reservation fee varies, and you'll need to pay a deposit. **Other locations** throughout the city.

CONSUME

H1898. *See p115.*

Hotels

THE BARRI GÒTIC

La Rambla is flanked by hotels ranging from no-frills to luxury, but the totally touristy environment – not to mention the noise – may prove a bit much for some people. The medieval labyrinth of the Gòtic conceals some cheaper alternatives, but bear in mind that old buildings can often be grotty rather than charming.

Expensive

H10 Racó del Pi

C/Pi 7 (93 342 61 90, www.h10hotels.es). Metro Liceu or Jaume I. **Rates** €70-€150 double. **Rooms** 37. **Credit** AmEx, DC, MC, V. **Map** p328 C4 ❶
Part of the H10 chain, the Racó del Pi gets top marks for location just next to the iconic Plaça del Pi, and also offers bright, spacious rooms with handsome terracotta-tiled bathrooms, unusual for this part of town. An elegant glass conservatory on the ground floor and a glass of cava on arrival are both nice touches, and occasional special offers can make it a good deal (prices can go as low as €69).
Bar. Disabled-adapted room. Internet (free wireless). No-smoking floors.
Other locations H10 Catalunya Plaza, Plaça Catalunya 7, Eixample (93 317 71 71); and throughout the city.

★ H1898

La Rambla 109 (93 552 95 52, www.hotel 1898.com). Metro Catalunya or Liceu. **Rates** €181-€490 double. **Rooms** 169. **Credit** AmEx, DC, MC, V. **Map** p328 B3 ❷
A dapper luxury hotel in a 19th-century building – the former Philippine Tobacco Company headquarters. Rooms are candy-striped; one floor is all perky green and white, another is red and white, and so on. The more expensive rooms have wooden-decked terraces, while some of the suites have private plunge pools. For those of lighter wallets, the rooftop deck with its navy-tiled pool and luxurious four-poster day beds elevates the experience considerably. *Photo p113.*
Bars (2). Business centre. Disabled-adapted rooms (4). Gym. Internet (free wireless). No-smoking hotel. Parking (€24.80). Pools (outdoor/indoor). Restaurant. Room service. Spa.

Hotel Barcelona Catedral

C/Capellans 4 (93 304 22 55, www.barcelona catedral.com). Metro Jaume I. **Rates** €160-€283 double. **Rooms** 80. **Credit** AmEx, DC, MC, V. **Map** p328 D4 ❸
This newcomer is sleek and relaxed, with a hip vibe. The Barcelona Catedral is the kind of place where Costes plays in a lobby that doubles as a funky lounge and cocktail bar. Rooms, while not particularly exciting, are bright and comfortable, with vast bathrooms and king-size beds. A garden terrace and a colourful rooftop deck with pool are added pluses.
Bar. Business centre. Disabled-adapted rooms (4). Gym. Internet (free wireless in business centre, otherwise €10.70). No-smoking floors (3). Parking (€33.50). Pool (outdoor). Restaurant (closed Aug). Room service.

Hotel Le Méridien Barcelona

La Rambla 111 (93 318 62 00, www.barcelona. lemeridien.com). Metro Liceu. **Rates** €189-€465 double. **Rooms** 233. **Credit** AmEx, DC, MC, V. **Map** p328 B3 ❹
After a €23-million refurbishment Le Méridien is now the poshest place on La Rambla, and it's fair to say that if you need to ask the price you probably can't afford it. In keeping with this, it has maintained its conservative look, opting for classy hardwood floors, polished marble and leather furnishings, along with Egyptian cotton bedlinen, rain showers and plasma-screen TVs. However, at this price you would expect more facilities: a rooftop, perhaps, or at least a terrace to sit on. Still, rooms come with iHome docking systems and you can rent iPhones with an interactive guide to Barcelona (€11.70/day). Guests are also given two tickets to the MACBA, and under-12s stay free.
Bar (Thur-Sat 10pm-1am). Disabled-adapted rooms (4). Gym. Internet (free Wi-Fi in public areas, €21/day in rooms). No-smoking floors. Parking (€35/day, €3/hour). Restaurant. Room service.

★ Hotel Neri

C/Sant Sever 5 (93 304 06 55, www.hotelneri. com). Metro Jaume I. **Rates** €275-€360 double. **Rooms** 22. **Credit** AmEx, DC, MC, V. **Map** p329 C5 ❺
One of the sexiest boutiques in town, this is the perfect treat for a naughty weekend, located in a former 18th-century palace. The vampish lobby-cum-library is decorated with flagstone floors and crushed red velvet chaises longues and lashings of gold leaf, even though the rooms are slightly more understated. Neutral tones, natural materials and rustic finishes (untreated wood and unpolished marble) stand in stylish contrast to lavish satins, sharp-edged design and high-tech perks (hi-fis, plasma-screen TVs). The mini bar stocks not only champagne, but candles and incense, and the lush rooftop garden features plenty of private nooks for dangerous liaisons.
Bar. Internet (free Wi-Fi). No-smoking rooms. Restaurant. Room service.

Hotel Petit Palace Opera Garden

C/Boquería 10 (93 302 00 92, www.hthoteles. com). Metro Liceu. **Rates** €110-€375 double. **Rooms** 61. **Credit** AmEx, DC, MC, V. **Map** p329 B5 ❻

A private mansion was completely gutted to create this minimalist hotel on a busy street just off La Rambla. The rooms are white and futuristic, with a different zingy colour on each floor and opera scores printed on the walls above the beds. Lamps and chairs lend a 1960s air. Some bathrooms have massage showers, others jacuzzi baths, and there's a computer in every room. Only breakfast is served in the chic dining room. There's a little-known public garden at the back: a real luxury in this densely packed area.
Disabled-adapted rooms (2). Internet (free wireless). No-smoking floors. Room service.

Moderate

★ Bonic Guesthouse
C/Josep Anselm Clavé 9, 1°-4ª (mobile 626 05 34 34, www.bonic-barcelona.com). Metro Drassanes. **Rates** €90-€95. **Rooms** 6. **No credit cards.** **Map** p329 B8 **❼**
Bonic is painted in daisy fresh colours with sunlight streaming through the windows and lots of meticulously restored original features, such as ornately tiled floors. Attention to detail is exceptional for the price, even with a recent change of management. Free newspapers and magazines, tea, coffee and water, and flowers in the three immaculate, communal bathrooms all add up to an experience that raises the budget bar considerably.
Internet (free wireless). No-smoking hotel.

Duc de la Victòria
C/Duc 15 (93 270 34 10, www.nh-hotels.com). Metro Catalunya. **Rates** €99-€250 double. **Rooms** 156. **Credit** AmEx, DC, MC, V. **Map** p328 C3 **❽**
The trusty NH chain, based in Spain but with properties all over the world, has high standards of comfort and service, and this good-value downtown branch is thankfully no exception to the rule. The rooms, with a blue-and-beige colour scheme, may not be very exciting, but the superior quality beds ensure a sound night's sleep. And note that it's just a stone's throw from La Rambla.
Disabled-adapted rooms (5). Internet (free wireless in lobby, rooms €5.90/hour, €10.60/day). No-smoking floors. Restaurant (only breakfast).

Hostal Jardí
Plaça Sant Josep Oriol 1 (93 301 59 00, www.hoteljardi-barcelona.com). Metro Liceu. **Rates** €65-€110 double. **Rooms** 44. **Credit** MC, V. **Map** p329 B5 **❾**
Despite its considerable fame, the best thing about the Hostal Jardí remains its location on one of the city's loveliest squares. Inside, however, it's a bit of a plain Jane, with overly bright lighting and stark decor. If you stay, the best rooms are on the top floor, with a balcony. Otherwise, expect something small,

and clinical, though all have en-suite bathrooms, and the place is sparkling clean.
Internet (free wireless in lobby). No-smoking hotel.

Hotel Duquesa de Cardona
Passeig Colom 12 (93 268 90 90, www.hduquesadecardona.com). Metro Drassanes or Jaume I. **Rates** €140-€265 double. **Rooms** 40. **Credit** AmEx, DC, MC, V. **Map** p329 C7 **❿**
This elegantly restored 16th-century palace retains many original features and is furnished with natural materials – wood, leather, silk and stone – that are complemented by a soft colour scheme reflecting the paintwork. The cosy bedrooms make it ideal for a romantic stay: particularly the deluxe rooms and junior suites on the higher floors, with views out across the harbour. Guests can sunbathe and linger over lunch on the decked roof terrace and then cool off in the mosaic-tiled plunge pool. The arcaded hotel restaurant serves a menu of modern Catalan dishes.
Business centre. Disabled-adapted room. Internet (free wireless). No-smoking floor. Pool (outdoor). Restaurant. Room service.

Hotel Medinaceli
Plaça del Duc de Medinaceli 8 (93 481 77 25, www.gargallohotels.com). Metro Drassanes. **Rates** €160-270 double. **Rooms** 44. **Credit** AmEx, DC, MC, V. **Map** p329 B8 **⓫**
The rooms in this restored palace near the harbour are done out in soothing rusty shades. Some of the bathrooms have jacuzzi baths, while others come with massage showers. Repro versions of the sofa Dalí created inspired by Mae West's lips decorate the lobby, to match the crimson velvet thrones in the first-floor courtyard. Staff are very helpful, but rooms overlooking the street can be noisy.
Bar. Disabled-adapted room(1). Internet (€12 wireless).

Marina View B&B
Passeig de Colom (93 317 59 20, mobile 93 268 90 70, www.marinaviewbcn.com). Metro Drassanes. **Rates** (incl breakfast) €80-€138 double. **Rooms** 6. **Credit** (deposit only) MC, V. **Map** p329 C8 **⓬**
Located in a 19th-century townhouse with views over the Port Vell, this simple little place is laid-back, friendly and fun, with nautically themed rooms such as 'Captain's Cabin' and 'Columbus' painted in sunshine colours. Marina View has got all the homely

CONSUME

details just right, such as the breakfast trolley loaded with fresh juice, coffee and croissants, as well as personalised service. It's a home as well as a hotel, so always call ahead rather than drop in off the street. *Internet (free wireless)*.

Budget

Hostal Fontanella
Via Laietana 71, 2° (93 317 59 43, www.hostal fontanella.com). Metro Urquinaona. **Rates** €59-€80 double. **Rooms** 11. **Credit** DC, MC, V. **Map** p328 D2 ⓭
The splendid Modernista lift lends a somewhat unjustified aura of grandeur to this 11-room *hostal*, where Laura Ashley devotees will feel totally at home amid the array of chintz, lace and dried flowers. The downside of the Fontanella's central location – on the thoroughfare bordering the Born, the Barri Gòtic and the Eixample – is that outward-facing rooms are abuzz with the sound of traffic. However, it's a clean and comfortable place, and the double-glazing makes the outdoors somewhat less present inside.
Internet (free wireless).

Hostal Lausanne
Portal de l'Àngel 24, 1° 1ª (93 302 11 39, www.hostalresidencialausanne.com). Metro Catalunya. **Rates** €48-€65 double. **Rooms** 17. **Credit** MC, V. **Map** p328 C3 ⓮
On one of downtown's busiest shopping streets, this *hostal* occupies the first floor of an impressive building. Unlike some *hostales*, the place feels spacious, with light pouring in from both ends of the building. Of the 17 basic rooms, four have en-suite bathrooms and some have balconies. It may be a bit dated, but it's friendly and safe, with a backpacker vibe. The street fills up during the day, but it's quiet at night. *Internet (free shared terminals)*.
Other locations Hostal Europa, C/Boquería 18, Barri Gòtic (93 318 76 20).

Hostal Rembrandt
C/Portaferrissa 23, pral (93 318 10 11, www.hostalrembrandt.com). Metro Liceu. **Rates** €45-€65 double. **Rooms** 26. **Credit** MC, V. **Map** p328 C4 ⓯
A charming 27-room *hostal* that is fairly stylish (for the price) with lots of wood panelling, soft lighting and a lift. A bonus is the pretty interior courtyard, which makes for a pleasant eating/relaxing area. Rooms out front can be a little noisy, but the passing stream of humanity means you'll never be bored. If the Rembrandt is fully booked, bear in mind that the same people also rent out apartments on nearby C/Canuda (€75-€150 for two people, minimum three-night stay at weekends, negotiable in low season). *Internet (free wireless, €3/hr shared terminal)*. *No-smoking hotel*.

Hostal Sol y K
C/Cervantes 2, 2°-1ª (93 318 81 48, www.solyk.com). Metro Jaume I or Liceu. **Rates** €60-€88 double. **Rooms** 14. **Credit** AmEx, DC, MC, V. **Map** p329 C6 ⓰
Bright and cheerful with some nice aesthetic touches (slate bathrooms and groovy leather bedheads), this *hostal* is a bargain for those who don't need any frills. There's no breakfast, and not all rooms are en suite, but all have washbasins, and the traditional, patterned tiles and exposed wood beams give the Sol y K plenty of character. Even though there is no breakfast service, free tea and coffee are available. Light sleepers would benefit from bringing a pair of earplugs with them, as noise carries from the street, and towels are for the skinny.
Internet (free wireless).

Pensió Alamar
C/Comtessa de Sobradiel 1, 1°-2ª (93 302 50 12, www.pensioalamar.com). Metro Jaume I or Liceu. **Rates** €36-€45 double. **Rooms** 12. **No credit cards**. **Map** p329 C6 ⓱
A basic, but tasteful family-run *hostal*. Beds are fresh and excellent quality, with crisp cotton sheets, and windows are double-glazed in order to keep noise to a minimum. The downside is that 12 rooms share two bathrooms among them. There are good discounts for longer stays, and larger rooms for families (or up to four). Single travellers are made welcome, with no supplement for occupying a double room, and guests can do laundry and cook in a well-equipped kitchen.
Internet (free wireless from March 2011).

Pensión Hostal Mari-Luz
C/Palau 4 (93 317 34 63, www.pension mariluz.com, www.apartmentsuniv.com). Metro Jaume I or Liceu. **Rates** €35-€62 double. **Rooms** 14. **Credit** MC, V. **Map** p329 C6 ⓲
The entrance and staircase of this 18th-century building are imposing, but you have to climb several flights of stairs to reach the Mari-Luz. The effort is worth it: the mismatched furniture and hotchpotch design are endearing and add character to the otherwise plain but quiet rooms, some of which face a plant-filled inner courtyard. There are dorms as well as double and triple rooms, and an equipped kitchen for guests' use. The owners also have small apartments in C/Unió in the Raval (€65-€100).
Internet (free wireless).
Other locations Pensión Fernando, C/Ferran 31, Barri Gòtic (93 301 79 93).

THE BORN & SANT PERE

New hotels are cropping up in revamped old buildings in these medieval areas. The Born is home to many restaurants, bars and boutiques.

CONSUME

Putting on the Ritz

How to live the high life at a low price.

W Hotel.

Can't afford to stay at a deluxe retreat? No matter: you can always pretend. In these tough economic times, many of Barcelona's swankiest hotels have started to welcome non-residents to their pools, bars and rooftops with open arms – providing, that is, you make the place look pretty.

For sheer class, you can't beat a drink at **Gran Hotel La Florida** (*see p137*), perched high above the city atop Tibidabo. The bar terraces tumble down the hillside amid scented gardens, the views of the city and the endless blue sea are extraordinary and the exertion of getting there is worth it for the reward of marvelling, if just for a moment, at how the other half use their expense accounts.

Acres of teak and groovy striped daybeds give **H1898** (*see p113*) the edge over the endless tourist traps below. Settle in for a fresh apple Martini or a frozen Daiquiri paired with fancy nibbles like mini duck burgers with foie and violet mustard, and veal with roast daikon and poppy flowers. Don't get any ideas about using the pool, though – it's strictly guests only.

Famous for its summer rooftop parties the Visit Up lounge at the **Hotel Pulitzer** (*see p131*) is also a great place to relax. Bamboo loungers, giant candles and a thickly planted desert garden could easily place it in Mexico or Marrakech, but the mood is distinctly Barcelonan, attracting as many locals as visiting guests.

One of the best-kept secret on the city's hotels scene, the rooftop of the otherwise dull-looking **Pullmann Barcelona Skipper** (*see p124*) has a wood deck and bumper-sized pool with fab views of Gehry's famed golden fish and the big blue. There's no fee for getting in, though you will be expected to drink something – in plastic beakers, alas. Still, it's a good bet if you want to escape the crowds on the beach.

As part of the sexiest hotel to open in the Catalan capital in years, the Ibiza-style beach terrace at the **W Hotel** (*see p132*) has quickly been adopted by the city's groovers and shakers. With white, four-poster day-beds, handsome waiter service and a pool the colour of grey goose vodka, don't even consider it without a Michael Kors bikini and a pair of retro Ray-Bans.

Expensive

Grand Hotel Central
Via Laietana 30 (93 295 79 00, www.grand hotelcentral.com). Metro Jaume I. **Rates** €125-€200 double. **Rooms** 147. **Credit** AmEx, DC, MC, V. **Map** p329 D5 ⓳

Another of the recent wave of Barcelona hotels to adhere to the unwritten design protocol that grey is the new black. The Central's shadowy, almost Hitchcockian corridors open up on to sleekly appointed rooms with interiors that feature flat-screen televisions, DVD players and Korres toiletries. However, it's worth bearing in mind that some guests have complained that the bathroom lighting is too dim. But the real charm of this establishment lies on the roof. Here you can sip a cocktail and admire the wonderful views while floating in the vertiginous infinity pool.
Bar. Business centre. Disabled-adapted rooms (4). Gym. Internet (€4 wireless). No-smoking floors. Parking (€28). Pool (outdoor). Room service.

Moderate

★ Banys Orientals
C/Argenteria 37 (93 268 84 60, www.hotelbanys orientals.com). Metro Jaume I. **Rates** €107 double. **Rooms** 56. **Credit** AmEx, DC, MC, V. **Map** p329 D6 ⓴

Banys Orientals is one of the best deals to be found in Barcelona. It exudes cool, from its location at the heart of the Born to the stylish shades-of-grey minimalism of its rooms, and nice touches such as complimentary mineral water on the landings and apples in the rooms. The main debit is the small size of some of the double rooms.
Disabled-adapted room. Internet (free wireless and free shared terminal). No-smoking floors. Restaurant.

Chic&Basic
C/Princesa 50 (93 295 46 52, www.chic andbasic.com). Metro Arc de Triomf or Jaume I. **Rates** €96-€118 double. **Rooms** 31. **Credit** AmEx, DC, MC, V. **Map** p329 F5 ㉑

This first-floor *hostal* takes white-on-white to extremes. Rooms come in sizes XL, L and M, with white cotton sheets, white floors, white walls, mirrored cornicing and glassed-in wet rooms in the centre for hosing yourself down. Elsewhere, the playful vibe continues throughout the establishment, with a lounge room furnished with fairytale sofas and pouffes; it also has tea- and coffee-making facilities, a fridge and a microwave. There are similarly designed apartments.
Disabled-adapted room. Gym. Internet (free wireless in public areas). No-smoking hotel. Restaurant.
Other locations Chic&basic Tallers, C/Tallers 82, Raval (93 302 51 83).

Grand Hotel Central.

CONSUME

Offset your
flight with
Trees for Cities
and make your
trip mean
something for
years to come

www.treesforcities.org/offset

Trees for Cities
Charity registration number 1032154

Ciutat Barcelona

C/Princesa 35 (93 269 74 75, www.ciutat barcelona.com). Metro Jaume I. **Rates** €90-€250 double. **Credit** AmEx, DC, MC, V. **Map** p329 E5 ㉒

The Ciutat Barcelona is a jolly, primary-coloured affair, which offers a refreshing contrast to the chocolate and charcoal shades of most of Barna's smart hotels. Retro shapes prevail in the furnishings and decorations, and rooms are very compact but reasonably comfortable places to stay. The big draw, however, is a swanky wood-decked roof terrace that is complete with shaded tables and a decent-sized plunge pool.

Disabled-adapted rooms (4). Internet (free high-speed in rooms, free wireless in lobby). No-smoking floors. Pool (outdoor). Room service.

Budget

Pensió 2000

C/Sant Pere Més Alt 6, 1° (93 310 74 66, www.pensio2000.com). Metro Urquinaona. **Rates** €56-€70 double. **Rooms** 6. **Credit** MC, V. **Map** p328 D3 ㉓

Pensió 2000 is a good-value *pension* located in a fine old building across from the Palau de la Música Catalana. Only two of the rooms are en suite, but the shared facilities are kept clean. The large rooms make it suitable for holidaying families. Call for details of special offers.

THE RAVAL

The Raval is the edgy neighbour of the Barri Gòtic, but recent regeneration means it's also the trendiest *barrio* for bars and restaurants, with a lively multicultural atmosphere.

Expensive

Casa Camper

C/Elisabets 11 (93 342 62 80, www.casa camper.com). Metro Catalunya. **Rates** (incl breakfast) €192-€305 double. **Rooms** 25. **Credit** AmEx, DC, MC, V. **Map** p328 A3 ㉔

Devised by the Mallorcan footwear giant, this is a holistic concept-fest of a hotel, designed by Ferran Amat of Vinçon fame. The place is quirky, and one of its unique selling points is a bedroom-living room arrangement, giving two spaces for the price of one. Less cleverly, the living rooms are across the corridor from the bedrooms, so in order to enjoy the cinema-sized TV screen and hammock you'll need to pack respectable pyjamas or risk the dash of shame. There are no minibars, but you can help yourself to free snacks and refreshments in the café whenever you fancy. *Photo p124.*

Bar. Business centre. Disabled-adapted room. Gym (from March 2011). Internet (free wireless). No-smoking hotel. Restaurant.

Moderate

Abba Rambla Hotel

C/Rambla del Raval 4 (93 505 54 00, www.abbaramblahotel.com). Metro Liceu or Sant Antoni. **Rates** €75-€225 double. **Rooms** 49. **Credit** AmEx, DC, MC, V. **Map** p326 E10 ㉕

The Abba Rambla is a comfortable and friendly base, although the modern rooms have an inescapably chain-hotel feel to them. More stylish are the ground-floor lounge and breakfast bar, where you eat perched on high stools. Some good offers are available online, particularly in the winter, so it's a place worth checking before booking.

Bar. Disabled-adapted room. Internet (€9 wireless). No-smoking floors. Parking €21.60.

★ Barceló Raval

Rambla del Raval 17-21 (93 320 14 90, 902 101 001, www.barceloraval.com). Metro Liceu. **Rates** €122-€215 double. **Rooms** 186. **Credit** AmEx, DC, MC, V. **Map** p326 E10 ㉖

This cylindrical building now dominates the Rambla del Raval and has become something of an icon of the *barrio*. A hip cocktail lounge designed by Jordi Galí and the avant-garde tapas bar, with DJs on Friday and Saturday nights, are upping the ante still more. The smart oval-shaped roof terrace offers 360° views (with key buildings usefully labelled from a viewing platform) and a plunge pool. Bedrooms are fairly uniform but airy and modern, with a technology port for all your multimedia needs and a Nespresso machine for those bleary mornings after.

Bar. Disabled-adapted rooms (4). Gym. Internet (free wireless). No-smoking floors. Pool (outdoor). Restaurant. Room service. Spa.

Hostal Gat Xino

C/Hospital 155 (93 324 88 33, www.gat accommodation.com). Metro Sant Antoni. **Rates** (incl breakfast) €65-€90 double. **Rooms** 35. **Credit** AmEx, DC, MC, V. **Map** p326 E10 ㉗

This is the second 'Gat' to open, and it has a similar cheap and chic vibe to the Gat Raval, with a bright breakfast room complete with apple-green polka-dot walls, a patio and a roof terrace with black beanbags. There's more bright green in the bedrooms (all of them en suite), with good beds, crisp white linen, flat-screen TVs and backlit panels of Raval scenes. The best rooms have large balconies. *Photo p130.*

Internet (free wireless). No-smoking hostal.

Hotel Ciutat Vella

C/Tallers 66 (93 481 37 99, www.hotel ciutatvella.com). Metro Catalunya or Universitat. **Rates** €70-€200 double. **Rooms** 40. **Credit** AmEx, DC, MC, V. **Map** p328 A2 ㉘

More *hostal*-like than the sister branch (Ciutat Barcelona; *see p123*) across town, this is a fun option when the budget's tight. Rooms and decor are done simply in white with splashes of pillar-box red.

Casa Camper. *See p123.*

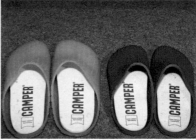

There's Wi-Fi and a hearty breakfast served in a lounge downstairs, free mineral water in the lobby and best of all a fabulously kitsch Astroturf rooftop terrace with hot tub, which, unlike most of the aquatic fun available in Barcelona, is open late enough to bathe under the stars.
Disabled-adapted room. Internet (free shared terminal, free wireless). No-smoking floors.

Hotel Curious

C/Carme 25 (93 301 44 84, www.hotelcurious. com). Metro Liceu. **Rates** (incl breakfast) €80-€105 double. **Rooms** 24. **Credit** AmEx, DC, MC, V. **Map** p328 A4 ㉙
Curious is an unusual new addition to the Raval, which takes a more art-based approach to design than is common in most other properties. The rather funky mauve-hued lobby is in total contrast to more monotone bedrooms, which have giant black and white prints depicting Barcelona *barrios* and other landscapes. Other hotels include Hostal Marenostrum (C/Sant Pau 2, 93 318 53 40).

Bar. Internet (free shared terminal, free wireless). Parking (€26.40).

Hotel Mesón Castilla

C/Valldonzella 5 (93 318 21 82, www.meson castilla.com). Metro Universitat. **Rates** (incl breakfast) €97-€130 double. **Rooms** 57. **Credit** AmEx, DC, MC, V. **Map** p328 A2 ㉚
If you want a change from modern design, check into this chocolate-box hotel, which opened in 1952. Before then, it belonged to an aristocratic Catalan family. The communal areas are full of antiques and artworks, while all rooms have tiled floors and are decorated with hand-painted furniture from Olot in northern Catalonia. The best rooms have terraces, and there is also a delightful plant-filled terrace off the breakfast room.
Internet (free wireless, shared terminal). Parking (€26).

Hotel Sant Agustí

Plaça Sant Agustí 3 (93 318 16 58, www.hotelsa.com). Metro Liceu. **Rates** (incl

breakfast) €75-€146 double. **Rooms** 82.
Credit AmEx, DC, MC, V. **Map** p329 A5 ③

With its sandstone walls and huge, arched windows that look out on to what has become a slightly insalubrious *plaça*, not to mention the pink-marble lobby filled with an array of forest-green furniture, this imposing establishment is the oldest hotel in town. Previously the convent of St Augustine, it was converted into a hotel in 1840. Rooms are spacious and comfortable, but there's no soundproofing. Good buffet breakfast.
Bar. Disabled-adapted rooms (3). Internet (free shared terminal, free wireless in rooms). Restaurant (dinner only).

Budget

Hostal Gat Raval

C/Joaquín Costa 44, 2° (93 481 66 70, www. gataccommodation.com). Metro Universitat. **Rates** €55-€70 double. **Credit** AmEx, DC, MC, V. **Map** p326 E9 ③

Smart, clean and stylish, with compact, reasonably bright rooms, each boasting a work by a local artist. Some rooms have balconies while others have views of the MACBA. The only downside is that nearly all the bathrooms are communal (though very clean) and there's no lift.
Internet (free wireless, shared terminal). No-smoking hotel.

Hostal La Palmera

C/Jerusalem 30 (93 317 09 97, www.hostal lapalmera.com). Metro Liceu. **Rates** (incl breakfast) €50-€55 double. **Rooms** 20.
Credit AmEx, MC, V. **Map** p328 A4 ③

With a great location behind La Boqueria, this well-run, basic *hostal* is a short stagger from some of Raval's trendiest bars, but is quiet at night. The decor is unremarkable, but rooms are light, airy and spotless, most have en-suite bathrooms and some have balconies overlooking the market.
Internet (free wireless).
Other locations Hostal Bertolin, C/Carme 116, 1°, Raval (93 329 06 47, reservations 93 317 09 97).

Hosteria Grau

C/Ramelleres 27 (93 301 81 35, www.hostal grau.com). Metro Catalunya. **Rates** €70-€105 double. **Rooms** 19. **Credit** AmEx, DC, MC, V. **Map** p328 B2 ③

This charming, family-run *hostal* oozes character, with a tiled spiral staircase and fabulous 1970s-style communal areas, including a lively café next door. The open fireplace is a winter luxury. Rooms are comfortable and fairly quiet; the cheaper ones share a bathroom. There are also six apartments on the top floor. A popular choice, so book well in advance.
Bar. Internet (free shared terminal, free wireless). No-smoking hotel. Parking (€24.60).

BARCELONETA & THE PORTS

Hotels are springing up along Barcelona's waterfront, particularly in the stretch between the Hotel Arts and the Fòrum that lies north of the city centre. These are mostly aimed at business travellers, so rates tend to fall at weekends and during holiday periods.

Expensive

Hotel Arts

C/Marina 19-21 (93 221 10 00, www. hotelartsbarcelona.com). Metro Ciutadella-Vila Olímpica. **Rates** €295-€425 double. **Rooms** 483. **Credit** AmEx, DC, MC, V. **Map** p327 K12 ③

The 44-storey, Ritz-Carlton-run Arts scores top marks for exemplary service. CD players, interactive TV, sea and city views and a 'Club' floor are just some of the perks that await. The avant-garde flower arrangements make the lobby a pleasant place to hang out rather than just pass through. Outdoors, the beachfront pool overlooks Frank Gehry's bronze fish sculpture, and a range of bars and restaurants cater to every taste. The spectacular duplex apartments have round-the-clock butlers and chef services, whereas the luxurious Six Senses Spa on floors 42 and 43 has fabulous views and is open to non-guests. In summer, a children's club will look after your offspring. *Photos p129.*
Bar (3). Business centre. Disabled-adapted rooms (8). Gym. Internet (free wireless in lobby, €25 wireless in rooms). No-smoking floors. Parking (€37.50). Pool (outdoor). Restaurants (4). Room service. Spa.

Pullmann Barcelona Skipper

Avda Litoral 10 (93 221 65 65, www.pullman hotels.com). Metro Ciutadella. **Rates** €165-€385 double. **Rooms** 241. **Credit** AmEx, DC, MC, V. **Map** p327 J12 ③

Situated near the Port Olimpic, the Skipper is a swish American-style five-star reeling in visiting long-weekenders with some good package deals. Think supersize rooms with slick touches like Egyptian cotton sheets and huge bathrooms. It's also good on outdoor space with a large heated pool for year round use, hammocks on the lawns, and a full-service spa. Additional treats include a lazy Sunday brunch, luxury rooftop pool and bar, and the AB Skipper yacht, which guests can charter for private use if they've left their boat at home.
Bars (3). Business centre. Disabled-adapted rooms (3). Gym. Internet (free wireless). No-smoking floors. Parking (€25). Pools (2, outdoor). Restaurants (2). Room service. Spa.

★ W Hotel

Plaça de la Rosa dels Vents 1 (93 295 28 00, www.whotels.com/barcelona). Metro Barceloneta,

Whatever your carbon footprint, we can reduce it

For over a decade we've been leading the way in carbon offsetting and carbon management.

In that time we've purchased carbon credits from over 200 projects spread across 6 continents. We work with over 300 major commercial clients and thousands of small and medium sized businesses, which rely upon our market-leading quality assurance programme, our experience and absolute commitment to deliver the right solution for each client.

Why not give us a call?

T: London (020) 7833 6000

www.CarbonNeutral.com

then bus 17. **Rates** €295-€645 double. **Rooms** 473. **Credit** AmEx, DC, MC, V. **Map** p326 G13 **37**
Barcelona's answer to Dubai's Burj Al Arab finally opened its doors in 2009 to a clamour of protest from local residents who feel it disrupts the view of the horizon. No one can deny it's a handsome building, however, and the lobby and terraces are master-pieces of design, as are the restaurant and tapas bar, overseen by masterchef Carles Abellan. Rooms are relatively simply done out, the better to appreciate the incredible views of the sea or city (request your preference when booking).
Bars (3). Business centre. Disabled-adapted rooms (6). Gym. Internet (free wireless in lobby, €19 wire-less in rooms). No-smoking rooms. Pool (outdoor). Parking (€27). Restaurants (2). Room service. Spa.

Moderate

Hotel 54
Passeig Joan de Borbó 54 (93 225 00 54, www.bestwesternhotel54.com). Metro Barceloneta. **Rates** €90-€300 double. **Rooms** 25. **Credit** AmEx, MC, V. **Map** p326 G13 **38**
It's been a long time coming, but finally the beach gets an affordable hotel in the shape of the 54. There's neon mood lighting above the bed, while muted tones of dove grey and charcoal against steel, blond-wood and glass give it a contemporary feel. It has one of the best roof terraces in the city for cock-tails, with great views of the port, and you can get tapas at Snack 54. It has been taken over by Best Western but little has changed.
Bar. Internet (free wireless). No-smoking floors. Parking (€20).

MONTJUÏC

Poble Sec is a quiet neighbourhood between Montjuïc mountain and the Avda Paral·lel.

Expensive

AC Miramar
Plaça Carlos Ibáñez 3, Passeig de Miramar (93 281 16 00, www.hotelmiramarbarcelona.com). Metro Paral·lel. **Rates** €135-€350 double. **Rooms** 75. **Credit** AmEx, DC, MC, V. **Map** p326 D12 **39**
The AC chain's flagship hotel is perched on top of Montjuïc, where the air's just a little bit fresher than in the city below and the view is fabulous. True, it has a slightly corporate air, what with its cham-pagne marble and cappuccino sofas, but there's a great deal to recommend the hotel nonetheless. Notable features include the scented orange-tree patio for drinks, a 'healthy' Mediterranean restau-rant, a pale turquoise pool illuminated by fibre-optics at night and English-style lawns. Bedrooms are fairly uniform, but it's worth opting for something smaller towards the top, which rewards with a hot tub on the terrace.

Bar. Disabled-adapted rooms (2). Gym. Internet (wireless). No-smoking hotel. Parking (€15 indoor, free outdoor). Pools (indoor & outdoor). Restaurant. Spa.

Moderate

Hotel Nuevo Triunfo
C/Cabanes 34 (93 442 59 33, www.hotel nuevotriunfo.com). Metro Paral·lel. **Rates** €80-€150 double. **Rooms** 40. **Credit** AmEx, MC, V. **Map** p326 E11 **40**
With 40 fresh, bright and spotless rooms, the Hotel Nuevo Triunfo is located in a peaceful street at the foot of Montjuïc. Rooms are bland but comfortable enough, and the four most desirable – two of which are singles – counteract the austerity of the sparse, modern fittings with their charming plant-filled ter-races. This is a worthwhile place to try should the other central hotels be full.
Disabled-adapted rooms (2). Internet (wireless €2.50/2hours, €6.50/day). No-smoking floors.

Budget

Hostal BCN Port
Avda Paral·lel 15 (93 324 95 00, www.hostal bcnport.com). Metro Drassanes or Paral·lel. **Rates** €59-€96 double. **Rooms** 32. **Credit** MC, V. **Map** p326 E12 **41**
A smart *hostal* near the ferry port, the BCN Port has rooms that are furnished in a chic contemporary style with not a hint of the kitsch decor prevalent in more traditional budget places. All the rooms have en-suite bathrooms, as well as televisions and air-conditioning. Check the website for discounts.
Disabled-adapted rooms (1). Internet (free wireless). No-smoking hotel. Parking (€15).

THE EIXAMPLE

The broad avenues forming the vast grid of streets of the Eixample district contain some of Barcelona's most expensive and fashionable hotels, along with some great budget options hidden away in Modernista buildings.

Expensive

Casanova BCN Hotel
Gran Via de les Corts Catalanes 559 (93 396 48 00, www.casanovabcnhotel.com). Metro Universitat or Urgell. **Rates** €105-€355 double. **Rooms** 124. **Credit** AmEx, DC, MC, V. **Map** p326 E8 **42**
Casanova is a smart hotel, aimed at business types but not without style. The charcoal grey and black decor with streaks of lime green is par for the course, but, each room has its own Nespresso machine, suites have two bathrooms, giant candles are scat-tered in the lounge areas and there's a small spa.

CONSUME

1000s of
things to do…

Plans for a rooftop pool have been put on hold for now. A Mexican-themed restaurant lends freshness to the usual tapas offerings, and DJs play in the bar on Friday and Saturday nights.
Bar. Disabled-adapted rooms (4). Internet (free high-speed in rooms, wireless €15/day, €9/hour, free shared terminal in lobby). No-smoking floors. Parking (€20). Restaurant (comida fusion mexicano-mediterránea). Spa.

Hotel Axel

C/Aribau 33 (93 323 93 93, www.axelhotels.com). Metro Universitat. **Rates** €109-€249 double. **Rooms** 105. **Credit** AmEx, DC, MC, V. **Map** p326 F8 ❹❸

Housed in a Modernista building, with multi-coloured tiles in the lobby and bright rooms with bleached floors, the Axel is a cornerstone of the 'Gaixample', as the area around the hotel is known. The good-looking staff sport T-shirts with the logo 'heterofriendly', and certainly everyone is made welcome. King-size beds come as standard, as do free mineral water and erotic artwork. The 'Superior' rooms have hydro-massage bathtubs and stained-glass gallery balconies. The Sky Bar on the rooftop is where it all happens, with a little pool, jacuzzi, sun deck, sauna and steam room. Non-guests are welcome to frequent the bar and roof terrace, where club nights are held, so there's always a bit of a buzz going on. Work to expand the hotel to 105 rooms should be finished by spring 2010.
Bar. Business centre. Disabled-adapted rooms (3). Gym. Internet (free wireless). No-smoking floors. Pool (outdoor). Restaurant. Room service. Spa.

Hotel Claris

C/Pau Claris 150 (93 487 62 62, www.derby hotels.com). Metro Passeig de Gràcia. **Rates** €135-€450 double. **Rooms** 120. **Credit** AmEx, DC, MC, V. **Map** p322 G7 ❹❹

Antiques and contemporary design merge behind the neo-classical exterior of the Claris, which contains the largest private collection of Egyptian art in Spain. Some bedrooms are on the small side, while others are duplex, but all have Chesterfield sofas and plenty of art. Warhol prints liven up the fashionable East 47 restaurant. The rooftop pool is just about big enough to swim in, with plenty of loungers, and a cocktail bar and DJ.
Business centre. Disabled-adapted rooms (8). Gym. Internet (€15 wireless). No-smoking floors. Parking (€23). Pool (outdoor). Restaurants (2). Room service. Spa.

Hotel Granados 83

C/Enric Granados 83 (93 492 96 70, www.derbyhotels.com). Metro Diagonal. **Rates** €120-€420 double. **Rooms** 70. **Credit** AmEx, DC, MC, V. **Map** p322 F7 ❹❺

The original ironwork structure of this former hospital contrives to lend an unexpectedly industrial

Hotel Arts. *See 125.*

CONSUME

CONSUME

Hotel Omm.

feel to the Granados 83. The hotel's variety of bare-bricked rooms include duplex and triplex versions, some with their own terraces and plunge pools. For mortals in the standard rooms, there's a rooftop pool and sun deck.

Bar. Business centre. Disabled-adapted rooms (2). Internet (€15 wireless). No-smoking hotel. Parking (€20). Pool (outdoor). Restaurant. Room service.

Hotel Jazz

C/Pelai 3 (93 552 96 96, www.nnhotels.com). Metro Catalunya. **Rates** €95-€330 double. **Rooms** 108. **Credit** AmEx, DC, MC, V. **Map** p328 A1 ④⑥

Rooms at the Hotel Jazz are super-stylish, in calming tones of, naturally, grey, beige and black, softened with parquet floors and spiced up with dapper pin-stripe cushions and splashes of funky colour. The beds are larger than is usual for a Barcelona hotel, and the bathrooms feature cool, polished black tiles. A rooftop pool and sun deck top things off nicely at this impressive place.

Bar-restaurant. Business centre. Disabled-adapted rooms (3). Internet (free shared terminals, free wireless in rooms). No-smoking hotel. Parking (€24). Pool (outdoor).

Other locations Hotel Barcelona Universal, Avda Paral·lel 76-78, Poble Sec (93 567 74 47); and throughout the city.

Hotel Majestic

Passeig de Gràcia 68 (93 488 17 17, www.hotelmajestic.es). Metro Passeig de Gràcia. **Rates** €229-€439 double. **Credit** AmEx, DC, MC, V. **Map** p322 G7 ④⑦

The Majestic has long been one of Barcelona's grandest hotels and is set to double in size in 2012. Behind a neo-classical façade lies a panoply of perks, such as a service that allows you to print a selection of the day's newspapers from all over the world from the comfort of the lobby. Its crowning achievement is the ninth floor, which has an apartment and a sumptuous Sagrada Família Suite with a private, outdoor jacuzzi. Non-guests can enjoy the high life in the rooftop pool and gym, which offer wonderful views out over the city while you sweat or swim. Rooms are suitably opulent, decorated with classical flair. The Drolma restaurant is one of the finest, and one of the priciest, in the city.

Bars (2). Business centre. Disabled-adapted rooms (4). Gym. Internet (€15 wireless). No-smoking floors. Parking (€25). Pool (outdoor). Restaurants (2). Room service. Spa.

★ Hotel Murmuri

Rambla Catalunya 104 (93 550 06 00, www.murmuri.com). Metro Diagonal. **Rates** €119-€510 double. **Rooms** 53. **Credit** AmEx, DC, MC, V. **Map** p322 G7 ④⑧

A sophisticated cut above its sister hotel, the Majestic, which stands just around the corner,

Murmuri exudes an effortless chic. Creamy tones with gilt trim and sculpted flower arrangements give the interior a cool and calm atmosphere, attracting a well-heeled and grown-up crowd. There's a lively lobby for drinks and a slick Thai restaurant, where you can enjoy dinner. Bedrooms are spacious and airy, and generously stocked with Molton Brown toiletries, and guests can use the pool and gym at its sister hotel, Majestic (*see left*). A victim of leaner economic times, the hotel also offers good deals on the website.

Bar. Business centre. Disabled-adapted rooms (2). Internet (€15/day, 10.60/hour wireless). No-smoking floors. Restaurant.

★ Hotel Omm

C/Rosselló 265 (93 445 40 00, www.hotelomm.es). Metro Diagonal. **Rates** €215-€380 double. **Rooms** 91. **Credit** AmEx, DC, MC, V. **Map** p322 G6 ④⑨

It was the Hotel Omm that redefined the hotel scene in the Eixample, establishing within the area a new breed of smart, sophisticated urban accommodation for discerning travellers. The hotel's bedrooms are light and bright, as opposed to black on black corridors, and enjoy what may well be the city's most comfortable beds and double bathrooms. Moo, the in-house restaurant, now boasts a Michelin star, but there's also a bistro alternative, as well as a wine and cocktail bar to enjoy during the evenings. An ultra trendy club occupies the perfectly soundproofed basement, along with a spa and hairdresser. Meanwhile, a bar and a pool area perch on the roof, offering views straight over the witchscarers of Gaudí's La Pedrera next door. For more on restaurant Moo, *see p161*.

Bars (2). Disabled-adapted rooms (2). Gym. Internet (free wireless). No-smoking floors. Pool (outdoor). Restaurant. Room service. Spa.

Hotel Pulitzer

C/Bergara 8 (93 481 67 67, www.hotelpulitzer.es). Metro Catalunya. **Rates** €99-€350 double. **Rooms** 92. **Credit** AmEx, DC, MC, V. **Map** p328 B2 ⑤⓪

Situated just off Plaça de Catalunya, the Hotel Pulitzer has become a popular place to meet before going out on a night out. A discreet façade reveals an impressive lobby that's stuffed with comfortable white leather sofas, a reading area overflowing with glossy picture books and a swanky bar and restaurant. The rooftop terrace is a fabulous spot for a cocktail, with squishy loungers, scented candles and tropical plants, and spectacular views across the heights of the city. The rooms themselves are not big, but they are sumptuously decorated and come complete with cool grey marble, fat fluffy pillows and kinky leather trim.

Bar. Disabled-adapted rooms (3). Internet (free wireless). No-smoking floors. Restaurant. Room service.

CONSUME

Mandarin Oriental

*Passeig de Gràcia 38-40 (93 151 88 88,
www.mandarinoriental.com/barcelona). Metro
Passeig de Gràcia.* **Rates** €325-€545. **Rooms** 98.
Credit AmEx, DC, MC, V. **Map** p322 G8 ⊕
Top Spanish designer Patricia Urquiola's high-
design Mandarin Oriental oozes old-style glamour
with a contemporary twist. Originally a bank, life
in the hotel centres around the old trading floor –
now a 'Mediterrasian' bistro – and the slick
Bankers Bar peopled by Catalan TV celebs down-
ing designer cocktails. Foodies get their kicks at
MOments, an all-Catalan eatery headed by multi-
Michelin starred Carme Ruscalleda's son Raül (and
which recently won a Michelin star), then relax on
the pretty Mimosa patio. Rooms are as plush as
you could hope for, big on bespoke Urquiola
pieces like 'Fat' sofas, cylindrical bathtubs and
'Caboche' chandeliers.
*Bar. Business centre. Disabled-adapted rooms (3).
Gym. Internet (€20 cable or wireless). No-smoking
hotel. Parking (€45). Pools (2). Restaurants (2).
Room service. Spa.*

Moderate

Hostal Barcelona Center Inn

*Gran Via de les Corts Catalanes 688, pral (93
265 25 60, www.hostalbarcelonacenter.com).
Metro Tetuán.* **Rates** €55-€75 double. **Rooms**
21. **Credit** MC, V. **Map** p327 H8 ⊕
Previously known as the Hostal D'Uxelles, this pretty,
tastefully decorated place has changed hands, but is
still a decent-enough place to stay and a bargain to
boot. The angels above reception are a hint of what's
to come within: Modernista tiles, cream walls with gilt-
framed mirrors, antique furnishings, canopies above
the beds and bright, Andaluz-tiled bathrooms (all en
suite). The best rooms have plant-filled balconies with
tables and chairs, where you can have breakfast. We
have heard complaints about noice, however.
*Internet (free wireless & free shared terminal).
No-smoking rooms (16). Room service.*
Other locations Gran Via de les Corts
Catalanes 667, entl 2ª, Eixample (93 265 25 60).

THE BEST HOTEL POOLS

AC MIRAMAR
Escape the slightly bland corporate interior.
See p127.

HOTEL ARTS
Great sea views from this high-end
enterprise. *See p125.*

W HOTEL
The US chain brings a little glamour to
the city. *See p125.*

Hostal Goya

*C/Pau Claris 74, 1º (93 302 25 65, www.
hostalgoya.com). Metro Urquinaona.* **Rates**
€97-€114 double. **Rooms** 19. **Credit** MC, V.
Map p328 D1 ⊕
Why can't all *hostales* be like this? Located in a typical Eixample building with fabulous tiled floors, the
bedrooms are done out in chocolates and creams,
with comfortable beds, chunky duvets and cushions;
the bathrooms are equally luxurious. The best rooms
either give on to the street or the terrace at the back.
The Goya is excellent value and a real gem. What's
more, guests leaving the city in the evening can still
use a bathroom to shower and change before they
go. That's service.
*Internet (free wireless & free shared terminal.).
No-smoking.*

Hotel Advance

*C/Sepulveda 180 (93 289 28 92, www.hotel
advance.com). Metro Universitat.* **Rates** €95-€370
double. **Rooms** 36. **Credit** AmEx, DC, MC, V.
Map p326 E9 ⊕
The Hotel Advance displays all the usual signs of
coolness in the lobby (dark paintwork, deep sofas, a
futuristic fireplace) but in reality it's a bit of a sleepy
hollow, making it a great retreat from the madness
of the town centre. Rooms are smart, comfortable
and very peaceful, bathrooms are bigger than average and there's a roof terrace for catching a few rays.
It doesn't have a bar, but friendly staff are happy to
share their local knowledge. Prices fluctuate a fair
amount, so keep an eye out for special offers.
*Disabled-adapted room. Internet (free wireless,
shared terminal €1/15min). No-smoking hotel.
Room service.*

Hotel Constanza

*C/Bruc 33 (93 270 19 10,
www.hotelconstanza.com). Metro Urquinaona.*
Rates €80-€170 double. **Rooms** 46. **Credit**
AmEx, MC, V. **Map** p328 E1 ⊕
This quiet and pleasant boutique has been around
for a few years now and continues to please. The
theme is oriental, with Japanese silk screens, orchid
and pebble prints and sleek teak furniture creating
an atmosphere of Zen-like calm. The best rooms are
at the back, some with smart walled-in terraces, and
it has comfortable single rooms. The Constanza also
does a good buffet breakfast.
*Disabled-adapted room (2). Internet (free wireless
in lobby, free high-speed in rooms). Free shared
terminal. No-smoking hotel. Restaurant.*

Hotel Soho

*Gran Via de les Corts Catalanes 543-545
(93 552 96 10, www.nnhotels.com). Metro
Urgell.* **Rates** €95-€280 double. **Rooms** 51.
Credit AmEx, DC, MC, V. **Map** p326 E8 ⊕
The Soho lives up to its Manhattan namesake in that
it has the feel of a New York village loft. A duplex-

Shoestring Style

How to find a little more tastefulness for a little less money.

Barcelona's lower-bracket hotels have come a long way from the dowdy *pensiones* and fleabitten *hostales* of old. In their wake are a new cluster of style-conscious budget options for the globetrotter who just wants to have fun.

CHIC&BASIC

Designed around the premise that sexy is cool, these M, L and XL (a nod, apparently, to condom sizes), white-on-white bedrooms ooze raunchiness. Check in to spice up your sex life, and when you stop doing that, hang with the beautiful people in the 'white bar' below.

High point The location and the *Alice in Wonderland* decor.

Low point The strange plastic curtains in the doorways.

▶ *See p121.*

Chic&Basic.

HOSTAL GAT RAVAL

Located just off La Rambla and a stone's throw from the city's modern art museum (MACBA), the Gat Raval has everything an art fan could hope for: clean lines, slick decor refreshed with splashes of citric colours, and the works of local artists and photographers adorning the walls.

High point The funky roof terrace and breakfast patio.

Low point The staff can be a little unhelpful at times.

▶ *See p125.*

MARKET HOTEL

Fans of the regular mini-break get to feel like locals in this off-the-beaten-path pad near the Sant Antoni market. An early adopter of the 'Mediterrasian' trend, the Market Hotel's rooms sport repro lacquered Chinese furniture and a red-on-black colour scheme combined with a typically laid-back Spanish air.

High point The four-poster beds and the bargain bistro.

Low point The front rooms are noisy.

▶ *See p135.*

Market Hotel.

ROOM-MATE EMMA

The newest of the budget boutiques, Emma is delightfully unstuffy. Think Stanley Kubrick does Ikea with some cool architectural details such as the central atrium and glass lift, black-out curtains in the boudoirs and a general sympathy for the fact that you're likely be out dancing until dawn.

High point The lavish breakfast buffet.

Low point Some bedrooms have no natural light.

▶ *See p135.*

Room-mate Emma.

CONSUME

The5rooms.

height lobby filled with the light of numerous glass art installations leads into a comfortable basement business space with library, desks, sofas, a small terrace and free internet. On the first floor there's a breakfast room and bar, and there's a plunge pool on the roof. Generously proportioned bedrooms have been done out in tasteful olive greens and wood, with gargantuan beds, plasma-screen TVs and glass bathrooms by Philippe Starck. The best have spacious terraces. It's trendy, but not achingly so and has a loyal following. Book well in advance.

Bar. Business centre. Disabled-adapted rooms (2). Internet (free wireless). No-smoking hotel. Pool (outdoor). Parking (€25).

★ Market Hotel

Passatge Sant Antoni Abat 10 (93 325 12 05, www.markethotel.com.es). Metro Sant Antoni. **Rates** €69-€138 double. **Rooms** 58. **Credit** AmEx, MC, DC, V. **Map** p326 D9 ⑤⑦

The people who brought us the wildly successful Quinze Nits chain of restaurants have gone on to apply their low-budget, high-design approach to this hotel. The monochrome rooms, though not huge, are comfortable and stylish for the price, and downstairs is a handsome and keenly priced restaurant, typical of the group. What's more, the nearby Mercat Sant Antoni is closed for two years, thus ensuring you won't be woken at dawn by shouting stallholders.

Disabled-adapted rooms. Internet (free wireless & free shared terminal). Restaurant. Parking (€18).

The5rooms

C/Pau Claris 72 (93 342 78 80, www.the5rooms.com). Metro Catalunya or Urquinaona. **Rates** (incl breakfast) €146-€178 double. **Rooms** 12. **Credit** MC, V. **Map** p328 D1 ⑤⑧

The5rooms is a chic and comfortable B&B in a handsome building, where the delightful Jessica Delgado makes every effort to encourage guests to feel at home. Books and magazines are dotted around the stylish sitting areas and bedrooms, and breakfast is served at any time of day. There are now two apartments (€189 for two, €232 for four) in the neighbouring building and seven rooms were added in 2009, though the name has remained the same.

Internet (free wireless). No-smoking hotel.

Room-mate Emma

C/Rosselló 205 (93 238 56 06, www.room-mate hotels.com). Metro Diagonal. **Rates** €66-€143 double. **Rooms** 56. **Credit** AmEx, DC, MC, V. **Map** p322 F6 ⑤⑨

The arrival of 'Emma' is a boon for the design-conscious and cash-strapped. The hotel reflects a fictional personality, as do all in the chain, in this case a graphic designer with aspirations to creating the next space hotel. The hotel's undulating ceilings, walls studded with sequins and mood lighting add va-va-voom. Rooms are small – if you value space,

check into the suite (€200) with a private terrace and hot tub – but the pay-off is soft, bouncy beds, power showers and a proper breakfast served until noon.

Disabled-adapted rooms (2). Internet (free wireless & free shared terminal).

★ Villa Emilia

C/Calàbria 115-117 (93 252 52 85, www. hotelvillaemilia.com). Metro Rocafort. **Rates** €95-€370 double. **Rooms** 53. **Credit** AmEx, DC, MC, V. **Map** p325 D8 ⑥⓪

A great value hotel that makes being located a little away from the action well worth it. There's not much to discover in the vicinity but Emilia compensates with the glam Zinc Bar in the lobby with black chandeliers and red velvet sofas, where you can snack on quality tapas washed down with local wine and vermouth. The pièce de résistance, however, is the open-air lounge on the rooftop, with plush sofas, candles, a well-stocked bar and a buzzer for service. The rooms are decent with large comfy beds, and decor that aims for a good night's sleep rather than design awards. Tea and biscuits are laid on at 5pm.

Bar. Disabled-adapted rooms (2). Internet (free wireless & free shared terminal). No-smoking hotel. Restaurant.

Budget

★ Hostal L'Antic Espai

Gran Via de les Corts Catalanes 660, pral (93 304 19 45, www.anticespai.com). Metro Passeig de Gràcia or Urquinaona. **Rates** €110-€160 double. **Rooms** 10. **Credit** MC, V. **Map** p326 G8 ⑥①

A real find for lovers of character places and fans of Almodóvar-style chintz. Each room is individually decorated and rammed with antiques, be it an ornately carved wooden bedhead, a teardrop chandelier, a faux Louis XV dresser or a silken throw. All have en-suite bathrooms and a little 21st-century gadgetry such as plasma TVs and free Wi-Fi, some have balconies and there is also a patio somewhat bizarrely planted with silk flowers.

Internet (free wireless). No-smoking hostal. Free movies. Parking (€34) al lado del hotel.

Hostal Central Barcelona

C/Diputació 346, pral 2ª (93 245 19 81, www. hostalcentralbarcelona.com). Metro Tetuán. **Rates** (incl breakfast) €55-€82 double. **Rooms** 20. **Credit** MC, V. **Map** p327 J8 ⑥②

Lodging at the Central, spread across two floors of an old Modernista building, is like staying in a rambling flat rather than an *hostal*. Rooms have original tiling and high ceilings, but are kitted out with air-conditioning and double glazing. Most have en-suite facilities, but the modern glass-brick cubicles in some eat up bedroom space. Clean and friendly, this is a bargain for budget travellers and a metro ride away from most sights.

Internet (free wireless). No-smoking.

Hostal Eden

C/Balmes 55, pral 1ª (93 452 66 20, www.hostal eden.net). Metro Passeig de Gràcia or Universitat. **Rates** €55-€70 double. **Rooms** 35. **Credit** AmEx, MC, V. **Map** p322 F8 ⑥

Located across three floors of a Modernista building, this warm and relaxed *hostal* with friendly, helpful staff offers free internet access and has a sunny patio with a shower for you to cool off. The best rooms have marble bathrooms with corner baths; rooms 114 and 115, at the rear of the property, are quiet and boast large windows overlooking the hotel's patio. *Internet (free wireless in lobby and some rooms). No-smoking rooms.*

★ Hostal Girona

C/Girona 24, 1º 1ª (93 265 02 59, www.hostal girona.com). Metro Urquinaona. **Rates** €65-€89 double. **Rooms** 26. **Credit** AmEx, DC, MC, V. **Map** p328 F1 ⑥

A gem of an *hostal*, filled with antiques, chandeliers and oriental rugs. The rooms may be on the simple side, but all have charm to spare, with tall windows, pretty paintwork (gilt detail on the ceiling roses) and tiled floors. It's worth splashing out on rooms in the refurbished wing, with en-suite bathrooms, although the rooms in the older wing are good too, and some have en-suite showers. Brighter, outward-facing rooms have small balconies overlooking C/Girona or bigger balconies on to a huge and quiet patio. *Internet (free wireless). Parking.*

Hostal San Remo

C/Ausiàs Marc 19, 1º-2ª (93 302 19 89, www.hostalsanremo.com). Metro Urquinaona. **Rates** €48-€65 double. **Rooms** 7. **Credit** MC, V. **Map** p328 E2 ⑥

Staying in this bright, neat and peaceful apartment feels a bit like staying with an amenable relative of the family. The friendly owner Rosa and her fluffy white dog live on site and take good care of their guests at this hostal All seven of the rooms have air-conditioning, shiny bedspreads and en-suite bathrooms, and most have double glazing and a little balcony to give you fresh air. *No-smoking hostal.*

Residencia Australia

Ronda Universitat 11, 4º 1ª (93 317 41 77, www.residenciaustralia.com). Metro Universitat. **Rates** €44-€85 double. **Rooms** 4. **Credit** MC, V. **Map** p328 B1 ⑥

Maria, the owner of Residencia Australia, quit Spain for Oz during the 1950s and only returned after Franco's death to carry on the family business and open this small, friendly *pensión*. The home-from-home feel makes for a pleasant stay. There are just four cute rooms (one en suite); all are cosy, clean and simply furnished. There is a minimum two-night stay at weekends. The family also has two apartments nearby, which can be booked if rooms are full (€60-€88 two people). *Internet (free wireless). No-smoking hotel.*

ME Barcelona.

GRÀCIA

Gràcia is off the beaten tourist track, which only adds to its allure. Its narrow streets and leafy squares have a villagey feel, and there are more and more interesting restaurants, shops and night-time activities to test out.

Expensive

Casa Fuster

Passeig de Gràcia 132 (93 255 30 00, www.hotelcasafuster.com). Metro Diagonal. **Rates** €160-€340 double. **Rooms** 105. **Credit** AmEx, DC, MC, V. **Map** p322 G6 ⑥⑦

There was a great deal of talk about the Fuster when it first opened. Many complained that this historic building should have been preserved as a public space. The famed Café Viennese answers that demand somewhat, though when a cup of tea costs €15 you won't find many locals drinking it. What is so appealing for the luxury end of the market, however, is the air of exclusivity that envelops you on arrival. Service is spot on, rooms – while rather small – feel regal in their dove grey and purples, and there are fresh flowers every day. The rooftop pool has spectacular views, while the gourmet restaurant has a clubby, insider feel.

Business centre. Disabled-adapted rooms (5). Gym. Internet (free wireless). No-smoking floors. Parking (€28). Pool. Restaurant. Room service.

Moderate

Hotel Confort

Travessera de Gràcia 72 (93 238 68 28, www.bestwesternhotelconfortgolf.com). Metro Diagonal or Fontana. **Rates** €55-€235 double. **Rooms** 36. **Credit** AmEx, DC, MC, V. **Map** p322 F5 ⑥⑧

The Confort is light years ahead of other similar establishments, with 36 simple but smart, modern bedrooms with curvy, light wood furnishings and gleaming marble bathrooms. All the rooms get lots of light, thanks to several interior patios. There's a bright dining room and lounge, with a large terrace upon which new owners Best Western have created a minuscule golf course.

Disabled-adapted room. Internet (free wireless & free shared terminal in lobby).

Budget

Hostal HMB

C/Francisco Giner 5 (93 368 20 13, www.hostal hmb.com). Metro Diagonal. **Rates** €55-€74 double. **Rooms** 28. **Credit** DC, MC, V. **Map** p322 G6 ⑥⑨

The spick and span HMB opened a few years ago and immediately proved a good addition to local budget hotels. The *hostal* is on the first floor (there's

a lift), and the 13 rooms have shiny tiled floors and furniture, flat-screen TVs and good lighting. All rooms have private bathrooms with decent showers. Bright contemporary art and design adorns the lobby and corridors.

Internet (free wireless).

OTHER DISTRICTS

Sants is convenient if you have an early train to catch, and it's pleasantly far from the crowds that fill the rest of the city. Poblenou has the added advantage of proximity to the beach.

Expensive

ABaC Restaurant Hotel

Avda Tibidabo 1, Tibidabo (93 319 66 00, www.abacbarcelona.com). FGC Tibidabo. **Rates** €225-€320 double. **Rooms** 15. **Credit** AmEx, DC, MC, V.

This swanky new uptown hotel combines a 19th-century villa with a state-of-the-art glass pavilion clad in teak lattices, giving it a modern Japanese air. The 15 bedrooms feature luxuries such as an Hermès welcome pack and jacuzzi with chromotherapy. Combined with perfectly manicured lawns, a Michelin-starred restaurant of the same name, and a white-on-white cocktail lounge in the basement, ABaC is now one of the classiest addresses in which to stay in Barcelona.

Bar. Internet (free wireless). No-smoking hotel. Parking (free). Restaurant. Room service. Spa.

Gran Hotel La Florida

Carretera de Vallvidrera al Tibidabo 83-93, Tibidabo (93 259 30 00, www.hotellaflorida.com). FGC Peu del Funicular. **Rates** €400 double. **Rooms** 70. **Credit** AmEx, DC, MC, V.

From 1925 to the 1950s, this was Barcelona's grandest hotel, frequented by royalty and stars. It has lavish suites, private terraces and gardens, a five-star restaurant, a summer outdoor nightclub, and a luxury spa. Perched as it is on Tibidabo, La Florida offers bracing walks in the hills and breathtaking 360° views, especially from the jaw-dropping infinity pool (with a heated indoor part for winter dips). It's a good choice if you want to relax in opulent style (guests even have free use of a laptop) and spend most evenings in the hotel. Getting a cab from town at night can be tricky.

Bar. Disabled-adapted rooms (2). Gym. Internet (free wireless, 2 free laptops). No-smoking floors. Parking (€21). Pool (indoor & outdoor). Restaurant. Room service. Spa.

ME Barcelona

C/Pere IV 272-286, Poblenou (93 367 20 50, www.mebymelia.com). Metro Poblenou. **Rates** €183-€190 double. **Rooms** 259. **Credit** AmEx, DC, MC, V.

CONSUME

ME Barcelona pierces the skyline here like a silver needle, and takes five-star luxury to the next level by offering a 'lifestyle experience'. It was designed by the French architect Dominique Perrault, and attracts urban thrill-seekers, who are drawn to its views, its entertainment room (with Wii and PlayStation), its 'Aura Managers' (some might call them 'concierges') and its immaculately designed interiors. Its restaurant recently won a Michelin star. *Photo p136.*
Bars (2). Business centre. Disabled-adapted rooms (4). Internet (free wireless). Gym. No-smoking floors. Parking (€25). Pool (outdoor). Restaurants (2). Room service. Spa.

Moderate

Anita's B&B
C/August Font 24, Tibidabo (93 254 67 93, www.anitasbarcelona.com) Metro Penitents then bus 124. **Rates** (incl breakfast) €69-€88 double. **Rooms** 3. **No credit cards.**
A true retreat, this friendly bed and breakfast property out in Tibidabo offers a home-style experience and is ideal if you are looking to experience a more peaceful city break. The centre is about 20 minutes away by taxi, but the air is that bit fresher and the views are fabulous (all rooms have a balcony and en suite bathrooms). Bedrooms are tastefully decorated, with cosy quilts and flowers, communal areas are wellstocked with guide books and magazines, and the breakfast is among the best in the city. Children are made particularly welcome, and cots, bottle-warmers and strollers can be provided.
Internet (free wireless). Room service.

Petit Hotel
C/Laforja 67, 1°-2ª, Sant Gervasi (93 202 36 63, www.petit-hotel.net). FGC Muntaner. **Rates** €72-€122 double. **Rooms** 4. **Credit** MC, V. **Map** p322 E5 ⑩
This charming and convivial B&B in Sant Gervasi has four neat, fresh bedrooms set around the comfy and softly lit lounge. Although only two of the rooms are en suite, the others have large, immaculate modern bathrooms located just outside. The owners, Rosa and Leo, are happy to chat to guests and provide information on the city. Breakfast, which is better than in many hotels, is served 8.30am-1.30pm.
Internet (free wireless & free shared terminal).

Budget

★ Barcelona Urbany
Avda Meridiana 97 (93 245 84 14, www.barcelonaurbany.com). Metro Clot. **Rates** (incl breakfast) €15-€25 dorm; €57-€85 double. **Beds** 400. **Credit** MC, V.
Forget the institutional youth hostels of old, with their mouldy showers, grubby sheets and threadbare towels – the Urbany has brought a paradigm shift in the market. For as little as €15 you can lie in

a clean and comfy dorm bed surfing the net, watch DVDs in a common room, have a free swim in a nearby pool or take a jacuzzi. Linen and a blanket are included and towels and hairdryers for hire.
Bar. Disabled-adapted room (3). Internet (free wireless). No-smoking hostel. Restaurant.

Hostal Poblenou
C/Taulat 30, Poblenou (93 221 26 01, www.hostalpoblenou.com). Metro Poblenou. **Rates** (incl breakfast) €65-€85 double. **Rooms** 10. **Credit** MC, V.
Poblenou is a delightful *hostal* in an elegant restored building. The rooms are light and airy with their own bathrooms, and breakfast is served on a sunny terrace. Guests can help themselves to tea, coffee and mineral water at no extra cost. *Photo p141.*
Internet (shared terminal, free wireless).

Hostal Sofia
Avda Roma 1-3 entl, Sants (93 419 50 40, www.hostalsofia.es). Metro Sants Estaciò. **Rates** €40-€60 double. **Rooms** 17. **Credit** DC, MC, V. **Map** p325 C7 ⑪
The 17 basic rooms of Hostal Sofia are a very sound budget option if an early train or quick stopover forces you to spend the night in the city. Some rooms have en-suite bathrooms. As the *hostal* is on the first floor and traffic is constant, outward-facing rooms are usually very noisy.

Apartment Hotels

Barcelona Center Plaza
C/Ronda Sant Pere 38, 1° 1ª (93 315 07 42, www.barcelonacenterplaza.com). Metro Urquinaona. **Rates** €60-€80/2 people. **Credit** MC, V. **Map** p328 E2 ⑫
All studios have a properly equipped kitchen and a dining area. Some of the decor is a bit nursery-school (fluffy clouds painted above the bed), but on the whole it's very comfortable and nicely done. There is another branch at C/Comtal 9 called Barcelona Center House, currently closed for renovations. A fee of €20 applies for check-in after 11pm.
Internet (free wireless).

Bòria
C/Bòria 24-26 (93 295 58 93, www.boriabcn.com). Metro Jaume I. **Rates** €119-€299/2 people (€54 extra adult). **Rooms** 9. **Credit** AmEx, DC, MC, V. **Map** p329 D5 ⑬
Located in an 18th-century palace, Bòria is half hotel, half apartment, with sophisticated loft-style rooms and suites with polished wood floors, plush rugs and designer fixtures and fittings, as well as cleverly incorporated kitchens, dining areas and office space. Communal zones include a smart and sleek library downstairs, and a wood-decked roof terrace.
Internet (free wireless).

Hispanos Siete Suiza
C/Sicilia 255, Eixample (93 208 20 51, www.
hispanos7suiza.com). Metro Sagrada Família.
Rates (incl breakfast) €120-€210/1-2 people;
€190-€250/3 people; €210-€280/4 people.
Apartments 19. **Credit** AmEx, DC, MC, V.
Map p323 J7 ⓴

Lovers of vintage automobiles will get a kick out of
the Hispanos Siete Suiza, named after the seven finely
restored pre-war motors that take up much of the
lobby of this property. The 19 elegant, spacious apartments each have a kitchen and sitting area with parquet floors, a terrace and two bedrooms. Profits go to
the cancer research foundation running the hotel.
Bar. Disabled-adapted room. Free high-speed inter-
net. Parking (€25.15). Restaurant.

Apartment & Room Rentals

Short-term apartment rental is an expanding
market. People who've visited the city several
times, or who want to spend longer than a few
days here, are increasingly opting for self-
catering accommodation. Some firms rent their
own apartments; others act as intermediaries
between apartment owners and visitors.

When renting, it pays to check the small
print (payment methods, deposits, cancellation
fees, etc) and what's included (cleaning,
towels and so on) before booking. Note that
apartments offered for rental tend to be small.
In addition to the outfit listed below, check the
gay-operated www.outlet4spain.com and the
following firms:

www.rentthesun.com
www.inside-bcn.com
www.oh-barcelona.com
www.barcelona-home.com
www.destinationbcn.com
www.rentaflatinbarcelona.com
www.friendlyrentals.com
www.apartmentsbcn.net
www.flatsbydays.com

In addition, www.habitservei.com can help to
find rooms in shared flats, and www.loquo.com
functions as a sort of Iberian Craig's List.

Barcelona-Home
C/Viladomat 89-95, Ent 3 (93 423 34 73,
www.barcelona-home.com). **Open** 10.30am-6pm
Mon-Fri. **Rates** vary. **Credit** AmEx, DC, MC, V.
Map p325 D9 ⓻

A reputable company staffed by knowledgeable
young people, Barcelona-Home aims to solve accommodation problems and provides guided tours, airport transfers, language courses and whatever else
clients might need. Apartment rental prices are reasonable considering the level of service, and the website is a great starting point for city information.

Youth Hostels

The fleapit dormitories of yesteryear are no
more, and Barcelona's new breed of youth
hostels are a colourful and clean bunch in
some great locations.

Increasingly, in addition to dorm rooms,
many hostels now have single or double rooms
to rent, often at eminently reasonable prices.

For more information on hostelling and HI
cards, see www.hihostels.com.

Alberg Mare de Déu de Montserrat
Passeig de la Mare de Déu del Coll 41-51, Gràcia
(93 210 51 51/93 483 83 63, www.tujuca.com).
Metro Vallcarca. **Open** *Reception* 24 hours daily.
Rates (incl breakfast) € 16.75-€21.75 person.
Credit DC, MC, V.

Located in a magnificent building north of the centre,
this 214-bed hostel boasts an architectural edge, with
original features such as Modernista tilework, whim-
sical plaster carvings and stained-glass windows,
not to mention the peaceful gardens. Hostelling
International cards are obligatory, but can be purchased here for €5 (under-29s) or €12 (over-29s).
Disabled-adapted room. Internet (€1.50/hr shared
terminals & free wireless) . No-smoking hostel.
Parking (free). Restaurant.

Barcelona Mar Youth Hostel
C/Sant Pau 80, Raval (93 324 85 30,
www.barcelonamar.com). Metro Paral·lel.
Open 24hrs daily. **Rates** (incl breakfast)
€13-€27/person. *Sheets* €2.50/person per stay.
Credit AmEx, DC, MC, V. **Map** p326 E11 ⓺

With its pleasant communal areas, sparkling wash-
rooms and handy facilities, this fine youth hostel is
certainly good value. There are no individual rooms,
only dormitories that are neatly stacked with bunk
beds (150 in total), but there are areas that can be
curtained off for privacy.
Disabled-adapted room. Internet
(free shared terminal). No-smoking hostel.
Other locations Alfonso XIII 28, Badalona (93
399 14 20, www.barcelonadream.net); Barcelona
Sound, Nou de la Rambla 91, Raval (93 185 08 00,
www.barcelonasoundhostel.com).

Hostal Poblenou. *See p139.*

Center Ramblas Youth Hostel

*C/Hospital 63, Raval (93 412 40 69,
www.center-ramblas.com). Metro Liceu.*
Open 24hrs daily. **Rates** (incl breakfast)
€17-€22/person under-25s; €19-€26/person
over-26s. Extra €2 without HI Card.*Towels*
€2/person. **Credit** MC, V. **Map** p328 A4 🟡
This friendly hostel has 201 beds, in dorms sleeping
three to ten people. Facilities include free internet
access, a communal fridge, microwave and lockers.
It's a good place to make friends, but beds sell out
fast, so book a space at least two weeks in advance.
*Disabled-adapted room. Internet (free terminal
& wireless). Lockers (free). No-smoking hostel.*

Centric Point

*Passeig de Gràcia 33, Eixample (93 215 65 38,
www.centricpointhostel.com, www.equity-point.com).
Metro Passeig de Gràcia.* **Open** 24hrs daily.
Rates (incl breakfast) €14-€30/person dorm;
€43-€57/person double; €67-€95 single. *Sheets,
blankets & towels* €2/person (incl in singles &
doubles). **Credit** DC, MC, V. **Map** p322 G8 🟡
The newest addition to the Equity Point group goes
upmarket, with more than 400 beds in an impressive
Modernista building, which is situated in one of the
swankiest locations in the city. There are singles,
doubles and dorms, mostly with en-suite facilities.
There is free internet access, satellite TV and breakfast. Lots of information on Barcelona is available.
*Disabled-adapted room. Internet (free wireless).
Lockers (free with own padlock).
No-smoking hostel.*

Gothic Point

*C/Vigatans 5, Born (93 268 78 08, www.
gothicpoint.com, www.equity-point.com). Metro
Jaume I.* **Open** 24hrs daily. **Rates** (incl breakfast)
€17-€25/person; €35/person single/double.
Sheets, blankets & towels €2/person per stay.
Credit AmEx, DC, MC, V. **Map** p329 D6 🟡
Belonging to the same group as Centric Point, this
friendly 154-bed hostel has an Asian feel. Dorms
(six to 14 beds) are cramped and an undersheet
and pillowcase are provided. There are washing
machines and dryers, a microwave and fridge.
Disabled-adapted room. Free internet. No-smoking.
Other locations Sea Point, Plaça del Mar 1-4,
Barceloneta (93 224 70 75, www.seapoint
hostel.com, www.equity-point.com).

Itaca Alberg-Hostel

*C/Ripoll 21, Barri Gòtic (93 301 97 51,
www.itacahostel.com). Metro Catalunya or
Urquinaona.* **Open** *Reception* 24hrs daily.
Rates (incl sheets) €16-€26/person dorm;
€50-€60 twin. **Credit** MC, V. **Map** p328 D4 🟡
Although the Itaca Alberg-Hostel is in the centre,
this is a laid-back place where you can recharge your
batteries. The hotel has a homely atmosphere, as
seen in its murals, sofas and lobby music; there's a
communal kitchen, a breakfast room and shelves of
books and games. Its 34 beds are in four cheerful
and airy dorms, all of which feature balconies.
*Internet (80¢/30min shared terminal, free
wireless). No-smoking hostel.*

Campsites

For more on campsites in striking distance of
Barcelona, get the *Catalunya Campings* or the
Campsites Close to Barcelona guide (available
in a PDF format at www.turismepropbarcelona.
cat/en/camping) and www.campingsonline.com.

Camping Masnou

*Carretera N2, km 633, El Masnou (93 555 15
03).* **Open** *Reception* Oct-May 9am-noon, 3-7pm
daily. June-Sept 8am-10pm daily. *Campsite* 7am-
11.30pm daily. **Rates** €7/person; €5.50 1-10s;
free under-1s; €7 car, €9.50 caravan, €13.50
camper; €5.50 electricity. **Credit** MC, V.
Alongside the tents there's space for camper vans,
plus a pool, supermarket, restaurant and bar.

Tres Estrellas

*Carretera C-31, km 186.2, Gavà (93 633 06 37,
www.camping3estrellas.com).* **Open** *Reception*
mid Mar-mid Oct 9am-9pm daily. *Campsite*
24hrs daily. Closed mid Oct-mid Mar. **Rates**
€6-€8/person; €5-€6 3-10s; free under-3s;
€8-€9 car/caravan; €6 electricity. **Credit** MC, V.
The campsite is by the beach, 12km from Barcelona.
There's a regular bus service into town.

CONSUME

Restaurants

From Gallic gems to gastro genius.

Catalonia, and the rest of the culinary world, gasped in horror at the recent announcement that from 2012 Ferran Adrià is to close his globally fêted restaurant, El Bulli, for a couple of years – and then only open it to a privileged handpicked few. Philosophical types, however, might say the restaurant's work is done.

Spain's culinary revolution has been one of the world's most significant gastronomic shake-ups in recent years, and Adrià's hot jellies, foams and edible clingfilms provided much of the impetus. Barcelona has greeted this new dawn with open arms, and the city's chefs now give the Basques a run for their money when it comes to unrestrained creativity in tandem with the dogged pursuit of ever more superior produce. Mass immigration has also played its part, adding ethnic variety to a culinary scene that offers both tradition and adventure.

THE LOCAL SCENE

At the top end of the scale, the tendrils of influence unfurling from überchef Adrià and his Costa Brava restaurant cannot be overestimated. Many of the city's top chefs, most notably Carles Abellan at Comerç 24 (*see p151*), have done training stints in Adrià's kitchen, a fact often reflected in the experimental nature of their dishes, while Adrià's influence is equally evident in the menus of dozens of other eateries.

More traditional restaurants remain, of course, but they've been joined of late by a number of places offering cuisine from around the world. It's become increasingly easy to find a plate of *momo* dumplings, hand-rolled *maki*, Peking duck or a *masala dosa* in the city. Hell, there's even a fish and chip shop.

What happens when

Lunch starts at around 1.30pm or 2pm and continues until roughly 3.30pm or 4pm; dinner is served from about 9pm until 11.30pm or midnight. Some restaurants open earlier in the evening, but arriving before 9.30pm or 10pm generally means you'll be dining alone or in the company of foreign tourists.

Booking a table is generally a good idea at weekends, and also on Monday lunchtimes, when few restaurants are open. Many also close for lengthy holidays, including about a week over Easter, two or three weeks in August or early September, and often the first week in January. We have listed closures of more than a week where possible, but it's always wise to call ahead during the summer.

Prices & payment

Eating out in Barcelona is not as cheap as it used to be, but low mark-ups on wines keep the costs reasonable for northern Europeans and Americans. For a cheap lunch, *see p166* **Lunch Crunched**.

Laws governing the issue of prices are routinely flouted, but, legally, menus must declare if the eight per cent IVA (VAT) is included in prices or not (it rarely is, but we have included it in the prices below), and also if there is a cover charge (such a thing is officially illegal, but is generally expressed as a charge for bread). For details on tipping etiquette in the city, *see p148* **Inside Track**.

> ❶ Blue numbers given in this chapter correspond to the location of each restaurant as marked on the street maps. *See pp321-329.*

We've used the € symbol to indicate not only where a restaurant's main courses are low-priced, but where the mark-up on drinks is reasonably low, and where there's no cover charge (or a very small one).

Restaurants

THE BARRI GÒTIC

★ Cafè de l'Acadèmia

C/Lledó 1 (93 319 82 53). Metro Jaume I. **Open** 1.30-4pm, 8.30-11.30pm Mon-Fri. Closed Aug. **Main courses** €15. **Set lunch** €10.50-€15 **Credit** DC, MC, V. **Map** p329 D6 ❶ **Catalan**
An assured approach to the classics of Catalan cuisine, combined with sunny tables on the pretty Plaça Sant Just, make this one of the best-value restaurants around. The brick-walled dining room gets full and the tables are close together, so it doesn't really work for a date, but it's an animated spot for a power breakfast among the suits from nearby City Hall. Eat à la carte for quail stuffed with duck's liver and *botifarra* with wild mushroom sauce, or duck confit with poached onion and orange sauce.

★ € Can Culleretes

C/Quintana 5 (93 317 30 22, www.culleretes.com). Metro Liceu. **Open** 1.30-4pm, 9-11pm Tue-Sat; 1.30 4pm Sun. Closed mid July-mid Aug. **Main courses** €9.50. **Set lunch** €12.50-€15.50 Mon-Fri. **Set dinner** €23-€29 daily. **Credit** MC, V. **Map** p329 B5 ❷ **Catalan**
The rambling dining rooms at the 'house of teaspoons' have been packing 'em in since 1786. The

secret to this restaurant's longevity is a straightforward one: honest, hearty cooking and decent wine served at the lowest possible prices. Under huge oil paintings and a thousand signed black-and-white photos, diners munch sticky boar stew, tender pork with prunes and dates, goose with apples, partridge escabeche and superbly fresh seafood.

El Gran Café

C/Avinyó 9 (93 318 79 86, www.restaurant elgrancafe.com). Metro Liceu. **Open** 1-4.30pm, 7.30pm-midnight daily. **Main courses** €15. **Set lunch** €11.25 Mon-Fri. **Credit** AmEx, DC, MC, V. **Map** p329 C6 ❸ **Mediterranean**
The fluted columns, bronze nymphs, suspended globe lamps and wood panelling help replicate a classic Parisian vibe, and the cornerstones of brasserie cuisine – onion soup, duck magret, tarte tatin and even crêpes suzette – are all present and correct. The imaginative Catalan dishes spliced into the menu also work, but the distinctly non-Gallic attitude towards the hastily assembled set lunch is less convincing.

CONSUME

Matsuri. *See p147.*

Menu Glossary

The essential list of gastronomic terms and vocabulary.

CONSUME

CATALAN	SPANISH	ENGLISH
ESSENTIAL TERMINOLOGY		
una cullera	*una cuchara*	a spoon
una forquilla	*un tenedor*	a fork
un ganivet	*un cuchillo*	a knife
una ampolla de	*una botella de*	a bottle of
un/a altre/a	*otro/otra*	another (one)
més	*más*	more
pa	*pan*	bread
oli d'oliva	*aceite de oliva*	olive oil
sal i pebre	*sal y pimienta*	salt and pepper
amanida	*ensalada*	salad
truita	*tortilla*	omelette
(note: **truita** can also mean 'trout')		
la nota	*la cuenta*	the bill
un cendrer	*un cenicero*	an ashtray
vi negre/ rosat/blanc	*vino tinto/rosado/blanco*	red/rosé/ white wine
bon profit	*que aproveche*	enjoy your meal
sóc...	*soy...*	I'm a...
vegetarià/ ana	*vegetariano/ a*	vegetarian
diabètic/a	*diabético/a*	diabetic
COOKING TERMS		
a la brasa	*a la brasa*	chargrilled
a la graella/ planxa	*a la plancha*	cooked on a hot plate
a la romana	*a la romana*	fried in batter
al forn	*al horno*	baked
al vapor	*al vapor*	steamed
fregit	*frito*	fried
rostit	*asado*	roast
ben fet	*bien hecho*	well done
a punt	*medio hecho*	medium
poc fet	*poco hecho*	rare
CARN I AVIRAM	**CARNE Y AVES**	**MEAT & POULTRY**
ànec	*pato*	duck
bou	*buey*	beef
cabrit	*cabrito*	kid
colomí	*pichón*	pigeon
conill	*conejo*	rabbit
embotits	*embutidos*	cold cuts
fetge	*hígado*	liver
gall dindi	*pavo*	turkey
garrí	*cochinillo*	suckling pig
guatlla	*codorniz*	quail

CATALAN	SPANISH	ENGLISH
llebre	*liebre*	hare
llengua	*lengua*	tongue
llom	*lomo*	loin (usually pork)
oca	*oca*	goose
ous	*huevos*	eggs
perdiu	*perdiz*	partridge
pernil (serrà)	*jamón*	dry-cured ham
pernil dolç	*jamón york*	cooked ham
peus de porc	*manos de cerdo*	pigs' trotters
pintada	*gallina de Guinea*	guinea fowl
pollastre	*pollo*	chicken
porc	*cerdo*	pork
porc senglar	*jabalí*	wild boar
vedella	*ternera*	veal
xai/be	*cordero*	lamb
PEIX I MARISC	**PESCADO Y MARISCOS**	**FISH & SEAFOOD**
anxoves	*anchoas*	anchovies
bacallà	*bacalao*	salt cod
besuc	*besugo*	sea bream
caballa	*verat*	mackerel
calamarsos	*calamares*	squid
cloïsses	*almejas*	clams
cranc	*cangrejo*	crab
escamarlans	*cigalas*	crayfish
escopinyes	*berberechos*	cockles
espardenyes	*espardeñas*	sea cucumbers
gambes	*gambas*	prawns
llagosta	*langosta*	spiny lobster
llagostins	*langostinos*	langoustines
llamàntol	*bogavante*	lobster
llenguado	*lenguado*	sole
llobarro	*lubina*	sea bass
lluç	*merluza*	hake
moll	*salmonete*	red mullet
musclos	*mejillones*	mussels
navalles	*navajas*	razor clams
percebes	*percebes*	barnacles
pop	*pulpo*	octopus
rap	*rape*	monkfish
rèmol	*rodaballo*	turbot
salmó	*salmón*	salmon
sardines	*sardinas*	sardines
sípia	*sepia*	cuttlefish
tallarines	*tallarinas*	wedge clams

CATALAN	SPANISH	ENGLISH
tonyina	*atún*	tuna
truita	*trucha*	trout
(note: **truita** can also mean 'omelette')		

VERDURES LEGUMBRES VEGETABLES

CATALAN	SPANISH	ENGLISH
albergínia	*berenjena*	aubergine
all	*ajo*	garlic
alvocat	*aguacate*	avocado
bolets	*setas*	wild mushrooms
carbassons	*calabacines*	courgettes
carxofes	*alcahofas*	artichokes
ceba	*cebolla*	onion
cigrons	*garbanzos*	chickpeas
col	*col*	cabbage
enciam	*lechuga*	lettuce
endívies	*endivias*	chicory
espinacs	*espinacas*	spinach
mongetes blanques	*judías blancas*	haricot beans
mongetes verdes	*judías verdes*	French beans
pastanagues	*zanahorias*	carrots
patates	*patatas*	potatoes
pebrots	*pimientos*	peppers
pèsols	*guisantes*	peas

CATALAN	SPANISH	ENGLISH
porros	*puerros*	leek
tomàquets	*tomates*	tomatoes
xampinyons	*champiñones*	mushrooms

POSTRES POSTRES DESSERTS

CATALAN	SPANISH	ENGLISH
flam	*flan*	crème caramel
formatge	*queso*	cheese
gelat	*helado*	ice-cream
música	*música*	dried fruit and nuts, with muscatel
pastis	*pastel*	cake
tarta	*tarta*	tart

FRUITA FRUTA FRUIT

CATALAN	SPANISH	ENGLISH
figues	*higos*	figs
gerds	*frambuesas*	raspberries
maduixes	*fresas*	strawberries
pera	*pera*	pear
pinya	*piña*	pineapple
plàtan	*plátano*	banana
poma	*manzana*	apple
préssec	*melocotón*	peach
prunes	*ciruelas*	plums

CONSUME

Discover the world's greatest cities

Available at **timeout.com/shop**

€ Machiroku

C/Moles 21 (93 412 60 82). Metro Catalunya or Urquinaona. **Open** 1.30-3.30pm, 8.30-11.30pm Mon-Fri; 8.30-11.30pm Sat. Closed Aug. **Main courses** €10. **Set lunch** €8.50-€11.90 Mon-Fri. **No credit cards. Map** p328 D3 **❹ Japanese**

A cosy, modest space decorated with Japanese wall hangings and prints. Service is charming and friendly and the various set menus at lunchtime offer good value, featuring rice and miso soup and then a choice of sushi, teriyaki, *yakinuku* (chargrilled beef) or a bento box with vegetable and prawn tempura. The short wine list has some excellent options.

Matsuri

Plaça Regomir 1 (93 268 15 35). Metro Jaume I. **Open** 8pm-midnight daily. **Main courses** €17. **Credit** MC, V. **Map** p329 C6 **❺ Asian**

This eaterie is painted in tasteful shades of ochre and terracotta, with the obligatory trickling fountain, wooden carvings and wall-hung candles, but saved from eastern cliché by some occidental jazz in the background. Reasonably priced tom yam soup and pad Thai feature, while less predictable choices include *pho bo* – a Vietnamese broth with meat and spices, and *sake niku*, a delicious beef dish with wok-fried broccoli and a lightly perfumed soy sauce. *Photo p143.*

€ Mercè Vins

C/Amargós 1 (93 302 60 56). Metro Urquinaona. **Open** 8am-4pm Mon-Fri. **Set lunch** €10. Closed 2wks Aug. **Credit** AmEx, MC, V. **Map** p328 D3 **❻ Catalan**

Set in the heart of the Barri Gòtic, this cosy, lunchtimes only restaurant is aimed at office workers. Dishes on the *menú del día* change daily, but might include a pumpkin soup or inventive salad, followed by *botifarra* with sautéed garlic potatoes. Dessert regulars are flat, sweet *coca* bread with a glass of muscatel, chocolate flan or figgy pudding. In the morning, it opens for breakfast, which here tends to be *pa amb tomàquet* (bread rubbed with tomato) topped with cheese or ham.

€ Mesón Jesús

C/Cecs de la Boqueria 4 (93 317 46 98). Metro Jaume I or Liceu. **Open** 1-4pm, 8-11pm Mon-Fri. Closed Aug. **Main courses** €12. **Set lunch** €11.50 Mon-Fri. **Set dinner** €18 Mon-Fri. **Credit** MC, V. **Map** p329 B5 **❼ Spanish**

Old-school Castilian is a surprisingly uncommon look among Barcelona's restaurants, and the gingham tablecloths, oak barrels and cartwheels hung at Mesón Jesús are a novelty. The menu is limited and never changes, but the dishes are good and inexpensive to boot – try the sautéed green beans with ham to start, then the superb grilled prawns or a tasty *zarzuela* (fish stew). The waitresses are cheerful with a largely non-Spanish-speaking clientele, and especially obliging when it comes to dealing with children.

El Paraguayo

C/Parc 1 (93 302 14 41). Metro Drassanes. **Open** 1-4pm, 8pm-midnight Tue-Sun. **Main courses** €17. **Set lunch** €12 Tue-Fri. **Credit** AmEx, DC, MC, V. **Map** p329 B8 **❽ Paraguayan**

The only way to go at El Paraguayo, and indeed at most South American restaurants, is to order a juicy steak, a bottle of good, cheap house Rioja and a bowl of piping hot yucca chips. The rest is a menu filler. As to which steak, a helpful chart walks you through the various cuts, most of them unfamiliar to European butchers; a *bife de chorizo* should satisfy even the ravenous. The place itself is cosy and wood-panelled, brightened with Botero-esque oil paintings of buxom madams and their dapper admirers.

€ Peimong

C/Templers 6-10 (93 318 28 73). Metro Jaume I. **Open** 1-4pm, 8-11.30pm Tue-Sat; 1-4pm Sun. Closed 2wks Aug. **Main courses** €8. **Credit** DC, MC, V. **Map** p329 C6 **❾ Peruvian**

Not, perhaps, the fanciest-looking restaurant around (think Peruvian gimcracks, strip lighting and tapestries of Macchu Pichu) or indeed the fanciest-looking food, but it certainly is tasty. Start with a pisco sour and a dish of chunky yucca chips, or perhaps some spicy corn tamales. Next, move on to ceviche for an explosion of lime and coriander; or the satisfying *lomo saltado* – pork fried with onions, tomatoes and coriander. Service is friendly and there are two types of Peruvian beer, plus (for the very nostalgic or the hypoglycaemic) Inca Kola.

Els Quatre Gats

C/Montsió 3 (93 302 41 40, www.4gats.com). Metro Catalunya. **Open** 1pm-1am daily. **Main courses** €18. **Set lunch** €14.95 Mon-Fri; €25.90 Sat. **Credit** DC, MC, V. **Map** p328 C3 **❿ Catalan**

Dazzling in its design, Els Quatre Gats is an unmissable stop for those interested in Modernista architecture and indeed the art of the period, being the former regular meeting place of Picasso and other artistic luminaries. Nowadays, it chiefly caters to tourists, and is no crucible for Catalan gastronomy – nor is it cheap. There is, however, a more reasonably priced and generously portioned set lunch, and when it's all over you can buy the T-shirt. *Photo p149.*

▶ *To appreciate the building without forking out for dinner, visit its café; see p169.*

€ Les Quinze Nits

Plaça Reial 6 (93 317 30 75, www.lesquinzenits.com). Metro Liceu. **Open** 1-3.45pm, 8-11.30pm daily. **Main courses** €10. **Set lunch** €8.95 Mon-Fri. **Credit** AmEx, MC, V. **Map** p329 B6 **⓫ Spanish**

The staggering success of the Quinze Nits enterprise (there are countless branches here in Barcelona and in Madrid, and a handful of hotels) is down to one concept: style on a budget. All the restaurants have a certain Manhattan chic, yet you'll struggle to spend

CONSUME

Els Quatre Gats.

CONSUME

much more than €20 a head. The food plays second fiddle and is a hit-and-miss affair, but order simple dishes and at these prices you can't go far wrong. The queues tend to be shorter at the other branches. **Other locations** throughout the city.

★ Shunka

C/Sagristans 5 (93 412 49 91). Metro Jaume I. **Open** 1.30-3.15pm, 8.30-11.15pm Tue-Sun. Closed Aug & 10 days at Christmas. **Main courses** €17. **Credit** AmEx, DC, MC, V. **Map** p328 D4 ⓬ **Japanese**

The speciality here is prime-grade *toro*, fatty and deliciously creamy tuna belly. It's wildly expensive as a main, but you can sample it as *nigiri-zushi*. The house salad with raw fish also makes for a zingy starter, then you'll find all the usual staples of the sushi menu, along with heartier options such as the *udon kakiage*, a filling broth of langoustine tempura, vegetables and noodles.

▶ *A new and more upmarket branch, Koy Shunka, recently opened round the corner at C/Copons 7 (93 412 79 39).*

INSIDE TRACK TOP TIPS

Catalans, and the Spanish in general, tend to tip very little, often rounding up to the nearest euro, but tourists should let their conscience decide.

Taxidermista

Plaça Reial 8 (93 412 45 36, www.taxidermista restaurant.com). Metro Liceu. **Open** 1.30-4pm, 7.30pm-12.30am Tue-Sun. Closed 2wks Jan. **Main courses** €15. **Set lunch** €10.50 Tue-Fri. **Set dinner** €24. **Credit** AmEx, DC, MC, V. **Map** p329 B6 ⓭ **Mediterranean**

When this was a taxidermist's, Dali ordered 200,000 ants, a tiger, a lion and a rhinoceros, which was wheeled into the Plaça Reial so he could be photographed atop the beast. Those who leave here stuffed are mostly tourists, but standards are high. À la carte offerings include foie gras with quince jelly and langoustine ravioli with seafood sauce, and fusion elements (wok-fried spaghetti with vegetables). It stays opens as a café in the afternoons. *Photo p150.*

Tokyo

C/Comtal 20 (93 317 61 80). Metro Catalunya. **Open** 1.30-4pm, 8-11pm Mon-Sat. Closed Aug. **Main courses** €15. **Set lunch** €12 Mon-Thur. **Credit** AmEx, MC, V. **Map** p328 D3 ⓮ **Japanese**

A small, simple space, where suspended beams, plastic plants and slatted partitions are used to clever effect and the walls lined with photos and drawings from grateful clients. The speciality is *edomae* (hand-rolled *nigiri-zushi*), but the meat and vegetable sukiyaki, which is cooked at your table, is also good, while the *menú* of sushi and tempura is great value. The *daifuku* (red bean) and *midori* (green tea) *mochi* rolls to finish are something of an acquired taste.

THE BORN & SANT PERE

★ El Atril

C/Carders 23 (93 310 12 20, www.atril barcelona.com). Metro Jaume I. **Open** 6pm-midnight Monday; noon-12.30pm Tue-Sun. **Main courses** €12.50. **Set lunch** €10.80 Tue-Fri; €12.80 Sat, €11.50 Sun (brunch). **Credit** DC, MC, V. **Map** p329 E5 ⓯ **Global**

El Atril's few tables require a reservation on most nights thanks to some reliably good cooking, traversing a range of cuisines. On the tapas menu, fried green plantains with coriander and lime mayonnaise sit alongside *botifarra* with caramelised onions, while a catholic selection of main courses includes a bowl of Belgian-style mussels and chips and a kangaroo burger. There is live music from Thursday to Sunday, and tables outside on the Plaça Sant Cugat.

▶ *If you can't get in on concert nights, you can catch the same bands at Ácoma; see p168.*

Big Fish

C/Comercial 9 (93 268 17 28, www.bigfish.cat). Metro Jaume I. **Open** 1.30-4pm, 8.30pm-midnight Tue-Sun. **Main courses** €20. **Set lunch** €18 Tue-Fri. **Credit** AmEx, MC, V. **Map** p329 F6 ⓰ **Fish**

Catalan Dishes

A primer of local cuisine.

Here is a selection of dishes considered classically Catalan. It's also worth noting that many dishes apparently from other cuisines – risotto, canelloni, ravioli – are entrenched in the Catalan culinary tradition. Two names borrowed from the French are foie (as opposed to *fetge/hígado* or foie gras), which has come to mean hare, duck or goose liver *mi-cuit* with liqueur, salt and sugar; and *coulant*, like a small soufflé but melting in the centre. For a full glossary of food terms, *see pp144-145.*

a la llauna 'in the tin' – baked on a metal tray with garlic, tomato, paprika and wine
allioli garlic crushed with olive oil to form a mayonnaise-like texture, similar to *aïoli*
amanida catalana/*ensalada catalana* mixed salad with a range of cold meats
arròs negre/*arroz negro* 'black rice', seafood rice cooked in squid ink
botifarra/*butifarra* Catalan sausage; variants include *botifarra negre* (blood sausage) and *blanca* (mixed with egg)
botifarra amb mongetes/*butifarra con judías* sausage with haricot beans
calçots variety of large spring onion, only available from December to spring, and eaten chargrilled with *romesco* sauce
carn d'olla traditional Christmas dish of various meats stewed with *escudella* (see below), then served separately
conill amb cargols/*conejo con caracoles* rabbit with snails
crema catalana cold custardy dessert with burned sugar topping, similar to crème brûlée
escalivada grilled and peeled peppers, onions and aubergine
escudella winter stew of meat and vegetables
espinacs a la catalana/*espinacas a la catalana* spinach fried in olive oil with garlic, raisins and pine nuts
esqueixada summer salad of shredded, marinated salt cod with onions, olives and tomato
fideuà/*fideuá* paella made with vermicelli instead of rice
mar i muntanya a traditional Catalan combination of meat and seafood, such as lobster and chicken in the same dish
mel i mató curd cheese with honey
pa amb tomàquet/*pan con tomate* bread with tomato, oil and salt

picada mix of nuts, garlic, parsley, bread, chocolate and little chilli peppers, often used to enrich and thicken dishes
romesco a spicy sauce from the coast south of Barcelona, made with crushed almonds and hazelnuts, tomatoes, oil and a special type of red pepper (*nyora*)
samfaina a mix of onion, garlic, aubergine and red and green peppers (like ratatouille)
sarsuela/*zarzuela* fish and seafood stew
sofregit a base for many sauces, made with caramelised onion, tomato and olive oil, occasionally with sugar
sípia amb mandonguilles/*sepia con albóndigas* cuttlefish with meatballs
suquet de peix/*suquet de pescado* stew made with fish (generally monkfish), shellfish, and potatoes
torrades/*tostadas* toasted *pa amb tomàquet*
xató salad containing tuna, anchovies and cod, with a *romesco*-type sauce

CONSUME

Taxidermista. See p148.

Sumptuously designed in a Manhattan style, with leather Chesterfields, cascading lampshades and a gilt-edged fireplace, Big Fish doubles as a Mediterranean fish restaurant and sushi bar. The food is good to excellent and the experience is hard to fault – except, perhaps, for the noise levels. Tables are very close together and the music is jacked up to club volume by about 11pm, at which point the waiting staff give up straining to hear you and bring you what they feel you'd probably like.

★ Cal Pep
Plaça de les Olles 8 (93 310 79 61, www. calpep.com). Metro Barceloneta. **Open** 7.30-11.30pm Mon; 1-3.45pm, 7.30-11.30pm Tue-Fri; 1-3.45pm Sat. Closed Aug and Easter wk. **Main courses** €15. **Credit** DC, MC, V. **Map** p329 E7 ⑰ **Seafood**
As much tapas bar as restaurant, Cal Pep is always packed with people: get here early for the coveted seats at the front. There is a cosy dining room at the back, but it's a shame to miss the show. The affable Pep will take the order, steering neophytes towards the *trifásico* – a mélange of fried whitebait, squid rings and shrimp. Other favourites include the exquisite little *tallarines* (wedge clams), and *botifarra* sausage with beans. For afters, squeeze in four shot glasses of foam – coconut with rum, coffee, *crema catalana* and lemon.

Casa Delfín
Passeig del Born 36 (93 319 50 88). Metro Barceloneta or Jaume I. **Open** 8am-1am daily. **Main courses** €10. **Credit** AmEx, DC, MC, V. **Map** p329 F6 ⑱ **Catalan**

Locals were heartbroken when the old, beloved Casa Delfín served its last plate of fried sardines, but it has scrubbed up very nicely indeed in its new incarnation. Meticulous attention has been paid to respecting traditional Catalan recipes, with a rich and sticky *suquet* (fish stew) and excellent 'mountain' lamb with wild mushrooms. Brit owner Kate has left her imprint, however, and you'll also find the best Eton Mess this side of Windsor.

Comerç 24
C/Comerç 24 (93 319 21 02, www.comerc24. com). Metro Arc de Triomf or Jaume I. **Open** 1.30-3.30pm, 8.30-11pm Tue-Sat. **Main courses** (tapas) €12. **Credit** DC, MC, V. **Map** p328 F4 ⑲ **Catalan**
Carles Abellan trained under Ferran Adrià, and ploughs his own, very successful furrow in this urbane and sexy restaurant. A selection of tiny, playful dishes changes seasonally for the most part, but normally includes the ever popular 'Kinder egg' (lined with truffle) and the tuna sashimi and seaweed on a wafer-thin pizza crust. Adrià's latest discoveries continue to affect Abellan's menu, so recently he's been embracing all things Eastern, with tuna *dashi* soup and so on.
▶ *For details of Tapaç24, Carles Abellan's take on trad tapas, see p181.*

Diez
C/Mercaders 10 (93 310 21 79). Metro Jaume I. **Open** 1.30-4pm Mon-Tue; 1.30-4pm, 8.30pm-12.30am Wed-Sat. Closed 2wks Aug. **Main courses** €13. **Set lunch** €10 Mon-Sat. **Credit** AmEx, MC, V. **Map** p329 D5 ⑳ **Global**

CONSUME

Low ceilings, Gothic arches, subtle lighting and handsome flower arrangements make dining in this former stables a cosy affair. The menu is almost as enticing, with a creative edge that works in a roast fennel and orange salad but can verge on the fussy – as in the *escalivada* (roast veg) with fried filo and a goat's cheese foam. As this guide went to press, we heard a rumour that the place was about to be refurbished, due to reopen under the name 'Arcano' at some point in 2011.

★ € Mosquito

C/Carders 46 (93 268 75 69, www.mosquito tapas.com). Metro Arc de Triomf or Jaume I. **Open** 7pm-1am Mon-Wed; 1pm-1am Thur-Sun. **Main courses** (tapas) €3.30. **Credit** MC, V. **Map** p328 F4 ㉑ **Asian**

Mosquito's latest speciality in the world of Asian tapas is Chinese dumplings in myriad forms. Of the new dishes, the *xiaolong bao* (steamed pork dumplings) and crispy duck are more than toothsome, and regulars will be happy to see that the crunchy potato *chaat* heads up the list. Mosquito also has excellent beers, some of which are brewed especially for the restaurant; the *trigo* (wheat) beer is especially good.

Mundial Bar

Plaça Sant Agustí Vell 1 (93 319 90 56). Metro Arc de Triomf or Jaume I. **Open** 9pm-midnight Tue; 1-4pm, 9pm-midnight Wed-Sat; 1-3.30pm, 8.30pm-11pm Sun. Closed 3wks Aug. **Main courses** €17. **Credit** MC, V. **Map** p328 F4 ㉒ **Seafood**

Since 1925, this venerable family establishment has been dishing up no-frills platters of seafood, cheeseboards and the odd slice of cured meat. Colourful tiles add charm to the rather basic decoration, but it's not as cheap as it looks. People come for the steaming piles of fresh razor clams, shrimp, oysters, fiddler crabs and the like, but there's also plenty of tinned produce, so check the bar displays to see exactly which is which.

★ € La Paradeta

C/Comercial 7 (93 268 19 39, www.laparadeta. com). Metro Arc de Triomf or Jaume I. **Open** 8-11.30pm Tue-Fri; 1-4pm, 8pm-midnight Sat; 1-4pm Sun. **Main courses** €10. **No credit cards. Map** p329 F6 ㉓ **Seafood**

Superb seafood, served in a refectory-style fashion. Choose from glistening mounds of clams, mussels, squid, spider crabs and other fresh treats, decide how you would like it cooked (grilled, steamed or *a la marinera*), pick a sauce (Marie Rose, spicy local *romesco*, *all i oli* or onion), buy a drink and wait for your number to be called. A great – and cheap – experience for anyone who is not too grand to clear away their own plate. **Other locations** Ptge Simó 18, Eixample (93 450 01 91); C/Riego 27, Sants (93 431 90 59).

Patxoca

C/Mercaders 28 (93 319 20 29). Metro Jaume I or Urquinaona. **Open** 9am-1am Mon-Thur; 9am-2am Fri; 12.30pm-2am Sat. **Main courses** €13.20. **Set lunch** €10 Mon-Fri. **Credit** MC, V. **Map** p329 D5 ㉔ **Catalan**

Describing itself as '*agroecològic*', Patxoca endeavours to source produce locally (with the curious omission of most of its wines) and buys organic wherever feasible. The cornerstones of Catalan soul food are all present, from *cap i pota* (stew of calves' head and meat) to salt cod, while homesick Brits can take comfort in a local take on shepherd's pie (*pastis de vedella*) or cauliflower cheese. There are tables outside next to a small playground.

Picnic

C/Comerç 1 (93 511 66 61, www.picnic-restaurant.com). Metro Arc de Triomf or Jaume I. **Open** 12.30pm-5pm, Sun; 12.30pm-5pm, 8.30pm-12.30am Tue-Sat. **Main courses** €6.50 (half-portions). **Set lunch** €7.50 (2 courses), €11.50 (3 courses). **Credit** MC, V. **Map** p328 F4 ㉕ **Chilean/American**

Picnic took over this modest space in 2010 and gave it a rigorous makeover – while the exterior is still rather unlovely, inside it's a welcoming space, with country-kitchen bar stools, dramatic flower arrangements and lounge-y music. The food is influenced by the deep South and beyond, with corn chowder, fried green tomatoes and some tasty little crab cakes with fennel salad and crème fraîche, all served in half-portions. At weekends, there's an excellent brunch: get there early for any chance of a table.

THE RAVAL

Au Port de la Lune

Plaça Sant Galdric s/n (93 270 38 19). Metro Liceu. **Open** 1.30-4pm, 9pm-midnight Mon, Wed-Sat; 1.30-4pm Tue, Sun. **Main courses** €13. **Set lunch** €15 Mon-Sat. **Set dinner** €25 daily. **No credit cards. Map** p328 B4. ㉖ **French**

A tomato's toss from the Boqueria market is this sunny little French bistro, chipped and battered in parts but ultimately charming. The menu, too, is a mix of delightful (oysters, rillettes with endive, cassoulet, clafoutis) and ever-so-slightly shabby (bought-in chocolate mousse in a plastic tub). Still, it's difficult not to feel reassured under a blackboard that reads 'There is no ketchup and no Coke, and there never will be'.

★ Biblioteca

C/Junta de Comerç 28 (93 412 62 21, www.bibliotecarestaurant.com). Metro Liceu. **Open** 8-11.30pm Mon-Sat. Closed 2wks Aug. **Main courses** €13. **Credit** AmEx, MC, V. **Map** p329 A5 ㉗ **Mediterranean**

This tranquil, elegant space features beige, minimalist decor and a striking display of cookbooks. From

Pla dels Àngels. *See p155*.

Bocuse to Bourdain, all the books are for sale, and their various influences collide in the menu. Increasingly, though, it draws from the Catalan culinary canon, with a good *esqueixada* (salt cod salad) or a reasonable onion *coca* (flat, crispy bread) with anchovies to start, followed by gamier mains that might include venison pie or pig's trotters stuffed with prunes.

Dos Trece
C/Carme 40 (93 301 73 06, www.dostrece.net). *Metro Liceu.* **Open** 10am-2am Mon-Thur; 10am-3am Fri-Sun. **Main courses** €12. **Set lunch** €10.50 Mon-Thur; €12 Fri-Sun. **Credit** AmEx, DC, MC, V. **Map** p328 A4 **㉙ Global**
Thanks to a recent easing of the council's draconian measures to cut down live music in the city, Dos Trece's cosy basement space once again jumps to DJs and jam sessions. Earlier in the evening, however, it functions as another dining room – this one with cushions and candles for post-prandial lounging. Apart from a little fusion confusion (ceviche with nachos, and all manner of things served with yucca chips), the food is not half bad for the price, and includes one of the few decent burgers to be enjoyed in Barcelona.

€ Elisabets
C/Elisabets 2-4 (93 317 58 26). Metro Catalunya. **Open** 7.30am-11pm Mon-Thur, Sat; 7.30am-2am Fri. Closed 3wks Aug. **Set lunch** €10.25 Mon-Fri; €10.75 Sat. **Set dinner** €14 Fri. **No credit cards. Map** p328 B3 **㉙ Catalan**
Also open in the mornings for breakfast, and late night for drinking at the bar, Elisabets maintains a sociable local feel, despite the recent gentrification of its street. Dinner, served only on Fridays, is actually a selection of tapas; otherwise, only the set lunch or myriad *bocadillos* are served. The lunch deal is terrific value, however, with osso buco, vegetable and chickpea stew, baked cod with garlic and parsley, and roast pork knuckle all making regular appearances on the menu.

€ Las Fernández
C/Carretes 11 (93 443 20 43). Metro Paral·lel. **Open** 9pm-1am Tue-Sun. Closed 2wks Aug. **Main courses** €11.35. **Credit** DC, MC, V. **Map** p326 E10 **㉚ Spanish**
An inviting entrance, pillar-box red, is a beacon of cheer on one of Barcelona's less salubrious streets. Inside, the three Fernández sisters have created a bright and unpretentious bar/restaurant that specialises in wine and food from their native León. Alongside *cecina* (dried venison), gammon and sausages from the region are lighter, Mediterranean dishes and generous salads; smoked salmon with mustard and dill; pasta filled with wild mushrooms; and sardines with a citrus escabeche. When booking, be warned that there are two separate sittings – 9.15pm and 11.20pm.

€ Juicy Jones
C/Hospital 74 (93 443 90 82). Metro Liceu. **Open** 1pm-5pm, 8pm-midnight daily. **Main courses** €6. **Set lunch** €8.50 daily. **Credit** MC, V. **Map** p326 F10 **㉛ Vegetarian**
Alongside its two menus, one European and one Indian, this colourful vegan restaurant has an inventive list of juices and smoothies, salads and filled baguettes. While its heart is in the right place, it's mostly aimed at backpackers and staffed, it would seem, by somewhat clueless language-exchange students (don't expect a speedy lunch). Bring a book. **Other locations** C/Cardenal Casañas 7, Barri Gòtic (93 302 43 30).

★ Mam i Teca
C/Lluna 4 (93 441 33 35). Metro Sant Antoni. **Open** 1-4pm, 8pm-midnight Mon, Wed-Fri, Sun; 8.30pm-midnight Sat. **Main courses** €11. **No credit cards. Map** p326 E10 **㉜ Catalan**
This bright little tapas restaurant only has four tables, so it pays to reserve in advance. All the usual tapas, from anchovies to cured meats, are rigorously sourced, and complemented by superb daily specials such as organic lamb chops, pork confit and scrambled egg with asparagus and shrimp. Note that the restaurant is closed on Tuesday.

Organic
C/Junta de Comerç 11 (93 301 09 02, www.antoniaorganickitchen.com). Metro Liceu. **Open** 1pm-5pm, 6pm-midnight daily. **Main courses** €11. **Set lunch** €10 Mon-Fri; €12 Sat, Sun. **Set dinner** €15. **Credit** AmEx, DC, MC, V. **Map** p329 A5 **㉝ Vegetarian**
The last word in refectory chic, Organic is better designed and lighter in spirit ('Don't panic, it's organic!') than the majority of the city's vegetarian spots. The friendly staff will usher you inside and give you a rundown on the options: an all-you-can-eat salad bar, a combined salad bar and main course, or the full whammy – salad, soup, main course and dessert. Beware the extras, drinks and so on, which can hitch up the prices considerably.
▶ *There is now a combined takeaway and organic tapas bar at C/Xuclà 15, Raval (93 318 49 30) and a takeaway stand at the back of the Boqueria market (stalls 972, 973, 974).*

€ Pla dels Àngels
C/Ferlandina 23 (93 329 40 47, www.semproniana.net). Metro Universitat. **Open** 1.30-4pm, 9-11.30pm daily. **Main courses** €8. **Set lunch** €6.50-€10 Mon-Fri. **Set dinner** €15 daily. **Credit** DC, MC, V. **Map** p326 F9 **㉞ Mediterranean**
Appropriately, given its position opposite MACBA, Pla dels Àngels is a riot of colour and chimera, something that also translates to its menu. The range of salads on offer might include mango, yoghurt and mint oil, or radicchio, serrano ham and roast

CONSUME

peppers, followed by a short list of pasta and gnocchi and a couple of meat dishes. The cheap set lunch includes two courses and a glass of wine. *Photo p153.*

Ravalo

Plaça Emili Vendrell 1 (93 442 01 00). Metro Sant Antoni. **Open** 1-4pm, 8pm-midnight Tue-Thur; 1-4pm, 8pm-12.30am, Fri, Sat; 8pm-midnight Sun. **Main courses** €9.90. **Set lunch** €9.50 Mon-Fri; €11 Sat. **Credit** MC, V. **Map** p326 E10 ⑤ **Pizza**

Perfect for fans of the thin and the crispy, Ravalo's table-dwarfing pizzas take some beating, thanks to flour (and a chef) imported from Naples. Most of the pizzas come with the cornerstone toppings you'd expect in any pizzeria; less familiar offerings include the Pizza Soufflé, which comes filled with ham, mushrooms and an eggy mousse (better than it sounds). The restaurant's terrace, overlooking a quiet square, is open year-round.
▶ *You can also order a pizza from the adjacent cocktail bar, Invisible, owned by the same people.*

Sésamo

C/Sant Antoni Abat 52 (93 441 64 11). Metro Sant Antoni. **Open** 8pm-midnight Tue-Sun. Closed Aug. **Main courses** €12. **Credit** MC, V. **Map** p326 E10 ⑥ **Vegetarian**

Sésamo's experiment in Argentinian grilled meats was a short-lived one, and now the restaurant is back to what it does best: creative vegetarian dishes (even though you will find a few cold cuts), served in a buzzing atmosphere. Options might include curry with dahl and wild rice, crunchy polenta with baked pumpkin, gorgonzola and radicchio, or a delicious selection of Japanese tapas.

Silenus

C/Àngels 8 (93 302 26 80, www.silenus.es). Metro Liceu. **Open** 1.30-4pm, 8.30-11.30pm Mon-Thur; 1.30-4pm, 8.30pm-midnight Fri, Sat. **Main courses** €14. **Set lunch** €14 Mon-Sat. **Credit** AmEx, DC, MC, V. **Map** p328 A3 ⑦ **Mediterranean**

Named after one of the drunken followers of Dionysus, Silenus is nonetheless all about restraint. Its quiet dining room has an air of scuffed elegance, with carefully chipped and stained walls whereon the ghost of a clock is projected and the faded leaves of a book float up on high. The food, too, is artistically presented. It's not especially cheap, but the set lunch is generally a good bet, offering dishes from Caesar salad to crunchy gnocchi with creamed spinach or spicy *botifarra* with puréed potatoes.

Los Toreros

C/Xuclà 3-5 (93 318 23 25). Metro Catalunya or Liceu. **Open** 6pm-midnight Mon-Wed, Sun; 6pm-1am Thur-Sat. **Main courses** €7.15. **Set dinner** €19.25, €19.90 daily. **No credit cards.** **Map** p326 F10 ⑧ **Spanish**

For many diners this will be the Spanish experience they were after: a warren of yellowing dining rooms, the walls lined with bullfighting posters and memorabilia, including a huge stuffed bull's head, a riotous atmosphere, delightfully friendly waiters, and carafes of cheap and decent house red. Most go for the set meals, which generally comprise old-school starters (melon with ham, *arroz cubano*) followed by grilled meats, but there's also a long list of tapas, paella and some generous salads.

La Verònica

Rambla de Raval 2-4 (93 329 33 03). Metro Liceu. **Open** *Sept-July* noon-5pm, 7pm-midnight Mon-Wed; noon-5pm, 7pm-12.30am Thur; noon-5pm, 7pm-1am Fri; noon-1am Sat; noon-midnight Sun. *Aug* 7pm-12.30am Mon-Thur, Sun; 7pm-1am Fri, Sat. **Main courses** €12. **Set lunch** €10 Mon-Fri. **Credit** MC, V. **Map** 342 E10 ⑨ **Pizza**

La Verònica's shortcomings (huge popularity with young foreigners, minuscule spacing between tables) are all but hidden by night, when candles add a cosy glow to the red, orange and yellow paintwork. Its pizzas are crisp and healthy, and come with such toppings as smoked salmon, or apple, gorgonzola and mozzarella. Salads include the Nabocondensor, a colourful tumble of parsnip, cucumber and apple.

La Xina

C/Pintor Fortuny 3 (93 342 96 28, www.grupotragaluz.com). Metro Catalunya. **Open** 1-11.30pm Mon-Thur, Sun; 1-12.30am Fri-Sat. **Main courses** €17.50. **Set lunch** €15 Mon-Fri. **Credit** AmEx, DC, MC, V. **Map** p328 B3 ⑩ **Chinese**

La Xina's Shanghai chic owes much to Alan Yau's Hakkasan, in London, with its lacquered teak screens, satin and velvet seating and club lighting – nothing less than you'd expect from the team behind the Tragaluz restaurants (*see p162*). Straightforward Chinese food is hard to find in Barcelona, and La Xina does little to buck the trend with its carpaccios and Madras curry. That said, the restaurant serves decent dim sum, and plenty of healthy vegetarian wok dishes and salads.
▶ *Around the corner is Bar Lobo (see p177), run by the same owners and good for a post-dinner drink.*

BARCELONETA & THE PORTS

Agua

Passeig Marítim 30 (93 225 12 72, www.grupotragaluz.com). Metro Barceloneta or bus |45, 57, 59, 157. **Open** 1-3.45pm, 8-11.30pm Mon-Thur, Sun; 1-4.30pm, 8pm-12.30am Fri, Sat. **Main courses** €15. **Credit** AmEx, DC, MC, V. **Map** p327 J13 ⑪ **Mediterranean**

Agua's main draw is its large terrace overlooking the beach, although the relaxed dining room is usually buzzing. The menu rarely changes, regardless of the time of year, but regulars never tire of the competently executed monkfish tail with *sofregit*, the risotto with partridge, and the fresh pasta with juicy prawns. Scrummy puddings include marron glacé mousse and sour apple sorbet. It's advisable to book ahead, especially during the summer months and at weekends.

Bestial

C/Ramón Trias Fargas 2-4 (93 224 04 07, www.grupotragaluz.com). Metro Barceloneta. **Open** 1-3.45pm, 8-11.30pm Mon-Thur, Sun; 1-3.45pm, 8pm-12.30am Fri, Sat. **Main courses** €16.50. **Set lunch** €17 (€5 terrace supplement) Mon-Fri. **Credit** AmEx, DC, MC, V. **Map** p327 K13 **42** **Italian**

A peerless spot for alfresco seaside dining, with tiered wooden decking and ancient olive trees framing a pleasant eating area. Bestial's dining room is also a stylish affair, with black-clad waiters sashaying along sleek runways, their trays held high. The food is of a modern Italian flavour: dainty mini-pizzas, rocket salad with parma ham and a lightly poached egg, tuna with black olive risotto and all the delicious puddings that you could ever hope to find – panna cotta, tiramisu and limoncello sorbet. At weekends, a DJ takes to the decks and drinks are served until 2am.

★ Can Majó

C/Almirall Aixada 23 (93 221 54 55). Metro Barceloneta. **Open** 1-4pm, 8-11.30pm Tue-Sat; 1-4pm Sun. **Main courses** €21. **Credit** AmEx, MC, V. **Map** p327 H13 **43** **Seafood**

Famous for its fresh from-the-nets selection of oysters, scallops, Galician clams, whelks and just about any other mollusc that you might care to mention. Even though the menu reads much as you would expect of a Barceloneta seafood restaurant, with plates of shellfish or (exemplary) fish soup as starters, followed by rich paellas and exquisitely tasty *fideuà*, the quality is a cut above the norm. Sit inside the dapper white and cornflower dining room, or across the road on the terrace, gazing out towards the beautiful view of the sea.

Can Ramonet

C/Maquinista 17 (93 319 30 64, www.can ramonet.com). Metro Barceloneta. **Open** noon-midnight daily. Closed 2wks Jan, 1 wk Christmas. **Main courses** €20. **Set lunch** €27 Mon-Fri. **Credit** DC, MC, V. **Map** p327 H12 **44** **Seafood**

Tucked away in the *barrio* of Barceloneta, this quaint, rose-coloured space with two quiet terraces is mostly overlooked by tourists, and consequently suffers none of the drop in standards of some of the paella joints on the seafront. Spectacular displays of fresh seafood show what's on offer that day, but it's also worth sampling the velvety fish soup and the generous paellas.

Other locations El Nou Ramonet, C/Carbonell 5, Barceloneta (93 268 33 13)

Can Solé

C/Sant Carles 4 (93 221 50 12, www.cansole.cat). Metro Barceloneta. **Open** 1.30-4pm, 8-11pm Tue-Sat; 1.30-4pm Sun. Closed 2wks Aug. **Main courses** €20. **Credit** AmEx, DC, MC, V. **Map** p326 H13 **45** **Seafood**

Portly, jovial waiters have been charming moneyed regulars for more than a hundred years at Can Solé. Over the course of time, many of these diners have added to the framed photos, sketches and paintings that line the sky-blue walls. What continues to lure them is the freshest shellfish (share a plate of *chipirones* in onion and garlic, Cantabrian anchovies or red shrimp to start) and fillets of wild turbot, lobster stews and sticky paellas. Beware the steeply priced extras (coffee, cover).

€ Itztli

C/Sant Miquel 60 (93 225 63 63, www.itztli.es). Metro Barceloneta. **Open** 1-11pm Tue-Sun. **Main courses** €4.50. **Credit** AmEx, MC, V. **Map** p326 H13 **46** **Mexican**

Fortify yourself following an afternoon on the beach with a takeaway chicken burrito from this nearby Mexican snack bar. Keenly priced at around the €4 mark, burritos also come with beef, chilli con carne or veg, as do tacos. Also on offer are quesadillas, wraps, nachos and salads, and there's a good selection of Mexican beers, tinned goods and fiery chilli sauces for sale.

★ Kaiku

Plaça del Mar 1 (93 221 90 82). Metro Barceloneta. **Open** 1-3.30pm Tue-Sun. Closed 3wks Aug & 1wk Dec. **Main courses** €15. **Set lunch** €11 Tue-Fri. **Credit** MC, V. **Map** p326 G13 **47** **Seafood**

With its simple look, missable façade and paper tablecloths, Kaiku looks a world apart from the upmarket seafood restaurants that pepper this *barrio*, but its dishes are sophisticated takes on the seaside classics. At Kaiku, a salad starter comes with shavings of foie gras or red fruit vinaigrette, and paella is given a rich and earthy spin with wild mushrooms. Book ahead, particularly for any chance of reserving one of the terrace tables that looks out across the lovely beach.

Set Portes

Passeig Isabel II 14 (93 319 30 33, www. 7portes.com). Metro Barceloneta. **Open** 1pm-1am daily. **Main courses** €20. **Credit** AmEx, DC, MC, V. **Map** p329 E7 **48** **Seafood**

The eponymous seven doors open on to as many dining salons, all kitted out in elegant 19th-century decor. Long-aproned waiters bring regional dishes, served in vast portions, including a stewy fish *zarzuela* with half a lobster, a different paella daily (shellfish, for example, or rabbit and snails), a wide array of fresh seafood, and heavier dishes such as herbed black-bean stew with pork sausage, and

CONSUME

orujo sorbet to finish. Reservations are available only for certain tables; otherwise, make sure that you get there early for dinner.

El Suquet de l'Almirall
Passeig Joan de Borbó 65 (93 221 62 33, www.suquetdelalmirall.com). Metro Barceloneta. **Open** 1.15-4pm, 8.30-11pm Tue-Sat; 1.15-4pm Sun. Closed 2wks Aug. **Main courses** €22. **Credit** MC, V. **Map** p326 G13 **49** **Seafood**
One of the famous beachfront *xiringuitos* that was moved and refurbished in preparation for the 1992 Olympic Games, El Suquet remains a friendly and family-run concern despite the smart decor and mid-scale business lunchers. The fishy favourites range from *xató* salad to *arròs negre* and include a variety of set menus, such as the 'blind' selection of tapas, a gargantuan taster menu and, most popular of all, the *pica-pica*, which includes roast red peppers with anchovies, a bowl of steamed cockles and clams, and a heap of *fideuà* accompanied by lobster.

MONTJUÏC & POBLE SEC

La Bella Napoli
C/Margarit 12 (93 442 50 56). Metro Paral·lel. **Open** 1.30-4pm, 8.30pm-midnight Tue-Sun. **Main courses** €12. **Credit** DC, MC, V. **Map** p325 D10 **50** **Italian**
La Bella Napoli's welcoming Neapolitan waiters can talk you through the long, long list of antipasti and pasta dishes, and you certainly can't go wrong by opting for one of the crispy baked pizzas. These include the Sofia Loren, complete with provolone, basil, bresaola, cherry tomatoes, rocket and parmesan). The speciality beer is the light and delicious Moretti, the wine list is all-Italian; in fact, the only thing that lacks authenticity is the catalogue of pre-made ice-cream desserts. There is own-made tiramisu, but you have to ask.

La Font del Gat
Passeig Santa Madrona 28 (93 289 04 04). Funicular Parc Montjuïc or bus 50, 55. **Open** 1-4pm Tue-Sun. Closed 3wks Aug, 2wks Christmas. **Main courses** €17.50. **Set lunch** €12.85 Tue-Fri. **Credit** MC, V. **Map** p325 B11 **51** **Catalan**
La Font del Gat is a welcome watering hole located high on Montjuïc, between the Miró and ethnological museums. The small, informal-looking restaurant has a surprisingly sophisticated menu: ravioli with truffles and wild mushrooms, for example, or foie gras with Modena caramel. However, most punters come to this restaurant for the set lunch: try starting with the scrambled egg with Catalan sausage and peppers or a salad, follow it with baked cod or chicken with pine nuts and basil, and finish it with fruit or a simple dessert. To reserve a table outside, a surcharge is payable.
▶ *For more information on the Fundació Joan Miró, see p85.*

Cinc Sentits. *See p161.*

★ Tapioles 53
C/Tapioles 53 (93 329 22 38, www.tapioles 53.com). Metro Paral·lel or Poble Sec. **Open** 9-10.30pm Tue-Sat. Closed Aug. **Set dinner** €38, €58. **Credit** MC, V. **Map** p325 D11 **52** **Mediterranean**
Tucked down a residential Poble Sec street, behind a doorbell and slatted blinds, Tapioles manages to be elegant and homely at the same time, with accomplished but unpretentious food. The menu changes daily, but has included gnocchi with goat's cheese and sage butter; boeuf bourguignon; fresh pasta with baby broad beans and artichokes; rose-water rice pudding with pomegranate, and ginger and mascarpone cheesecake in recent times. The freshest produce is purchased every day and cooked according to demand, so booking ahead is obligatory.

Tatami Room
C/Poeta Cabanyes 22 (93 329 67 40, www. thetatamiroom.net). Metro Paral·lel. **Open** 7pm-1am daily. **Main course** (tapas) €4. **Credit** MC, V. **53** **Japanese**
Opened in December 2010 by a trio of Japanophile Brits, the Tatami Room is based on the concept of izakayas – which nearly equate to the idea of tapas bars, only with more comfortable areas of seating. Downstairs in a cosy basement-bar there are sunken tables and tatami mats to sit on (your footwear stays in a neat space underneath), at which you can chow down on shared plates of grilled yakitori brochettes, sashimi, tempura, noodle and rice dishes.

CONSUME

THE EIXAMPLE

Alkimia

C/Indústria 79 (93 207 61 15). Metro Joanic or Sagrada Família. **Open** 1.30-3.30pm, 8.30-11pm Mon-Fri. Closed 3wks Aug. **Main courses** €33.50. **Credit** DC, MC, V. **Map** p323 J6 **54**
Catalan

Even before Alkimia was awarded its Michelin star it was notoriously tricky to get a table and these days it hasn't got any easier. Chef Jordi Vilà is hugely respected, and turns out complex dishes that play with Spanish classics – for instance, liquid *pa amb tomàquet* with *fuet* sausage, wild rice with crayfish and strips of tuna on a bed of foamed mustard. There is also an enviably stocked wine cellar. What is lacking, however, is a great deal of warmth in either the minimalist dining room or from the occasionally tight-lipped waiting staff.

Casa Calvet

C/Casp 48 (93 412 40 12). Metro Urquinaona. **Open** 1-3.30pm, 8.30-11pm Mon-Sat. Closed 2-3 wks Aug. **Main courses** €28.50. **Set lunch** €40 Mon-Sat. **Credit** AmEx, DC, MC, V. **Map** p328 E1 **55 Catalan**

Casa Calvet allows the time-strapped visitor to sample some excellent cooking and appreciate the

Casa Calvet.

master of Modernisme at the same time. One of Gaudí's more understated buildings from the outside, Casa Calvet has an interior full of glorious detail in the carpentry, stained glass and tiles. The food is up to par, with surprising combinations almost always hitting the mark: sole with pistachio sauce and sautéed aubergine; scallops with black olive tapenade and wild mushroom croquettes; and roast beef with apple sauce and truffled potatoes. The puddings are superb – try the anis-flavoured orange cream with fresh cheese (*crema de naranja al parfume de anís con queso fresco*).

★ Cinc Sentits

C/Aribau 58 (93 323 94 90, www.cincsentits.com). Metro Passeig de Gràcia or Universitat. **Open** 1.30-3pm, 8.30-10.30pm Tue-Sat. Closed 2wks Aug. **Main courses** €22.50. **Set menu** (lunch and dinner) €49, €79. **Set lunch** €32.40 Mon-Fri. **Credit** AmEx, MC, V. **Map** p322 F7 ❺❻ **Catalan**
Talented Canadian-Catalan chef Jordi Artal shows respect for local classics (flat *coca* bread with foie gras and crispy leeks, duck magret with apple), while adding a personal touch in dishes such as a Palamós prawn in *ajoblanco* (garlic soup) with cherries and an ice-cream made from their stones. To finish, save room for the artisanal Catalan cheeses or the 'false egg' with white chocolate around a passionfruit yolk. Cinc Sentits has finally been acknowledged by the Michelin men with a long overdue star, but this is still one of the more affordable of the city's top-end restaurants. *Photo p159.*

Fonda Gaig

C/Còrsega 200 (93 453 20 20, www.fonda gaig.com). Metro Hospital-Clínic. **Open** 1.30-3.30pm, 9-11pm Tue-Sat; 1.30-3.30pm Sun. **Main courses** €20. **Credit** AmEx, DC, MC, V. **Map** p322 E6. ❺❼ **Catalan**
It's currently all the rage for Barna's top chefs to set up more affordable offshoots, and this one is under the guiding hand of Carles Gaig. The Fonda Gaig schtick, like that at Petit Comité (*see p162*), is a return to grandmotherly Catalan basics, and the favourite dish here is the *canelons* – hearty, steaming tubes of pasta filled with shredded beef and topped with a fragrant béchamel. The various dining rooms manage to be both modern and wonderfully comfortable, with red leather armchairs, careful soundproofing and mellow lighting.

Gresca

C/Provença 230 (93 451 61 93, www.gresca.net). Metro Diagonal or FGC Provença. **Open** 1.30-3.30pm, 8.30-10.30pm Mon-Fri; 8.30-10.30pm Sat. Closed 2wks Aug. **Credit** MC, V. **Map** p322 F7 ❺❽ **Modern European**
A potentially great restaurant, let down by a dining room rendered clamorous by a steel floor. The lighting, too, is a bit spotty and unforgiving; still, sympathetic, if harried, service and excellent food go

some way towards smoothing what, with luck, are teething troubles. There is a classy wine list, sensibly organised by style, but the real highlights are dishes such as foamed egg on a bed of jamón ibérico, fennel and courgette, or puddings like the *coca* bread with roquefort and lychee and apple sorbet. This restaurant is one to watch.

★ Manairó

C/Diputació 424 (93 231 00 57, www.manairo. com). Metro Monumental. **Open** 1.30-4pm, 8.30-11pm Mon-Sat. **Main courses** €30. **Set lunch** €35 Mon-Fri. **Credit** AmEx, MC, V. **Map** p323 K8 ❺❾ **Catalan**
If you're curious to try some of the more extreme experiences in postmodern haute cuisine (we're talking tripe and brains rather than the latest flights of fancy from the Blumenthal school), Manairó is the place to start. Its divine tasting menu takes in small portions of Catalan specialities such as *cap i pota* (a stew of calves' head and feet) and langoustine with *botifarra* sausage and cod tripe, and renders them so delicately that even the most squeamish diner will be seduced. Other star turns include a 'false' anchovy – actually a long strip of marinated tuna dotted prettily with pearls of red vermouth.

★ Moo

C/Rosselló 265 (93 445 40 00, www.hotelomm.es). Metro Diagonal. **Open** 1.30-3.45pm, 8.30-10.45pm Mon-Sat. Closed Aug. **Main courses** €20. **Set lunch** €45. **Credit** AmEx, DC, MC, V. **Map** p322 G6 ❻⓪ **Catalan**
The tables at Moo are as desirable as the rooms in its parent, Hotel Omm. The cooking, overseen by the celebrated Roca brothers, is some of the most exciting in the city, presenting classics such as a chocolatey hare royale with as much aplomb as more fanciful numbers such as a gold-plated quail's egg yolk on a bed of puréed, truffled potato. There are various tasting menus, at different prices, and particular wines (from a list of 500) are suggested to go with every course; Moo's sommelier is considered to be one of Spain's best.
▶ *For more on the Hotel Omm, see p131. The Rocas also run a restaurant in Girona.*

Noti

C/Roger de Llúria 35 (93 342 66 73, www. noti-universal.com). Metro Passeig de Gràcia or Urquinaona. **Open** 1.30-3.30pm, 8.30-11.30pm Mon-Fri; 8.30pm-midnight Sat. **Main courses** €25. **Set lunch** €14, €19, €24 Mon-Fri. **Set dinner** €36 Mon-Sat. **Credit** AmEx, DC, MC, V. **Map** p326 G8 ❻❶ **Bistro**
Housed in the former offices of *El Noticiero* newspaper, Noti pulls in a glamorous selection of the great and the good with its globetrotting selection of dishes. Centrally positioned tables surrounded by reflective glass and gold panelling make celebrity-spotting unavoidable, but other excellent reasons

CONSUME

for coming to this restaurant include steak tartare, squid stuffed with pigs' trotters and a good selection of French cheeses.

Petit Comité

Ptge de la Concepció 13 (93 550 06 20, www.petitcomite.cat). Metro Diagonal. **Open** 1pm-4pm, 8pm-midnight daily. **Main courses** €21.50. **Credit** AmEx, DC, MC, V. **Map** p322 G7 **62** Catalan

Said to be the mentor of überchef Ferran Adrià, Fermí Puig has enjoyed years of quiet success with the moneyed classes at Drolma in the Hotel Majestic. This bistro is Puig's attempt to open up to a less élite public, serving more affordable versions of the Catalan classics; *suquet* (fish and potato stew), pig's trotters with spinach and pine nuts, and so on. However, be warned: it's not obvious from the menu that dishes are small and meant to be ordered in a tapas style, so for all the good intentions behind the concept, this is still not an especially cheap option for your evening meal.

★ Routa

C/Enric Granados 10 (93 451 19 97, www.restaurant-routa.com). Metro Passeig de Gràcia or Plaça Universitat. **Open** 7.30-11pm Tue-Sat. **Main courses** €23.50. **Credit** MC, V. **Map** p322 F8 **63** Scandinavian

The young, talented Finnish chefs at Barcelona's first high-level Scando restaurant employ traditional techniques of smoking, salting and pickling to create delicacies such as smoked herring ravioli with ice-cream, or sweetbreads with horseradish jelly and beetroot risotto. Everything about the decor (or lack of it) yells Scandinavian style, from the whitewashed walls and floor to the curtain of cut-out snowflakes dividing the dining room from the bar. For most people, this will be a very tasty journey through the unknown, finishing in more familiar territory with some elaborate petits fours.

★ La Taverna del Clínic

C/Rosselló 155 (93 410 42 21, http://lataverna delclinic.com). Metro Hospital Clínic or Diagonal. **Open** 7.30am-1.30am Mon-Sat. **Main courses** (tapas) €7. **Credit** AmEx, MC, V. **Map** p322 E6 **64** Spanish

La Taverna del Clínic sums up much that is good about the Spanish sense of priorities. The lighting is hideous, the decor is cheap and crappy, the television is permanently on, the walls and floor are tiled in the ugliest terrazzo imaginable, and yet the loving care that goes into the food is the match of many a luxury dining room. The menu concept lies somewhere between tapas and restaurant, so you will probably need to order a stack of dishes to share among friends. Try the creamy morels with foie; a sticky oxtail stew made with Priorat wine; or a tiny skillet of chips, fried egg and crispy *jamón*. The octopus 'igloo' is also superb.

Tintoreria Dontell

C/Aribau 55, Eixample (93 452 07 20, www.tintoreriadontell.com). Metro Universitat. **Open** 1-4pm, 8.30pm-2am daily. **Main courses** €18. **Credit** MC, V. **Map** p322 F7 **65** Mediterranean

See right **Shhh... You Know Where.**

Tragaluz

Ptge de la Concepció 5 (93 487 01 96, www.grupo-tragaluz.com). Metro Diagonal. **Open** Sept-July 1.30-4pm, 8.30pm-midnight daily. *Aug* 1.30-4pm, 8.30pm-midnight Mon-Fri; 8.30pm-midnight Sat. **Main courses** €23. **Set lunch** €20 Mon-Fri. **Credit** AmEx, DC, MC, V. **Map** p322 G7 **66** Mediterranean

The stylish flagship for this extraordinarily successful restaurant group has weathered the city's culinary revolution exceptionally well over recent years, and is still covering fresh ground on the Mediterranean creative scene. Although the food certainly doesn't come cheaply, and the wine mark-up is particularly hard to swallow, there is no faulting the tuna tataki served with a cardamom wafer and a dollop of ratatouille-like pisto; monkfish tail in a sweet tomato *sofregit* with black olive oil; or juicy braised oxtail with cabbage. At the time of writing, the restaurant was closed for renovations, and scheduled to reopen in February 2011.

► *For other restaurants in the Tragaluz group, see Agua (see p156) and Bestial (see p157).*

€ Ty-Bihan

Ptge Lluís Pellicer 13 (93 410 90 02, www.tybihan.com). Metro Hospital Clínic. **Open** 1.30-3.30pm Mon; 1.30-3.30pm, 8.30-11.30pm Tue-Fri; 8.30-11.30pm Sat. Closed 3wks Aug. **Main courses** €7.50. **Set lunch** €11.50 Mon-Fri. **Credit** MC, V. **Map** p322 E6 **67** French

A small restaurant and centre for all things Breton, with live music playing on Wednesday evenings. There is a blend of specialities from across the region, with Spanish produce in starters such as *andouille* sausage and *membrillo* (quince jelly), but from there onwards, it's French cuisine all the way. Gallic specialities include a range of sweet and savoury *galettes* (crêpes made with buckwheat flour), some scrumptious little blinis (try them smothered with strawberry jam and cream) or crêpes suzettes served in a pool of flaming Grand Marnier. The Petite menu will take care of *les enfants*, while a bowl or two of Breton cider will certainly take care of the grown-ups.

★ Windsor

C/Còrsega 286 (93 415 84 83, www.restaurant windsor.com). Metro Diagonal. **Open** 1.30-4pm, 8.30pm-midnight Mon-Fri; 8.30pm-midnight Sat. Closed Aug. **Main courses** €21. **Set lunch** €29.50 Mon-Fri. **Credit** AmEx, DC, MC, V. **Map** p322 F6 **68** Catalan

CONSUME

Shhh… You Know Where

Take a look behind closed doors for the best restaurants in Barcelona.

Anyone who's ever been to Cuba knows that in some countries the best food is served behind closed doors. The vogueish breed of restaurants having a fashion moment in Barcelona right now does not always see a closed door as good enough cover, however, and you might find one behind a shop, a bar or even, say, a drycleaner's.

This last is the case of Tintoreria Dontell (geddit?), a startlingly glitzy eaterie entered by keying in a code to open a door behind racks of freshly laundered jackets. A long corridor lined with white leather sofas and adorned with chandeliers leads to a cavernous and dimly lit dining room with an open kitchen down one side.

It drips with sugar-daddy glamour and the quality of the food, quite honestly, comes

as something of a surprise. Original and brave combinations, such as lamb sweetbreads with langoustines, come in half or full portions, beautifully presented and cooked with aplomb. Including a bottle from a very decently priced wine list, the bill comes to around €40 to €50 a head.

Other clandestine dining rooms around town currently include Speakeasy, which is entered through the kitchen at Dry Martini (*see p181*), and works hard to replicate the elegant jazz vibe of the era of Prohibition, and Mutis, above Bar Mut (*see p180*), where live music and cabaret complement some creative cooking, plated up for the cognoscenti. You heard it here first.

▶ Tintoreria Dontell (*see p162*).

Although it is let down slightly by a smart but drab dining room, and a clientele formed, in great part, by English-speaking business executives, Windsor nevertheless serves some of the most creative and uplifting food around. Most dishes riff on the cornerstones of Catalan cuisine – pigs' trotters stuffed with *cap i pota*, squab risotto and so on – whereas others have a lighter, Mediterranean feel: turbot with orange risotto and citrus powder, or salt cod with stewed tomatoes and olives.

▶ *Dry Martini (see p181) is a few minutes' walk away, and the perfect place for a cocktail before or after dinner.*

GRÀCIA

Botafumeiro

C/Gran de Gràcia 81 (93 218 42 30, www. botafumeiro.es). Metro Fontana. **Open** 1pm-1am daily. **Main courses** €26. **Credit** AmEx, DC, MC, V. **Map** p322 G5 ⑳ **Seafood**

The speciality at this vast Galician restaurant is seafood in every shape and form, served with military precision by a fleet of nautically clad waiters. The sole cooked in cava with prawns is superb, as are more humble dishes such as a cabbage and pork broth typical of the region. The platter of seafood (for two) is an excellent introduction to the various molluscs of the Spanish coastline. It can be hard to get a table at peak times, but the kitchen is open throughout the day.

€ Cantina Machito
C/Torrijos 47 (93 217 34 14). Metro Joanic.
Open 1-4pm, 7pm-1.30am daily. **Main courses** €11. **Credit** MC, V. **Map** p323 H5 **⓻** **Mexican**
The red and blue colour scheme, tissue paper bunting and chaotic hubbub make this a little slice of old Mexico. The minuscule writing on the menu and low lighting make for some guesswork when placing your order (the covered patio at the back is brighter), but the choices are standard enough – quesadillas, tacos, ceviche and enchiladas – with a couple of surprises, such as the tasting platter of insects. The *'aguas'* are refreshing on summer nights – iced water with lime and honey; pineapple and mint, and other fruit. Service can be slow and the kitchen a little heavy-handed with the sauces, but the portions are huge and prices reasonable.

Envalira
Plaça del Sol 13 (93 218 58 13). Metro Fontana.
Open 1.30-4pm, 9pm-midnight Tue-Sat; 1.30-5pm Sun. Closed Aug, 1wk Christmas, 1wk Easter.
Main courses €12. **Credit** MC, V. **Map** p322 G5 **⓺** **Spanish**
Most regions of Spain are represented at this deeply traditional restaurant. There is a particular emphasis on Galicia (*caldeirada gallega* is a hearty fish stew, *lacón con grelos* is gammon with turnip tops and *tarta de Santiago* is an almond cake), but the Basque oxtail stew is also a tasty dish. The dining room could use a lick of paint and some subtlety in its lighting; arrive early for the more comfortable leather banquettes at the front of the restaurant, and book ahead at weekends.
▶ *If the puddings on offer don't tempt you, stroll down to the excellent Gelateria Caffeteria Italiana (see p183).*

★ € Himali
C/Milà i Fontanals 68 (93 285 15 68). Metro Joanic. **Open** 1-4.30pm, 8pm-midnight Tue-Sun.
Main courses €9.50. **Set lunch** €9.90 Tue-Fri.
Credit AmEx, MC, V. **Map** p323 H6 **⓻**
Nepalese
A comic metaphor for modern-day Barcelona, Himali moved into what was a local boozer, but has retained the silhouettes of famous Catalans – Dalí and Montserrat Caballé among them – on the windows; inside, meanwhile, there are Nepalese prayer flags and tourist posters of the Himalayas. The alien and impenetrable menu looks a little daunting at first glance, but the waiters are helpful with their recommendations. Alternatively, you could start your meal with *momo* dumplings or Nepalese soup, followed by *mugliaco kukhura* (barbecued butter chicken in creamy tomato sauce) or *khasi masala*

tarkari (baked spicy lamb). All dishes include rice and nan bread as accompaniments.

Mesopotamia
C/Verdi 65 (93 237 15 63). Metro Fontana.
Open 8.30-10.45pm Tue-Thur; 8.30-11.30pm Fri-Sat. Closed 2wks Sept, 2wks Dec. **Main courses** €13.20 **Set dinner** €30 Tue-Sat.
No credit cards. Map p323 H4 **⓻** **Iraqi**
The policy at Barcelona's only Iraqi restaurant is to have everything on the menu at the same price, so that the cost won't hold anybody back from ordering what they want. The menu is based on Arab 'staff of life' foods, such as yoghurt and rice. Best value is the enormous taster menu, which includes great Lebanese wines, a variety of dips for your *riqaq* bread, bulgur wheat with aromatic roast meats and vegetables, sticky baklava and Arabic teas. Also good are the potato croquettes stuffed with minced meat, almonds and dried fruit.

€ Octubre
C/Julián Romea 18 (93 218 25 18). Metro Diagonal/FGC Gràcia. **Open** 1.30-3.30pm, 9-11pm Mon-Fri; 9-11pm Sat. Closed Aug, 1wk Easter.
Main courses €10.75. **Credit** MC, V. **Map** p322 F5 **⓻** **Catalan**
Time stands still in this quiet little spot, with its quaint old-fashioned decor, swathes of lace and brown table linen. Time often stands still, in fact, between placing an order and receiving any food, but this is all part of Octubre's sleepy charm. Also contributing to its appeal is a roll-call of reasonably priced, mainly Catalan dishes: squid stuffed with meatballs on a bed of *samfaina (see p149)*; pig's trotter with fried cabbage and potato, and cod with a nut crust and pumpkin purée.

San Kil
C/Legalitat 22 (93 284 41 79). Metro Joanic.
Open 1-3pm, 8.30pm-midnight Mon-Sat. Closed 2wks Aug. **Main courses** €12. **Credit** DC, MC, V. **Map** p323 J4 **⓻** **Korean**
If you've never eaten Korean food before, it would probably pay to gen up before you head to this jolly but no-frills restaurant. *Panch'an* (on the house) is served first: four dishes containing vegetable appetisers, one of which will be tangy *kimch'i* (fermented cabbage with chilli). Or you could try the *empanadas* (fried dumplings, strictly speaking Chinese, but tasty). Then try *pulgogi* (beef served sizzling at the table and eaten rolled into lettuce leaves) and maybe the mouth-watering seafood omelette. Finish up with a shot of soju rice wine for the full experience.

★ Shojiro
C/Ros de Olano 11 (93 415 65 48). Metro Fontana. **Open** 1.30-3.15pm, 9-11.30pm Tue-Sat.
Closed Aug & 1wk Easter. **Set lunch** €18.50 (all incl) Tue-Fri. **Set dinner** €35 (food only).
Credit MC, V. **Map** p322 G5 **⓻** **Japanese**

Cantina Machito.

Lunch Crunched

How to find the best wallet-friendly pit stops in town.

One of Franco's better ideas was to introduce the *menú del día,* a cheap, fixed-price menu that would provide sustenance to the workers and increase productivity by ensuring that they weren't required to travel home for lunch. In Franco's day, it was (inevitably) obligatory, but the tradition lives on and all but the high-end restaurants normally provide one.

The *menú* (*menú* is not to be confused with the menu, which is *la carta*) usually costs around €10, and includes a starter, a main course, pudding, bread and either water, wine or beer. While it can be a bargain, it should not be considered a tasting menu (more upmarket places might also offer a *menú degustación*) or a showcase for the chef's greatest hits. In standard places the starter might be a mixed salad (the iceberg, tomato, grated carrot and tinned tuna mix is omnipresent) or soup, with unadorned meat as a main (you might get potatoes) and a typically custardy dessert – often *flan* (like crème caramel) or *crema catalana* (more like crème brulée.

Many places will show a bit more creativity, though you may have to shell out an extra euro or two. Some of the best

include Cafè de l'Acadèmia (*see p143*); Mercè Vins (*see p147*); El Atril (*see p148*); Big Fish (*see p148*); Kaiku (*see p157*); and Hisop (*see p167*).

A curious but surprisingly successful mix of Catalan and Japanese applies to the decor as much as the food at Shojiro, with mosaic flooring and dark-green paintwork setting off a clean feng-shuied look. It only serves set meals (water, wine, coffee and tax are included in lunch). So, after an amuse-bouche, there may be foie steamed with *umeshu* (plum wine), mackerel cooked with miso and white aubergine, followed by venison with wild mushrooms and black basil. Two puddings are included in the price.

La Singular

C/Francisco Giner 50 (93 237 50 98). Metro Diagonal or Fontana. **Open** 1.30-4pm, 9pm-midnight Mon-Thur; 1.30-4pm, 9pm-1am Fri; 9pm-1am Sat. Closed last wk Aug & 1st wk Sept. **Main courses** €12.90. **Set lunch** €10 Mon-Fri. **Credit** MC, V. **Map** p322 G6 ⑦ **Mediterranean**
While this is often described as a lesbian-friendly restaurant, in fact that's the least noteworthy thing about it, and all are made welcome. Most come here for the good-value set lunch (salads and light pasta dishes to start, followed by dishes such as roast beef carpaccio with red cabbage and onion) in snug surroundings of red walls with pale green woodwork

and a tiny, leafy patio. It can get noisy when full, so it's best to come early and beat the rush. Reservations are necessary for a table on Friday and Saturday nights.

OTHER DISTRICTS

Can Travi Nou

C/Jorge Manrique s/n, Parc de la Vall de Hebron, Horta (93 428 03 01, www.gruptravi.com). Metro Horta or Montbau. **Open** 1.30-4pm, 8.30-11pm Mon-Sat; 1.30-4pm Sun. **Main courses** €22. **Credit** AmEx, DC, MC, V. **Catalan**
An ancient rambling farmhouse clad in bougainvillea, perched high above the city, Can Travi Nou offers wonderfully rustic dining rooms with roaring log fires in the winter, whereas in the summer the action moves out to a covered terrace in a bosky, candlelit garden. The food is hearty, traditional Catalan cuisine, even though it's a little expensive for what it is, and suffers from the sheer volume being churned out of the kitchen. Puddings are better and served with a *porrón* (a glass jug with a drinking spout) of muscatel. But CTN is really all about location, location, location.

Hisop

Passatge Marimon 9, Sant Gervasi (93 241 32 33, www.hisop.com). Metro Diagonal or Hospital Clínic. **Open** 1.30-3.30pm, 8.30-11pm Mon-Fri; 9-11pm Sat. Closed 3wks Aug. **Main courses** €22.75. **Set lunch** €26.75 Mon-Fri. **Set dinner** €26.75 Mon-Thur. **Credit** AmEx, DC, MC, V. **Map** p322 E5 ⑳ **Mediterranean**

Run by two young, enthusiastic and talented chefs, Hisop aims to bring serious dining to the non-expense-account masses by keeping its prices low and its service approachable – here's hoping its shiny new Michelin star doesn't change all that. The €52 tasting menu is a popular choice among diners; dishes vary according to the season, but often include their rich 'monkfish royale' (which is served with its liver, a cocoa-based sauce and tiny pearls of saffron) and a pistachio soufflé with Kaffir lime ice-cream and rocket 'soup'.

Icho

C/Deu i Mata 69-95, Les Corts (93 444 33 70, www.ichobcnjapones.com). Metro Maria Cristina. **Open** 1.30-3.30pm Mon; 1.30-4pm, 9-11.30pm Tue-Sat. Closed Aug. **Main courses** €20. **Set lunch** €33 Mon-Fri. **Credit** AmEx, MC, V. **Map** p321 C5 ⑳ **Japanese/Spanish**

In a coolly designed space under the NH Constanza, Icho (in Japanese it means gingko tree, of which three graceful examples sit outside) fuses Japanese with Spanish cooking. This really shouldn't work, but somehow does, beautifully – perhaps because you can offset the digestive demands of tender suckling pig and pumpkin pureé with a platter of sushi, or balance a starter of foie and eel with tuna tartare and creamed tofu with wasabi.

La Parra

C/Joanot Martorell 3, Sants (93 332 51 34). Metro Hostafrancs. **Open** 8.30pm-12.30am Tue Fri; 1.30 4.30pm, 8.30pm-12.30am Sat; 1.30-4.30pm Sun. Closed Aug. **Main courses** €16. **Credit** MC, V. **Map** p325 B7 ⑳ **Catalan**

A charming converted 19th-century coaching inn with a shady, vine-covered terrace. The open wood grill sizzles with various parts of goat, pig, rabbit and cow, as well as a few more off-piste items such as deer and even foal. Huge, oozing steaks are slapped on to wooden boards and accompanied by baked potatoes, calçots (large spring onions), grilled vegetables and *allioli*, with jugs of local wines from the giant barrels.

★ Els Pescadors

Plaça Prim 1, Poblenou (93 225 20 18, www.elspescadors.com). Metro Poblenou. **Open** 1-3.45pm, 8pm-11.30pm daily. **Main courses** €25. **Credit** MC, V. **Seafood**

In a forgotten, almost rustic square of Poblenou lies this first-rate fish restaurant, with tables under the canopy formed by two huge and ancient *ombú* trees.

Suspend your disbelief with the crunchy sardine skeletons that arrive as an aperitif (trust us, they are delicious), and move on to tasty fried chipirones, followed by cod and pepper paella or creamy rice accompanied by prawns and smoked cheese. Creative desserts include the likes of strawberry gelatine 'spaghetti' in a citric soup. The waiters are masters of their art.

★ El Petit Bangkok

C/Saragossa 87, Sant Gervasi (mobile 616 185 196). Metro Lesseps/FGC Plaça Molina. **Open** 7.30pm-midnight Tue-Thur; 1-3.30pm, 8pm-12.30am Fri-Sat. **Main courses** €8.50. **Credit** MC, V. **Map** p322 F3 ⑳ **Thai**

Unlike most Thai restaurants in Barcelona, with their trickling fountains, garlanded Buddhas and leafy settings, Petit Bangkok is cramped, bright, bare and a pain to get to. Unlike most Thai restaurants in Barcelona, however, Petit Bangkok serves really excellent food – authentic, hot and fantastically cheap dishes, ranging from an aromatic tom yam soup to spicy duck rolls. Because of this, reservations are usually essential.

La Venta

Plaça Doctor Andreu, Tibidabo (93 212 64 55, www.restaurantelaventa.com). FGC Avda Tibidabo, then Tramvia Blau or bus 179. **Open** 1.30-3.15pm, 9-11.30pm daily. **Main courses** €18. **Credit** AmEx, DC, MC, V. **Mediterranean**

La Venta's pretty Moorish-influenced interior plays second fiddle to the terrace during every season: shaded by day and uncovered by night in summer, sealed and warmed with a wood-burning stove in winter. Of the food, complex starters include lentil and spider crab salad; sea urchins au gratin (a must); and langoustine ravioli, filled with leek and foie mousse. Simpler but high-quality mains run from rack of lamb to delicate monkfish in filo pastry with pesto. Friendly service is a bonus.

OUT OF TOWN

★ El Bulli

Cala Montjoi (972 15 04 57, www.elbulli.com). **Open** Mid June to Christmas only. Hours vary weekly, see website for details. Closed Jan-mid June. **Set dinner** €230. **Credit** AmEx, DC, MC, V.

Darling of the Sunday newspapers, El Bulli is possibly the most talked-about restaurant in the world today; therefore it merits a mention here, despite its location up on the Costa Brava. There is only a *degustación*, and diners must arrive by 8.30pm if they are to finish the 30 or so courses by midnight. Eating dinner is an extraordinary experience, occasionally exalted and frequently frustrating: diners are cossetted like guinea pigs, their reactions are scanned by the maître d' and the great Ferran Adrià himself. The restaurant is set to close in 2012, so reserve your space now.

Cafés, Tapas & Bars

Pintxos, strong coffee and liberal measures keep the city buzzing.

From the sheer number of bars in Barcelona (the highest per capita of anywhere in the world), it would be easy to infer that Catalans were heavy drinkers. In fact, the opposite is true. The bars, which run the gamut from fiercely lit, zinc-countered old men's social clubs to ersatz Maghrebi lounges with sofas and hookahs, exist to facilitate conversation and social interaction, not drunkenness and fighting. Mind you, that means that alcohol is a constant accompaniment throughout the day starting, perhaps, with a thoughtful shot of anís with a morning coffee and

ending with *la penúltima*, the final drink of the night with friends (*última* is never uttered, and to do so would be bad luck), with all manner of snifters in between.

WHAT TO ORDER

If you ask for a *caña*, you'll be given a small draught beer; a *jarra* is closer to a pint. Ask for a *cerveza*, and you'll be given a bottle. The local Damm beer is ubiquitous: Estrella, a strong lager, is the most popular variety; stronger yet is Voll Damm; and the dark version is Bock Damm. Moritz beer, also local and with a fruitier, more natural flavour, has made a comeback. Shandy (*clara*) is also popular.

Among wines, Rioja is well known, but there are many excellent wines from other regions in the north of Spain, such as the Priorat in Catalonia, Navarra or Ribera del Duero. Most wine drunk here is red (*negre/tinto*), but Galicia produces good whites too, including a slightly sparkling and very refreshing wine called *vino turbio*. Of course, Catalonia has its many cavas, running from *semi-sec* (which is 'half-dry', but actually pretty sweet) to *brut nature* (very dry).

Spanish coffee is very strong and generally excellent. There are three basic types: *café solo* (*cafè sol* in Catalan, also known simply as '*café*'), a small black coffee equivalent to an espresso; *cortado/tallat*, the same but with a little milk; and *café con leche/cafè amb llet*, the

same with more milk. Cappuccino has yet to catch on. Then there's *café americano* (a tall black coffee diluted with more water) and spiked coffee (a *carajillo*, which is a short, black coffee with a liberal dash of brandy). If you want another type of liqueur, you must be specific: *carajillo de ron* (rum), say, or *carajillo de whisky*. A *trifásico* is a *carajillo* with a layer of milk. Decaffeinated coffee (*descafeinado*) is widely available and usually very good, but ask for it *de máquina* (from the machine) unless you want a sachet of Nescafé and a cup of milk.

Tea, on the other hand, is pretty poor. If you can't live without it, ask for cold milk on the side ('*leche fría aparte*') or run the risk of getting a glass of hot milk and a teabag. Basic herbal teas, such as chamomile (*manzanilla*), limeflower (*tila*) and mint (*menta*), are common.

Except in busy bars or when sitting outside you won't usually be required to pay until you leave. To get a waiter's attention, a loud but polite '*oiga*' or, in Catalan, '*escolti*' is acceptable.

THE BARRI GÒTIC
Cafés

Ácoma
C/Boqueria 21 (93 301 75 97, www.acomacafe. com). Metro Liceu. **Open** 9am-midnight daily. **Credit** AmEx, MC, V. **Map** p345 B5 ❶
A regular enough looking bar from the street, Ácoma is almost unique in the Old City for its sheltered patio at the back. Here there are tables in the

---

❶ Green numbers given in this chapter correspond to the location of each café, bar and tapas bar on the street maps. *See pp321-329.*

---

shade of an orange tree and the rear of the Santa Maria del Pi church, and a small pond from which bemused fish and turtles can observe singer-songwriters and small groups perform for a young and merry foreign crowd. Salads, burgers, burritos and the like are served from midday to 11.30pm.

★ Café de l'Opera

La Rambla 74 (93 317 75 85, www.cafeopera bcn.com). Metro Liceu. **Open** 8am-2.30am Mon-Fri, Sun; 8am-3am Sat. **Credit** (over €20) MC, V. **Map** p345 B5 **②**

Cast-iron pillars, etched mirrors and bucolic murals create an air of fading grandeur at Café de l'Opera, which now seems incongruous among the fast-food joints and tawdry souvenir shops on La Rambla. Coffee, hot chocolate, pastries and a handful of tapas are served by attentive bow-tied waiters to a largely tourist clientele, but given the atmosphere (and the opposition), there's no better place for a coffee on the city's most celebrated boulevard.

Čaj Chai

C/Sant Domènec del Call 12 (93 301 95 92). Metro Jaume I. **Open** 3-10pm Mon; 10.30am-10.30pm Tue-Sun. **Credit** MC, V. **Map** p345 C5 **③**

A cosy tearoom, where first-flush Darjeeling is approached with the reverence afforded to a Château d'Yquem. A range of leaves comes with tasting notes describing not only the origins, but giving suggestions for maximum enjoyment – Waternymph (an aromatic Oolong), for example, is apparently the ideal tea for those moments 'when your thoughts have been interrupted'. In summer, iced teas are accompanied by a dollop of sorbet.

La Clandestina

Baixada Viladecols 2 (93 319 05 33). Metro Jaume I. **Open** 10am-10pm Mon-Thur; 10am-midnight Fri, Sat; 11am-10pm Sun. **No credit cards. Map** p345 D6 **④**

What used to be a slightly hippie tearoom in which dreadlocked students would sip masala chai and lassi while reminiscing about their trip to Rajasthan is now a slightly hippie tearoom where young professionals take advantage of free Wi-Fi and ponder the decent art (all for sale). It's still a very relaxed vibe, however, especially when friends are sharing a hookah of apple, peach or strawberry tobacco.

La Granja

C/Banys Nous 4 (93 302 69 75). Metro Liceu. **Open** *May-July, Sept* 9.30am-1.30pm, 5-9.30pm Mon-Sat. *Oct-Apr* 9.30am-1.30pm, 5-9.30pm Mon-Sat; 5-9pm Sun. Closed Aug. **No credit cards. Map** p345 C5 **⑤**

La Granja is an old-fashioned café filled with yellowing photos and antiques, which has its very own section of Roman wall. You can stand your spoon in the tarry-thick hot chocolate, which won't

be to all tastes, but the *xocolata amb café*, a mocha espresso, or the *xocolata picant*, chocolate with chilli, pack a mid-afternoon energy punch.

★ Milk

C/Gignas 21 (93 268 09 22, www.milkbarcelona. com). Metro Jaume I. **Open** 6pm-3am Mon-Wed; 10am-3pm Thur-Sun. **Credit** AmEx, MC, V. **Map** p345 D7 **⑥**

Still unchallenged in the Old City in its provision of a decent brunch, Milk's fry-ups, pancakes and smoothies are now available from Thursday to Sunday. Its candlelit, low-key baroque look, charming service and cheap prices make it a good bet at any time, with solid, home-made bistro grub ranging from Caesar salad to fish and chips.

► *Milk's owners also run Marmalade, a flash bar in the Raval (C/Riera Alta 4-6, 93 442 39 66).*

Els Quatre Gats

C/Montsió 3 bis (93 302 41 40, www.4gats.com). Metro Catalunya. **Open** 10am-2.30am Mon-Wed; 10am-3am Thur-Sat; noon-midnight Sun. **Credit** MC, V. **Map** p344 C3 **⑦**

The essence of fin-de-siècle Barcelona, the 'Four Cats' was designed by Modernista heavyweight Puig i Cadafalch and patronised by the cultural glitterati of the era – most notably Picasso, who hung out here with Modernista painters Santiago Rusiñol and Ramon Casas. These days it's mostly frequented by tourists, but an essential stop nonetheless.

Schilling

C/Ferran 23 (93 317 67 87, www.cafe schilling.com). Metro Liceu. **Open** 11am-2am Mon-Thur; 10am-2.30am Fri, Sat; noon-midnight Sun. **Credit** AmEx, DC, MC, V. **Map** p345 B5 **⑧**

Schilling's large windows on to the main thoroughfare connecting La Rambla with the Plaça Sant Jaume were once *the* spot to see and be seen. Although it's lost some of its cachet, it's still undeniably elegant, the high ceilings, bookshelves and traditional air contrasting with the fiercely modern young waiting staff. Weave through to the back for more intimate seating.

Tapas

★ Bar Celta

C/Mercè 16 (93 315 00 06). Metro Drassanes. **Open** noon-midnight Tue-Sun. **Credit** AmEx, MC, V. **Map** p345 C7 **⑨**

Celta's unapologetically '60s interior is fiercely lit, noisy and not recommended for anyone feeling a bit rough. It is, however, one of the more authentic experiences to be had in the Gòtic. A Galician tapas bar, it specialises in food from the region, such as *lacón con grelos* (boiled gammon with turnip tops) and good seafood, accompanied by crisp Albariño wine served in traditional white ceramic bowls.

CONSUME

El Portalón

★ Bar Pinotxo

La Boqueria 466-467, La Rambla 89 (mobile 647 869 821). Metro Liceu. **Open** 6am-4pm Mon-Sat. **No credit cards. Map** p344 B4 ⑩

Just inside the entrance of the Boqueria, on the right-hand side, is this essential market bar. It's run by Juanito, one of the city's best-loved figures. In the early morning the place is popular with ravenous night owls on their way home and, at lunchtime, foodies in the know. Various tapas are available, along with excellent daily specials such as tuna casserole or scrambled eggs with clams.

▶ *La Boqueria is one of Europe's best food markets; see p198 and p199.*

Cervecería Taller de Tapas

C/Comtal 28 (93 481 62 33, www.tallerde tapas.com). Metro Catalunya. **Open** 9am-2am Mon-Sat; 10am-midnight Sun. **Credit** AmEx, MC, V. **Map** p344 D3 ⑪

Although strictly speaking a tapas bar, with a wide range and a useful menu in English, the Cervecería has tried to fill a gap in the market by providing a reasonable selection of beers from around the world. The list provides a refreshing alternative to the ubiquitous Estrella, with Argentine Quilmes, Brazilian Brahma (this one, admittedly, via Luton), Bass Pale Ale, Leffe and Hoegaarden, among others.

Onofre

C/Magdalenes 19 (93 317 69 37, www.onofre.net). Metro Urquinaona. **Open** 10am-5pm, 7.30pm-midnight Mon-Sat. Closed Aug. **Credit** MC, V. **Map** p344 D3 ⑫

It's tiny and not especially well known, but Onofre has a following for impeccably sourced wines, cured

meats, pâtés, hams and artisanal cheeses from around the country. It provides more elaborate dishes, too, such as a scallop gratin with caramelised onion, or a pear tatin with melted goat's cheese and *sobrassada* sausage.

El Portalón

C/Banys Nous 20 (93 302 11 87). Metro Liceu. **Open** 8.45am-11.30pm Mon-Sat. Closed Aug. **Credit** MC, V. **Map** p345 C5 ⑬

A rare pocket of authenticity in the touristy Barri Gòtic neighbourhood, this traditional tapas bar is located in what were once medieval stables, and the place seems to have inherited the ancient dust. The tapas list is long, however, and the *torrades* are good: toasted bread topped with juicy red peppers and anchovies, cheese, ham… or whatever takes your fancy. The house wine comes in terracotta jugs.

Taller de Tapas

Plaça Sant Josep Oriol 9 (93 301 80 20, www.tallerdetapas.com). Metro Liceu. **Open** noon-midnight Mon-Thur, Sun; noon-1am Fri, Sat. **Credit** AmEx, MC, V. **Map** p345 B5 ⑭

At its best, Taller de Tapas is an easy, multilingual environment, with plentiful outdoor seating and a good selection of tapas, from heavenly razor clams to local wild mushrooms. At busy periods, however, the service can be a little hurried and unhelpful, with dishes prepared in haste and orders confused, so it pays to avoid the lunchtime and evening rush hours.

Other locations C/Argenteria 51, Born (93 268 85 59).

★ La Vinateria del Call
C/Sant Domènec del Call 9 (93 302 60 92).
Metro Jaume I or Liceu. **Open** 8pm-midnight
daily. **Credit** MC, V. **Map** p345 C5

An atmospheric little bar, with a real commitment
to the sourcing of its wine, hams and cheeses, and
excellent home-made dishes, including a delicious
fig ice-cream. Despite the antique fittings and dusty
bottles, the staff are – like the music they play –
young and lively; some speak English.

Bars

★ Ginger
C/Palma de Sant Just 1 (93 310 53 09,
www.ginger.cat). Metro Jaume I. **Open** 7pm-
2.30am Tue-Thur; 7pm-3am Fri, Sat. Closed
3wks Aug. **Credit** MC, V. **Map** p345 D6

Ginger manages to be all things to all punters: a
swish art deco cocktail bar with comfortable butter-
cup yellow banquettes; purveyor of fine tapas and
excellent wines; and, above all, a superbly relaxed
place to chat and listen to music. Admittedly the for-
eigner quotient has risen in recent years, but it would
be short-sighted to dismiss this little gem of
Barcelona nightlife for that.

Ice-cream

Gelaaati!
C/Llibreteria 7 (93 310 50 45). Metro Jaume I.
Open 9.30am-midnight daily. Closed mid Jan-mid
Feb. **No credit cards. Map** p345 D5

The ice-cream at Gelaaati! is made on the premises
each day, using natural ingredients – no colourings,
no preservatives. Especially good are the hazelnut,

pistachio and raspberry flavour ice-creams; more
unusual varieties include the healthy-sounding
soya bean, celery and avocado.

THE BORN & SANT PERE
Cafés

Bar del Convent
Plaça de l'Acadèmia (93 256 50 17, www.
bardelconvent.com). Metro Arc de Triomf or
Jaume I. **Open** 10am-10pm Mon-Thur; 10am-
11pm Fri; 1pm 11pm Sat. **No credit cards.**
Map p345 F5

The 14th-century Convent de Sant Agustí has had
a new lease of life in recent years with James
Turrell's fabulous 'light sculpture' surrounding
the C/Comerç entrance, and a dynamic civic
centre. This secluded little café is in the cloister.
Croissants, pastries and light dishes are available
all day, and bands, DJs, storytellers and other
performers appear on occasional Friday or
Saturday nights.

La Báscula
C/Flassaders 30 (93 319 98 66). Metro Jaume I.
Open 1pm-11.30pm Wed-Sun. **No credit cards.**
Map p345 E6

After a sustained campaign, the threat of demolition
has been lifted from this former chocolate factory
turned café. Just as well, since it's a real find, with
good vegetarian food and a large dining room out
back. An impressive list of drinks runs from chai to
Glühwein, taking in cocktails, milkshakes, smoothies and iced tea, and the pasta and cakes are as good
as you'll find anywhere.

Bags packed, milk cancelled, house raised on stilts.

You've packed the suntan lotion, the snorkel set, the stay-pressed shirts. Just one more thing left to do – your bit for climate change. In some of the world's poorest countries, changing weather patterns are destroying lives.

You can help people to deal with the extreme effects of climate change. Raising houses in flood-prone regions is just one life-saving solution.

**Climate change costs lives.
Give £5 and let's sort it *Here & Now***

www.oxfam.org.uk/climate-change

Oxfam is a registered charity in
England and Wales (No.202918)
and Scotland (SCO039042). Oxfam GB
is a member of Oxfam International.

Be Humankind ☹ Oxfam

Drac Café

*Parc de la Ciutadella, Passeig Lluís Companys
entrance (93 310 76 06, www.draccafe.com).
Metro Arc de Triomf.* **Open** *Mar-Nov* 9am-9pm
Tue-Sun. **No credit cards. Map** p343 H10 ⓴
With this alfresco terrace café, the Parc de la
Ciutadella has a healthy alternative to the *kioskos*
serving overpriced beer and bags of rainbow pop-
corn. Not much more than a *kiosko* itself, the friendly
'Dragon Café' serves breakfast all day, along with
salads, nachos, guacamole and houmous, served
tapas-style. To guard against the perils of outdoor
eating, the tables are warmed by gas heaters in winter and cooled with 'vaporisers' in summer.

★ En Petit Comité

*C/Lluís el Piadós 2 (93 269 13 35, www.
enpetitcomite.es). Metro Arc de Triomf.*
Open 10am-midnight Tue-Thur; 10am-2.30am
Fri, Sat; noon-midnight Sun. **Credit** MC, V.
Map p344 F3 ㉑
The peaceful Plaça Sant Pere has never been well
served with good places to eat or drink, so this
relaxed, sunny and spacious new café has been joy-
fully received in the neighbourhood. French cheeses
and charcuterie are the mainstays of the kitchen,
served for the most part on toasted bread with a
well-dressed salad.

Tapas

Bar del Pla

C/Montcada 2 (93 268 30 03). Metro Jaume I.
Open noon-11pm Tue-Thur, Sun; noon-midnight
Fri, Sat. **Credit** MC, V. **Map** p345 E5 ㉒
Positioned somewhere between a French bistro and
a tapas bar, the Bar del Pla serves tapas or *raciones*
(divine pig's trotters with foie, outstanding *pa amb
tomàquet*). Drinks include Mahou on tap (a fine beer,
often ignored here because it's from Madrid), plus
some good wines by the glass.
Other locations Pla, C/Bellafila 5, Barri Gòtic (93
412 65 52).

El Bitxo

*C/Verdaguer i Callís 9 (93 268 17 08). Metro
Urquinaona.* **Open** 1pm-1am Tue-Thur; 1pm-2am
Fri, Sat; 7.30pm-1am Sun. **No credit cards.**
Map p344 D3 ㉓
This small, lively tapas bar specialises in excellent
cheese and charcuterie from the small Catalan village of Oix, along with more outré fare such as
salmon sashimi with a coffee reduction. The wine
list is steadily increasing and now has around 30
suggestions, all of them good. Being so close to the
Palau de la Música, the bar can get packed in the
early evening before concerts.

★ Euskal Etxea

*Placeta Montcada 1-3 (93 310 21 85,
http://euskaletxeak.org). Metro Barceloneta or*

Jaume I. **Open** *Bar* 10am-12.30am Mon-Fri,
Sun; 10am-1.30am Sat. *Restaurant* 1-4pm,
8pm-midnight daily. **Credit** AmEx, MC, V.
Map p345 E6 ㉔
A Basque cultural centre and the best of the
city's many *pintxo* bars. Help yourself to dainty
jamón serrano croissants, chicken tempura with
saffron mayonnaise, melted provolone with mango
and crispy ham, or a mini-brochette of pork. Hang
on to the toothpicks spearing each one: they'll
be counted up and charged for at the end. In addition to the tapas bar, there is also a dining room
at the back.

Bars

Casa Paco

*C/Allada-Vermell 10 (93 295 51 18). Metro
Arc de Triomf or Jaume I.* **Open** *May-Oct*
9.30am-2am Mon-Thur; 9.30am-3am Fri; 1pm-
3am Sat. *Nov-Apr* 6pm-2am Tue-Thur; 6pm-
3am Fri, Sat. **No credit cards.**
Map p345 F5 ㉕
Not much more than a hole-in-the-wall with a handful of zinc tables outside, Casa Paco is the improbable nerve centre for a young and thrusting scene that
attracts DJs from the higher echelons of cool. In the
daytime, mind you, it's simply a nice place for parents to sit on the terrace and have a cheeky beer in
the sunshine while their children amuse themselves
in the playground in front.

GMT

*C/Rec 24 (93 310 10 27). Metro Barceloneta
or Jaume I.* **Open** 10pm-3am daily. **No credit
cards. Map** p345 F6 ㉖
On quiet nights, this discreet little wood-panelled
cocktail bar, its long mahogany counter burnished
by the same well-clad elbows for years, has something of an Edward Hopper feel. Friday and
Saturday nights are an altogether different proposition, however, and you'll need to make yourself
noticed to get a drink from the unsmiling bar staff.
It's been snappily renamed as GMT but it's still better known as Gimlet.

Mudanzas

*C/Vidrieria 15 (93 319 11 37). Metro Barceloneta
or Jaume I.* **Open** 10am-3am daily. **Credit** AmEx,
MC, V. **Map** p345 E6 ㉗

CONSUME

INSIDE TRACK
BETTER IN THAN OUT

Most bars and cafés charge a supplement for terrace tables. Some also operate a three-tier system, depending on whether you're sitting down, standing at the bar, or outside.

Eternally popular with all ages and nationalities, Mudanzas has a beguiling, old-fashioned look, with marble-topped tables, a black-and-white chequered floor and a rack of newspapers and magazines, many of them in English. Its main drawback used to be that it got very smoky in the winter months, which of course is a thing of the past with the new legislation.

La Vinya del Senyor

Plaça Santa Maria 5 (93 310 33 79). Metro Barceloneta or Jaume I. **Open** noon-1am Mon-Thur; noon-2am Fri, Sat; noon-midnight Sun. **Credit** (over €10) AmEx, MC, V. **Map** p345 E7 ㉘

Though many pull up a chair simply to appreciate the splendours of Santa Maria del Mar's Gothic façade, it's a case to take up the tables of the 'Vineyard of the Lord' without sampling a few of the excellent vintages on its list, along with some top-quality cheeses, hams and other tapas.

El Xampanyet

C/Montcada 22 (93 319 70 03). Metro Jaume I. **Open** noon-3.30pm, 7-11pm Tue-Sat; noon-3.30pm Sun. Closed 2wks Aug. **Credit** MC, V. **Map** p345 E6 ㉙

The eponymous bubbly is actually a pretty low-grade cava, if truth be told, but a drinkable enough accompaniment to the house tapa; a saucer of Cantabrian anchovies. Lined with beautiful coloured tiles, barrels and antique curios, the bar chiefly functions as a little slice of Barcelona history, and has been in the hands of the same family since the 1930s.

Takeaway

★ Bacoa

C/Colomines 2 (93 268 95 48). Metro Jaume I. **Open** 1-11pm Tue-Thur; 1pm-midnight Fri, Sat. **No credit cards.** **Map** p345 E5 ㉚

This gourmet burger bar opened in 2010 and set off a wave of similar places, none of which is quite as good. Succulent char-grilled half-pounders are loaded up with Manchego cheese, caramelised onions and a whole load of more outré toppings (try the Swiss, with rösti and gruyère, or the Japanese with teriyaki sauce).

THE RAVAL
Cafés

Bar Kasparo

Plaça Vicenç Martorell 4 (93 302 20 72). Metro Catalunya. **Open** 9am-10pm Tue-Sat. Closed mid Dec-mid Jan. **No credit cards.** **Map** p344 B2 ㉛

Still the best of the various café terraces around the edges of the quiet, traffic-free Plaça Vicenç Martorell, Kasparo serves tapas, *bocadillos*, salads and a varying selection of more substantial dishes, available all day. There is no indoor seating, so this is more of a warm weather proposition.

Bar Mendizábal

C/Junta de Comerç 2 (no phone). Metro Liceu. **Open** 8.30am-midnight daily. **No credit cards.** **Map** p344 A4 ㉜

Considered something of a classic, Bar Mendizábal has been around for decades, its multicoloured tiles and serving hatch a feature in thousands of holiday snaps. Strictly speaking it's little more than a hole in the wall, whence juices, sandwiches and soup are ordered, and carried across to a terrace on the other side of the road. Hours may vary according to the weather.

Buenas Migas

Plaça Bonsuccés 6 (93 318 37 08). Metro Liceu. **Open** 8am-midnight daily. **Credit** AmEx, MC, V. **Map** p344 B3 ㉝

A doggedly wholesome place, all red gingham and pine and chewy spinach tart. The speciality is tasty focaccia with various toppings, along with the usual high-fibre, low-fun cakes you expect to find in a vegetarian café. Its terrace sprawls across the wide pavement and continues across the street.

Other locations Baixada de Santa Clara 2, off Plaça del Rei, Barri Gòtic (93 319 13 80); Plaça del Mar, Barceloneta (93 221 63 16).

★ Granja M Viader

C/Xuclà 4-6 (93 318 34 86, www.granja viader.cat). Metro Liceu. **Open** 5-8.30pm Mon; 9am-1.30pm, 5-8.30pm Tue-Sat. Closed 1wk Aug. **Credit** AmEx, MC, V. **Map** p344 B3 ㉞

The chocolate milk drink Cacaolat was invented in this old *granja* in 1931, and it's still on offer, along with strawberry and banana milkshakes, *orxata* (tiger nut milk) and hot chocolate. It's an evocative, charming place with century-old fittings and enamel adverts, but the waiters refuse to be hurried.

El Jardí

C/Hospital 56 (93 329 15 50, www.eljardi barcelona.es). Metro Liceu. **Open** 9am-11pm Mon-Sat. **Credit** (over €10) AmEx, MC, V. **Map** p344 A4 ㉟

The courtyard of the Gothic Antic Hospital is a tranquil, tree-lined spot a million miles from the hustle of C/Hospital. Terrace café El Jardi has two separate bars – go to the lesser-known one, further from the entrance, for more chance of a table. Breakfast pastries and all the usual tapas are present and correct, along with pasta dishes, quiches and salads.

Olivia

C/Pintor Fortuny 22 (93 318 63 80). Metro Catalunya. **Open** *Oct-May* 9am-9pm daily. *June-Sept* 9am-9pm Mon-Sat. **No credit cards.** **Map** p344 A3 ㊱
The love of a good home-made carrot cake knows no international boundaries, and Olivia sees a good

mix of races (not to mention ages and sexualities). Its other universally admired facets include hot ciabatta sandwiches (try avocado, brie and sun-dried tomato); great breakasts; Illy coffee; fruit smoothies; and Miles Davis on the stereo.

Tapas

Resolis

C/Riera Baixa 22 (93 441 29 48). Metro Liceu. **Open** 5pm-1am daily. **Credit** MC, V. **Map** p342 E10 ㊲
A favourite with traders from along the C/Riera Baixa, Resolis blends a trad look and run-of-the-mill tapas (tortilla, Manchego cheese, prawns)

Pick up a Pintxo

Pintxos reign over tapas in Barcelona.

The custom of giving a free tapa, or just a saucer of crisps or olives, is almost unheard of in Catalonia, and hopping from bar to bar is not as popular as it is in other regions. What has caught on big-time in Barcelona, though, are *pintxo* bars. A *pintxo* consists of some ingenious culinary combination on a small slice of bread: platters of them are generally brought out at particular times, often around 1pm and again at 8pm. *Pintxos* come impaled with toothpicks, which you keep on your plate, so that the barman can tally them at the end. The Brits and other tourists hold the worst reputation for abusing this eminently civilised system by 'forgetting' to hand over all their toothpicks.

Without a decent grasp of the language, tapas bars can be quite intimidating unless you know exactly what you want. Some of the more standard offerings include *tortilla* (potato omelette), *patatas bravas* (fried potatoes in a spicy sauce), *ensaladilla ruso* (Russian salad), *champiñones al ajillo* (mushrooms fried in garlic), *pinchos morunos* (small pork skewers), *gambas al ajillo* (prawns and garlic), *mejillones a la marinera* (mussels in a tomato and onion sauce), *chocos* (squid fried in batter), *almejas al vapor* (steamed clams with garlic and parsley), *pulpo* (octopus) and *pimientos del padrón* (little green peppers, one or two of which will kick like a mule).

CONSUME

WHEREVER CRIMES AGAINST HUMANITY ARE PERPETRATED.

Across borders and above politics.
Against the most heinous abuses
and the most dangerous oppressors.
From conduct in wartime
to economic, social, and cultural rights.
Everywhere we go,
we build an unimpeachable case
for change and advocate action
at the highest levels.

HUMAN RIGHTS WATCH TYRANNY HAS A WITNESS

WWW.HRW.ORG

HUMA
RIGHT
WATC

with an immaculate selection of vinyl and some fanciful foodstuffs (salmon ceviche). In the summer months, its serving hatch to the alley alongside is thronged.

Els Tres Tombs
Ronda Sant Antoni 2 (93 443 41 11). Metro Sant Antoni. **Open** 6am-2.30am Mon-Thur, Sun; 6am-3am Fri, Sat. **Credit** AmEx, MC, V. **Map** p342 E10 ⓷⓷

Not, perhaps, the most inspired tapas bar in town, with its overcooked *patatas bravas*, sweaty Manchego and vile loos, but Els Tres Tombs is still a long-time favourite for its pavement terrace and proximity to the Sunday morning book market. The *tres tombs* in question are nothing more ghoulish than the 'three turns' of the area performed by a procession of men on horseback during the Festa dels Tres Tombs in January.

Bars

Bar Lobo
C/Pintor Fortuny 3 (93 481 53 46, www.grupo tragaluz.com). Metro Catalunya. **Open** 9am-midnight daily. **Credit** AmEx, MC, V. **Map** p344 B3 ⓷⓽

The watchword is moody (not least among the waiting staff) in this stark, monochrome space, with punky artwork from celebrated graffiti artists. It comes alive with DJs and studied lounging at night, however, and by day its terrace is a peaceful space for coffee or breakfast, given the proximity to La Rambla. Recent changes have brought about more of a focus on food, and lunchtimes can get packed.

★ Boadas
C/Tallers 1 (93 318 95 92). Metro Catalunya. **Open** noon-2am Mon-Thur; noon 3am Fri, Sat. **No credit cards. Map** p344 B3 ⓸⓪

Set up in 1933 by Miguel Boadas, born to Catalan parents in Havana (where he became the first barman at the legendary La Floridita), this classic cocktail bar has changed little since Hemingway used to come here. In a move to deter the hordes of rubbernecking tourists, it has instituted a dress code.

Cafè de les Delicies
Rambla del Raval 47 (93 441 57 14). Metro Liceu. **Open** 8am-11pm Mon-Wed; 8am-1am Thur; 8am-3am Fri, Sat; 11am-1am Sun. Closed 2wks mid Aug. **No credit cards. Map** p342 E10 ⓸⓵

After an overhaul in the kitchen, the delightful Cafè de les Delicies is now serving breakfast, along with tapas and light dishes, in its dining room at the back. Off the corridor there's a snug with armchairs, but otherwise the buzzing front bar is the place to be, with its theatre-set mezzanine, '70s jukebox, shelves of books and reams of club flyers.

★ Las Guindas
C/Sant Pau 126 (mobile 670 437 709). Metro Paral·lel. **Open** 7pm-2.30am Mon-Thur, Sun; 7pm-3am Fri, Sat. **No credit cards. Map** p342 E11 ⓸⓶

Las Guindas is a long narrow bar with a crimson-hued retro look, a deeply funky mural and DJs fighting for turntable space to show off their vinyl acquisitions from the '50s to the '70s. Monday night is rockabilly night, but the rest of the week you're as likely to hear northern soul or boogaloo. For all this, Las Guindas is refreshingly attitude free. There are plans to start opening all day Sunday for brunch.

London Bar
C/Nou de la Rambla 34 (93 318 52 61). Metro Liceu. **Open** 2pm-3am Mon-Thur; 2pm-3.30am Fri, Sat. **Credit** AmEx, MC, V. **Map** p345 A6 ⓸⓷

Since it had its live music licence revoked, this classic old bar has had to rely on its pool table or the odd football match to entertain its patrons. The TV screen is hidden at the back, however, and easily avoided; there is much else to feast your eyes on, from the period posters to the graceful swirls of the nicotine-stained turn-of-the-century woodwork.

★ Marsella
C/Sant Pau 65 (93 442 72 63). Metro Liceu. **Open** 10pm-2.30am Mon-Thur; 10pm-3am Fri, Sat. **No credit cards. Map** p342 E11 ⓸⓸

This place was opened in 1820 by a native of Marseilles – who may just have changed the course of Barcelona's artistic history by introducing absinthe, still a mainstay of the bar's delights. Untapped 100-year old bottles of the stuff sit in glass cabinets alongside old mirrors and William Morris curtains, probably covered in the same dust kicked up by Picasso and Gaudi.

★ Quiet Man
C/Marqués de Barberà 11 (93 412 12 19). Metro Liceu. **Open** 6pm-2am Mon-Thur; 1pm-3am Fri-Sun. **Credit** AmEx, MC, V. **Map** p345 A6 ⓸⓹

One of the first and best of the city's many Oirish pubs, the Quiet Man is a peaceful place with wooden floors and stalls, which mostly eschews the beautiful game for occasional poetry readings and pool tournaments. There is Guinness (properly poured) and Murphy's, and you're just as likely to see Catalans as homesick expats or tourists.

BARCELONETA & THE PORTS

Cafés

1881
Plaça Pau Vila 3 (93 221 00 50, www. gruposagardi.com). Metro Barceloneta. **Open** 9.30am-midnight Mon-Thur, Sun; 9.30am-1am Fri, Sat. **Credit** AmEx, MC, V. **Map** p345 E8 ⓸⓺

CONSUME

There's no need to buy a ticket to the Museu d'Història de Catalunya to make the most of this little-known rooftop museum café with fabulous views. The set lunches don't break any ground gastronomically speaking, but are reasonable enough; or you can take coffee and a croissant to the vast terrace and watch the boats bobbing in the harbour.

Filferro

C/Sant Carles 29 (93 221 98 36). Metro Barceloneta. **Open** 10am-1am Tue-Thur, Sun; 10am-2am Fri, Sat. **No credit cards. Map** p343 E7 ⓐ

Simply but edgily decorated with cascades of red 1950s lampshades and rusted iron balustrades, this Italian-owned café is a restful, sunny spot for breakfast, lunch or tapas, with tables outside on a quiet square. As well as a decent range of fresh fruit juices (try the Trifàsic, with carrot, pear and lemon), there are pastries, toasted sandwiches, pasta and salads. ▶ *Alongside Filferro's terrace tables is a playground to keep the little ones happy.*

Tapas

Can Ganassa

Plaça de la Barceloneta 6 (93 221 75 86. www.canganassa.com). Metro Barceloneta. **Open** 9am-mid Tue-Sun. **Credit** (over €6) MC, V. **Map** p343 H13 ⓐ

It's chaotic, it's noisy, it's full of gruff old men competing to be heard above the fruit machines – it's great. And besides, there are tables outside. Good tapas are nearly all on display, so you don't need to worry about flexing your Catalan, just point. Try the 'bomba Ganassa'; a huge potato and bacon croquette served with allioli and a fiery chilli sauce.

★ La Cova Fumada

C/Baluard 56 (93 221 40 61). Metro Barceloneta. **Open** 9am-3.15pm Mon-Wed; 9am-3.15pm, 6-8.15pm Thur, Fri; 9am-1.15pm Sat. Closed Aug. **No credit cards. Map** p343 H13 ⓐ

An authentic family-run *bodega*, hugely popular with local workers, where you'll need to arrive early for a cramped and possibly shared table. Said to be the birthplace of the spicy potato *bomba*, La Cova Fumada also turns out a great tomato and onion salad, delicious chickpeas with *morcilla* (black pudding) and unbeatable marinated sardines.

El Vaso de Oro

C/Balboa 6 (93 319 30 98). Metro Barceloneta. **Open** noon-11.45pm daily. Closed Sept. **No credit cards. Map** p343 H12 ⓐ

The enormous popularity of this long, narrow cruise ship style bar tells you everything you need to know about the tapas, but it also means that he who hesitates is lost when it comes to ordering. Elbow out a space and demand, loudly, *chorizitos, patatas bravas, solomillo* (cubed steak) or *atún* (tuna, which here

comes spicy). The beer (its storage, handling and pouring) is also a point of great pride.

Bars

The loud, tacky bars lining the Port Olímpic draw a mixture of drunken stag parties staring at the go-go girls and curious locals staring at the drunken stag parties.

★ Can Paixano

C/Reina Cristina 7 (93 310 08 39, www.can paixano.com). Metro Barceloneta. **Open** 9am-10.30pm Mon-Sat. Closed 3wks Aug-Sept. **No credit cards. Map** p345 E8 ⓐ

The 'Champagne Bar', as it's invariably known, has a huge following among young Catalans and the legion foreigners who think they discovered it first. It can be impossible to talk, get your order heard or move your elbows, yet it's always mobbed for its age-old look and atmosphere, dirt-cheap bottles of house cava and (literally) obligatory sausage butties.

MONTJUÏC & POBLE SEC

Cafés

Bar Seco

Passeig Montjuïc 74 (93 329 63 74). Metro Paral·lel. **Open** 9am-8pm Mon-Wed; 9am-1am Thur; 10am-1.30am Fri, Sat; 10am-midnight Sun. Closed 2wks Aug. **No credit cards. Map** p341 D11 ⓐ

The 'Dry Bar' is, in fact, anything but, and its ethically friendly choices range from local beers and organic wines to fair-trade Brazilian *cachaça*. It opened a few years ago, and despite a quiet location rapidly gathered a following for the quality of its Italian-Spanish vegetarian dishes and tapas, its fresh milkshakes and a heavenly home-made chocolate and almond cake. Those who run it are keen advocates of the Slow Food Movement.

Tapas

★ Quimet i Quimet

C/Poeta Cabanyes 25 (93 442 31 42). Metro Paral·lel. **Open** noon-4pm, 7-10.30pm Mon-Fri; noon-4pm Sat. Closed Aug. **Credit** MC, V. **Map** p341 D11 ⓐ

Packed to the rafters with dusty bottles of wine, this classic but minuscule bar makes up for in tapas what it lacks in space. The specialities are *conservas* (shellfish preserved in tins), which aren't always to non-Spanish tastes, but the *montaditos*, sculpted tapas served on bread, are spectacular. Try salmon sashimi with cream cheese, honey and soy, or cod, passata and black olive pâté. Get there early for any chance of a surface on which to put your drink.

Tickets

Avda Paral·lel 164 (93 292 42 50, www.tickets bar.es). Metro Poble Sec. **Open** visit website for details. **Map** p341 C9 ⑭
Superchef Ferran Adrià's new tapas venture hadn't quite opened as this guide went to press, but is set to be the next big thing and thus worth inclusion here. A large space, it will house a dining room where avant-garde tapas will be served, and, alongside, a small bar (named 41°) for cocktails and fancy bar snacks.

Bars

★ La Caseta del Migdia

Mirador del Migdia, Passeig del Migdia (mobile 617 956 572). Bus 55 or funicular, then 10min walk. Follow signs to Mirador de Montjuïc. **Open** *June-Sept* 8pm-1am Wed-Fri; noon-2am Sat; noon-1am Sun. *Oct-May* noon-sunset Sat, Sun. **No credit cards**. **Map** p341 A12 ⑮
Completely alfresco, high up in a clearing among the pines, this is a magical space, scattered with deckchairs, hammocks and candlelit tables. Rather surreally, DJs spinning funk, rare groove and lounge alternate with a faltering string quartet; food is grilled sausages and salad, plus a few rice dishes. To find it, cut through the Brossa gardens from the funicular and follow the Camí del Mar footpath south around the castle. Be aware it's a lot cooler up here than in town.

THE EIXAMPLE

Cafés

Bauma

C/Roger de Llúria 124 (93 207 54 31). Metro Diagonal. **Open** 8.30am-midnight Mon-Fri, Sun. **Credit** AmEx, DC, MC, V. **Map** p338 G6 ⑯
An old-style café-bar that's good for lazy Sunday mornings, with its battered leather seats, ceiling fans and shady tables outside, although staff can sometimes be less than friendly. There's a decent list of *bocadillos* and tapas, along with well-priced, substantial dishes such as baked cod and wild boar stew served from the adjoining restaurant.

Café del Centre

C/Girona 69 (93 488 11 01). Metro Girona. **Open** 8am-11pm Mon-Fri; 5pm-midnight Sat. Closed 2wks Aug. **Credit** MC, V. **Map** p343 H8 ⑰
The oldest in the Eixample, and possibly the only one of its type left in the city, with a delightfully dusty air, Modernista wooden banquettes, walls stained with the nicotine of ages and marble tables sitting on a chipped chequered floor that almost certainly dates back to the bar's opening in 1873. The Café del Centre is still in the hands of the same fam-

Can Paixano.

Bar Mut.

ily, whose youngest members' attempts to instigate change don't seem to have progressed much beyond a list of fruit teas.

Dolso

C/València 227 (mobile 679 140 730). Metro Passeig de Gràcia. **Open** 9am-9pm Mon; 9am-11pm Tue-Thur; 9am-1am Fri, Sat. **Credit** AmEx, MC, V. **Map** p338 F7 ⑱

Heaven on earth for the sweet of tooth, Dolso is a 'pudding café', where even the fabulously on-trend retro baroque wallpaper is chocolate-coloured. Desserts run from light (a gin and tonic rendered in clear jelly, lemon sorbet, candied peel and juniper berries) to wickedly indulgent (chocolate fondant with sherry reduction and passion fruit sorbet). A short range of sandwiches and topped ciabatta keeps the spoilsports happy.

★ Federal

C/Parlament 39 (93 187 36 07, www.federal cafe.es). Metro Sant Antoni. **Open** 8am-10pm Tue-Thur; 8am-1am Fri, Sat; 9am-5.30pm Sun. Closed 1wk Easter, 2wks Christmas, 1wk Aug. **Credit** AmEx, MC, V. **Map** p342 D10 ⑲

Australian-run Federal exudes a breezy oceanside chic not often seen in Sant Antoni – a barrio of old-timers and market-goers. Spacious, open to the street and crowned with a pretty little roof garden, it offers own-made cupcakes, excellent brunch (try the skillet of eggs, pancetta, caramelised onion and crème fraîche) and copies of the *New Yorker* to leaf through.

Velódromo

C/Muntaner 213 (93 430 60 22). Metro Hospital Clínic. **Open** 6am-3am daily. **Credit** AmEx, MC, V. **Map** p338 E6 ⑳

For most of the 20th century this was a favoured meeting place of the Catalan intelligentsia, underground political groups and the 1960s artistic group known as La Gauche Divine. It lay fallow during the noughties, but its elegant art deco interior was dusted off and gussied up thanks to a collaboration between chef Carles Abellan (*see p151* Comerç 24) and Moritz beer. There's a long list of tapas and larger dishes, along with excellent coffee and bathrooms that pay technicolour homage to Paul Smith.

Tapas

Bar Mut

C/Pau Claris 192 (93 217 43 38). Metro Diagonal. **Open** noon-11pm Tue, Wed; noon-midnight Thur-Sat; noon-4pm Sun. **Credit** AmEx, MC, V. **Map** p338 G6 ㉛

Bar Mut has an ineffably Gallic feel, with its etched glass, bronze fittings, *chanteuses* on the sound system, and (whisper it) Paris prices. The tapas are undeniably superior, however, running from a carpaccio of sea urchin to fried eggs with foie. Other sophisticated food for the soul to look out for includes haricot beans with wild mushrooms and *morcilla* or poached egg with chips and chorizo sauce. In a word? *Formidable.*

▶ *The same owner also operates Bar del Pla (see p173), which brings a similar idea to the Old City, albeit a more down-to-earth version.*

La Bodegueta

Rambla de Catalunya 100 (93 215 48 94). Metro Diagonal. **Open** 7am-1.30am Mon-Sat; 6pm-1am Sun. **Credit** MC, V. **Map** p338 G7 ㉜

This delightful old *bodega*, with a pretty tiled floor, is dusty and welcoming, supplying students, businessmen and pretty much everyone in between with reasonably priced wine, vermouth on tap and prime-quality tapas. The emphasis is placed on locally sourced products (try Montserrat tomatoes with tuna), among old favourites such as *patatas bravas*. Expect smoking and shouting aplenty.

Cervesería Catalana

C/Mallorca 236 (93 216 03 68). Metro Passeig de Gràcia. **Open** 8am-1.30am Mon-Fri daily. **Credit** AmEx, MC, V. **Map** p338 F7 ⓺

The 'Catalan Beerhouse' lives up to its name with a winning selection of brews from around the world, but the real reason to come is the tapas. A vast array is yours for the pointing; only hot *montaditos*, such as bacon, cheese and dates, have to be ordered from the kitchen. Arrive early for a seat at the bar, and even earlier for a pavement table.

★ Tapaç24

C/Diputació 269 (93 488 09 77, www. carlesabellan.com). Metro Passeig de Gràcia. **Open** 9am-midnight Mon-Sat. **Credit** MC, V. **Map** p342 G8 ⓺

Another nu-trad tapas bar focusing on excellent quality produce. Among the oxtail stews, fried prawns and cod croquettes, however, fans of chef Carles Abellan will also find playful snacks more in keeping with his signature style. The McFoie Burger is an exercise in fast-food heaven, as is the Bikini, a small version of his take on the ham and cheese toastie, his comes with truffle.

► *To sample Abellan's cooking in more formal surroundings, visit Comerç 24; see p151.*

Bars

★ Dry Martini

C/Aribau 162-166 (93 217 50 72). FGC Provença. **Open** 1pm-2.30am Mon-Fri; 6.30pm-2.30am Sat. **Credit** AmEx, MC, V. **Map** p338 F6 ⓺

A shrine to the famous cocktail, which is honoured in Martini-related artwork and served in a hundred forms. All the trappings of a traditional cocktail bar are here (bow-tied staff, leather banquettes, antiques and wooden cabinets displaying a century's worth of bottles) but there's a notable lack of stuffiness, and the musical selection owes more to trip hop than middle-aged crowd-pleasers.

Xix Bar

C/Rocafort 19 (93 423 43 14, www.xixbar.com). Metro Poble Sec. **Open** 5pm-2.30am Mon-Thur; 5pm-3am Fri; 5pm-3am Sat. **Credit** MC, V. **Map** p341 D9 ⓺

Xix (pronounced 'chicks', and a play on the street number, among other things) is a newish, unconventional cocktail bar in the candlelit surroundings of a prettily tiled former *granja* (milk bar). It's exceedingly cosy and just a little bit scruffy, which makes the list of 20 brands of gin all the more unexpected.

Ice-cream

Cremeria Toscana

C/Muntaner 161 (93 539 38 25). Metro Hospital Clínic or FGC Provença. **Open** *Apr-Oct* 1pm-midnight Tue-Sun. *Nov-Mar* 1pm-9pm Tue-Sun. **No credit cards.** **Map** p338 E6 ⓺

In this charming little ice-cream parlour, with its antique-strewn mezzanine, around 20 authentically Italian flavours are made daily, ranging from zingy mandarin to impossibly creamy coconut. '*I dopocena*' ('after dinner') are miniature gourmet sundaes, mixing – among others – parmesan and pear flavours; mascarpone and tiramisu; chocolate and pistachio, or liquorice and mint.

Other locations C/Canvis Vells 2, Born (93 268 07 29).

GRÀCIA

Cafés

A Casa Portuguesa

C/Verdi 58 (93 368 35 28, www.acasa portuguesa.com). Metro Fontana. **Open** 5pm-midnight Tue-Fri; 11am-3pm, 5pm-midnight Sat, Sun. **Credit** AmEx, MC, V. **Map** p339 H5 ⓺

Fado provides the soundtrack at this mellow, tile-floored café-cum-deli, which is dedicated to all things nice from Portugal. Sit down with a coffee and a freshly made pastéis de Belém (little custard tarts with a dusting of cinnamon), or linger over a glass

Cervesería Catalana.

CONSUME

CONSUME

Pop Go the '80s

The decade that style forgot was actually a time of real creativity in Barcelona.

The pre-Olympic years were heady ones in Barcelona. The city was quivering with the prospect of hosting the 1992 Games, Irish pubs and sports bars had yet to appear, and simply being 'foreign' guaranteed you entrance into the VIP section of the city's swankiest clubs. It was also a time of immense creativity, and while architects, town planners and engineers occupied themselves with ringroads and levelling the Raval, designers focused their attentions on installing their artistic visions inside bars. The 'design bar' was born.

Often featuring stainless-steel seating, fibre optics and transparent loos, the design bar was devised to put the 'wow' into watering hole. The mother of them all was (and perhaps still is) the **Torres de Ávila** at the Poble Espanyol. Designed by Alfredo Arribas and Javier Mariscal (who would become a world-famous designer), the Torre was a barrage of PoMo excess, set over various pot-holed levels. Wire sculptures and shattered glass tables jutted from the walls, and the dancefloor was a mezzanine that hung precariously from the upper level.

Another favourite was **Nick Havanna** (C/Rosselló 208, mobile 625 149 339), designed by Eduardo Samsó. Here clients sat on rusted-metal saddle stools at the cow-skin covered bar, watched MTV on a wall lined in TV screens and danced under an enormous swinging pendulum. It still exists in somewhat subdued form, as does **KGB** (*see p249*), which broke new ground with its industrial chic in the '80s. Others included Zsa Zsa, which had mesmerising

light-pulsating walls; at Seltz every inch was covered in backlit variations of the Martini brand's typography.

The following years, or the decade of minimalism, were not kind to the design bar. In 1992, renowned art critic Robert Hughes wrote that the Torre de Ávila's 'sheer awfulness may entitle it to preservation'. He was only partly right: it's still there – albeit without some of its more outré elements. Other design bars have disappeared completely, and become fallen angels to the tyranny of design itself.

of wine and some nibbles. In the deli section, you can choose from a great selection of wines, preserves, pâtés, jams and cheeses. Check the website for wine tastings and other special events.

▶ *The same owners are opening a wine shop and delicatessen nearby at C/Oro 8 in early 2011.*

Flash Flash

C/Granada del Penedès 25 (93 237 09 90). FGC Gràcia. **Open** 11pm-1.30am daily. **Credit** AmEx, DC, MC, V. **Map** p338 F5 ⑥⑨

Opened back in 1970, this bar was a design sensation in its day, with its white leatherette banquettes and walls imprinted with silhouettes of a life-size, frolicking, Twiggy-like model. The owners

describe it as a *tortilleria*, with 60 or so tortilla variations available, alongside a list of child-friendly dishes and adult-friendly cocktails.

La Nena

C/Ramón y Cajal 36 (93 285 14 76). Metro Fontana or Joanic. **Open** 9am-2pm, 4-10pm Mon-Wed; 10am-10.30pm Thur-Sun. Closed Aug. **No credit cards. Map** p339 H5 ⑦⓪

With whitewashed stone walls, piles of books and games, and a gaily painted table-and-chair set for children, La Nena is wonderfully cosy – or would be if the staff would only lighten up. The speciality is sugar and spice and all things nice; waffles, crêpes, hot chocolate, fresh juices and ice-cream. Savoury delights include sandwiches and toasted bread with various toppings. Note there is no alcohol and that, rather infuriatingly, it's closed at lunchtime.

Tapas

★ Sureny
Plaça de la Revolució 17 (93 213 75 56).
Metro Fontana or Joanic. **Open** *Sept-June* 1-
3.30pm Mon; 1-3.30pm, 8pm-midnight Tue-Thur;
1-4pm, 8.30pm-1am Fri; 8.30pm-1am Sat; 8pm-
midnight Sun. *July, Aug* 8pm-midnight Tue-
Thur; 8.30pm-1am Fri, Sat; 8pm-midnight Sun.
Closed 2wks Christmas. **Credit** MC, V.
Map p339 H5 ⑦
A well-kept gastronomic secret, Sureny boasts
superb gourmet tapas and waiters who know what
they're about. In addition to the usual run-of-the-mill
tortilla 'n' calamares fare found in tapas bars everywhere, look out for dishes such as tuna marinated in
ginger and soy sauce, partridge, venison and other
game when in season, and a sublime duck foie with
redcurrant sauce.
▶ *To round off an evening of tapas with some*
spectacular ice-cream, cross the square to the
Gelateria Caffetteria Italiana (see below).

Bars

Châtelet
C/Torrijos 54 (93 284 95 90). Metro Fontana.
Open 6pm-2.30am Mon-Thur, Sun, 6pm 3am Fri,
Sat. **No credit cards. Map** p339 H5 .
Crammed with funkily mismatched flea market
finds, old movie posters, and chandeliers, the
Châtelet is part of a small gracienc chain of bars with
a Parisian flavour. It has the edge over the others
thanks to its corner location just a block from the
Verdi art cinema, with huge windows that open up
completely in summer. Comfy sofas and armchairs
plus occasional film screenings make this a favourite
with an artsy, studenty crowd.

Ice-cream

★ Gelateria Caffetteria Italiana
Plaça Revolució 2 (93 210 23 39). Metro
Fontana or Joanic. **Open** *Summer* 2pm-1am
daily. *Winter* 3pm-8pm daily. **No credit cards.**
Map p339 H5 ⑦
Run by an Italian mother and daughter, the Gelateria
Caffetteria Italiana is famous for its own-recipe dark
chocolate ice-cream – which invariably sells out
every night. Other freshly made, additive-free
flavours include fig, strawberry and peach: basically, whatever fruit happens to be in season. There
are tables outside on the square, if you're lucky
enough to get one – the Italiana is one of the hottest
tickets in town on balmy summer evenings, so be
prepared to queue.
Other locations Placeta Montcada 12, Born
(93 319 81 83).

OTHER DISTRICTS
Cafés

Café Berlin
C/Muntaner 240-242, Sant Gervasi (93 200 65
42). Metro Diagonal. **Open** 10am-2am Mon-Thur;
10am-3am Fri-Sat. **Credit** MC, V. **Map** p338 E5 ⑦
Downstairs in the basement, the low sofas fill up
with amorous couples, while upstairs everything is
sleek and light, with brushed steel, dark leather and
a Klimt-like mural. A rack of newspapers and plentiful sunlight make Berlin popular for coffee or
snacks all day; as well as tapas, there are pasta
dishes, *bocadillos* and cheesecake. Note the 20% surcharge for pavement tables.

Fragments Café
Plaça de la Concòrdia 12, Les Corts (93 419 96
13, www.fragmentscafe.com). Metro Les Corts or
Maria Cristina. **Open** 1.15pm-1am Tue, Wed;
1.15pm-2am Thur, Fri; 11.30am-2am Sat; 11.30am-
1am Sun. Closed 2wks Christmas, 2wks Aug.
Credit V. **Map** p337 B5 ⑦
A tapas bar with a smart, classy look in the one
remaining pocket of charm left in the neighbourhood
of Les Corts. Sit at the tables in the square or the
bar's garden at the back (candlelit at night), and
order some *vermut* (on tap here) and *gildas*
(anchovies with chilli) before you so much as begin
to peruse the menu. There are scrambled eggs with
foie, juicy steaks, home-made pasta and cherry
crumble to finish. Be warned that prices can be a bit
steep for what are quite small portions.

Tapas

L'Esquinica
Passeig Fabra i Puig 296, Horta (93 358 25 19).
Metro Virrei Amat or Vilapicina. **Open** 8am-
midnight Tue-Fri; 8am-4pm, 6.30pm-midnight Sat;
8am-4pm Sun. Closed last 2wks Aug. **Credit** V.
Think of it not as a trek, but as a quest; queues outside are testament to the great value of the tapas. On
especially busy nights you'll be asked to take a number, supermarket-style. Waiters will advise first-
timers to start with *chocos* (creamy squid rings),
patatas bravas with *allioli*, *llonganissa* sausage and
tigres (stuffed mussels). After which the world is
your oyster, cockle or clam.

Quimet d'Horta
Plaça Eivissa 10, Horta (93 358 19 16). Metro
Horta. **Open** 9am-midnight Mon-Thur, Sun; 9am-
12.30 Fri, Sat. Closed Aug. **Credit** MC, V.
Sadly, Juanito the house parrot has gone to the great
perch in the sky (though his image remains on the
menu), but the same regulars have been coming to
Quimet for decades, to chew the fat over a beer in
the sunshine. Ciabatta sandwiches are a speciality,
and come with every filling imaginable.

Shops & Services

Small specialist shops still rule in Barcelona.

As with most other major cities, the call of the mall grows ever stronger in Barcelona. However, although the credit crunch has picked off many small start-ups, plenty of alternatives remain. Barcelona is still known for its old specialist shops, many family-run for generations; there's nowhere better to browse for just the right kind of pork sausage or votive candle. Fashion is another strong point: head up Passeig de Gràcia and beyond to the Avda Diagonal for high fashion and couture, or trawl the Born, the Raval and Gràcia for an ever-changing line-up of local designers selling from hole-in-the-wall shops. Indeed, the centre of Barcelona is so crammed with retail outlets that it can feel like one enormous open-air department store.

SHOPPING PRACTICALITIES

Most shops don't open until 10am and then close for lunch from 2pm; after lunch, they're usually open from 5pm until about 8pm. Many small shops also close on Saturday afternoons and all day on Monday. Note that if you're paying by credit card, you usually have to show photographic ID, such as a passport or a driving licence.

The rate of sales tax (IVA) depends on the type of product: it's currently eight per cent on food and 18 per cent on most other items. In any of the 700 or so shops that display a Tax-Free Shopping sticker on their door, non-EU residents can request a Tax-Free Cheque on purchases of more than €90.15 (call Spain Refund, 91 523 70 04, www.spainrefund.com; or Global Refund, 91 761 37 02, www.global refund.com, for further information). Before leaving the EU, these must be stamped at customs (at Barcelona airport, it's located in Terminal 2A by the Arrivals gate) and can immediately be reclaimed in cash at the adjacent branch of La Caixa bank (or from refund offices in your home country).

Bargain hunters should note that sales (*rebaixes/rebajas*) begin after the retail orgy of Christmas and Epiphany, running from 7 January to mid February, and again during July and August.

Returning goods, even when they're faulty, can be difficult. For consumer rights, *see p297*.

General

DEPARTMENT STORES

El Corte Inglés

Plaça Catalunya 14, Eixample (93 306 38 00, www.elcorteingles.es). Metro Catalunya. **Open** 10am-10pm Mon-Sat. **Credit** AmEx, DC, MC, V. **Map** p328 C2.

This monolith sits on Plaça Catalunya and stocks all the major international brand names, along with plenty of Spanish labels. This branch is the place for toiletries, cosmetics, clothes and homewares. It also houses a well-stocked but pricey supermarket and a gourmet food store, plus services ranging from key-cutting to currency exchange; on the top floor, there's a restaurant with great views (but service station-style food). The Portal de l'Àngel branch stocks CDs, DVDs, books, electronic equipment, stationery and sports gear. There are fashion and accessories geared to a younger market on the ground floor.

Other locations Avda Diagonal 471-473, Eixample (93 493 48 00); Avda Diagonal 617, Eixample (93 366 71 00); L'Illa (sports clothing only), Avda Diagonal 545, Eixample (93 363 80 90); Avda Portal de l'Àngel 19-21, Plaça Catalunya, Eixample (93 306 38 00).

MALLS

★ Barcelona Glòries

Avda Diagonal 208, Eixample (93 486 04 04, www.lesglories.com). Metro Glòries. **Open** *Shops*

10am-10pm Mon-Sat. *Food court & entertainment* 10am-1am daily. **Map** p327 L8.

Since opening in 1995, this mall, office and leisure centre has become a focus of local life. There's a seven-screen cinema (foreign films are mostly dubbed into Spanish) and more than 220 shops, including a Carrefour supermarket, an H&M, a Mango and a Disney Store, facing on to a large, café-filled square decorated with jets of coloured water. Family-friendly attractions include a free pram-lending service, play areas, and entertainment such as bouncy castles and trampolines.

Diagonal Mar

Avda Diagonal 3, Poblenou (93 567 76 37, www.diagonalmar.com). Metro El Maresme-Fòrum. **Open** *Shops* 10am-10pm Mon-Sat. *Food court & entertainment* 10am-midnight Mon-Thur; 10am-1am Fri, Sat; noon-midnight Sun.

This three-level mall at the sea end of Avda Diagonal has an airy marine theme and a sea-facing roof terrace filled with cafés and restaurants of the fast-food variety. As well as major anchors, such as an Alcampo supermarket, Zara and FNAC, there's a particular emphasis on children's clothes and toy shops, plus plenty of smaller global brands (Miss Sixty to Swarovski). Extras include a wheelchair-lending service and golf carts in which to drive your purchases to your car; for the kids, there's a crèche, a play area and miniature cars for hourly rental.

▶ *The centre provides 30 minutes of free Wi-Fi.*

L'Illa

Avda Diagonal 545-557, Eixample (93 444 00 00, www.lilla.com). Metro Maria Cristina. **Open** 10am-9.30pm Mon-Sat. *Supermarket & food court* 9.30am-9.30pm Mon-Sat. **Map** p321 C4.

This monolithic mall is designed to look like the Rockefeller Center fallen on its side, stretching 334m (1,100ft) along Avda Diagonal. It features all the usual fashion favourites but also has a good range of renowned Catalan brands, such as Camper, Custo and Antonio Miró. L'Illa has been gaining a good reputation for its food, with specialist gourmet food stalls and interesting eateries such as sushi and oyster bars.

Maremagnum

Moll d'Espanya 5, Port Vell (93 225 81 00, www.maremagnum.es). Metro Drassanes. **Open** *Shops* 10am-10pm daily. *Food court & entertainment* 11am-2am daily. **Map** p326 F12.

When Viaplana and Piñon's black-mirrored shopping and leisure centre opened in 1995, it was *the* place to hang out. After years of declining popularity, it's ditched most of the bars and discos and taken a step upmarket: residents now include the likes of chocolate shop Xocoa, Calvin Klein and boudoirish Lollipops, which deals in Parisian accessories. All the high-street staples are present (Mango, H&M, Women's Secret) and the ground floor focuses on the family market, with sweets, children's clothes and a Barça shop. There's also a Starbucks and a handful of tapas restaurants.

CONSUME

Maremagnum.

Pedralbes Centre
*Avda Diagonal 609-615, Pedralbes (93 410 68
21, www.pedralbescentre.com). Metro Maria
Cristina.* **Open** *Shops* 10am-9pm Mon-Sat.
Food court 9.30am-9pm Mon-Sat. **Map** p321 B4.
When this black Rubik's Cube of a building opened
in the early '90s, it caused such excitement that it
even inspired a short-lived TV soap of the same
name. The mall's focus is on upmarket clothes,
accessories and homewares, with plenty of local
names such as Elena Miró, Majoral jewellers and
Luis Guirau in among the likes of Hello Kitty and
Timberland. The cafés and restaurants appeal to
ladies who lunch, with salad buffets, gourmet tapas,
a Bubó pâtisserie, along with a crèche, regular catwalk shows and art exhibitions. In winter, the mall's
plaza is transformed into an ice rink.

MARKETS

The Modernista **Sant Antoni** market is
currently closed for refurbishment. The
stalls have been housed in a temporary site on
Ronda Sant Antoni, where C/Villarroel meets
C/Riera Alta.

Other general markets include **Del Ninot**
(C/Mallorca 133, Eixample, 93 453 65 12, closed
Sun) and **La Barceloneta** (Plaça Font 1,
Barceloneta, 93 221 64 71, closed Sun). Also
look out for the **book and coin market** (*see
p187*), food markets (*see p198*) and the **Fira
de Santa Llúcia** Christmas market.

The city is home to a number of artisan food
fairs, similar in spirit to farmers' markets in the
UK. The most central is at picturesque **Plaça
del Pi**, held on the first and third weekends of
the month (Friday to Sunday) and during local
fiestas. For **La Boqueria** food market, *see
p198 and p199* **Market Picks**. See also
www.bcn.cat/mercatsmunicipals for details
of the 40 permanent neighbourhood markets
around the city.

Specialist
BOOKS & MAGAZINES

A glut of shops specialising in comics, film
and other visual arts can be found on Passeig
de Sant Joan in the Arc de Triomf area.
Elsewhere, **Kowasa** (C/Mallorca 235,
Eixample, 93 215 80 58, www.kowasa.com)
runs fine exhibitions in addition to holding an
extensive stock of books about photography.
For books on Catalonia, head to the **Llibreria
de la Generalitat** (La Rambla 118, 93 302 64
62). The venerable **FNAC** (El Triangle, Plaça
Catalunya 4, 93 344 18 00, www.fnac.es) has
a large selection of English-language books
on the second floor.

English language

BCN Books
*C/Roger de Llúria 118, Eixample (93 457 76 92,
www.bcnbooks.com). Metro Diagonal.* **Open** *July,
Aug* 10am-8pm Mon-Fri. *Sept-June* 10am-8pm
Mon-Fri; 10am-2pm Sat. **Credit** MC, V. **Map**
p322 G7.
This well-stocked English-language bookstore has
a wide range of learning and teaching materials for
all ages. There's also a decent selection of contemporary and classic fiction, a good kids' section, some
travel guides and plenty of dictionaries.
Other locations C/Amigó 81, Eixample
(93 200 79 53).

Casa del Libro
*C/Passeig de Gràcia 62, Eixample (93 272 34 80,
www.casadellibro.com). Metro Passeig de Gràcia.*
Open 9.30am-9.30pm Mon-Sat. **Credit** AmEx,
DC, MC, V. **Map** p322 G7.
Part of a well-established Spanish chain, the Casa
del Libro bookstore offers a diverse assortment
of titles that includes some English-language
fiction. Glossy, Barcelona-themed coffee-table
tomes with good gift potential sit by the front right-
hand entrance.

Hibernian Books
*C/Montseny 17, Gràcia (93 217 47 96,
www.hibernian-books.com). Metro Fontana.*
Open 4-8.30pm Mon; 10.30am-8.30pm Tue-Sat.
No credit cards. Map p322 G5.
With its air of pleasantly dusty intellectualism,
Hibernian feels like a proper British second-hand
bookshop. There are books for all tastes, from
beautifully bound early editions to classic Penguin
paperbacks, biographies, cookbooks and so
on, more than 30,000 titles in all. Part-exchange is
possible here.

Specialist

★ Altaïr
*Gran Via de les Corts Catalanes 616, Eixample
(93 342 71 71, www.altair.es). Metro Universitat.*
Open 10am-8.30pm Mon-Sat. **Credit** AmEx, DC,
MC, V. **Map** p326 F8.
Every aspect of travel is covered in this, the largest
travel bookshop in Europe. You can pick up guides

INSIDE TRACK MUSEUM SHOPS

Some of the best places in which to find
great presents, or books on art, design
and architecture are museum stores.
In particular, try the **MACBA** (*see p72*),
CaixaForum (*see p84*) and the **Museu
d'Història de Barcelona** (*see p59*).

CONSUME (margin)

Where to Shop

Barcelona's best shopping neighbourhoods in brief.

THE BARRI GOTIC

The Saturday-afternoon hordes head to the big-name chain stores that line Avda Portal de l'Àngel and C/Portaferrissa, but there are plenty of less mainstream retail options. It's possible to spend hours browsing antiques on C/Banys Nous, where tiny shops specialise in furniture, posters or textiles. The streets around Plaça Sant Jaume house some lovely, old-fashioned stores selling hats, candles, traditional toys and stationery. For something more modern, try the independent boutiques on C/Avinyó, which offer affordable, streetwise fashion and household items with a twist.

THE BORN & SANT PERE

The streets leading off the Passeig del Born are a warren of stylish little boutiques offering quality, rather than quantity. Hip music, intimidating sales assistants and heartbreaking prices are part of the shopping experience, but so are gorgeous clothing, shoes and accessories from a clique of fast-rising local and international designers. Nearby C/Argenteria was named after its denizen silversmiths, and a handful of shops there follow the tradition, selling affordable, if mainstream, trinkets.

THE RAVAL

The Raval's shopping, concentrated on the streets between the Boqueria market and Plaça dels Angels, has a youthful bent: head to C/Riera Baixa and C/Tallers for second-hand clothing and streetwear, and C/Bonsuccès for specialist record shops. C/Doctor Dou and C/Elisabets feature some trendy boutiques and shoe shops; the latter also has a couple of design stores. C/Pelai, along the Raval's top edge, has an impressive number of shoe stores.

BARCELONETA & THE PORTS

Barcelona's seafront shopping is concentrated in the shopping centre of Maremàgnum, which houses a large, if sterile, confection of high-street fashion stores that are at least open late.

THE EIXAMPLE

Passeig de Gràcia is home to enough high-fashion and statement jewellery to satisfy even a footballer's wife. Chanel, Dior, Cartier and friends are present and correct, as are Spanish luxury brands Tous, Loewe and, on adjacent Consell de Cent, Catalan fashion hero Antoni Miró. A stone's throw away, the tree-lined Rambla de Catalunya offers high-street fashion.

GRÀCIA & OTHER DISTRICTS

Independent shops rule in bohemian Gràcia: head to the bottom end of C/Verdi or the streets around Plaça Rius i Taulet for quirky little boutiques selling clothing, accessories and gifts. Local design collective Ruta Gràcia (www.rutagracia.com) lists dozens of independent retailers on its website.

to free eating in Barcelona, academic tomes on geolinguistics, handbooks on successful outdoor sex and CDs of tribal and world music. Of course, all the less arcane publications are also here: maps for hikers, travel guidebooks, multilingual dictionaries, travel diaries, atlases and equipment such as mosquito nets.

▶ *For more travel-related shops and services, see p206.*

Book & Coin Market

C/Comte Borrell with C/Tamarit, Eixample (93 423 42 87). Metro Sant Antoni. **Open** 9am-2.30pm (approx) Sun. **No credit cards.** **Map** p326 D9.

The Sant Antoni market is being refurbished (it's due to reopen in 2012), but the Sunday book market remains, housing tables packed with every manner of reading material from arcane old tomes to well-

pawed bodice-rippers and yellowing comics. There are also stacks of coins and more contemporary merchandise such as music, software and posters. Arrive early to beat the crowds.

Continuarà

Via Laietana 29, Barri Gòtic (93 310 43 52, www.continuara.org). Metro Jaume I. **Open** 10.30am-2.30pm, 4-9pm Mon-Sat. **Credit** DC, MC, V. **Map** p329 D5.

The comic scene is big in Spain, and this two-storey shop has been serving Barcelona's substantial geek community since 1980. The ground floor has both national and imported comics and comix, principally in English and French, along with plenty of posters, DVDs, CDs and figurines. The first floor is a temple to manga and Amerimanga, with a huge selection of Japanese merchandise.

Discover the city from your back pocket

Essential for your weekend break, over 30 top cities available.

CHILDREN
General

The third floor of the Plaça Catalunya branch of the **El Corte Inglés** department store (*see p184*) has a large selection of clothes, toys and baby equipment, while **Galeries Maldà** (C/Portaferrissa 22, no phone, Barri Gòtic) is a small shopping centre with plenty of kids' shops.

Chicco
Ronda Sant Pere 13, Eixample (93 301 49 76, www.chicco.es). Metro Catalunya. **Open** 10am-8.30pm Mon-Fri; 10am-9pm Sat. **Credit** AmEx, DC, MC, V. **Map** p328 D2.
The market leader in Spain, this colourful store has every conceivable babycare item, from dummies and high chairs to bottle-warmers and travel cots. Its clothes and shoes are practical and well designed, and made for children up to eight years old.
Other locations Diagonal Mar, Avda Diagonal 3, Poblenou (93 356 03 74),

Fashion

Larger branches of **Zara** have decent clothes sections. **Kiddy's Class**, which has branches all over town, sells exclusively Zara's children's clothing. For cheapo kids' shoes and casual clothes, head to **Decathlon** (*see p206*).

Mujer
C/Carders 28, Sant Pere (93 315 15 31, www.mujermamabebe.blogspot.com). Metro Jaume I. **Open** 11am-3pm, 5-8pm Mon-Fri; 11am-8pm Sat. Closed last 2wks Aug. **Credit** MC, V. **Map** p329 F5.
Run by the energetic Lulu, Mujer is the local nerve centre for expat parents. It stocks imported funky baby gear from the likes of Cath Kidston or Twisted Twee and is the perfect place to pick up a tiny Metallica T-Shirt or an AC/DC one-size. There's also a range of maternity wear, baby accessories, books, toys and a chill-out space for playing and breastfeeding in comfort. Lulu also runs regular sessions of happy clapping, baby massage and the like.

★ Du Pareil au Même
Rambla Catalunya 95, Eixample (93 487 14 49, www.dpam.com). Metro Diagonal/FGC Provença. **Open** 10am-8.30pm Mon-Sat. **Credit** AmEx, DC, MC. V. **Map** p322 F7.
This French chain stocks everything a pint-sized fashionista might need, though the girls do a bit better than the boys. Newborns to 14-year-olds are served with a covetable range of funky, bright and well-designed clothes at great prices.

Toys

Imaginarium
Passeig de Gràcia 103, Eixample (93 272 57 10, www.imaginarium.es). Metro Diagonal. **Open** 10am-8pm Mon-Thur, 10am-9pm Fri, Sat. **Credit** MC, V. **Map** p322 G6.
As well as the endless racks of the excellent toys that made Imaginarium famous, the new three-floor flagship store for Spain's biggest toy chain has a hairdresser's, shoe department, computer zone, a multilingual book department (including a solid English-language selection) and a play area and reading corner. The friendly assistants run regular craft activities, balloon-bending sessions and puppet shows, while the top floor Saborea café has organic food in appropriately small portions.
Other locations throughout the city.

★ El Ingenio
C/Rauric 6, Barri Gòtic (93 317 71 38, www.el-ingenio.com). Metro Liceu. **Open** 10am-1.30pm, 4.15-8pm Mon-Fri; 11am-2pm, 5-8.30pm Sat. **Credit** (purchases over €6) MC, V. **Map** p329 B5.
At once enchanting and disturbing, El Ingenio's handcrafted toys, tricks and costumes are reminders of a pre-digital world where people made their own entertainment. Its cabinets are full of practical jokes and curious toys; its fascinating workshop produces the oversized heads and garish costumes used in Barcelona's traditional festivities.

Joguines Monforte
Plaça Sant Josep Oriol 3, Barri Gòtic (93 318 22 85, www.joguinesmonforte.com). Metro Liceu. **Open** 9.30am-1.30pm, 4-8pm Mon-Fri; 10am-2pm, 4.30-8.30pm Sat. **Credit** MC, V. **Map** p329 B5.
This venerable toy shop has been selling traditional toys, board games and everything you need for a game of billiards since 1840. Try the Spanish version of snakes and ladders (*el joc de l'oca*, or the 'goose game') and ludo (*parxís*), along with chess, jigsaws, painted tin toys and outdoor games such as croquet and skittles.

ELECTRONICS & PHOTOGRAPHY

The area around Ronda Sant Antoni is the best place to go if you're looking for hardware for your PC. **Life Informática** (C/Sepúlveda 173, Sant Antoni, 93 390 02 30, www.life informatica.com) is good for parts; **PC City** (C/Casanova 2, Eixample, 902 10 03 02, www.pccity.es) is a reliable option for hardware. For photography, if **Casanova Foto** (*see p191*) doesn't have what you need, try **ARPI** (La Rambla 38-40, Barri Gòtic, 93 301 74 04, www.arpi.es), which has a wide range but poor service.

CONSUME

CONSUME

Finding an Outlet

Budget fashion fixes.

With all the talk of *la crisis* and the global recession, frugality is back in fashion. Bargain-hunters will find the best pickings along C/Girona, particularly between Gran Vía and C/Ali Bei: top addresses include the **Mango** outlet at No.37 (93 412 29 35, www.mangooutlet.es); gorgeous eveningwear and accessories from **Etxart & Panno** (*pictured*) at No.40 (93 232 80 45, www.etxartpanno.com); and slinky designs from Catalan label **Javier Samorra** at No.38 (93 231 49 21, www.javier samorra.com). Just off C/Girona, the **Desigual Outlet** (C/Diputació 323, 93 2720 66, www.desigual.com) offers the signature bright prints at bargain prices. A few blocks west, rummage through piles of colourful, funky street fashion and accessories from Basque label **Skunkfunk** (Ronda Sant Pere 31, 93 412 02 23, www.skunkfunk.com).

For pile-it-high, sell-it-cheap fashion, make for **Lefties** (Plaça Universitat 11, 93 317 50 70, www.lefties.com), the Zara outlet store, which stocks slightly faulty or end-of-line clothes and accessories for men, women and children (new stock arrives on Mondays and Thursdays). There's another branch in the Maremagnum shopping mall (93 225 81 00, www.maremagnum.com), which, as every *barcelonin* shopaholic knows, is open every day of the year.

Committed fashionistas should check out the three-day biannual sales (usually held in August and November – check websites for details) organised by some stores. **Santa Eulalia** (*see p192*), has Balenciaga, Lanvin and all the top couture labels for less than half price. The original but wearable footwear designed by **Vialis** (C/Botànica 131, L'Hospitalet, 93 264 00 58, www.vialis.es) attracts lengthy queues of discerning women looking for discounts of up to 70 per cent on its colourful shoes, sandals and boots.

The Holy Grail for luxury-loving but light-walleted shoppers, however, is the **La Roca Village** (93 842 39 00, www.larocavillage. com), a massive designer outlet mall located 37 kilometres north-east of Barcelona. The Shopping Express bus leaves Plaça Catalunya daily at 10am, 4pm and 6pm, returning at 3pm, 7pm and 9pm (€12 return). There are about 100 stores, with most of the top brands represented, including Versace, Dolce & Gabbana, Comptoir des Cotonniers, Hoss Intropia, Loewe, Farrutx, Nike and Petit Bateau.

The considerably smaller – if more centrally located – **Heron City** mall (Passeig Andreu Nin 31, Nou Barris, 902 401 144, www.heroncitybarcelona.com) has outlets from high-street fashion labels like Desigual, Mango and Lefties (Zara), as well as shoes for kids at Querolet.

BCN Computers

C/Mozart 26, Gràcia (93 217 61 66, www.bcn-computers.es). Metro Fontana. **Open** 10am-2pm, 4-8pm Mon-Fri, open Sat with appointment. **No credit cards. Map** p322 G6.
Everything for Macs and PCs: software in English; hardware and software installations; repairs for personal computers and laptops, and ADSL support. There's English-speaking customer service; unlike many local shops, staff offer a free evaluation of your computer's problems when you take it for repair.

Casanova Fotografia

C/Pelai 18, Raval (93 302 73 63, www.casanova foto.com). Metro Universitat. **Open** 10am-2pm, 4.30-8.30pm Mon-Fri; 10am-2pm, 5-8.30pm Sat. **Credit** MC, V. **Map** p328 B1.
An extensive stock of new and second-hand digital and film equipment: camera bodies, lenses, tripods, darkroom gear, bags and more. There's also a slow but thorough repair lab, and a full range of processing services for film and digital photos.
Other locations Ronda Universitat 35, Eixample, 93 302 73 63.

CTA Serveis

C/Consell de Cent 382, Eixample (93 244 03 50, www.cta.es). Metro Girona. **Open** 9am-2pm, 4-7pm Mon-Fri. Closed 3wks Aug. **Credit** MC, V. **Map** p327 H8.
Computer installation and repairs for Macs.

FASHION

Designer

More off grid options include the recent arrival of 'pop-up shops', or 'guerrilla shops' as they're known here. These include everything from tiny set-ups in private flats – such as **El Vestidor** (C/Portaferrissa 25, Barri Gòtic, open 11am-8pm Sat, Sun), which shows clothes by 12 emerging local designers – to one-offs such as the architect-designed installation **Fashion Pop-Up**, held occasionally at the Maremagnum centre (*see p185*), with more established names such as Txell Miras and El Delgado Buil.

Antonio Miró

Rambla Catalunya 125, Eixample (93 238 99 42, www.antoniomiro.es). Metro Diagonal. **Open** 10.30am-8.30pm Mon-Sat. **Credit** AmEx, DC, MC, V. **Map** p322 G8.
Miró famously likes to cause a stir on the catwalk, using illegal immigrants and even local prisoners to model his wares. His clothes, however, for men and women, couldn't be less controversial, with sober, almost uniform-like designs in muted tones. His diffusion line, Miró jeans, is more relaxed and playful.

Como Agua de Mayo

C/Argenteria 43, Born (93 310 64 41, www.comoaguademayo.com). Metro Jaume I. **Open** 10am-8.30pm Mon-Fri; 10am-9pm Sat. **Credit** AmEx, DC, MC, V. **Map** p329 E6.
A temple for coquettish Carrie Bradshaw style on a mid-range budget. Think lots of mixing and matching of patterns with plenty of candy-bright shoes. Labels include Masscob, Mariona Gen and Miriam Ocáriz; footwear comes courtesy of Otto et Moi, Pedro Garcia and Chie Mihara. If the door is shut, you'll need to buzz to get in.
Other locations C/Banys Nous 17, Barri Gòtic (93 412 31 72).

★ Custo Barcelona

Plaça de les Olles 7, Born (93 268 78 93, www.custo-barcelona.com). Metro Jaume I. **Open** 10am-9pm Mon-Sat; noon-8pm Sun. **Credit** AmEx, DC, MC, V. **Map** p329 E7.
The Custo look is synonymous with Barcelona style, and the loud, cut-and-paste print T-shirts have spawned a thousand imitations. Custodio Dalmau's signature prints can now be found on everything from coats to jeans to swimwear for both men and women, but a T-shirt is still the most highly prized (and highly priced) souvenir for visiting fashionistas. There's also a Custo Vintage (Plaça del Pi 2, Barri Gòtic, 93 304 27 53), with clothes from past seasons.
Other locations C/Ferran 36, Barri Gòtic (93 342 66 98); La Rambla 109, Barri Gòtic (93 481 39 30); L'Illa, Avda Diagonal 545-557, Eixample (93 322 26 62).

Jean-Pierre Bua

Avda Diagonal 469, Eixample (93 439 71 00, www.jeanpierrebua.com). Bus 6, 7, 15, 33, 34, 67, 68/tram T1, T2, T3. **Open** 10am-2pm, 4.30-8.30pm Mon-Sat. **Credit** AmEx, DC, MC, V. **Map** p322 E5.
The clothes are the highest of high-end fashion, the assistants are model-beautiful, and the shop itself has the air of a runway at a Paris catwalk show. No inferiority complexes are allowed: if you have the money, the figure and the label knowledge (and *only* if), come to worship at the altar of Miu Miu, Dries van Noten and many more. Next door at No.467 is the new Jean-Pierre Symbol, with three floors of what they term 'alternative' clothing.

★ Josep Font

C/Provença 304, Eixample (93 487 21 10, www.josepfont.com). Metro Diagonal. **Open** Sept-July 3.30-8.30pm Mon; 10am-8.30pm Tue-Sat. Closed Aug. **Credit** AmEx, DC, MC, V. **Map** p322 G7.
Tomboys should turn away now: Josep Font's romantic and feminine designs are dripping with ribbons and ruffles. And yet for all that, they never stray into Barbara Cartland territory. Look for cute

CONSUME

'50s-inspired shorts suits, floral maxi dresses and sumptuous materials, from shimmery silks to mille-feuille chiffon, all temptingly displayed in a quirked-up art nouveau space.

Miriam Ponsa

C/Princesa 14, Born (93 295 55 62, www.miriamponsa.com). Metro Jaume I. **Open** 11am-8.30pm Mon-Sat. **Credit** AmEx, DC, MC, V. **Map** p329 E5.

Miriam Ponsa's designs are squarely aimed at affluent young urbanites with a taste for stripped-down, quasi-Japanese style. The clothes are generally loose fitting and with a strong vertical silhouette while materials can get pretty quirky; you might find yourself wondering how a T-shirt splattered in dripped latex or a hole-punched grey leather waistcoat could ever look so good.

Other locations C/Elisabets 20, Raval (93 412 33 81).

MTX Barcelona

C/Rec 32, Born (93 319 43 44, www.mertxehernandez.com). Metro Barceloneta. **Open** 11am-9pm Mon-Sat. **Credit** DC, MC, V. **Map** p329 F6.

Right now, nobody in Barcelona is hipper than local designer Mertxe Hernández. Her clothes have the distinction of being utterly different but immediately recognisable: colourful, multi-layered textiles, slashed and restructured to make a kind of soft and feminine body armour. Mertxe has also made the tourist T-shirt sexy: you can also find her sharp designs in the shops at La Pedrera, the Liceu opera house and the Museu Picasso. One Wednesday a month, the shop is given over showcasing an up-and-coming artist.

★ Santa Eulalia

Passeig de Gràcia 93, Eixample (93 215 06 74, www.santaeulalia.com). Metro Diagonal. **Open** 10am-8.30pm Mon-Sat. **Credit** AmEx, DC, MC, V. **Map** p322 G6.

Barcelona's oldest design house and a pioneer in the local catwalk scene, Santa Eulalia was founded in 1843 and remains a seriously upmarket proposition. The prêt-à-porter selection at the shop is fresh and up-to-the-minute and includes labels such as

Balenciaga, Jimmy Choo, Stella McCartney and Ann Demeulemeester. Services include bespoke tailoring and wedding wear for grooms. The C/Pau Casals branch is for men only.

Other locations C/Pau Casals 8, Eixample (93 201 70 51).

Discount

One of Barcelona's hotspots for bargain clothes shopping is C/Girona. In particular, the two blocks between C/Ausiàs Marc and Gran Via de les Corts Catalanes are lined with remainder stores and factory outlets of fluctuating quality. **Mango Outlet** (C/Girona 37, 93 412 29 35), crammed with last season's unsold stock, outshines most of the competition.

Elsewhere, **Lefties** (Plaça Universitat 11, 93 317 50 70) is a remainder store crammed with discounted items for men, women and children from the Inditex stable (which includes Zara, Pull & Bear and Bershka). There is also a branch in Maremagnum. The Desigual fashion chain has an outlet called **Almazén** (C/Diputació 323, Eixample, 93 272 00 66).

See also p190 **Finding an Outlet.**

Espacio de Creadores

C/Comtal 22, Barri Gòtic (93 318 03 31). Metro Urquinaona. **Open** 10am-8.30pm Mon-Sat. **Credit** AmEx, DC, MC, V. **Map** p328 D3.

This elegant boutique specialises in end-of-line clothing for women designed by respected Spanish names such as Josep Font, Purificación García, Jordi Labanda, Etxart & Panno at discount prices. Smart styles predominate; eveningwear is upstairs.

General

Adolfo Domínguez

C/Ribera 16, Born (93 319 21 59, www.adolfodominguez.com). Metro Barceloneta. **Open** 10am-8.30pm Mon-Sat. **Credit** AmEx, DC, MC, V. **Map** p329 F7.

The women's department has finally caught up with the men's tailoring that for many years was Domínguez's forte, particularly his elegantly cut suits and shirts. Expect to find sharp, flattering jackets along with surprisingly adventurous separates in luxurious materials and well-made shoes and bags. The more casual U de Adolfo Domínguez line courts well-to-do youths, but doesn't quite attain the effortless panache of its grown-up precursor. This under-visited two-storey flagship store is supplemented by several others around the city.

Other locations Passeig de Gràcia 32, Eixample (93 487 41 70); Passeig de Gràcia 89, Eixample (93 487 48 89); Avda Diagonal 490, Gràcia (93 416 17 16); and throughout the city.

CONSUME

The Retro Route

A retail tour of the Raval.

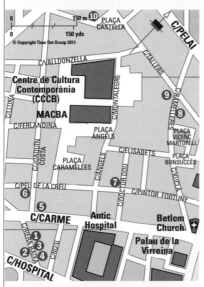

The epicentre for retro junkies in Barcelona has long been Raval's C/Riera Baixa, where dealers put out racks of clothing on Saturdays at flea market prices. You won't find many of those at **Lailo ❶** (No.20, 93 441 37 49) but rather good quality, genuine 20th-century vintage, some from the 1940s. You can almost feel the static from the racks of crimplene when you walk into **Smart & Clean ❷** (No.7, 93 441 87 64), which specialises in 1960s and '70s mod clobber.

Billie Jean ❸ (No.16, 93 324 84 48) sells party dresses from c.1980 and occasion ensembles with a few more recent designer pieces thrown into the eclectic mix. By contrast, **Cañero ❹** (No.6-8, 93 443 90 12) is pure pot luck: styles and eras are piled on top of each other, and nothing has a price tag. However, a few minutes of digging might unearth such goodies as an Italian silk dress for €20.

Around the corner, **Wilde ❺** (C/Joaquín Costa 2, mobile 654 455 057) only stocks vintage glasses, with frames ranging from Dame Edna-ish cat's eyes to original Ray-Bans. Opposite, **Vintage Barcelona ❻** (No.3, 93 443 86 44) is a spacious emporium with clothing laid out according

to 'look' (note to Goths: head straight to the rear) and a fabulous range of tomato-red, white and blue Italian sailor shirts.

Venture further north to two of the best vintage destinations in the city. **Blow by Le Swing ❼** (C/Doctor Dou 11, 93 302 36 98) caters to disco divas and Barbie girls, with a glittering array of top-flight couture at surprisingly reasonable prices. Baubles, bags, beads and all sorts of feathered and fascinating millinery complement the frocks and there's a selection of mid-century modern furniture and objects. **Produit National Brut ❽** (C/Ramalleres 16-20, 93 268 27 55) stocks very feminine 1970s floral apparel, pert knits, customised pieces and its own-label jewellery.

The upper swathe of the Raval remains the grunge-tinged stomping ground of the city's counterculture, particularly around C/Tallers. Scottish-owned **Retro City ❾** (No.47, no phone) pulls in the punters with its arrays of military jackets and old-skool Adidas, while you'll need a bucketload of patience at the enormous **Holala! Plaza + Gallery ❿** (Plaça Castella 2, 93 302 05 93) if you're going to rifle through the good, the bad and the ugly of its all-era used clothing.

Lailo

CONSUME

Cortefiel

Avda Portal de l'Àngel 38, Barri Gòtic (93 301 07 00, www.cortefiel.com). Metro Catalunya. **Open** 10am-8.30pm Mon-Sat. **Credit** AmEx, DC, MC, V. **Map** p328 C3.

Cortefiel is a popular chain that casts a wider net than Mango or Zara, and its fine tailored jackets and elegant, mature renditions of current trends appeal to a variety of women (from conservative students to fashion-conscious fiftysomethings). If you like a bit of glitz, take a peek at the swankier Pedro del Hierro collection downstairs. Both labels have less prominent, but successful, menswear lines.

Other locations L'Illa, Avda Diagonal 545-557, Eixample (93 419 58 25); Avda Diagonal 399 (93 218 59 21) and throughout the city.

Free

C/Ramelleres 5, Raval (93 301 61 15, www.freeskate.com). Metro Catalunya. **Open** 11.30am-8.30pm Mon-Sat. **Credit** MC,V. **Map** p328 B3.

A skate emporium that has grown exponentially to cater Barcelona's expanding population of enthusiasts. For boys, there's casualwear from Stüssy, Carhartt et al; girls get plenty of Compobella and Loreak Mendian. The requisite chunky or retro footwear comes courtesy of Vans, Vision and Etnies.

Other locations C/Viladomat 319, Eixample (93 321 72 90); Passeig Bonanova 63, Sarrià (93 212 30 57).

Ivo & Co

C/Rec 20, Born (93 268 33 31). Metro Arc de Triomf or Jaume I. **Open** 11am-3pm, 5-9pm Mon-Sat. **Credit** MC, V. **Map** p329 F6.

If Cath Kidston were given free rein to create a fairytale Christmas in a Provençal farmhouse, the result would be something like Ivo & Co. This branch has wooden toys, knitted dolls, hand-stitched bunting and polka dots a go-go, while the branch opposite (Plaça Comercial 3, 93 268 86 31) focuses on homeware, with vintage-style crockery and wallpaper, table linen, hand-painted coat hangers and etched wine goblets.

On Land

C/Princesa 25, Born (93 310 02 11, www.on-land.com). Metro Jaume I. **Open** 5-8.30pm Mon; 11am-2pm, 5-8.30pm Tue-Fri; 11am-8.30pm Sat. Closed 1wk Aug. **Credit** AmEx, DC, MC, V. **Map** p329 E5.

This little oasis of urban cool has all you need to hold your head up high against the Barcelona hip squad: bags and wallets by Becksöndergaard and Can't Go Naked; cute skirts by y-dress; loose cotton trousers by IKKS; covetable T-shirts by Fresh from the Lab.

Other locations C/València 273, Eixample (93 215 56 25).

▶ *Just down the street is the similarly fashionable Miriam Ponsa; see 192*

Used & vintage

The Raval is the area to head for vintage clothing (*see p193* **The Retro Route**).

FASHION ACCESSORIES & SERVICES

Cleaning & repairs

Any shop marked '*rapid*' or '*rápido*' does shoe repairs and key cutting; **El Corte Inglés** (*see p184*) has both in the basement.

La Hermosa

C/Formatgeria 3, Born (93 319 97 26). Metro Jaume I. **Open** 10am-9pm Mon-Sat. **No credit cards**. **Map** p329 E6.

There's no self-service here, but the drop-off laundry service is €15 for 8kg, €22 for 14kg. Dry-cleaning takes two to three days.

LavaXpres

C/Ferlandina 34, Raval (93 318 30 18, www.lavaexpress.com). Metro Sant Antoni or Universitat. **Open** 8am-10pm daily. **No credit cards**. **Map** p326 E9.

This self-service launderette is open 365 days a year. There are machines that take 18kg of washing – plenty big enough for a rucksack-full of dirty clothes. Smaller 9kg loads cost €3.50. Pre-paid cards, available in the launderettes, offer discounts.

Other locations C/Nou de Sant Francesc 5, Barri Gòtic; C/Carders 29, Born; Passeig Elisabets 3, Raval; Avda Paral·lel 101, Poble Sec.

Hats

Hatquarters

Plaça de la Llana 6, Born (93 310 18 02). Metro Jaume I. **Open** noon-9pm Mon-Sat. **Credit** AmEx, DC, MC, V. **Map** p329 E5.

You won't find anything as vulgar as a tourist sombrero at Chad Weidmar's tiny temple to the titfer. From raffia and tweed cadet caps, leather bucket hats to felt fedoras – by Goorin Bros, Cassel Goorin and Sant Cassel – the simple application of any piece of headwear in this shop will get you past the toughest nightclub bouncer in town. Nowadays, there is also a selection of Mayans shoes.

Other locations L Illa, Avda Diagonal 545-557, Eixample (93 444 00 00).

Sombreria Obach

C/Call 2, Barri Gòtic (93 318 40 94). Metro Jaume I or Liceu. **Open** *Oct-July* 9.30am-1.30pm, 4-8pm Mon-Fri; 10am-2pm, 4.30-8pm Sat. *Aug, Sept* 9.30am-1.30pm, 4-8pm Mon-Fri; 10am-2pm Sat. **Credit** MC, V. **Map** p329 C5.

Now in the hands of the fourth generation of the same family, Sombreria Obach's old-fashioned display windows are worth seeing for themselves: Kangol's mohair berets share space with fedoras, while monteras (matador's caps with Mickey Mouse ears) face off with *barrets* (traditional red Catalan hats).

Jewellery

The Born's C/Argenteria takes its name from the numerous silversmiths who established themselves here in the 15th century. Even today, the street and the surrounding area are home to a number of shops selling silver jewellery, such as **Joid'art** (Passeig del Born 2, 93 295 43 48, www.joidart.com), which is part of a successful chain that has pretty, affordable pieces in its shops throughout Barcelona. Nearby, boutiques such as **Ad Láter** (C/Ases 1, 93 310 66 00) or **Alea Majoral Galería de Joyas** (C/Argenteria 66, 93 310 13 73, www.aleagaleria.com) exhibit pieces by innovative local jewellery designers.

Upmarket jewellers naturally gravitate towards the city's glamorous shopping districts, such as Passeig de Gràcia and Avda Diagonal.

Bagués

Passeig de Gràcia 41, Eixample (93 216 01 73, www.bagues.com). Metro Passeig de Gràcia. **Open** *Sept-July* 10am-8.30pm Mon-Fri; 10am-1.30pm, 5-8.30pm Sat. *Aug* 10am-1.30pm, 4.30-8.30pm Mon-Fri; 10am-1.30pm Sat. **Credit** AmEx, DC, MC, V. **Map** p322 G8.

Lluís Masriera, the original master jeweller of the house, created revolutionary pieces using a 'translucid enamel' technique at the start of the 20th century. His signature motifs, the art nouveau favourites of flowers, insects and birds, are reflected in today's designs.
▶ *Bagués is housed in the Modernista palace Casa Amatller, now open for tours; see p92.*

Helena Rohner

C/Espaseria 13, Born (93 319 88 79, www. helenarohner.com). Metro Barceloneta. **Open** 11am-2.30pm, 5-8.30pm Mon-Fri; noon-3pm, 5-9pm Sat. Closed 2wks Aug. **Credit** AmEx, DC, MC, V. **Map** p329 E7.

The style is *Barbarella*-at-the-boardroom in the boutique of one of Spain's most successful jewellery designers. Spare clean lines in gold or silver wrap around big, smooth chunks of ebony, coral, porcelain or even wood to create a look that's sleek but funky. Big rings are a speciality.

Lingerie & underwear

Rambla de Catalunya is a mecca for underwear shoppers, with boutiques such as **La Perla** (No.88, 93 467 71 49). There's inexpensive swimwear and underwear at high-street chains such as **Oysho** (No.75, 93 487 49 80, www.oysho.com), from the same stable as Zara. **Vanity Fair** (No.11, 93 317 65 45, www.vanityfair.es) strikes a happy medium with reasonably priced Spanish labels and its own range. **El Corte Inglés** (*see p184*) has men's and women's underwear.

★ Le Boudoir

C/Canuda 21, Barri Gòtic (93 302 52 81, www.leboudoir.net). Metro Catalunya.

CONSUME

Le Boudoir.

Open 11am-8.30pm Mon-Fri; 11am-9pm
Sat. **Credit** DC, MC, V. **Map** p328 C3.
Think Dita Von Teese in an 18th-century French
boudoir: feather boas, stockings, masks, gloves and,
of course, racks of sexy bras, knickers, basques and
suspender belts. To show you how to use it all, the
shop runs regular striptease classes.

Janina

*Rambla de Catalunya 94, Eixample (93 215
04 84). Metro Diagonal/FGC Provença.* **Open**
Sept-July 10am-8.30pm Mon-Sat. *Aug* 10am-2pm,
5-8.30pm Mon-Sat. **Credit** AmEx, MC, V.
Map p322 G7.
Janina offers good-quality women's underwear
and nightwear by Calvin Klein, Christian Dior, La
Perla and others. Some larger sizes are stocked;
alternatively, bras can be sent to a seamstress to be
altered overnight.
Other locations Avda Pau Casals 8, Eixample
(93 202 06 93).

Women's Secret

*C/Portaferrissa 7-9, Barri Gòtic (93 318 92
42/www.womensecret.com). Metro Liceu.* **Open**
10am-9pm Mon-Sat. **Credit** AmEx, DC, MC, V.
Map p328 B4.
There are some sexy pieces at Women's Secret, but
the stock is mostly versatile bras, brightly printed
cotton pyjamas and nighties, and a colourful line of
under/outerwear in cartoonish stylings: skimpy
shorts, miniskirts and vest tops.
Other locations Avda Portal de l'Àngel, Barri
Gòtic (93 318 70 55); and throughout the city.

Luggage

Capricho de Muñeca

*C/Brosoli 1, Born (93 319 58 91, www.capricho
demuneca.com). Metro Jaume I.* **Open** 5-8.30pm
Mon; noon-3pm, 5-8.30pm Tue-Sat. **Credit** MC,
V. **Map** p329 E6.
Soft leather handbags in cherry reds, parma violet
and grass green made by hand just upstairs by
designer Lisa Lempp. Sizes range from the cute and
petit to the luxuriously large. Belts and wallets complement the handbags.

Casa Antich

*C/Consolat del Mar 27-31, Born (93 310
43 91, www.casaantich.com). Metro Jaume I.*
Open 9am-8.30pm Mon-Fri; 9.30am-8.30pm
Sat. **Credit** AmEx, DC, MC, V.
Map p329 D7.
A luggage shop that, in levels of service and size of
stock, recalls the golden age of travel. Here you can
still purchase trunks for an Atlantic crossing, and
ladies' vanity cases that would be perfect for a
sojourn on the Orient Express. But you'll also find
computer cases, backpacks and shoulder bags from
the likes of Kipling and Mandarina Duck.

Scarves & textiles

Textiles were once one of Barcelona's main
industries. It's a legacy visible in many of the
street names of the Born, where you'll find
the highest concentration of textile shops
and workshops in the city.

Almacenes del Pilar

*C/Boqueria 43, Barri Gòtic (93 317 79 84,
www.almacenesdelpilar.com). Metro Liceu.*
Open 10am-2pm, 4-8pm Mon-Sat. Closed
2wks Aug. **Credit** AmEx, DC, MC, V.
Map p329 B5.
An array of fabrics and accessories for traditional
Spanish costumes is on display in this colourful,
shambolic interior, dating all the way back to 1886.
Making your way through bolts of material, you'll
find the richly hued brocades used for Valencian *fall-
era* outfits and other rudiments of folkloric dress
from various parts of the country. Lace *mantillas*,
and the high combs over which they are worn,
are stocked, along with fringed, hand-embroidered
pure silk m antones dem anilla (shawls) and colourful
wooden fans.

Alonso

*C/Santa Anna 27, Barri Gòtic (93 317 60 85,
www.tiendacenter.com). Metro Liceu.* **Open** 10am-
8pm Mon-Sat. Closed 1wk Sept. **Credit** DC, MC,
V. **Map** p328 C3.
Elegant Catalan ladies have come to Alonso for
those important finishing touches for their outfit for
more than a century. Behind the Modernista façade
lie soft gloves in leather and lace, intricate fans, both
traditional and modern, and scarves made from
mohair and silk.

Shoes

In summer, people of all ages wear *abarcas*,
sloppy, peep-toe leather shoes from Menorca,
or the traditional Catalan *espardenyes*,
espadrilles of hemp and canvas. Footwear
outlets line the main shopping strips, such
as Avda Portal de l'Àngel or C/Pelai; chains
include **Casas Sabaters** (along with their
U-Casas shops aimed at younger fashionistas
and Casas International for top-line names)
Royalty, **Querol**, **Tascón** and **Vogue**,
which have huge but similar collections.

Camper

*C/Pelai 13-37, Eixample (93 302 41 24,
www.camper.com). Metro Catalunya.* **Open**
10am-10pm Mon-Sat. **Credit** AmEx, DC, MC, V.
Map p328 B2.
Mallorca-based eco shoe company Camper has sexed
up its ladies' line in recent years. Each year, the label
seems to flirt more with high heels (albeit rubbery
wedgy ones) and girly straps. Of course, it still has

its classic round-toed and clod-heeled classics, and the guys still have their iconic bowling shoes. But Camper is definitely worth another look if you've previously dismissed it.

Other locations Plaça del Àngels 6, Raval (93 342 41 41); Passeig de Gràcia 100, Eixample (93 467 41 48); and throughout the city.

Czar

Passeig del Born 20, Born (93 310 72 22). Metro Jaume I. **Open** 4-10pm Mon; noon-9pm Tue-Sat. **Credit** MC, V. **Map** p329 E6.

The hippest trainers are presented here as if they're valuable pieces in a museum: you should be able to find an Adidas Originals or Vision Streetwear pair to suit even the most demanding of street feet. The collection is aimed chiefly at men, but girls have a small and sassy range at the back.

Èstro

C/Flassaders 33, Born (93 310 40 77). Metro Jaume I. **Open** 5-9pm Mon, 11-2pm, 5-9pm Tue-Sat. **Credit** AmEx, DC, MC, V. **Map** p329 E6.

This narrow street is full of original fashion boutiques, but Èstro stands out for its small but exquisite collection of footwear for men and women. All beautifully made by hand from soft, supple leather, the range includes high-heeled knee boots in rich berry shades for women to contemporary takes on the Oxford shoe for men. There is also a small selection of bags, belts and clothes.

La Manual Alpargatera

C/Avinyó 7, Barri Gòtic (93 301 01 72, www.lamanual.net). Metro Liceu. **Open** Jan-Sept, Dec 9.30am-1.30pm, 4.30-8pm Mon-Fri; 10am-1.30pm, 4.30-8pm Sat. Oct, Nov 9.30am-1.30pm, 4.30-8.30pm Mon-Fri; 10am-1.30pm Sat. **Credit** AmEx, DC, MC, V. **Map** p329 C6.

La Manual Alpargatera opened in 1910, stocking handmade espadrilles. The store has shod such luminaries as Pope John Paul II and Jack Nicholson during its years of service – be warned, however, that these names are good indications of the kind of styles you'll find on sale. However, for a basic beach shoe, the prices are astoundingly low (the standard espadrille is €8.70).

Muxart

Rambla de Catalunya 47, Eixample (93 467 74 23, www.muxart.com). Metro Passeig de Gràcia. **Open** 10am-8.30pm Mon-Sat. **Credit** AmEx, DC, MC, V. **Map** p322 F8.

Muxart sells shoes around which to build an outfit. The materials are refined, and the styles are sharp, avant-garde and blatantly not designed to be hidden under a pair of baggy beige slacks. Lines for men and women are complemented by equally creative and attractive bags and accessories.

U-Casas

C/Espaseria 4, Born (93 310 00 46, www.casasclub.com). Metro Jaume I. **Open** 10.30am-8.30pm Mon-Thur; 10.30am-9pm Fri, Sat. **Credit** MC, V. **Map** p329 E7.

The pared-down, post-industrial decor so beloved of this neighbourhood provides the perfect backdrop for bright and quirky shoes. Strange heels and toes are still enjoying their moment in the sun, and after trying on all those snub-nosed winklepickers and rubber wedgies from the likes of Helmut Lang, Fly, Fornarina and Irregular Choice, you can rest your weary pins on the giant, shoe-shaped chaise longue.

FOOD & DRINK

Drinks

Lavinia

Avda Diagonal 605, Eixample (93 363 44 45, www.lavinia.es). Metro Maria Cristina. **Open** 10am-9pm Mon-Sat. **Credit** AmEx, DC, MC, V. **Map** p322 D5.

This ultra-slick store houses the largest selection of wines in Europe. Knowledgeable, polyglot staff happily talk customers through the thousands of horizontally displayed Spanish and international wines, including exceptional vintages and special editions at good prices. They'll also help you put together cases to send home, and let you try before you buy.

▶ *For more on Catalan wine, see pp46-49.*

Torres

C/Nou de la Rambla 25, Raval (93 317 32 34, www.vinosencasa.com). Metro Drassanes or Liceu. **Open** 9am-2pm, 4-9pm Mon-Sat. **Credit** MC, V. **Map** p329 A6.

Torres's shiny shop is a bit out of place in the run-down end of the Raval, but it's worth a visit. There's a good range of Spanish wines, along with interesting beers and spirits from elsewhere, including black Mallorcan absinthe. Prices are competitive.

★ Vila Viniteca

C/Agullers 7, Born (902 32 77 77, www.vilaviniteca.es). Metro Jaume I. **Open** Sept-June 8.30am-8.30pm Mon-Sat. July, Aug 8.30am-8.30pm Mon-Fri; 8.30am-2pm Sat. **Credit** DC, MC, V. **Map** p329 D7.

Whether you want to blow €1,245 on a magnum of 2003 L'Ermita or just snag a €5 bottle of table wine, you'll find something to drink. The selection here is mostly Spanish and Catalan, but does cover international favourites. The new food shop next door at No.9 stocks fine cheeses, cured meats and oils.

Other locations Vinacoteca, València 595, Eixample (93 232 58 35).

CONSUME

CONSUME

General

The supermarket in the basement of **El Corte Inglés** (*see p184*) in Plaça Catalunya has a gourmet section of local and foreign specialities.

Carrefour Express
La Rambla 113, Barri Gòtic (93 302 48 24).
Metro Catalunya. **Open** 10am-10pm Mon-Sat.
Credit AmEx, MC, V. **Map** p328 B3.
The opening hours, the chemist and the unbeatable location make up for the slight shabbiness, the confusing layout and the agonising checkout queues.

Colmado Quilez
Rambla Catalunya 63, Eixample (93 215 23 56).
Metro Passeig de Gràcia. **Open** *Jan-mid Oct* 9am-2pm, 4.30-8.30pm Mon-Fri; 9am-2pm Sat. *Mid Oct-Dec* 9am-2pm, 4.30-8.30pm Mon-Sat. **Credit** MC, V. **Map** p322 F/G8.
Colmados – old-school grocery stores – are relics of the old way of shopping before the invasion of the supermarket. This is one of the few surviving examples in the Modernista Eixample, with floor-to-ceiling shelves stacked full of gourmet treats: local preserved funghi in cute mushroom-shaped bottles (Delicias del Bosque), and the store's own-label caviar, cava, saffron and anchovies.

Markets

Mercat Santa Caterina (Avda Francesc Cambó, 93 319 57 40, www.mercatsanta caterina.net), in a remarkable Gaudiesque building by the late Enric Miralles, is also worthy of note.
For more on general markets, *see p186*.

★ La Boqueria
La Rambla 89, Raval (93 318 25 84, www.boqueria.info). Metro Liceu. **Open** 8am-8pm Mon-Sat. **Map** p328 A/B4.
Thronged with tourists searching for a little bit of Barcelona's gastro magic, and usually ending up with a pre-sliced quarter of overpriced pineapple, Europe's biggest food market is still an essential stop. Admire the orderly stacks of ridged Montserrat tomatoes, the wet sacks of snails and the oozing razor clams on the fish stalls. If you can't or don't want to cook it all yourself, you can eat instead at several market tapas bars.
If you visit in the morning, you'll see the best produce, including the smallholders' fruit and vegetable stalls in the little square attached to the C/Carme side of the market, where prices tend to be cheaper. But if you come only to ogle, remember that this is where locals come to shop. Don't touch what you don't want to buy, ask before taking photos and watch out for vicious old ladies with ankle-destroying wheeled shopping bags.

Specialist

La Botifarreria de Santa Maria
C/Santa Maria 4, Born (93 319 91 23, www.labotifarreria.com). Metro Barceloneta or Jaume I. **Open** 8.30am-2.30pm, 5-8.30pm Mon-Fri; 8.30am-3pm Sat. Closed Aug. **Credit** MC, V. **Map** p329 E7.
In this charming old shop, metres and metres of the typical Catalan *botifarra* sausage are made anew every day, along with unusual variations (cider, squid, Cabrales cheese, even chocolate). Before Lent, look out for the traditional yellowy egg *botifarras*. Other porky treats on offer include farmhouse pâtés, top quality acorn-fed ham and some of the most unusual types of local cured sausages such as *xolís*.

★ Caelum
C/Palla 8, Barri Gòtic (93 302 69 93, www.caelumbarcelona.com). Metro Liceu. **Open** 10.30am-8.30pm Mon-Thur; 10.30am-11pm Fri, Sat; 11.30am-9pm Sun. Closed 2wks Aug. **Credit** AmEx, DC, MC, V (shop only). **Map** p328 C4.
Spain's monks and nuns have a naughty sideline in sweets including '*pets de monja*' (little chocolate biscuits known as 'nuns' farts') candied saints' bones, and drinkable goodies such as eucalyptus and orange liqueur, all beautifully packaged. If you'd like to sample before committing to a whole box of Santa Teresa's sugared egg yolks, there's a café downstairs on the site of the medieval Jewish thermal baths.

La Campana
C/Princesa 36, Born (93 319 72 96). Metro Jaume I. **Open** 10am-9pm daily. **Credit** AmEx, MC, V. **Map** p329 E5.
Founded in 1922, this lovely old shop in the Born sells *turrons*, blocks of nougat traditionally eaten at Christmas. They come in two types: soft (Xixona) or hard and brittle (Alicant). In the summer, there's also *orxata*, an ice-cold drink made from tiger nuts; there are also wide ranges of ice-creams and pralines.
▶ *Just round the corner (C/Flassaders 15, Born, 93 268 18 44) is a branch with outdoor seating.*

★ Casa Gispert
C/Sombrerers 23, Born (93 319 75 35, www.casagispert.com). Metro Jaume I. **Open** *Jan-Sept* 9.30am-2pm, 4-7.30pm Tue-Fri; 10am-2pm, 5-8pm Sat. *Oct-Dec* 9.30am-2pm, 4-7.30pm Mon-Fri; 10am-2pm, 5-8pm Sat. **Credit** MC, V. **Map** p329 E6.
Another Born favourite, Casa Gispert radiates a warmth that has something to do with more than just its original wood-fired nut and coffee roaster. Like a stage-set version of an olde school shoppe, its wooden cabinets and shelves groan with the finest and most fragrant nuts, herbs, spices, preserves, sauces, oils and seasonings. The pre-packed

Market Picks

Ten things to look out for in La Boqueria market.

CONSUME

BACALLÀ SALAT

Dried, salted cod has been a staple in Catalonia for centuries, and entire stalls in the Boqueria are given over to this simple foodstuff. Try it in *esqueixada*, a salad of tomatoes, onions and black olives topped with *bacallà*.

BOLETS

Catalans are mad for mushrooms, and Bolets Petràs (stall Nos.867 and 870) is a mecca for fresh and dried funghi of all kinds, including meaty *rovellons*, slender *camagrocs* and succulent *llenegues*.

BULL

Catalans take pride in their *embotits* (charcuterie), and the curiously misshapen, roundish *bull* is a beloved local speciality. Some recipes call for head and tongue to be used in the recipe.

CALÇOTS

Midway between a leek and an onion in both appearance and taste, calçots are traditionally eaten at mass barbecues called *calçotades*. Shuck off the charred skin and dunk the stem in *romesco* sauce.

CARGOLS

The humble Catalan snail is a traditional component of several country dishes, particularly *cargols a la llauna* (oven-baked snails). Delicious dipped in *alioli* or *romesco* sauce.

CODONYAT

Dense, reddish slabs of tart quince jelly are usually found alongside cheese at market stalls, and are the ideal accompaniment to the Catalan curd cheese, *mató*, or a hunk of Manchego.

MONTSERRAT TOMATOES

These giant, bulging tomatoes may not look very pretty, but they are beloved by local foodies for their intense flavour and dense flesh.

PERCEBES

There are plenty of strange aquatic creatures to gawp at in the Boqueria, but *percebes* – knobbly goose-neck barnacles scraped from Galician cliffs – might be the strangest of all.

PEUS DE PORC

No part of the pig goes to waste in Catalunya, and you'll see the chunky trotters (alongside snouts and offal) at most butchers' stalls. Try them stewed with snails or tripe, or even *rebossat* (tossed in breadcrumbs and fried), then dusted with sugar.

TRIPAS

Those long, greyish-white, frilly things displayed at butchers' stalls are tripe (pigs' intestines), a traditional ingredient of the classic Catalan dish *cap i pota* ('head and foot').

Arlequí Màscares

kits for making local specialities such as *panellets* (Halloween bonbons) make great gifts.

Escribà

Gran Via de les Corts Catalanes 546, Eixample (93 454 75 35, www.escriba.es). Metro Urgell. **Open** 8am-3pm, 5-9pm Mon-Fri; 8am-9pm Sat, Sun. **Credit** MC, V. **Map** p326 E8.
Antoni Escribà, the 'Mozart of Chocolate', died in 2004, but his legacy lives on. His team produces jaw-dropping creations for Easter, from a chocolate Grand Canyon to a life-size model of Michelangelo's *David*. The smaller miracles include cherry liqueur encased in red chocolate lips. The Rambla branch is situated in a pretty Modernista building.
Other locations La Rambla 83, Raval (93 301 60 27)
► *To see more of Escribà's chocolate sculptures, visit the Museu de la Xocolata; see p64.*

★ Formatgeria La Seu

C/Dagueria 16, Barri Gòtic (93 412 65 48, www.formatgerialaseu.com). Metro Jaume I. **Open** 10am-2pm, 5-8pm Tue-Thur; 10am-3.30pm, 5-8pm Fri, Sat. Closed Aug. **No credit cards.** **Map** p329 D6.
Spain has long neglected its cheese heritage, to the point where this is the only shop in the country to specialise in Spanish-only farmhouse cheeses. Scottish owner Katherine McLaughlin hand-picks her wares, such as a manchego that knocks the socks off anything you'll find in the market or the truly strange Catalan *tupí*. She also stocks six varieties of cheese ice-cream and some excellent value olive oils. Her taster plate of three cheeses and a glass of wine for just a few euros is a great way to explore what's on offer.

★ Jamonísimo

C/Provença 85, Eixample (93 439 08 47, www.jamonisimo.com). Metro Entença. **Open** 9.30am-2.30pm, 5-9pm Mon-Sat. **Credit** AmEx, MC, V. **Map** p322 D7.
This is where Ferran Adrià buys his ham: simply the best available acorn-fed Iberian hams, made by artisans who control the entire process from breeding to curing. The dedicated and passionate salesmen are also happy to talk you through the purchase of *jamón* paraphernalia such as leg holders and knives, and there are tables where you can try a 'plate of three textures' or divine ham croquettes matched with great Spanish wines.
Other locations C/Muntaner 328 (93 209 15 62).

Olive

Plaça de les Olles 2, Born (93 310 58 83). Metro Barceloneta. **Open** 10am-9pm Mon-Sat; 2-9pm Sun. **Credit** MC, V. **Map** p329 E7.
Buying from small-scale producers of olive oil-based delicacies in Provence, Tuscany and Spain, this French chain has ventured below the Pyrenees. As well as oils, fruit vinegars, compotes and a cornucopia of other mouthwatering delights, it has gorgeously packaged soap, candles and cosmetics.

Papabubble

C/Ample 28, Barri Gòtic (93 268 86 25, www.papabubble.com). Metro Barceloneta or Drassanes. **Open** 10am-2pm, 4-8.30pm Mon-Fri; 10am-8.30pm Sat. Closed 2wks Aug. **Credit** AmEx, MC, V. **Map** p329 C7.
Push through the crowds to watch the candymen stretch, roll and chop their kaleidoscopic rock candy into lollies, sticks, humbugs and novelty sculptures. The goodies come in any flavour from strawberry to lavender or passion fruit.

GIFTS & SOUVENIRS

Arlequí Màscares

C/Princesa 7, Born (93 268 27 52, www. arlequimask.com). Metro Jaume I. **Open** 10.30am-8.30pm Mon-Sat; 10.30am-4.30pm Sun. **Credit** MC, V. **Map** p329 D5.
The walls in this lovely shop are dripping with masks, crafted from papier mâché and leather. Whether gilt-laden or in feathered commedia dell'arte style, simple Greek tragicomedy styles or traditional Japanese or Catalan varieties, they make striking fancy dress or decorative staples. Other trinkets and toys include finger puppets, mirrors and ornamental boxes.

Other locations Plaça Sant Josep Oriol 8, Barri Gòtic (93 317 24 29); C/Caballeros 10, Poble Espanyol (93 426 21 69).

Cereria Subirà

Baixada de Llibreteria 7, Barri Gotic (93 315 26 06). Metro Jaume I. **Open** 9am-1.30pm, 4-7.30pm Mon-Fri; 9am-1.30pm Sat. **Credit** DC, MC, V. **Map** p329 D5.

With a staircase fit for a full swish from Scarlett O'Hara, this exquisite candle shop dates back to the pre-electric days of 1716 when candles were an everyday necessity at home and in church. These days, the votive candles sit next to novelties such as After Eight-scented candles and candles in the shape of the Sagrada Família, alongside related goods such as garden torches and oil burners.

Dos i Una

C/Rosselló 275, Eixample (93 217 70 32). Metro Diagonal. **Open** 10.30am-2pm, 5-8.30pm Mon-Sat. **Credit** AmEx, DC, MC, V. **Map** p322 G6.

The first ever design shop in Barcelona (est. 1977) and an early patron of celebrated designer Javier Mariscal, Dos i Una stocks good quality designer frippery such as retro, round-cornered postcards in glorious technicolor, cheese graters in the shape of flamenco dancers, flower-shaped tea cups, chrome cuckoo clocks, colourful prints and jewellery.

Flora Albaicín

C/Canuda 3, Barri Gòtic (93 302 10 35). Metro Catalunya. **Open** 10.30am-1pm, 5-8pm Mon-Sat. **Credit** AmEx, MC, V. **Map** p328 B3.

This tiny boutique is bursting at the seams with brightly coloured flamenco frocks, polka-dotted shoes, head combs, bangles, shawls and everything else you need to dance the *sevillanas* in style.
▶ *Shop here before going to the nearby Feria de Abril de Catalunya (see p208 Calendar).*

★ Herboristeria del Rei

C/Vidre 1, Barri Gòtic (93 318 05 12). Metro Liceu. **Open** 4-8pm Tue-Fri, 10am-8pm Sat. Closed 2wks Aug. **Credit** MC, V. **Map** p329 B6.

Designed by a theatre set designer in the 1860s, this atmospheric shop hides myriad herbs, infusions, ointments and unguents for health and beauty. More up-to-date stock includes vegetarian foods, organic olive oils and organic mueslis; it's also a good place to buy saffron.

★ El Rei de la Màgia

C/Princesa 11, Born (93 319 39 20, www. elreidelamagia.com). Metro Jaume I. **Open** Sept-June 11am-2pm, 5-8pm Mon-Fri; 11am-2pm Sat. July, Aug 11am-2pm, 5-8pm Mon-Fri. **Credit** MC, V. **Map** p329 E5.

Cut someone in half, make a rabbit disappear or try out any number of other professional-quality stage illusions at the beautiful old 'King of Magic.' Less ambitious tricksters can practise their sleight of hand with the huge range of whoopee cushions, squirty flowers and itching powder.
▶ *The same people run the Museu de la Màgia; see p217.*

Xilografies

C/Freneria 1, Barri Gòtic (93 315 07 58). Metro Jaume I. **Open** 9am-1pm Mon-Sat. Closed Aug. **No credit cards. Map** p329 D5.

Using painstakingly detailed 18th-century carved boxwood blocks that have been passed down in her family for generations (some of which are displayed in a glass cabinet in this tiny shop), Maria creates *ex libris* stickers for books, bookmarks, notepaper, address books and prints. She also sells pens, birthday cards, prints of 18th-century maps and reproduction pocket sundials.

Flowers

The 18 flower stalls dotting the Rambla de les Flors originated from the old custom of Boqueria market traders giving a free flower to their customers. There are also stands at the **Mercat de la Concepció** (C/Aragó 311, Eixample, 93 457 53 29, www.laconcepcio.com), on the corner of C/València and C/Bruc (map p323 H7), some of which are open all night. Many local florists also offer the Interflora delivery service.

Flors Navarro

C/València 320, Eixample (93 457 40 99, www.floresnavarro.com). Metro Verdaguer. **Open** 24hrs daily. **Credit** AmEx, MC, V. **Map** p322 H7.

At Flors Navarro, fresh-cut blooms, pretty house plants and stunning bouquets are available to buy 24 hours a day. A dozen red roses can be delivered anywhere in the city, until 10pm, for €36.

HEALTH & BEAUTY
Hairdressers

Bot Peluqueria

C/Bot 4, Barri Gòtic (93 342 63 39, www.bot-hair.com). Metro Jaume I. **Open** 10am-8pm Mon-Sat. **Credit** MC, V. **Map** p328 B4.

José Juan Guzmán has styled everyone from Ferran Adrià to Ricky Martin, and regularly works on fashion shoots for the likes of *Marie Claire*. He's behind Bot, an ultra-hip hair salon, where the red-painted walls are hung with enormous black-and-white photos of giggling young models. A simple cut will set you back a hefty €29, but the friendly atmosphere means you'll never be pressured to try a style you don't want. Beauty treatments are also available.

CONSUME

Llongueras

*Passeig de Gràcia 78, Eixample (93 215 41 75,
www.llongueras.com). Metro Passeig de Gràcia.*
Open *Sept-June* 9am-7pm Mon-Sat. *July, Aug*
9am-6pm Mon-Fri; 9am-1pm Sat. **Credit** AmEx,
DC, MC, V. **Map** p322 G7.
A safe bet for all ages, this pricey Catalan chain has
well-trained stylists who take the time to give a
proper consultation, wash and massage. The cuts
are up-to-the-minute but as natural as possible.
Other locations throughout the city.

Raffel Pagès

*C/Canuda 22, Barri Gòtic (93 301 25 99,
www.raffelpages.com). Metro Catalunya.* **Open**
9am-8pm Mon-Fri; 9am-2pm Sat. **Credit** MC, V.
Map p328 C3.
The huge advantage of this chain is you don't neces-
sarily need appointments: whenever you feel the
spontaneous need for a change of style, you can simply wander right in. With a whole army of stylists
waiting to pounce, there's never a queue; although
service won't be particularly personalised or linger-
ing, it will be professional, competent and well priced.
Other locations throughout the city.

Opticians

+Visión

*El Triangle, Plaça Catalunya 4, Eixample (93
304 16 40, www.masvision.es). Metro Catalunya.*
Open 10am-10pm Mon-Sat. **Credit** AmEx, DC,
MC, V. **Map** p328 B2.
There are some English-speaking staff at this handy
optical superstore. It's occasionally possible to get a
test without an appointment.

Pharmacies

Pharmacies *(farmàcies/farmàcias)* are signalled
by large green and red neon crosses. About a
dozen operate around the clock, while more
have late opening hours; some of the most
central are listed below.

The full list of pharmacies that stay open late
and/or all night is posted on every pharmacy
door and in the local papers. You can also call
two helplines, 010 and 098, for information.
Late-night pharmacies may appear closed, but
you'll get help by knocking on the shutters.

Farmàcia Álvarez

*Passeig de Gràcia 26, Eixample (93 302 11 24).
Metro Passeig de Gràcia.* **Open** 8am-10.30pm
Mon-Thur; 8am-midnight Fri; 9am-midnight Sat.
Credit MC, V. **Map** p326 G8.

Farmàcia Cervera

*C/Muntaner 254, Eixample (93 200 09 96).
Metro Diagonal/FGC Gràcia.* **Open** 24hrs daily.
Credit AmEx, MC, V. **Map** p322 E5.

Farmàcia Clapés

*La Rambla 98, Barri Gòtic (93 301 28 43).
Metro Liceu.* **Open** 24hrs daily. **Credit** AmEx,
MC, V. **Map** p328 B4.

Farmàcia Vilar

*Vestíbule, Estació de Sants, Sants (93 490 92 07).
Metro Sants Estació.* **Open** 7am-10.30pm Mon-Fri;
8am-10.30pm Sat, Sun. **Credit** AmEx, MC, V.
Map p325 B7.

Shops

Alongside Sephora, which should be your
first port of call, the ground floor of **El
Corte Inglés** *(see p184)* also has a good
range of toiletries.

Sephora

*El Triangle, C/Pelai 13-37, Eixample (93 306
39 00, www.sephora.es). Metro Catalunya.* **Open**
10am-10pm Mon-Sat. **Credit** AmEx, DC, MC, V.
Map p328 B2.
Of all Barcelona's beauty options, Sephora is your
best bet for unfettered playing around with scents and
make-up. Products include most of the usual mid- to
high-end brands; there are also handy beauty tools,
such as eyebrow tweezers and pencil sharpeners.
Other locations throughout the city.

Spas & salons

★ Aire de Barcelona

*Passeig Picasso 22, Born (902 555 789,
www.airedebarcelona.com). Metro Arc de Triomf
or Jaume I.* **Open** 10am midnight Mon, Tue,
Sun; 10am-2am Wed-Sat. *Baths* (90 mins) €28;
(incl 15-min massage) €39. **Credit** MC, V.
Map p327 H11.
Opened in 2008, these subterranean, bare-bricked
Arab baths are superbly relaxing, and offer a range
of extra massages in addition to the basic package
of hot and cold pools, jacuzzi, salt-water pool, ham-
mam and relaxation zone. Entrance is offered every
two hours from 10am (you get 90 minutes) and
reservations are advisable. If you've left your
swimsuit at home, you can borrow one, or buy
one for €10.

Instituto Francis

*Ronda de Sant Pere 18, Eixample (93 317 78
08, www.institutofrancis.com). Metro Catalunya.*
Open 9.30am-8pm Mon-Fri; 9am-4pm Sat.
Credit DC, MC, V. **Map** p328 D2.
Europe's largest beauty centre has seven floors and
more than 50 staff all dedicated to making you beautiful – inside and out. As well as offering all the usual
facials, massages, anti-cellulite treatments and man-
icures, the institute specialises in depilation, home-
opathic therapies and non-surgical procedures such
as teeth whitening and micropigmentation.

CONSUME

HOUSE & HOME

Antiques

If you don't mind haggling, dealers set up stands at Port Vell at weekends. C/Palla is the main focus for antiques in the Barri Gòtic; however, they're of variable quality. Dazzlingly expensive antiques can be found on C/Consell de Cent in the Eixample; there are more affordable goodies around C/Dos de Maig, near Els Encants flea market (*see right*). Other worthwhile markets include the **stamp and coin market** on Plaça Reial (9am-2.30pm Sun), and the weekly **book and coin market** (*see p187*).

Antiques Market

Plaça Nova, Barri Gòtic (no phone). Metro Jaume I. **Open** 9am-7pm Thur. Closed 3wks Aug. **No credit cards. Map** p328 C4.

Thanks in part to its location in front of the cathedral, this market charges prices that are targeted at tourists – be prepared to haggle. The set-up dates from the Middle Ages, but antiques generally consist of smaller and more modern items: sepia postcards, *manila* shawls, pocket watches, typewriters, lace, cameras and jewellery, among bibelots and bric-a-brac. In the first week of August, and from 27 November to 20 December, the market is held at Avda Portal de l'Àngel.

L'Arca de l'Àvia

C/Banys Nous 20, Barri Gòtic (93 302 15 98, www.larcadelavia.com). Metro Liceu.

Open 10.30am-2pm, 5-8.30pm Mon-Fri; 11am-2pm Sat. Closed 1wk Aug. **Credit** AmEx, DC, MC, V. **Map** p329 C5.

Specialising in antique textiles, the 'Grandmother's Ark' smells wonderfully of cloves and freshly ironed linen and is bursting with both antique and reproduction curtains, bedlinen, tablecloths, clothes and a snowstorm of handmade lace. It's particularly popular with brides seeking original lace veils and vintage dresses (there's a tailoring service), and is also the perfect place to go in search of a jaw-dropping lace *mantilla* (headdress) or lavishly embroidered *mantones* (fringed silk shawls).

Bulevard dels Antiquaris

Passeig de Gràcia 55, Eixample (93 215 44 99, www.bulevarddelsantiquaris.com). Metro Passeig de Gràcia. **Open** 10am-2pm, 5-8.30pm Mon-Sat. **Credit** AmEx, MC, V. **Map** p322 G7.

This small antiques 'mall' is one of the most convenient and safest places to shop for antiques in Barcelona (experts inspect every object for authenticity). Miró and Tapies fans can buy limited-edition prints at March (No.42). Check out the style of ethnic art that influenced the likes of Miró at Raquel Montagut (No.11), where you can pick up a Nigerian funeral urn. Collectors will love the antique playthings at Tric Trac (No.43) and Govary's (No.54).

Els Encants

C/Dos de Maig 177-187, Plaça de les Glòries, Eixample (93 246 30 30, www.encantsbcn.com). Metro Glòries. **Open** 9am-5pm Mon, Wed, Fri, Sat. *Auctions* 7-9am Mon, Wed, Fri. **No credit cards. Map** p327 L8.

Vinçon.

CONSUME

The new location of this open-air flea market has been up in the air for years, but the Ajuntament now has plans to house it alongside the Teatre Nacional de Catalunya in 2011. For now, the market remains a chaotic antidote to the Glòries mall next door with its stew of shouts, musty smells and teetering piles of everything from old horseshoes and Barça memorabilia to cheap electrical gadgets, religious relics and ancient Spanish schoolbooks.

If you want to buy furniture at a decent price, join the commercial buyers at the auctions from 7am, or arrive at noon, when unsold stuff drops in price. Don't forget to check out the vast warehouses on the market's outskirts, where you may find a bargain. Avoid Saturdays, when prices shoot up and the crowds move in, and be on your guard for pickpockets and short-changing.

General

★ Vinçon
Passeig de Gràcia 96, Eixample (93 215 60 50, www.vincon.com). Metro Diagonal. **Open** 10am-8.30pm Mon-Sat. **Credit** AmEx, DC, MC, V. **Map** p322 G6.
This is one of the vital organs that keeps Barcelona's reputation as a city of cutting-edge design alive. The building itself is a monument to the history of local design: the upstairs furniture showroom is surrounded by Modernista glory (and you get a peek at Gaudí's La Pedrera); downstairs in the kitchen, bathroom, garden and other departments, everything is black, minimalist and hip. Although not cheap, almost everything you buy here is, or will be, a design classic, whether it's a Bonet armchair or the so-called 'perfect' corkscrew.
Other locations TinçÇon, C/Rosselló 246, Eixample (93 215 60 50); KitchenÇon, C/Rosselló 246, Eixample (93 215 60 50).

MUSIC & ENTERTAINMENT

C/Tallers, C/Valldonzella, C/Bonsuccès and C/Riera Baixa in the Raval are dotted with music shops catering to all tastes and formats, with plenty of sheet music and instruments. Mainstream music selections are found in the huge Avda Portal de l'Àngel branch of **El Corte Inglés** (*see p184*) and, more cheaply, at **FNAC** (El Triangle, Plaça Catalunya 4, 93 344 18 00, www.fnac.es), which also has world music and acres of classical.

CDs & records

Casa Beethoven
La Rambla 97, Raval (93 301 48 26, www.casabeethoven.com). Metro Liceu. **Open** 9am-2pm, 4-8pm Mon-Fri; 9am-2pm, 5-8pm Sat. Closed 3wks Aug. **Credit** AmEx, DC, MC, V. **Map** p328 B4.
The sheet music and songbooks on sale in this old shop in the Raval cover the gamut from Wagner to the White Stripes, with a concentration on opera. Books cover music history and theory, while CDs are particularly strong on both modern and classical Spanish music.

Discos Castelló
C/Tallers 3 & 7, Raval (93 302 59 46, http://castellodiscos.com). Metro Catalunya. **Open** 10am-8.30pm Mon-Sat. **Credit** MC, V. **Map** p328 B2.
Discos Castelló is a long-established and very reputable music store in the Raval. The shop at No.3 is devoted to classical music; the largest shop, at no.7, covers pretty much everything else; including hip hop, pop, rock, jazz, electronica and ethnic music, as well as a range of T-shirts and bags. Vinyl is also bought and sold.

Discos Juandó
C/Giralt el Pellisser 2B, Sant Pere (93 319 16 74). Metro Jaume I. **Open** 10am-2pm, 4-8pm Mon-Sat. **Credit** MC, V. **Map** p329 E4.
An old-school vinyl store specialising in soul and jazz but with a decent range of most other styles up to and including '80s new wave. Take a seat and flick through some copies of Record Collector, or peruse such oddities as the 'nude' section – albums with naked women on the front. Just don't come looking for techno or happy house.

Gong
C/Consell de Cent 343, Eixample (93 215 34 31, www.gongdiscos.com). Metro Passeig de Gràcia. **Open** 10am-9pm Mon-Sat. **Credit** AmEx, MC, V. **Map** p322 G8.
An unglamorous but serious record shop chain with a wide range of stock, which also stretches to DVDs, books and video games. Bargain-hunters can flick through the always extensive cheapies rack (and a big box of old vinyl records). Gong is a reliable source of concert tickets and information.
Other locations Barcelona Glòries, Avda Diagonal 208, Eixample (93 486 00 28); Fabra i Puig 50, (93 311 44 61).

CONSUME

Instruments

Guitar Shop

C/Tallers 27, 46 & 61, Raval (93 412 19 19, 93 412 66 22, 93 317 50 50, www.guitarshop.es). Metro Catalunya. **Open** 10am-2pm, 4.30-8.30pm Mon-Sat. **Credit** AmEx, DC, MC, V. **Map** p328 B2.

A mecca for fretheads, this trio of shops has all the goodies: cedarwood Antonio Aparicio classical guitars, Prudencio Saez flamenco guitars, and cheap Admiras. At No.27, there's a whole host of vintage Fenders, '80s Marshall amps and the like; bargain-hunters can browse the second-hand gear at No.61.

SPORT & FITNESS

In addition to the stores listed below, the tourist shops on La Rambla stock a huge range of football strips.

La Botiga del Barça

Maremagnum, Moll d'Espanya, Port Vell (93 225 80 45). Metro Drassanes. **Open** 10am-10pm daily. **Credit** AmEx, DC, MC, V. **Map** p326 F12.

Everything for the well-dressed Barça fan, from the standard blue and burgundy strips to scarves, hats, crested ties and even underpants, plus calendars, shirts printed with your name, shield-embossed ashtrays, beach towels and so on.

Other locations C/Jaume I 18, Barri Gòtic (93 269 15 32); Ronda Universitat 37-39, Barri Gòtic (93 318 64 77); Museu del FC Barcelona, Nou Camp (93 409 02 71).

Decathlon

C/Canuda 20, Barri Gòtic (93 342 61 61, www.decathlon.es). Metro Catalunya. **Open** 9.30am-9.30pm Mon-Sat. **Credit**, MC, V. **Map** p328 C3.

Whether you need boxing gloves or a bicycle lock, this multi-storey French chain will probably be able to see you right. Additional services include bike repair and hire, and team kit stamping.

Other locations L'Illa, Avda Diagonal 545-557, Eixample (93 444 01 54); Gran Via 2, Gran Via de les Corts Catalanes 75-97 L'Hospitalet de Llobregat (93 259 15 92).

TICKETS

FNAC (El Triangle, Plaça Catalunya 4, 93 344 18 00, www.fnac.es) has a very efficient ticket desk situated on its ground floor, covering everything from theme parks to gigs. Concert tickets for smaller venues are often sold in record shops and at the venues themselves; check street posters around the city for details.

For Barça tickets, *see below and p262.*

ServiCaixa – La Caixa

902 332 211, www.servicaixa.com. **Credit** AmEx, MC, V.

Use the special ServiCaixa cashpoints (you'll find them in most larger branches of La Caixa), dial the phone number, or check the website to buy tickets for cinemas, concerts, plays, museums, amusement parks and Barça games. You'll need to show the card with which you made the payment when you collect the tickets; check the pick-up deadline.

Telentrada – Caixa Catalunya

902 101 212, www.telentrada.com. **Credit** MC, V.

Tickets for theatre performances, cinemas (including shows at the IMAX), concerts, museums and sights over the phone, online from the website above, or even over the counter at any branch of the Caixa Catalunya savings bank. Tickets can be collected from either Caixa Catalunya cashpoints or the tourist office at Plaça Catalunya.

TRAVELLERS' NEEDS

FNAC (El Triangle, Plaça Catalunya 4, 93 344 18 00, 902 10 06 32, www.fnac.es) and **El Corte Inglés** (*see p184*) both have travel agencies, and www.rumbo.es is also worth checking if you're planning a trip abroad. If you're after new luggage, try **Casa Antich** (*see p196*).

If you have items to send overseas, post offices will send anything weighing up to 30 kilos. For shipping larger boxes and items, contact **FedEx** (902 100 871, 91 329 87 00, www.fedex.com); for other couriers and shippers, *see pxxx.*

Halcón Viajes

C/Aribau 34, Eixample (93 454 59 95, 902 300 600, www.halconviajes.com). Metro Universitat. **Open** 9am-1.30pm, 4.30-8pm Mon-Fri; 9am-1pm Sat. **Credit** AmEx, DC, MC, V. **Map** p322 F8.

This mammoth chain has exclusive deals with Air Europa and Globalia, among others, and can offer highly competitive rates in most areas. Service tends to be quite brisk but efficient.

Other locations throughout the city.

Orixà Viatges

Altaïr, Gran Via de les Corts Catalanes 616, Eixample (93 342 66 26, www.orixa.com). Metro Universitat. **Open** Mid July-mid May 10am-2pm, 4.30-7.30pm Mon-Fri. May-July 10am-2pm, 4.30-7.30pm Mon-Fri; 10am-1pm Sat. **Credit** MC, V. **Map** p326 F8.

Located within the Altaïr travel bookshop, this agency specialises in group and adventure tours in exotic locations, although it also provides all the standard travel services you would expect. English-speaking agents are available.

Other locations C/Aragó 227, Eixample (93 487 00 22).

Arts & Entertainment

Gran Teatre del Liceu. *See p253.*

Calendar

A plan for all seasons.

The Catalans' seemingly endless enthusiasm for festivals and parties means that there's scarcely a week in the year that doesn't include at least a couple. These range from the full-on traditional knees-up, with giants, dwarfs and dragons wheeling through fireworks, to gentle street fairs selling artisanal honey and sausages, and perhaps laying on a bouncy castle.

The array of religious events and old-fashioned pageants, all of which spotlight what makes Catalonia unique, are supplemented by a wide variety of more modern celebrations. You're just as likely to stumble across a festival of rock documentaries, graffiti art, hip hop or cyber sculpture as you are to see a traditional parade: Sónar alone attracts 80,000 people each year.

ARTS & ENTERTAINMENT

LOCAL TRADITION

The key annual events are September's **Festes de la Mercè**, the main city celebrations that offer a wild variety of events. The Mercè and the other 30 or so neighbourhood *festes* share many traditional ingredients: dwarfs, *castellers* (human castles), and *gegants* (huge papier-mâché/fibreglass giants dressed as princesses, fishermen, sultans and even topless chorus girls), and two unique exercises: the *correfoc* and the *sardana*.

The **correfoc** ('fire run') is a frenzy of pyromania. Groups of horned devils dance through the streets, brandishing tridents that spout fireworks and generally flouting every safety rule in the book. Protected by cotton caps and long sleeves, the more daring onlookers try to stop the devils and touch the fire-breathing dragons being dragged along in their wake.

The orderly antidote to this pandemonium is the **sardana**, Catalonia's folk dance. Watching the dancers executing their fussy little hops and

steps in a large circle, it's hard to believe that *sardanes* were once banned as a vestige of pagan witchcraft. The music is similarly restrained; a reedy noise played by an 11-piece *cobla* band. The *sardana* is much harder than it looks, and the joy lies in taking part rather than watching. To try your luck, check out the *sardanes populars* held in front of the cathedral (noon-2pm Sun Jan-Aug & Dec; 6-8pm Sat, noon-2pm Sun Sept-Nov) and in the Plaça Sant Jaume (6pm Sun Oct-July), or see www.fed.sardanista.cat for monthly displays around the city (*see also p57* **You Put Your Left Leg In**).

INFORMATION

Organisers are prone to change dates. For more information, try tourist offices, the city's information line (010) and the cultural agenda section at www.bcn.cat. Newspapers also carry details, especially in their Friday or Saturday supplements. Events listed below that include public holidays, when most of the city's shops, bars and restaurants close, are marked ★.

> **INSIDE TRACK**
> **FURTHER INFORMATION**
>
> For music festivals, *see p237-238*; for art festivals, *see p225*; for film festivals, *see p224*. For full listings of venues mentioned here, see their entries in the guide.

EVENTS

Spring

Festes de Sant Medir de Gràcia
Gràcia to Sant Cugat & back (www.santmedir. org). Starting point Metro Fontana. **Date** 3 Mar. **Map** p338 G4/5 & p339 H4/5.

On or around the feast day of St Emeterius (Sant Medir in Catalan), for almost 200 years colourfully decorated horse-drawn carts have gathered around the Plaça Trilla to ride up to his hermitage in the Collserola hills. The most popular element are the carts that circle the streets of Gràcia and shower the crowd with 100 tons of blessed boiled sweets.

El Feile
Various venues (93 423 76 68, www.elfeile.com). **Date** wk of 17 Mar.
This Saint Patrick's celebration of all things Gaelic has become an established part of the Barcelona calendar in its short life. It embraces music, dance and stand-up comedy, as well as sports such as Gaelic football, rugby and hurling.
► *The celebrations are enjoyed with particular enthusiasm at the Quiet Man pub; see p177.*

Kosmopolis
CCCB (see p72, www.cccb.org/kosmopolis). **Date** 24-26 Mar 2011. **Map** p344 A2.
Subtitled the 'International Literature Festival', the Kosmopolis runs every two years and explores every aspect of the written word (and indeed the oral

tradition), with conferences, workshops and readings. In 2011, Jonathan Safran Foer, Paul Auster and Ian McEwan are slated to appear, alongside mostly local authors.

Setmana Santa* (Holy Week)
Date wk leading up to Easter.
Easter for Catalans is a relatively sober affair, with none of the pageantry embraced by their southern cousins. The main event is the blessing of the palms on *diumenge de rams* (Palm Sunday). Crowds surge into the cathedral clutching bleached palm fronds bought from stalls around the city; these are then used to bring luck to households. On Good Friday, a series of small processions and blessings takes place in front of the cathedral. On Easter Sunday, godparents dole out the *mones*: chocolate confections, more elaborate than humble Easter eggs.

Fira de la Terra
Parc de la Ciutadella and Passeig Lluís Companys, Born (www.diadelaterra.org). Metro Arc de Triomf. **Date** 16, 17 Apr 2011. **Map** p343 H/J 10/11.

Fun for Free

Enjoy the city without spending a cent.

As the planet continues to struggle in the tentacles of *la crisis*, holidays have taken a hit for almost everyone – but Barcelona is one city that offers plenty for free. From **La Mercè** (*see p213*) to **Sant Joan** (*see p211*), none of the city's many street festivals charges admission, and anyone can enjoy the parades, music and fireworks.

Rock and pop are free during the **BAM**, free classical music and jazz come courtesy of **Música als Parcs** (*see p212*) and dance fans can get a free fix at the **Dies de Dansa** (*see p256*). For free family entertainment, try **Fira de la Terra** (*see above*), **Festa Major de Gràcia** (*see p212*) and **Santa Eulàlia** (*see p215*), which offer clowns and circus acts, play tents, bouncy castles and the like. The queen of freebies, however, is the **Montjuïc de Nit** (*see p212*) where, from dusk 'til dawn, everything is free, from theatre, music and film to swimming and astronomy sessions.

Festivals are also good for snagging free snacks: there's *botifarra* sausage dished out in the Boqueria for **Carnaval** (*see p215*); cups of hot chocolate at Santa Eulàlia; and hot chocolate with fried batter *xurros* at the Festes de Gràcia. The **Festes de Sant Medir** (*see p208*) bring bag-loads

of blessed boiled sweets, and there's free food-tasting at Montjuïc de Nit.

As a new initiative, all municipal museums (see www.bcn.cat for a list) are free on Sunday afternoons, along with the feast days of Sant Eulàlia, La Mercè and **Sant Jordi** (*see p210*), as well as the **Dia Internacional dels Museus** (*see p211*). At the **MACBA** (*see p72*), the first day of any new exhibition is free, while other museums have set days for free entry.

The permanent collections of all the municipal museums are free on the first Sunday of each month, as is the **Monestir de Pedralbes** (*see p106*). Exceptions are: the **Museu de l'Història de Barcelona** (*see p53*), which is free from 4-8pm on the first Saturday of the month; the **Jardí Botanic** (*see p85*), which is free on the last Sunday of the month; the **CCCB** (*see p72*), free on the first Wednesday of the month; and the **Museu Marítim** (*see p78*), free from 3pm on the first Saturday of the month. In addition to the first Sunday of the month, the **Museu Frederic Marès** (*see p59*) is also free on Wednesdays from 3-7pm, and the **Museu d'Història de Catalunya** (*see p77*) is also free on September 11 (the Diada) and 24 (the Mercè).

ARTS & ENTERTAINMENT

The Fira de la Terra is a two-day eco-festival to celebrate Earth Day (22 April), although it's normally held on the nearest weekend to the actual day. There are handicrafts, food stalls and performances, along with talks on environmental issues. Most of the activities are aimed at children.

▶ *For more on the Parc de la Ciutadella, see p69.*

Sant Jordi

La Rambla & all over Barcelona (www.bcn.cat/stjordi). **Date** 23 Apr.
On the feast day of Sant Jordi (St George), the patron saint of Catalonia, nearly every building bears the red and gold Catalan flag, while bakeries sell Sant Jordi bread streaked with red *sobrassada* pâté. Red roses decorate the Palau de la Generalitat and the city's many statues and paintings of George in all his dragon-slaying glory.

It's said that as the drops of the dragon's blood fell, they turned into red flowers – and for more than five centuries, this has been the Catalan version of St Valentine's Day. Men traditionally gave women a rose tied to an ear of wheat, and women reciprocated with a book; this is also the 'Day of the Book'. It accounts for an amazing 10% of Catalonia's annual book sales, and street stalls and bookshops give good discounts.

★ Feria de Abril de Catalunya

Fòrum area (www.fecac.com). Metro El Maresme-Fòrum. **Date** 29 Apr-8 May 2011.
A pale imitation of Seville's grand Feria de Abril, this week-long, sprawling and joyously tacky event is still a whole heap of fun, especially for fans of fried squid and candyfloss. The rows of decorated marquees are a sea of polka dots, as young and old twirl on and off the stages, and onlookers glug

European Commissions

A new festival Europes aspires to build cultural bridges between nations.

Launched in autumn 2010 and set to become a regular feature on the city's calendar, **Europes** has as its wildly ambitious aim an exploration of the continents' latest trends in art, architecture, theatre, dance, film, food, music, literature and – for any miscellanea that might have dropped through the cracks – 'cultural thought'.

Held over 25 days in October and November, it involved over 250 activities, held in 200 different locations. These ranged from the soundscapes of the Orchestra of Chaos at the Museu Picasso to author John Banville giving a talk in a local library to the north of the city. A surprise hit was the talk given by Eugen Gomringer, considered to be one of the creators of 'concrete' or 'shape' poetry, and a double bill of Romanian cinema pulled an equally impressive crowd. There were three days of debates on cultural themes, and a abundance of performances in different genres, most notably at the Liceu opera house, the Mercat de les Flors and the CaixaForum.

One of the pillars of the festival is considered to be the showcasing of young art students from across Europe, and organisers La Fábrica (www.lafabrica.com) created a slightly unfortunately named, if well-intentioned, scheme: Bed Sharing. This involved Catalan students supplying accommodation to their counterparts from the rest of Europe for the run of the festival, on the understanding this would be reciprocated in the future.

▶ www.europes-festival.eu

manzanilla sherry and scarf some of the greasiest food imaginable. It's great for children, and there's a funfair.

Dia del Treball* (May Day)
Various venues. **Date** 1 May.
A day of demonstrations and marches led by trade unionists representing various left-wing organisations. The main routes cover Plaça da la Universitat, Via Laietana, Passeig de Gràcia, Passeig Sant Joan and Plaça Sant Jaume.

Sant Ponç
C/Hospital. Metro Liceu. **Date** 11 May.
Map p344 A4.
A street market held in honour of the patron saint of beekeepers and herbalists, and ablaze with candied fruit, fresh herbs, natural infusions, honey and honeycomb, most of it straight off the farmer's cart.

Barcelona Poesia & Festival Internacional de Poesia
All over Barcelona (93 316 10 00, www.bcn.cat/barcelonapoesia). **Date** 11-17 May 2011.
This poetry festival started in 1393 as the courtly Jocs Florals (Floral Games), named after the prizes: a silver violet for third prize; a golden rose as second; and, naturally, a real flower for the winner. The games died out in the 15th century but were resuscitated in 1859 as a vehicle for the promotion of the Catalan language. Prizes went to the most suitably florid paeans to the motherland; these days, Spanish is permitted, as are Basque and Galician. Many languages can be heard at the International Poetry Festival.

Festa Major de Nou Barris
All over Nou Barris (www.bcn.cat/noubarris). Metro Virrei Amat. **Date** mid May.
What the humble neighbourhood of Nou Barris lacks in landmark architecture, it makes up for with vim. Along with some great cultural programming, it has a very lively *festa major*, attracting top-notch local bands, along with the usual parades and street fairs. The Nou Barris flamenco festival runs concomitantly, and also brings in some big names.

Dia Internacional dels Museus
All over Barcelona (http://icom.museum/imd.html, www.bcn.cat/lanitdelsmuseus). **Date** mid May.
Masterminded by the International Council of Museums, this worldwide day of free museum entrance has an annual theme with related activites; in 2010 this will be 'Museums and Social Harmony'. Note that the recommended date is 18 May, but this can vary from year to year.
▶ *La Nit dels Museus is a new initiative, where 21 museums offer free entry on the previous night from 7pm to 1am.*

La Tamborinada
Parc de la Ciutadella, Born (93 414 72 01, www.fundaciolaroda.cat). Metro Ciutadella-Vila Olímpica. **Date** late May.
Aimed at children, this vibrant one-day festival fills the Ciutadella park with concerts, workshops and circus performances. Games and entertainments run from snakes and ladders to a towering wall for rock-climbing.

Festa dels Cors de la Barceloneta
Barceloneta. **Date** weekend of Whitsun.
Map p343 H12/13.
In a Pentecostal tradition dating back 150 years, more than 20 choirs of workers parade through the streets of the *barrio* in elaborate costumes garlanded with objects typical of their profession – nets and oars for a fisherman, cereal boxes and sausages for a grocer – on the Saturday morning before Whitsun. They then pile into coaches and take off on a weekend jolly, returning for more parading, fireworks and revelry on Monday evening.

★ L'Ou Com Balla
Ateneu Barcelonès, C/Canuda 6; Casa de l'Ardiaca, C/Santa Llúcia 1; Cathedral cloisters; Museu Frederic Marès; all in Barri Gòtic (information Institut de Cultura 93 301 77 75, www.bcn.cat/icub). **Date** early June.
L'Ou Com Balla (the 'dancing egg') is a local Corpus Christi tradition dating from 1637: a hollowed-out eggshell is set spinning and bobbing in apparent *perpetuum mobile* on the spout of various fountains, garlanded for the occasion with flowers. The Sunday Corpus Christi procession leaves from the cathedral in the early evening; on the Saturday, there's free entry to the Ajuntament, the Palau Centelles behind it and the Museu d'Història de Barcelona, along with *sardanes* (circle dances) at 7pm outside the cathedral.

Summer

★ Sant Joan*
All over Barcelona. **Date** night of 23 June.
In the weeks leading up to the feast of St John, the streets become a terrifying war zone of firecrackers and cowering dogs. This is mere limbering up for the main event – on the night of 23 June there are bonfires and firework displays all over the city, but especially the beach, running until dawn. Cava is the traditional tipple, and piles of *coca* – flat, crispy bread topped with candied fruit – are consumed. Special metro and FGC trains run all night and the 24th is a much-needed holiday.

Festa de la Música
All over Barcelona (93 316 10 00, www.bcn.cat/festadelamusica). **Date** late June.
Started in France in 1982 and now celebrated in more than 100 countries, the three-day Festival of Music

sees amateur musicians from 100 countries take to the streets. All events are free, and you're as likely to see a child slapping a bongo as a first-rate blues band, symphony orchestra or choir.

Gran Trobada d'Havaneres

Passeig Joan de Borbó, Barceloneta (93 319 98 46, www.amicshavaneres.com). Metro Barceloneta. **Date** last Sat in June. **Map** p345 E7/8.
The barnacled legacy of Catalonia's old trade links with Cuba, *havaneres* are melancholy 19th-century shanties accompanied by accordion and guitar. The main event is at the port town of Calella de Palafrugells, but the Barcelona satellite is no less fun. Performances by groups dressed in stripy shirts, with salty sea-dog names such as Peix Fregit (fried fish) and Xarxa (fishing net), are followed by *cremat* (flaming spiced rum) and fireworks.

★ Música als Parcs

93 413 24 00, www.bcn.cat/parcsijardins. **Date** June-Aug.
This series of free, alfresco concerts runs throughout the summer months in some of Barcelona's loveliest parks. It comprises two cycles; there's jazz from June to August on Wednesdays and Fridays at 10pm in Ciutadella park in front of the fountain and, in July, young musicians perform a varied classical concert programme from Thursday to Saturday in various parks. A municipal band boosts the programme on occasional Thursdays with crowd-pleasers from Gershwin, *West Side Story* and the like.

★ Festival del Grec

Various venues (93 316 10 00, www.bcn.cat/grec). **Tickets** vary. **Date** late June-early Aug.
Named after the Greek amphitheatre (Teatre Grec) that forms such an integral part of its programming, this is the major cultural festival of the year. It brings together dozens of shows from around the world, encompassing dance, music, theatre and circus. Increasingly there are performances in English, with Catalan surtitles.

★ Montjuïc de Nit

Montjuïc (www.bcn.cat/cultura/montjuicnit). **Date** 2 July 2011.
In line with other 'White Night' or 'Nuit Blanche' events across Europe, Barcelona has laid on its own night of dusk-to-dawn entertainment, all of it free. While Rome, Paris, Brussels and others hold theirs in early October, the date was felt to be uncomfortably close to the Mercè celebrations. Instead, a quiet weekend in July was picked for a vibrant selection of music, theatre, dance, cinema and art, with Montjuïc's museums staying open until 3am or so.

Festa Major del Raval

www.bcn.cat/cultura. Metro Drassanes or Liceu. **Date** mid-late July.

INSIDE TRACK
TEARS OF SAINT EULALIA

Almost without fail, the clear blue skies of a Barcelona September fill with clouds over the few days of the Mercè festival. These raindrops are known as the 'Tears of Santa Eulàlia', and are said to express her sadness that, as joint patron saint of the city, she was overlooked and Mercè chosen for the big bash of the year.

Over three days, entertainments include giants, a fleamarket, children's workshops and free concerts on the Rambla del Raval. This particular *festa major* prides itself on multiculturalism, with music from around the world and ethnic food stalls.

Nits d'Estiu CaixaForum

CaixaForum (93 476 86 00, www.fundacio.lacaixa.es). **Date** every Wed in July, Aug.
Many museums hold a Nits de Estiu (Summer Nights) programme in July and August, but CaixaForum has one of the best. All exhibitions are open until midnight, and there are concerts of varying stripes, films (€2) and other activities.

Festa de Sant Roc

Various venues around Plaça Nova, Barri Gòtic (010, www.bcn.cat). Metro Jaume I. **Date** 12-16 Aug. **Map** p344 C4.
The Festa de Sant Roc, celebrated every year since 1589, is the Barri Gòtic's street party. It's hard to beat for lovers of Catalan traditions: there are parades with the giants and fat heads, *sardana* dancing and 19th-century street games. The festivities, which centre around the Plaça Nova in front of the cathedral, conclude with a *correfoc* and fireworks.

★ Festa Major de Gràcia

All over Gràcia (93 459 30 80, www.festamajordegracia.cat). Metro Fontana. **Date** 3rd wk in Aug. **Map** p338 G4/5 & p339 H4/5.
The main event at Gràcia's extravagant *festa major* is its street competition, where residents transform some 25 streets into pirate ships, rainforests and Jurassic landscapes. The festival opens with giants and castles in Plaça Rius i Taulet, and climaxes with a *correfoc* and a *castell de focs* (castle of fireworks). In between, there are some 600 activities, from concerts to *sardanes* and bouncy castles. Recent years have been marred by vandalism and late-night scuffles with the police.

Festa Major de Sants

All over Sants (93 490 62 14/www.festamajor desants.net). Metro Plaça de Sants or Sants Estació. **Date** last wk in Aug.

One of the lesser-known *festes majors*, Sants has a traditional flavour, with floral offerings to images of St Bartholomew at the local church and the market. Major events, such as the *correfoc* on the night of the 24th, can be found in the Parc de l'Espanya Industrial; others are held at Plaça del Centre, C/Sant Antoni, Plaça de la Farga and Plaça Joan Peiro, behind Sants station.

Autumn

Diada Nacional de Catalunya*
All over Barcelona. **Date** 11 Sept.
Catalan National Day commemorates Barcelona's capitulation to the Bourbon army in the 1714 War of the Spanish Succession, a bitter defeat that led to the repression of many Catalan institutions. It's lost some of its vigour but is still a day for national re-affirmation, with the Catalan flag flying on buses and balconies. There are marches throughout the city, the centre being the statue of Rafael Casanova (who directed the resistance) on the Ronda Sant Pere.
▶ *Many make a pilgrimage to the monastery at Montserrat, Catalonia's spiritual heart.*

★ Festival Asia
Various venues (www.festivalasia.es).
Tickets vary. **Date** 2wks in Sept.
This week of twirling saris, Chinese acrobats, music, workshops and stalls from 17 Asian countries, has expanded from its base at the Mercat de les Flors to take in a number of venues, including the MACBA

(*see p72*) and the CCCB (*see p72*). The festival now runs with the Festes de la Mercè; *see below*.

★ Festes de la Mercè★
All over Barcelona (www.bcn.cat/merce).
Date wk of 24 Sept.
This week-long event in honour of the patron saint of the city, Our Lady of Mercy, opens with giants, dragons and *capgrosses* in the Plaça Sant Jaume. It's followed by more than 600 events including *sardanes* and *correfocs* (a tamer version for children, followed by the biggest and wildest of the year on the Saturday night). Other highlights include dazzling fireworks displays, free concerts, a seafront air show, sporting events including a swim across the port and a regatta, and a heap of activities for children. The pressure on the centre has been eased of late: many events are now staged up at Montjuïc castle or in the former textile factory, Fabra i Coats, in Sant Andreu. Even so, around 100,000 people descend on the Barri Gòtic to watch the final parade.

Mostra de Vins i Caves de Catalunya
Moll de la Fusta, Port Vell (93 552 48 00, www.mostradevinsicaves.cat). Metro Drassanes.
Date Thur-Sun during Festes de la Mercè, Sept.
Map p342 F12.
This outdoor wine and cava fair has been running since 1980 and now showcases more than 400 labels from around 50 Catalan *bodegas*. Big names include Torres, Freixenet, Codorníu, Pinord and Mont Marçal; also on show are fine cheeses and

Open House BCN. *See p214.*

ARTS & ENTERTAINMENT

charcuterie. Ten wine or cava tastings with a free glass cost €6; four food tastings cost €5.

Festa Major de la Barceloneta

All over Barceloneta (93 221 72 44, www.cascantic.net/web). Metro Barceloneta. **Date** late Sept/early Oct. **Map** p343 H12/13.

This tightly knit maritime community throws itself into the local *festes* with incredible gusto. The fun kicks off with fireworks on the beach, a 24-hour football tournament, *falcons* (acrobatic groups), *sardana* dancing and a free tasting of traditional crispy *coca* bread washed down with muscatel, and ends with more of the same ten days later. In between, expect parades, music, fire-breathing dragons, open-air cinema and bouncy castles. Look out, too, for a character called General Bum Bum, who parades with a wooden cannon but stops periodically to fire sweets into crowds of scrabbling children.

Open House BCN

All over Barcelona (93 310 61 19, www.48hopenhousebarcelona.org). **Date** 2 days mid Oct.

In line with the Open House weekend held in many countries, Barcelona launched its own event in 2010. Over 150 architecturally important or historically interesting buildings were opened to the public, but know that queues were very long. Arrive early to put your name on a list. *Photo p213.*

Europes

All over Barcelona (93 329 22 37, www.europes-festival.eu). **Date** Oct-Nov. *See p210* **European Commissions**.

La Castanyada*

All over Barcelona. **Date** 31 Oct-1 Nov.

All Saints' Day and the evening before are known as the Castanyada, after the traditional treats of *castanyes* (roast chestnuts) – consumed along with *moniatos* (roast sweet potatoes) and *panellets* (small almond balls covered in pine nuts). The imported tradition of Halloween has grown in popularity of late, and there are now several celebrations around town. Tots Sants (All Saints') is also known as the Dia dels Difunts (Day of the Dead); the snacks switch

---

INSIDE TRACK
IT COULD BE YOU

Spaniards love their lotteries, but the favourite of them all is the Christmas El Gordo, the largest in the world and one of the most anxiously anticipated events of the year; the average Spaniard spends €20 a year on it. Tickets are on sale at every street corner from about August, and the results are drawn on 22 December.

---

to white, bone-shaped *ossos de sant* cakes. Thousands visit local cemeteries over the weekend to sprinkle the graves with holy water, leave flowers, hold vigils, and honour and pray for the dead.

Winter

★ Fira de Santa Llúcia

Pla de la Seu & Avda de la Catedral (010, www.bcn.cat/nadal). Metro Jaume I. **Open** 10.30am-8.30pm Mon-Sat; 10.30am-9.30pm. **Date** 3-23 Dec. **Map** p344-p345 D4/5.

Dating from 1786, this traditional Christmas fair has expanded to more than 300 stalls, selling all manner of handcrafted Christmas decorations and gifts, along with mistletoe, poinsettias and Christmas trees. The most popular figure on sale for Nativity scenes is the curious Catalan figure of the *caganer* (crapper), a small figure crouching over a steaming turd with his trousers around his ankles. Kids line up for a go on the giant *caga tió*, a huge, smiley-faced 'shitting log' that poops out pressies upon being beaten viciously by a stick; smaller versions are on sale at the stalls. There's also a Nativity scene contest, musical parades and exhibitions, including the popular life-size Nativity scene in Plaça Sant Jaume.

Fira de Sant Eloi

C/Argenteria, Born (93 319 84 51, www.acar.cat). **Open** 11am-9pm daily **Date** 1-24 Dec. **Map** p345 D6.

Neither as sprawling nor as lively as the Fira de Santa Llúcia (*see above*), this Christmas street fair nonetheless has some pretty handmade gifts, from leather bags and hand-painted ceramics to puppets. There are musical performances from 6-8pm.

Nadal* & Sant Esteve*
(Christmas Day & Boxing Day)

Dates 25 & 26 Dec.

The Catalan equivalent of the Christmas midnight Mass is the *missa del gall* (cockerel's mass), held at dawn. Later, the whole family enjoys a traditional Christmas feast of *escudella i carn d'olla* (a meaty stew), seafood and roast truffled turkey, finishing off with great ingots of *turrón*. The *caga tió* (*see above*; Fira de Santa Llúcia) gives small gifts, but the real booty doesn't arrive until the night of 5 January.

El Dia dels Sants Innocents

Date 28 Dec.

The name is an incongruous reference to King Herod's Massacre of the Innocents, but in fact this is a cheerful local version of April Fool's Day, with cut-out newspaper figures attached to the backs of unsuspecting victims. The media also introduces fake stories into the day's coverage.

Cap d'Any* (New Year's Eve)

Date 31 Dec & 1 Jan.

Santa
Eulàlia.

In Spain, New Year's Eve tends to be a time for family dinners, with most people emerging to party after midnight, but there is always a group of revellers to be found in Plaça Catalunya. The drill is to wear red underwear for luck in the coming year, and to eat 12 grapes, one for each chime of the clock, at midnight. It's harder than you'd think, and tinned, pre-peeled versions are available. During the day, look out for L'Home dels Nassos, the man who has as many noses as days the year has left (it being the last day, the sly old fox has only one) who parades and throws sweets to the children.

★ Cavalcada dels Reis
www.bcn.cat/nadal.
Date 5 Jan, 5-9pm.
Epiphany is the big Christmas event here, and is marked by the Kings' Parade. Melchior, Gaspar and Balthasar arrive aboard the Santa Eulàlia boat at the bottom of La Rambla before beginning a grand parade around town with a retinue of acrobats, circus clowns and child elves. The route is published in the newspapers, but normally starts at the lower entrance of Ciutadella, running up C/Marquès de l'Argentera and Via Laietana. Later that night, children leave their shoes out on the balcony stuffed with hay for the kings' camels; in the morning, they're either full of presents or edible sugar coal depending on their behaviour the previous year. The following day is a holiday.

★ Festa dels Tres Tombs
Sant Antoni. Metro Sant Antoni.
Date around 17 Jan. **Map** p342 E10.
St Anthony's day, naturally enough, also marks the *festa major* of the district; all the usual ingredients of music and *gegants* here include a monstrous, symbolic, fire-breathing pig – the form the devil took when tempting the saint. Anthony is patron saint of animals, and on his feast day it's still the custom to bring pets to the church of St Anthony to be blessed. Afterwards, horsemen ride three circuits (*tres tombs*) in a formal procession from Ronda Sant Antoni, through Plaça Catalunya, down La Rambla and along C/Nou de la Rambla.
► *A good vantage point is the bar Els Tres Tombs; see p177.*

Sa Pobla a Gràcia
Gràcia, around Plaça del Diamant, Plaça Rius i Taulet, C/Verdi, C/Joan Blanques, C/Llibertat (www.bcn.cat). Metro Fontana. **Date** around 29-30 Jan. **Map** p338 G4/5.
Another celebration in honour of St Anthony, who is one of the world's most venerated saints, this one imported from Mallorca. Two days of Balearic folk festivities see street bonfires, parades of dragons and giants, and candlelit singing (in *mallorquín*) in the Plaça del Diamant.

★ Santa Eulàlia
All over Barcelona. **Date** around 12 Feb.
The city's blowout winter festival is in honour of Santa Eulàlia (Laia), who met her end at the hands of the Romans after enduring terrible tortures. Barcelona's co-patron saint, she is a particular favourite with children. Her feast day on 12 February kicks off with a ceremony in Plaça Sant Jaume, followed by music, *sardanes* and parades, with Masses and children's choral concerts held in the churches and cathedral. In the evening, the female giants gather in Plaça Sant Josep Oriol, then go to throw flowers on the Baixada de Santa Eulàlia before a final boogie in the Plaça Sant Jaume. The Ajuntament and the cathedral crypt (where she's buried) are free and open to the public, as are more than 30 museums. The festival closes on Sunday evening with *correfocs* (for adults and children) centred around the cathedral.

Carnaval (Carnival)
All over Barcelona (www.bcn.cat/carnaval).
Date Shrove Tuesday & Ash Wednesday.
The city drops everything for this last big hurrah of overeating, overdrinking and underdressing prior to Lent. The celebrations begin on Dijous Gras (Mardi Gras) with the appearance of pot-bellied King Carnestoltes – the masked personification of the carnival spirit. That's followed by the grand weekend parade, masked balls, *fartaneres* (neighbourhood feasts, typically with lots of pork), food fights and a giant *botifarrada* (sausage barbecue) on La Rambla, with most of the kids and market traders in fancy dress.

ARTS & ENTERTAINMENT

Children

Kids tag along with grown-ups in Barcelona.

The key to your children having a good time in Barcelona is your own flexibility; if you can adapt to later bedtimes and having them eat out without worrying about mess or noise, you'll all have a better time for it. You'd also do well to get used to complete strangers striking up conversations with your kids, because other people's children are considered public property round these parts.

In common with most Mediterranean countries, Spain tends to expect kids to rub along with whatever the adults are up to, so you won't find a dazzling range of child-oriented attractions. But Barcelona is a natural playground, and small children are as delighted by its spooky medieval alleys after dark as they are with its sandy beaches by day.

PRACTICALITIES

Public transport is free for under-fours. An increasing number of metro stations have lifts; see the maps (*pp334-335*). Officially, pushchairs are supposed to be folded on the metro, but most people just grapple with the obstacle course and the guards don't interfere. All buses are low enough to wheel buggies straight on.

There are listings for kids at www.timeout.cat and www.toctoc.cat (both in Catalan only); www.kidsinbarcelona.com is a reliable source for all kinds of information in English. Lulu at Mujer (*see p189*) has also become a de facto information service for English-speaking mums.

ENTERTAINMENT

Attractions

The two most child-friendly attractions are the excellent **Zoo** and the marginally less exciting **Aquarium**. The **Magic Fountain** (Font Mágica; *see p85*) is also a huge hit; and a simple stroll down **La Rambla**, past the living statues, entertainers, artists and general hubbub, can be a good bet. Fun transport options include the two cable car systems, the **Tramvia Blau** (Blue Tram, *see p106*) and the **rickshaws**.

There isn't a multitude of museums aimed at kids; one of the better ones is **CosmoCaixa**, the science museum. A must-see for junior footy

fiends is the **Museu FC Barcelona** (*see p103*), where kids can walk from the dressing rooms through the tunnel and take a few steps on the pitch. The fake Spanish village of **Poble Espanyol** (*see p83*) also has a certain appeal.

★ L'Aquàrium

Moll d'Espanya, Port Vell (93 221 74 74, www.aquariumbcn.com). Metro Barceloneta or Drassanes. **Open** *Oct-May* 9.30am-9pm Mon-Fri; 9.30am-9.30pm Sat, Sun. *June, Sept* 9.30am-9.30pm daily. *July, Aug* 9.30am-11pm daily. **Admission** €17.75; €12.75-€14.75 reductions; free under-4s. **Credit** AmEx, MC, V. **Map** p326 G13.

The main draw here is the Oceanari, a giant shark-infested tank traversed via a glass tunnel on a slow-moving conveyor belt. Other aquaria house shoals of kaleidoscopic fish where kids can play 'hunt Nemo'. The upstairs section is devoted to children. For pre-schoolers, Explora! has 50 knobs-and-whistles style activities, such as turning a crank to see how ducks' feet move underwater or climbing inside a mini-submarine; unfortunately, much of the equipment is looking a bit the worse for wear. Older children should head to Planet Aqua – an extraordinary, split-level circular space with Humboldt penguins.

★ CosmoCaixa

C/Teodor Roviralta 47-51, Zona Alta (93 212 60 50, www.cosmocaixa.com). Bus 17, 22, 58/FGC Avda Tibidabo. **Open** *July-mid Sept* 10am-8pm daily. *Mid Sept-June* 10am-8pm Tue-Sun. **Admission** €3; €2 reductions; free under-3s

& 1st Sun of mth. *Planetarium, Toca Toca!* €2;
€1.50 reductions; free under-8s. **Credit** MC, V.
Child-specific attractions at the science museum
include the Bubble Planetarium (a digital 3D simu-
lation of the universe); the Toca Toca! space where
supervisors guide the exploration of natural phe-
nomena such as tarantulas and snakes, and the
candy-bright Javier Mariscal-designed spaces of Clik
(for three- to six-year-olds) and Flash (for seven- to
nine-year-olds), where children learn how to generate
electricity and how a kaleidoscope works.
▶ *Check the constantly changing timetable for
Planetarium and Toca Toca! online.*

Museu de Cera

*Ptge de la Banca 7, Barri Gòtic (93 317 26 49,
www.museocerabcn.com). Metro Drassanes.*
Open *Mid July-mid Sept* 10am-10pm daily. *Mid
Sept-mid July* 10am-1.30pm, 4-7.30pm Mon-Fri;
11am-2pm, 4.30-8.30pm Sat, Sun. **Admission**
€15; €9 reductions; free under-5s. **Credit** MC, V.
Map p329 B7.
Madame Tussauds it ain't, but the Wax Museum is
an enjoyable enough way to pass a rainy afternoon,
particulary if you have small children, who love the
'underwater' section (a submarine and creaky old
ship). Be warned that the exhibits are very dated,
and a curious mix of historical and 1980s (19th-
century composers alongside ET, *Star Wars* characters, JR from *Dallas* and Lady Di).
▶ *Want more kitsch? Visit the adjacent 'enchanted
forest' café, El Bosc de les Fades.*

Museu de la Màgia

*C/Jonqueres 15, Born (93 319 39 20, www.
elreydelamagia.com). Metro Jaume I* **Open**
Show 6pm Sat; noon Sun. Closed July-Sept.
Admission €8. **No credit cards. Map** p329 B3.
This collector's gallery of 19th- and 20th-century
tricks and posters from the magic shop El Rei de la
Màgia will enchant any budding magicians. To see
some live sleight of hand, book for the shows; places
are limited. They're not in English, but they are very
visual, so it doesn't matter too much.

Museu de la Xocolata

*C/Comerç 36, Born (93 268 78 78, www.museu
delaxocolata.cat). Metro Arc de Triomf or Jaume I.*
Open 10am-7pm Mon-Sat; 10am-3pm Sun.

CosmoCaixa.

Admission €4.30; €3.65 reductions; free under-
7s. **Credit** MC, V (minimum €10). **Map** p329 F5.
The best-smelling museum in town draws chocoholics
of all ages to its collection of chocolate sculptures made
by Barcelona's master *pastissers* for the Easter competition; these range from multicoloured models of
Gaudí's Casa Batlló to characters from the latest Pixar
film. Audio-visual shows and touch-screen computers
help children make their way through what would otherwise be the rather dry history of the cocoa bean.
Reserve in advance for weekend chocolate figurine-
making courses and lessons in cooking desserts.

Platja de l'Eixample

*Jardins de la Torre de les Aïgues, C/Roger de
Llúria 56 interior, Eixample (93 291 62 60,
mobile 637 40 28 66). Metro Girona.* **Open** *End
June-Aug* 10am-8pm Mon-Sat; 10am-3pm Sun.
Admission €1.40; free under-1s & over-65s.
No credit cards. Map p322 G8.
In the summer, this leafy inner patio becomes the
'Eixample Beach', an oasis for the under-sevens.
There's a knee-high wading pool, plenty of sand
with buckets and spades provided, trees for shade
and a water tower in the centre, along with outdoor
showers, changing tents and toilets.
▶ *For an outdoor, free pool for older children,
visit Parc de la Creueta del Coll; see p105.*

INSIDE TRACK TRAVEL LIGHT

If you don't have space in your suitcase
for all the Barbie dolls and potties, or
your low-cost airline won't allow you to
bring a pushchair, help is at hand. All
these things and more are for hire at
www.buggyingbcn.com or www.baby
travelling.com.

ARTS & ENTERTAINMENT

Tibidabo Funfair

Plaça del Tibidabo 3-4, Tibidabo (93 211 79 42, www.tibidabo.net). FGC Avda Tibidabo & funicular. **Open** *check website.* **Admission** *Camí del Cel* Mar-Dec €11.10 adults; €7 under 120cm; free under 90cm. *Parc d'Atraccions* (unlimited rides) €25.20, €9 under 120cm, free under 90cm. **Credit** MC, V.

This hilltop fairground, dating from 1889, is investing millions in getting itself bang up to date, with the terrifying freefall Pendulum and a hot-air balloon style ride for smaller children. Adrenalin freaks are delighted with the new 80km-per-hour rollercoaster, and the many other attractions include a house of horrors, bumper cars and the emblematic Avió, the world's first popular flight simulator when it was built in 1928. Don't miss the antique mechanical puppets and contraptions at the Museu d'Autòmats, and there are hourly puppet shows at the Marionetàrium (from 1pm). At the weekends, there are circus parades at the end of the day and, in summer, *correfocs* (fire runs – parades where participants let off fireworks) and street theatre.

The opening hours are fiendishly complex and vary from week to week (check the website), but roughly speaking what's now known as the Camí del Cel (this includes the more traditional rides, such as the carousel, the Avió, and so on) is open daily, while the Parc d'Atraccions (including the rollercoaster) is open at weekends.

★ Zoo

Parc de la Ciutadella, Born (93 225 67 80, www.zoobarcelona.com). Metro Barceloneta or Ciutadella-Vila Olímpica. **Open** *Jan-Mar, Oct-Dec* 10am-5.30pm daily. *Apr-mid May, mid Sept-Oct* 10am-7pm daily. *Mid May-mid Sept* 10am-8pm daily. **Admission** €16.50; €9.90 3-12s; free under-3s. **Credit** AmEx, MC, V. **Map** p327 J11/12.

The dolphin shows are the big draw, but the decently sized zoo has plenty of other animals, all of whom look happy enough in reasonably sized enclosures and the city's comfortable climate. Favourites include giant hippos, the prehistoric-looking rhino, sea lions, elephants, giraffes, lions and tigers. Child-friendly features include a farmyard zoo, pony rides, picnic areas and two excellent playgrounds. If all that walking is too much, there's a zoo 'train'. Bear in mind that on hot days many of the animals are sleeping and out of sight, and when the temperature drops below 13° many are kept inside.

Festivals

The **Festes de Santa Eulàlia** in February are specially geared towards children, with hands-on activities and even a mini *correfoc* (fire-run). **La Mercè** and the local *festes majors* of each area also have plenty of parades and music; the decorated streets of **Festa Major de Gràcia** are especially popular with younger children,

and there are bouncy castles, circus performers and storytelling in many of the district's squares. More hits include the carnival parades of **Carnestoltes** or gathering sweets from the streets at the **Festes de Sant Medir de Gràcia**. Christmas traditions are also very child-centred (and scatological), with racks of pooping logs and crouching *caganers* (nativity scene figures with their trousers round their ankles) at the Santa Llúcia market. The Three Kings' procession on 5 January is also a guaranteed hit. For all, *see pp208-215*.

Music, film & theatre

The **Auditori** (*see p253*) and the **Palau de la Música** (*see p254*) often run cycles of family concerts, normally at weekends and during the holidays. English-language children's theatre is rare, with the exception of the Christmas pantomime, but **La Puntual** (C/Allada Vermell 15, Born, mobile 639 30 53 53, www.lapuntual. info) is a little puppet theatre that often has

Tibidabo Funfair.

language-free shows. To catch a film in English, the best bet is the huge **Yelmo Icària Cineplex** (*see p222*) for mainstream blockbusters, while the **Filmoteca de la Generalitat** (*see p223*) shows original-language children's films on occasional Sundays at 5pm. On a rainy or cold day, the **IMAX Port Vell** (*see p223*) is a good, if pricey, standby, although the films are only shown in Spanish and Catalan.

PARKS

The **Parc de la Ciutadella** (*see p69*) has shady gardens, a giant mammoth sculpture, play parks, picnic areas, rowing boats and a zoo, which provide a packed day out. Gaudí's quirky **Park Güell** (*see p101*) makes up for its lack of grass with bright gingerbread houses and winding coloured benches. High above the city, the **Parc de la Creueta del Coll** (*see p105*) has a large playground, table-tennis tables, a picnic area and great views, and the large artificial lake is filled up in summer for use as an outdoor public swimming pool. The delightful **Parc del Laberint** (*see p110*) has hidden benches and elfin tables, picnic areas and a deceptively difficult maze, while the **Jardins de la Tamarita** (*see p104*) form a tranquil dog-free enclave of swings and slides hidden away next to the stop for the Tramvia Blau. The lovely **Parc del Castell de l'Oreneta** (Camí de Can Caralleu & Ptge Blada, Zona Alta, 93 413 24 80) has great views, picnic areas, pony rides for three- to 12-year-olds at weekends (10am-2pm, €6) and a miniature train on Sundays (€1.20). The largest of them all is the **Parc de Collserola** (*see p104*), perfect for young nature lovers. The beachfront esplanades are ideal places for bicycle riding.

EATING & DRINKING

It's rare to find a children's menu in Barcelona, but many restaurants will provide smaller portions on request. That said, there's little need to do so when children and tapas were so clearly made for each other. Basque *pintxo* bars such as **Euskal Etxea** (*see p173*) are an even better option, as children can simply serve themselves from the food that is laid out, waiting for hungry young mouths, on the bar. An important point to remember for families with early-eating children is that most restaurants in Barcelona don't serve lunch before 1.30pm or dinner before 9pm, so play it like the locals and encourage a siesta followed by tea at 5pm so the children can hold out for a late dinner. However, if the children need a snack, there are plenty of options available: **Bar Mendizábal** (*see*

Take a Swing

Barca's best playgrounds.

Urban minibreaks are not always the easiest getaways, with small children less interested in Goya's darker moments than climbing trees; but help is at hand. Though Barcelona's green spaces are few and far between, you are rarely more than five minutes' walk from the nearest set of swings, some set in the most incongruous of places.

The undisputed favourite is the playground between the boating lake and the school in the Parc de la Ciutadella. Early mornings and lunchtimes it's nice enough, with a little slide, couple of swings, a sand pit and some rocks for clambering over, but from 11am to 2pm and again from 5.30 to 8pm it becomes a *ludoteca*, a free playspace where the two much-loved monitors, Beatriz and Fátima (aided by the children), bring armfuls of toys, trikes, buckets and spades, balls, Spacehoppers and dolls' prams outside for everyone to play with. There is also a Wendy house, a huge blackboard with chalks and, occasionally during the summer, a paddling pool.

It can get crowded at peak times, but there's a quieter, quirky playground on the other side of the school buildings, with a climbing slope, a large basket swing (really designed for disabled children, but a hit with all kids) and a board for learning Braille.

p174) is good for fresh juices and healthy sandwiches, and there's all-day pizza at **Al Passatore** (Pla del Palau 8, Born, 93 319 78 51). For relaxing in the sun (near a playground), you could try the outdoor terraces at **Bar Kasparo** (*see p174*), **Casa Paco** (*see p173*) or **Filferro** (*see p178*). The café **1881** (*see p177*), at the Catalan history museum, has fantastic views and plenty of terrace space on which to play. There's also lots of safe open space in which to play around the beachfront terraces.

OUT OF TOWN

Catalunya en Miniatura

Can Balasch de Baix, Torrelles de Llobregat (93 689 09 60, www.catalunyaenminiatura.com). By car A2 south to Sant Vicens dels Horts then left to Torrelles de Llobregat (5km/3 miles). By bus 62 Soler i Sauret (info 93 632 51 33) from Travessera de les Corts. **Open** *July, Aug* 10am-8pm daily. *Oct-Feb* 10am-6pm Tue-Sun. *Mar-June, Sept* 10am-7pm daily. **Admission** €11; €8 reductions; free under-4s. **Credit** AmEx, MC, V.

Highlights of these tiny renderings of 170 of Catalonia's most emblematic sights include a miniature Montserrat, Girona cathedral and everything Gaudí ever laid a finger on. An appropriately munchkin-sized train circles part of the complex, and there's a picnic area and playground.

Illa Fantasia

Finca Mas Brassó, Vilassar de Dalt (93 751 45 53, www.illafantasia.com). By car NII north to Premià de Mar then left (24km/15 miles). **Open** *June-mid Sept* 10am-7pm daily. Closed mid Sept-May. **Admission** *One day* €19.80; €15 under-140cm. *Half day (from 2pm)* €16, €13 under-140cm. Free under-1m. **Credit** AmEx, MC, V.

A large water park with foam slides, kamikaze-style rides and rubber-dinghy chutes, along with pools, a restaurant, supermarket and a range of activities. There's also a picnic/barbecue area in a pine grove.

Port Aventura

977 77 90 90, www.portaventura.es. Train from Passeig de Gràcia (approx 1hr30mins). **Open** *Mid Mar-mid June, mid Sept-Oct* 10am-7pm daily. *Mid June-mid Sept* 10am-midnight daily. *Nov, Dec* 10am-6pm Fri; 10am-7pm Sat, Sun. **Admission** €44; €35 reductions. *Night ticket* (7pm-midnight) €25; €20.50 reductions; free under-4s. **Credit** AmEx, MC, V.

A theme park with some 90 rides spread across five internationally themed areas (Mexico, the Wild West, China, Polynesia and the Mediterranean), while Popeye and the Pink Panther roam the time-

INSIDE TRACK ALL CHANGE

Nappy-changing rooms and special breastfeeding areas are not widely provided. There are mother-and-baby facilities in El Corte Inglés (*see p184*), the airport, the large shopping malls and Poble Espanyol, but be warned that most nappy changes occur in the car or the pram; breastfeeding in public is totally accepted, as long as you are discreet.

space continuum in order to hug your kids. The truly stomach-curdling Dragon Khan rollercoaster is one of the park's highlights for older kids; for the little ones, there's the usual slew of carousels and spinning teacups. There are also 100 daily live shows and a spectacular lakeside Fiesta Aventura with lights, music and fireworks.

BABYSITTING & CHILDCARE

Canguro Gigante

Passeig de Sant Gervasi 16-20, Sant Gervasi (93 211 69 61). FGC Avda Tibidabo. **Open** 9am-8pm Mon-Fri. Closed Aug. **Rates** from €6/hr. **No credit cards.**

A daycare centre for children aged one to 11. Meals are available. Some English is spoken.

Cinc Serveis

C/Pelai 50, 3º, 1ª, Eixample (93 412 56 76, 24hr mobile 639 361 111, www.5serveis.com). Metro Catalunya. **Open** 9.30am-1.30pm, 4.30-8.30pm Mon-Fri. **No credit cards.** **Map** p328 B2.

The basic rate after 8pm is €11 per hour, plus the cost of the sitter's taxi home. Long-term rates are cheaper and vary according to the age of the child.

Happy Parc

C/Pau Claris 97, Eixample (93 317 86 60, www.happyparc.com). Metro Passeig de Gràcia. **Open** *Sept-June* 5-9pm Mon-Fri; 11am-9pm Sat, Sun. Closed last 2wks Aug. **Rates** €4; parents free. **No credit cards.** **Map** p326 G8.

Ball pools, twister slides and more are on offer at this giant indoor fun park and drop-in daycare centre for children up to ten years old (maximum height 1.45m/4ft 7in). Note that kids have to bring socks.

Tender Loving Canguros

Information mobile 647 605 989, www.tl canguros.com. **Open** 9am-9pm Mon-Sat. **No credit cards.**

English resident Lucie Bloor provides long- and short-term nannies and babysitters. All speak fluent English. Prices start at €8 an hour; the agency fee is €15 per session.

ARTS & ENTERTAINMENT

Film

Feature comforts.

Barcelona cinemas were up in arms in 2010 over the Generalitat's proposal for a new law that would require them to show 50 per cent of all films dubbed or subtitled into Catalan. Owners feared that audiences would dwindle and, more importantly, that distributors would ultimately avoid the region, considering the translation process to be simply too much trouble. It's just the latest headache affecting the Catalan film industry: institutional and financial support is often easier for films shot in the Catalan language, but in addition to limiting the scope for casting, the use of Catalan can simply drive audiences away.

Even so, the city still provides a magnificent backdrop for filmmakers of all stripes, most memorably in recent years for Woody Allen and his *Vicky Cristina Barcelona*. There was outcry at the time over the Ajuntament's vast subsidy to the director, but the publicity generated seems to have justified the outlay.

LOCAL MOVIEMAKERS

The paramount figure of Spanish cinema, both at home and abroad, continues to be Pedro Almodóvar, whose films invariably shoot to the top of the charts. However, Barcelona-born Isabel Coixet has also found success with her mainstream films, many of which have featured Hollywood-friendly actors and an English script (*My Life Without Me*, *The Secret Life of Words*). Alejandro Amenábar (*The Others*, *The Sea Inside*) is another Spanish director who has found global recognition through English-language movies. And even genre-hopping wild child Álex de la Iglesia (*Perdita Durango*, *The Perpect Crime*) returned to the language of Shakespeare for his last film, *Oxford Murders*.

From the next generation of film-makers, Fernando León de Aranoa (*Barrio*, *Mondays in the Sun*, *Princesas*) has built an impressive body of work as a Loach-esque social realist, though with greater doses of well-observed naturalist comedy. Equally distinctive are the many ethereal dreamscapes created by director Julio Medem, in films including *Cows*, *Lovers of the Arctic Circle*, *Sex and Lucia* and *Chaotic Ana*. One Barcelona-born director worth looking out for is José Luis Guerin, whose last film, *In the City of Sylvia*, met with worldwide acclaim.

SEEING FILMS

Release dates vary widely. Blockbusters are usually released more or less simultaneously worldwide, but smaller productions can take up to three years to arrive at cinemas, long after they're available on DVD. The dubbing of films into Catalan often plays a part in delays.

Newspapers carry full details of all cinema screenings, as does the weekly *Time Out Barcelona* magazine and its online version at www.timeout.cat. Subtitled (as opposed to dubbed) films are marked VO or VOSE (for '*versió original subtitulada en espanyol*'). Some larger cinemas open at 11am, but most have their first screenings around 4pm. Evening showings start around 7.30-8.30pm; later screenings usually begin at 10.15-10.45pm. On Fridays and Saturdays, many cinemas have a late-night session starting around 1am. Weekend evenings can be very crowded, especially for recent releases, so turn up early.

INSIDE TRACK
CHEAP FLICKS
All cinemas have a discounted night (the *dia de l'espectador*). In most cinemas it's Monday, but occasionally it's Wednesday.

You can buy tickets for some cinemas online, via their website, at www.entradas.com or at ServiCaixa (*see p206*).

ORIGINAL-LANGUAGE CINEMAS

Casablanca-Kaplan

Passeig de Gràcia 115, Eixample (93 218 43 45).
Metro Diagonal. **Tickets** *Mon* €5. *Tue-Sun* €6.80.
No credit cards. Map p322 G6.
Two 180-seater auditoriums offer a mix of local films, world cinema and Hollywood blockbusters.

Cinemes Méliès

C/Villarroel 102, Eixample (93 451 00 51,
www.cinesmelies.net). Metro Urgell. **Tickets** *Mon*
€4. *Tue-Sun* €6. **No credit cards. Map** p322 E8.
This small, two-screen cinema is the nearest that Barcelona comes to an arthouse theatre, with an idiosyncratic roster of accessible classics alongside more recent films that aren't quite commercial enough for general release. This is the place to bone up on your Wilder, Antonioni, Hitchcock and others, with up to eight films per week.

Renoir-Floridablanca

C/Floridablanca 135, Eixample (93 228 93 93,
www.cinesrenoir.com). Metro Sant Antoni.

Filmoteca de la Generalitat.

Tickets *Mon* €5.70. *Tue-Fri* €7. *Sat, Sun*
€7.50. **Credit** AmEx, MC, V. **Map** p326 E9.
This, the more central of the Renoir cinemas, screens up to eight independent, offbeat American, British and Spanish films per day, though note that programming tends towards the worthy.
Other locations Renoir-Les Corts, C/Eugeni d'Ors 12, Les Corts (93 490 55 10).

Verdi

C/Verdi 32, Gràcia (93 238 79 90, www.
cines-verdi.com). Metro Fontana. **Tickets** *1st*
screening Tue-Fri, all screenings Mon €5.50.
Tue-Fri €7.50. *Sat, Sun* €8. **Credit** AmEx,
MC, V. **Map** p323 H5.
The five-screen Verdi and Verdi Park, its four-screen annexe on the next street, have transformed this corner of Gràcia with a diverse programme of independent, mainly European and Asian cinema. At peak times, chaos reigns; arrive early and make sure you don't confuse the line to enter for the line to buy tickets, which can stretch to Madrid on rainy Sundays.
Other locations Verdi Park, C/Torrijos 49, Gràcia (93 238 79 90).

Yelmo Icària Cineplex

C/Salvador Espriu 61, Vila Olímpica
(information 93 221 75 85, tickets 902 22 09
22, www.yelmocines.es). Metro Ciutadella-Vila
Olímpica. **Tickets** *Mon* €6. *Tue-Sun* €7.50; €6
reductions & all before 3pm. **Credit** AmEx, MC,
V. **Map** p327 K12.
This vast multiplex has all the atmosphere of the near-empty mall that surrounds it. But what it lacks in charm, it makes up for in choice, with 15 screens offering blockbusters plus mainstream foreign and Spanish releases. Weekends are seat-specific, so queues tend to be slow-moving; it's worth booking your seat online before you go.

SPECIALIST CINEMAS

Some bars screen films while they serve drinks. **Planeta Rai** (C/Carders 12, Born, 93 268 13 21, www.pangea.org/rai, closed Aug) shows European *cine d'auteur* twice a week, on Tuesdays and Thursdays (free). **V.O.s** (Plaça Cardona 4, Sant Gervasi, mobile 651 970 971, www.vosbar.cat) is a more upmarket bar showing retrospectives of Cary Grant and the like.

Cinema Maldà

C/Pi 5, Barri Gòtic (93 317 85 29, http://
cinemamalda.net). Metro Catalunya or Liceu.
Tickets *Mon* €5.50. *Tue-Thur* €7.50.
Fri-Sun €7.80. **No credit cards. Map** p328 C4.
In its latest incarnation, the well-loved Cinema Maldà is now showing indie and arthouse films, alongside more commercial fare.

ARTS & ENTERTAINMENT

Sala Montjuïc. *See p224.*

Filmoteca de la Generalitat

*Avda Sarrià 31-33, Eixample (93 410 75 90,
http://cultura.gencat.net/filmo). Metro Hospital
Clínic.* **Tickets** €2.70; €2 reductions; €18 for
10 films. **Credit** (block tickets only) MC, V.
Map p322 D5.

The government-funded Filmoteca is a little dry for
some tastes, offering comprehensive seasons of
cinema's more recondite auteurs alongside better-
known classics. Overlapping cycles last two or three
weeks, with each film screened at least twice at different times. Books of ten tickets bring down the
price per film to a negligible amount. The 'Filmo'
also runs an excellent library of film-related books,
videos and magazines at Portal Santa Madrona 6-8
(93 316 27 80), just off La Rambla.

▶ *In 2011, La Filmo is due to move to new
premises in the Raval. Check website for details.*

IMAX Port Vell

*Moll d'Espanya, Port Vell (93 225 11 11,
www.imaxportvell.com). Metro Barceloneta
or Drassanes.* **Tickets** *Mon, Tue, Thur-Sun*
€8.70-€10. *Wed* €7.70-€9. **Credit** MC, V.
Map p326 G12.

The predictable programming (sharks, dinosaurs,
adventure sports) lets down the IMAX experience.
Note that not all films are in 3-D.

FESTIVALS

Though none of Barcelona's festivals is as big or brash as **Sitges'** (*see below*), they all show interesting work. In addition to those below, regular festivals include: International Short Films (April), Women's (June), Animation (June), Jewish (July), Gay & Lesbian (July and October), Open Air Shorts (September), Documentaries (February and October), Human Rights (October), and African (November). OVNI, an alternative video festival, takes place every 18 months, in early spring and late autumn; the next is scheduled for autumn 2011.

Gandules
CCCB (see p72) (93 306 41 00, www.cccb.org). **Date** *Aug* 10pm Tue-Thur. **Admission** free.
A series of films are screened in the deckchair-strewn patio of the CCCB. It gets extremely crowded, so arrive early for any chance of a seat.

In-Edit Beefeater Festival
Aribau Multicines, C/Aribau 8-10 & Aribau Club, Gran Via 565-567 (902 424 243, www.in-edit.beefeater.es). **Date** Last week Oct. **Tickets** €5 (1 film); €30 (6 films).
A well-regarded cinema festival of musical documentaries, featuring genres from jazz to flamenco.

Barcelona Asian Film Festival
Various venues (www.baff-bcn.org). **Date** Late Apr-early May. **Tickets** free-€6.50. *10 films* €25.
Some of the sharpest and most broad-ranging programming of any of the city's film festivals.

Sala Montjuïc
Castell de Montjuïc (www.salamontjuic.org). **Date** July-early Aug. **Admission** €5.
A blend of classics and recent independent cinema shown three times a week throughout July, transforming the grassy moat of the castle into an outdoor cinema. Bring a picnic and turn up early for the jazz band; deckchairs are available for €3. A bus service runs from Espanya metro from 8.30-9.30pm and after the film. *Photo p223.*

L'Alternativa
Various venues (www.alternativa.cccb.org). **Date** Nov. **Tickets** free-€4.50. *10 films* €25.
A week-long festival showcasing independent, mostly European cinema.

Sitges Festival Internacional de Cinema de Catalunya
Various venues (93 894 99 90, www.cinemasitges.com.) **Date** Oct. **Tickets** €6-€8.
See below **Oh, the horror!**

Oh, the horror!

Sitges' week-long film festival is a must for all types of star gazer.

If rattling doorknobs, piercing screams, spilling guts and headless wraiths are your thing, then there's only one place for you to be when October comes around – the **Sitges International Fantasy Film Festival of Catalonia**. What began modestly in 1968 as a week of fantasy and horror movies has become one of the most well-respected genre festivals in the world. It now attracts A-list stars such as Jodie Foster, Viggo Mortensen, Quentin Tarantino and Woody

Harrelson, while at the same time staying small and intimate enough to attract local fans. Fans and stars mix in the bar and garden of the Hotel Meliá, the festival's focal point.

The Sitges Official Selection has provided the European première for films such as John Carpenter's latest, *The Ward* – a supernatural horror thriller set in a psychiatric hospital and starring Amber Heard. Another film to get its European première in 2010 was *Vanishing on 7th Street* by Brad Anderson, winner of the best director award at Sitges 2001 for *Session 9*, while there were special screenings in Barcelona of films not yet released in Spain, such as Christopher Nolan's *Inception*. There are also conferences and appearances from the leading figures in the rarefied world of genre filmmaking.

During the festival, a special late-night train service returns to Barcelona after the final screening of the evening.
• www.sitgesfilmfestival.com

Galleries

The art world is a stage in Barcelona.

Public sponsorship for art and art festivals remains scarce, so Barcelona's arts scene has tried to insert itself into other large-scale performance events. Film festivals such as April's Mecal (www.mecalbcn.org) incorporate an art film section, while experimental art and audiovisual work by groups such as graphic designers No-domain feature at music festival Sónar. Look past the on-stage action at La Fura dels Baus shows, meanwhile, and you will see spectacular stage sets by German-born local Roland Olbeter. There's mediocrity on the local scene, but there's also a good deal of excellent art on display. Visit the galleries below are all reliable sources of the latter.

THE LOCAL SCENE

The contemporary art scene has lightened up since the 1980s and '90s, when any gallery that was serious about selling paintings had to elbow its way on to a small section of C/Consell de Cent in the Eixample and show works by famous names of the time. These days, the art scene is much more relaxed, and keen to experiment with what it sells and where it sells it in the city.

In the spruced-up Raval, you will find that the **Àngels Barcelona** and **NoguerasBlanchard** host lively, contemporary shows and the occasional performance. Local artists and the city's many street artists are given support by **ADN**, whereas **Loft** and **Tasneem** are refreshingly non-Eurocentric. Of the locally based artists, look out in particular for the Catalan artists Alicia Framis, Frederic Amat and Ester Partegàs, Scottish artist Jo Milne, Briton Hannah Collins and Dutchman Bert van Zelm.

Gallery listings appear in the *Guía del Ocio* and *Time Out Barcelona* magazines. Note that public exhibition spaces and galleries are covered in this guide under 'Sightseeing', while commercial galleries are listed below.

About the author

Alex Phillips has lived in Barcelona for a decade. She writes on cultural matters for the local English-language press.

Festivals

Entrepreneurial individuals are always prepared to invest in the local art scene, and a keen public audience swarm to springtime events such as May's video art fair **Loop** (www.loop-barcelona.com) and international contemporary art fair **Swab** (www.swab.es – 26-29 May 2011), which is open to all and provides a much-needed platform for new artists.

Later in the year, November offers the chance to check out the latest progeny of the union between mind and machine at pioneer cyber-art festival **Art Futura** (www.artfutura.org). In December, there's **Drap Art** (93 268 48 89, www.drapart.org): also held at CCCB (*see p72*), it's an international creative recycling festival, with concerts, performances, workshops and a Christmas market.

COMMERCIAL GALLERIES
The Barri Gòtic

Local dealer **Artur Ramón** (C/Palla 23 & 25, 93 302 59 70, www.arturamon.com) has various outlets on C/Palla, near the cathedral; at No.23, stock includes lithographs by Picasso, Mariano Fortuny and Joan Serrà.

Galería Trama

C/Petritxol 8 (93 317 48 77, www.galeria trama.com). Metro Liceu. **Open** 10.30am-2pm,

4-8pm Tue-Fri; 10.30am-2pm, 4.30-8.30pm Sat. Closed Aug. **Credit** AmEx, MC, V. **Map** p328 B4. This unassuming space is the contemporary arm of Sala Parés, which is just opposite, and quietly displays some fabulous paintings, photography and media work. Aziz & Cucher, Jo Milne and Julio Vaquero are among the featured artists.

★ Loft Barcelona
C/Ample 5 (93 318 24 77, www.espace-ample.com). Metro Drassanes or Jaume I. **Open** 5-8.30pm Tue-Sat. **Credit** AmEx, MC, V. **Map** p329 B7.
When Loft opened in 2003, the local scene didn't know what to make of French collector Bertrand Cheuvreux's quirky space, then dedicated solely to contemporary Chinese art. Since then, local interest in China, and in international art in general, has shot up, and this wonderful haven, with a lovely patio out the back, has come into its own, lending intriguing, ingenious and often hilarious works to big shows. Increasingly, the focus has branched out from China to contemporary art from other countries. *Photo p228.*

★ Sala Parés
C/Petritxol 5 (93 318 70 20, www.salapares.com). Metro Liceu. **Open** 4-8pm Mon; 10.30am-2pm, 4-8pm Tue-Fri; 10.30am-2pm, 4.30-8.30pm Sat; 11am-2pm Sun. Closed 3wks Aug. **Credit** AmEx, MC, V. **Map** p328 B4.
The elegant Sala Parés, founded in 1840, is a grand, two-tier space that smells deliciously of wood varnish and oil paint. Conservative figurative and historical paintings are the mainstay, although it was also here that a young Picasso had his very first solo show in 1905. In September, Sala Parés hosts the Young Painters' Prize.

The Born

Galería Maeght
C/Montcada 25 (93 310 42 45). Metro Jaume I. **Open** 10am-2pm, 4-7pm Tue-Fri; 10am-2pm Sat. Closed 3wks Aug. **Credit** AmEx, MC, V. **Map** p329 E6.
The sister ship of the prestigious French gallery, Galería Maeght occupies what was once a Renaissance palace on the elegant C/Montcada. The exterior grandeur fades inside, although the taupe paintwork and worn carpets seem appropriate for sombre Spanish greats such as Antoni Tàpies, Eduardo Arroyo and Pablo Palazuelo.

The Raval

Art/design bookshop **Ras** (C/Doctor Dou 10, 93 412 71 99, www.actar.es) is good for a browse. Check out the gallery at the back.

Àngels Barcelona
C/Pintor Fortuny 27 (93 412 54 00, www.angels barcelona.com). Metro Catalunya. **Open** noon-2pm, 5-8.30pm Tue-Sat. Closed Aug. **No credit cards. Map** p328 A3.
Hurrah to local gallery owner and entrepreneur Emilio Álvarez for keeping the Barcelona contemporary art world alive – and its various factions talking to one another. This smart space shows photography and video pieces, and hosts the occasional performance. Nearby Room Service (C/Àngels 16, 93 302 10 16), is dedicated to furniture design, while Álvarez's restaurant Carmelitas shows lo-fi video art at mealtimes (C/Doctor Dou 1, 93 412 46 84, www.carmelitasgallery.com).

Galería Trama. *See p225.*

INSIDE TRACK AFTER HOURS

In the evenings, local artists hang out in **Saladestar** (C/Martínez de la Rosa 40, Gràcia, www.saladestar.com, 93 218 39 20) and **Miscelänea** (C/Guardia 10, Raval, 93 317 93 98, www.miscelanea.info). The latter incorporates exhibition spaces and a cinema.

Galería NoguerasBlanchard

C/Xuclà 7 (93 342 57 21, www.nogueras blanchard.com). Metro Liceu. **Open** 10.30am-7pm Tue-Sat. Closed Aug. **No credit cards.** **Map** p326 F10.
This gallery occupies a sociable slot on C/Xucla, and is famed locally for the prowling kitty-cats painted on the wall outside. Alex Nogueras and Rebecca Blanchard have proven themselves adept at talent-spotting: artists Marine Hugonnier and Ignacio Uriarte regularly feature, while Cuban artist Wilfredo Prieto is their *nom célèbre*, having won the Cartier Award in 2008.

The Eixample

Established galleries reside on C/Consell de Cent, between Rambla de Catalunya and Balmes. **Galeria Carles Taché** (C/Consell de Cent 290, 93 487 88 36, www.carlestache.com) is where you can purchase and lug home that Tony Cragg sculpture you've always wanted. The two branches of **Galeria Joan Prats** (Rambla Catalunya 54, 93 216 02 90 and C/Balmes 54, 93 488 13 98, www.galeriajoanprats.com) are also top-notch. Further along, towards the university, gallery/showroom **A34** (C/Aribau 34, 93 451 55 79) hosts a few impressive shows a year: past offerings have run from Picasso sketches to Hiroshi Sugimoto's photography.

Galeria ADN

C/Enric Granados 49 (93 451 00 64, www.adngaleria.com). Metro Passeig de Gràcia. **Open** 10am-2pm, 4-8pm Mon-Fri; 11am-2pm, 5-8.30pm Sat. Closed Aug. **Credit** AmEx, MC, V. **Map** p322 F7.
ADN (DNA in English) favours less established contemporary artists, half of whom are locally based. Collective shows can be hit-and-miss affairs so far as quality is concerned, but are good to check out if you're hungry for raw talent. (It once showed the video work of Alejandro Vidal, later swiped by posher gallery Joan Prats.) ADN supports the worthy social projects of young architect Sergio Cirugeda, who creates ingenious foldable homes that clamp to buildings or nestle in trees.

Galeria Estrany · De La Mota

Ptge Mercader 18 (93 215 70 51, www.estranydelamota.com). FGC Provença. **Open** *July* 10.30am-1.30pm, 4.30-8.30pm Mon-Fri. *Sept-June* 10.30am-1.30pm, 4.30-8.30pm Tue-Sat. Closed Aug. **Credit** MC, V. **Map** p322 F7.
This cavernous basement is one of the most intriguing art spaces in the city. It hosts outstanding contemporary exhibitions, particularly in photography and film, from the likes of Finnish artist Esko Männikkö and Scottish film buff Douglas Gordon.

Galeria Joan Gaspar

Plaça Doctor Letamendi 1 (93 323 08 48, www.galeriajoangaspar.com). Metro Universitat. **Open** *July-Sept* 10.30am-1.30pm, 5-8pm Tue-Fri. *Oct-June* 5-8pm Mon; 10.30am-1.30pm, 5-8pm Tue-Fri; 10.30am-1.30pm. **Credit** AmEx, MC, V. **Map** p322 F8.
This is the present location of the celebrated Sala Gaspar, which in 1960, in the throes of the Franco era, mounted a solo show of the paintings of the exiled Pablo Picasso; queues stretched down the block, and all the celebrities of Barcelona rebelliously attended. Nowadays, Joan Miró and Antoni Clavé are on display, among others.

Galeria Toni Tàpies

C/Consell de Cent 282 (93 487 64 02, www.tonitapies.com). Metro Passeig de Gràcia. **Open** *July, Sept* 10am-2pm, 4-8pm Tue-Fri. *Oct-June* 10am-2pm, 4-8pm Tue-Fri; 11am-2pm, 5-8.30pm Sat. Closed Aug. **Credit** AmEx, MC, V. **Map** p326 F8.
Owned by the son of the famous painter, Tàpies hosts a classy mix of locals and internationals, the excellent video work of Portuguese artist João Onofre and local artist Tere Recarens included.
▶ *On a related note, visit the Fundació Antoni Tàpies; see p94.*

Kowasa Gallery

C/Mallorca 235 (93 487 35 88, www.kowasa. com/ gallery). Metro Passeig de Gràcia. **Open** 4.30-8.30pm Tue-Sat. Closed Aug. **Credit** AmEx, DC, MC, V. **Map** p322 F7.
A must for photography fans, Kowasa Gallery, above a bookshop, exhibits historical and contemporary photography. Oriol Maspons, Ramon Masats, Joan Colom and Eugeni Forcano set the standards for contemporary Catalans, such as Toni Catany.

ProjecteSD

Ptge Mercader 8 (93 488 13 60, www.projectesd. com). FGC Provença. **Open** 11am-7pm Tue-Sat. Closed Aug. **No credit cards.** **Map** p322 F7.
Silvia Dauder's penchant for innovative photography and film is sculpted into subtle, provocative and highly original shows. Limited-edition artists' texts, detailed explanations in English and Silvia's own bilingual talents complement the exhibitions.

ARTS & ENTERTAINMENT

Loft Barcelona. *See p226.*

You will enter intrigued, but emerge informed after visiting the show. Look out for Patricia Dauder, Pieter Vermeersch and Asier Mendizábal.

Gràcia & Zona Alta

Galería Alejandro Sales

C/Julián Romea 16, Gràcia (93 415 20 54, www.alejandrosales.com). FGC Gràcia. **Open** July, Sept 11am-2pm, 5-8pm Tue-Fri. Oct-June 11am-2pm, 5-8pm Tue-Sat. Closed Aug. **No credit cards. Map** p322 F5.

Alejandro Sales's contemplative, sophisticated exhibitions are given the space and tranquillity that they deserve at this gallery. The high-profile painters José Cobo, Eduard Arbos and Pep Duran are regular exhibitors here.

▶ *The excellent Fundació Foto Colectània is on the same street; see p101.*

Galeria H2O

C/Verdi 152, Gràcia (93 415 18 01, www.h2o.es). Metro Lesseps. **Open** July 4-8pm Tue-Fri. Sept-June 4-8pm Tue-Fri; 11am-1pm Sat. Closed Aug. **No credit cards. Map** p323 H4.

Local architect Joaquim Ruiz Millet and writer Ana Planella collaborated on the foundation of this friendly Gràcia gallery in 1989. Design and photography exhibitions and book publications feature prominently on the agenda.

Tasneem Gallery

C/Castellnou 51, Zona Alta (93 252 35 78, www.tasneemgallery.com). FGC Tres Torres. **Open** 10am-2pm, 4-8pm Tue-Fri; 10am-2pm Sat. Closed 3wks Aug. **Credit** MC, V.

International development consultant Tasneem Salam has opened this welcome addition to the gallery scene in the uptown *barrio* of Tres Torres. The gallery displays all kinds of contemporary African and Asian art, whether it is photography, paintings or furniture.

THE FRINGE

Active artists' collectives include **Art Liv** (www.artliv.org), **Gràcia Arts Project** (www.graciaartsproject.com) and **La Xina ART** (www.laxinaart.org). Barri Gòtic's **Tallers Oberts** (www.tallersoberts.org) sees artists opening their studios to the public for two weekends in May/June, while **Barcelona Creativa** (www.barcelonacreativa.info) offers an electronic classified ads page aimed at promoting creative projects. Civic centres can be supportive of new projects, Poblenou's **Centre Civic Can Felipa** (C/Pallars 277, 93 256 38 40, www.bcn.cat/canfelipa) particularly so.

Established production centre **Hangar** (Passatge del Marquès de Santa Isabel 40, Poblenou, 93 308 40 41, www.hangar.org) has a limited number of studios and offers workshops and exchanges; it's a good place to get details.

NIU

C/Almogàvers 208, Poblenou (93 356 88 11, www.niubcn.com). Metro Llacuna. **Open** June, July, Sept 5-10pm Tue-Sat. Oct-May 5-10pm Tue-Sun. Closed Aug. **Credit** MC, V. **Map** p327 off L10.

NIU is a buzzing centre for media and audio-visual art, incorporating a small exhibition space, live music, conferences, workshops and information on a kaleidoscopic array of musical and art events.

CLASSES

For those inspired to create, **Masia Can Serrat** (93 771 00 37, www.canserrat.org), in Montserrat Natural Park, offers board, lodging and studio space. For courses in life drawing, painting or sculpture in the city centre, try **Cercle Artístic de Sant Lluc** (93 302 45 79, www.santlluc.cat), although you must register with the group to attend.

Gay & Lesbian

All fun and games.

Gay Catalans are hugely proud of the scene in Barcelona, although Londoners and Berliners might find it a little quiet. Nonetheless, the city thrusts its credentials into the faces of visitors with bars, clubs, hotels and festivals… and that's before you reach the beautiful beach town of Sitges, probably the gayest village in Europe and just a short train ride down the coast. The sea change since Franco's death (homosexuality was illegal until 1978) has brought about gay marriage and adoption, gay hotels, the staging of the gay and lesbian EuroGames, and even a gay circus (www.myspace.com/gaycircus). Queer Catalonia has never had it so good.

THE LOCAL SCENE

The scene – *el ambiente* in Spanish – is mostly limited to a small and otherwise unremarkable area in the Eixample. Bordered by the streets Diputació, Villarroel, Aragó and Balmes, it's delightfully if dizzily called the **Gaixample**. But there are also shops and bars throughout the Old City, along with alfresco cruising behind Plaça d'Espanya in the leafy shadows of Montjuïc. There's also the aesthetically challenged 'Chernobyl beach': take the train or tram to **Sant Adrià de Besòs** and wander about in front of the three huge cooling towers.

That said, most of the city's nightlife is pretty mixed, and there's a lot of fun to be had off the official scene – a keen ear to the ground and the occasional flyer will often deliver an embarrassment of riches. Don't worry about dress codes: you can wear anything or almost nothing. The summer's fiestas at shacks on gay-friendly Mar Bella beach are a particularly fine example of minimum advertising, maximum raving. For more on nightlife, *see pp236-50*.

For more information, pick up free copies of gay rag *Shanguide* in bars and gay shops around town, or have a look on: www.shangay.com, www.60by80.com/barcelona, www.barcelonagay.com, www.guiagaybarcelona.es, www.bolloandbutter.com and www.catalunya-lgbt.cat.

Festivals

For **Carnival** in February (*see p215*), head to Sitges, but Barcelona takes over in summer. At the end of June, **Gay Pride** (www.pridebarcelona.org) usually centres on the Plaça Universitat, with parades and concerts; in late July/early August, **Circuit** includes parties, cinema and cultural offerings from flamenco to gay art (*see p232* **The Party Circuit**). The **Mostra Internacional de Cinema Gai i Lesbià** film festival (www.cinemalambda.com) is also held in July. In winter, the highlight is the **Matinée Winter Festival** (www.matineewinterfestival.com), a huge New Year's Day party in the Pabellò Olímpic de Badalona.

BARS

The Gaixample

The bars mentioned below have proved more durable than most, given the fickle nature of the local scene in Barcelona. However, we advise you to ask around about a venue – is it still worth visiting, is it still open? – before shelling out on a cab fare and making a special journey.

About the authors

Roberto Rama and Dylan Simanowitz have lived, worked and partied in Barcelona for the last six years.

Átame

El Cangrejo

C/Villarroel 86 (mobile 625 779 393). Metro Universitat or Urgell. **Open** 10.30pm-3am daily. **Credit** AmEx, V. **Map** p326 E8.

If you can ignore first impressions based on the decor (which looks as if the art nouveau architect Gaudí sneezed violently), you'll find a lively and friendly bar at El Cangrejo. It tends to attract a younger crowd, similar to that of the original Cangrejo in the Raval.

Col·lectiu Gai de Barcelona

Ptge Valeri Serra 23 (93 453 41 25, www. colectiugai.org). Metro Universitat or Urgell. **Open** 7-9.30pm Mon-Thur; 7-9.30pm, 11pm-3am Fri, Sat. **No credit cards. Map** p326 E8.

This is a good place to come to find out information about the city; the headquarters of this local gay association is home to an easygoing, quiet and unpretentious bar, with cheap and cheerful drinks and few tourists.

Dietrich

C/Consell de Cent 255 (93 451 77 07, www.facebook.com/dietrichcafe.com). Metro Universitat. **Open** *Apr-Oct* 10.30pm-3am daily. *Nov-Mar* 10.30pm-3am Fri-Sat. **Credit** MC, V. **Map** p326 E8.

A classic club – although somewhat careworn – Dietrich generally attracts a mixed and lively crowd of punters. A whirl of activity occupies a friendly environment. Acrobats and drag artists perform on the dancefloor here, and the amiable international bar crew speak English.

► *Átame, two doors down at No.257, is run by the same people, and is very relaxed.*

★ Lust

C/Casanova 75 (93 451 14 19). Metro Universitat. **Open** 9pm-2.30am Tue-Sun. **Credit** MC, V. **Map** p326 E8.

A low-lit, loft-style space, Lust has massive abstract prints swirled across the walls and a big dancefloor (for a bar). It attracts a relaxed but good-looking crowd, with fewer pretensions than the preening Muscle Marys next door at BimBamBum Zeltas (*see below*). The cocktails are prepared with more care than many a Gaixample hangout, but be warned: prices are high.

Museum Bar

C/Sepúlveda 171 (mobile 625 779 393). Metro Sant Antoni. **Open** *Apr-Oct* 10.30pm-3am Mon, Wed-Sat. *Nov-Mar* 10.30pm-3am daily. **Credit** AmEx, MC, V. **Map** p326 E9.

Over-the-top, tongue-in-cheek, and fabulously faux baroque is the theme at this trendy music bar, where the video screens are surrounded by huge gilded frames and classical statues pose at the entrance. Rihanna, Beyoncé and other lamé-clad pop divas will get you warmed up for the long night ahead.

► *The same owner recently opened Museum Retro nearby at C/Urgell 106.*

People Lounge

C/Villarroel 71 (93 532 77 43, www.people bcn.com). Metro Universitat or Urgell. **Open** 8pm-3am Mon-Thur; 8pm-3.30am 7.30pm-3am Fri-Sat; Sun **No credit cards. Map** p326 E8.

People Lounge offers a good alternative if you're tired of trekking around from bar to bar listening to non-stop Europop. Decked out as a facsimile of an posh English pub, with big plush sofas and chandeliers, it attracts a mature, smartly dressed crowd and has plenty of space to sit, have a drink and chat.

Plata Bar

C/Consell de Cent 233 (93 452 46 36). Metro Universitat. **Open** *Nov-Feb* 7pm-2.30am Wed-Sun. *Mar-Oct* 7pm-2.30am daily. **Credit** MC, V. **Map** p326 E8.

This lively cocktail bar comes into its own on warm evenings, when the bar is completely open to the street. Take your pick from the standard cocktail menu, grab a seat and watch the world pass by.

Punto BCN

C/Muntaner 63-65 (no phone, www.arena disco.com). Metro Universitat. **Open** 6pm-2am daily. **No credit cards. Map** p326 E8.

Punto BCN is a Gaixample staple and the first gay bar in town. It's fiercely unstylish, but friendly and down to earth. It's also one of the few places where you'll find anybody early on. Tables on the mezzanine give a good view of the crowd, so you can take your pick before the object of your affections heads off into the night.

▶ *Free passes to the Arena clubs (see p232) are available behind the bar.*

BimBamBum Zeltas

C/Casanova 75 (93 454 19 02). Metro Universitat. **Open** 11pm-3am daily. **Credit** MC, V. **Map** p326 E8.

Zeltas is one of the more stylish of the Gaixample's bars. Open every day, it only really comes into its own later on in the week, when the trendy young guapos show their appreciation for the DJs' tunes (mainly funky house) by squashing each other on the mini dancefloor.

The rest of the city

Schilling (*see p169*), **La Concha** (*see p241*) and **Zelig** (C/Carme 116, no phone), though not exclusively gay, are all worth a visit. During the long summer months, though, the action moves to the shore. The *xiringuitos* (beach bars) on Mar Bella are the places to be, especially the first on this stretch (with the sea to your right): it's called **El Dulce Deseo de Lorenzo** (www.lorenzo.chiringuitogay.com).

La Bata de Boatiné

C/Robadors 23, Raval (93 317 17 38). Metro Liceu. **Open** 10pm-3am Wed-Sat; 10pm-2.30am Sun. **No credit cards. Map** p329 A5.

The rapid redevelopment and gentrification of the area make one wonder how long this grungy, semi-underground bar can survive, but for now La Bata still holds pride of place on the alternative BCN gay scene. Cheap drinks mean it can get

packed, so fight your way down the long narrow bar to where the action is – if you dare.

New Chaps

Avda Diagonal 365, Eixample (93 215 53 65, www.newchaps.com). Metro Diagonal or Verdaguer. **Open** 9pm-3am Mon-Wed; 7pm-3am Thur, Sun; 9pm-3.30am Fri, Sat. **No credit cards. Map** p322 G6.

The more mature clientele that frequents this sex bar avoids studying the rather bizarre collection of objects hung around the place and instead heads directly for the busy darkroom downstairs. If you're tempted to join them, make sure you check in your valuables first.

La Penúltima

C/Riera Alta 40, Raval (mobile 645 427 310, www.myspace.com/lapenu). Metro Sant Antoni. **Open** 7pm-2am Tue, Wed, Sun; 7pm-2.30am Thur; 7pm-3am Fri, Sat. **No credit cards. Map** p326 E9.

This slightly kitsch former bodega, where ancient barrels of wine contrast with glass-fronted displays of Barbie dolls, makes a comforting change from the muscle-bound posing bars of the Gaixample. A mixed and friendly establishment, it's one of the few places populated before midnight.

Punto BCN.

ARTS & ENTERTAINMENT

The Party Circuit

Summer hits a high note with a leading LGBT festival.

Get the shirts off and the baby oil on: it's time for Barcelona's biggest gay festival. But this one is about much more than showing off your six-pack on the dancefloor. In just three years, the **Circuit Festival** has grown so popular that it now stretches over nine days (usually in late July and early August) and encompasses no fewer than three festivals in one: Circuit for gay men, Girlie Circuit for lesbians and bisexuals, and Circuit Bear, for the bears and chasers out there. All three are open to any homo-friendly person who is sufficiently buffed, hairy or brave enough to give it a go.

Circuit, Girlie and Bear each have their own specific programme of after-dark clubs, parties and shows but share many of the daytime events. Among them is the notorious Circuit Water Park Day, when some 10,000 participants take over the Illa Fantasia water park for 24 hours of aquatic madness and DJs.

Circuit was born in 2008, as an initiative of the entrepreneurial Matinee Group. With over 50,000 participants from 50 countries, the event has become the most international LGBT festival in Europe, and no wonder: it's a smooth operation, with user-friendly packages including hotels, apartments, a flight selector, private transport to events and advance ticket sales available on the website. Parties are scattered among a variety of iconic gay venues in and around the city, ranging from Gaixample clubs such as D-Boy to Mar Bella beach and the nearby town of Sitges, with additional hosting from the likes of The Week (Brazil), Work (New York), Megawoof and Salvation (London) and La Leche! (Barcelona).

The festival is also gaining ground away from the dancefloor, with sports events organised by the Panteres Grogues (Yellow Panthers, the local LGBT sports association), theatre and movie screenings (in collaboration with the Cinema Maldà). On the more serious side, there are also workshops on the prevention of HIV or homophobic bullying, and art exhibitions covering topics such as the body as a creative space and the history of homosexuality.

▶ *www.circuitfestival.net.*

CLUBS

Spain's recent anti-smoking laws have resulted in many clubs having a tiny, packed smokers' dancefloor and a larger non-smoking area which is pretty empty.

The Gaixample

Arena

Classic *C/Diputació 233.* **Madre** *C/Balmes 32.* **Open** *12.30-5.30am Fri, Sat.* **Map** p322 F8.
VIP & Dandy *Gran Via de les Corts Catalanes 593.* **Open** *Winter* 1am-6am Fri-Sat.
All *93 487 83 42, www.arenadisco.com. Metro Universitat.* **Admission** (incl 1 drink) €6 Mon-Fri; €12 Sat. **No credit cards.**
Map p326 F8.

The four Arena clubs are still packing them in every week, with a huge variety of punters. The unique selling point is that you pay once, get your hand stamped and can then flit between all four clubs. Madre is the biggest and most full-on venue of the quartet, with thumping house music and a darkroom. There are shows and strippers at the beginning of the week, but Wednesday's semi-riotous foam parties in July and August are where all the action takes place. VIP doesn't take itself too seriously and is popular with just about everyone, from mixed gangs of Erasmus students to parties of thirtysomethings down from Sabadell, all getting busy to Snoop Dogg and vintage Mariah Carey. Classic is similarly mixed, if even cheesier, playing mostly handbag, and, finally, Dandy bangs away with vintage chart hits.

▶ *Admission is also good for lesbian club Aire; see right.*

★ Metro

C/Sepúlveda 185 (93 323 52 27, www. metrodiscobcn.com). Metro Universitat.
Open *1-5am Mon; midnight-5am Tue-Thur, Sun;. midnight-6am Fri-Sat.* **Admission** (incl 1 drink) €15. **Credit** MC, V. **Map** p326 E9.

Metro's popularity seldom wanes, whatever the time of year. The club is particularly packed at the weekends, which makes the smaller of the two dancefloors, specialising in Latin beats, something of a challenge for more flamboyant dancers to navigate. The larger one is a space to dance to more traditional house music. The corridor-like darkroom is where the real action takes place, though. Among other nocturnal delights there are strippers, drag queen acts and, yes, bingo. *Photo p235.*

The rest of the city

Ácido Óxido

C/Joaquín Costa 61, Raval (93 412 26 21).
Metro Universitat. **Open** 6-11am daily.
No credit cards. Map p328 E9.
If you are having one of those nights when you just
have to keep going (or you haven't picked up your
energy levels yet), stagger into this wildly popular
'after-hours' joint. The venue claims to have the
darkest darkroom in town.

★ D-Boy

Ronda Sant Pere 19-21, Eixample (93 318 06 86,
www.matineegroup.com). Metro Urquinaona.
Open midnight-6am Fri-Sat; 11.30pm-5.30am Sun.
Admission (incl 1 drink) €18; €15 with flyer.
Credit (bar only) AmEx, MC, V. **Map** p328 E2.
The much-loved Salvation reopened, after a €2m
makeover and much fanfare, as D-Boy. With two
spaces, one for house and another for deep house,
and a huge darkroom, it's kept its megatron and go-
gos; you can be the judge of whether adding a few
pink lasers gives a club the right to have an attitude
and pricing policy that might exceed its actual
charms. Absolutely no women. Ever.

LESBIAN BARS & NIGHTCLUBS

Barcelona's lesbian scene doesn't seem to have
much consistency, with bars struggling to
survive amid constant changes of ownership.
On the other hand, there are several thriving
groups that organise regular parties, including
Nextown Ladys (www.nextownladys.com),
which runs a women-only Saturday event at
Lolita's (Ptge Domingo 3, no phone,
www.lolitasbarcelona.com), and **Silk**
(http://silkbcn.spaces.live.com). Check online for
details of the activities and events they arrange.

You'll also find lesbians in some of the
spots favoured by gay men, such as **Arena**
(*see p232*) or **La Bata de Boatiné** (*see p231*).
The second *xiringuito* on Mar Bella beach
functions as a lesbian meeting place – at its
liveliest on Sunday evenings, when it becomes
El Misterioso Secreto de Amparo
(www.amparo.chiringuitolesbico.com).
Admission to the bars listed below is free,
unless otherwise stated.

Aire

C/València 236, Eixample (93 454 63 94,
www.arenadisco.com). Metro Passeig de Gràcia.
Open 11pm-3am Thur-Sat. **Admission**
(incl 1 drink) €5 Fri; €6 Sat. **No credit cards.**
Map p322 F7.
The girly outpost of the Arena group is the city's
largest lesbian club, and as such sees a decent variety of girls (and their male friends, by invitation)
head down to shoot pool and dance to pop, house

and 1980s classics. On the first Sunday of the month,
there's a women-only strip show.
▶ *The admission price to gay megaclub Arena (see*
left) also allows for entry here.

★ Can Fly

Baixada de Viladecols 6, Barri Gòtic (mobile 675
618 473). Metro Jaume I. **Open** 5pm-2am Mon-
Thur, Sun; 5pm-3am Fri, Sat. **Admission** free.
No credit cards. Map p329 D6.
Patchwork graffiti meets rustic in this café/bar. If
you don't want to wait until midnight to get your
evening started, this is a cosy spot to start with a
drink, a tapa and a flirt. Friendly staff, who welcome
all comers, femme or butch, lesbian or straight.
There are also outdoor tables in a pretty square.

RESTAURANTS

In addition to the establishments below, plenty
of mixed restaurants in Barcelona have large
gay followings. Among the most popular are
the Barri Gòtic's **La Verònica** (*see p156*)
nd **Venus Delicatessen** (C/Avinyó 25, 93 301
15 85). **La Singular** (*see p166*) in Gràcia is
popular with lesbians, while **Zoologic**
(C/Casanova 30, Eixample, 93 453 52 49,
www.zoologicrestaurant.com) is popular with
all sorts for its over-the-top drag cabarets.

El Bierzo a Tope

C/Diputació 159, Eixample (93 453 70 45). Metro
Universitat. **Open** 8am-midnight Mon Sat. **Main**
courses €12.50. **Set menu** €9 Mon-Fri, €12.50
Fri dinner & Sat. **Credit** MC, V. **Map** p326 E8.
Serving traditional Spanish fare from León, in large
portions and at reasonable prices, this restaurant is
popular with bears and their admirers. Good-value
set menus are served all day.

Castro

C/Casanova 85, Eixample (93 323 67 84,
www.castro-barcelona.es). Metro Universitat.
Open 1-4.30pm, 8pm-12.30am Mon-Sat;
8pm-midnight Sun. **Main courses** €14.
Set lunch €10 Mon-Sat. **Set dinner** €20-€30
daily. **Credit** MC, V. **Map** p326 E8.
Still ahead of the crowd as far as gay restaurants go,
Castro continues to provide imaginative dishes such
as kangaroo with eucalyptus sauce and blackberry
tartlet, or venison in balsamic vinegar, all served by
the cutest of staff.

Iurantia

C/Casanova 42, Eixample (93 454 78 87,
www.iurantia.com). Metro Universitat. **Open**
1.30-4pm, 9pm-midnight Mon-Fri; 9pm-midnight
Sat. **Main courses** €11.50. **Set lunch** €10 Mon-
Fri. **Credit** AmEx, MC, V. **Map** p326 E8.
Although this is not a gay restaurant as such,
Iurantia's Gaixample location ensures it's frequented

ARTS & ENTERTAINMENT

by a stylish crowd, who are keen on the slick red paint job, downbeat tunes and the menu, which varies from imaginative fusion – octopus carpaccio – to popular and fairly priced pasta and pizzas. Leave room for the own-made bitter chocolate truffles with a touch of mint.

SHOPS & SERVICES

General shops

★ Antinous Libreria Café

C/Josep Anselm Clavé 6, Barri Gòtic (93 301 90 70, www.antinouslibros.com). Metro Drassanes. **Open** 10.30am-2pm, 5-8.30pm Mon-Fri; noon-2pm, 5-8.30pm Sat. **Credit** AmEx, MC, V. **Map** p329 B7.

This large, bright bookshop has an appealing café at the back – an ideal spot in which to check out your purchases (DVDs to postcards, poetry to magazines, art to comics). The shop also has a great selection of nude photobooks.

Complices

C/Cervantes 4, Barri Gòtic (93 412 72 83, www.libreriacomplices.com). Metro Jaume I. **Open** 10.30am-8pm Mon-Fri; 12.30-8pm Sat. **Credit** AmEx, MC, V. **Map** p329 C6.

Barcelona's oldest gay bookshop is run by a helpful lesbian duo who stock a variety of literature and films, from highbrow paperback classics (some available in English) and *Queer as Folk* box sets to porn mags and DVDs.

D'Arness

C/Villarroel 43, Eixample (www.d-arness. com). Metro Urgell. **Open** 5-9pm Mon-Sat. **Credit** MC, V. **Map** p326 E8.

This small specialist leather shop has all the gear you could possibly need. From 10.30pm, Wednesday to Sunday, the back room becomes a members-only sex bar (join at the door).

Ovlas

C/Aribau 31, Eixample (93 268 76 91, www.ovlasbarcelona.com). Metro Universitat. **Open** 11am-9pm Mon-Sat. **Credit** AmEx, MC, V. **Map** p326 F8.

This large space keeps Barcelona's boys in lurid briefs, singlets and revealing garments, making it a perfect one-stop shop for a weekend break in Sitges.

INSIDE TRACK TICKETS & INFO

Part bar and part ticket outlet, **Matinée Corner** (C/Consell de Cent 253, Eixample, no phone) is the place to get information and buy tickets for all the big gay events.

Hairdressers

Esclusif

C/Diputació 159, Eixample (93 454 24 10). Metro Urgell. **Open** 4-8pm Mon; 11am-8.30pm Tue-Sat. **Credit** V. **Map** p326 E8.

A gay hairdressing salon for boys and girls.
► *For more hairdressers, see p202.*

Saunas

At both of the establishments listed below, you'll find plenty of showers, steam rooms and dry saunas, along with bars and colourful porn lounges. On arrival, you'll be supplied with a locker key, towel and flip-flops.

Corinto

C/Pelai 62, Eixample (93 318 64 22, www. pases.com). Metro Catalunya. **Open** noon-5am Mon-Thur; 24hrs Fri-Sun. **Admission** €15.50. **Credit** AmEx, MC, V. **Map** p328 B2.

Nothing really changes at the Corinto, smack in the centre, and it still remains the most popular place for tourists to go get busy, aided by some fine vistas of Plaça Catalunya and La Rambla.

Sauna Casanova

C/Casanova 57, Eixample (93 323 78 60, www.pases.com). Metro Urgell. **Open** 24hrs daily. **Admission** €14-€18. **Credit** MC, V. **Map** p326 E8.

Casanova still attracts plenty of well-muscled eye candy for the visitor. It's at its busiest on Tuesday and Thursday evenings, every night after the clubs close and all day Sunday.

Sex shops

The following gay-oriented sex shops have viewing cabins for DVDs.

Nostromo

C/Diputació 208, Eixample (93 451 33 23). Metro Universitat. **Open** 11am-11pm Mon-Fri; 3-11pm Sat, Sun. **No credit cards. Map** p326 E8.

Zeus

C/Riera Alta 20, Raval (93 442 97 95, www.zeusgayshop.com). Metro Sant Antoni. **Open** 10am-9pm Mon-Sat. **Credit** MC, V. **Map** p326 E10.

SITGES

To the surprise of many, Sitges is charmingly pretty and family-oriented during the day. But its Jekyll and Hyde character is revealed during hot summer nights, when the town is bustling with partygoers. The small gay beach in the centre is where to preen and be seen. If you

Metro. *See p232.*

would rather not have to stare directly into your neighbour's armpit, hit the seafront and walk right for an hour or so until you reach the nudist beach (with corresponding cruising ground behind).

Accommodation

August can be a nightmare, so booking three months in advance is advisable for anything decent. This goes in particular for **El Xalet** and its sister **Hotel Noucentista** (for both, C/Illa de Cuba 35, 93 811 00 70, www.elxalet.com, rates €60-€100 incl breakfast) both of which occupy Modernista palaces and are furnished with period furniture. Almost next door is **Hotel Liberty** (C/Illa de Cuba 45, 93 811 08 72, www.libertyhotelsitges.com, rates €68-€135 incl breakfast), with spacious rooms, a lush garden and, if you feel like splashing out, a luxury penthouse with two terraces overlooking the town. The owners also have 41 apartments for rent; for details, see www.staysitges.com.

The romantics' choice, naturally, is the **Hotel Romàntic**, a beautifully restored 19th-century house with a secluded palm-filled garden (C/Sant Isidre 33, 93 894 83 75, www.hotelromantic.com, rates €58-€132.50 incl breakfast, closed late Oct- Easter). In a quieter residential area is the welcoming, French-run **Hotel Los Globos** (Avda Nuestra Señora de Montserrat 43, 93 894 93 74, www.hotellosglobos.com, rates €64-€106 incl breakfast), recently renovated with new bathrooms and with a balcony or private garden for each room. The friendly Peter and Rico at **RAS** (mobile 607 14 94 51, www. raservice.com) may be able to help you out with information or hotel bookings if you're stuck.

Bars & nightclubs

Sitges has a definite circuit, which begins around midnight with a drink at one of the many pavement cafés on C/Primer de Maig, aka Sin Street, or for the girls at **Mari Pili** (C/Joan Tarrida Ferratges 14, no phone). The next move is to one of the earlier bars (they start filling up around 1.30am). For those who want to dance, both **Organic** (C/Bonaire 15, no phone, www.theorganicdanceclub.com) and **Trailer** (C/Angel Vidal 36, 93 894 04 01, www.trailerdisco.com) are in the centre of town. Otherwise, head out to **L'Atlantida** at Platja les Coves (93 453 05 10, www.club atlantida.com, summer only) on foot (20 mins), by taxi or on board the free bus from the Calipolis hotel. For other night-time activities, just head for the beach.

Restaurants

For such a popular town, Sitges lacks good restaurants. Still, if you are looking for a particularly gay experience and aren't too bothered about the food, try **Parrots Restaurant** (C/Joan Tarrida 18, 93 811 12 19, www.parrotsrestaurant.com, mains €16, closed Nov-Dec).

Music & Nightlife

Barcelona is the party destination for those in the know

Barcelona makes no claims to be a party capital, despite a somewhat unwarranted reputation as such, but there is a reason that stag parties and night owls from around the globe head here in such numbers. There isn't the 24-hour, seven-days-a-week party vibe that you'll find in Ibiza, but there's an energy and creativity in the local nightlife that isn't found anywhere else.

It's a mood that's made and fostered by a population who party well, know when to go for it and when to call it quits, when to buy you a beer and when to leave you alone, when to clap and when to soft-shoe... but who most of all understand that going out is a necessary part of life that should be done right if it's to be done at all.

THE LOCAL SCENE

Millions of words have been spent lamenting the clubs and bars that have fallen victim to the municipal government's recent anti-noise campaign, but visitors don't lack opportunities for after-dark indulgence. There are superclubs hosting superstar DJs and tiny venues playing the latest electro. There are lounge clubs and gilded ballrooms, *salsatecas* and Brazilian samba bars, seductive tango emporiums and alternative nights offering anything from northern soul to Bollywood bhangra.

Going out happens late here, with people rarely meeting for a drink much before 11pm – if they do, it's a pre-dinner thing. Bars tend to close around 2am, or 3am at weekends, and it's only after this that the clubs get going, so many offer reduced entrance fees or free drinks to those willing to be seen inside before 1am. And if you're still raring to go at 6am, just ask around – more often than not there'll be an after-party party catering to the truly brave.

Traditionally, you had to head uptown to hit the posh clubs, but the Port Olímpic is putting on some serious competition with places such as **Club Catwalk** and **CDLC** luring the *pijos* (well-groomed uptowners) downtown. There are also nightly beach parties running up and down the coast from Bogatell to Mataró through the summer. Meanwhile, you'll find smaller venues pulsating with life in the Barri Gòtic, particularly around the Plaça Reial

and C/Escudellers. Across La Rambla, in the Raval, you can skulk in the grittier, grungier places, though even this neighbourhood hasn't proven impervious to gentrification, and a number of upmarket nightspots have lately sprung up on C/Joaquín Costa and between the kebab joints of the Rambla del Raval. If street beers, dogs and vintage sweaters are your thing, Gràcia is heaven – though in truth it's better for drinking than it is for dancing.

Live music

While the licensing battles between club owners and the town hall continue to inspire apocalyptic images in the local media, the rumours of the death of the city's music scene are gradually fading away. In a long-awaited move, officials have simplified convoluted licensing laws and offered financial support to those owners willing to go some way towards meeting the objections of local residents by soundproofing their spaces.

There's further evidence that all is not as bad as it seems: local acts continue to pop up, their success and profligacy attesting to Barcelona's tenacious relevancy on the wider Spanish music scene. Electro group Love of Lesbian, recently rebounded trip-hop pioneers Najwajean,

About the author
Katie Addleman is a writer and former deputy editor of Barcelona Metropolitan magazine.

Cineplexx & the Odeons, and Catalan folk popsters Manel are some names to look out for. There are also more active metal-core bands than you can shake a death rattle at, if that's your thing, and a slew of internationally minded musicians drawing from a blend of rock, flamenco, hip hop and various South American, Asian and African styles of music; the best known among them are Ojos de Brujo, Raval's 08001 and CaboSanRoque.

Some of the main music venues for seeing international names (as well as hotly tipped unknowns and locals) are the multi-faceted **Razzmatazz**, **Bikini** and the old dancehall **Sala Apolo**. The first hosts both cutting-edge live and electronic music, while the latter specialises in feel-happy DJs and special theme nights. You can catch occasional visits by pop-rock superstars in Montjuïc's sports stadiums – one of which has become the **Barcelona Teatre Musical** (C/Joaquim Blume s/n, 93 423 15 21) – at Vall d'Hebron, or even way out in **Badalona's Palau Olímpic**.

Advance information

For concert information, see *Time Out Barcelona* or the Friday papers, which usually include listings supplements. Look in bars and music shops for free magazines such as *Go*, *AB*, *Mondo Sonoro* (all mostly independent pop/rock/electronica) and *Batonga!* (which covers world music). *Punto H* and *Suite* are good for keeping abreast of the club scene.

For more, see www.infoconcerts.cat, www.atiza.com, www.salirenbarcelona.com, www.barcelonarocks.com and www.clubbing spain.com. For more on the city's many music festivals, try www.festivales.com and www.whatsonwhen.com.

FESTIVALS

Other festivals to look out for include **Flamenco Ciutat Vella** (*see p260*), **Festa de la Música** (*see p211*), **Festival del Grec** (*see p212*) and **Festival Asia** (*see p213*).

Festival Internacional de Percussió
L'Auditori (see p253). **Tickets** €15.
Date Feb.
The name may be a slight misnomer, since most of the acts of the International Percussion Festival are actually Catalan, but it's none the worse for that. At the end of the festival, CDs are made featuring those artists who have performed.

Festival Guitarra
Various venues (93 481 70 40, www.the project.cat). **Tickets** €15-€120. **Date** Feb-June.

This prestigious festival of guitars has the ability to attract world-class players. Previous guests have included Pat Metheny and Paco de Lucía. Styles span everything from flamenco to Latin sounds, classical guitar and gypsy jazz.

Primavera Sound
Poble Espanyol (see p83) & Parc del Fòrum (www.primaverasound.com). **Tickets** 5 days €145. **Date** 25-29 May 2011.
Fast stealing Sónar's thunder, this four-day music festival is one of the best in Spain. Credit for its success is due to its range of genres. There are rafts of electronica acts, DJs and local bands, plus a record fair and the Soundtrack Film Festival. In 2011, the line-up includes Belle & Sebastian, Fleet Foxes, Pulp and the Flaming Lips.

★ Sónar
93 320 81 63, www.sonar.es. **Tickets** €155.
Date 16-18 June 2011.
The three-day International Festival of Advanced Music and Multimedia Art (or Sónar, as it's more snappily known) remains a must for anyone into electronic music, urban art and media technologies. The event is divided into two parts. SónarDay comprises multimedia art, record fairs, conferences, exhibitions and sound labs around the CCCB, while DJs play. Later, SónarNight means a scramble for the desperately overcrowded shuttle bus from the bottom of La Rambla out to the vast hangars of the site in Hospitalet (tip: share a cab between four – it'll cost you the same), where concerts and DJs are spread over SónarClub, SónarPark and SónarPub.
▶ *A new addition to the festival is SónarKids (€18, €12 under-15s, www.sonarkids.com), with music, workshops and puppet shows on the Sunday at the SónarDay site.*

Els Concerts de l'Estiu
Poble Espanyol, Avda Francesc Ferrer i Guàrdia 13 (93 508 63 00, www.poble-espanyol.com). *Metro Espanya.* **Tickets** €18-€55. **Date** July.
'Summer Concerts' is a varied programme up in the cool alfresco environs of the Poble Espanyol, Kings of Convenience, Seal, Bob Dylan and Erikah Badu have all played.

Cruïlla BCN
Parc del Fòrum (no phone, www.cruilla barcelona.com). Metro El Maresme-Fòrum. **Tickets** *Two days* €68. *One day* €37. **Date** 2 days mid July.
Cruïlla snuck quietly on to the scene in 2008 with an unassuming clutch of bands, before launching into something quite special two years later. In 2010, the line-up included Ben Harper, the Wailers, Femi Kuti and Eli Paperboy Reed, but the real strength is in the choice of excellent local bands – the Pinker Tones, Muchachito Bombo Infierno, Macaco and Love of Lesbian.

ARTS & ENTERTAINMENT

San Miguel Mas i Mas Festival

Various venues (93 319 17 89,
www.masimas.com). **Tickets** €5-€30.
Date late July-Aug.
This tasteful music festival stretches over the summer months, and has gone from concentrating on Latin sounds to providing a little bit of everything. Concerts take place at various venues, including the Palau de la Música (*see p254*).

Festival L'Hora del Jazz

Various venues (93 268 47 36, www.amjm.org).
Tickets vary. **Date** Sept.
A month-long festival of local jazz acts, with free daytime concerts taking place in the Plaça Vilà de Gràcia on Sunday lunchtimes and various venues during the week at night. Some night-time concerts are also free of charge.

Barcelona Acció Musical (BAM)

Various venues (010, www.bcn.cat/bam/2011).
Date during the Festes de la Mercè, Sept.
BAM stages free concerts, often showcasing jazz and singer-songwriters, on Plaça del Rei; more famous names perform outside the cathedral, with dance acts on show at the Fòrum and rumba at Portal de la Pau (near the Museu Marítim). The prime mover of what's known as *so Barcelona* (Barcelona Sound), BAM promotes leftfield *mestissa* (vaguely, ethnic fusion) in its mission to provide 'music without frontiers'.

LEM Festival

Various venues, Gràcia (93 238 40 38,
www.gracia-territori.com). **Tickets** free-€6.
Date Oct.
A month-long, well-organised festival of multimedia art and experimental music. It mostly covers electronica, but also includes jazz and rock. Concerts are generally free.

MPB

Various venues (972 864 561,
www.festivalmpb.com). Metro Catalunya.
Date Oct.
Not to be confused with Brazilian pop genre MPB, the festival of Música Popular de Barcelona celebrates every kind of music but classical heard in the city. Venues including L'Auditori (*see p253*) and Luz de Gas (*see p248*) reverberate to sounds from gypsy punk to cumbia.

INSIDE TRACK TICKETS, PLEASE

You can get information and tickets from Telentrada, ServiCaixa and FNAC (for all, *see 206*). Specialist record shops, such as those on C/Tallers in the Raval, are good for info and flyers.

Festival de Músiques del Món

L'Auditori (see p253). Metro Marina.
Tickets €15-€30. **Date** 2wks Oct.
Staged every October, this world music festival has been scaled down over recent years, as a result of the global economic downturn. However, you still might catch a Mongolian throat-singer or Turkish whirling dervishes, alongside such home-grown talents as flamenco singer Miguel Poveda, who is a regular at this event.

Festival de Tardor Ribermúsica

Various venues, Born (93 319 3089,
www.ribermusica.org). Metro Barceloneta or Jaume I. **Date** 4 days mid Oct.
A lively autumn music festival that boasts more than 100 free performances around the Born, and fills the squares, bars, galleries, shops, churches and clubs with concerts of all stripes.

Festival Internacional de Jazz de Barcelona

Various venues (93 481 70 40, www.
barcelonajazzfestival.com). **Tickets** varies.
Date Oct-Nov.
One of Europe's most well-respected jazz festivals has grown to embrace everything from bebop to gospel, around a core of mainstream performers that have included Chick Corea, Wayne Shorter, Bebo Valdés, Al Green, Herbie Hancock, Caetano Veloso and even Katie Melua. Venues included in the festival's programme range from the Palau de la Música, Luz de Gas and Razzmatazz to L'Auditori; there are also big-band concerts and swing dancing in the Ciutadella park.

Els Grans del Gospel

Various venues (93 481 70 40,
www.theproject.cat). **Tickets** €15-€44. **Date** Dec.
A three-week festival of international gospel music, born of the gospel section of the International Jazz Festival (*see above*), which eventually became popular enough to stand alone.

VENUES
The Barri Gòtic

Barcelona Pipa Club

Plaça Reial 3, pral (93 301 11 65,
www.bpipaclub.com). Metro Liceu.
Open 11pm-3am daily. **Admission** free.
No credit cards. Map p329 B6.
This converted flat on Plaça Reial is decorated with oak, velvet, Sherlock Holmes-style memorabilia and a bar that's often impossible to get anywhere near, despite the prices. For all its genteel decor, the Barcelona Pipa Club has a semi-underground quality and is rammed with young Americans and their Catalan friends. Ring the bell downstairs to get into this establishment.

Barcelona Pipa Club.

★ Harlem Jazz Club

C/Comtessa de Sobradiel 8 (972 864 561,
www.harlemjazzclub.es). Metro Jaume I.
Open *July-Sept* 8pm-4am Tue-Thur; 8pm-5am Fri,
Sat. *Oct-June* 8pm-4am Tue-Thur, Sun; 8pm-5am
Fri, Sat. **Gigs** 10.30pm, midnight Tue-Thur, Sun;
11.30pm, 1am Fri, Sat. Closed 2wks Aug.
Admission €5 (incl 1 drink) Tue-Thur, Sun;
€5 Fri, Sat. **No credit cards. Map** p329 C6.
A hangout for not-so-cashed-up musicians, buffs
and students alike. A lot of local history has gone
down at Harlem, and some of the city's great talents
have emerged here. Jazz, klezmer, funk and flamenco
get a run in a venue that holds no musical prejudices.

★ Jamboree/Los Tarantos

Plaça Reial 17 (93 319 17 89,
www.masimas.com). Metro Liceu. **Open** 1-5am
Mon-Thur, Sun; 1-6am Fri, Sat. **Shows** *Jamboree*
9pm, 11pm daily. *Los Tarantos* 8.30pm, 9.30pm,
10.30pm daily. **Admission** *Shows* €13. *Club* €8.
Credit MC, V. **Map** p329 B6.
Every night, the cave-like Jamboree hosts jazz, Latin
or blues gigs by mainly Spanish groups – on
Mondays, in particular, the popular WTF jazz jam
session is crammed with a young local crowd.
Upstairs, slicker sister venue Los Tarantos stages
flamenco performances, then joins forces with
Jamboree to become one fun, cheesy club later on in
the evening. You'll need to leave the venue and pay
again, but admission serves for both spaces.

La Macarena

C/Nou de Sant Francesc 5 (no phone,
www.macarenaclub.com). Metro Drassanes.
Open midnight-4.30am Mon-Thur, Sun, midnight-
5am Fri, Sat. **Admission** free before 1.30am; €6
afterwards (but can vary). **No credit cards.**
Map p329 B7.
La Macarena is smaller than your apartment but has
big-club pretensions in the best sense. The music is
minimal electro selected by resident DJs and the
occasional big-name guests and is complemented by
a kicking sound system. Be warned that you should
watch your bag and your drink.

★ Marula Café

C/Escudellers 49 (93 318 76 90,
www.marulacafe.com). **Open** 11pm-5am Mon-
Thur, Sun; 11.30pm-6am Fri; 9.30pm-6am Sat.
Admission free-€10 (incl 1 drink). **Credit** MC, V.
Map p329 B6.
Grown-up clubbers were thrilled when the popular
Marula Café in Madrid announced it was opening a
sister club in Barcelona, and it hasn't disappointed.
The musical policy is what is known in Spain, some-
what uncomfortably, as *música negra* – a fairly use-
less label that in this case ranges from Sly and the
Family Stone to Michael Jackson via Fela Kuti, but
is a byword for quality and danceability. On
Saturday nights musicians play from about 9.30pm.
Admission is fairly randomly charged, but seems
not to apply if there's no queue.

El Paraigua

*C/Pas de l'Ensenyança 2 (93 302 11 31,
www.elparaigua.com). Metro Jaume I or
Liceu.* **Open** 9.30am-midnight Mon-Thur;
9.30am-3am Fri; 11am-3am Sat; noon-midnight
Sun. **Admission** free. **Credit** AmEx, MC, V.
Map p329 C6.

Upstairs is a beautifully elegant Modernista cocktail
bar, mirrored and wood-panelled, whereas downstairs is a cosy vaulted space framed by bare-brick
walls, which sees some of Barcelona's most promising new bands performing on Friday and Saturday
nights. El Paraigua seems to hold a particularly
special appeal for expat musicians. The music programme in any given month might include an Irish
soul singer, a British funk band and a mixed-nation-
ality cappella group.

Sidecar Factory Club

*Plaça Reial 7 (93 302 15 86, www.sidecar.es).
Metro Liceu.* **Open** 7pm-5am Mon-Thur;
7pm-6am Fri, Sat. **Admission** (incl 1 drink)
€5-€9. **Gigs** €6-€20. **No credit cards**.
Map p329 B6.

The Sidecar Factory Club still has all the ballsy attitude of the spit 'n' sawdust rock club that it used to
be. Its programming, which includes breakbeat,
indie, electro and live performances, has changed a
bit over recent times, but continues to pack in the
local indie kids and Interrailers to its bare-bricked,
barrel-vaulted basement.

The Born & Sant Pere

Club Mix

*C/Comerç 21 (93 319 46 96, www.clubmix
bcn.com). Metro Jaume I.* **Open** *Apr-Sept*
9pm-3am Tue-Thur; 9pm-4am Fri, Sat. *Oct-
Mar* 9pm-3am Wed-Thur; 9pm-4am Fri, Sat.
Admission free. **Credit** MC, V.
Map p329 F5.

With an interior designed by local tastemaker Silvia
Prada, a fashionable postcode and a menu of delicate
finger foods, Mix attracts a professional, stylish
crowd who enjoy both an after-work cocktail and an
after-dinner piss-up. DJs play funk, soul and world
beat on Thursdays, and safe and sophisticated rare
groove the rest of the time. There's live bossa nova
and jazz on Tuesdays.

★ Diobar

*C/Marquès de l'Argentera 27 (93 268 76 90).
Metro Barceloneta.* **Open** 11.30pm-3.30am
Thur-Sat. **Admission** free. **Credit** MC, V.
Map p329 F7.

The basement of a Greek restaurant is the unlikely
setting for this cosy and wildly popular club. There's
no plate-throwing but instead, from Thursday
through to Saturday night, it becomes a temple of
funk, soul and assorted Latin beats as DJ Fred Spider
hits the decks.

▶ *For something to eat beforehand, try Dionisus,
the Greek restaurant upstairs.*

Sidecar Factory Club.

The Raval

23 Robador

C/Robador 23 (no phone). Metro Liceu.
Open 6pm-3am daily. **Admission** free.
No credit cards. Map p329 A5.
Inside this stone-walled and smoke-filled lounge,
Raval denizens dig the jazz jam on Wednesdays, jazz
bands on Thursdays, the flamenco on Saturdays and
Sundays and, in between times, DJs playing a genre-
defying range of music (Joy Division and DJ Shadow
on the same night). A manga-style mural on the back
wall, by one of Barna's many graffiti artists, adds to
the underground appeal.

Aurora

*C/Aurora 7 (mobile 627 217 637). Metro
Paral·lel.* **Open** 8.30pm-2.30am Mon-Thur,
Sun; 8.30pm-3am Fri, Sat. **Admission** free.
No credit cards. Map p326 E10.
DIY-stylish, low-lit and cheap. Aurora's regulars
chat over *cañas* during the week and bounce around
the wee dancefloor downstairs at weekends. The
smiling, chatty bar staff tune the stereo to 'reggae'
and 'T-Rex' and keep your cocktail topped up until
you wander out to the Rambla de Raval, looking to
satisfy your craving for late-night döner kebab.

Bar Pastis

*C/Santa Mònica 4 (mobile 634 938 422,
www.barpastis.com). Metro Drassanes.*
Open 7pm-2.30am Tue-Thur, Sun; 7pm-3.30am
Fri, Sat. **Admission** free. **Credit** AmEx, MC, V.
Map p329 A7.
This quintessentially Gallic bar once served pastis
to visiting sailors and denizens of the Chino underworld. It still has a louche feel, with floor-to-ceiling
clippings and oil paintings, Piaf on the stereo and
paper cranes swaying from the ceiling. There's
live music every night (see the website for details).

Big Bang

*C/Botella 7 (no phone, www.bigbangbcn.net).
Metro Liceu or Sant Antoni.* **Open** *Bar* 9.30pm-
2.30am Tue-Thur, Sun; 9.30pm-3am Fri, Sat.
Gigs around 10pm-1am Fri, Sat. *Jam session*
10.30pm-1am Sun. **Admission** *Bar & jam
sessions* free. *Gigs* prices vary. **No credit cards.**
Map p326 E10.
Big Bang is decked out like a New York jazz club,
circa 1930, with the low-lit smokiness and bar stool
seating that implies. The diner-style tiled floor leads
from the bar to the tiny stage, where groups of talented musicians play swing, rock 'n' roll, bebop and
every other vintage genre that should never have
gone out of style. Bring your Stetson and a few euros
for beer; shows are almost always free.

★ La Concha

*C/Guàrdia 14 (93 302 4118). Metro
Drassanes.* **Open** 5pm-2.30am Mon-Thur, Sun;

Learn the Lingo

A good-time glossary.

If you've plans to sample Barcelona's
somewhat erratic nightlife, it's important
to know your *cul* (arse) from your *chulo*
(arrogant idiot). Nightlife slang can be
coarse and insulting. Both Catalan and
Spanish terms are used willy-nilly and
sometimes combined. Handy expressions
such as *(no) sóc gay* are universally
understood. So if you still '*tens ganas*'
(are up for it), here are a few pointers
to get you on your way.

EXPRESSING INTENTIONS

sortir	to go out
anar de festa/juerga	to go out partying
anar de farra	to go on a big night out
agafar un pet	to get totally drunk
lligar	to pull
intentar lligar	chat up, or try to pull
fer un clau	(very vulgar indeed) to have sex

THE VENUE – EL LLOC

brut	dirty
cutre	shabby
guarro	seedy
de moda	trendy/flashy
de gom a gom (Cat)/ a tope (Sp)	packed
una estafa (Cat)/ un timo (Sp)	a rip-off

THE CLIENTELE

golfo/golfa	shameless/up for anything/slapper
friqui	freak
pijo	posh
cursi (Sp)	cheesy
hortera (Sp)	flashy, tasteless

THE EXPERIENCE

chupitos	shots
dos per un	cheap drinks (lit. 'two for one')
un pitillo	a cigarette
un after	a late-night/early-morning bar

THE POST MORTEM

nit en blanc	sleepless night
liarse	to get 'lost' in the night
tornar de dia	get back in daylight
empalmar	to stay out all night

ARTS & ENTERTAINMENT

Get the local experience

Over 50 of the world's top destinations available.

5pm-3am Fri, Sat. **Admission** free.
No credit cards. Map p329 A6.
Papered with posters of vintage Spanish sexpot Sara Montiel and filled with hookah smoke and the sounds of Bollywood balladry, La Concha is a gem of dusty fabulousness that stands in direct contrast to all the slick and pretentious glamour of most of the newer late-night bars. The venue is under Moroccan ownership and there's now tea and baklava in the afternoon.

Guru

C/Nou de la Rambla 22 (mobile 661 646 161, www.guru-barcelona.com). Metro Liceu.
Open 10pm-3am daily. **Admission** free.
No credit cards. Map p329 A6.
Guru has its eyes set on becoming the latest addition to the Raval bar scene's sleekification, but – palm trees and mood lighting aside – you can't help thinking that, with its white padded walls, it looks rather like a rest room for the suicidal. The venue hasn't yet achieved the exclusive status it's aiming for and, as such, cosmo-sipping, black-clad Parisians are still having to deal with gangs of tipsy Scousers hopping about to live salsa.

Jazz Sí Club

C/Requesens 2 (93 329 00 20, www.tallerde musics.com/jazzsi-club). Metro Sant Antoni.
Open 7.45-10.30pm Tue; 8.30-11pm Mon, Wed-Fri; 7.45-11pm Sat; 6.30-10pm Sun. **Admission** (incl 1 drink) €5-€8. **No credit cards.**
Map p326 E10.
Tucked into a Raval side street, with cheap shows every night and cheap bar grub, this truly authentic place is worth seeking out during your stay in the city. Since it functions as both a venue for known-in-the-scene locals and an auditorium for students of the music school across the street, it's packed to the brim with students, teachers, music lovers and players. Nights vary between jazz, flamenco and Cuban, and there are jam sessions on Tuesdays and Saturdays.

Moog

C/Arc del Teatre 3 (93 301 72 82, www. masimas.com). Metro Drassanes. **Open** midnight-5am Mon-Thur, Sun; midnight-6am Fri, Sat. **Admission** €15. **Credit** MC, V.
Map p329 A7.
Moog is a curious club: long, narrow and enclosed, with the air conditioner pumping; the experience of partying here is like dancing on a dimly lit aeroplane. The two floors are rather hilariously divided along gender lines: girls shake to pop and 1980s music upstairs, whereas boys tune in to non-stop hard house and techno downstairs. As well as classic soundtracks, there are occasional rock gigs. The Moog is packed seven days a week, and Angel Molina, Laurent Garnier and Jeff Mills have all played here at some point.

Barceloneta & the Ports

Around the quayside of the Port Olímpic, you will find dance bars interspersed with seafood restaurants and mock-Irish pubs, with video screens and go-gos in abundance. It makes little difference which you choose.

CDLC

Passeig Marítim 32 (93 224 04 70, www.cdlcbarcelona.com). Metro Ciutadella-Vila Olímpica. **Open** noon-3.30am daily. **Admission** free. **Credit** AmEx, MC, V. **Map** p327 J13.
Carpe Diem Lounge Club, to give the venue its full name, remains at the forefront of Barcelona's splash-the-cash, see-and-be-seen celeb circuit: the white beds flanking the dancefloor, guarded by a clip-boarded hostess, are perfect for showing everyone who's the daddy. Alternatively, for those not celebrating recently signed, six-figure record deals, funky house and a busy terrace provide an opportunity for mere mortals (and models) to mingle and discuss who's going to finance their next drink and, secondly, how to get chatting to whichever member of the Barça team has just walked in.

Club Catwalk

C/Ramón Trias Fargas s/n (93 221 61 61, www.clubcatwalk.net). Metro Ciutadella-Vila Olímpica. **Open** midnight-6am Thur-Sun.
Admission (incl 1 drink) €12-€20.
Credit AmEx, MC, V. **Map** p327 K12.
Maybe it's the name or maybe it's the location, but most of the Catwalk queue seems to think they're headed straight for the VIP room – that's crisp white collars and gold for the boys and short, short skirts for the girls. Inside it's suitably snazzy; upstairs there's R&B and hip hop, but the main house room is where most of the action is, with everything from electro-house to minimal beats. *Photo p244.*
Warm up with a louche cocktail at CDLC while you're waiting for Catwalk to open; see above.

Le Kasbah

Plaça Pau Vilà 1 (Palau del Mar) (mobile 667 166 783, www.ottozutz.com). Metro Barceloneta. **Open** *Oct-May* midnight-3.30am Wed-Sat. *June-Sept* midnight-3.30am daily.
Admission free. **Credit** MC, V.
Map p329 E8.

INSIDE TRACK GET THE WORM

If you turn up to Barcelona clubs much before about 1am, you'll probably have the place to yourself. On the other hand, you're also more likely to get in for free, and drinks are occasionally cheaper, depending on the hour.

ARTS & ENTERTAINMENT

A white awning over terrace tables heralds the entrance to this decidedly louche bar, which lies behind the Palau de Mar. Inside, a North African harem look seduces a young and up-for-it crowd of tourists and students on to its plush cushions for a cocktail or two before they depart for other venues. But as the night progresses, so does the music, from chilling out tunes in the early evening to full-on boogie after midnight.

Mondo

Edifici IMAX, Moll d'Espanya (93 221 39 11, www.mondobcn.com). Metro Barceloneta or Drassanes. **Open** 11.30pm-3.30am Wed-Sat. **Credit** AmEx, MC, V. **Map** p326 G12.

If you plan on visiting Mondo, we suggest that you arrive in style. Go for a yacht or a Jaguar – anything less might not get you past the door. Once you're inside the establishment, an upmarket dining experience alongside a window of spectacular views of the port precede late-night caviar and champagne house parties with DJs from Hed Kandi and Hotel Costes. Meanwhile, a number of intimate VIP rooms provide privacy, pleasure and prestige.

★ Sala Monasterio

Passeig Isabel II 4 (93 319 19 88, www.sala monasterio.com). Metro Barceloneta. **Open** 9.30pm-2.30am Mon-Thur, Sun; 9.30pm-3am Fri, Sat. **Admission** free-€6. **No credit cards**. **Map** p329 E7.

The entrance to Sala Monasterio is easily missed; go in past the bar at street level and descend to this low-ceilinged, bare-brick cavern to hear all nature of jamming and live music on a great sound system. There is a diverse line-up throughout the week. Singer-songwriters play on Monday and rock jams on Tuesday. Wednesday sees Brazilian music here, Thursday blues jams, and a jazz jam usually takes place on Sunday nights. Friday and Saturday tend to be reserved for a more eclectic range of gigs, from Catalan rock to Bowie tribute bands.

Club Catwalk. *See p243.*

ARTS & ENTERTAINMENT

Le Kasbah. See p243.

Montjuïc & Poble Sec

La [2]

*C/Nou de la Rambla 111 (93 441 40 01,
www.sala-apolo.com). Metro Paral·lel.* **Open**
Concerts 8pm daily. *Club* midnight-6am Mon,
Tue; 12.30-6am Wed-Sat. **Admission** €6-€25.
Credit AmEx, MC, V. **Map** p326 E11.
La [2] has excellent sound, an intimate layout and
the only hip flamenco night in the city (Mondays
from May to September). The music is reliably good,
with performances by more cultish artists than those
that play next door. Punters can stay on for indie-
rock club Nitsa.
► *Can't get in here? Sala Apolo is next door;
see below.*

Bar Só-ló

*C/Margarit 18 (no phone, http://solobar.
wordpress.com). Metro Paral·lel or Poble Sec.*
Open 6pm-2am Wed, Thur, Sun; 6pm-2.30am
Fri, Sat. **Admission** free. **No credit cards**.
Map p325 D10.
Remember university? Lazy conversations, mindless
tooling around on someone's guitar… Relive the
glory at this sprawling but oddly cosy bar near the
buzzing C/Blai, where stacked up board games and
seemingly half-finished art projects comprise the
student-living decor. Nightly shows run from blues
spectaculars to didgeridoo trios, and there's a big
screen for live football and rugby.

Barcelona Rouge

*C/Poeta Cabanyes 21 (93 442 49 85).
Metro Paral·lel. Open* 7pm-2.30am Wed, Sun;
7pm-3am Thur-Sat. **Admission** free.
No credit cards. Map p326 D11.
Ah – comfy. This is a pretty place done up with
throw rugs, vintage lamps that don't do a whole lot
(the lighting concept is the uncomplicated 'dark') and
dusty sofas. Later in the night it gets packed with
singing, decked-out thirtysomethings who don't
mind getting tipsy in a place where it costs quite a
bit of coin to do so. There are occasional live shows
(normally Sundays).

Maumau

*C/Fontrodona 35 (93 441 80 15, www.maumau
barcelona.com). Metro Paral·lel.* **Open** 11pm-
2.30am Thur-Sat. Closed Aug. **Credit** AmEx,
MC, V. **Map** p326 D11.
Ring the bell by the anonymous grey door. You no
longer have to pay to get in, but the membership
card gets some good discounts for cinemas, clubs
and so on (see the website). Inside, a large warehouse
space is humanised with colourful projections,
Ikea-style sofas and scatter cushions, and a friendly,
laid-back crowd. These days Maumau has taken a
step upmarket and is more of a lounge bar, and its
latest speciality is the G&T, with 25 different types
of gin available.

Sala Apolo

*C/Nou de la Rambla 113 (93 441 40 01,
www.sala-apolo.com). Metro Paral·lel.* **Open**
Concerts 8.30pm daily. *Club* midnight-6am
Mon-Sat. **Admission** *Concerts* varies. *Club*
(incl 1 drink) €13 Mon; €12 Tue; €10 Wed,
Thur; €15 Fri, Sat. **Credit** MC, V.
Map p326 E11.

Midnight Feasts

Late-night snacks for the journey home.

It's 6am on a Saturday morning, you've just fallen out of a club and you're jonesing for something greasy. What to do?

Just off La Rambla, the Boqueria market opens at 7am, but the stallholders are there at 6am, tucking into huge slices of *tortilla* at the **Bar Boqueria** (Stand 282, 93 412 64 62). If you can hold out until 7am, sophisticated drunks with a gourmet palate (and slightly deeper pockets) can tuck into a fresh baguette filled with artichoke *tortilla* – or a whopping *esmorzar de forquilla* (literally, 'fork breakfast'), which might be sausage and beans, or scrambled eggs with chorizo at the **Bar Pinotxo** (*see p170*).

For something considerably more upmarket, try **Velódromo** (*see p180*), a cult café-bar which has recently reopened as a gourmet tapas bar with extended hours under the direction of Michelin-starred chef Carles Abellán. Also uptown, the old-fashioned **Bar París** (C/París 46, 93 322 41 52) was once a post-party classic, but has reduced its hours considerably under the city-wide crackdown on bars. Still, if you're in the neighbourhood when the doors open at 7am, a mountain of eggs and bacon, or a baguette stuffed with a greasy slab of pork and some cheese, might just hit the spot nicely.

Back downtown, the **Bar Estudiantil** (Plaça Universitat 12, 93 302 31 25) is another classic, and is probably the only place in town with a packed-out terrace at 8am on summer weekends. Not far away,

Els Tres Tombs (*see p177*), an old-timer bar which sits opposite the Mercat Sant Antoni, opens at 6am, and is another favourite for bleary-eyed party animals warding off hangovers with piles of fried food.

If you've been out partying in Poblenou or on the beaches, a visit to the **Churrería Argiles** (Plaça Marina s/n, 93 234 43 07) is in order. Famous for its time-warp 1970s decor and the prominently displayed photograph of the Catalan President bestowing a diploma in making of *churros* (fried batter sticks) on the owner, it has a massive cult following among *barcelonin* youth. An order of chips smothered in mayonnaise and ketchup, along with a large beer, should keep the party going for another hour or two.

Sala Apolo, one of Barcelona's most popular clubs, is a 1940s dancehall, with all that implies for atmosphere (good) and acoustics (bad). Live acts range from Toots & the Maytals to Killing Joke, but note that buying tickets for the band doesn't include admission to the club night: you'll need to re-enter for that, and pay an extra charge. On Wednesdays, the DJs offer African and Latin rhythms; on Thursdays, it's funk, Brazilian, hip hop and reggae; and Fridays and Saturdays are an extravaganza of bleeping electronica.

▶ *Look out for monthly burlesque night Taboo.*

★ La Terrrazza

Poble Espanyol, Avda Francesc Ferrer i Guàrdia 13 (93 272 49 80, www.laterrrazza.com). Metro Espanya. **Open** *May-mid Oct* midnight-6am Thur-Sat. **Admission** (incl 1 drink) €18. **Credit** AmEx, MC, V. **Map** p325 B9.

Gorgeous, glamorous and popular (with the young, hair-gel-and-heels brigade), La Terrrazza is a nightclub that Hollywood might dream of. Wander through the night-time silence of Poble Espanyol to the starry patio that is the dancefloor for one of the more surreal experiences that it's possible to have with an highly priced G&T in your hand. Gazebos, lookouts and erotic paintings add to the magic, and if the music is mostly crowd-pleasing house tunes (the occasional big-name DJ, though no one truly fabulous), so what? That's not really what you came for.

Tinta Roja

C/Creu dels Molers 17 (93 443 32 43, www.tintaroja.net). Metro Poble Sec. **Open** 8.30pm-2am Thur; 8.30pm-3am Fri, Sat. Closed 2wks Aug. **Admission** free. **No credit cards. Map** p325 D10.

A smooth and mysterious bar, once a dairy farm, lent a Buenos Aires bordello/theatre/circus/cabaret vibe by plush red velvet sofas, smoochy niches and an ancient ticket booth. It's an atmospheric place to go for a late-ish drink, and it's open from 9-11pm for tango classes on Wednesday nights.

The Eixample

Antilla BCN Latin Club

C/Aragó 141 (93 451 45 64, www.antilla salsa.com). Metro Urgell. **Open** 11.30pm-4am Wed; 11pm-5am Thur; 11.30pm-6am Fri, Sat; 9pm-1am Sun. *Gigs* around 12.30am Wed, Thur. **Admission** free Wed, Thur, Sun; (incl 1 drink) €10 Fri, Sat. **No credit cards. Map** p326 E8.

This Caribbean cultural centre hosts exhibitions, publishes its own magazine (*Antilla News*) and offers Latin dance classes. But when the sun goes down all cultural pretensions go out the window – it's a hedonistic jungle in there. Salsa shows by entire orchestras and DJs playing rumba, merengue and *son* until six in the morning will spin your head and parch your throat until the only word you can croak is 'mojito'.

Astoria

C/París 193-197 (93 414 63 62, www.grupo costaeste.com). Metro Diagonal. **Open** 11.30pm-2.30am Tue-Thur, Sun; 11.30pm-3.30am Fri, Sat. Closed Aug. **Admission** free. **Credit** AmEx, MC, V. **Map** p322 F6.

Opium offers a break from the norm. For a start, the club is housed in a converted 1950s cinema, which means the projections arc actually watchable. There are three bars and plenty of comfortable seating, along with a small dancefloor; if you're very wonder-

ful, you may get to sit on a heart-shaped cushion in the tiny VIP area. With all this going for it, Astoria has inevitably become the domain of Barcelona's moneyed classes. Drinks are dearer upstairs.

Bucaro

C/Aribau 195 (93 209 65 62, www.grupo costaeste.com/bucaro). FGC Provença. **Open** 11.30pm-4.30am Mon-Thur; 11pm-6am Fri, Sat. **Admission** free before 1am; (incl 1 drink) €12 after. **Credit** AmEx, MC, V. **Map** p322 F6.

Looking a tad jaded, Bucaro's white leather sofas and pouffes still manage to pull a crowd of glamour pusses, who stalk their prey from the mezzanine. There's chill-out and jazz in the bar at the front and house for the dancefloor at the back. Drinks are a couple of euros more expensive if you're sitting at a table. Dress code is smart.

▶ *If you like it here, try Astoria, which is run by the same people; see p247.*

City Hall

Rambla Catalunya 2-4 (93 317 21 77, www.grupo-ottozutz.com). Metro Catalunya. **Open** 10.30pm-6am daily. **Admission** (incl 1 drink) €12. Free before 2.30am with flyer. **Credit** (door only) AmEx, MC, V. **Map** p328 C1.

City Hall ain't big, but it is popular. The music is mixed, from deep house to electro rock, and there's an older post-(pre-?) work crowd joining the young, tanned and skinny to show the dancefloors some love. Outside, the terrace is a melting pot of tourists and locals, who rub shoulders under the watchful (and anti-pot-smoking) eye of the bouncer. *Photo p248.*

▶ *Flyers for City Hall are easy to find in bars and shops around town, and will get you in free.*

Sala Apolo. *See p245.*

City Hall. *See p247.*

Danzarama

Gran Via de les Corts Catalanes 604 (93 342 52 70, www.danzarama.com). Metro Universitat. **Open** midnight-2am Mon-Thur, Sun; midnight-3am Fri, Sat. **Admission** free. **Credit** AmEx, MC, V. **Map** p326 F8.

Danzarama starts the night as a flash restaurant – we're talking white sofas swinging from the ceiling – and then becomes a club at midnight. With no entry charge and lots of tables, Danzarama has become a popular pre-party venue, and thumping tunes make up for the club-priced drinks.

Discothèque

C/Tarragona 141-147 (93 426 84 44, www.discotheque.info). Metro Tarragona. **Open** midnight-6am Fri-Sat; 8pm-midnight Sun. **Admission** (incl 1 drink) €12-€15. **Credit** MC, V. **Map** p325 C8.

Phenomenally successful in the early noughties, big D is back in a new location. The club has adopted a purse-friendly, all-inclusive policy, with student night on Thursdays and special deals on drinks. Ibizan-style 'tea dance' Café Olé attracts a munificent crowd on Sundays.

Distrito Diagonal

Avda Diagonal 442 (mobile 607 11 36 02, www.distritodiagonal.com). Metro Diagonal. **Open** midnight-6am Fri, Sat. **Admission** free before 3am; (incl 1 drink) €15 after. **No credit cards. Map** p322 G6.

Distrito Diagonal attracts a slightly older crowd with an easygoing atmosphere. The venue is bathed in red light, sounds run from from nu jazz to deep

house, and there are plenty of chairs to sink into. It's become a sought-after place for small promoters and one-off parties, which means the tunes can veer anywhere from Bollywood to hip hop.

Luz de Gas

C/Muntaner 246 (93 209 77 11, www.luz degas.com). FGC Muntaner. **Open** *Club* 1-5.30am daily. *Gigs* 9pm, 11pm daily. **Admission** *Club* (incl 1 drink) €18. *Gigs* vary. **Credit** AmEx, MC, V. **Map** p322 E5.

This lovingly renovated old music hall, garnished with chandeliers and classical friezes, is a mainstay on the live music scene and is one classy joint. In between visits from international artists and benefit concerts for local causes, you will find nightly residencies: blues on Mondays, Dixieland jazz on Tuesdays, disco on Wednesdays, pop-rock on Thursdays, soul on Fridays and vintage and Spanish rock on weekends.

Monk Barcelona

C/Pau Claris 92 (93 318 42 52, www.monk barcelona.com). Metro Catalunya. **Open** midnight-3am daily. **Admission** free. **Credit** AmEx, MC, V. **Map** p328 D1.

The centre of Barcelona is strangely devoid of glamorous nightspots – or at least it was until Buda came along. A restaurant early on, which turns into a nightclub at midnight, it has lots of throne-style furniture and gilded wallpaper, topped off with a colossal chandelier. The laid-back staff (dancing on the bar seems completely acceptable here) and upbeat house music make it an excellent spot for drinks and an ogle.

ARTS & ENTERTAINMENT

Gràcia

Heliogabal

C/Ramón y Cajal 80 (no phone, www.helio gabal.com). Metro Joanic. **Open** 9pm-2am Mon-Wed, Sun; 9pm-3am Thur-Sat. *Concerts* 10pm. **Admission** free-€10. **No credit cards.** **Map** p323 H5.

Loved by habitués of the Gràcia arts scene, this low-key bar and performance venue is filled to bursting with neighbourhood cutie pies in cool T-shirts who just really adore live poetry. Events change nightly, running from live music to film screenings, art openings and readings, and programming focuses mostly on local talents. On concert nights arrive early for an 'at-least-I'm-not-standing' folding chair.

KGB

C/Alegre de Dalt 55 (93 210 59 06, www.sala kgb.net). Metro Joanic. **Open** 1-6am Thur-Sat. **Admission**(incl 1 drink) €12. *Gigs* varies. **Credit** AmEx, MC, V. **Map** p323 J4.

KGB is a cavern-like space that was, in its heyday, the rock 'n' roll disco barn capital of the city, and *'un after'* where Sidecar heads would bolt at 6am on the weekend. It still remains loud, whether featuring concerts or DJ sessions. Thursday's concerts tend towards pop rock, which then continues for the DJ sets, while the occasional weekend gigs vary but are followed by tech-house.

▶ *KGB was one of the original 'design bars';* see p182 **Pop Go the '80s**.

Vinilo

C/Matilde 2 (mobile 626 464 759, http://vinilus.blogspot.com). Metro Fontana. **Open** 7pm-2am Mon-Thur; 7pm-3am Fri, Sat; 7pm-12.30am Sun. **Admission** free. **No credit cards. Map** p322 G5.

Run by an affably hip family, Vinilo seems like an artist's den masquerading as a neighbourhood bar. The walls are papered with original prints and concert posters; a silent TV plays '80s cartoons on loop and the beer selection is nothing to scoff at. But it's the music that makes it: Sufjan Stevens, Coco Rosie, Leonard Cohen… You'll wish you lived here.

Other districts

Bikini

Avda Diagonal 547, Les Corts (93 322 08 00, www.bikinibcn.com). Metro Les Corts or Maria Cristina. **Open** *Club* midnight-5am Wed-Sat. **Admission** (incl 1 drink) €15. **Credit** MC, V. **Map** p321 C5.

Bikini lost some muscle in recent years, with the big-name stars it once booked replaced by little-knowns and ageing rockers. In 2010, however, programming had really picked up, with gigs from Richard Hawley, Florence and the Machine and Cornershop. Gigs are staged with the professional vigour of gold-ticket shows, and the club nights that follow are legendary. Divide your time between the rooms playing hip hop, pop, lounge or Latin sounds.

Elephant. *See p250.*

Elephant

Passeig dels Til·lers 1, Pedralbes (93 334 02 58, www.elephantbcn.com). Metro Palau Reial. **Open** 11.30pm-4.30am Thur-Sat. **Admission** free. **Credit** AmEx, MC, V. **Map** 337 A2.

If you have a Porsche and a model girlfriend, this is where you meet your peers. Housed in a converted mansion, Elephant is as elegant and hi-design as its customers. The big attraction is the outdoor bar and terrace dancefloor – though the low-key, low-volume (due to the neighbours' complaints) house music doesn't inspire much hands-in-the-air action. *Photo p249.*

★ Liquid

Centre Poliesportiu L'Hospitalet Nord, Avda Manuel Azaña 21-23, L'Hospitalet (no phone, www.liquidbcn.com). Metro Zona Universitària. **Open** *mid June-Aug* midnight-5.30am Sun. **Admission** (incl 1 drink) €15. **Credit** MC, V.

In an almost-criminal strike against the morale of the working population (or the sobriety of Monday mornings), this summer-only clubbing classic hosts the best of the best in European electronica – on Sundays. Miss Kitten, DJ Hell, Sascha Funke and the Hacker all passed through last year to 'party in the pool'. Yes, that's right; it's a swimming pool.

Mirablau

Plaça Doctor Andreu, Tibidabo (93 418 58 79). FGC Avda Tibidabo then Tramvia Blau. **Open** 11am-4.30am Mon-Wed, Sun; 11am-6am Thur-Sat. **Admission** free. **Credit** AmEx, MC, V.

It doesn't get any more uptown than this, geographically and socially. Located at the top of Tibidabo, this small bar is packed with the high rollers of Barcelona, from local footballers living on the hill to international businessmen on the company card. They're drawn here for the view and the artificial wind that sweeps through the tropical shrubbery outside on hot summer nights.

Otto Zutz

C/Lincoln 15 (93 238 07 22, www.ottozutz. com). FGC Gràcia. **Open** midnight-5am Wed; midnight-6am Thur-Sat. **Admission** (incl 1 drink) €20. **Credit** AmEx, MC, V. **Map** p322 F4.

Otto Zutz should have been great. Located away from the maddening crowds of the old quarter in a three-floor former textile factory that oozes character, the initial concept held potential in abundance. But it got lost somewhere amongst the pretentious staff, mediocre house and bad R&B music. Fortunately, the crowd doesn't seem to notice – this place sure can pack in the punters, especially when it comes to those who are young and dolled-up. Flyers are ubiquitous.

★ Razzmatazz

C/Almogàvers 122 (93 320 82 00, www.sala razzmatazz.com). Metro Bogatell or Marina. **Open** *Concerts* vary. *Club* 1-6am Fri, Sat. **Admission** *Concerts* varies. *Club* (incl 1 drink) €15. **Credit** MC, V. **Map** p327 L10.

This monstrous club's five distinct spaces form the night-time playground of seemingly all young Barcelona. There's indie rock in Razz Club, tech-house in the Loft, techno pop in Lolita, electro pop in the Pop Bar and electro rock in the Rex Room. Live acts run from Arctic Monkeys to Banarama. The price of admission will get you into all five rooms (no matter what's on in each), though the gigs are normally ticketed separately.

Sala BeCool

Plaça Joan Llongueras 5 (93 362 04 13, www.salabecool.com). Metro Hospital Clínic. **Open** *Gigs* 10pm Thur-Sat. *Club* midnight-5am Thur; 1am-6am Fri, Sat. **Admission** *Gigs* varies. *Club* (incl 1 drink) €12. **Credit** AmEx, MC, V. **Map** p322 D5.

The latest from Berlin's minimal electro scene reaches Barcelona via this uptown concert hall. After the live shows by local rock stars or international indie success stories, a packed and music-loving crowd throbs to sophisticated electronica and its bizarre attendant visuals. Upstairs, in the Red Room, DJs playing indie pop rock provide an alternative to the pounding beats of the main room.

Sala Salamandra

Avda Carrilet 301, L'Hospitalet (93 337 06 02, www.salamandra.cat). Metro Avda Carrilet. **Open** *Concerts* 9.30pm. *Club* midnight-7am Fri, Sat. **Admission** *Gigs* prices vary. *Club* (incl 1 drink) €8; free before 2am. **Credit** MC, V.

If you're willing to travel 30 minutes on the metro to L'Hospitalet, do it for a night at this 500-person venue-cum-nightclub, which regularly hosts the best local artists, including Macaco, Muchachito Bombo Infierno and Kinky Beat. Local and visiting DJs take over after the shows, and it's worth sticking around; the music stays fun, the crowd local, the atmosphere unpretentious and the drinks fairly cheap.

Universal

C/Marià Cubí 182 bis-184 (93 201 35 96). FGC Muntaner. **Open** 11pm-3.30am Mon-Thur; 11pm-5.30am Fri, Sat. **Admission** free Mon-Thur; free before 1am (incl 1 drink), €15 after 1am Fri, Sat. **Credit** AmEx, MC, V. **Map** p322 E5.

One of the few clubs in Barcelona that caters to an older, well-dressed crowd, Universal doesn't charge admission, but the drink prices are pretty steep. Upstairs is a chill-out area, complete with aquatic slide projections, while downstairs sports a sharper look. Later, the music moves from downtempo to soft house, which works the crowd up to a gentle shimmy.

Performing Arts

Rich pickings for music lovers.

Barcelona has a remarkable musical heritage and now, finally, it has performance venues to match. Mayor Jordi Hereu has vowed to defy the economic crisis and invest not only in protecting the arts, but in creating innovative centres to develop and encourage new forms of expression in music, dance and theatre. And the rich pickings are not accessible only to Spanish- or Catalan-speakers, thanks to the tradition of physical spectacle that began in the Franco years when the Catalan language was banned.

Meanwhile, three of the city's most venerable institutions – the Liceu opera house, the Auditori concert hall and the extraordinary, century-old Palau de la Música Catalana – are in rude health, with increasingly diverse programming.

ARTS & ENTERTAINMENT

Classical Music & Opera

The best news about the local music scene is that confidence is high and programmes are increasingly well rounded. Although the canon still reigns at the Liceu, contemporary productions, local works and some adventurous formats add a bit of risk to its classical repertoire. The **Conservatori** – part of the Liceu – offers its own programme of chamber operas, recitals and contemporary compositions in a subterranean auditorium. Smaller venues such as **Auditori Axa** host fewer regular concerts, although those that are staged are generally of a high standard.

The main musical season runs from September to June (see below for exceptions). During this time, the city orchestra, the **OBC**, plays weekly at the Auditori, which also regularly hosts resident contemporary orchestra **BCN 216**. The Liceu stages a different opera every three or four weeks. Both the **Auditori** and the **Palau de la Música** hold several concert cycles of various genres, either programmed by the venues or by independent promoters (Ibercamera, Euroconcert or Promoconcert are the most high-profile).

From June to August, many concerts take place outdoors. **Música als Parcs** (*photo p252*) is a programme of some 50 evening concerts hosted in a number of parks across the city (www.parcsijardins.cat).

Additionally, various museums, among them the **Fundació Miró** (*see p85*) and the **CaixaForum** (*see p84*) also hold occasional small outdoor concerts. From October to May, Euroconcert (www.euroconcert.org) organises a monthly free organ recital at the cathedral, which is usually held on the second Wednesday of the month at 8pm.

INFORMATION & TICKETS

The *Informatiu Musical*, put together by Amics de la Música (93 268 01 22, www.amicsmusica.org), lists concerts in all genres on its website. Weekly entertainment guide *Guía del Ocio* (in Spanish) has a music section, as does the weekly *Time Out Barcelona* (www.timeout.cat), in Catalan; both *El País* and *La Vanguardia* list forthcoming concerts. For children's events try www.toc-toc.cat. The council website, www.bcn.cat/cultura, also has details of many forthcoming events. Tickets for most major venues can be bought by phone or online from venues, or from Telentrada or ServiCaixa (*see p206*).

FESTIVALS

For more festivals taking place in Barcelona, including performances of classical music, see

Música als Parcs. *See p251.*

Festa de la Música, Festival del Grec
and **Música als Parcs** (*p212*).

Tradicionàrius
*Centre Artesà Tradicionàrius, Travessia de
Sant Antoni 6-8 & various venues in Gràcia
(93 218 44 85, www.tradicionarius.cat). Metro
Fontana.* **Date** mid Jan-mid Apr. **Tickets** €12.
Credit MC, V. **Map** p322 G5.
A spirited folk festival that is held mainly in
the above auditorium, even though some concerts
take place in public squares and market places
dotted around Gràcia. Acts are mostly local
but there are occasional visits from international
musicians or dance troupes.

AvuiMúsica
*Associació Catalana de Compositors, Passeig
Colom 6, Espai IV, Barri Gòtic (93 268 37 19,
www.accompositors.com). Metro Jaume I.*
Date Mar-mid July. **Tickets** €9; €4.50
reductions. **No credit cards. Map** p329 D7.

**INSIDE TRACK
SEASIDE SOUNDS**

In summer, as the city empties out and
the Catalans head to their (many, many)
second homes, there are countless music
festivals along the Costa Dorada and,
particularly, the Costa Brava. Especially
worth checking out are the festivals in the
towns of Vilabertrán, Perelada, Cadaqués
and Torroella de Montgrí.

Not so much a festival as a season of small-scale
contemporary concerts run by the Association of
Catalan Composers and held at various venues
around the city. Members of the association are well
represented and include local Grammy-nominated
composer Joan Albert Amargós.

Festival de Música Antiga
L'Auditori (see p253). **Tickets** vary.
Date 2wks Apr.
Go for Baroque at the Festival of Early Music, which
features well-known performers from around the
world. The accompanying free concerts of El Fringe
festival are held over three days in outdoor spaces
around the Barri Gòtic and offer young performers
an opportunity to perform alongside more established musicians.

LEM
*Various venues in Gràcia (93 238 40 38,
www.gracia-territori.com).* **Date** Oct.
Tickets free-€6.
The main focus of the dynamic Gràcia Territori
Sonor collective is the month-long LEM festival in
autumn. Held in various venues, it's a rambling
series of musical happenings, many experimental,
improvised and electronic; most are free. Larger-
scale events are held at MACBA (*see p72* La Pedrera
(*see p97*) and CaixaForum (*see p84*).

VENUES

In addition to the venues listed over the next
few pages, several churches also hold concerts.
Not only are the acoustics (usually) excellent,
but the spaces suit sacred music. The most

popular church is **Santa Maria del Mar** (*see p69*) in the Born, where Handel's *Messiah* draws the crowds at Christmas, but the more atmospheric are smaller chapels such as **Santa Maria del Pi** (*see p53*), **Sant Felip Neri** (*see p37*) and **Santa Anna** (*see p54*), as well as the gorgeous Gothic convent in Pedralbes (*see p106*). Concerts run from Renaissance music to gospel, with everything in between.

Ateneu Barcelonès

C/Canuda 6 (93 343 61 21, www.ateneubcn.org). **Metro** *Liceu.* **Open** (office) 10am-2pm, 4-7pm Mon-Thur; 10am-2pm Fri. **Tickets** vary. **No credit cards. Map** p328 C3

This fine old library hosts occasional concerts, either in its leafy central patio or an auditorium. Worth looking out for is the '30 Minuts de Música' cycle from September to December. Organised by the Fundació Mas i Mas (www.fundaciomasimas.org), it's a series of half-hour concerts, mostly chamber music, with promising young musicians and the odd big name.

★ L'Auditori

C/Lepant 150, Eixample (93 247 93 00, www. auditori.cat). **Metro** *Marina.* **Open** *Information* 8am-10pm daily. *Box office* 3-9pm Mon-Sat; 1hr before performance Sun. Closed Aug. **Tickets** vary. **Credit** MC, V. **Map** p327 K9.

Designed by architect Rafael Moneo and directed by the affable Joan Oller, L'Auditori tries to offer something to everyone. The 2,400-seat Pau Casals hall, dedicated to the Catalan cellist, provides a stable home for city orchestra OBC, now under the baton of conductor Eiji Oue (although it frequently performs with guest conductors). It's also a place for the revered Jordi Savall to straddle his *viola da gamba* in an excellent series of early music concerts called El So Original, running from October to April. A more intimate 600-seat chamber space, which is dedicated to choir leader Oriol Martorell, has a more diverse programme incorporating contemporary and world music, whereas experimental and children's work is staged in a 400-seat space named after jazz pianist Tete Montoliu. A late-night bus service connects the Auditori with Plaça Catalunya following evening performances.

★ Gran Teatre del Liceu

La Rambla 51-59, Barri Gòtic (93 485 99 13, www.liceubarcelona.cat). **Metro** *Liceu.* **Open** *Information* 11am-2pm, 3-8pm Mon-Fri. *Box office* 1.30-8pm Mon-Fri; 1hr before performance Sat, Sun. Closed 2wks Aug. **Tickets** vary. **Credit** AmEx, MC, V. **Map** p329 B5.

Since it opened in 1847, two fires, a bombing and financial crisis have failed to quash the spirit and splendour of the Liceu, one of the most prestigious venues in the world. A restrained façade opens into a 2,292-seat auditorium of red plush, gold leaf and ornate carvings. The latest mod cons include seat-back subtitles in various languages that complement the Catalan surtitles above the stage. Under the stewardship of artistic director Joan Matabosch and musical director Sebastian Weigle, the Liceu has consolidated its programming policy, mixing co-productions with leading international opera houses with in-house productions. Classical, full-length opera is the staple – the 2010 schedule included Strauss's *Der Rosenkavalier*, Britten's *War Requiem* and, from London's Royal Ballet, a production of *Sleeping Beauty* – but opera and classics also feature.

L'Auditori.

ARTS & ENTERTAINMENT

ARTS & ENTERTAINMENT

Gran Teatre del Liceu. See p253.

A large basement bar hosts pre-performance talks and recitals, as well as children's shows and other musical events. The Espai Liceu is a 50-seat auditorium with a regular programme of screenings of past operas, while the swish six-floor Conservatori (C/Nou de la Rambla 82-88, 93 327 12 00, www.conservatori-liceu.es), which is part of the Liceu, lends its 400-seater basement auditorium to classical and contemporary concerts, small-scale operas and jazz.

★ Palau de la Música Catalana
C/Sant Francesc de Paula 2, Sant Pere (93 295 72 00, www.palaumusica.org). Metro Urquinaona.
Box office 10am-9pm Mon-Sat; 2hrs before performance Sun. Closed Aug for concerts.
Tickets vary. **Credit** AmEx, MC, V.
Map p328 E3.
This extraordinary visual explosion of Modernista architectural flights of fancy is a UNESCO World Heritage site. Built in 1908 by Lluís Domènech i Montaner, it's certainly one of the most spectacular music venues anywhere and much work has been done to improve its acoustics. A 21st-century extension has added a terrace, a restaurant and a subterranean hall. The Palau has seen some of the best international performers over the years, including the likes of Leonard Bernstein and Daniel Barenboim.
▶ *For more on this spectacular building, see p64 and p69.*

ORCHESTRAS & ENSEMBLES

BCN 216
93 487 87 81, www.bcn216.com.
This small but prolific ensemble is resident in L'Auditori and maintains a strong commitment to contemporary music of all types, from solo works to pieces requiring 40 musicians.

La Capella Reial de Catalunya, Le Concert des Nations & Hespèrion XXI
93 580 60 69, www.alia-vox.com.
The popularity of Catalonia's rich heritage in early music is due in large part to the efforts of the indefatigable Jordi Savall, the driving force behind these three interlinked musical groups which, between them, play around 300 concerts a year worldwide. La Capella Reial specialises in Catalan and Spanish Renaissance and Baroque music; Le Concert des Nations is a period-instrument ensemble playing orchestral and symphonic work from 1600 to 1850; and Hespèrion XXI plays pre-1800 European music.

Diapasón
mobile 605 081 060.
Diapasón is a septet specialising in Erik Satie and the more playful works of contemporary classical music. The group is led by composer/performer Domènec González de la Rubia.

Grup XXI
93 285 14 87,www.grup21music.com.
A contemporary music ensemble led by American flautist Peter Bacchus. The group has premiered international works as well as promoting Spanish and Catalan composers.

Orfeó Català
93 295 72 00, www.palaumusica.org.
The Orfeó Català began life as one of 150 choral groups that sprang up as part of the patriotic and social renewal movements in the late 19th century

and, due to its success, was banned by Franco after the Civil War as a possible focus of Catalan nationalism. While it's no longer as pre-eminent on the musical scene as it once was, the group still stages around 25 performances a year, giving a cappella concerts, as well as providing a choir for the Orquestra Simfònica and other Catalan orchestras. The largely amateur group also includes a small professional nucleus, the Cor de Cambra del Palau de la Música, which gives 50 performances a year.

Orquestra Simfònica de Barcelona i Nacional de Catalunya (OBC)
93 247 93 00, www.obc.cat.
The Orquestra Simfònica de Barcelona is the busiest orchestra in the city, performing at the Auditori almost every weekend of the season. The orchestra provides a fairly standard gallop through the symphonic repertoire, though Japanese director Eiji Oue has brought in a more adventurous programme. The orchestra is also committed to new Catalan composers, commissioning two works a year.

Orquestra Simfònica del Vallès
93 727 03 00, www.osvalles.com.
This provincial orchestra, based in the nearby town of Sabadell, performs regularly in Barcelona, often at the Palau de la Música Catalana, where it plays a dozen symphonic concerts each season.

Orquestra Simfònica i Cor del Gran Teatre del Liceu
93 485 99 13, www.liceubarcelona.com.
As well as a roster of operas every season, there's also a programme of concerts and recitals, and half a dozen colourful mini operas aimed at children (or their bigger brethren), including *The Little Chimney Sweep* and *Peter and the Wolf*.

Trio Kandinsky
93 301 98 97, www.triokandinsky.com.
Formed in 1999, the Trio Kandinsky has an excellent reputation, performing contemporary repertoire as well as the classical canon.

Theatre & Dance

Catalan theatre was banned under Franco. After his death, troupes surged on to the streets, luring audiences with the spectacular and the daring. However, the excitement of the 1980s fizzled in the '90s, when groups became tired of the nomadic life and despondent with the lack of funding and dearth of performance spaces. The survivors were those companies such as Els Comediants and La Fura dels Baus, who stuck to the attention-seeking style of street theatre. The 21st century has been a little kinder, and the current city council has put culture as a process and not just a product back

on the agenda. This has led to the availability of public cash for organisations that support creation, such as L'Estruch (www.sabadell.cat) and La Caldera (www.lacaldera.info), theatre groups AreaTangent (www.areatangent.com) and Conservas (http://conservas.tk) and dance collective La Porta (www.laportabcn.com). The funding system is notoriously complicated, however, with groups or projects having to piece together minimal grants from an array of sources: municipal and city, public and private. It's hoped that the recent establishment of a Catalan arts council, the **Consell Nacional de la Cultura i de les Arts** (CoNCA, 93 316 27 86, www.gencat.cat) can bring some coherence.

Today, most Barcelona theatre is in Catalan, although Spanish works tour, and Teatre Lliure offers surtitles in English for major productions. In the world of dance, performers such as the Compañía Nacional de Danza (directed by the revered Nacho Duato) fill grand venues such as the Teatre Nacional and the Liceu. Companies such as Sol Picó and Erre que Erre usually run a new show every year, as do Mudances and Gelabert-Azzopardi. Main shows start around 9-10pm. On Sundays, there are morning matinées aimed at family audiences and earlier evening shows at around 5-6.30pm; most theatres around the city are dark on Monday.

Festival del Grec. *See p252.*

ARTS & ENTERTAINMENT

Advance bookings are best made through ServiCaixa or Telentrada. The best places to find information are *Guia del Ocio*, *Time Out Barcelona* magazine and the *cartelera* (listings) pages of the newspapers. Online, check www.teatral.net and www.teatrebcn.com; for dance, try www.dansacat.org. You can also visit Canal Cultura at www.bcn.cat/cultura.

FESTIVALS

The **Grec Festival** (*see p83*) attracts major international acts in theatre and dance, some of which appear in an open-air amphitheatre on Montjuïc. The performing arts festival **Escena Poblenou** (www.escenapoblenou.com) merits a trip to the beachside barrio in mid October, while in summer, **Dies de Dansa** is three days of free, open-air national and international dance in public sites such as the CCCB or the MACBA patios.

New companies in the city can launch their work at the **Mostra de Teatre** (93 443 38 19, www.mostradeteatredebarcelona.com) in October and November, when they're assigned two nights apiece and judged by a panel.

Dies de Dansa

Various venues. Information Associació Marató de l'Espectacle (93 268 18 68, www.marato.com).
Date early July.
Under the umbrella of the Grec Festival, this four-day Festival of Dance is free, with shows on the terraces of the CCCB, MACBA, CaixaForum, Museu Picasso and Fundació Miró. A special programme for 2011 celebrates its 20th anniversary.

★ Dansalona

Various venues. Information 93 485 1377.
Date late Aug to late Sept.
A new festival incorporating every kind of dance, from ballet to hip hop, performed by local and international groups. Shows in 2010 incorporated a solo piece in a hotel room and a huge choreographed public event in the Parc de la Ciutadella.

La Mercè Arts de Carrer

Various venues (www.bcn.cat/merce).
Date late Sept.
Free three-day street performance festival.

MAJOR VENUES

Large-scale commercial productions are shown in **Teatre Condal** (Avda Paral·lel 91, Poble Sec, 93 442 31 32, www.teatrecondal.com), the **Borràs** (Plaça Urquinaona 9, Eixample, 93 412 15 82), and the **Tívoli** (C/Casp 8-10, Eixample, 93 412 20 63). For more information on these two latter venues, see www.grupbalana.com. The **Monumental** bullring (*see p261*) and the

Barcelona Teatre Musical (C/Guàrdia Urbana 7, Montjuïc, 93 423 15 41) are used for mega-shows and musicals.

★ Mercat de les Flors

Plaça Margarida Xirgu, C/Lleida 59, Poble Sec (93 426 18 75, www.mercatflors.org). Metro Poble Sec. **Box office** 1hr before show. Advance tickets also available from Palau de la Virreina (*see p61*). **Tickets** vary. **No credit cards. Map** p325 C10.
British theatre director Peter Brook is credited with transforming this former flower market into a venue for the performing arts in 1985, when he was looking for a place to stage his legendary production of the *Mahabharata*. After decades of fairly diffuse programming, the Mercat has finally focused in on national and international contemporary dance, and offers a strong programme that experiments with unusual formats and mixes in new technologies and live music. The venue also supports emerging dancers, producing the BCSTX cycle in May/June.

Teatre Lliure

Passeig de Santa Madrona 40-46, Poble Sec (93 289 27 70, www.teatrelliure.com). Metro Poble Sec. **Box office** 9am-8pm Mon-Fri; 2hrs before show Sat, Sun. **Credit** MC, V. **Map** p325 C10.
Under its young and dynamic director, Àlex Rigola, the Teatre Lliure's main and mini stage host an adventurous array of theatre and dance that occasionally spills on to the square outside. Bigger theatre shows are surtitled in English on Thursdays and Saturdays.

Teatre Nacional de Catalunya (TNC)

Plaça de les Arts 1, Eixample (93 306 57 00, www.tnc.cat). Metro Glòries. **Box office** 3-8pm Wed-Fri; 3-9.30pm Sat; 3-6pm Sun. Closed Aug. **Credit** MC, V. **Map** p327 K9.
The Generalitat-funded theatre, which was designed by Ricardo Bofill in a neo-classical style, boasts a vast airy lobby and three fabulous performance spaces. Director Sergi Belbel has opted for a good mix of contemporary and classical pieces and incorporated a fine contemporary dance programme, divided between a main stage and smaller stage. Works by new writers are normally performed in the more experimental Sala Tallers.

Teatre Poliorama

La Rambla 115, Barri Gòtic (93 317 75 99, www.teatrepoliorama.com). Metro Catalunya. **Box office** 5-8pm Wed-Sun. Closed 2wks Aug. **Tickets** vary. **Credit** MC, V. **Map** p328 B3.
Run by private producers 3xtr3s, this once adventurous theatre now puts on predominantly mainstream comedies and musicals such as *Spamalot*, along with the occasional piece of serious theatre. It also stages a long-running and incredibly popular opera and flamenco show.

Setting Sail

The launch of music hall El Molino.

In its heyday, **El Molino** – a 110-year-old music hall fronted with a weather-beaten windmill – was one of a dozen on Paral·lel, an avenue that boasted a backstreet Broadway appeal. In 1908, it was renamed Petit Moulin Rouge after the Parisian club, in 1929 it gained its sails and in 1936 tossed the 'Petit'. El Molino once offered naughty spectacles, complete with vedettes, and attracted illustrious clientele including Italian filmmaker Federico Fellini. It managed to thwart the censorship of dictator General Franco, with only 'Rouge' dropped from its name when Barcelona's signs were purged of their communist associations. Its condition deteriorated, and it closed in 1997.

El Molino's present owners have retained El Molino's basic function as a musical theatre, lit up with neon and with red-rimmed sails that rotate during performances. A new silver building billows from the back; inside there is a bar with a view and space for one-off cultural events. Architects BOPBAA have maintained the original interior structure of the theatre itself, which, as if to compensate for El Molino's cream-washed façade, is redder than ever. The venue has a capacity of 250 and seats are at tables. Alcohol is served during performances, as is a set menu.

The inaugural show *Made In Paral·lel* revived El Molino's cabaret past with a corsets-and-feathers extravaganza that will continue into 2011. While owners evaluate whether cabaret can kick it like before, however, the programme is variable. Flamenco is set for Tuesday nights: Poco Ruido y Mucho Duende comes under the artistic direction of flamenco singer Mayte Martín and guests include acclaimed *cantaor* Enrique Morente. A burlesque festival in May and a tango festival in September also draw big names into the little windmill. On Saturday nights, Los Unique Saturdays is run by veteran DJ Raúl Orellana, with select club DJs spinning from 1am to 4am.
▶ C/Vila i Vilà 99 (93 205 91 11, www.elmolinobcn.com).

Teatre Romea

C/Hospital 51, Raval (information 93 301 55 04, www.teatreromea.com). Metro Liceu. **Box office** 4.30-8pm Tue-Sun. **Tickets** vary. **Credit** (phone bookings only) AmEx, DC, MC, V. **Map** p328 A4.
The fertile imagination of artistic director Calixto Bieito runs rampant at Romea, although his infamous theatre of the senses can prove wearisome at times. Bieito looks toward contemporary European theatre for inspiration, even though most works are performed in Catalan.

ALTERNATIVE THEATRES

There are a number of smaller theatres in Barcelona struggling to secure funding and audiences. Survivors are **Tantarantana** (C/Flors 22, Raval, 93 441 70 22, www. tantarantana.com), the tiny **Espai Escènic Joan Brossa** (C/Allada-Vermell 13, Born, 93 310 13 64, www.espaibrossa.com) and the **L'Antic Teatre** (C/Verdaguer i Callis 12, Born, 93 315 23 54, www.anticteatre.com). Additionally, **Versus Teatre** (C/Castillejos 179, Eixample, 93 603 51 52, www.versus teatre.com) and **Sala Muntaner** (C/Muntaner 4, Eixample, 93 451 57 52, www.salamuntaner. com) often produce interesting work.

The **Teatre de la Riereta** (C/Reina Amalia 3, Raval, 93 442 98 44, www.la riereta.es) hosts English works, as does **Cafè-Teatre Llantiol** (C/Riereta 7, Raval, 93 329 90 09, www.llantiol.com), which occasionally holds Giggling Guiri comedy nights in English.

Sala Beckett

C/Alegre de Dalt 55 bis, Gràcia (93 284 53 12, www.salabeckett.cat). Metro Joanic. **Box office** 8pm until end of performance. **No credit cards**. **Map** p323 J4.
This small but important venue was founded by the Samuel Beckett-inspired Teatro Fronterizo group, which is run by playwright José Sanchis Sinisterra. Although he is no longer based at the theatre, his influence continues to prevail. High rental costs and bigger ambitions may mean, however, that Sala Beckett is on the move in the future. Check the website for updates.

THEATRE COMPANIES

As well as those reviewed below, companies to watch out for include the satirical troupe **The Chanclettes** (www. thechanclettes. com) and **Dagoll Dagom** (www.dagolldagom.com). Longstanding troupe **Els Joglars** (www. elsjoglars.com) was founded 40 years ago by Albert Boadella, who was imprisoned by Franco for his political stance but is currently in self-imposed exile from Catalonia after some high-profile spats regarding the regional government's linguistic policy.

For English-language theatre in Barcelona, *see p259* **English Channelled**.

Els Comediants

www.comediants.com.
Els Comediants has its roots in *commedia dell'arte* and street performance; its mix of mime, circus, music, storytelling and fireworks is as likely to appear on the street to celebrate a national holiday as at any major theatre festival.

La Cubana

www.lacubana.es.
La Cubana's shows have a popular appeal and cartoonish quality, using multimedia effects, camp music and audience participation.

La Fura dels Baus

www.lafura.com.
This ostentatious troupe started out on the streets of Barcelona in the 1980s with a donkey, a cart and nihilistic ideas, but now tours the world with high-tech, polemical productions. Former founder member – and ex-abattoir employee – Marcel·li Antúnez Roca follows a similar vein in his solo shows.

Tricicle

93 317 4747, www.tricicle.com.
Local boys Carles Sans, Paco Mir and Joan Gràcia founded this mime trio some 30 years ago. The goofy, clean-cut humour appeals to the Spanish taste for slapstick, and children love it as well. They are regulars at El Petit Liceu and have, among other feats, managed to bring Monty Python's *Spamalot* to a local audience.

DANCE COMPANIES

In addition to those listed below, groups worth seeing include **Group Búbulus** (www.bubulus.net) and Toni Mira's company **Nats Nus** (www.natsnus.com). Its highly successful offshoot **Nats Nens** produces contemporary dance shows for children. For a comprehensive list, check www.companyiesdansa.info.

Compañia Mar Gómez

www.danzamargomez.com.
Compañia Mar Gómez provides a mix of contemporary dance and theatre with a wicked sense of humour and good music.

Erre que Erre

www.errequeerredanza.net.
This excellent collective of younger dancers transforms complex ideas into contemplative performances, complete with well-measured doses of theatre and original music.

Pure Spectacle

The visual glory of Catalan theatre.

In a city so proud of its language and culture, it's no surprise that the majority of plays here are performed in Catalan. However, that's no reason for visiting theatre buffs who don't speak the lingo to miss curtain up.

Subtitling plays into English has fallen out of fashion of late, with just Teatre Lliure's March/April production of Chekhov's *The Three Sisters* scheduled for special treatment in 2011 as we went to press; but Catalan theatre is notoriously visual as a result of groups like **La Fura dels Baus** and **Els Comediants** (for both, *see p255*) finding new ways to tell their stories when Catalan was banned under Franco. Both companies are often away on tour, but if you get the chance to see them perform, expect big, ballsy, punch-you-in-the-face spectacle and little or no dialogue. Meanwhile, **Teatro de los Sentidos** (www.teatrodelossentidos.com)

takes audiences on a memorable, though sometimes odorous, journey of the senses.

Professional English-language theatre is thin on the ground, but an enthusiastic amateur scene fills the void, especially during June and November. Tucked away on a Raval backstreet, the **Teatre La Riereta** (*see pxx*) attracts English-speaking people and was the venue of choice for Jo Marvel's directorial debut, *The Snapping Turtle's Lament*, in 2010. This fell under the umbrella of the **Jocular Theatre** (www.joculartheatre.com), known for its dark comedies and for being the most prolific of English-language companies.

But look out for the **12x12** theatre company (http://teatro12x12.blogspot.com) and the **Prostíbulo Poético** ('poetry brothel', http://poetrybrothelbarcelona.blogspot.com), whose poetry-reading 'prostitutes' occasionally get kinky and turn tricks in English.

Gelabert-Azzopardi
www.gelabertazzopardi.com.
Expect fluid, poetic performances from Barcelona's Cesc Gelabert and Londoner Lydia Azzopardi.

Mal Pelo
www.malpelo.org.
Maria Muñoz and Pep Ramis incorporate images and text into their shows.

Marta Carrasco
www.martacarrasco.com.
Veteran dancer Marta Carrasco has choreographed many plays and musicals over the years. Lavish costumes and extravagant set designs define her elegant performances.

Mudances
www.margarit-mudances.com.

Director Àngels Margarit and his dancers create melodic work drawing on world music and dance. The company produces pieces for family audiences.

Raravis-Andrés Corchero-Rosa Muñoz
http://raravisdanza.com.
Quirky Raravis is the dancers' dance company – minimalist and delightfully inventive.

Sol Picó
www.solpico.com.
Charismatic Sol Picó mixes up the genres and adds a touch of humour.

FLAMENCO

Local *cantaors* (flamenco singers), such as Miguel Poveda, play to sell-out crowds at the **Palau de la Música** or smaller venues such as **Luz de Gas** (*see p248*), as do singers and guitarists from the south Paco de Lucía,

El Tablao de Carmen.

Diego de Cigala or Vicente Amigo. Dancers, including Rafael Amargo, appear at the **Liceu**.

The Friday night flamenco performances that take place at the restaurant **Nervion** (C/Princesa 2, Born, 93 315 21 03, www.restaurantenervion.com, closed end Aug, 1st wk Sept) seem to be aimed at tourists, but they are a cheaper night out than the established *tablaos*: if you don't eat at the venue, entry is €12 and includes a drink; €35 gets you dinner and a show. **Flamenco Barcelona** (mobile 622 517 065, www.flamencobarcelona.com) organises flamenco events along with flamenco guitar, singing and dance courses.

El Tablao de Carmen
Poble Espanyol, Avda Francesc Ferrer i Guàrdia 13), Montjuïc (93 325 68 95, www.tablaodecarmen. com). Metro Espanya. **Open** 6-8.30pm, 9-11pm Tue-Sun. **Shows** 6.45pm, 10pm Tue-Sun. **Admission** show & 1 drink €35; show & tapas €45; show & dinner €69. **Credit** AmEx, DC, MC, V. **Map** p325 A9.
This rather sanitised version of the flamenco *tablao* resides in faux-Andalucían surroundings in the Poble Espanyol. You will find stars and young talent here on a regular basis, showcasing flamenco singing, dancing and music. It's advisable to book (up to a week ahead in summer). The admission fee includes entry to the Poble Espanyol after 7pm.

Los Tarantos
Plaça Reial 17, Barri Gòtic (93 318 30 67, www.masimas.com/tarantos). Metro Liceu. **Open** 8-11pm daily. *Shows* 8.30pm, 9.30pm, 10.30pm daily. **Admission** €7; €6 online. **Credit** MC, V. **Map** p329 A3.
This flamenco *tablao* has presented many top stars to a wide audience over the years, as well as offering some *rumba catalana*. Now Los Tarantos caters mainly to the tourist trade.

FESTIVALS

De Cajón!
Various venues (www.theproject.cat).
Tickets vary. **Date** Feb-Apr.
This high-quality mini festival has snagged some of Barcelona's top venues to showcase spectacular flamenco talents such as *cantaor* Antonio Vargas 'Potito', flamenco pianist Diego Amador and the world-famous guitarist Paco de Lucía.

Flamenco Ciutat Vella
CCCB (see p72) (93 443 43 46, www.flamenco ciutatvella.com). Metro Catalunya. **Tickets** €10-€20. **Date** mid May. **Map** p328 A2.
Although there are plenty of traditional performers featured in this four-day festival, hard-line flamenco purists should be warned that it includes DJs fusing the Andalucían music with anything from electronica to jazz and rock.

Sport & Fitness

It's not just about Barça – but it sometimes feels like it.

Although there are topics of conversation in Barcelona bars that don't involve sporting activity, they are few and far between. Catalans are an active lot and love *excursionisme* (basically, heading out to the hills at weekends to do anything from cycling to parapenting) as much as they love spectactor sports.

Foremost among these, of course, is football. Catalans are obsessed with soccer and proud of the status of their biggest football team. Rather than being the plaything of a rich oligarch, Barça literally belongs to the fans: the team has more than 163,000 members, which means that more than one in ten *barcelonins* has a say in the running of the club. But you'll see the passion for sport all over town throughout the year, from lycra-clad granddads reliving the latest Tour de France to ambitious young lads dreaming of becoming the next Rafa Nadal.

SPECTATOR SPORTS

Sport in the city is not only about the beautiful game. Barcelona took advantage of the 1992 Olympics to equip itself with facilities that put larger cities to shame. As a result, big events such as the World Swimming Championships have passed through town with great success.

Tickets for big games can often be bought by credit card from ServiCaixa or Telentrada (*see p206*). Check www.agendabcn.com or see newspapers such as *El Mundo Deportivo* for event details.

Basketball

The ACB, Europe's most competitive league, runs from September to early June. Matches are played on weekend evenings, with European matches played midweek.

AXA FC Barcelona

Palau Blaugrana, Avda Aristides Maillol s/n, Les Corts (93 496 36 00, www.fcbarcelona.cat). Metro Collblanc or Palau Reial. **Ticket office** 10am-6.15pm Mon-Sat; 10am-1.30pm Sun; also 2hrs before a game. **Tickets** vary. **Credit** AmEx, MC, V.

About the author

Daniel Campi is a journalist and writer who has lived and worked in Barcelona since 1991.

From its heyday in the 1980s, when matches were played at the massive Sant Jordi stadium, Barcelona basketball has slipped in status. The team's triumph in the 2003 Euroleague, the basketball equivalent of the Champions League, was expected to herald a renaissance. But as the fortunes of Barça football soared with the arrival of president Joan Laporta, the basketball team lost all its best players. A new team was built around Juan Carlos 'The Bomb' Navarro and Australian forward David Anderson; it remains to be seen if this will help the team to more success.

Bullfighting

Plaza de Toros Monumental

Gran Via de les Corts Catalanes 749, Eixample (93 245 58 04, 93 215 95 70). Metro Monumental. **Open** *Bullfights* Apr-Sept 6-7pm Sun. *Museum* Apr-Sept 11am-2pm, 4-8pm Mon-Sat; 11am-1pm Sun. **Admission** *Bullfights* vary. Advance tickets available from ServiCaixa. *Museum* €6; €5 reductions. **Credit** (fights only) MC, V. **Map** p327 K8.

With the bullfighting ban in Catalonia coming into play in 2012, bullfights in Barcelona are becoming increasingly tired affairs. However, there are occasional *corridas* worth seeing; they take place on Sundays in summer in the impressive Modernista Plaza de Toros Monumental, the city's only bullring.

INSIDE TRACK
TICKETS PLEASE

Getting tickets for a Barça match can be a lottery. Around 4,000 tickets usually go on sale on the day of the match: phone to find out when, and join the queue an hour or so beforehand at the intersection of Avda Arístides Maillol and Travessera de les Corts. 'Rented out' seats go on sale from these offices and can also be bought via ServiCaixa. If there are none left, buy a *reventa* ticket from the touts at the gates.

Football

While FC Barcelona fight it out for the *Primera Liga* title every year, usually with arch rivals Real Madrid, RCD Espanyol have managed to establish themselves as a reliable mid-table team with regular finishes in the top half of the league. The season runs from the last weekend in August to May, with games played late on Saturday evening or Sunday afternoon; check the press for details, and keep checking as kick-off times can change. Europa (in Gràcia) and Júpiter (in Poblenou) are decent semi-pro teams.

FC Barcelona

Camp Nou, Travessera de les Corts 63-71, Les Corts (93 496 36 00, www.fcbarcelona.cat). Metro Collblanc or Palau Reial. **Ticket office** 10am-6.15pm Mon-Sat; 10am-1.30pm Sun; from 11am match days. **Tickets** vary. Advance tickets for league games available from ServiCaixa; *see also above* **Inside Track**. **Credit** AmEx, DC, MC, V. **Map** p321 A4.

No club in football history has achieved what Pep Guardiola's men managed in 2009: six tournaments, six trophies. This 'annus memorabilis' climaxed in December with the FIFA World Club Cup win over Estudiantes, the tactics-obsessed young coach telling his players: 'Lose and you'll still be the best team in the world; win, and you'll be eternal.' Like Guardiola himself, seven of the Champions League-winning XI were formed at FCB's youth system, including Xavi, Iniesta and Lionel Messi. 'Some clubs buy superstars; we make them,' boasted club president Joan Laporta, whose term ran out in summer 2010. His greatest achievement may be yet to come: persuading Guardiola to sign a new contract.

RCD Espanyol

Avda Baix Llobregat 100, Cornellà (93 292 77 00, www.rcdespanyol.com). Metro Cornellà Riera. **Ticket office** times vary, check website. **Tickets** €45-€90. **Credit** V.

Always the bridesmaids, 2007 UEFA Cup runners-up RCD Espanyol began 2009-10 with a new stadium,

the Estadi Cornellà-El Prat, and a settled side. Regulars such as Luis Garcia, Ivan de la Peña and Raúl Tamudo have given the Parakeets a sense of continuity, although there's an inevitability about RCD's mid-table mediocrity in the constant shadow of FC Barcelona. Tickets are available up to four days before the game, via ServiCaixa or the ticket office.

Other events

Marató Barcelona

902 43 11 763, www.barcelonamarato.es. **Date** 6 Mar. **Fee** €70.
Barcelona's annual marathon starts and ends at Plaça Espanya.

Tennis

Reial Club de Tennis Barcelona-1899, C/Bosch i Gimpera 5, Les Corts (93 203 78 52, www. rctb1899.es, www.barcelonaopenbancosabadell. com). FGC Reina Elisenda or bus 63, 78. **Open** 8.30am-1.30pm, 3.30-6.30pm Mon-Fri. **Tickets** vary. **Credit** AmEx, MC, V. **Map** p321 B2.
The annual Open Seat Comte de Godó tournament in Pedralbes is considered one of the ATP circuit's most important clay-court tournaments. Rafa Nadal won the tournament every year from 2005 to 2009.

La Cursa del Corte Inglés

www.cursaelcorteingles.net. **Date** May.
Barcelona's seven-mile fun run is free to enter, and attracts over 50,000 participants.

Motorsports

Circuit de Catalunya, Ctra de Parets del Vallès a Granollers, Montmeló (93 571 97 77, www.circuit cat.com). By car C17 north to Parets del Vallès exit (20km/13 miles). **Times & tickets** vary; tickets from ServiCaixa. **Credit** MC, V.
Barcelona boasts one of the world's best racing circuits at Montmeló. The Spanish Grand Prix is now a huge event and tickets can be hard to come by, so book well in advance. Barcelona is also crazy about motorbikes, with local boys Dani Pedrosa and Toni Elias competing for the Moto GP, which also stops off at the Montmeló circuit.

Caminada Internacional de Barcelona

934 02 30 00, 010, www.euro-senders.com/ internacional. **Date** mid Oct.
The International Walk is conducted along several different routes of a variety of lengths.

ACTIVE SPORTS & FITNESS

The 237 municipally run facilities include an excellent network of *poliesportius* (sports centres). One-day entry tickets are usually available, but should the great outdoors prove irresistible, you can just head to the beach: there's a free outdoor gym and table-tennis

Profile Pep Guardiola

FC Barça's coach has the Midas touch.

Most managers at the upper echelons of the Champions League circuit are seen-it-all septuagenarians, seldom wont to risk all on home-grown talent. Barcelona boss Pep Guardiola, at 38 the youngest coach to win the Champions League, is different. The team's home-grown heroes – Xavi, Iniesta, Busquets et al – are all cut from the same cloth as Guardiola, and all share the same heritage: one created by Johan Cruyff. It was the former Barcelona player and manager who first noticed a teenage Pep running out for Barça's youth side, and whispered that he should be moved to a pivotal position in the middle. By 1990, this Santpedor-born son from a modest family had made Cruyff's Dream Team to be.

Cruyff's side won the Spanish title four years running, winning the European Cup for the first time in 1992. Under Cruyff, Guardiola went on to win two more league titles, until a calf problem led to long absences and, eventually, a transfer. Just as injury cut Guardiola down, so Barcelona's hegemony collapsed following Cruyff's controversial departure. A few years later, however, the club's new bosses, doubtless listening to a now-back-in-favour Cruyff, appointed Guardiola as the replacement for Frank Rijkaard as coach.

Taking over at the start of the 2008-09 season, Guardiola announced the departure of former totems Ronaldinho, Lilian Thuram, Deco and Samuel Eto'o (although the latter stayed to partner Lionel Messi and Thierry Henry in attack). A 4-3-3 midfield engine of Xavi, Iniesta and Busquets provided the engine for a team that, in Guardiola's first season, swept all before them, winning the Spanish Liga, the

Spanish Copa del Rey and the Champions League.

November 2009 saw Real Madrid look for revenge over their arch-rivals at the season's first Gran Clásico, with Real's big signings Cristiano Ronaldo and Kaká thrown before 98,772 baying *blaugranas*. A superb goal from Zlatan Ibrahimovic, Guardiola's inspired pre-season replacement for Eto'o, gave Barça the win. And then, a month later, Messi scored the extra-time winner in Abu Dhabi to make Barcelona World Club champions. Pep the manager had gone one better than Pep the player.

ARTS & ENTERTAINMENT

Sport & Fitness

table at Barceloneta, and the sea is warm enough for swimming from May to October. All beaches have wheelchair ramps, and most of the city's pools are fully equipped for disabled people.

Servei d'Informació Esportiva
93 402 30 00, www.bcn.cat/esports.
The Ajuntament's sports' information service. Call for information but note that not all staff speak English. Alternatively, consult the Ajuntament's listings on the Esports section of its website, www.bcn.cat.

Bowling

Bowling Pedralbes
Avda Dr Marañón 11, Les Corts (93 333 03 52, www.bowlingpedralbes.com). Metro Collblanc or Maria Cristina. **Open** 10am-1.30am Mon-Thur; 10am-3.30am Fri, Sat; 10am-11.30pm Sun. *Aug* open only from 5pm daily. **Rates** €2.20-€5/person. **Credit** MC, V.
There are 14 lanes to try for that perfect 300, in an alley that hosts international tournaments. Early afternoons are quiet; otherwise, sit at the bar and wait to be paged. Shoe hire is available (€1), as are pool, snooker and *futbolín* (table football).

Cycling

The city council has been encouraging cycling as an environmentally conscious solution to Barcelona's traffic congestion problems – not least through the introduction of the successful Bicing scheme (www.bicing.cat), where bikes can be picked up and dropped off around town. In theory, membership of the scheme is restricted to residents, but many tourists have got round that by 'borrowing' addresses in town for registration.

The city has an efficient and ever-expanding network of cycle lanes, while the seafront is a good bet for leisure cycling; otherwise, try the spectacular Carretera de les Aigües, a flat gravel road that skirts along the side of Collserola mountain. To avoid a killer climb, take your bike on the FGC to Peu del Funicular station, then take the Funicular de Vallvidreira to the midway stop. For serious mountain biking, check http://amicsbici.pangea.org, which also has information on when you can take your bike on public transport.

For suggested bike rides around the city, *see p77, p87 and p97.*

Probike
C/Viladomat 310, Eixample (93 419 78 89, www.probike.es). Metro Hospital Clínic. **Open** 10am-8.30pm Mon-Sat. **No credit cards. Map** p322 E6.

The Probike club organises regular excursions, from day trips to a more challenging summertime cross-Pyrenees run. Its centre, which has a broad range of equipment plus maps and information on all manner of routes, is a magnet for local mountain bikers.

Football

Barcelona International Football League
www.bifl.info.
Matches, of Sunday League standard, are generally played at weekends from September to June among teams of expats and locals. New players are welcome (especially if they know how to kick a ball).

Golf

Catalonia has been a popular golfing-holiday destination for years. Visitors to Barcelona hoping to swing a club or two should book in advance; courses can often be full at weekends.

Club de Golf Sant Cugat
C/Villa 79, Sant Cugat del Vallès (93 674 39 08, www.golfsantcugat.com). By train FGC from Plaça Catalunya to Sant Cugat, by car Túnel de Vallvidrera (C16) to Valldoreix. **Open** 8am-8.30pm Mon-Fri; 8am-9pm Sat, Sun. **Rates** *Non-members* €72 Mon; €100 Tue-Thur; €150 Fri-Sun. **Club hire** €40. **Credit** MC, V.
Designed by Harry S Colt back in 1917, the oldest golf course in Catalonia is a tight, varied 18-hole set-up that's challenging enough to host professional tournaments. There's a restaurant and swimming pool on site. You may be asked to pay a membership fee depending on the time of year: call ahead.

Gyms & fitness centres

Sports centres run by the city council are cheaper and more user-friendly than most private clubs in the city. Phone the council's sport information service, Servei d'Informació Esportiva (*see above*), for prices and locations.

Centres de Fitness DiR
C/Casp 34, Eixample (93 301 62 09, 902 10 19 79, www.dir.cat). Metro Urquinaona. **Open** 7am-11pm Mon-Fri; 9am-8pm Sat; 9am-3pm Sun. **Rates** from €18 a day. **Credit** MC, V. **Map** p328 D1.
This plush, well-organised, private chain has 12 fitness centres. Additional installations vary from a huge outdoor pool (at DiR Diagonal) to a squash centre (DiR Campus).
Other locations DiR Campus, Avda Dr Marañón 17, Les Corts (93 448 41 41); DiR Diagonal, C/Ganduxer 25-27, Eixample (93 202 22 02); and throughout the city.

Club de Natació Atlètic Barceloneta.

Europolis

Travessera de les Corts 252-254, Les Corts (93 363 29 92, www.europolis.cat). Metro Les Corts. **Open** 7am-11pm Mon-Fri; 8am-8pm Sat; 9am-3pm Sun. **Rates** *Non-members* €10.60/day; €5.50 reductions. *Membership* varies. **Credit** V. **Map** p321 B5.

As large and well equipped as any private gym in town, Europolis centres are municipally owned but run by the British chain Holmes Place. They provide exercise machines, as well as pools, classes, trainers and weight-lifting gear.

Other locations 4 C/Sardenya 549-553, Gràcia (93 210 07 66).

Ice skating

FC Barcelona Pista de Gel

Camp Nou, entrance 7 or 9, Avda Joan XXIII, Les Corts (93 496 36 30, www.fcbarcelona.com). Metro Collblanc or Maria Cristina. **Open** *Sept-June* 10am-2pm, 4-6pm Mon-Thur; 10am-2pm, 4-8pm Fri; 11am-2pm, 5-8.30pm Sat, Sun. *July* 10am-1pm, 5pm-8.30pm. Closed Aug. **Rates** (incl skates) €11.80. **Credit** MC, V. **Map** p321 A4.

This functional rink is situated next to the Camp Nou complex, which makes it a perfect place for the non-football fans in the family to spend 90 minutes or more. Gloves are obligatory, and on sale at €2.60 a pair. The rink is also used for ice-hockey matches.

Skating Roger de Flor

C/Roger de Flor 168, Eixample (93 245 28 00, www.skatingclub.cat). Metro Tetuan. **Open** *July-mid Sept* 10.30am-1.30pm, 5-9pm Mon-Fri, Sun; 10.30am-2pm, 4.30-9.30pm Sat. *Mid Sept-June* 10.30am-1.30pm, 5-9pm daily. **Rates** (incl skates) €13.70. **Credit** MC, V. **Map** p323 J8.

A family-oriented ice rink off Avda Diagonal in the Eixample. Gloves (€3) are compulsory. Any non-skaters in a group can get in for €1 and then have use of the café.

In-line skating

The **APB** (Asociacion de Patinadores de Barcelona, www.patinar-bcn.com) organises skating convoys: beginners meet at the Fòrum at 10.15pm on Fridays. Pro skaters hook up at Plaça Catalunya at 10.30pm on Thursday and follow an 'unofficial' route. Visit www.sat.org.es/bcnskates for details. **RODATS** (635 629 948, www.rodats.com/tours) organises skating convoys and classes at four levels of difficulty (€10 per 90-minute class, and monthly courses for €23, €8 for equipment).

Going it alone, you're not officially allowed on roads or cycle paths, and the speed limit is ten kilometres/hour. The pedestrian broadways of Rambla de Catalunya, Avda Diagonal and Passeig Marítim are popular haunts.

Running

The seafront and the Parc de la Ciutadella are good locations. If you can handle the climb, or use other transport for the ascent, there are scenic runs on Montjuïc – especially around the castle and Olympic stadium – or try Park Güell/Carmel hills and Collserola.

Sailing

Base Nàutica de la Mar Bella

Avda Litoral, between Platja Bogatell & Platja de Mar Bella, Poblenou (93 221 04 32, www.base nautica.org). Metro Poblenou. **Open** *Apr-Aug* 10am-8pm daily. *Sept-Oct* 10am-7pm daily. *Nov-Mar* 10am-5.30pm daily. **Rates** *Windsurfing* €187/10hr

---

INSIDE TRACK HIT THE SANDS

Combine a jog along the beach with a workout on the various bars, poles and benches built for the purpose on a spit in front of the Hospital del Mar.

Club Tennis Pompeia.

course; €23/hr equipment hire. *Catamaran* €218/12hr course. *Kayak* €24/10hr course; €14.25-€23.80/hr equipment hire. **Credit** MC, V. The Base Nàutica hires catamarans and windsurf gear to those with experience. There's a proficiency test for windsurfing held on Fridays at 4 or 5pm (€20 fee). You can hire a kayak without a test. There are also different options available for intensive or longer-term sailing proficiency courses.

Skiing

The best bet for a skiing day trip is the resort of La Molina (972 89 20 31, www.lamolina.cat). A RENFE train from Plaça Catalunya at 7.05am or 9.22am (€7.50 single, €15 return) takes you to the train station (get off at La Molina), then catch a bus up to the resort. A day's *forfait* will set you back around €39, or you can buy combined return train ticket and *forfait* for around €42. Trains return at 4.55pm and 7.15pm (check the timetable in the station or www.renfe.es). There are runs to suit all.

Swimming

The city has a large number of municipal pools, many of which are outdoors. For a list, contact the Servei d'Informació Esportiva (*see p264*). Flip-flops and swimming caps are generally obligatory. There are also more than three miles of beach, patrolled in summer by lifeguards.

Club de Natació Atlètic Barceloneta

Plaça del Mar, Barceloneta (93 221 00 10, www.cnab.org). Metro Barceloneta then bus 17, 39, 64. **Open** *Oct-mid May* 6.30am-11pm Mon-Fri; 7am-11pm Sat; 8am-5pm Sun. *Mid may-Sept* 6.30am-11pm Mon-Fri; 7am-11pm Sat; 8am-8pm Sun. **Admission** *Non-members* €10.55/day. **Membership** €35.70/mth, plus €71 joining fee. **Credit** AmEx, DC, MC, V. **Map** p326 G13. This beachside centre has an indoor pool and two outdoor pools (one heated), as well as sauna (which costs extra) and gym facilities. There's a *frontón* (Spanish ball-sports court), if you fancy a go at the world's fastest sport: *jai alai*, a fierce Basque game that lies between squash and handball.

Poliesportiu Marítim

Passeig Marítim 33-35, Barceloneta (93 224 04 40, www.claror.cat). Metro Ciutadella-Vila Olímpica. **Open** *Sept-July* 7am-midnight Mon-Fri; 8am-9pm Sat; 8am-4pm Sun. *Aug* 7am-10.30pm Mon-Fri; 8am-9pm Sat; 8am-3pm Sun. **Admission** *Non-members* €15.40 Mon-Fri; €18.30 Sat, Sun; 5-visit pass €63.70; 10-visit pass €112. **Credit** MC, V. **Map** p327 K13. This spa centre specialises in thalassotherapy; there are seven saltwater pools of differing temperatures, including one with waterfalls to massage shoulders, and an icy plunge-pool. There's also a sauna, a steam room and a slab of hot marble on which to rest weary bones that have been over exerted in the jacuzzi.

Tennis

Club Tennis Pompeia

C/Foixarda, Montjuïc (93 325 13 48). Bus 13, 50. **Open** 8am-10pm daily. **Rates** *Non-members* €16/hr; €4.80 floodlights. €154 3-month pass. **No credit cards**. There are good rates for non-members at this pleasant club above the Poble Espanyol, with its seven clay courts and free racket hire.

Yoga

Yoga Studio

Plaça Universitat 4, 1º, 2ª, Eixample (93 451 29 28, www.yogastudio.es). Metro Universitat. **Open** See website for timetable. **Credit** MC, V. **Map** p326 F9. Xavi and Pilar offer a wide variety of yoga styles, from hatha to ashtanga. The centre runs one-off classes for €14, plus week- and month-long courses.

Escapes & Excursions

Getting Started

Plan your escape from the city.

Just two hours separate sand from snow in this part of the world. But that's not all: a gastronomic heritage, pretty villages, fine wines and amazing festivals only add to the appeal of Catalonia.

The **Palau Robert** tourist centre (*see p304*) is a hub of useful information about the region. Catalunya Turisme (www.catalunyaturisme.com) is another thorough guide. And for details of Catalonia's wide and varied network of *casacases de pagès* (country houses or old farmhouses for rent), see the publication *Generalitat's Residències – Casa de pagès*.

ESCAPES & EXCURSIONS

GETTING AROUND

Public transport is good, but you'll need a car for far-flung destinations. For more on getting around, see the Generalitat's ww.mobilitat.org.

By bus

The **Estació d'Autobusos Barcelona-Nord** (C/Ali Bei 80, map p343 J9) is the principal bus station for services in Catalonia. Timetables and other information for all companies are available at 902 26 06 06 and www.barcelonanord.com.

By road

Over the last few years, Spain's roads have undergone a gradual process of renaming, and many maps are out of date. Road signs should include both new and old names, but signage isn't always clear. Plan your route in advance.

Roads beginning C1 run north–south; C2 run east–west; and C3 run parallel to the coast. Driving in or out of Barcelona, you'll come across either the **Ronda de Dalt**, along the edge of Tibidabo, or the **Ronda Litoral** along the coast, meeting north and south of the city. They intersect with several motorways (*autopistes*): the C31 (heading up the coast from Mataró); the C17/AP7 (to Girona and France) and the C58 (Sabadell, Manresa), which run into Avda Meridiana; the AP2 (Lleida, Madrid), a continuation of Avda Diagonal that connects with the AP7 south (Tarragona, Valencia); and the C32 to Sitges, reached from the Gran Via. All are toll roads, and are often expensive; when possible, we've given toll-free alternatives. The

Túnel de Vallvidrera, the continuation of Via Augusta under Collserola to Sant Cugat, has a high toll, as does the **Túnel de Cadí**, through the mountains south of Puigcerdà. For more on tolls, call 902 20 03 20 or see www.autopistas.com.

By train

All **RENFE** trains (902 320 320, www.renfe.es) stop at **Sants** station, and some at **Passeig de Gràcia** (Girona, Figueres, south coast), **Estació de França** (south coast) or **Plaça Catalunya** (Vic, Puigcerdà). RENFE's local and suburban trains (*rodalies/cercanías*) are integrated into the metro and bus fares system (*see p293*); tickets for them are sold at separate windows.

Catalan Government Railways (**FGC**) serves destinations from **Plaça d'Espanya** and **Plaça Catalunya**. FGC information is available on 93 205 15 15 and at www.fgc.net.

On foot

Catalonia's hills and low mountain ranges are great for hiking and biking. In many places, it's made easier by GR (*gran recorregut*) long-distance footpaths, marked with red-and-white signs; they may have inns, campsites or basic refuges en route. Good places for walking within reach of the city include the **Parc de Collserola** (*see p104*), **Montserrat** (*see p286*) and **La Garrotxa** (*see p272*). Another useful Generalitat website, www.turismedecatalunya.com, has good information on walks. For detailed walking maps, try **Altaïr** (*see p186*) or **Llibreria Quera** (C/Petritxol 2, 93 318 07 43).

Escapes

Avoid the resorts and you'll find plenty that appeals beyond the city.

In this section, we look at some of the farther-flung parts of Catalonia, places that reward a stay of a couple of days or more. There's skiing to be had at **Puigcerdà**; hiking through the beech forest of **La Garrotxa** or along the route of **Cistercian** monasteries; birdwatching at the **Ebre Delta**; and cycling along the region's disused railway tracks. Hedonists will make straight for the **Costa Brava**: some to the frenetic resorts of the south, others to the quieter villages of its upper reaches, a landscape loved by Dalí and peppered with spaces dedicated to his work.

The Delta Blues
TORTOSA & THE EBRE DELTA

Southern Catalonia has an entirely different flavour to the North, and is still little visited by outsiders. An appealing way to investigate its untapped charms is by starting at the town of **Tortosa**, the capital of the Baix Ebre, and using it as a base from which to explore the surrounding delta.

Tortosa itself is an attractive place in its own right. Built on the site of a Roman temple, the town's magnificent Gothic cathedral is ringed by medieval alleyways; traces of the town's Jewish and Arab quarters can still be seen here (they're clearly signposted). There are also plenty of interesting Modernista buildings around the town. Among them are the colourful, Mudéjar-inspired pavilions of the former slaughterhouse (Escorxador), on the banks of the Ebre river.

Further inland, **Miravet** hangs suspended above the mighty Ebre, which you can still cross by car ferry. Within, the castle was rebuilt by the Knights Templar and is considered one of the best examples of their architectural prowess in Spain. Combined with its sleepy potters' quarter (eight workshops still operate) and its curiously Islamic flavour, it makes for an agreeable side trip.

Tortosa sits inland from the ecologically remarkable **Parc Natural del Delta de l'Ebre**. The towns of the delta are themselves nothing special, but the immense, flat, green expanses of wetlands, channels, dunes and still-productive rice fields are eerily beautiful.

It's this variety of habitat that makes the area such a popular birdwatching destination. Birdwatchers can hope to tick off over half the 600 bird species found in Europe at the site. The flocks of flamingos make a spectacular sight as they shuffle around filter-feeding; elsewhere, the wetlands are full of herons, great crested grebes, spoonbills and marsh harriers. For birding tours from Barcelona, see www.catalanbirdtours.com.

The town of **Deltebre** is the base for most park services; from here, it's easy to embark on day trips to the bird sanctuaries, especially the remote headland of **Punta de la Banya**. The delta's flatness also makes it an ideal place for walking or cycling; for bicycle hire, check at the tourist office in Deltebre. Small boats offer trips along the river from the north bank about eight kilometres east of Deltebre.

Eating, drinking & sleeping

Tortosa itself has a wonderful parador, **Castell de la Suda** (977 44 44 50, €105-€138), built on the site of a Moorish fortress with panoramic views of the countryside. See www.paradors.es for occasional offers. On a very different level, the southern edge of the Ebre delta holds Platja dels Eucaliptus, a wide, sweeping beach where you'll find the **Camping Eucaliptus** (977 47 90 46, www.campingeucaliptus.com, closed Oct-mid Mar, €4.85-€6.85/person; €6.85-€8.35/tent; €4.30-€5.75/car). Other options include **Hotel Rull** in Deltebre (Avda Esportiva 155, 977 48 77 28, www.hotelrull.com, €69.50-€96.30, mains €15), which organises occasional 'safaris', and the ecologically friendly **Delta Hotel** (Avda del Canal, Camí de la Illeta, 977 48 00 46, www.deltahotel.net, €74-€98); both operations also have restaurants.

Local culinary specialities include dishes made with delta rice, duck, frogs' legs and the curious *chapadillo* (sun-dried eels). You can try them all at **Galatxo** (C/Alfores s/n, Desembocadura Riu Ebre, 977 26 75 03, mains €15), at the mouth of the river. **L'Estany-Casa de Fusta** (l'Encanyissada s/n, 977 26 10 26, www.restaurantestany.com, mains €11) offers dishes such as stewed eel and wild duck in a traditional wood cabin.

Tourist information

Delta de l'Ebre *C/Doctor Marti Buera 22, Deltebre (977 48 96 79, www.parcsdecatalunya. net)*. **Open** *Oct-Apr* 10am-2pm, 3-6pm Mon-Sat; 10am-2pm Sun. *May-Sept* 10am-2pm, 3-7pm Mon-Sat; 10am-2pm Sun.
Tortosa *Plaça Carrilet 1 (977 44 96 48, www.turismetortosa.com)*. **Open** *Oct-Apr* 10am-1.30pm, 3.30-6.30pm Tue-Sat; 11am-1.30pm Sun. *May-Sept* 10am-1.30pm, 4.30-7.30pm Tue-Sat; 10am-1.30pm Sun.

Getting there

By train & bus RENFE from Sants or Passeig de Gràcia every 2hrs to Tortosa (journey time 2hrs 30mins) or L'Aldea (journey time 2hrs 30mins), then seven buses daily 8am-8.05pm (run by HIFE; 977 44 03 00, www.hife.es) to Deltebre.

A Monk's Life

FOLLOWING THE CISTERCIAN ROUTE

The coast around Barcelona is hugely popular, and as a result, much of the non-coastal countryside in the area consists of roads less travelled by the tourist hordes, and they make a lovely change from the crowded norms along the beaches and ports.

There's no better example of this than **La Ruta del Cister** (the Cisterian Route; www.larutadelcister.info). Connecting the wonderful Cistercian monasteries of Poblet, Santes Creus and Vallbona de les Monges, all of which can be visited on a single €9 ticket, the GR175 runs to more than 100 kilometres (62 miles), and offers a peaceful idyll for cyclists or ramblers. It may be located near Tarragona, but the route gives a completely different flavour of the region.

All three monasteries are easily accessible by car from **Montblanc**, 119 kilometres (74 miles) west of Barcelona and a beautiful town

in its own right. In the Middle Ages, it was one of Catalonia's most powerful centres, with an important Jewish community. Its past is today reflected in its narrow medieval streets, magnificent 13th-century town walls, and its churches, the **Palau Reial** and the **Palau del Castlà** (Chamberlain's Palace).

Poblet, to the west, was founded in 1151 as a royal residence and monastery. The remarkable complex includes a 14th-century **Gothic royal palace**, the 15th-century chapel of **Sant Jordi** and the main **church**, which houses the tombs of most of the count-kings of Barcelona.

Santes Creus, founded in 1158, grew into a small village when families moved into the old monks' residences in the 1800s. Fortified walls shelter the **Palau de l'Abat** (Abbot's Palace), a monumental fountain, a 12th-century church and a superb Gothic cloister and chapterhouse. Unlike the other two, it no longer has a religious community in residence.

Santa Maria de Vallbona, the third of these Cistercian houses, was, unlike the others, a convent for nuns. It has a fine part-Romanesque cloister but is less grand than the other two.

Monestir de Poblet *977 87 02 54, www. poblet.cat*. **Open** *Mid Mar-mid Oct* 10am-12.40pm, 3-5.25pm Mon-Sat; 10am-12.40pm, 3-5.25pm Sun. *Mid Oct-mid Mar* 10am-12.45pm, 3-5.25pm Sun. **Admission** €7; €3.50 reductions; free under-7s. **No credit cards**.
Monestir de Santa Maria de Vallbona *973 33 02 66, www.vallbona.com*. **Open** *Apr-Oct* 10.30am-1.30pm, 4.30-6.30pm Tue-Sat; noon-1.30pm, 4.30-6.30pm Sun. *Nov-Mar* 10.30am-1.30pm, 4.30-5.30pm Tue-Sat; noon-1.30pm, 4.30-5.30pm Sun. **Admission** €3.50; €2.50 reductions; free under-12s. **Credit** V.
Monestir de Santes Creus *977 63 83 29*. **Open** *June-Sept* 10am-6.30pm Tue-Sun. *Oct-May* 10am-5pm Tue-Sun. **Admission** €4.50; €3 reductions; free under-7s & Tue. **Credit** MC, V.

Eating, drinking & sleeping

In Montblanc, you'll need to book in advance in order to secure a room at the popular **Fonda dels Àngels** (Plaça dels Àngels 1, 977 86 01 73, www.fondadelsangels.com, closed Sun & 3wks Sept, €43.20, set menu €16 Mon-Fri, €23 Sat), which also has a great restaurant. The **Fonda Cal Colom** (C/Civaderia 5, 977 86 01 53, closed dinner Sun, all day Mon, 2wks Sept & 2wks Jan, mains €16, set lunch €15 Mon-Fri, set dinner €15 Fri, Sat) is a friendly old restaurant located behind the Plaça Major.

Blazing Trails

Disused railway tracks have been turned into hiking heaven.

Former Socialist prime minister Felipe González is something of a fallen idol in Spain, but one of his government's better ideas was the repurposing of the country's 1,800 kilometres of disused railway tracks as hiking and cycle paths, known as the **Vías Verdes** (www.viasverdes.com).

Three interlinking *vías* run 135 kilometres from **Ripoll** in the foothills of the Pyrenees (*see p274*) all the way to **Sant Feliu de Guíxols** (*see p276*) on the Costa Brava. En route they pass through some spectacular scenery, such as the **Núria gorge** (*see p274*), romantic medieval villages such as **Besalú** (*see p272*) and pretty coves including **Cala Giverola** just north of Sant Feliu. In addition, it's easy cycling country, particularly if you start at Olot and head downhill to the coast.

Ripoll to **Sant Joan de les Abadesses** (*see p274*) is known as the 'Iron and Coal route' because it once formed part of a railroad carrying coal from the mountains to Barcelona. It closed for good in 1985 and is the toughest section of the route, rising up just after Sant Joan de Abadesses to nearly 1,000 metres. After that, it's pretty much downhill once you get to Olot.

From **Olot** (*see p272*) to **Girona** and on to **Sant Feliu** are the 'Carrilet I and II routes', which follow a network of

narrow-gauge railway tracks that connected the small towns and villages of the region at the end of the 19th century. Think Hobbits' Shire, with smooth grit paths framed by mountains, deep green forest, rolling pasture, fields of maize and babbling brooks.

There are plenty of picnic spots and handily located bars and restaurants, as well as various possibilities for staying over en route – from smart country hotels and boutique townhouses to more basic campsites – if you want to spread it over a few days. Bike rentals are available from firms such as **ATMA** (Antiga Estació, Les Preses, 972 69 20 23, www.atma.cat); the English-speaking and very helpful **Cicloturisme i Medi Ambient** (C/Impressors Oliva 2, Girona, 972 22 10 47, www.cicloturisme.com); and **Cicles Tarrés** (Avda Girona 29, Olot, 972 26 99 78, closed 2wks July and 1 wk Sept); **Tornasol Aventura** (C/Progrés 14, Ripoll, 972 70 27 47, www.tornasol.com) offers packages including bikes, hotel and tours.

The **Greenway Guides** are available at tourist offices anywhere en route. They include maps, accommodation and camping tips, and services such as bike hire and trailer-taxis for you and your bike if you feel yourself running out of steam.

Besalú.

In L'Espluga de Francolí, en route to Poblet, the **Hostal del Senglar** (Plaça Montserrat Canals 1, 977 87 01 21, www.hostaldelsenglar.com, €58 room only or €75-€100 half board) is a great-value country hotel with lovely gardens, a swimming pool and an atmospheric if slightly pricey restaurant (mains €13). In Santes Creus the **Hostal Grau** (C/Pere El Gran 3, 977 63 83 11, closed mid Dec-mid Jan, 1 wk after 24 June €65, restaurant closed Sun eve, Mon & mid Dec-mid Jan, 1 wk after 24 June, mains €14) is a reasonable option, with good Catalan food, as is the **Restaurant Catalunya** (C/Abreda 2, 977 63 84 32, mains €14, set lunch €11 Mon-Fri, closed Wed).

Tourist information

Montblanc *Antiga Església de Sant Francesc (977 86 17 33, www.montblancmedieval.cat).* **Open** 10am-1.30pm, 3-6.30pm Mon-Sat; 10am-2pm Sun.

Getting there

By bus Hispano Igualadina (93 339 73 29, www.igualadina.net) runs a service to Montblanc from Sants station leaving at 4.50pm Mon-Fri (except Aug). More buses run from Valls and Tarragona.
By train RENFE trains leave from Sants or Passeig de Gràcia to Montblanc. There are five trains a day. The journey takes about 2hrs.

Low-key Catalonia
BESALÚ & OLOT

Besalú is one of Catalonia's loveliest towns, accessed by an impressive 12th-century fortified bridge spanning the Fluvià river. The town has, in the gentlest way, sold some of its soul to tourism, and these days piped music echoes through the cobbled streets.

Once home to a sizeable Jewish community, the town boasts the only remaining Jewish baths (*mikveh*) in Spain, dating back to the 13th century but only discovered in the 1960s. Charmingly, if the doors are locked when you arrive, the tourist office will give you a key so that you can let yourself in. Also worth a visit are the Romanesque church of Sant Pere and the arcaded Plaça de la Llibertat. The peculiar **Museu de Miniatures i Microminiatures** (Plaça Prat de Sant Pere 15, 972 59 18 42, www.museuminiaturesbesalu.com, €3.50, reductions €2.50, free under-8s) houses such curios as the Eiffel Tower atop a poppy seed.

West from here the N260 runs to **Olot**, past a spectacular view of **Castellfollit de la Roca**, a village perched on the edge of a precipitous crag. Olot is the capital of the Garrotxa region and is surrounded by 38 inactive volcanoes. An earthquake in 1427 destroyed most of its oldest architecture, but it does have impressive 18th-century and Modernista buildings. In the last century, it was home to a school of landscape painters: the local **Museu de la Garrotxa** (C/Hospice 8, 972 27 91 30, www.turismeolot.cat, closed Mon, admission €3) has works by them, along with Ramon Casas, Santiago Rusiñol and other Modernista artists.

Off the G1524 toward Banyoles, which boasts a magnificent lake, you'll see a vast beech forest, the **Fageda d'en Jordà**, immortalised by Catalan poet Joan Maragall, and the pretty, if touristy, village **Santa Pau**, with an impressive castle and arcaded squares.

Eating & drinking

Besalú is overflowing with good places to eat. The most famous is **Pont Vell** (C/Pont Vell 24, 972 59 10 27, www.restaurantpontvell.com, closed dinner Mon, all day Tue & mid Dec-mid Jan, mains €18), which offers a fine view of the bridge and a superb menu. The terrace of the **Cúria Reial** (Plaça de la Llibertat 8-9, 972 59 02 63, www.curiareial.com, closed dinner Mon, all day Tue & all Feb, mains €14) is more welcoming, with hearty cooking such as Garrotxa lamb stewed with dates.

Located on the edge of Olot, surrounded by woodland, **Font Moixina** (Paratge de la Moixina s/n, 972 26 10 00, www.font moixina.com, closed Tue & all Feb, mains €14) is owned by the same people as Cúria Reial in Besalú and specialises in local cuisine. **La Deu** (Ctra de la Deu, 972 26 10 04, www. ladeu.es, closed dinner Sun, mains €13.50, set lunch €11.40, €16, €25 Mon-Fri) specialises in *cuina volcánica*, which includes beef stewed in onions and beer.

North of the town is the **Restaurant Les Cols** (Crta de la Canya, 972 26 92 09, closed Sun, Mon, dinner Tue, 3wks Jan, 1wk July & 2wks Aug, mains €23) which is famed as much for its fabulous design as its food. The structure combines a Modernist dining room with an 18th-century farmhouse. It has a handful of glassed-in cubes in the garden for those who want to sleep.

Sleeping

In Besalú, the 19th-century **Hotel Fonda Siqués** (Avda Lluís Companys 6-8, 972 59 01 10, www.grupcalparent.com, €48-€65), offers clean, basic rooms and is located above a charming restaurant (set meal €11). More upmarket is **Els Jardins de la Martana** (C/Pont 2, 972 59 00 09, www.lamartana.com, €94-€105), an eccentric and somewhat jaded stately home with a magnificent wood-panelled library and maze-like terraces and gardens. For a proper treat, **Sant Ferriol Hotel and Spa** (Jardins de Sant Ferriol, 972 59 05 32, 972 59 03 31, www.santferriol.com, €150-€200) is a lovingly restored Catalan farmhouse with 12 spacious rooms, most with their own terrace, and surrounded by idyllic countryside.

In Olot, **La Perla** (Avda Santa Coloma 97, 972 26 23 26, www.laperlahotels.com, €73-€107) is a large hotel with a good restaurant. Otherwise, on the corner of Plaça Major, try **Pensió La Vila** (C/Sant Roc 1, 972 26 98 07, www.pensiolavila.com, €42 or €48 with

Coastal Calendar

Seasonal seaside events dot the year in Catalonia.

If there's one thing above all others at which the Spanish are world leaders, it's celebrating. The Barcelona calendar is full of fabulous festivals; *see pp208-215* for the best of them. And there are plenty more terrific events outside the city, especially up the coast towards France.

Some of the best coastal events are traditional. Held in Calella de Palafrugell on the first Saturday in July, Cantata de las Habaneras celebrates the return of native fishermen from the New World by singing shanties on the beach while sipping *cremat* (rum and sugar flambéed with coffee beans). And while the **Blanes Fireworks Festival** began in an official capacity 50 years ago, it dates back considerably longer. The spectacular event is held at the end of July; for details, call 972 33 03 48.

Others, though, are cultural. Between Calella and Blanes, the beachside town of Santa Susanna offers the unlikely prospect of a **Shakespeare Festival** (www.festival shakespeare.com). Launched in 2003 in collaboration with the Teatre Lliure in Barcelona, the festival runs over ten days in late July and early August; some performances are staged in English.

There's more culture further up the coast in Sant Feliu de Guíxols at **La Porta Ferrada** (www.portaferrada.com), held in July and August. One of the oldest arts festivals in Catalonia, it includes everything from flamenco to Herbie Hancock. And up in Palafrugell (also in July and August), the clifftop **Jardins de Cap Roig** (botanic gardens, http://jardins.caproig.cat) hosts dance, opera, jazz and classical music in a spectacular location.

breakfast), a modern and central place. South of Olot, in La Pinya, is **Mas Garganta** (972 27 12 89, www.masgarganta.com, closed mid-Dec to Easter, €84 with breakfast included, dinner €18), an 18th-century *masia* (farmhouse) with magnificent views that has walking tours in conjunction with two *masies* nearby.

Tourist information

Olot *C/Hospici 8 (972 26 01 41, www.turisme olot.cat).* Open *Apr-mid July, mid Sept-Oct* 10am-2pm, 4-7pm Mon-Sat, 10am-2pm Sun. *Mid July-mid Sept* 10am-8pm Mon-Sat, 10am-2pm Sun. *Nov-Mar* 9am-2pm, 4-6pm Mon-Fri; 10am-2pm, 4-6pm Sat; 10am-2pm Sun.

Getting there

By bus TEISA (93 215 35 66, www.teisa-bus.com) to Besalú and Olot from the corner of C/Pau Claris and C/Consell de Cent.

Nearing the Pyrenees
BERGA, PUIGCERDÀ, RIPOLL & AROUND

The popular approach to the Pyrenees from Barcelona is via **Berga**, famous for the frenzied festival of La Patum at Corpus Christi. Further north, the giant cliffs of the **Serra del Cadí**, one of the ranges of the Pyrenees foothills, loom above the town, but the blight of endless holiday apartment blocks has taken its toll on the charm of its old centre.

Far prettier is the little town of **Bagà**, north of here on the C17. With its partially preserved medieval walls around an atmospheric old quarter, Bagà marks the beginning of the **Parc Natural del Cadí-Moixeró**, a mountain park containing wildlife and forest reserves, and some 20 or so ancient villages. All retain some medieval architecture, and many offer stunning views. Picasso stayed and painted in the village of **Gósol** in 1906. Rising above this are the twin peaks of **Pedraforça**, practically a pilgrimage for hiking enthusiasts and well worth the effort (allow a full day to get up there and back).

Above Bagà, the C16 road enters the Túnel del Cadí to emerge into the wide, fertile plateau of the **Cerdanya**. The area has a clear geographical unity, but the French/Spanish border runs through its middle. **Puigcerdà**, the capital of the area (on the Spanish side), is a popular ski-resort town but not wildly exciting. There are many gentle hiking routes around here, which take in thermal spas and bald-headed peaks.

From here, you can head left after the Cadí tunnel to **La Seu d'Urgell**, **Sort** and on to the breathtaking highlands of the **Parc Nacional d'Aigüestortes**. A favourite for hikers in the spring and cross-country skiers in the winter, the steep wooded slopes give way to jade green lakes, giant waterfalls and lovely snowy peaks.

Alternatively, head south-east from Puigcerdà towards **Ribes de Freser**. This is the starting point for the narrow-gauge cog railway that runs via the pretty, if slightly gentrified, village of **Queralbs** along the Freser river up to the sanctuary of **Núria**, affording incredible views (€17.75-€21.25 return, reductions €10.65-€12.75, journey time 40 mins, closed 3wks Nov). The ticket includes a ride on the cable car once you reach Núria, plus admission to exhibitions in the sanctuary. Many choose to walk back to Queralbs (around two hours), following the path through dramatic rock formations, crumbling scree, pine-wooded slopes and dramatic, crashing waterfalls.

Núria itself nestles by a lake in a wide, flat valley at over 2,000 metres (6,500 feet), and was the first ski resort on this side of the border. Home to the second most famous of Catalonia's patron virgins, and a 12th-century wooden statue of the Madonna, it was a refuge and a place of pilgrimage long before then. The mostly 19th-century monastery that surrounds the shrine is nothing special, but its location is spectacular. It's a great day out, particularly if you have kids, for whom there are pony rides, playgrounds and acres of grassland.

There's more monastic history south of Ribes de Freser in **Ripoll**. The extraordinary **Santa Maria de Ripoll** was founded in 879 by Wilfred 'the Hairy', who's buried here. The church has a superb 12th-century stone portal, its carvings among the finest examples of Romanesque art in Catalonia. Wilfred also founded the monastery and town of **Sant Joan de les Abadesses**, ten kilometres east up the C26, worth a visit for its Gothic bridge as well as the 12th-century monastery buildings. Neither town holds much charm outside its monastery.

Eating, drinking & sleeping

In Bagà, the **Hotel Ca L'Amagat** (C/Clota 4, 93 824 41 60, www.hotelcalamagat.com, closed 1wk Dec & 1wk Jan, €58-€73) has rooms with large balconies, and a restaurant (closed Mon mid Sept-May, mains €15).

Puigcerdà has plenty of hotels in the town centre, including the small and charming **Avet Blau** (Plaça Santa Maria 14, 972 88 25 52,

€80-€110) and the lovely **Villa Paulita**
(Avda Pons i Gasch 15, 972 88 46 22, www.
hospes.es, €120-€225), right by the lake.
The **Hotel Rita-Belvedere** (C/Carmelites
6-8, 972 88 03 56, www.ritabelvedere.com,
open weekends only 6 Jan-Easter, daily
rest of year, €45-€56) has a small garden
and terrace with a great view. For French-
influenced cuisine, try **La Col d'Hivern**
(C/Baronia 7, 972 14 12 04, closed Mon-Wed,
set menu €18).

A little further out in Bolvir, the sumptuous
Torre del Remei (C/Camí Reial s/n, 972 14
01 82, www.torredelremei.com, €240-€800,
mains €26.50) also has one of the best (and
pricier) restaurants in the area. In Bellver, the
Fonda Biayna (C/Sant Roc 11, 973 51 04 75,
www.fondabiayna.com, €60 B&B, €80 half
board) is charming, with its sweet cornflower-
blue woodwork, a sunny bar and a lively feel.

Towards Aigüestortes, the best bet for
lodgings is Espot, which acts as a gateway to
the park. **Els Avets** (Port de la Bonaigua, Alt
Aneu, 973 62 63 55, www.elsavets.com, €120-
€150) is a pleasant place in which to combine
the great outdoors with a little modern comfort.
The hotel has information on adventure sports
in the region.

East in Ribes de Freser, the family-run
Hotel Els Caçadors (C/Balandrau 24-26,
972 72 77 22, www.hotelsderibes.com, closed
Nov, €50-€109) is the first eco-hotel in the
Pyrenees and has decent food and comfortable
rooms, including family rooms. **La Perdiu
Blanca** (C/Puigcerdà 5, 972 72 71 50, www.
laperdiublanca.com, closed Wed & Apr, mains
€11.50, set lunch €11.50 daily except Wed, set
dinner €17.50 daily except Wed) is a village
classic. Ribes also has a lovely, quiet campsite
with a small pool, **Camping Vall de Ribes**
(Ctra Pardines km 0.5, 972 72 88 20, www.
campingvallderibes.com, €5.70 per person,
€5.10 per tent).

In Queralbs, there's **Calamari Hostal
l'Avet** (C/Major 17-19, 972 72 73 77, closed
Mon Thur from Oct May, €80 half-board).
The one good place to eat in Queralbs is
La Plaça (Plaça de la Vila 2, 972 72 70 37,
closed Tue, closed 2wks July & 2wks Oct-
Nov, mains €8.50), which serves regional
specialities.

East of here in Camprodon, the **Hotel
Maristany** (Avda Maristany 20, 972 13 00
78, www.hotelmaristany.com, closed mid Dec-
Jan, €130) is unexpectedly smart, with formal
gardens filled with topiary and roses, and a
decent pool. It's a great treat after hiking,
especially combined with a creative dinner
at the romantic old **Can Po** (Ctra Beget
s/n, 972 74 10 45, closed Mon-Thur Sept-July,
mains €12.50).

Tossa del Mar. *See p276.*

Costa Brava.

Tourist information

Berga *C/Àngels 7 (93 821 13 84,*
www.turismeberga.cat). **Open** 10am-2pm,
6-8pm Mon-Sat; 11am-2pm, 6-8pm Sun.
Núria *Estació de Montanya del Vall de Núria*
(972 73 20 20, www.valldenuria.cat). **Open** *Mid*
July-mid Sept 8.30am-6.45pm daily. *Mid Sept-mid*
July 8.30am-5.45pm daily.
Puigcerdà *C/Querol 1 (972 88 05 42,*
www.puigcerda.cat). **Open** *Oct-May, Aug* 10am-
1pm, 4-7pm Mon-Fri; 10am-1pm, 4.30-7pm Sat;
10am-2pm Sun. *June, Sept* 10am-1pm, 4-7pm
Tue-Fri; 10am-2pm Sat.
Ribes de Freser *Plaça del Ajuntament 3 (972*
72 77 28, www.valldeflibes.cat). **Open** 10am-2pm,
5-8pm Tue-Sat; 10am-2pm Sun.

Getting there

By bus Alsina-Graëlls (93 265 68 66, 902 422
242, www.alsa.es) runs eight buses daily to
Berga from the corner of C/Balmes and Ronda
de Universitat 11-13 or the Estació del Nord;
journey time is about 2hrs. The same company
runs buses to Puigcerdà from Estació del Nord;
journey time is 3hrs. Otherwise, TEISA (93 215
35 66, www.teisa-bus.com) runs one bus a day
from the corner of C/Pau Claris and C/Consell
de Cent to Ripoll, Sant Joan de les Abadesses
and Camprodon.
By train Take RENFE from Sants or Plaça
Catalunya. The journey time to Ripoll is 2hrs;
to Puigcerdà, it's about 3hrs. For Queralbs and
Núria, change to the *cremallera* train in Ribes
de Freser.

Beauty and the Beasts
THE SOUTHERN COSTA BRAVA

In its heyday, the Costa Brava was the most
exclusive resort area in Spain, attracting film
stars, artists and writers to its sandy beaches.
By the 1970s, though, things had changed.
Encouraged by the local authorities, package
tours from the UK descended on the area, and
all manner of tacky restaurants and ugly
apartment blocks soon followed. The area,
which covers the stretch of coast between
Blanes and the French border, is blighted by its
reputation as the playground of unimaginative
British holidaymakers. However, there's plenty
to enjoy if you know where to stop.

Most of the good stuff is further north.
Ruined by holiday-home high-rises, the towns
of **Blanes** and **Lloret del Mar** boast enviable
locations but are really best avoided. Continue,
instead, to **Tossa del Mar** (*photo p275*) the
southern entry to the Costa Brava proper and
by far the loveliest town on this stretch. The
painter Marc Chagall once described it as a
'blue paradise'; Ava Gardner spent so much
time here with lover Frank Sinatra that they
erected a statue in her honour. The new town
has been constructed with little thought, but
Tossa has retained one of Spain's most
handsome medieval quarters.

The twisting 20-kilometre (12-mile) drive
through coastal pine forests from here to
Sant Feliu de Guíxols offers brief but
unforgettable views of the sea. And when you
arrive, Sant Feliu itself has superb Modernista

buildings along the Passeig Marítim. Other sights include the **Benedictine monastery** (Plaça Monestir, 972 82 15 75, closed Mon, admission free) that incorporates the celebrated Porta Ferrada, a tenth-century portico, and the town museum, which will house part of the Carmen Thyssen-Bornemisza Catalan art collection in late 2010. Sant Feliu also pulls in big names for an excellent music festival every summer. **Sant Pol** beach is three kilometres north of the crowded town sands, and offers more towel room.

Just north of Sant Pol, the GR92 path, or 'Camino de Ronda', starts out from below the Hostal de la Gavina in S'Agaró where Ava and Frank spent much of their time, and continues on along many secluded coves and rocky outlets for swimming. The sandy bay of **Sa Conca**, considered to be one of the most beautiful beaches on the Costa Brava, has a couple of good *xiringuitos* for a sardine lunch. From here, there's a tedious stretch through the ugly **Platja d'Aro** that then picks up all the way to **Torre Valentina**, from where you can catch a bus back. The walk is roughly ten kilometres in length.

Palamós has never really recovered from an attack by the infamous pirate Barba Roja (Redbeard) in 1543; the most exciting thing about the town is its famous and terrifyingly expensive giant red prawns. Continue, instead, to the area around **Palafrugell**, which has pretty villages built into its rocky coves. All of them make great bases for a little leisurely beach-hopping. The **Fundació Vila Casas** (Plaça Can Mario 7, 972 30 62 46,

www.fundaciovilacasas.com, closed Tue from mid June-mid Sept & Mon-Fri mid Sept-mid June) in Palafrugell itself houses a good collection of works by local artists and sculptors, and gives an idea of the kind of creativity the environment inspires.

Calella de Palafrugell, not to be confused with its ugly near-namesake down the coast, is a lively and attractive town sitting around a clear water bay. The cliff-top botanical gardens at **Cap Roig** (972 61 45 82, www.caproig.cat) host a wonderful music and arts festival every July and August, attracting names such as Caetano Veloso and London's Royal Ballet. Nearby **Llafranc** is not quite as pretty but has a long curved beach where you can swim between fishing boats in the bay.

Tamariu, known for its good seafood, is the perfect base for scuba-diving and fishing. Giro Náutic (www.gironautic.com) is a useful portal for all things aquatic in the area. Next up is **Aiguablava**, with its modern parador and white sandy beach, and **Fornells** – the town that inspired Norman Lewis' *Voices of the Old Sea*, now much changed. Both are accessible from **Begur**, as is the small **Aiguafreda**, a cove that's sheltered by pines.

Beyond the Ter estuary and the Montgri hills, which divide the Baix and Alt Empordà, is **L'Estartit**. This small resort town caters for tourists interested in exploring the **Illes Medes**, a group of rocky limestone outcrops. The biggest housed a British prison in the 19th century, but Les Illes are now home only to a unique ecosystem, an underwater paradise where divers can contemplate colourful coral

ESCAPES & EXCURSIONS

Cap de Creus. *See p280.*

and hundreds of different species of sea life. For a view of the islands, it's worth the climb up to the 12th-century **Castell de Montgrí**.

Eating & drinking

In Tossa, **Santa Marta** (C/Francesc Aromir 2, 972 34 04 72, www.restaurantsantamarta.com, closed Feb, mains €18) has a pretty terrace in the old town and specialises in Catalan cuisine. Upmarket **La Cuina de Can Simón** (C/Portal 24, 972 34 12 69, www.lacuinadecansimon.es, closed Tue year-round and Mon & Sun dinner from Oct-Feb, closed mid-Nov to mid-Mar except for 2wks around Christmas, mains €36.50) is more eccentric, but serves excellent fish dishes, as does **Can Pini** (C/Portal 14, 972 34 02 97, closed Mon Oct-Apr, mains €20, set lunch €18 daily).

In Sant Feliu de Guíxols, try the **Nàutic** (Port Esportiu, 972 32 13 36, closed Mon & Sun dinner from Oct-May, mains €10.50, set lunch €12.50 Tue-Fri, €19.75 Sat-Sun) in the Club Nàutic sailing club, for great views and superb seafood. Also with a sea view, **El Dorada Mar** (Passeig Presidente Irla 15, 972 32 62 86, closed Wed mid Sept-mid June, mains €15) has a more traditional take on rice and fish dishes.

Calella has the fashionable **Tragamar** (Platja de Canadell, 972 61 43 36, www. grupotragaluz.com, closed Nov-mid-Mar, mains €14.50. while in Llafranc, **El Simpson** (Passeig Cipsela 10, 972 30 11 57, closed mid Dec-Feb; Mon-Fri Mar-May & Oct; Wed June & Sept, mains €14) is justifiably famous for excellent seafood. In Tamariu, there's good seafood at the **Royal** on the beachfront (Passeig de Mar 9, 972 62 00 41, closed mid Dec-Feb; Mon-Fri Nov, Dec & Mar, mains €18), or succulent lamb at **El Mossec** (C/Pescadors 8, 972 62 03 27, closed lunchtimes and all day Wed June & Sept; open dinner Fri and Sat Oct-May, mains €12). In Aiguablava, the **Hotel Aiguablava** (Platja de Fornells, 972 62 20 58, www.aiguablava.com, closed mid Oct-mid Mar, €155-€265, mains €17.50) has an excellent beachfront restaurant.

Sleeping

In Tossa, the **Hotel Diana** (Plaça España 6, 972 34 18 86, www.hotelesdante.com, closed Nov-Mar, €99-€200) is situated in a Modernista building with a beautifully preserved marble staircase and tiled floors, though the interior decor is somewhat wanting. Bargain rooms are available at **Fonda Lluna** (C/Roqueta 20, 972 34 03 65, www.fondalluna.com, €40-€54).

In Sant Feliu de Guíxols, try the friendly **Hotel Plaça** (Plaça Mercat 22, 972 32 51 55, www.hotelplaza.org, €79.50-€103), close to the beach. North of Sant Feliu, in S'Agaró, the **Hostal de la Gavina** (Plaça de la Rosaleda, 972 32 11 00, www.lagavina.com, closed Oct-Apr, €245-€325) is a five-star in the European grand hotel tradition. Near the Platja d'Aro, **Mas Torrellas** (Ctra de Santa Cristina a Castell d'Aro km2, 972 83 75 26, www.mas torrellas.com, closed Oct-Feb, €64-€95) is an 18th-century farmhouse with bags of charm.

On the road to Palamós, the **Hostal del Sol** (Ctra de Palamós, 972 32 01 93, www.hostaldelsol.es, closed Oct-Mar, €65-€115), is located in a Modernista mansion with a swimming pool and live music on the terrace through the summer. You'll also find fashionable **La Malcontenta** (Platja de Castell 12, 972 31 23 30, www.lamalcontentahotel.com, €150-€315, closed Sun, Mon from Nov-Mar), which has a fabulous pool, plush beds and linen, and a designer air.

Llafranc has the famous **Hotel Llafranch** (Passeig de Cipsela 16, 972 30 02 08, www. hllafranch.com, closed Nov, €80-€164), which was a favourite haunt of Salvador Dalí and his cronies back in the 1960s. The **El Far de Sant Sebastià** (Platja de Llafranc s/n, 972 30 16 39, www.elfar.net, closed Jan, €195-€290), is a swanky address situated on the cliff tops. Alternatively, the friendly **Hotel Casamar** (C/Nero 3-11, 972 30 01 04, www.hotel casamar.net, closed Jan- Mar, €55-€130) is a good budget option, with recently renovated rooms.

Tamariu offers the chilled-out **Hotel Tamariu** (Passeig de Mar 2, 972 62 00 31, www.tamariu.com, closed mid Nov-mid Feb, €103-€157), and the **Hotel Hostalillo** (972 62 02 28, www.hotelhostalillo.com, closed Nov-Apr, €56-€92), located above the beach in the middle of pine forest. Aiguablava's modern parador is **Platja d'Aiguablava** (972 62 21 62, www.parador.es, €90-€204, half board obligatory in July and Aug, €282 for a double room).

Tourist information

L'Estartit *Passeig Marítim (972 75 19 10, www.visitestartit.com)*. **Open** *June, Sept* 9.30am-2pm, 4-8pm daily. *July, Aug* 9.30am-2pm, 4-9pm daily. *Oct-Apr* 9am-1pm, 3-6pm Mon-Fri, 10am-2pm, 3pm-6pm Sat, 10am-2pm Sun. *May* 9am-1pm, 4-7pm daily.

Palafrugell *C/Carrilet 2 (972 30 02 28, www.visitpalafrugell.cat)*. **Open** *Sept-June* 10am-1pm, 4-7pm daily. *July, Aug* 9am-9pm Mon-Sun.

Sant Feliu de Guíxols *Passeig del Mar 8-12 (972 82 00 51, www.guixols.cat)*. **Open** *Mid June-mid Sept* 10am-2pm, 4-8pm daily. *Mid Sept-mid June* 10am-1pm, 4-7pm Mon-Sat; 10am-2pm Sun.

Dalí's Designs

The life and works of the moustachioed one.

Pablo be damned. Sure, the artist has his admirers; and, in Barcelona, he's celebrated by a fine museum. But north-east of the city, close to the French border, another very different artist dominates: Salvador Dalí, who lived and worked in this corner of Catalonia. Several Dalí-related landmarks remain open to the public today.

Start just east of Girona at the 12th-century **Castell Gala-Dalí** (Plaça Gala Dalí, Púbol, 972 48 86 55, www.salvador-dali.org, closed Jan-mid Mar & Mon mid Sept-Dec & mid Mar-June, admission €8, €6 reductions, free under-9s) bought by Dalí to house his wife-muse Gala (who's buried here) in her later years. Relations were strained by the time she moved in: Dalí had to book appointments to see her, and the tomb that he prepared for himself lies empty (he changed his mind), guarded by a stuffed giraffe and two oversized chess knights.

Due north lies Figueres, the capital of the Alt Empordà region and Dalí's birthplace. The artist donated many of his works to the **Teatre-Museu Dalí** (Plaça Gala-Salvador Dalí 5, 972 67 75 00, www.salvador-dali.org,

closed Mon Oct-May, €11, €8 reductions; *photo above*), housed in the town's old theatre, and also redesigned the place, putting thousands of yellow loaves on the external walls and huge eggs on its towers. The highlight is the 3D room sized Mae West face, a collection of furniture arranged to look like the star when viewed from a certain angle; a plump red sofa takes the place of her famous pout. And if you're wondering what happened to Dalí's body after seeing the empty tomb at the Castell de Púbol, wonder no more: he's buried here.

East of here, on the coast, lies relatively isolated Cadaqués, another former Dalí haunt. The artist spent his childhood summers here, then brought his surrealist circle along and eventually built his home – now a museum – in nearby Port Lligat. The **Casa-Museu de Port Lligat** (972 25 10 15, www.salvador-dali.org, closed Mon 12 Feb-mid June, mid Sept-6 Jan, €11, €8 reductions; *photo p281*) is filled with zany furniture, peculiar fittings and stuffed animals, offering an extraordinary insight into the genius's lifestyle. Book ahead: only eight people are allowed in at a time.

Getting there

By bus Sarfa (902 30 20 25, www.sarfa.com) runs eight buses daily to Sant Feliu from Estació del Nord (journey time 1hr 25mins), and eight to Palafrugell (2hrs15mins); some continue to Begur. Change in Palafrugell or Torroella for L'Estartit.

The French Connection

THE NORTHERN COSTA BRAVA

By comparison to the coastal stretch further south, the northern end of the Costa Brava is quieter, more isolated and less developed. Sure, there are large tourists resorts here, and some fairly unseemly architectural development. But there's also plenty of well-preserved history, numerous beautiful landscapes and a wealth of opportunities to get away from it all.

One of the main sites of interest on this stretch is **Empúries**. Here, you'll find the remains of an ancient city dating back to 600 BC, when it was founded by the Phoenicians and before it was recolonised by the Greeks and finally the Romans. Today, ruins from all three periods – including a stunning mosaic of Medusa, as well as the layout of the original Greek harbour – are visible. It's quite a contrast with the overcrowded tourist resort of **Roses**, on the other side of the huge Golf de Roses, which has little to recommend it apart from a 16th-century citadel and the nearby legendary restaurant **El Bulli** (*see p180*) in Cala Montjoi.

From Roses, the road coils over the hills that form the **Cap de Creus** nature reserve, before dropping spectacularly down to **Cadaqués**, which has retained its charm thanks to a ban on the high-rise buildings that have blighted so much of the Spanish coastline. Dalí really put the place on the map; *see p279* **Dalí's Designs**.

On the north side of the cape, up in the windswept hills you'll find the remarkable **Sant Pere de Rodes** fortified abbey (972 38 75 59, closed Mon, admission €4.50, reductions €3, free Tue), the area's most accomplished example of Romanesque architecture. A further climb takes you up to the **Castell de Sant Salvador**, an imposing tenth-century castle that seems to grow out of the rock, with unparalleled views out over the Pyrenees to France, and back into Catalonia.

Heading back inland, the capital of the Alt Empordà region is **Figueres**, where Dalí was born and is buried in his own museum in the city's old theatre, the **Teatre-Museu Dalí** (*see p279* **Dalí's Designs**). It somewhat overshadows the city's other two fine museums: the **Museu de l'Empordà** (Rambla 2, 972 50 23 05, www.museuemporda.org, closed Mon,

admission €2, reductions €1), which gives an overview of the area's history, and the **Museu del Joguet** (C/Sant Pere 1, 972 50 45 85, www.mjc.cat, closed Mon Oct-May, admission €5, reductions €4, free under-5s, free Sun 11am-2pm), full of 19th- and early 20th-century toys, some of which belonged to Dalí and Miró.

Between Figueres and the sea sits the **Parc Natural dels Aiguamolls de l'Empordà**, a haven for rare birds that flock to the marshy lowlands at the mouth of the Fluvia river in spring and autumn. As well as flamingos and moustached warblers, this nature reserve is home to turtles, salamanders and otters.

Eating, drinking & sleeping

Next to the ruins in Empúries, the **Hostal Empúries** (Platja Portitxol, 972 77 02 07, www.hostalempuries.com, €105-€140, set menu €22) offers starchy white rooms and a new spa in a fantastic setting in front of the rocky beach. It serves good Mediterranean food all year round and arranges cookery courses. Near the beach in Sant Pere Pescador, **Ca la Caputxeta** (C/Disseminat 60, 972 25 03 10, www.caputxeta.com, €70-€85) has a lovely rustic feel and a laid-back vibe. Over the bay, a twisting drive from Roses, is the extraordinary and world-famous **El Bulli** (*see p180*). Reasonably nearby, sitting in a bay between Roses and Cadaqués, the **Hotel Cala Jóncols** (Ctra Vella de Roses a Cadaqués, 972 25 39 70, www.calajoncols.com, closed Nov-Mar, €102.50-€222 half-board per person) is isolated and no-frills. It's a blissful hideaway for those who can do without luxuries, though it does have a pool.

Cadaqués has few hotels, and most are closed in winter – call ahead. The **Hotel Rocamar** (C/Dr Bartomeus s/n 972 25 81 50, www.rocamar.com, €103-€228) is the finest hotel in Cadaqués and set away from the rest of the town, looking back over the bay. Alternatively, **Playa Sol** (Platja Pianc 3, 972 25 81 00, www.playasol.com, closed Jan-mid Feb & Dec, €77-€198) also overlooks the sea, but has more of a business feel. Smaller and slightly more basic is **Hotel Llané Petit** (Platja Llané Petit s/n, 972 25 10 20, www.llanepetit.com, closed Jan, €62-€161). It has a pretty terrace overlooking the bay, a pool, and simply decorated rooms.

Over the hill in Port Lligat, the two-star **Hotel Port Lligat** (972 25 81 62, www.port-lligat.net/hotel, closed 2wks Dec & 3wks Jan €73-€140) is right next door to the Dalí museum and has a boutiquey feel to it, while the **Hotel Calina** (Avda Salvador Dalí, 33, 972 25 88 51, www.hotelcalina.com, €71.50-€152) is more modern and more comfortable, and has a decent-sized swimming pool overlooking the

ESCAPES & EXCURSIONS

Casa-Museu de Port Lligat. *See p279.*

ESCAPES & EXCURSIONS

beach. **Restaurant Casa Nun** (Plaça Portitxó 6, 972 25 88 56, closed dinner Mon & and all day Tue-Thur Nov-Apr, mains €17) has a sea-facing terrace, lots of charm and good value set menus featuring boat-fresh fish. **Restaurant Can Rafa** (C/Passeig Marítim 7, 972 15 94 01, closed Dec; Wed Sept-June, mains €22) specialises in local lobster, while the pretty **Es Balconet** (C/Sant Antoni 2, 972 25 88 14, closed Tue and Jan, Feb & 2wks Nov, mains €16, set lunch €14.95 daily), up a winding street back from the bay, is good for paella. **Casa Anita** (C/Miguel Roset 16, 972 25 84 71, closed Mon and 3 wks Nov-Dec, mains €19) is fiercely popular (Dalí, no less, used to eat here back in the day) and serves excellent seafood.

In Figueres, the **Hotel Duran** (C/Lasauca 5, 972 50 12 50, www.hotelduran.com, €69-€99, set menu €20) was also an old haunt of Dalí, and exudes comfortable, battered elegance. The restaurant offers fine game and seafood. For clean and simple rooms, head for **La Barretina** (C/Lasauca 13, 972 67 64 12, www.hostallabarretina.com, €45-€48, set lunch €10 Mon-Fri). **President** (Avda Salvador Dalí 82, 972 50 17 00, www.hotelpresident.info, set lunch €15) offers solid Catalan fare and excellent seafood. C/Jonquera is the main drag for cheap *menús del día*, which you can sample at alfresco tables. A couple of kilometres west,

Mas Pau (Ctra de Figueres a Besalú, Avinyonet de Puigventós, 972 54 61 54, www.maspau.com, closed all Mon, lunch Tue, dinner Sun & Jan mid Mar, mains €25) is an excellent and creative restaurant.

Tourist information

Cadaqués *C/Cotxe 2A (972 25 83 15, www.cadaques.cat).* **Open** *June-Sept* 9am-9pm Mon-Sat; 10am-1pm, 5-8pm Sun. *Oct-May* 10am-1pm, 3-6pm Mon-Thur; 10am-1pm, 3-7pm Fri-Sat. **L'Escala** *Plaça de les Escoles 1 (972 77 06 03, www.lescala.cat).* **Open** *Mid June-mid Sept* 9am-8.30pm daily. *Mid Sept-mid June* 9am-1pm, 4-7pm Mon-Sat; 10am-1pm Sun. **Figueres** *Plaça del Sol s/n (972 50 31 55).* **Open** *July-Sept* 9am-8pm Mon-Sat; 10am-3pm Sun. *Oct-June* 10am-2pm, 4-7pm Mon-Fri; 10am-2pm Sat.

Getting there

By bus Sagales (902 26 06 06, www.sagales.com) runs several buses daily to Figueres from Estació del Nord (2hrs 30mins). Sarfa (902 30 20 25) runs one bus daily to Roses (2hrs 15mins) and one bus daily to Cadaqués (2hrs 45min).
By train RENFE from Sants or Passeig de Gràcia to Figueres (2hrs). Trains leave every hour.

Excursions

Beaches and ancient cities within striking distance of Barcelona.

Just a short ride from Barcelona, a very different atmosphere awaits – a world of monasteries, vineyards and market towns. You'll also find attractive and manageable cities such as **Girona** and **Tarragona**, better beaches such as those at **Sitges** or **Castelldefels** and, at **Colònia Güell**, more of Gaudí's fantastical creations. Hire a car and you'll have even more freedom to explore some of Catalonia's honey-coloured villages. But in many cases, the transport is part of the fun: take the cog-wheel train or cable car that ascends the mountain of **Montserrat** to its famous abbey.

Sandy Shores

ALONG THE COAST TO SITGES

The sands in Barcelona have become cleaner in recent years, but they can still seem grubby in comparison to those found a short train ride away. Either side of the city, up and down the coast, lie a number of beautiful beaches that make a welcome and relatively isolated break from the hurly-burly of the city itself. Add the cluster of small, handsome towns that adjoin the beaches, and you have plenty of reasons to make your escape for an afternoon or more.

About half an hour south from Passeig de Gràcia station, the **Castelldefels** is a broad strand of sand. The backdrop of urban sprawl is particularly unlovely, but there's plenty of towel space to compensate. The beach is also something of a mecca for kite-surfers, as well as other watersports. Try the **Escola Nàutica Garbí** (Passeig Marítim 271-275, mobile 609 752 175, www.escolagarbi.com) for equipment.

Two stops beyond the Castelldefels lies the tiny and relatively undiscovered port of **Garraf**. Its small curved beach is backed by green-and-white striped bathing huts, and the steep-sided mountains that surround it mean that development is not a worry. At the northern tip of the bay sits the **Celler de Garraf**, a magical Modernista creation built by Gaudí for the Güell family in 1895 but now home to a restaurant. Behind the village stretches the **Parc del Garraf** nature reserve, with hiking and biking trails (marked out on maps available from the tourist office in Sitges).

Further south along the coast, the pretty, whitewashed streets of **Sitges** do double-duty. In summer, they're packed with party-goers – since the 1960s, this has been Spain's principal gay resort, served by a hotchpotch of bars and discos (*see p252*). In winter, though, it's a different story: the scene is far more relaxed, and it's a mellow place for a getaway.

In the 19th century, the town was a fashionable retirement spot for local merchants who had made their fortunes in the Caribbean. More than 100 of the palaces owned by '*los americanos*', as they were known, are dotted around the centre of town. Pick up an excellent booklet from the tourist office, or take a tour of these houses with **Agis Sitges** (mobile 619 793 199, www.agisitges.com, €10) on Sundays.

Sitges's highest building, topping a rocky promontory, is the pretty 17th-century church of **Sant Bartomeu i Santa Tecla**, offering wonderful views of the sea. Behind the church is the extraordinary **Museu Cau Ferrat** (unfortunately closed for renovations until at least 2013); nearby is the **Palau Maricel** (C/Fonollar, 93 894 03 64, tours €10, booking essential), an old hospital that's been converted into a Modernista palace and is now used as a concert hall in summer. The building contains medieval and Baroque paintings and sensuous marble sculptures. Both are under wraps until 2011 while work is done to link the two buildings. Also worth a look is the **Museu Romàntic** in the handsome Casa Llopis (C/Sant Gaudenci 1, 93 894 29 69, closed Mon, €3.50), which portrays the lifestyle of the 19th-century family that once lived there.

Those who prefer messing about in boats are served well at the Port Esportiu Aiguadolç. The **Centro Náutico Aiguadolç-Vela** (93 811 31 05, www.advela.net) rents out sailing boats and organises sailing excursions; a private hour-long session costs €40. To escape the crowds on Platja de Sant Sebastià or those south of the town centre, head just beyond the Port of Aiguadolç to **Platja de Balmins**, a hidden oasis with an excellent restaurant (La Caleta, *see below*).

Eating & drinking

In Garraf, commandeer a terrace table at **Chiringuito del Garraf** (Avda Llorach 3, 93 632 00 16, www.restaurantlacupulagarraf.com, closed all day Wed-Fri & dinner Sat-Tue, except in July and Aug, mains €17) for a long, lazy lunch. The food is average but the location is unbeatable.

The restaurants in Sitges can be expensive (there's better value down the coast in the port of Vilanova i la Geltrú), but there are good options here. A fisherman's lunch of steamed mussels, clams, razor clams, and arròs negre doesn't come better than from friendly E l T am bucho (Port Alegre 49, Platja Sant Sebastià, 93 894 79 12, mains €22.50).

There's more seafood in the form of a tasting menu at **El Velero** (Passeig de la Ribera 38, 938 94 20 51, www.restaurantevelero.com, closed Mon, lunch Sun and 2wks Jan, mains €18), a real Sitges classic, and **La Caleta** (Platja del Balmins, 93 811 20 38, www.lacaleta desitges.es, closed Mon & Nov-Feb, mains €17), which offers great views and a more intimate vibe. R estaurant M aricel (Passeig de la Ribera 6, 93 894 20 54, www.maricel.es, mains €24) gives local produce an elegant twist. And be sure to leave time for a cava cocktail on the terrace at the delightful **Hotel Romàntic** (C/Sant Isidre 33, 93 894 83 75, www.hotel romantic.com, closed Nov-Mar.

Tourist information

Castelldefels *C/Pintor Serrasanta 4 (93 635 27 27, www.castelldefelsturismo.info).* **Open** *June-Sept* 10am-2pm, 4-8pm daily. *Oct-May* 9am-1pm, 3-6pm daily.
Sitges *Plaça Eduard Maristany 2 (93 894 42 51, www.sitgestur.com).* **Open** *mid June-mid Sept* 9am-8pm Mon-Sat. *Mid Sept-mid June* 9am-2pm, 4-6.30pm Mon-Sat.

Getting there

By bus Mon-Bus (93 893 70 60) runs a frequent service from 7.20am to 11.20pm to Sitges, and an

Sitges.

ESCAPES & EXCURSIONS

hourly night service between 12.13am and 3.13am to Ronda Universitat 33 in Barcelona.
By train Frequent trains leave from Passeig de Gràcia for Platja de Castelldefels (20mins) and Sitges (35mins), though not all stop at Castelldefels and Garraf.

From Ancient to Modern

TARRAGONA

Tárraco, as the Romans knew Tarragona, was once Catalonia's biggest powerhouse. Dating back to 218 BC, it was one of the first Roman cities to be built outside Italy; it was constructed with a flourish that ticked all the Roman boxes for hedonism, while also serving as a more sensible centre for commerce. The town is gradually being restored: modern-day Tarragona rather nattily integrates its crumbling ruins with modern town planning and an increasingly hip dining and wining scene. It's all far more appealing than the area's other main attraction: the ghastly but immensely popular **Port Aventura** theme park (977 77 90 90, www.portaventura.es), a short drive from the town.

The **Passeig Arqueològic** (Avda Catalunya, 977 24 57 96, €3), the path along the Roman walls that once ringed the city, has its entrance at **Portal del Roser**, one of three remaining towers. In the old part of town, Roman remains include the ancient Pretori – praetorium, used as both palace and government office, and reputed to have been the birthplace of Pontius Pilate. Nearby, the ruined **Circ Romans** (same admission ticket as Pretori, 977 23 01 71, €3) was where the chariot races were held, while the **Museu Nacional Arqueològic** (Plaça del Rei 5, 977 23 62 09, www.mnat.cat, closed Mon, €2.40) is home to an important collection of Roman artefacts and mosaics.

To see all of the **Catedral de Santa Maria**, not to mention an impressive collection of religious art and archaeological finds, you'll need a ticket for the **Museu Diocesà** (C/Claustre 5, 977 22 36 71, http://museu. diocesa.arquebisbattarragona.cat, closed Sun, €3.80 including audioguide, €1.20 kids 7-16; note that it's under renovation until 2012, though parts will be open). The cathedral was built on the site of a Roman temple to Jupiter, and is Catalonia's largest. The glorious cloister was built in the 12th and 13th centuries; the carvings alone are worth the trip.

Leading from the Old Town towards the sea, the **Passeig de las Palmeres** runs to the

Balcó del Mediterrani and overlooks the Roman **amphitheatre** (Parc del Miracle, 977 24 25 79). The same street also leads to the pedestrianised, shop-packed **Rambla Nova**, from where you can follow C/Canyelles to the **Fòrum** (C/Lleida, 977 24 25 01, €3) and the remains of the juridical basilica and Roman houses.

But while the town's history remains dominant, the biggest news in Tarragona in recent years has been the recent gentrification of **El Serrallo**. This old port area now boasts fountains and slick promenades, upmarket fish restaurants and, in one of the old warehouses, the **Museu del Port** (Refugi 2, Moll de Costa, 977 25 94 42, closed Mon, €3, free under-16s), displaying the usual maritime accoutrements.

Note: an all-in ticket for sites belonging to the Museu d'Història de Tarragona (MHT, www.museutgn.com) is €10 (€5 reductions, free under-16s).

Eating & drinking

In the old city, **Les Coques** (C/Sant Llorenc 15, 977 22 83 00, closed Sun, mains €18) serves traditional roast kid and cod dishes. For snacks, **Le Vin** (C/Méndez Núñez 10, 977 23 00 20, www.devins.es, closed Sun & dinner Wed, set lunch €16.85 Mon-Fri) is a new-wave tapas and wine bar showcasing the best of local produce in an upmarket setting.

In El Serrallo, the excellent **Restaurant Manolo** (C/Gravina 61-63, 977 22 34 84, closed Mon & dinner Sun, mains €21, set lunch €35 Tue-Fri) does superb fresh fish and seafood, while **Ca L'Eulàlia** (C/Sant Pere 23, 977 21 50 75, www.caleulaia.com) is small restaurant down a back street behind the port serving fresh seafood puts you right at the water's edge. Alternatively, head out of the centre to the west to **Sol-Ric** (Via Augusta 227, 977 23 20 32, closed Mon, dinner Sun & Christmas to Jan, mains €27) for sturdy post-hangover fodder.

Tourist information

Tarragona C/Major 39 (977 25 07 95, www. tarragonaturisme.cat). **Open** Mid Sept-mid June 10am-6pm Mon-Sat; 10am-2pm Sun. Mid June-mid Sept 10am-8pm Mon-Sat; 10am-2pm Sun.

Getting there

By bus Alsa (902 42 22 42, www.alsa.es) runs 7 buses daily from Barcelona Nord station, and one from Barcelona Sants station.
By train RENFE trains run from Sants or Passeig de Gràcia to Tarragona. Trains depart hourly (journey time 1hr 18mins).

Drink in the Scenery
WINE COUNTRY

An easy day trip south-west from Barcelona lie Catalonia's best-known wine regions, with a range of *denominaciones de origen* from the workaday **Penedès** to the prestigious **Priorat**. With numerous companies offering guided tours, and the wineries themselves now opening their doors to visitors, Spain is becoming a serious destination for oenophiles.

The **Penedès** comprises gently undulating hills and ancient Roman routes. It's the most accessible destination if you're limited to public transport – you can reach it in about an hour by train. At its heart is **Vilafranca**, a handsome medieval town with a lively Saturday market and the elegant 14th-century **Basílica de Santa Maria**. The town's wine museum, **Vinseum** (Plaça Jaume I 1-5, 93 890 05 82, www.vinseum.cat, closed Mon, admission €5, free 1st Sun of mth), has displays covering ancient winemaking tools, as well as a train for taking visitors out to the vineyards.

The two main wineries in the area are both owned by the Torres family and offer entertaining tours, but you'll need your own transport, or a taxi, to take you there. **Torres** (Finca El Maset, Pacs del Penedès, 93 817 74 87, www.torres.es; tours €6.10) is Penedès's largest winemaker; but for serious wine-lovers, the more cutting-edge **Jean León** (Pago Jean León, 93 899 55 12, www.jeanleon.com, admission €7, free under-18s, tours must be reserved in advance) has a sleek tasting room that looks on to a sea of vines. Nearby **Albet i Noya** (Can Vendrell de la Codina, Sant Pau d'Ordal, 93 899 48 12, www.albetinoya.com, tours €6) was Spain's first organic winery and now leads the way in restoring traditional, pre-phylloxera varietals to the area. And there's also **Can Ràfols dels Caus** (Avinyonet del Penedès, 93 897 00 13, www.canrafolsdelscaus.com, tours €15, booking necessary), which produces superb pinot noir and delightful pink bubbles and has just opened a cool new designer *bodega*.

North of here is **Sant Sadurní d'Anoia**, the capital of the Penedès cava industry: 90 per cent of Spain's cava is made here, a fact celebrated during Cava Week (www.cavatast.cat) every October. It's not a pretty town, but its wine producers are at least easily accessible on public transport. **Codorníu** (Avda Codorníu, 93 891 33 42, www.codorniu.com, admission €6, free under-3s, booking necessary), one of the largest producers, offers a theme-park style tour of its Modernista headquarters, designed by Puig i Cadafalch – a train takes visitors through parts of the 26 kilometres (16 miles) of underground cellars, finishing, of course, with a tasting. Elsewhere, **Freixenet** (C/Joan Sala 2, 93 891 70 96, www.freixenet.es, admission €6.10, booking necessary) is opposite

Catedral de Santa Maria.

ESCAPES & EXCURSIONS

Sant Sadurní station and offers free tours and tastings. You can combine a few of the wineries through **El Molí Tours** (www.elmolitours. com), which offers boozy sip-and-cycle day trips of the area.

The **Priorat** area is renowned for its full-bodied (and full-priced) red wines. Monks were producing wine here as long ago as the 11th century, but the area had been all but abandoned as a centre of viticulture when young winemaker **Álvaro Palacios** set up a tiny vineyard here in the late 1980s. He battled steep hills and a sceptical wine industry, but within a few years he won global acclaim; the region is now one of Spain's most exclusive.

The small **Alella** district, east of Barcelona, is best known for light, dry whites, but more important is **Terra Alta**: near the Priorat in Tarragona, with Gandesa as its capital, the area is famous for its heavy reds. **Montsant**, another local DO, is also growing in popularity.

Eating, drinking & sleeping

If you'd like to try terrific local wines in Vilafranca, head to the **Inzolia** wine bar and store (C/Palma 21, 93 818 19 38, www. inzolia.com, closed Sun). **El Purgatori Formatgeria** (Plaça Campanar 5, 93 892 12 63, closed lunch daily & Wed Sept-July, mains €9.50) serves *pa amb tomàquet* (bread with tomato) with charcuterie and cheese. One of the best places to eat in the Penedès is at **Cal Xim** (Plaça Subirats 5, Sant Pau d'Ordal, 93 899 30 92, www.calxim.com, closed dinner Mon-Thur, Sat, Sun, 1wk Aug & 1wk Sept, mains €16), a cheery, atmospheric spot popular with winemakers for its upmarket grilled meats. **Cal Blay** (C/Josep Rovira 27, Sant Sadurní, 93 891 00 32, www.calblay.com, closed dinner Mon-Thur & Sun, mains €15) is also excellent, serving new-wave dishes; there's a good value set lunch (€12 Mon-Fri) served in the shop-cum-café in front of the restaurant.

If you're here for an extended stay, the range of accommodation is broad. In the Penedès, the **Can Bonastre Wine Resort** (Masquefa, 93 772 87 67, www.canbonastre.com, €182-€278) stands testament to the boom in wine tourism, and even has a vinotherapy spa.

In the Priorat, **Hostal Sport** (C/Miquel Barceló 4-6, Falset, 977 83 00 78, www.hostal sport.com, €97.20-€145.80 incl breakfast) is a good town-based option. **Cal Llop** (C/Dalt 21, Gratallops, 977 83 95 02, www.cal-llop.com, €88-€157 incl breakfast, half-board available for €25 per person) offers boutique style, a modern mix of stone, wood and iron, cobalt walls and exotic flowers. Alternatively, **Mas Ardèvol** (Ctra Falset a Porrera km 5.3, mobile 630 324 578, www.masardevol.net, closed 2wks

Christmas, €85-€130, dinner €28) is more rustic, with cheerful decor and mature gardens. Both have good home cooking; alternatively, there's top-flight cuisine at **Irreductibles** (C/Font 38, Gratallops, 977 26 23 73, www. irreductibles.org, closed Tue, Wed & 2wks Feb, menu €42), the creation of acclaimed winemaker René Barbier Jr.

Tourist information

Falset *C/Bonaventura Pascó s/n (977 83 10 23, www.turismepriorat.org).* **Open** 10am-2pm, 4.30-6.30pm Mon-Sat; 11am-2pm Sun.
Sant Sadurní d'Anoia *C/Hospital 21 (93 891 31 88, www.cavatast.cat, www.turismesant sadurni.com).* **Open** *Sept-July* 10am-2pm, 4.30-6.30pm Tue-Fri; 10am-2pm Sat, Sun. *Aug* 10am-2pm Tue-Sun.
Vilafranca del Penedès *C/Cort 14 (93 818 12 54, www.turismevilafranca.com).* **Open** 4-7pm Mon; 9am-1pm, 4-7pm Tue-Fri; 9.30am-1.30pm, 4-7pm Sat; 10am-1pm Sun.

Getting there

By bus
Alt Penedès Hispano Igualadina (93 890 11 51, 902 29 29 00, www.igualdina.net) provides 8-10 buses daily to Vilafranca del Penedès from Sants. Hillsa (93 891 25 61, www.hillsabus.com) runs about 15 services daily to Sant Sadurní d'Anoia from the corner of C/Urgell and C/París.
Falset & Gandesa Hispano Igualadina (93 804 44 51). There are two buses daily from Sants.
By train Alt Penedès RENFE from Sants or Plaça Catalunya; trains hourly 6am-10pm (journey time 45mins), then taxi for Torres, Jean León and Codorníu.
Falset & Gandesa RENFE from Sants or Passeig de Gràcia to Marcà-Falset. Two trains daily (2hrs 14mins). For Gandesa, go to Mora la Nova (a further 20mins) and catch a bus.

Heaven and Hell
MONTSERRAT

It's unsurprising that Montserrat is seen as the spiritual heart of Catalonia. The vast bulbous-peaked sandstone mass, its name meaning 'jagged mountain', dominates the landscape to the west of Barcelona, its appearance lending it a mystical aura that's made it a centre of worship and veneration for centuries. These days, it's something of a tourist trap and gets unbearably crowded in the summer. But it's still a worthwhile excursion, if only for the views.

In the Middle Ages, Montserrat was an important pilgrimage destination, as the

Colònia Güell

Gaudí's unfinished yet fascinating church.

Just near Barcelona, on the western outskirts of Santa Coloma de Cervelló, stands the unusual **Colònia Güell** (C/Claudi Güell 6, 93 630 58 70, www.historia viva.net, €5, reductions €3.80, free under-10s). Textile baron Eusebi Güell commissioned Antoni Gaudí to build a garden city for the textile workers around the factory where they worked. Like so many of Gaudí's projects, it was never completed, in this case because Güell's funding ran dry – but Gaudí did finish the crypt of the church, an extraordinary achievement with a ribbed ceiling and twisted pillars, and textbook examples of Gaudí's use of the 'catenary' arch – so named for the form a chain takes when you let it hang. (You can see this most clearly in the model for the church in the Sagrada Família.) Note that the Colònia Güell is sometimes closed for private events (wedding, funeral, communion), so call ahead before making a special trip. Mass at Sat 8pm, Sun 11am and 1pm.

Benedictine monastery that sits near the top became the jewel in the crown of a politically independent fiefdom. Surrounded by a number of tiny chapels and hermitages, the monastery is still venerated by locals, who queue in the 16th-century basilica to say a prayer while kissing the orb held by **La Moreneta** (the Black Virgin). Open 7.30am-7.30pm daily, the basilica is at its most crowded around 1pm (Mon-Fri), when the celebrated boys' choir sings mass. Elsewhere in the monastery, there's a museum stocked with fine art by the likes of Picasso, Dalí, El Greco, Monet and Caravaggio, as well as collections of liturgical gold and silverware, archaeological finds and gifts for the Virgin.

If all this piety isn't to your taste, it's still worth the trip up the mountain by road,

cable car or rack railway. The tourist office gives details of walks to the various caves; among them is **Santa Cova** where the statue was discovered, reachable via the funicular or a 20-minute hike from the monastery. The most accessible hermitage is **Sant Joan**, also 20 minutes or a funicular ride away. But the most rewarding trek is the lengthy one to the 1,235-metre (4,053-foot) peak of **Sant Jeroni**, which offers 360-degree views from a vertigo-inducing platform.

Eating & drinking

Eat before you leave or bring something with you: the characterless, pricey restaurants on Montserrat are best avoided.

Montserrat. *See p286.*

Tourist information

Oficina de Turisme de Montserrat *Plaça de la Creu, Montserrat (93 877 77 77, www.montserrat visita.com).* **Open** *June-Sept* 9am-8pm daily. *Oct-May* 9am-6pm daily.

Getting there

By bus A Julià bus (93 490 40 00, www.autocares julia.es) leaves at 9.15am from Sants bus station and returns at 5pm (6pm July-Sept); journey time is 80mins.

By train FGC trains from Plaça d'Espanya run hourly from 8.36am to Montserrat-Aeri (1hr) for the cable car (every 15mins); or to Monistrol de Montserrat for the rack train (hourly) to the monastery. The last cable car/rack train is at 6pm. FGC offers all-inclusive packs which include train ticket, Cremallera, and admission to museum and exhibitions, see www.fgc.cat.

Country Life
VIC & AROUND

Just 45 minutes away by train from the centre of Barcelona, Vic provides a handy taste of Catalan rural life. The beech forests, medieval villages, steep gorges and Romanesque hermitages make this area rewarding to explore by car, on foot or by bicycle, but it's also a centre of both paragliding and hot air ballooning (for which see Osona Globus, 93 889 33 36, www.aircat.cat, €150-€160 per person).

At the town's heart is the impressive arcaded **Plaça Major**, home to a famous market (Tuesday and Saturday mornings) that's nearly as old as the town itself. It's good for picking up local basketware, terracotta pots and, of course, the town's famous *embotits* (cured sausages), which are among the best in Spain. The **Museu Episcopal** (Plaça del Bisbe Oliva 3, 93 886 93 60, www.museuepiscopal vic.com, closed Mon, admission €5, reductions €2.50, free under 10s) is worth a visit for its magnificent 12th-century murals and a superb collection of Romanesque and Gothic art.

There are also other architectural gems. In one corner of the market square is the Modernista Casa Comella; sgraffiti depicts the four seasons and was designed by Gaietà Buïgas, who was also responsible for the Monument a Colom in Barcelona. Vic also has many interesting churches, and the **Catedral de Sant Pere** contains Romanesque, Gothic and neo-classical elements, along with a set of dramatic 20th-century murals by Josep María Sert, who is buried here. The **Temple Romà**, rediscovered in 1882 when the 12th-century walls that surrounded it were knocked down, now houses a municipal gallery.

There's more of note outside the town. Following the C153 road towards Olot, **Rupit** is a lovely ancient village, built on the side of a medieval castle, its fairytale air enhanced by a precarious hanging bridge across the Ter gorge. Later building has been done so sympathetically to the style that it's difficult to tell the old from the new. Almost as lovely, and not quite as touristy, is nearby **Tavertet**.

Eating & drinking

The hotels in **Vic** are uninspiring; if you're here for a while, you're better off staying north around **Ripoll** (*see p274*). However, it does have several good restaurants, and some of the best charcuterie this side of France. **El Caliu** (C/Riera 13, 93 889 52 71, www.elcaliuvic.com, closed dinner Tue & Sun, all day Mon, set menu €10 Tue-Fri) specialises in traditional carns a la brasa, torrades, and so on. **Cardona 7** (C/Cardona 7, 93 886 38 15, tapas €7.50, closed lunch Tue-Fri, dinner Sun & all day Mon), serves new-wave tapas such as pig's trotter salad and salt cod in rosemary. **Boccatti** (C/Mossèn Josep Gudiol 21, 93 889 56 44, closed dinner Sun & Wed, all day Thur, mains €18) has surprisingly good seafood in an old-fashioned bar-restaurant run by a delightful husband-and-wife team.

Tourist information

Vic *C/Ciutat 4 (93 886 20 91, www.victurisme.cat).* **Open** 10am-2pm, 4-8pm Mon-Fri; 10am-2pm, 4-7pm Sat; 10.30am-1.30pm Sun.

Getting there

By bus Empresa Sagalés (902 13 00 14, 93 889 25 77) runs hourly buses from Estació del Nord and/or C/Casp 30 (journey time 1hr10mins) to Vic. For Rupit, take a local bus from Vic.
By train RENFE from Sants or Plaça Catalunya to Vic. Trains leave about every hour. Journey time is 1hr 20mins.

An Urban Getaway

GIRONA

For travellers in search of big-city facilities without big-city stress, Girona is a classy compromise. The city combines a healthy dose of culture with more hedonistic pursuits: within its beautifully restored medieval heart sits an imposing cathedral and some interesting museums. In addition, some of the region's best restaurants can be found here, along with a handful of smart bars.

The **River Onyar** divides the Old City from the new, and connects one to the other by the impressive Eiffel-designed bridge, the **Pont de les Peixateries**. A walk up the lively riverside **Rambla de la Llibertat** takes you towards the city's core and its one major landmark, the magnificent **cathedral** (Plaça del Catedral, 972 21 58 14, www.catedral degirona.org, €5, € 3 during mass, when you can only visit the treasury and cloister). The building's 1680 Baroque façade conceals a graceful Romanesque cloister and understated Gothic interior, which boasts the widest nave in Christendom. In the cathedral treasury is the stunning 12th-century **Tapestry of Creation** and the **Beatus**, an illuminated set of tenth-century manuscripts.

Before their expulsion in 1492, the city's many Jews had their own district: the Call, whose labyrinthine streets running off and around the C/Força are among the most beautifully preserved in Europe. The story of the community is told in the Jewish museum in the **Centre Bonastruc ça Porta** (C/Força 8,

Rupit.

ESCAPES & EXCURSIONS

Girona.

steps, **Le Bistrot** (Pujada Sant Domènec 4, 972 21 88 03, mains €8, menu €14 Mon-Fri, €20 Sat-Sun), offers a cheap, tasty set lunch in a pretty setting. The **Enoteca Gastaldi** (Plaça de Sant Pere 5, 972 00 35 38, closed Sat lunch & all day Sun, mains €15, set lunch menu €20 Mon-Fri, set dinner €30 Mon-Sat) has a pleasant walled terrace, and serves sophisticated tapas, such as baked artichoke hearts and spoonfuls of foie. **Mimolet** (C/Pou Rodó 12, 972 20 21 24, www.mimolet.net, closed Mon & Sun, set lunch €17.90 Tue-Fri, mains €18.50) is one of the city's most talked-about restaurants, serving excellent creative cooking and superb desserts.

The city's oldest restaurant is **Casa Marieta** (Plaça de la Independència 5-6, 972 20 10 16, www.casamarieta.com, closed Mon, mains €12), over the river from the old town. Also in the new town, an old Modernista flour factory houses **La Farinera** (Ptge Farinera Teixidor 4, 972 22 02 20, menu €9), which has good tapas.

Tourist information

Girona *C/Joan Maragall 2 (872 97 59 75, www.girona.cat/turisme).* **Open** 9am-8pm Mon-Sat; 9am-2pm Sun.

Getting there

By bus Sagalés (902 26 06 06, www.sagales.com) runs approximately five buses daily (three on Sun) from Estació del Nord.
By train RENFE from Sants or Passeig de Gràcia (approx 1hr20mins). Trains leave hourly, 6am-9.15pm.

972 21 67 61, www.girona.cat/call), built on the site of a 15th-century synagogue.

Heading north from here, the **Mudéjar Banys Àrabs** (C/Ferran el Catòlic, 972 21 32 62, www.banysarabs.cat) is actually a Christian creation, a 12th-century bathhouse blending Romanesque and Moorish architecture. The nearby monastery of **Sant Pere de Galligants** is a fine example of Romanesque architecture, its beautiful 12th-century cloister rich with intricate carvings. It also houses the **Museu Arqueològic** (C/Santa Llúcia 8, 972 20 26 32, www.mac.cat, closed Mon), which shows day-to-day objects from the Paleolithic to the Visigothic periods. Continuing from here, the **Passeig Arqueològic** runs along what's left of the old city walls, intact until 1892.

Eating & drinking

The best restaurant in town, and one of the best in Spain, is the **Celler de Can Roca** (C/Can Sunyer 48, 972 22 21 57, www.cellercanroca.com, closed Mon, Sun & 3wks Dec/Jan, mains €42). Located in a quiet suburb, it's been cited by *Restaurant* magazine as one of the world's best 100 restaurants for its innovative dishes. Booking is essential.

For more low-key dining, **Massana** (C/Bonastruc de Porta 10, 972 21 38 20, closed dinner Tue, all day Sun & 2wks Dec-Jan, 1wk Aug, mains €35) offers a more affordable alternative. Halfway up a medieval flight of

> ### INSIDE TRACK
> ### MAKING HISTORY
>
> For all Girona's handsome charm, it also boasts a couple of unusual museums that take very different approaches to the past. At the **Museu D'Història de la Ciutat** (C/Força 27, 972 22 22 29, www.girona.cat/museuciutat, closed Mon), housed in an 18th-century monastery, look out for the alcoves with ventilated seating on the ground floor: this is where the deceased monks were placed to dry out for two years, before their mummified corpses were put on display. And over at eccentric **Museu del Cinema** (C/Sèquia 1, 972 41 27 77, www.museudelcinema.org, closed Mon exc July and Aug), meanwhile, you'll find a fascinating collection of early animation techniques right through to those of the present day.

Directory

CCCB. *See p72.*

Getting Around

Barcelona's centre is compact and easily explored on foot. Bicycles are good for the Old City and port: there is a decent network of bike lanes across the city. The metro and bus systems are best for longer journeys. Cars can be a hindrance: there's little parking, and most of the city is given over to an array of one-way systems.

For transport outside Barcelona, *see p268.*

ARRIVING & LEAVING

By air

AEROPORT DE BARCELONA
902 40 47 04 , www.aena.es.
Barcelona's airport is at El Prat, south-west of the city. There are now two main terminals: the new Terminal 1 (known as T1), and Terminal 2 (T2). The latter comprises the old terminals formerly called A, B and C, and now called T2A, T2B and T2C. Tourist information desks can be found in T1 and T2B, and currency exchanges are in both terminals. The map (download it from www.emt-amb.com) details all bus and train routes to the airport.

Note that passengers travelling from T1 to countries outside the Schengen Agreement (including the UK and Ireland) cannot access the shopping and restaurant areas once they've passed through passport control. However, there is a café that's accessible to all.

AEROBÚS The airport bus (010, www.aerobusbcn.com) runs two routes from Plaça Catalunya: bus A1 for Terminal 1, and bus A2 for Terminal 2 (which makes two stops: at Terminals 2B and 2C; it's a 5- to 10-minute walk to Terminal 2A). Both services depart from Plaça Catalunya (in front of El Corte Inglés), with stops at C/Sepúlveda and Plaça Espanya. The A1 bus runs every 5-10mins, leaving the Plaça Catalunya 5.30am-12.30am daily, returning from the airport at 6.10am-1.05am daily. The A2 bus runs every 10-20mins, leaving the airport 6am-1am daily, returning from Plaça Catalunya 5.30am-12.30am daily. The trip (A1 and A2) takes 35-45mins. A single costs €5.05, a return (valid six days) costs €8.75.

CITY BUSES Bus 46 runs between Plaça Espanya and the airport every half hour. The service leaves from Plaça Espanya between 5am-12.15am daily. From the airport the first is at 5.30am and the last at 12.45am. Journey time is about 45mins.

At night, the N17 runs every 20 minutes between both airport terminals (from 9.50pm T1, from 10.01pm T2) and Plaça Catalunya (from 11pm), with several stops on the way, including Plaça d'Espanya and Plaça Universitat. Last departures are at 4.50am from T1, 5.01am from T2. Journey time is 45mins.

AIRPORT TRAINS The long overhead walkway between terminals 2A and 2B leads to the train station. The Cercanías train (R2 Nord) leaves the airport at 08 and 38 mins past the hour (except the first train, which leaves at 5.42am) until 11.38pm, stopping at Barcelona Sants and Passeig de Gràcia. Trains to the airport leave Barcelona Sants at 09 and 39 mins past the hour (except the first train, which leaves at 5.35am), until 11.09pm daily (7mins earlier from Passeig de Gràcia, departing at 02 and 28 mins past the hour). The journey takes 18-25mins and costs €1.60 one way (no return tickets). Tickets are valid only for 2hrs after purchase (902 32 03 20, www.renfe.es/cercanias. The T-10 Zone 1 metro pass (*see right*) is also valid.

TAXIS The basic taxi fare to town should be €20-€26, including a €3.10 airport supplement (the minimum fare from the airport is €20 including all supplements.) Fares are about 15 per cent higher after 8pm and at weekends. There is a €1 supplement for each large piece of luggage placed in the car boot. All licensed cab drivers use the ranks outside the terminals.

By bus

Most long-distance coaches (national and international) stop or terminate at Estació d'Autobusos Barcelona-Nord (C/Ali Bei 80, 902 26 06 06, www.barcelonanord.com, map p327 J9). The Estació d'Autobusos Barcelona-Sants at

C/Viriat is only a secondary stop for many coaches, though some international Eurolines services (93 367 44 00, www.eurolines.es) both begin and end at Sants.

By car

The easiest way to central Barcelona from almost all directions is the Ronda Litoral, the coastal half of the ring road. Take exit 21 (Paral·lel) if you're coming from the south, or exit 22 (Via Laietana) from the north. Motorways also feed into Avda Diagonal, Avda Meridiana and Gran Via, which all lead to the city centre. Tolls are charged on most of the main approach routes, payable in cash (the lane marked 'manual'; motorbikes are charged half) or by credit card ('automatic'). For more on driving in Barcelona, *see pp294-295.*

By rail

Most long-distance services run by the Spanish state railway company RENFE leave from Barcelona-Sants station, easily reached by metro. A few services from the French border or south to Tarragona stop at the Estació de França in the Born, which is otherwise sparsely served. Many trains stop at Passeig de Gràcia, which can be the handiest for the city centre and also has a metro stop.

RENFE operate the high-speed service AVE (Alta Velocidad) between Barcelona Sants station and Madrid, via Zaragoza, Lleida and Camp de Tarragona. Travelling at speeds averaging 300km per hour, AVE whisks travellers to the capital in about 2hrs 50mins. A single ticket to Madrid starts from €115 but there are special deals if you book online and in advance.

RENFE *902 320 320, www. renfe.es.* **Open** 24hrs daily. **Credit** AmEx, MC, V.
Some English-speaking operators. RENFE tickets can be bought online, at stations and travel agents, or reserved over the phone, and either collected from ticket machines at the train station or delivered for a small fee.

By sea

Balearic Islands ferries dock at the Moll de Barcelona quay, at the bottom of Avda Paral·lel; Acciona Trasmediterránea (902 45 46 45, www.trasmediterranea.es) is the main operator.

Grimaldi Lines runs a ferry a day from Monday to Saturday (also on Sundays in August) between Barcelona and Civitavecchia (near Rome), which also stops at Porto Torres in Sardinia, as well as a service to Livorno (Tuscany) three times a week (902 53 13 33, www.grimaldi-ferries.com).

Cruise ships use several berths around the harbour. The PortBus shuttle service (93 415 60 20) runs every 15 mins between them and the bottom of La Rambla when ships are in port.

MAPS

For street, local train and metro maps, *see pp320-335*. Tourist offices provide a reasonable free street map, or a better-quality map for €1. Metro maps (ask for *un plano/un plànol del metro*) are available free at all metro stations; bus maps can be obtained from the main Oficines d'Informació Turística (*see p304*). There's also an excellent interactive street map at www.bcn.cat/guia.

PUBLIC TRANSPORT

Barcelona's public transport is now highly integrated, with units on multi-journey tickets valid for up to three changes of transport (within 75mins) on bus, tram, local train and metro lines. The metro is generally the quickest and easiest way of getting around the city. All metro lines operate from 5am to midnight Monday to Thursday, Sunday and public holidays; 5am to 2am on Friday; and non-stop on Saturday. Buses run all night, to areas not covered by the metro system. Local buses and the metro are run by the city transport authority (TMB). Two underground lines connect with the metro, run by Catalan government railways, the FGC. One runs north from Plaça Catalunya; the other west from Plaça d'Espanya to Cornellà. There are six tramlines following two main routes (www.trambcn.com), though they're of limited use to visitors.

FGC INFORMATION *Vestíbule, Plaça Catalunya FGC station (93 205 15 15, www.fgc.net)*. **Open** 7am-9pm Mon-Fri. **Map** p328 C1. **Other locations** FGC Plaça d'Espanya. **Open** 9am-2pm, 4pm-7pm Mon-Fri.

TMB INFORMATION *Main vestíbule, Metro Universitat, Eixample (93 318 70 74, www.tmb.net)*. **Open** 8am-8pm Mon-Fri. **Map** p328 A1. **Other locations** vestíbule, Metro Sants Estació and Sagrada Família; vestíbule, Metro Diagonal, Metro Sagrera.

Fares & tickets

Journeys in the Barcelona urban area have a flat fare of €1.40, but multi-journey tickets (*targetes/tarjetas*) are better value. The basic ten-trip *targeta* is the T-10 (*Te-Deu* in Catalan, *Te-Diez* in Spanish), which can be shared by any number of people travelling simultaneously; the ticket is validated in the machines on the metro, train or bus once per person per journey.

Along with the other integrated *targetes* listed below, the T-10 offers access to all five of the city's main transport systems (local RENFE and FGC trains within the main metropolitan area, the metro, the tram and buses). To transfer, insert your card into a machine a second time; unless 75mins have elapsed since your last journey, no other unit will be deducted. Single tickets do not allow free transfers.

You can buy T-10s in newsagents and Servi-Caixa cashpoints, as well as on the metro and train systems (from machines or the ticket office), but not on buses. More expensive versions of all *targetes* take you to the outer zones of the metropolitan region, but the prices listed below will get you anywhere in central Barcelona, and to the key sights on the outskirts of the city itself.

INTEGRATED TARGETES

T-10 Valid for ten trips; each strip can be shared by two or more people. €7.95.
T-Dia A one-day travelcard. €6.
T-Mes Valid for any 30-day period. €49.30.
T-Trimestre Valid for three months. €135.50.
T-50/30 Gives 50 trips in any 30-day period; but can only be used by one person. €32.40.
T-Familiar Gives 70 trips in any 30-day period; can be shared. €46.75.
T-Jove Valid for three months; for under-21s, or students under 25. €115.

OTHER TARGETES

2, 3, 4 & 5 Dies Two-, three-, four- and five-day travelcards on

the metro, buses and FGC trains. Also sold at tourist offices. €11.20, €15.90, €20.40 and €24.10.
Barcelona Card A tourist scheme offering unlimited use of public transport for up to five days (www.barcelonacard.com).

Buses

Many bus routes originate in or pass through Plaça Catalunya, Plaça Universitat and Plaça Urquinaona. However, they often run along parallel streets, due to the city's one-way system. Not all stops are labelled, and street signs are not always easy to locate.

Most routes run 5.30am-11.30pm daily except Sundays. There's usually a bus every 10-15mins, but they're less frequent before 8am, after 9pm and on Saturdays. On Sundays, buses are less frequent still; a few do not run at all. Only single tickets can be bought from the driver; if you have a *targeta*, insert it into the machine behind the driver as you board.

NIGHT BUSES There are 17 urban night bus (*Nitbus*) routes (010, or EMT), most running from around 10.30-11.30pm to 4.30-6am nightly, with buses every 20-30mins, plus an hourly bus to the airport; *see left*. Most pass through Plaça Catalunya. Fares and *targetes* are as for daytime buses. Plaça Catalunya is also the terminus of all night bus services linking Barcelona with more distant parts of its metropolitan area.

Local trains

Regional trains to Sabadell, Terrassa and other towns beyond Tibidabo depart from FGC Plaça Catalunya, those for Montserrat from FGC Plaça d'Espanya.

All trains on the RENFE local network ('Rodalies/Cercanías') stop at Sants but can also be caught at either Plaça Catalunya and Arc de Triomf (for Vic and the Pyrenees, Manresa, the Penedès and Costa del Maresme) or Passeig de Gràcia (for the southern coastal line to Sitges and the Girona-Figueres line north).

Metro

The metro is the easiest way to get around Barcelona. There are eight lines, each colour coded. For tickets and running times, *see above*; for a map, *see pp334-335*.

Trams

Lines T1, T2 and T3 go from Plaça Francesc Macià, Zona Alta, to the outskirts of the city. T4 is the most useful line for visitors and runs from Ciutadella-Vila Olímpica (also a metro stop), via Glòries and the Fòrum. T5 and T6 run north to Badalona.

All trams are fully accessible for wheelchair-users and are part of the integrated TMB *targeta* system. You can buy integrated tickets and single tickets from the machines at tram stops.

TRAM INFORMATION *Trambaix (902 19 32 75, www.trambcn.com).* **Open** *July, Aug* Mon-Fri 8am-3pm. *Sept-June* 9am-2pm, 4-7pm Mon-Thur; 9am-2pm Fri.

TAXIS

It's usually easy to find one of the 10,500 black-and-yellow taxis. There are ranks at railway and bus stations, in main squares and throughout the city, but taxis can also be hailed on the street when they show a green light on the roof and a sign saying *lliure/libre* ('free') behind the windscreen. Information on taxi fares, ranks and regulations can be found at www.taxibarcelona.cat.

Fares

Current rates and supplements are shown inside cabs on a sticker on the rear side window (in English). The basic fare for a taxi hailed in the street is €2, which is what the meter should register when you set off. The basic rates (90¢/km) apply 8am-8pm Mon-Fri; at other times, including public holidays, the rate is €1.15/km.

There are supplements for luggage (€1), for the airport (€3.10), Sants train station (€2.10), and the port (€2.10), and for nights such as New Year's Eve (€3.10), as well as a waiting charge. Taxi drivers are not required to carry more than €20 in change; few accept credit cards. There is a €2 supplement from midnight to 6am on Friday, Saturday and Sunday. And if a public holiday falls on one of these days, there's an additional €3.10 supplement.

Radio cabs

These companies take bookings 24 hours daily. Phone cabs start the meter when a call is answered but, by the time it picks you up, it should not display more than €3.40

(€4.20 at night, weekends or public holidays). Note that a minimum fare applies for radio cabs (€7). Supplements are added at the end of the journey.

BARNATAXI 93 322 22 22.
FONO-TAXI 93 300 11 00.
RÀDIO TAXI '033' or 93 303 30 33.
SERVI-TAXI 93 330 03 00.
TAXI GROC 93 358 11 11.
TAXI MIRAMAR 93 433 10 20.

Receipts & complaints

To get a receipt, ask for *un rebut/un recibo*. It should include the fare, the taxi number, the driver's NIF (tax) number, the licence plate, the driver's signature and the date; if you have a complaint insist on all these, and the more details (time, route) the better. Complaints must be filed in writing to the Institut Metropolità del Taxi (93 223 51 51 ext 2168, www.taxibarcelona.cat).

DRIVING

For information (only in Catalan or Spanish) on driving in Catalonia, call the Servei Català de Trànsit (93 567 40 00); the local government's information line (012), which has English speakers; or see www.gencat.net/transit. Driving in the city can be intimidating and time-consuming. If you do drive:
● Keep your driving licence, vehicle registration and insurance documents with you at all times.
● Do not leave anything of value, including car radios, in your car. Foreign plates can attract thieves.
● Be on your guard at motorway service areas, and take care to avoid thieves in the city who may try to make you stop, perhaps by indicating you have a flat tyre.

Breakdown services

If you're planning to take a car, join a motoring organisation such as the AA (www.theaa.com) or the RAC (www.rac.co.uk) in the UK, which usually have reciprocal agreements.

RACE (REAL AUTOMÓVIL CLUB DE ESPAÑA) *902 40 45 45, 24hr help 902 30 05 05, or 91 593 33 33 from abroad, www.race.es.*

Car & motorbike hire

Car hire is relatively pricey, but it's a competitive market, so shop around. Ideally, you want unlimited mileage, VAT (IVA) included and full insurance cover (*seguro sense*

risc/seguro todo riesgo) rather than the third-party minimum (*seguro obligatori/seguro obligatorio*). You'll need a credit card as a guarantee. Most companies require you to have had a licence for at least a year; many also enforce a minimum age limit.

EUROPCAR *Plaça dels Països Catalans, Sants (93 491 48 22, reservations 902 10 50 30, www.europcar.com). Metro Sants Estació.* **Open** 7am-11pm Mon-Fri; 8am-10pm Sat, Sun. **Credit** AmEx, MC, V. **Map** p325 B7.
Other locations Airport terminals 1 and 2B (902 105 055); C/Viladomat 214, Eixample (93 439 84 03); Gran Via de les Corts Catalanes 680, Eixample (93 302 05 43).
MOTISSIMO *C/Comandante Benítez 25, Sants (93 490 84 01, www.motissimo.es). Metro Badal.* **Open** 9am-1.30pm, 4-8pm Mon-Fri; 9am-1.30pm Sat. **Credit** AmEx, MC, V. **Map** p321 A5.
PEPECAR *C/Rivadeneyra, underground car park (807 41 42 43, www.pepecar.com). Metro Catalunya.* **Open** 8am-8pm Mon-Sat; 8am-10pm Sun. **Credit** AmEx, MC, V. **Map** p328 C2.
VANGUARD *C/Viladomat 297, Eixample (93 439 38 80, www.vanguardrent.com). Metro Hospital Clínic.* **Open** 8am-1.30pm, 4-7.30pm Mon-Fri; 9am-1pm Sat, Sun. **Credit** MC, V. **Map** p321 D6.

Legal requirements

For driving laws and regulations (in Spanish), see the Ministry of Interior's website (www.dgt.es).

Parking

Parking is fiendishly complicated and municipal police are quick to hand out tickets or tow cars. In some parts of the Old City, access is limited to residents for much of the day. In some Old City streets, time-controlled bollards pop up, meaning your car may get stuck. Never park in front of doors marked 'Gual Permanent', indicating an entry with 24-hour right of access.

PAY & DISPLAY AREAS The Àrea Verda contains zones only for use of residents (most of the Old City and centre of Gràcia – look out for 'Àrea residents' signs). Elsewhere in central Barcelona, non-residents pay €2.42/hr with a 1hr, 2hr or 3hr maximum stay.

If you overstay by no more than an hour, you can cancel the fine by paying an extra €6; to do so, press

Anul·lar denùncia on the machine, insert €6, then press Ticket. Some machines accept cards (AmEx, MC, V); none accepts notes or gives change. For information, check www.bcn.cat/areaverda or call 010. There's a drop-in centre for queries on the ground floor of the Ajuntament building on Plaça Carles Pi i Sunyer 8-10, open 8.30am-5.30pm Mon-Fri.

CAR PARKS Car parks (*parkings*) are signalled by a white 'P' on a blue sign. Those run by SABA (Plaça Catalunya, Plaça Urquinaona, Rambla de Catalunya, Avda Catedral, airport and elsewhere; 93 230 56 00, 902 28 30 80, www.saba.es) cost around €2.75/hr. Discount and long-stay passes (from 6-12hrs) are available in packs of 10 units. SMASSA car parks (Plaça Catalunya 23, C/Hospital 25-29, Avda Francesc Cambó 10, Passeig de Gràcia 60 and elsewhere; 93 409 20 21, www.bsmsa.cat/mobilitat, for location of car parks, see www.ona parcar.bcn.es) cost €2.30-€2.80/hr.

TOWED VEHICLES If police tow your car, they should leave a triangular sticker on the pavement where it was. The sticker should let you know to which pound it's been taken. If not, call 901 513 151; staff generally don't speak English. Recovering your vehicle within 4hrs costs €150.70, with each extra hour costing €1.96, or €19.50/day. You'll also have to pay a fine. You'll need your passport and documentation, or rental contract, to prove ownership. www.bsmsa.cat has information in Catalan and Spanish.

CYCLING

There's a network of bike lanes (*carrils bici*) along major avenues and alongside the seafront; local authorities are very keen to promote cycling. Be warned that bike theft is rife: always carry a good lock. For information see www.bcn.cat/bicicleta. There are bike hire shops all over the city; also, *see below* **Un Cotxe Menys**.

TOURS

Another way to get around is to hire a Trixi rickshaw (www.trixi.com). Running 11am-8pm, March to November, and costing €10 per half-hour, they can be hailed on the street, or by calling 93 310 13 79. There are several tours, including a 15min Barri Gòtic tour and a 90min Gaudí tour (€25 for two people).

By bike

UN COTXE MENYS *C/Esparteria 3, Born (93 268 21 05, www.bicicletabarcelona.com). Metro Jaume I.* **Open** 10am-7pm daily. **Tours** 11am daily, plus *Apr-Sept* 4.30pm Mon, Fri-Sun. **Rates** *Tours* €22. **Hire** €5 1hr; €10 half-day; €15 1 day; €55 1wk. **No credit cards. Map** p329 E7. Meet in Plaça Sant Jaume and then head to the nearby shop for bikes and helmets followed by a three-hour English-speaking tour.

FAT TIRE BIKE TOURS *C/Escudellers 48 (93 301 36 12, http://fattirebiketours.com/barcelona). Metro Drassanes.* **Tours** *Feb-mid Apr, Nov-mid Dec* 11am daily. *Mid Apr-Oct* 11am, 4pm daily. **Rates** *Tours* €22. **Hire** €6/2 hrs; €10/5hrs; €15/1 day. **Credit** MC, V (tours only). **Map** p329 C6. Tours meet in Plaça Sant Jaume and last over four hours, taking in the Old City, Sagrada Família, Ciutadella park and the beach.

By bus

BARCELONA CITY TOURS *93 261 56 79, www.barcelonacity tour.cat.* **Tours** *Nov-May* 9am-7pm daily; every 15-20mins. *June-Oct* 9am-8pm daily; every 8-10mins. **Tickets** *1 day* €23; €14-€18 reductions. *2 days* €30; €18-€22 reductions. Free under-4s. Available on bus. **Credit** MC, V. Though more frequent, off-season, than rival Bus Turístic, there are no discounts offered to attractions. There are two routes: the East route takes in Montjuïc, Camp Nou and La Pedrera; the West route takes in the seafront and the Fòrum, the Sagrada Família and La Pedrera. Both circuits take around 2hrs. **BUS TURÍSTIC** *93 285 38 32, www.tmb.net.* **Tours** *Apr-Oct* 9am-8pm daily; approx every 6-10mins. *Nov-Mar* 9am-7pm daily; approx every 25mins. **Tickets** *1 day* €23; €14 reductions. *2 days* €30; €18 reductions. Free under-4s. Available from tourist office (credit MC, V) or on bus (no credit cards). Bus Turístic (white and blue, with colourful images of the sights) runs three circular routes. Tickets are valid for all routes and ticket-holders get discount vouchers for a range of attractions. **BUS TURÍSTIC DE NIT** *93 285 38 32, www.tmb.net.* **Tours** *June-Sept* 9.30pm (boarding from 9.10pm) Fri-Sun. **Tickets** €17; €10 reductions. Available from tourist offices or on bus. **No credit cards.**

The night tour bus (with guided commentary) is designed to show off the illuminations of the city.

On foot

BARCELONA WALKING TOURS *93 285 38 32, www.barcelona turisme.com.* **Tours** (in English) *Gothic* 10am daily. *Picasso* 4pm Tue, Thur, Sat. *Modernisme June–Sept* 6pm Fri, Sat. *Oct-May* 4pm Fri, Sat. *Marina* 10am Fri, Sat. *Gourmet* 10am Fri, Sat. **Tickets** *Gothic, Modernisme* €12.50; €5 reductions. *Picasso, Gourmet* (reservations essential) €19; €7 reductions. *Marina* €16; €6 reductions. **No credit cards. Map** p328 C2. Tours take 90mins to 2hrs, excluding the museum trip. Modernisme, Gourmet and Picasso tours start in the underground tourist office in Plaça Catalunya; Marina tour starts at the Mirador de Colom, Plaça Portal de la Pau. Gothic tour starts at the tourist office in the Ajuntament, Plaça Sant Jaume. There is a 10% discount for booking online. Also offer shopping tours, literary tours, a guided tour of Park Güell, night tours of the Gothic Quarter, and a scenic Collserola tour; check website for details. **MY FAVOURITE THINGS** *mobile 637 265 405, www.myft.net.* Unusual outings (€26) that include walking tours for families with children, urban design tours, and romantic tours for couples, plus a one-day wine tasting tour in the Priorat (€155) **RUTA DEL MODERNISME** *93 317 76 52, www.rutadelmodernisme. com.* **Rates** €12. Not so much a route as a guidebook to 115 Modernista buildings, giving discounts on entry. It's available at the Plaça Catalunya tourist office (*see p304*), the Hospital Sant Pau and the Pavellons Güell.

By scooter

BARCELONA SCOOTER TOURS *Cooltra Motos, Passeig Joan de Borbó 80-84, Barceloneta (93 221 40 70, www.cooltra.com). Metro Barceloneta.* **Tours** 10.30am Sat, 3.30pm Thur. **Rates** €50 3hr30min tour; €99 *Shadow of the Wind* 7hr tour. **Hire** €35 for 24hrs, inc basic insurance. **Credit** AmEx, MC, V. **Map** p326 G13. There's a 4hr tour, a shorter express ('highlights') tour, a tour on a Harley-Davidson and a full-day *Shadow of the Wind* tour. Note that you must have at least three years' driving experience. Book 24hrs ahead.

DIRECTORY

Resources A-Z

DIRECTORY

ADDRESSES

Most apartment addresses consist of a street name followed by a street number, floor level and flat number, in that order. So, to go to C/València 246, 2º 3ª, find No.246, go to the second floor and find the door marked 3 or 3ª. Ground-floor flats are usually called *baixos* or *bajos* (often abbreviated bxs/bjos); one floor up, the *entresol/entresuelo* (entl), and the next is often the *principal* (pral). Confusingly, numbered floors start here: first, second, up to the *àtic/ático* at the top. Addresses occasionally point out whether a property number is on the left- or right-hand side of the street; 'right' is *dreta/derecha* (dta/dcha) and 'left' is *esquerra/izquierda* (esq/izq).

AGE RESTRICTIONS

Buying/drinking alcohol 18.
Driving 18.
Smoking 18.
Sex (hetero- and homosexual) 13.

ATTITUDE & ETIQUETTE

The Catalans are generally less guarded about personal space than people in Britain or the US. The common greeting between members of the opposite sex and between two women, even the first time that the two parties have met, is a kiss on both cheeks. Men usually greet each other by shaking hands. Don't be surprised if people bump into you on the street, or crowd or push past you on the bus or metro without apologising: it's not seen as rude.

Contrary to appearances, Catalans have an advanced queuing culture. They may not stand in an orderly line, but they're normally

very aware of when it's their turn, particularly at market stalls. The standard drill is to ask when you arrive, *¿Qui es l'últim/la última?* ('Who's last?'), and say *jo* ('me') to the next person who asks.

BUSINESS

Admin services

The *gestoria*, a Spanish institution is designed to lighten the weight of local bureaucracy by dealing with it for you. A combination of bookkeeper, lawyer and business adviser, a good *gestor* can be helpful in handling paperwork.
CMB ASSESSORS *C/Aribau 226, pral 2ª, Eixample (93 209 67 88). Metro Diagonal/FGC Gràcia.* **Open** *Oct-June* 9am-2pm, 4-7pm Mon-Fri; *July-Sept* 9am-2pm, 4-7pm Mon-Thur; 9pm-2pm Fri. Closed 2wks Aug. **Map** p322 F5.
Lawyers, economists and a *gestoria*.
MARTIN HOWARD ASSOCIATES *C/Aribau 177, entl 1ª, Eixample (93 202 25 34, www.mhasoc.com).* **Open** *Sept-July* 9am-6pm Mon-Thur; 9am-2pm Fri. *Aug* 8am-3pm Mon-Fri. **Map** p322 F5.
Tax and accounts from British accountant Alex Martin.

Conventions & conferences

BARCELONA CONVENTION BUREAU *Rambla Catalunya 123, pral, Eixample (93 368 97 00, www.barcelonaturisme.com). Metro Diagonal.* **Open** *Sept-mid June* 9am-2.30pm, 3.30-6.30pm Mon-Thur; 9am-3pm Fri. *Mid June-Aug* 8am-3pm Mon-Fri. **Map** p322 F6.
FIRA DE BARCELONA *Avda Reina Maria Cristina, Montjuïc (93 233 20 00, www.firabcn.cat). Metro Espanya.* **Open** *Mid Sept-*

mid June 9am-1.30pm, 3.30-5.30pm Mon-Fri. *Mid June-mid Sept* 9am-2pm Mon-Fri. **Map** p325 B9.
One of Europe's largest exhibition complexes.
WORLD TRADE CENTER *Moll de Barcelona 1a, Edifici Est, (93 508 88 88, www.wtcbarcelona.com). Metro Drassanes.* **Open** 8.30am-7pm Mon-Fri. **Map** p326 F13.
130,000sq m (72,624sq ft) of office space in a modern complex.

Courier services

ESTACIÓ D'AUTOBUSOS BARCELONA-NORD *C/Alí Bei 80, Eixample (93 232 43 29). Metro Arc de Triomf.* **Open** 7.30am-2.30pm, 4.30-7.30pm Mon-Fri. **No credit cards**. **Map** p327 J9.
MISSATGERS TRÈVOL *C/Antonio Ricardos 14, La Sagrera (93 498 80 70, www.trevol.com). Metro Sagrera.* **Open** 8am-7pm Mon-Thur, 8am-5pm Fri. **No credit cards**.
SEUR *93 336 85 85, www.seur.es.* **Open** 8.30am-7pm Mon-Fri. **Credit** V.
UPS *902 88 88 20, www.ups.com.* **Open** 8am-8pm Mon-Fri; 9am-2pm Sat. **Credit** AmEx, MC, V.

Office services

See p189 for computer shops.

CENTRO DE NEGOCIOS *C/Pau Claris 97, 4º 1ª, Eixample (93 304 38 58, www.centro-negocios.com). Metro Passeig de Gràcia.* **Open** *Sept-July* 8am-9pm Mon-Fri. *Aug* 9am-2pm Mon-Fri. **No credit cards**. **Map** p326 G8.
Desks in shared offices, mailboxes, meeting rooms, secretarial services and administrative services.

MICRORENT *C/Rosselló 35, Eixample (93 363 32 50, www. microrent.es). Metro Entença.* **Open** *Sept-June* 9am-6pm Mon-Fri. *July, Aug* 8am-3pm Mon-Fri. **No credit cards. Map** p325 C6. Computer and audiovisual equipment for rent.

Translators

For more, see www.act.es.

DUUAL *C/Aragó 336, Eixample (93 566 01 01, www.duual.com). Metro Girona.* **Open** *Sept-June* 9am-2pm, 4-7pm Mon-Thur; 9am-2pm Fri. *July* 8.30am-3pm Mon-Fri. Closed 3wks Aug. **No credit cards. Map** p323 H8.
TRADUIT *(93 898 60 50, www. traduit.com).* **Credit** MC, V. Internet/phone enquiries only.

Useful organisations

AJUNTAMENT DE BARCELONA *Plaça Sant Miquel 4-5, Barri Gòtic (information 010, 93 402 70 00, www.bcn.cat). Metro Jaume I.* **Open** *Sept-June* 8.30am-5.30pm Mon-Fri. *Aug* 8.15am-2.15pm Mon-Fri. **Map** p329 C6. The city council.
BORSA DE VALORS DE BARCELONA *Passeig de Gràcia 19, Eixample (93 401 35 55, www.borsabcn.es). Metro Passeig de Gràcia.* **Open** *Reception* 9am-5.30pm Mon-Fri. *Library* 10am-1pm Mon-Tue. **Map** p328 C1. The stock exchange.
GENERALITAT DE CATALUNYA *Information 012 (from outside Catalonia 902 400 012)/new businesses 902 20 15 20, www.gencat.net.* The Catalan government.

CONSULATES

AUSTRALIAN CONSULATE *Avda Diagonal 458, 3°, Eixample (93 490 90 13, www.spain.embassy. gov.au). Metro Diagonal.* **Open** 10am-noon Mon-Fri. Closed Aug. **Map** p322 G6.
BRITISH CONSULATE *Avda Diagonal 477, 13°, Eixample (93 366 62 00, www.ukinspain.com). Metro Hospital Clínic.* **Open** 8.30am-1.30pm Mon-Fri (telephone hours 8am-4pm). **Map** p322 E5.
CANADIAN CONSULATE *Plaça Catalunya 9, 1° (93 412 72 36, www.canadainternational.gc.ca). Metro Catalunya.* **Open** 9am-12.30pm Mon-Fri.
IRISH CONSULATE *Gran Via Carles III 94, 10°, Les Corts*

(93 491 50 21). Metro Maria Cristina. **Open** 10am-1pm Mon-Fri. **Map** p321 B4.
NEW ZEALAND CONSULATE *Travessera de Gràcia 64, 2°, Gràcia (93 209 03 99). Metro Diagonal.* **Open** 9am-2pm, 4-7pm Mon-Fri. **Map** p322 F5.
US CONSULATE *Passeig Reina Elisenda 23, Sarrià (93 280 22 27, www.embusa.es). FGC Reina Elisenda.* **Open** 9am-1pm Mon-Fri. **Map** p321 B1.

CONSUMER

Ask for a complaint form (*full de reclamació/hoja de reclamación*), which many businesses and all shops, bars and restaurants are required to keep. Leave one copy with the business. Take the other forms to the consumer office.

OFICINA MUNICIPAL D'INFORMACIÓ AL CONSUMIDOR *Ronda de Sant Pau 43-45, Barri Gòtic (93 402 78 41, www.omic.bcn.es). Metro Sant Antoni.* **Open** 9am-5pm Mon-Thur, 9am-2pm Fri. **Map** p326 E10. The official centre for consumer advice and complaints follow-up.
TELÈFON DE CONSULTA DEL CONSUMIDOR *012.* **Open** 24hrs. Consumer advice.

CUSTOMS

Custom declarations are not usually necessary if you arrive from another EU country and are carrying legal goods for personal use. The amounts given below are guidelines only: if you come close to the maximums in several categories, you may have to explain your personal habits.

● 800 cigarettes, 400 small cigars, 200 cigars or 1kg loose tobacco.
● 10 litres of spirits (more than 22% alcohol), 20 litres of spirits (less than 22% alcohol), 90 litres of wine (or 60 litres of sparkling wine) or 110 litres of beer.
Coming from a non-EU country or the Canary Islands, you can bring:
● 200 cigarettes, 100 small cigars, 50 regular cigars or 250g (8.82oz) of tobacco.
● 1 litre of spirits (more than 22% alcohol) or 2 litres of wine or beer (less than 22% alcohol).
● 50g (1.76oz) of perfume.
● 500g coffee; 100g tea.
Visitors can also carry up to €6,000 in cash without having to declare it. Non-EU residents can reclaim VAT (IVA) on some large

purchases when they leave. For details, *see p184.*

DISABLED

The website at www.accessible barcelona.com, run by a British expat wheelchair-user living in Barcelona, is a useful resource. It also provides reviews of accessible accommodation, and has an apartment adapted for wheelchair-users available for rent. Although many sights claim to be accessible, you may still need assistance. Phoning ahead to check is always a good idea. Another useful resource is the Catalan government's website www.turismeperatothom.com, which describes accessible accommodation, sights, and transport in Barcelona and throughout Catalonia.

INSTITUT MUNICIPAL DE PERSONES AMB DISCAPACITAT *C/València 344, Eixample (93 413 27 75, www.bcn.cat/accessible). Metro Girona.* **Open** 9am-2pm Mon-Fri. **Map** p323 H7
The official city organisation for the disabled has information on access to venues and transport, and can provide a map with wheelchair-friendly itineraries. Call in advance to make an appointment. There are some English speakers available.

Transport

Access for disabled people to local transport is improving but still leaves much to be desired. For wheelchair-users, buses and taxis are usually the best bet. For transport information, call TMB (93 318 70 74) or 010. Transport maps, which can be picked up from transport information offices and some metro stations, indicate wheelchair access points and adapted bus routes.
For a list of accessible metro stations and bus lines, check www.tmb.cat and click on Transport for Everyone, or see the maps on pp350-352. However, even those stations with lifts can sometimes prove inaccessible, so wheelchair-users are advised to avoid the metro altogether.

BUSES All the Aerobús airport buses, night buses, standard buses and the open-topped tourist buses are fully accessible, though you may need assistance with the steep ramps. Press the blue button with the wheelchair symbol to alert the driver before your stop.

DIRECTORY

DIRECTORY

METRO & FGC Only L2, L9 and L11 have lifts and ramps at all stations. On L1, L3, L4 and L5 some stations have lifts. There is usually a step on to the train, the size of which varies; some assistance may be required. The Montjuïc funicular railway is fully wheelchair-adapted. Accessible FGC stations include Provença, Muntaner and Avda Tibidabo. The FGC infrastructures at Catalunya and Espanya stations are accessible, but interchanges with metro lines are not.

RENFE TRAINS Sants and Plaça Catalunya stations are wheelchair-accessible, but the trains are not. If you go to the Atenció al Viajero office ahead of time, help on the platform can be arranged.

TAXIS All taxi drivers are officially required to transport wheelchairs and guide dogs for no extra charge, but cars can be small, and the willingness of drivers to co-operate varies widely. Special minibus taxis adapted for wheelchairs can be ordered from the Taxi Amic service.

TAXI AMIC *93 420 80 88, www.taxi-amic-adaptat.com.* **Open** 7am-11pm Mon-Fri; 9am-10pm Sat, Sun.
Fares are the same as for regular cabs, but there is a minimum fare of €12.60 for Barcelona city (€14 at weekends), and more for the surrounding areas.

TRAMS All tram lines throughout Barcelona are fully accessible for wheelchair-users, with ramps that can access all platforms. Watch out for the symbol on each platform that indicates where the wheelchair-accessible doors will be situated.

Wheelchair-friendly museums & galleries

All of the below should be accessible to wheelchair users:

Disseny Hub Barcelona; CCCB; CaixaForum; Espai Gaudí – La Pedrera; Fundació Joan Miró; Fundació Antoni Tàpies; MNAC; Museu Barbier-Mueller d'Art Precolombi; Museu Frederic Marès; Museu d'Arqueologia de Catalunya; Museu del Calçat; Museu de Cera; Museu del Temple Expiatori de la Sagrada Família; Museu d'Història de Catalunya; Museu d'Història de Barcelona; Museu de la Ciència – CosmoCaixa; Museu de la Xocolata; Museu Frederic Marès; Museu Picasso; Palau de la Música; Palau de la Virreina.

DRUGS

Many people smoke cannabis fairly openly in Spain, but possession or consumption in public is illegal. In private, the law is contradictory: smoking is OK, but you can be nabbed for possession or distribution. Enforcement is often not the highest of police priorities, but you could theoretically receive a fine. Larger amounts entail a fine and, in extreme cases, prison. Smoking in bars is also prohibited. Cocaine is also common in Spain, but if you are caught in possession of this or any other Class A drug, you are looking at a hefty fine, and possibly a long prison sentence.

ELECTRICITY

The standard voltage in Spain is 220V. Plugs are of the two-round-pin type. You'll need a plug adaptor to use British-bought electrical devices. If you have US (110V) equipment, you will need a current transformer as well as an adaptor.

EMERGENCIES

EMERGENCY SERVICES *112.*
Police, fire or ambulance.
AMBULANCE/AMBULÀNCIA *061.*
For hospitals and other health services, *see below.*
FIRE/BOMBERS/BOMBEROS *080.*
MOSSOS D'ESQUADRA *088.*
Catalan police force.

GAY & LESBIAN

CASAL LAMBDA *C/Verdaguer i Callís 10, Sant Pere (93 319 55 50, www.lambda.cat).* Metro Urquinaona. **Open** 5-9pm Mon-Sat. Closed Aug. **Map** p328 D4.
Gay cultural organisation.
COORDINADORA GAI-LESBIANA *C/Violant d'Hongria Reina d'Aragó 156, Sants (93 298 00 29, www.cogailes.org).* Metro Plaça del Centre. **Open** 10am-7pm Mon-Fri. Closed Aug. **Map** p325 A7.
This gay umbrella group works with the Ajuntament on concerns for the gay, bisexual and transsexual communities. Its Telèfon Rosa service (900 601 601, open 6-10pm daily) gives help or advice and is open all year round.
FRONT D'ALLIBERAMENT GAI DE CATALUNYA *C/Verdi 88, Gràcia (93 217 26 69, www.fagc.org).* Metro Fontana. **Open** 7-9pm Mon-Fri. **Map** p323 H4.

A vocal group that produces the *Debat Gai* information bulletin.

HEALTH

Visitors can obtain emergency care through the public health service, Servei Catalá de la Salut. EU nationals are entitled to free basic medical attention if they have the European Emergency Health Card (Tarjeta Sanitaria Europea), also known as the Health Insurance Card. This replaced the E111 form and is valid for one year. Contact the health service in your country of residence for details. If you don't have one but can get one sent or faxed within a few days, you will be exempt from charges. Citizens of certain other countries that have a special agreement with Spain, among them several Latin American states, can also have access to free care.

For general details on healthcare, check the website www.gencat.net/temes/eng/salut.htm, or call the Catalan government's 24-hour health information line on 902 11 14 44 (press 2 for information) or the Instituto Nacional de Seguridad Social on 901 50 20 50 (press 3 for information), www.seg-social.es.

For non-emergencies, it's usually quicker to use private travel insurance rather than the state system. Similarly, non-EU nationals with private medical insurance can also make use of state health services on a paying basis, but private clinics are generally simpler.

Accident & emergency

In an emergency, go to the casualty department (*Urgències*) of any of the main public hospitals in the city (including those below). All are open 24hrs daily. The most central are the Clínic, which also has a first-aid centre for less serious emergencies two blocks away (C/València 184, 93 227 93 00, open 8.30am-10pm daily) and Perecamps. Call 061 or 112 for an ambulance.

CENTRE D'URGÈNCIES PERECAMPS *Avda Drassanes 13-15, Raval (93 441 06 00).* Metro Drassanes or Paral·lel. **Map** p326 E11.
HOSPITAL CLÍNIC *C/Villarroel 170, Eixample (93 227 54 00).* Metro Hospital Clínic. **Map** p322 E6.
HOSPITAL DOS DE MAIG *C/Dos de Maig 301, Eixample (93 507 27*

00). Metro Sant Pau-Dos de Maig or Cartagena. **Map** p323 L6.
HOSPITAL DEL MAR *Passeig Marítim 25-29, Barceloneta (93 248 30 00). Metro Ciutadella-Vila Olímpica.* **Map** p327 J12.
HOSPITAL DE SANT PAU *C/Sant Quintí 89, Eixample (93 291 90 00). Metro Hospital de Sant Pau-Guinardó.* **Map** p323 L5.

Complementary medicine

INTEGRAL: CENTRE MÈDIC I DE SALUT *C/Diputació 321, 1º 1ª, Eixample (93 467 74 20, www.integralcentremedic.com). Metro Girona.* **Open** (by appointment only) 9am-3pm, 4-9pm Mon-Fri. Closed Aug. **Map** p323 H8.

Contraception

All pharmacies sell condoms (*condoms/preservativos*) and other forms of contraception including pills (*la píndola/la píldora*), which can be bought without a prescription. You'll generally need a prescription to get the morning-after pill (*la píndola del dia seguent/la píldora del día siguiente*) but some CAP health centres (*see below*) will dispense it free themselves. Many bars and clubs have condom vending machines.

CENTRE JOVE D'ANTICONCEPCIÓ I SEXUALITAT *C/La Granja 19-21, Gràcia (93 415 10 00, www.centre jove.org). Metro Lesseps.* **Open** noon-7pm Mon-Thur; 10am-2pm Fri. Closed 2wks Aug. **Map** p323 H4.
A family-planning centre aimed at young people (under-25s).

Dentists

Most dentistry is not covered by the Spanish public health service (to which EU citizens have access). Check the classified ads in *Metropolitan* (*see p301*) for English-speaking dentists.

INSTITUT ODONTOLÒGIC CALÀBRIA *Avda Madrid 141-145, Eixample (93 439 45 00, www.ioa.es). Metro Entença.* **Open** 10am-1pm, 3-8pm Mon-Fri. **Credit** MC, V. **Map** p325 C6.
These well-equipped clinics provide a complete range of dental services. Some staff speak English. **Other locations** Institut Odontològic Sagrada Família, C/Sardenya 319, Eixample (93 457

04 53); Institut Odontològic, C/Diputació 238, Eixample (93 342 64 00).

Doctors

A **Centre d'Assistència Primària** (CAP) is a local health centre (aka am bulatori/ am bulatorio), where you should be seen fairly quickly by a doctor, but you may need an appointment. There are around 55 in total across Barcelona; see www.bcn.cat for a full list of all locations.

CAP CASC ANTIC *C/Rec Comtal 24, Sant Pere (93 310 50 98). Metro Arc de Triomf.* **Open** 9am-8pm Mon-Fri; (emergencies only) 9am-5pm Sat. **Map** p328 F4.
CAP DOCTOR LLUÍS SAYÉ *C/Torres i Amat 8, Raval (93 301 27 05). Metro Universitat.* **Open** 8am-8pm Mon-Fri; (emergencies only) 9am-5pm Sat. **Map** p328 A1.
CAP DRASSANES *Avda Drassanes 17-21, Raval (93 329 44 95). Metro Drassanes.* **Open** 8am-8pm Mon-Fri; (emergencies only) 9am-5pm Sat. **Map** p326 E11.
CAP VILA OLÍMPICA *C/Joan Miró 17, Vila Olímpica (93 221 37 85). Metro Ciutadella-Vila Olímpica or Marina.* **Open** 8am-8pm Mon-Fri; (emergencies only) 9am-5pm Sat. **Map** p327 K11.
GOOGOL MEDICAL CENTRE *Gran Via Carles III 37-39, Eixample (93 330 24 12/mobile 627 669 524, www.googol mediualcentre.com). Metro Les Corts.* **Open** 10am-6pm Mon-Fri. **Map** p321 A5.
An English-speaking clinic.
DR MARY MCCARTHY *C/Aribau 215, pral 1ª, Eixample (93 200 29 24/mobile 607 220 040). FGC Gràcia/bus 14, 58, 64.* **Open** by appointment. **Map** p322 F5.
Dr McCarthy is an internal medicine specialist from the US.

Hospitals

See left **Accident & emergency**.

Opticians

See p203.

Pharmacies

See p203.

STDs, HIV & AIDS

Free, anonymous blood tests for HIV and other STDs are given at the Unidad de Infección de Transmisión Sexual (93 441 46 12) at CAP Drassanes (*see below*). HIV tests are also available at the Coordinadora Gai-Lesbiana (*see left*), at the Asociació Ciutadana Antisida de Catalunya (C/Lluna 11, Raval, 93 317 05 05, www.acasc.info) and at BCN Checkpoint (C/Comte Borrell 164-166, 93 318 20 56, www.bcncheckpoint.com, closed Aug).

GTT (GRUPO DE TRABAJO SOBRE TRATAMIENTOS DEL VIH), *C/Sardenya 259, Eixample (93 208 08 45, www.gtt-vih.org). Metro Sagrada Família.* **Open** *8am–6pm Mon-Fri.* Support and advice for people with HIV and AIDS. Call 93 458 26 41 for information on treatment.
AIDS INFORMATION LINE *Freephone 900 21 22 22.* **Open** *Mid Sept-May* 8am-5.30pm Mon-Thur; 8am-3pm Fri. *June-mid Sept* 8am-3pm Mon-Fri.

HELPLINES

ALCOHOLICS ANONYMOUS *93 317 77 77, www.alcoholicos-anonimos.org, www.aaspain.org.* **Open** 10am-1pm, 5-8pm Mon-Fri.
NARCOTICS ANONYMOUS *902 11 41 47, www.na-esp.org.* **Open** hours vary.
TELÈFON DE L'ESPERANÇA *93 414 48 48, www.telefono esperanza.com.* **Open** 24hrs daily. Counselling and specialist help groups, from psychiatric to legal.

ID

From the age of 14, Spaniards are legally obliged to carry their DNI (identity card). Foreigners are also meant to carry an ID card or passport, and are in theory subject to a fine – in practice, you're more likely to get a warning. If you don't want to carry it around with you (wisely, given the prevalence of petty crime), it's a good idea to carry a photocopy or a driver's licence instead: technically, it's not legal, but usually acceptable. ID is needed to check into a hotel, hire a car, pay with a card in shops and exchange or pay with travellers' cheques.

DIRECTORY

INSURANCE

For health care and EU nationals, *see left*. Some non-EU countries have reciprocal health-care agreements with Spain, but for most travellers, it's usually more convenient to have private travel insurance, which will also, of course, cover you in case of theft and flight problems.

INTERNET

Despite relatively high costs, Spain boasts a high concentration of internet users, and there are internet centres all over Barcelona. Most libraries (*see below*) have free internet points and wireless access for public use, although you may have to join the library first. The city council provides free Wi-Fi access in about 200 public spaces, including parks, museums, beaches, cultural centres and markets (all signposted with a white diamond with a blue 'W' in the centre). The service is usually available daily 8am-8pm with some exceptions, and there's a 1hr browsing limit at some types of location. A full list (with map) of the Wi-Fi access points, as well as a comprehensive service guide is available at www.bcn.cat/barcelonawifi.

ALSUR CAFÉ *C/Sant Pere Més Alt 4, Sant Pere (93 310 12 86, www.alsurcafe.com). Metro Urquinaona.* **Open** 10am-1am Mon-Thur; 10am-3am Fri, Sat; 10am-1.30am Sun. **No credit cards. Map** p328 D4.
BORNET INTERNET CAFÈ *C/Barra de Ferro 3, Born (93 268 15 07, www.bornet-bcn.com). Metro Jaume I.* **Open** 10am-11pm Mon-Fri; noon-11pm Sat, Sun. **Rates** €2.80/hr. **Credit** (for payments over €5) AmEx, MC, V. **Map** p329 E6.

LANGUAGE

See pp308-309 for vocabulary; see p303 for classes.

LEFT LUGGAGE

Look for signs to the *consigna*.

AEROPORT DEL PRAT Terminal 1. Open 24hrs daily. **Rates** €3.80-4.90/day.
ESTACIÓ D'AUTOBUSOS BARCELONA-NORD C/Ali Bei 80, Eixample. Metro Arc de Triomf.

Open 24hrs daily. **Rates** €3-€4.50/day. **Map** p327 E5.
TRAIN STATIONS SANTS-ESTACIÓ Open 6am-11.45pm daily. **Rates** €3-€4.50/day. **Map** p325 A4.
Some smaller railway stations also have left-luggage lockers.

LEGAL HELP

Consulates (*see p297*) can help tourists in emergencies, and recommend lawyers.

MARTI & ASSOCIATS *Avda Diagonal 584, pral 1ª, Eixample (93 201 62 66, www.marti lawyers.com). Bus 6, 7, 15, 33, 34.* **Open** *Sept-July* 9am-8pm Mon-Thur; 9am-7pm Fri. *Aug* 9am-2pm, 4-7pm Mon-Thur, 9am-2pm Fri. **Map** p322 E5.

LIBRARIES

There's a network of public libraries around the city that offers free internet access, some English novels and information on cultural activities. Membership is free. Opening times are generally 10am-2pm, 4-8.30pm Mon-Sat. See www.bcn.cat/icub/biblioteques or call 93 316 10 00 for details.

Private libraries (*see below*) are better stocked but generally require paid membership to use their facilities.

ATENEU BARCELONÈS *C/Canuda 6, Barri Gòtic (93 343 61 21, www.ateneubcn.org). Metro Catalunya.* **Open** 9am-10.30pm daily. **Map** p328 C3.
The city's best private library, plus a wonderfully peaceful interior garden patio and a quiet bar. Membership is €27 a month, plus a €60 joining fee.
BIBLIOTECA DE CATALUNYA *C/Hospital 56, Raval (93 270 23 00, www.bnc.cat). Metro Liceu.* **Open** 9am-8pm Mon-Fri; 9am-2pm Sat. **Map** p328 A4.
The Catalan national collection is housed in the medieval Hospital de la Santa Creu. Readers' cards are required, but free one-day research visits are allowed for over-18s (call in advance; take your passport!).
BRITISH COUNCIL/INSTITUT BRITÀNIC *C/Amigó 83, Zona Alta (93 241 97 11, www.british council.org). FGC Muntaner.* **Open** *Sept-July* 9.30am-9pm Mon-Fri; 10.30pm-2pm Sat (also 3.30-6.30pm for students). **Map** p322 E4.

Membership is obligatory for use of the library and borrowing materials. The charge is €62 a year.
MEDIATECA *CaixaForum, Avda Marquès de Comillas 6-8, Montjuïc (902 22 30 40, 93 476 86 51, www.mediatecaonline.net). Metro Espanya.* **Open** *Sept-July* 10am-8pm Mon-Sat; *Aug* 4pm-8pm Mon-Fri. **Map** p325 B9.
You can borrow books, magazines, CDs, etc. Membership is €6 (€3 reductions). The lending desk is open 10am-7.30pm Mon-Sat (or 4-7.30pm Aug).

LOST PROPERTY

If you lose something at the airport, report it to the lost property centre (Oficina d'Objectes Perduts, in T1, 93 259 64 40). If you have mislaid anything on a train, look for the Atenció al Passatger desk or Cap d'Estació office at the nearest station to where your property went astray. Call ahead to the destination station, or call station information and ask for *objetos perdidos*.

MUNICIPAL LOST PROPERTY OFFICE *Oficina de Troballes, Plaça Carles Pi i Sunyer 8-10, Barri Gòtic (93 413 20 31, 010). Metro Catalunya or Jaume I.* **Open** 9am-2pm Mon-Fri. **Map** p328 C4.
All documentation or valuables found on city public transport and taxis, or picked up by the police in the street, should eventually find their way to this Ajuntament office, just off Avda Portal de l'Àngel.
TMB LOST PROPERTY OFFICE *Diagonal metro station, L5 entrance (93 318 70 74, www.tmb.net).* **Open** 8am-8pm Mon-Fri. **Map** p322 G6.
Items found on most public transport services are sent to this office, then transferred to the municipal office (*see above*) on Mondays and Thursdays. If the item was lost on a tram, call 902 193 275; on FGC trains, 93 205 15 15; for taxis, call 902 10 15 64.

MEDIA

Spanish and Catalan newspapers tend to favour serious and lengthy political commentary. There are no sensationalist tabloids in Spain: for scandal, the *prensa rosa* ('pink press', or gossip magazines) is the place to look. Television channels, though, go straight for the mass market, with junk television (*telebasura*) prevalent. Catalan is the dominant language on both radio and TV, less so in print.

Daily newspapers

Free daily papers of reasonable quality, such as *20 Minutes* and *Metro*, are handed out in the city centre every morning. The dailies tend to the high brow. Spanish readers can try *ABC*, *El Mundo*, *El País* and *La Vanguardia*; those conversant in Catalan have *Avui* and one of the editions of *El Periódico*.

English language

Foreign newspapers are available at most kiosks on La Rambla and Passeig de Gràcia, along with FNAC (*see p186*).
BARCELONA CONNECT A small free magazine with tips for travellers (www.barcelona connect.com).
BARCELONA METROPOLITAN A free monthly magazine for English-speaking locals, distributed in bars and other anglophone hangouts (www.barcelona-metropolitan.com).
CATALONIA TODAY English-language monthly with a round-up of local news and cultural events (www.cataloniatoday.cat). A PDF version is available for €36 a year.

Listings & classifieds

The main papers have daily 'what's on' listings, with entertainment supplements on Fridays (most run TV schedules on Saturdays). For monthly listings, see *Metropolitan* or the handy *Butxaca*, (www.butxaca.com) which can be picked up in cultural information centres, such as Palau de la Virreina on La Rambla; and freebies such as *Mondo Sonoro* (www.mondo sonoro.com) or GO (www.go-mag.com), which can be found in bars and music shops. Of the dailies, *La Vanguardia* has the best classifieds; you can also consult it at www.clasificados.es. www.infojobs.net is a popular resource for job vacancies.

GUÍA DEL OCIO A weekly listings magazine, published every Friday, in Spanish, with the odd page in English (www.guiadelociobcn.com).
TIME OUT BARCELONA A comprehensive weekly listings magazine in Catalan.

Radio

There are vast numbers of local, regional and national stations, with the Catalan language having a high profile. Catalunya Música (101.5 FM) is mainly classical and jazz, while Flaix FM (105.7 FM) provides news and music. For something a little more alternative, try Radio Bronka (104.5 FM) or Radio 3 (98.7 FM), which has a wonderfully varied music policy. You can listen to the BBC World Service on shortwave on 15485, 9410, 12095 and 6195 KHz, depending on the time of day.

Television

The emphasis of Spanish television is on mass entertainment, with Catalan channels only marginally better. Films are mainly dubbed and advertising is interminable. The best of the bunch may be Barcelona TV, which produces the city's most groundbreaking viewing. Also worth a look is La2 ('La Dos'), which is often compared to BBC2, with good late-night movies and documentaries.

MONEY

Spain's currency is the euro. Each euro (€) is divided into 100 cents (¢), known as *céntims/céntimos*. Notes come in denominations of €500, €200, €100, €50, €20, €10 and €5. Due to the increasing circulation of counterfeit notes, smaller businesses may be reluctant to accept anything larger than €50.

Banks & currency exchanges

Banks (*bancos*) and savings banks (*caixes d'estalvis/cajas de ahorros*) usually accept euro travellers' cheques for a commission, but they tend to refuse any kind of personal cheque except one issued by that bank. Some bureaux de change (*cambios*) don't charge commission, but rates are worse. Obtaining money through ATMs (which are everywhere) with a debit or credit card is the easiest option, despite the fees often charged.

BANK HOURS Banks are normally open between 8.30am and 2pm Mon-Fri. From October to April, most branches also open between 8.30am and 1pm on Saturdays.

From October to May many savings banks (normally beginning 'Caixa' or 'Caja') are also open late on Thursdays, 4.30-7.45pm.
OUT-OF-HOURS BANKING Foreign exchange offices at the airport are in terminals 1 (open 7am-10pm) and 2B (open 7am-8.30pm). Others in the centre open late: some on La Rambla open until midnight, later between July and September. At Sants, change money at La Caixa (8am-8pm daily), there's another change point at Plaça Cataluñya 7. At the airport and outside some banks are automatic exchange machines that accept notes in major currencies.

Credit & debit cards

Major credit cards are accepted in hotels, shops, restaurants and other places (metro ticket machines and pay-and-display parking machines, for instance). American Express cards are less frequently accepted than MasterCard and Visa. Many debit cards from other European countries may also be accepted. You can withdraw cash with major cards from ATMs, and banks will also advance cash against a credit card.
  Note: you need photographic ID (a passport, driving licence or something similar) when using a credit or debit card in a shop, but it's usually not required for payment in a restaurant.

LOST/STOLEN CARDS All lines have English-speaking staff and are open 24 hours daily. Maestro do not have a Spanish helpline.
American Express 902 37 56 37.
Diners Club 902 40 11 12.
MasterCard 900 97 12 31.
Visa 900 99 11 24.

Tax

The standard rate for sales tax (IVA) is 18%; this drops to 8% in hotels and restaurants, and 4% on some books. IVA may or may not be included in listed prices at restaurants, and it usually isn't included in rates quoted at hotels. If it's not, the expression IVA *no inclòs/incluido* (sales tax not included) should appear after the price. Beware of this when getting quotes on expensive items.
  In shops displaying a 'Tax-Free Shopping' sticker, non-EU residents can reclaim tax on large purchases when leaving the country.

DIRECTORY

DIRECTORY

OPENING TIMES

Most shops open from 9/10am to 1/2pm, and then 4/5pm to 8/9pm, Monday to Saturday. Many smaller businesses don't reopen on Saturday afternoons. All-day opening (10am to 8pm or 9pm) is becoming more common, especially for larger and more central establishments.

Markets open at 7/8am; most stalls are shut by 2pm, although many open on Fridays and Saturdays until 8pm.

Note that in summer, many of Barcelona's shops and restaurants shut for all or part of August (we have noted this where possible in our listings). Some businesses work a shortened day from June to September, from 8am or 9am until 3pm. Many museums close one day each week, usually on Mondays.

POLICE

Barcelona has several police forces: the Mossos d'Esquadra (in a uniform of navy and light blue with red trim), the Guàrdia Urbana (municipal police – navy and pale blue), the Policía Nacional (national police – darker blue uniforms and white shirts, or blue, combat-style gear). The Mossos are the Catalan government's police force and are taking over from the other two police forces but the GU and the PN will keep control of certain matters, like immigration and terrorism, which are dealt with by central government.

The Guàrdia Civil is a paramilitary force with green uniforms, policing highways, customs posts, government buildings and rural areas.

Reporting a crime

If you're robbed or attacked, report the incident as soon as possible at the nearest police station (*comisaría*), or dial 112. In the centre, the most convenient is the 24-hour Guàrdia Urbana station (La Rambla 43, Barri Gòtic, 092 or 93 256 24 30), which often has English-speaking officers on duty; they may transfer you to the Mossos d'Esquadra (C/Nou de la Rambla 76-80, Raval, 088 or 93 306 23 00) to report the crime formally. To do this, you'll need to make an official statement (*denuncia*). It's highly improbable that you will recover your property, but you need

the *denuncia* to make an insurance claim. You can also make this statement over the phone or online (902 10 21 12, www.policia.es), apart from crimes involving violence, or if the perpetrator has been identified. You'll still have to go to the *comisaría* within 72 hours to sign the *denuncia*, but you'll be able to skip some queues.

POSTAL SERVICES

Letters and postcards weighing up to 20g cost 34¢ within Spain; 64¢ to the rest of Europe; 78¢ to the rest of the world; prices normally rise on 1 January. It's usually easiest to buy stamps at *estancs* (*see below*). Mail sent abroad is slow: five to six working days in Europe, eight to ten to the USA. Postboxes in the street are yellow, sometimes with a white or blue horn insignia. For information on postal services, ring 902 19 71 97 or see www.correos.es. **CORREU CENTRAL** *Plaça Antonio López, Barri Gòtic* (93 486 80 50). *Metro Barceloneta or Jaume I.* **Open** 8.30am-9.30pm Mon-Fri; 8.30am-2pm Sat. **Map** p329 D7. Take a ticket from the machine as you enter and wait your turn. Apart from the typical postal services, fax-sending and receiving is offered (with the option of courier delivery in Spain, using the Burofax option). To send something express delivery, ask for *urgente*.
Other locations Ronda Universitat 23 & C/Aragó 282, Eixample (both 8.30am-8.30pm Mon-Fri, 9.30am-1pm Sat); and throughout the city.

ESTANCS/ESTANCOS

Government-run tobacco shops, which are known as *estancs/estancos* (at times, just *tabac*) and identified by a brown-and-yellow sign, are important institutions in Spain. As well as tobacco – still popular in the country – they supply postage stamps, public transport *targetes* and phonecards.
POST BOXES A PO box (*apartado postal*) address costs €65.49 annually.
POSTE RESTANTE Poste restante letters should be sent to Lista de Correos, 08080 Barcelona, Spain. Pick-up is from the main post office (*see above*); you'll need your passport when coming to claim your mail.

RELIGION

ANGLICAN: ST GEORGE'S CHURCH *C/Horaci 38, Zona Alta (93 417 88 67, www.st-georges-*

church.com). FGC Avda Tibidabo.
Main service 11am Sun.
An Anglican/Episcopalian church with a mixed congregation. Activities include the Alpha course (directed at faith-seekers), a women's club, bridge and Sunday school. See website for details.
ROMAN CATHOLIC: PARRÒQUIA MARIA REINA *Ctra d'Esplugues 103, Zona Alta (93 203 41 15). Metro Maria Cristina/bus 22, 63, 75.* **Mass** 10.30pm Sun. Closed Aug. **Map** p321 A1. Mass is said in English at the above time on Sunday.
JEWISH ORTHODOX: SINAGOGA DE BARCELONA & COMUNITAT ISRAELITA DE BARCELONA *C/Avenir 24, Zona Alta (93 200 85 13, www.cibonline.org). FGC Gràcia.* **Prayers** call for times. **Map** p322 F5.
MUSLIM: MOSQUE ISLAMIC CULTURAL COUNCIL OF CATALUNYA *C/Nou de Sadurní 9, entl, Raval (93 301 08 31, www.consellislamic.org). Metro Liceu.* Phone or see website for information on local services. **Map** p326 E10.

SAFETY & SECURITY

Pickpocketing and bagsnatching are epidemic in Barcelona, with tourists a prime target. Be especially careful around the Old City, particularly La Rambla, as well as at stations and on public transport, the airport train being a favourite. However, thieves go anywhere tourists go, including parks, beaches and internet cafés. Most street crime is aimed at the inattentive, and can be avoided by taking precautions:
● Avoid giving invitations: don't keep wallets in accessible pockets, keep your bags closed and in front of you. When you stop, put bags down where you can always see them (or hold them on your lap).
● Don't flash wads of cash or fancy cameras.
● In busy streets or crowded places, keep an eye on what is happening around you. If you're suspicious of someone, move somewhere else.
● As a rule, Barcelona street thieves tend to use stealth and surprise rather than violence. However, muggings and knife threats do sometimes occur. Avoid deserted streets in the city centre if you're on your own at night, and offer no resistance when threatened.
● Don't carry more money and valuables than you need: use your

hotel's safe deposit facilities, and take out travel insurance.

SMOKING

Since January 2011, smoking has been banned in enclosed public areas. Most hotels have non-smoking rooms or floors; although if you ask for a non-smoking room, some hotels may just give you a room that has had the ashtray removed.

STUDY

Catalonia is generally well disposed towards the European Union, and the vast majority of foreign students who come to Spain under the EU's Erasmus scheme are studying at Catalan universities or colleges. Catalan is usually the language spoken in these universities, although some lecturers are more relaxed than others about the use of Castilian in class for the first few months.

SECRETARIA GENERAL DE JOVENTUT – PUNT D'INFORMACIÓ JUVENIL
C/Calabria 147-C/Rocafort 116, Eixample (reception 93 483 83 83/information 93 483 83 84, www.gencat.net/joventut). Metro Rocafort. **Open** *Oct-May* 9.30am-2pm, 3-7pm Mon-Thur, 9.30am-2pm Fri. *July, Sept* 9.30am-2pm, Mon, Wed, Fri; 9.30am-2pm, 4.30-8.30pm Tue, Thur. *Aug* 9.30am-2pm Mon-Fri. Closed 1wk Aug. **Map** p325 D8. Generalitat-run centre with a number of services: information for young people on travel, work and study.

Language classes

If you plan to stay in bilingual Barcelona for a while, you may want (or need) to learn some Catalan. The city is also a popular location for those coming to the country to study Spanish. See http://centrosasociados.cervantes.es for schools recommended by Spain's official language institute, the Instituto Cervantes.

BABYLON IDIOMAS *C/Bruc 65, pral 1ª, Eixample (93 467 36 36, www.babylon-idiomas.com). Metro Girona.* **Open** 8.30am-7.30pm Mon-Fri. **Credit** MC, V. **Map** p328 H8. Small groups (up to ten people) run at all levels of Spanish.
CONSORCI PER A LA NORMALITZACIÓ LINGÜÍSTICA *C/Carabassa 15, Barri Gòtic (93*

412 72 24, www.cpnl.cat). Metro Drassanes. **Open** 9am-12pm Mon, Wed-Fri, 9am–12pm, 4pm–8pm Tue. **No credit cards. Map** p329 B5.
The Generalitat organisation for the promotion of the Catalan language has centres around the city offering Catalan courses for non-Spanish speakers at very low prices or even for free (level one). The basic classes are held at the C/Avinyó venue.
Other locations C/Avinyó 52, Barri Gòtic (902 07 50 60); C/Mallorca 115, entl 1ª, Eixample (93 451 24 45); and throughout the city.
ESCOLA OFICIAL D'IDIOMES DE BARCELONA – DRASSANES *Avda Drassanes, Raval (93 324 93 30, www.eoibd.es). Metro Drassanes.* **Open** *Sept-June* 8.30am-9pm Mon-Fri. **Map** p326 E11. This state-run school has semi-intensive four-month courses, starting in October and February (enrolment tends to be in either September or January, check the website for details), at all levels in Spanish, Catalan, French and other languages.
Other locations Escola Oficial, Avda del Jordà 18, Vall d'Hebrón (93 418 74 85, 93 418 68 33).
ESTUDIOS HISPÁNICOS DE LA UNIVERSITAT DE BARCELONA *Gran Via de les Corts Catalanes 585, Eixample (93 403 55 19, www.eh.ub.es). Metro Universitat.* **Open** information (Pati de Ciències entrance) *mid June-Aug* 9am-2pm Mon-Fri. *Sept-mid June* 9am-8pm Mon-Thur; 9am-2pm Fri. **Credit** AmEx, DC, MC, V. **Map** p326 F8. Intensive, fortnight, three-month and year-long Spanish language and culture courses.
INTERNATIONAL HOUSE *C/Trafalgar 14, Eixample (93 268 45 11, www.ihes.com/bcn). Metro Urquinaona.* **Open** 8am-9pm Mon-Fri; 10am-1.30pm Sat. **Map** p328 E3. Intensive Spanish courses running all year round.

TELEPHONES

Phonecards and phone centres give cheaper call rates, especially for international calls.

Dialling & codes

Normal Spanish phone numbers have nine digits; the area code (93 in the province of Barcelona) must be dialled with all calls, both local and long-distance. Spanish mobile

numbers always begin with 6. Numbers starting 900 are freephone lines, while other 90 numbers are special-rate services. Those starting with 80 are high-rate lines and can only be called from within Spain.

International & long-distance calls

To make an international call, dial 00 and then the country code, followed by the area code (omitting the first zero in UK numbers), and then the number. Country codes are as follows:

AUSTRALIA 61.
CANADA 1.
IRISH REPUBLIC 353.
NEW ZEALAND 64.
SOUTH AFRICA 27.
UNITED KINGDOM 44.
USA 1.

To phone Spain from abroad, dial 00, followed by 34, followed by the number.

Mobile phones

The mobile phone, or *móvil*, is omnipresent in Spain. Calls are paid for either through direct debit or by using prepaid phones, topped up with vouchers. Most mobiles from other European countries can be used in Spain, but you may need to set this up before you leave. You may be charged international roaming rates even when making a local call, and you will be charged for incoming calls. Not all US handsets are GSM-compatible; check with your service provider before you leave.
If you're staying more than a few weeks, it may work out cheaper to buy a pay-as-you-go package when you arrive, from places such as FNAC (*see p186*), or buy a local SIM card for your own phone. These usually include a little credit, which you can then top up (from newsagents, cash machines and *estancs*).

Operator services & useful phone numbers

Operators normally speak Catalan and Spanish only, except for international operators, most of whom speak English.

GENERAL INFORMATION (BARCELONA) 010 (24hrs daily). From outside Catalonia, but within Spain, call 807 117 700.

DIRECTORY

INTERNATIONAL DIRECTORY ENQUIRIES 11825.
INTERNATIONAL OPERATOR FOR REVERSE CHARGE CALLS 1408.
NATIONAL DIRECTORY ENQUIRIES 11818 (Telefónica, the cheapest, and free from public phones) or 11888 (*Yellow Pages*, more expensive, or free on www.paginasamarillas.com), among others.
NATIONAL OPERATOR FOR REVERSE CHARGE CALLS 1409.
TELEPHONE FAULTS SERVICE (Telefónica) 1002.
TIME 1212.
WAKE-UP CALLS 1212. After the message, key in the time at which you wish to be woken, in the 24hr clock, in four figures: for example, 0830 for 8.30am, 2030 for 8.30pm.
WEATHER 1212.

Phone centres

Phone centres (*locutoris*) are full of small booths where you can sit down and pay at the end. They offer cheap calls and avoid the need for change. Concentrated particularly in streets such as C/Sant Pau and C/Hospital in the Raval, and along C/Carders-C/Corders in Sant Pere, they generally offer other services too, including international money transfer, currency exchange and internet access.

CATY MULTISERVICIOS
C/Villaroel 14, Eixample (93 289 22 76). Metro Sant Antoni. Open 9am-10pm daily. **No credit cards.** **Map** p326 E9.
LOCUTORIO *C/Hospital 17, Raval (93 318 97 39). Metro Liceu.* **Open** 9am-10pm daily. **No credit cards.** **Map** p328 A2.

Public phones

The most common type of payphone in Barcelona accepts coins (5¢ and up), phonecards and credit cards. There is a multilingual digital display (press 'L' to change language) and written instructions in English and other languages. Take plenty of small coins with you. For the first minute of a daytime call to a landline, you'll be charged around 20¢; to a mobile phone around 55¢; and to a 902 number around 70¢. Calls to directory enquiries on 11818 are free from payphones, but you'll usually have to insert a coin to make the call (it will be returned when you hang up). If you're still

in credit at the end of your call, you can make further calls by pushing the 'R' button and dialling again. Bars and cafés often have payphones, but these can be more expensive than street booths.

Telefónica phonecards (*targetes telefónica/tarjetas telefónica*) are sold at newsstands and *estancs* (*see p302*). Other cards sold at phone centres, shops and newsstands give cheaper rates on all but local calls. This latter type of card contains a toll-free number to call from any phone.

TIME

The local time is one hour ahead of Greenwich Mean Time, six hours ahead of US Eastern Standard Time and nine hours ahead of Pacific Standard Time. Daylight saving time runs concurrently with the United Kingdom: clocks go back in October and forward in March.

TIPPING

There are no rules for tipping in Barcelona, but locals don't tip much. It's fair to leave five to ten per cent in restaurants, unless the service has been bad. People sometimes leave a little change in bars. In taxis, tipping is not standard, but many people round up to the nearest 50¢. It's usual to tip hotel porters.

TOILETS

The problem of people urinating in the streets of the Old City has pressed the Ajuntament into introducing more public toilets. There are 24-hour public toilets in Plaça del Teatre, just off La Rambla, and more at the top of C/dels Àngels, opposite MACBA. Most of the main railway stations have clean toilets. Parks such as Ciutadella and Güell have a few dotted about, but you need a 20¢ coin to use them. The beach at Barceloneta has six (heavily in demand) Portaloos; there are five further up at the beach at Sant Sebastià, and in season there are also toilets open under the boardwalk, along the beach towards the Port Olímpic. Most bar and café owners don't mind if you use their toilets (you may have to ask for the key), although some in the centre and at the beach are less amenable. Fast-food restaurants are good standbys.

Toilets are known as *serveis*, *banys* or *lavabos* (in Catalan) or *servicios*, *aseos*, *baños* or *lavabos* (in Spanish).

In bars or restaurants, the ladies' is generally denoted by a D (*dones/damas*), and occasionally by an M (*mujeres*) or S (*señoras*) on the door; while the men's mostly say H (*homes/hombres*) or C (*caballeros*).

TOURIST INFORMATION

010 PHONELINE Open 24hrs daily.
This city-run information line is aimed mainly at locals, but it does an impeccable job of answering all kinds of queries. There are sometimes English-speaking operators available. Call 807 117 700 from outside Catalonia but within Spain.
CENTRE D'INFORMACIÓ DE LA VIRREINA *Palau de la Virreina, La Rambla 99, Barri Gòtic (93 316 10 00, www.bcn.cat/cultura). Metro Liceu.* **Open** 10am-8.30pm daily (information office and ticket sales). **Map** p328 B4.
The information office of the city's culture department has details of shows, exhibitions and special events.
OFICINES D'INFORMACIÓ TURÍSTICA *Plaça Catalunya, Eixample (information 93 285 38 34, bookings 93 285 38 33, www.bcn.cat, www.barcelona turisme.com). Metro Catalunya.* **Open** *Office* 9am-9pm daily. *Call centre* 8am-8pm Mon-Fri. **Map** p328 C2.
The main office of the city tourist board is underground on the El Corte Inglés/south side of the square: look for the big red signs with 'i' superimposed in white. It has information, money exchange, a shop and a hotel booking service, and sells phonecards and tickets for shows, sights and public transport.
Other locations C/Ciutat 2 (ground floor of Ajuntament), Barri Gòtic; C/Sardenya (opposite the Sagrada Família), Eixample; Plaça Portal de la Pau (opposite Monument a Colom), Port Vell; Sants station; La Rambla 115, Barri Gòtic; corner of Plaça d'Espanya and Avda Maria Cristina, Eixample; airport.
PALAU ROBERT *Passeig de Gràcia 107, Eixample (93 238 80 91/92/93, www.gencat.net/probert, www.catalunyaturisme.com). Metro Diagonal.* **Open** 10am-7pm Mon-Sat; 10am-2.30pm Sun. **Map** p322 G7.
The Generalitat's centre for tourists is at the junction of Passeig de Gràcia and Avda Diagonal. It has maps and other essentials for Barcelona, but its speciality is a

huge range of information in different media for attractions to be found elsewhere in Catalonia. It also sometimes hosts interesting exhibitions on local art, culture, gastronomy and nature and has a pleasant garden out back.
Other locations Airport terminals 1 (93 478 47 04) and 2B (93 478 05 65), open 9am-9pm daily.

VISAS & IMMIGRATION

Spain is one of the European Union countries that's covered by the Schengen Agreement, which led to common visa regulations and limited border controls among member states that were signatories in the agreement. However, neither the UK nor the Republic of Ireland are signatories in this agreement; nationals of those countries will need their passports. Most European Union citizens, as well as Norwegian and Icelandic nationals, only need a national identity card.

Visas are not required for citizens of the United States, Canada, Australia and New Zealand who are arriving for stays of up to 90 days and not for work or study. Citizens of South Africa and other countries need visas to enter Spain; approach Spanish consulates and embassies in other countries for information. Visa regulations do change, so check before leaving home.

WATER

Tap water is drinkable in Barcelona, but it tastes of chlorine. Bottled water is what you will be served if you ask for *un aigua/agua* in a bar or restaurant; *fresca* is cold, *natural* is at room temperature. *Sin gas* is still water, *con gas* sparkling.

WHEN TO GO

Barcelona is usually agreeable year-round, though the humidity in summer can be debilitating, particularly when it's overcast. Many shops, bars and restaurants close (especially during August). Public transport and cinemas can overcompensate for the summer heat with bracing air-conditioning.

Climate

Spring is unpredictable: warm, sunny days can alternate with winds and showers. Temperatures in May and June are pretty much perfect; the city is especially lively around 23 June, when locals

celebrate the beginning of summer with all kinds of fireworks and fiestas. July and August can be unpleasant, as the summer heat and humidity kick in and make many locals leave town. Autumn weather is generally warm and fresh, with heavy downpours common around October. Crisp, cool sunshine is normal from December to February. Snow is very rare.

Public holidays

Most shops, banks and offices, and many bars and restaurants, close on public holidays (*festius/ festivos*), and public transport is limited. Many take long weekends whenever a major holiday comes along. If the holiday coincides with, say, a Tuesday or a Thursday, many people will take the Monday or Friday off: this is what is known as a *pont/puente*.

NEW YEAR'S DAY/ANY NOU 1 Jan
THREE KINGS/REIS MAGS 6 Jan
GOOD FRIDAY/DIVENDRES SANT
EASTER MONDAY/DILLUNS DE PASQUA
MAY (LABOUR) DAY/FESTA DEL TREBALL 1 May
MON AFTER WHITSUN/ SEGONA PASCUA 1 June
SANT JOAN 24 June
VERGE DE L'ASSUMPCIÓ 15 Aug
DIADA DE CATALUNYA 11 Sept
LA MERCÈ 24 Sept
DIA DE LA HISPANITAT 12 Oct
ALL SAINTS' DAY/ TOTS SANTS 1 Nov
CONSTITUTION DAY/DÍA DE LA CONSTITUCIÓN 6 Dec
LA IMMACULADA 8 Dec
CHRISTMAS DAY/NADAL 25 Dec
BOXING DAY/SANT ESTEVE 26 Dec

WORKING & LIVING

Common recourses for English speakers in Barcelona are to find work in the tourist sector (often seasonal and outside the city), in a downtown bar or teaching English in the numerous language schools. For the latter, it helps to have the TEFL (Teaching English as a Foreign Language) qualifications; these can be gained in reputable institutions in the city as well as in your home country. Bear in mind that teaching work dries up in June until the end of summer, usually September, although it's possible to find intensive teaching courses during July. The number of jobs in call centres for English speakers and other foreigners has also rocketed of late.

Queries regarding residency and legal requirements for foreigners who are working in Spain can be addressed to the Ministry of Interior's helpline 060 (where there are English-speaking operators).

EU citizens

EU citizens living in Spain for more than three months are no longer issued with a resident's card (*tarjeta de residencia*) but need to have ID or a passport from their own country.

Non-EU citizens

While in Spain on a tourist visa, you are not legally allowed to work. Those wanting a work permit officially need to be made a job offer while still in their home country. The process is lengthy and not all applications are successful. If you do get lucky, you can then apply for residency at a Spanish consulate in your home country.

THE LOCAL CLIMATE

Average temperatures and monthly rainfall in Barcelona.

	High (°C/°F)	Low (°C/°F)	Rainfall (mm/in)
Jan	13 / 56	6 / 43	44 / 1.7
Feb	15 / 59	7 / 45	36 / 1.4
Mar	16 / 61	8 / 47	48 / 1.9
Apr	18 / 64	10 / 50	51 / 2.0
May	21 / 70	14 / 57	57 / 2.2
June	24 / 76	17 / 63	38 / 1.5
July	27 / 81	20 / 67	22 / 0.9
Aug	29 / 84	20 / 67	66 / 2.6
Sept	25 / 78	18 / 64	79 / 3.1
Oct	22 / 71	14 / 57	94 / 3.7
Nov	17 / 63	9 / 49	74 / 2.9
Dec	15 / 59	7 / 45	50 / 2.0

DIRECTORY

timeout.com/travel
Get the local experience

Dream deli counter at Franchi, in the Prati district, **Rome**

© Gianluca Moggi

Further Reference

BOOKS

Food & drink

Colman Andrews
Catalan Cuisine
A mine of information on food and more (with usable recipes).
Anya von Bremzen
The New Spanish Table
A guide to Spanish staples with some entertaining anecdotes.
Alan Davidson *Tio Pepe Guide to the Seafood of Spain and Portugal*
An excellent pocket-sized guide to Spain's fishy delights.

Guides & walks

J Amelang, X Gil & GW McDonogh *Twelve Walks Through Barcelona's Past*
Well-thought-out walks, organised by historical theme.
Xavier Güell *Gaudí Guide*
A handy guide, with good background on the architect's work.
Juliet Pomés Leiz & Ricardo Feriche *Barcelona Design Guide*
An engaging listing of everything ever considered 'designer' in BCN.

Context & culture

Jimmy Burns
Barça: A People's Passion
The first full-scale history in English of one of the world's most storied football clubs.
JH Elliott
The Revolt of the Catalans
A fascinating, detailed account of the Guerra dels Segadors and the Catalan revolt of the 1640s.
Felipe Fernández Armesto
Barcelona: A Thousand Years of the City's Past
A solid history.
Ronald Fraser *Blood of Spain*
A vivid oral history of the Spanish Civil War.
Gijs van Hensbergen *Gaudí*
A thorough account of his life.
John Hooper *The New Spaniards*
An incisive and very readable survey of the changes in Spanish society since the death of Franco.
Robert Hughes *Barcelona*
The most comprehensive single book about Barcelona.
Temma Kaplan
Red City, Blue Period: Social Movements in Picasso's Barcelona
The interplay of avant-garde art and avant-garde politics in the 1900s.
George Orwell
Homage to Catalonia
Barcelona in revolution.
Abel Paz
Durruti, The People Armed
The legendary Barcelona anarchist.
Ignasi Solà-Morales *Fin de Siècle Architecture in Barcelona*
A wide-ranging description of the city's Modernista heritage.
Colm Tóibín *Homage to Barcelona*
An evocative and perceptive journey around the city.
Manuel Vázquez Montalbán
Barcelonas
Idiosyncratic, insightful reflections.
Rainer Zerbst *Antoni Gaudí*
A lavishly illustrated survey.

Literature

Pere Calders *The Virgin of the Railway and Other Stories*
Quirky stories by a Catalan writer who spent years in exile in Mexico.
Victor Català *Solitude*
This masterpiece by female novelist Caterina Albert shocked readers in 1905 with its open, modern treatment of female sexuality.
Ildefonso Falcones
Cathedral of the Sea
A hugely popular historical novel, centred on the basilica of Santa Maria del Mar in the Born.
Juan Marsé *The Fallen*
The classic novel of survival in the city during the long posguerra.
Joanot Martorell & Joan Martí de Gualba *Tirant lo Blanc*
The first European prose novel, from 1490: a rambling, bawdy, shaggy-dog story of travels, romances and chivalric adventures.
Eduardo Mendoza *City of Marvels; Year of the Flood*
A sweeping saga of the city between its great Exhibitions in 1888 and 1929; a more recent novel of passions in the city of the 1950s.
Maria-Antònia Oliver
Antipodes; Study in Lilac
Two adventures of Barcelona's first feminist detective.
Mercè Rodoreda
The Time of the Doves; My Cristina and Other Stories
A translation of Plaça del Diamant, the most widely read of all Catalan novels; plus a collection of similarly bittersweet short tales.
Carlos Ruiz Zafón
Shadow of the Wind
An enjoyable neo-Gothic melodrama set in post-war Barcelona.
Manuel Vázquez Montalbán
The Angst-Ridden Executive; An Olympic Death; Southern Seas
Three thrillers starring detective and gourmet Pepe Carvalho.

MUSIC

Lluís Llach
An icon of the 1960s and '70s protest against the Franco regime.
Manel
Four folky Barcelona popsters enjoying a fashion moment.
Maria del Mar Bonet
Though from Mallorca, del Mar Bonet sings in Catalan and specialises in her own compositions, North African music and Mallorcan music.
Mayte Martín
Virtuoso flamenco/bolero singer.
Angel Molina
Leading local DJ with an international reputation.
Ojos de Brujo
Proponents of *rumba catalana*.
The Pinker Tones
A chirpy Barcelona duo spanning lounge, electro, funk and pop.
Pep Sala
Excellent musician and survivor of the successful Catalan group Sau.

WEBSITES

www.barcelonareporter.com
Local news items in English.
www.barcelonarocks.com
Music listings and news.
www.barcelonaturisme.com
Official tourist authority info.
www.bcn.cat The city council's information-packed website.
www.bcn.cat/guia Excellent interactive Barcelona street maps.
www.enciclopedia.cat
Catalan history and geography. Also in English.
www.lecool.com Youth-oriented round-up of offbeat cultural events.
www.mobilitat.net Generalitat's website about getting from A to B in Catalonia, by bus, car or train.
www.renfe.es Spanish railways.
www.timeout.cat Comprehensive local listings magazine, in Catalan.
www.timeout.com/barcelona
The online city guide.

DIRECTORY

Spanish Vocabulary

Spanish is generally referred to as *castellano* (Castilian) rather than *español*. Many locals prefer to speak Catalan, but everyone in the city can also speak Spanish, and will switch to it if visitors show signs of linguistic jitters. The Spanish familiar form for 'you' – *tú* – is used very freely, but it's safer to use the more formal *usted* with older people and strangers (verbs below are given in the *usted* form). For menu terms, *see pp144-145*.

PRONUNCIATION

● c before an **i** or an **e** and **z** are like th in thin
● c in all other cases is as in cat
● g before an **i** or an **e** and **j** are pronounced with a guttural **h**-sound that doesn't exist in English – like ch in Scottish 'loch', but much harder
● g in all other cases is as in get
● h at the beginning of a word is normally silent
● ll is pronounced almost like a **y**
● ñ is like **ny** in canyon
● a single **r** at the beginning of a word and **rr** elsewhere are heavily rolled
● v is more like an English **b**
● In words ending with a vowel, **n** or **s**, the penultimate syllable is stressed: eg *barato, viven, habitaciones.*
● In words ending with any other consonant, the last syllable is stressed: eg *exterior, universidad.*
● An accent marks the stressed syllable in words that depart from these rules: eg *estación, tónica.*

BASICS

● **please** *por favor*; **thank you (very much)** *(muchas) gracias*; **you're welcome** *de nada*
● **hello** *hola*; **hello** (when answering the phone) *hola, diga*
● **goodbye/see you later** *adiós/hasta luego*
● **excuse me/sorry** *perdón*;
● **excuse me, please** *oiga* (the standard way to attract attention, politely; literally, 'hear me')
● **OK/fine**/(to a waiter) **that's enough** *vale*
● **open** *abierto*; **closed** *cerrado*
● **entrance** *entrada*; **exit** *salida*
● **very** *muy*; **and** *y*; **or** *o*; **with** *con*; **without** *sin*; **enough** *bastante*

MORE EXPRESSIONS

● **good morning/good day** *buenos días*; **good afternoon/good evening** *buenas tardes*; **good evening** (after dark)/**good night** *buenas noches*
● **do you speak English?** *¿habla inglés?*; **I'm sorry, I don't speak Spanish** *lo siento, no hablo castellano*; **I don't understand** *no lo entiendo*; **speak more slowly, please** *hable más despacio, por favor*; **wait a moment** *espere un momento*; **how do you say that in Catalan?** *¿Cómo se dice eso en catalán?*
● **what's your name?** *¿cómo se llama?* **my name is...** *me llamo...*
● **Sir/Mr** *señor* (sr); **Madam/Mrs** *señora* (sra); **Miss** *señorita* (srta)
● **where is...?** *¿dónde está...?*; **why?** *¿porqué?*; **who?** *¿quién?*; **when?** *¿cuándo?*; **what?** *¿qué?*; **where?** *¿dónde?*; **how?** *¿cómo?*; **who is it?** *¿quién es?*; **is/are there any...?** *¿hay...?*
● **what time does it open/close?** *¿a qué hora abre/cierra?*
● **pull** *tirar*; **push** *empujar*
● **I would like** *quiero*; **how many would you like?** *¿cuántos quiere?*; **how much is it?** *¿cuánto vale?*
● **price** *precio*; **free** *gratis*; **discount** *descuento*; **do you have any change?** *¿tiene cambio?*
● **I don't want** *no quiero*; **I like** *me gusta*; **I don't like** *no me gusta*
● **good** *bueno/a*; **bad** *malo/a*; **well/badly** *bien/mal*; **small** *pequeño/a*; **big** *gran, grande*; **expensive** *caro/a*; **cheap** *barato/a*; **hot** (food, drink) *caliente*; **cold** *frío/a*;
● **bank** *banco*; **to rent** *alquilar*; **(for) rent, rental** (en) *alquiler*; **post office** *correos*; **stamp** *sello*; **postcard** *postal*; **toilet** *el baño, el servicio, el lavabo*
● **airport** *aeropuerto*; **rail station** *estación de ferrocarril/estación de RENFE* (Spanish railways); **metro station** *estación de metro*; **car** *coche*; **bus** *autobús*; **train** *tren*; **bus stop** *parada de autobus*; **the next stop** *la próxima parada*; **a ticket** *un billete*; **return** *de ida y vuelta*
● **excuse me, do you know the way to...?** *¿oiga, señor/señora, sabe cómo llegar a...?*
● **left** *izquierda*; **right** *derecha*

● **here** *aquí*; **there** *allí*; **straight on** *recto*; **near** *cerca*; **far** *lejos*; **it is far?** *¿está lejos?*

ACCOMMODATION

● **do you have a double/single room for tonight?** *¿tiene una habitación doble/para una persona/para esta noche?*
● **we have a booking** *tenemos reserva*; **an inside/outside room** *una habitación interior/exterior*
● **with/without bathroom** *con/sin baño*; **shower** *ducha*; **double bed** *cama de matrimonio*; **with twin beds** *con dos camas*; **breakfast included** *desayuno incluido*; **air-conditioning** *aire acondicionado*

TIME

● **now** *ahora*; **later** *más tarde*
● **yesterday** *ayer*; **today** *hoy*; **tomorrow** *mañana*; **tomorrow morning** *mañana por la mañana*
● **morning** *la mañana*; **midday** *mediodía*; **afternoon/evening** *la tarde*; **night** *la noche*
● **at what time...?** *¿a qué hora...?*

NUMBERS

● **0** *cero*; **1** *un, uno, una*; **2** *dos*; **3** *tres*; **4** *cuatro*; **5** *cinco*; **6** *seis*; **7** *siete*; **8** *ocho*; **9** *nueve*; **10** *diez*; **11** *once*; **12** *doce*; **13** *trece*; **14** *catorce*; **15** *quince*; **16** *dieciséis*; **17** *diecisiete*; **18** *dieciocho*; **19** *diecinueve*; **20** *veinte*; **21** *veintiuno*; **22** *veintidós*; **30** *treinta*; **40** *cuarenta*; **50** *cincuenta*; **60** *sesenta*; **70** *setenta*; **80** *ochenta*; **90** *noventa*; **100** *cien*; **200** *doscientos*; **1,000** *mil*; **1,000,000** *un millón*

DATES & SEASONS

● **Monday** *lunes*; **Tuesday** *martes*; **Wednesday** *miércoles*; **Thursday** *jueves*; **Friday** *viernes*; **Saturday** *sábado*; **Sunday** *domingo*
● **January** *enero*; **February** *febrero*; **March** *marzo*; **April** *abril*; **May** *mayo*; **June** *junio*; **July** *julio*; **August** *agosto*; **September** *septiembre*; **October** *octubre*; **November** *noviembre*; **December** *diciembre*
● **spring** *primavera*; **summer** *verano*; **autumn** *otoño*; **winter** *invierno*

Catalan Vocabulary

Over a third of Barcelona residents use Catalan as their everyday language, around 70 per cent speak it fluently, and more than 90 per cent understand it. If you take an interest and learn a few phrases, it is likely to be appreciated.

Catalan phonetics are different from those of Spanish, with a wider range of vowel sounds and soft consonants. Catalans use the familiar (*tu*) rather than the polite (*vostè*) forms of the second person freely, but for convenience, verbs are given here in the polite form. For menu terms, *see pp144-145.*

PRONUNCIATION

● In Catalan, words are run together, so *si us plau* (please) is more like sees-plow.
● ç, and c before an i or an e, are like a soft s, as in sit; c in all other cases is as in cat
● e, when unstressed as in *cerveses* (beers), or Jaume I, is a weak sound, like centre or comfortable
● g before i or e and j are pronounced like s in pleasure; tg and tj are similar to dg in badge
● g after an i at the end of a word (Puig) is a hard ch sound, as in watch; otherwise, g is as in get
● h is silent
● ll is somewhere between the y in yes and the lll in million
● l·l has a slightly stronger stress on a single l sound; paral·lel sounds similar to the English parallel
● o at the end of a word is like the u sound in flu; ó at the end of a word is similar to the o in tomato; ò is like the o in hot
● r beginning a word and rr are heavily rolled; but at the end of many words is almost silent, so *carrer* (street) sounds like carr-ay
● s at the beginning and end of words and ss between vowels are soft, as in sit; a single s between two vowels is a z sound, as in zoo
● t after l or n at the end of a word is almost silent
● v is more like an English b
● x is at the beginning of a word, or after a consonant or the letter i, is like the sh in shoe, at other times like the English expert
● y after an n at the end of a word or in nys is not a vowel but adds a nasal stress and a y-sound to the n

BASICS

● please *si us plau;* thank you (very much) *(moltes) gràcies;* very good/great/OK *molt bé;* you're welcome *de res*
● hello *hola;* hello (when answering the phone) *hola, digui'm*
● goodbye/see you later *adéu/fins després*
● excuse me/sorry *perdoni/disculpi;* excuse me, please *escolti* (literally, 'listen to me'); OK/fine *val/d'acord*
● open *obert;* closed *tancat;* entrance *entrada;* exit *sortida;* very *molt;* and *i;* or *o;* with *amb;* without *sense;* enough *prou*

MORE EXPRESSIONS

● good morning, good day *bon dia;* good afternoon/evening *bona tarda;* good evening (after dark), good night *bona nit*
● do you speak English? *parla anglès?;* I'm sorry, I don't speak Catalan *ho sento, no parlo català;* I don't understand *no ho entenc;* speak more slowly, please *parli més a poc a poc, si us plau;* can you say that in Spanish, please? *m'ho pot dir en castellà, si us plau?;* how do you say that in Catalan? *còm es diu això en català?*
● what's your name? *com es diu?;* my name is… *em dic…*
● Sir/Mr *senyor (sr);* Madam/Mrs *senyora (sra);* Miss *senyoreta (srta)*
● where is…? *on és…?;* why? *per què?;* who? *qui?;* when? *quan?;* what? *què?;* where? *on?;* how? *com?;* who is it? *qui és?;* is/are there any…? *hi ha…?/n'hi ha de…?*
● I would like… *vull…* (literally, 'I want'); how would you like? *quants en vol?;* how much is it? *quant val?*
● price *preu;* free *gratuit/de franc;* change, exchange *canvi*
● I don't want *no vull;* I like *m'agrada;* I don't like *no m'agrada*
● good *bo/bona;* bad *dolent/a;* well/badly *bé/malament;* small *petit/a;* big *gran;* expensive *car/a;* cheap *barat/a;* hot (food, drink) *calent/a;* cold *fred/a*
● toilet *el bany/el servei/ el lavabo*

AIRPORT / TRANSPORT

● airport *aeroport;* rail station *estació de tren/estació de RENFE* (Spanish railways); metro station *estació de metro*
● car *cotxe;* bus *autobús;* train *tren;* bus stop *parada d'autobús;* the next stop *la propera parada*
● a ticket *un bitllet;* return *d'anada i tornada*
● left *esquerra;* right *dreta*
● here *aquí;* there *allà;* straight on *tot recte;* near *a prop;* far *lluny;* at the corner *a la cantonada;* as far as *fins a;* towards *cap a;* is it far? *és lluny?*

TIME

● now *ara;* later *més tard*
● yesterday *ahir;* today *avui;* tomorrow *demà;* tomorrow morning *demà pel matí*
● morning *el matí;* midday *migdia;* afternoon *la tarda;* evening *el vespre;* night *la nit;* late night (roughly, 1-6am) *la matinada*
● at what time…? *a quina hora…?;* in an hour *en una hora;* at 2 *a les dues*

NUMBERS

● 0 *zero;* 1 *u, un, una;* 2 *dos, dues;* 3 *tres;* 4 *quatre;* 5 *cinc;* 6 *sis;* 7 *set;* 8 *vuit;* 9 *nou;* 10 *deu;* 11 *onze;* 12 *dotze;* 13 *tretze;* 14 *catorze;* 15 *quinze;* 16 *setze;* 17 *disset;* 18 *divuit;* 19 *dinou;* 20 *vint;* 21 *vint-i-u;* 22 *vint-i-dos, vint-i-dues;* 30 *trenta;* 40 *quaranta;* 50 *cinquanta;* 60 *seixanta;* 70 *setanta;* 80 *vuitanta;* 90 *noranta;* 100 *cent;* 200 *dos-cents, dues-centes;* 1,000 *mil;* 1,000,000 *un milió*

DATES & SEASONS

● Monday *dilluns;* Tuesday *dimarts;* Wednesday *dimecres;* Thursday *dijous;* Friday *divendres;* Saturday *dissabte;* Sunday *diumenge*
● January *gener;* February *febrer;* March *març;* April *abril;* May *maig;* June *juny;* July *juliol;* August *agost;* September *setembre;* October *octubre;* November *novembre;* December *desembre*
● spring *primavera;* summer *estiu;* autumn *tardor;* winter *hivern*

Content Index

INDEX

Venue Index

INDEX

Advertisers' Index

Please refer to the relevant pages for contact details.

INDEX

Maps

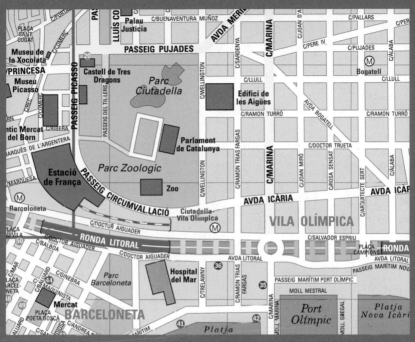

Major sight or landmark . . . .

Hospital or college . . . .

Railway station . . . .

Parks . . . .

River . . . .

Carretera . . . .

Main road . . . .

Main road tunnel . . . .

Pedestrian road . . . .

Airport . . . . ✈

Church . . . . ✚

Metro station, FGC station . . . . Ⓜ 🌀

Area name . . . . **EIXAMPLE**

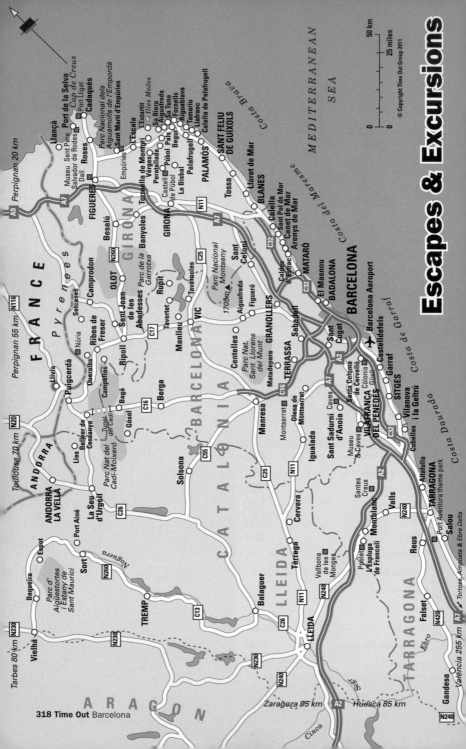

Escapes & Excursions

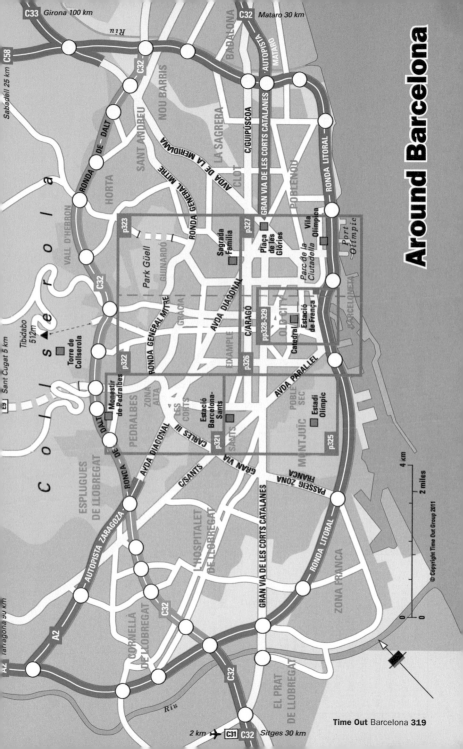

Around Barcelona

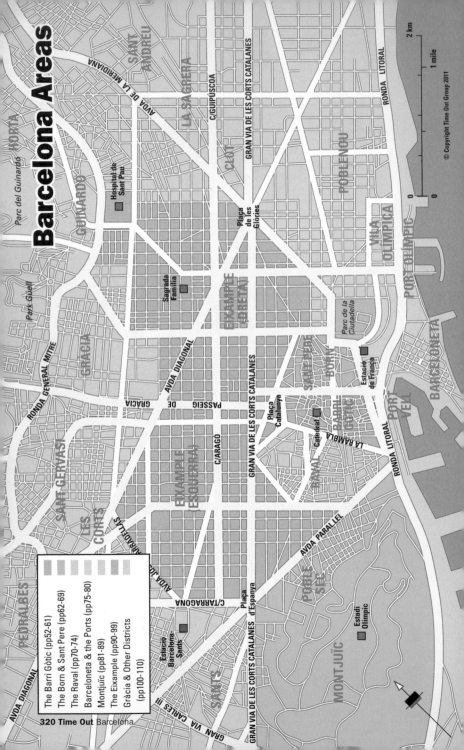

Barcelona Areas

The Barri Gòtic (pp52-61)
The Born & Sant Pere (pp62-69)
The Raval (pp70-74)
Barceloneta & the Ports (pp75-80)
Montjuïc (pp81-89)
The Eixample (pp90-99)
Gràcia & Other Districts (pp100-110)

320 Time Out Barcelona

© Copyright Time Out Group 2011

2 km
1 mile

HORTA
Parc del Guinardó
GUINARDÓ
Parc Güell
SANT ANDREU
AVDA DE LA MERIDIANA
LA SAGRERA
C/GUIPÚSCOA
GRAN VIA DE LES CORTS CATALANES
CLOT
Hospital de Sant Pau
Sagrada Família
EIXAMPLE (DRETA)
Plaça de les Glòries
POBLENOU
VILA OLÍMPICA
PORT OLÍMPIC
GRÀCIA
AVDA DIAGONAL
PASSEIG DE GRÀCIA
Parc de la Ciutadella
BARCELONETA
SANT GERVASI
RONDA GENERAL MITRE
C/ARAGÓ
GRAN VIA DE LES CORTS CATALANES
SANT PERE
BORN
Estació de França
PORT VELL
Plaça Catalunya
BARRI GÒTIC
Catedral
LA RAMBLA
RAVAL
RONDA LITORAL
EIXAMPLE (ESQUERRA)
LES CORTS
AVDA JOSEP TARRADELLAS
PEDRALBES
AVDA DIAGONAL
SANTS
GRAN VIA CARLES III
Estació Barcelona-Sants
C/TARRAGONA
Plaça d'Espanya
GRAN VIA DE LES CORTS CATALANES
AVDA PARAL·LEL
POBLE SEC
Estadi Olímpic
MONTJUÏC

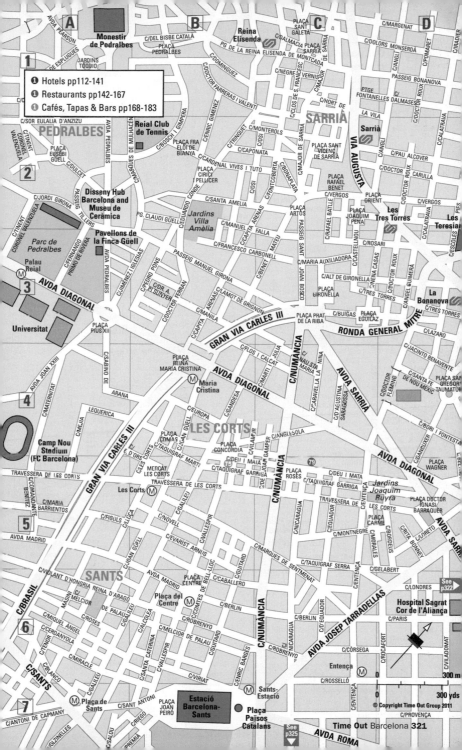

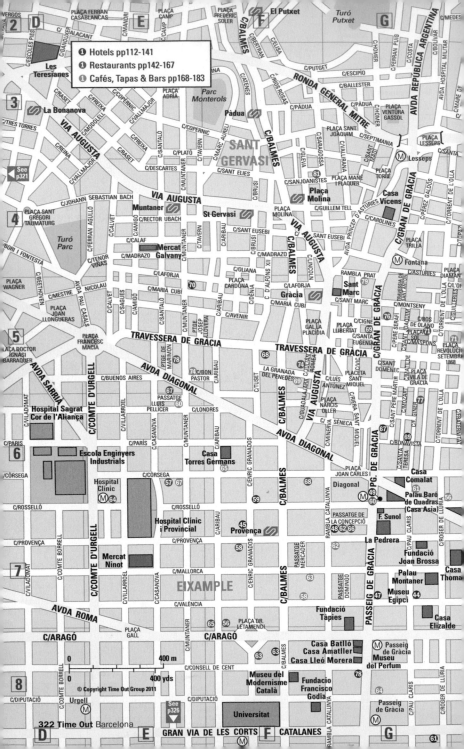

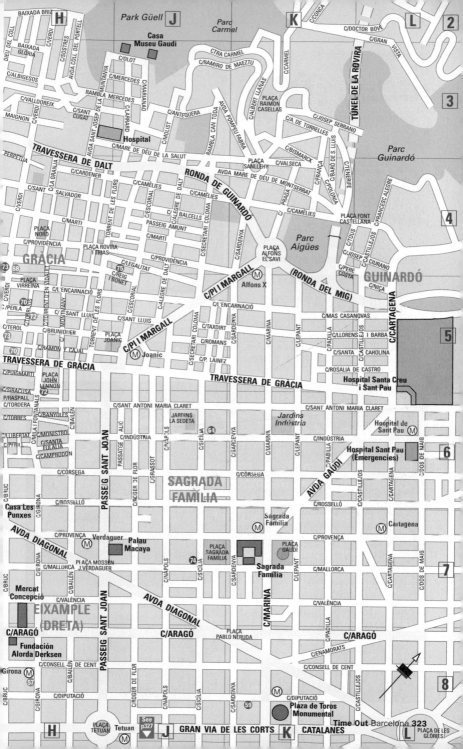

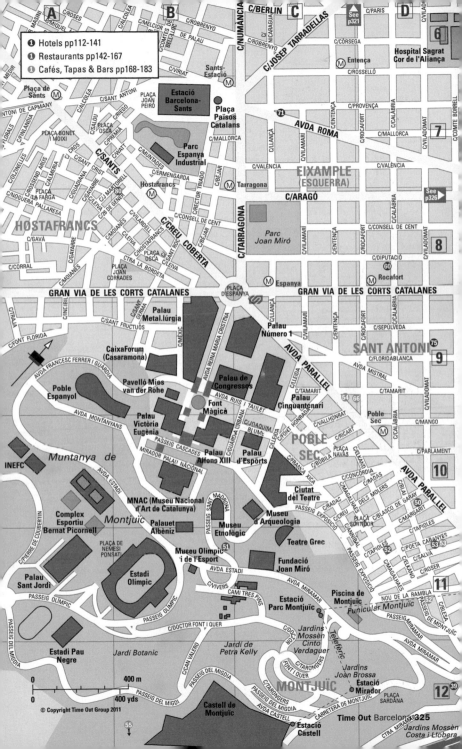

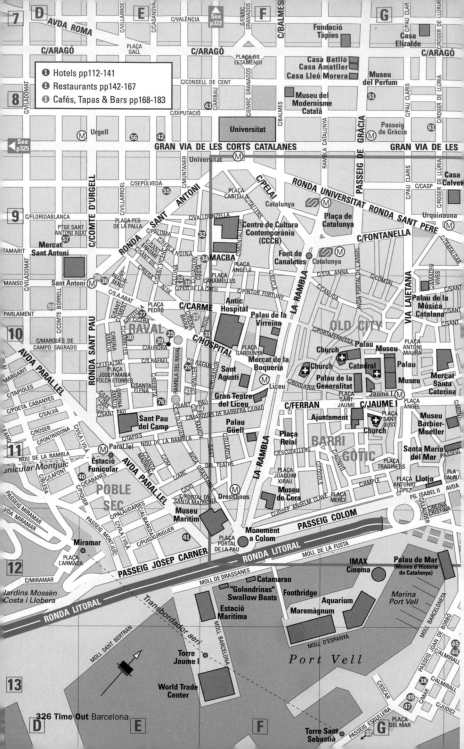

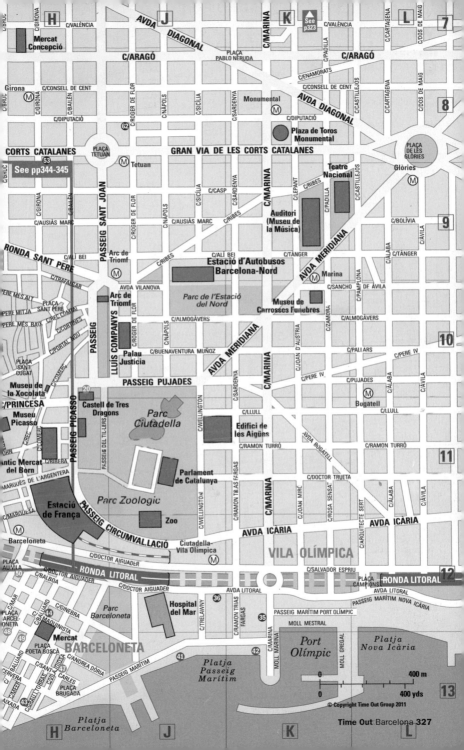

H
C/BRUC
C/GIRONA
J
AVDA
DIAGONAL
C/VALÈNCIA
K
See
p323
C/MARINA
L
C/DOS DE MAIG
C/VALÈNCIA
7

Mercat
Concepció

C/ARAGÓ

C/ARAGÓ

PLAÇA
PABLO NERUDA

C/PADILLA

C/ENAMORATS

8

Girona
C/CONSELL DE CENT
C/BAILEN

C/DIPUTACIÓ

C/SICILIA

C/ROGER DE FLOR

C/NÀPOLS

62

C/GIRONA

C/CONSELL DE CENT

AVDA DIAGONAL

C/SARDENYA

Monumental
M

C/DIPUTACIÓ

C/CASTILLEJOS

C/CARTAGENA

PLAÇA
DE LES
GLÒRIES

CORTS CATALANES

PLAÇA
TETUAN

GRAN VIA DE LES CORTS CATALANES

Plaza de Toros
Monumental

Glòries

M

See pp344-345
53

M Tetuan

C/GIRONA
C/BAILEN

PASSEIG SANT JOAN

C/SICILIA

C/CASP

C/SARDENYA

C/RIBES

Teatre
Nacional

C/CASTILLEJOS

9

C/AUSIÀS MARC

C/NÀPOLS

C/ROGER DE FLOR

C/AUSIÀS MARC

Auditori
(Museu de
la Música)

C/PADILLA

C/BOLÍVIA

C/ALABA

C/TÀNGER

RONDA SANT PERE

C/ALÍ BEI

Arc de
Triomf

M

C/RIBES

C/ALÍ BEI

C/TÀNGER

AVDA MERIDIANA

C/ÀVILA

C/TRAFALGAR

'ERE MÉS ALT

PLAÇA
SANT PERE

'ERE MITJA

'ERE MÉS BAIX

C/CORTINES

C/PORTAL NOU

Arc de
Triomf

AVDA VILANOVA

Estació d'Autobusos
Barcelona-Nord

C/SANCHO

M Marina

DE ÀVILA
C/PAMPLONA

PASSEIG LLUÍS COMPANYS

Parc de l'Estació
del Nord

Museu de
Carrosses Fúnebres

C/ZAMORA

C/ALMOGÀVERS

PLAÇA
SANT CUGAT

C/ROGER DE FLOR

C/NÀPOLS

C/ALMOGÀVERS

Palau
Justicia

C/BUENAVENTURA MUÑOZ

C/JOAN D'ÀUSTRIA

C/PERE IV

10

Museu de
la Xocolata

20

PASSEIG PICASSO

PASSEIG PUJADES

C/SARDENYA

C/PERE IV

C/PALLARS

C/PERE IV

C/ALABA

C/ÀVILA

C/PRINCESA

Castell de Tres
Dragons

PASSEIG DEL TILLERS

Parc
Ciutadella

C/WELLINGTON

C/LLULL

Edifici de
les Aigües

Bogatell

M

11

Museu
Picasso

C/MONTCADA

C/LLULL

antic Mercat
del Born

C/RIBERA

Parlament
de Catalunya

C/RAMON TURRÓ

AVDA BOGATELL

C/RAMON TURRÓ

MARQUÉS DE L'ARGENTERA

Parc Zoologic

C/RAMON TRIAS FARGAS

C/DOCTOR TRUETA

Estació
de França

PASSEIG CIRCUMVAL·LACIÓ

Zoo

C/WELLINGTON

C/MARINA

C/JOAN MIRÓ

C/ROSA SENSAT

C/ARQUITECTE SERT

C/ALABA

C/ÀVILA

M

Barceloneta

Ciutadella-
Vila Olímpica

AVDA ICÀRIA

AVDA ICÀRIA

PLAÇA
AU VILA

C/DOCTOR AIGUADER

RONDA LITORAL

M

VILA OLÍMPICA

C/SALVADOR ESPRIU

PLAÇA
CAMPIONS

RONDA LITORAL

12

50

C/DOCTOR AIGUADER

C/BALBOA

C/DOCTOR AIGUADER

AVDA LITORAL

RONDA LITORAL

PASSEIG MARÍTIM NOVA ICÀRIA

C/MAR

C/GINEBRA

Parc
Barceloneta

Hospital
del Mar

36

C/TRELAWNY

C/RAMON TRIAS FARGAS

35

PASSEIG MARÍTIM PORT OLÍMPIC

PLAÇA
ARCELO-
NETA

C/BALUARD

C/MAQUINISTA

MOLL MESTRAL

48

49

Mercat

C/SANT
CARLES

BARCELONETA

41

42

C/MARINA
MOLL MARINA

Port
Olímpic

MOLL GREGAL

Platja
Nova Icària

PLAÇA
POETA BOSCÀ

C/ANDREA DÓRIA

PASSEIG MARÍTIM

Platja
Passeig
Marítim

MOLL MESTRAL

CERVERA

C/SANT

C/GRAU I TORRES

PLAÇA
BRUGADA

43

Platja
Barceloneta

400 m

0

400 yds

© Copyright Time Out Group 2011

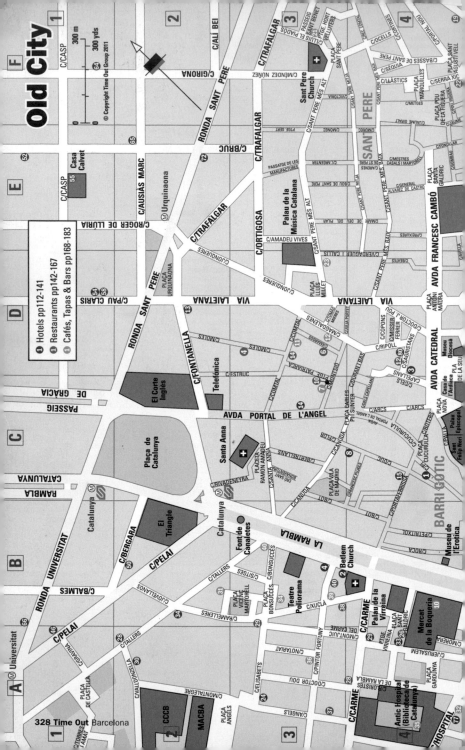

Street Index

STREET INDEX

STREET INDEX

Mar Mediterrània

ATM

TMB Transports Metropolitans de Barcelona

Metro

Renfe Local Trains

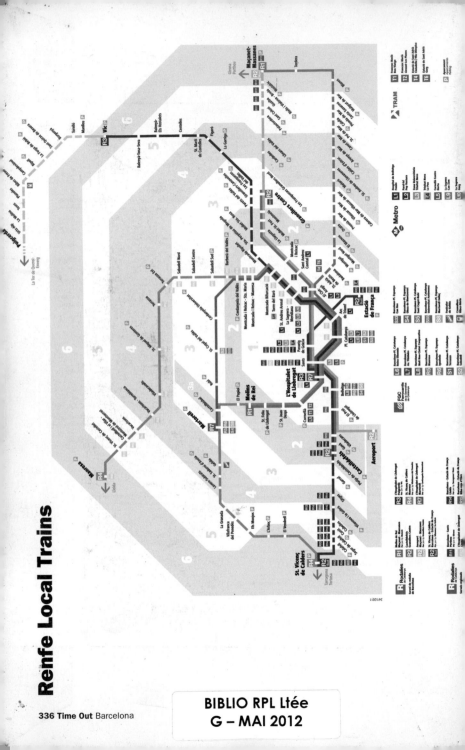